DIVINATION,
AND THE END OF TH

MW01004105

This book offers a comprehensive assessment of the intersection between Roman politics, culture and divination in the late Republic. It discusses how the practice of divination developed at a time of great political and social change and explores the evidence for a critical reflection and debate on the limits of divination and prediction in the second and first centuries BC. Divination was a central feature in the workings of the Roman government and this book explores the ways in which it changed under the pressure of factors of socio-political complexity and disruption. It discusses the ways in which the problem of the prediction of the future is constructed in the literature of the period. Finally, it explores the impact that the emergence of the Augustan regime had on the place of divination in Rome and the role that divinatory themes had in shaping the ideology of the new regime.

FEDERICO SANTANGELO is Lecturer in Ancient History at New-castle University. His previous publications include *Sulla, the Elites and the Empire. A Study of Roman Policies in Italy and the Greek East* (2007).

DIVINATION, PREDICTION AND THE END OF THE ROMAN REPUBLIC

FEDERICO SANTANGELO

CAMBRIDGE
UNIVERSITY PRESS

CAMBRIDGE
UNIVERSITY PRESS

University Printing House, Cambridge CB2 8BS, United Kingdom

One Liberty Plaza, 20th Floor, New York, NY 10006, USA

477 Williamstown Road, Port Melbourne, VIC 3207, Australia

314-321, 3rd Floor, Plot 3, Splendor Forum, Jasola District Centre, New Delhi - 110025, India

103 Penang Road, #05-06/07, Visioncrest Commercial, Singapore 238467

Cambridge University Press is part of the University of Cambridge.

It furthers the University's mission by disseminating knowledge in the pursuit of education, learning and research at the highest international levels of excellence.

www.cambridge.org
Information on this title: www.cambridge.org/9781009296359

First published 2013
3rd printing 2014
First paperback edition 2022

A catalogue record for this publication is available from the British Library

Library of Congress Cataloging in Publication data
Santangelo, Federico.
Divination, prediction and the end of the Roman Republic / Federico Santangelo.
pages   cm
Includes bibliographical references and index.
ISBN 978-1-107-02684-1 (hardback)
1. Rome – History – Republic, 265–30 B.C.   2. Divination – Rome.   3. Rome – Politics and government – 510–30 B.C.   4. Political culture – Rome – History.   5. Social change – Rome – History.   I. Title.
DG254.S253   2013
937′.09 – dc23   2012048526

ISBN 978-1-107-02684-1 Hardback
ISBN 978-1-009-29635-9 Paperback

LER

Contents

vii

Illustrations

Thanks are due to the Deutsches Archäologisches Institut, Rom for kindly providing photographs and permissions.

Acknowledgments

It is a pleasure to acknowledge the many debts that I have contracted as I have been working on this book.

The completion of the project was made possible by the generosity of two institutions: the Arts and Humanities Research Council, which awarded me an Early Career Fellowship, and my own academic home, Newcastle University, which granted me a semester of research leave.

Errietta Bissa, Dominique Briquel, Michael Crawford, Angelo Giavatto, Ingo Gildenhard, Ulrich Gotter, Tim Kirk, Stefan Maul, Don Miller, John Moles, Fiona Noble, John North, Martin O'Kane, Jonathan Powell, Thilo Rising, Alessandro Schiesaro, Tony Spawforth, Naomi Standen, Olga Tellegen-Couperus, Kai Trampedach, Sam Turner and Jaap Wisse offered advice and support at various stages. José Joaquín Caerols, David Engels, Ulrich Gotter, Alex Nice, Jörg Rüpke, Susan Satterfield, Alexander Thein, David Wardle and Peter Wiseman generously shared unpublished work. I had the good fortune to be able to present aspects of my research on Roman divination to a number of audiences: a panel on Cicero at a Classical Association Conference in Birmingham, a conference on law and religion in the Roman Republic at Tilburg University, a Cicero Awayday in Newcastle, and research seminars in Lampeter, Philadelphia, Cardiff, Swansea, Manchester, Newcastle, Heidelberg, Konstanz and Durham. I have greatly benefited from the comments I received on those occasions.

I am very grateful to the friends and colleagues, some close to home, some far afield, who took upon themselves the burden of reading drafts of the whole manuscript: Massimiliano Di Fazio, Charlotte Greenacre, Jerzy Linderski, Jeremy Paterson, James Richardson, Federico Russo and Susan Satterfield. Two readers for Cambridge University Press provided very rich and stimulating comments on an early version.

Michael Sharp has been an extraordinarily supportive publisher all the way through. Gillian Dadd, Elizabeth Spicer and Christina Sarigiannidou have provided invaluable guidance at the final stages in the preparation of the manuscript. Frances Brown has turned the copyediting process into a very enjoyable undertaking.

Most of the research towards this book was done in two libraries: the Robinson Library at Newcastle University and the Library of the Institute of Classical Studies in London. It would not have been possible without the assistance and expertise of the staff at those institutions. Jackie Dunn in Newcastle and Sue Willetts in London deserve special mention for their efficiency and cheerfulness in dealing with even the most abstruse queries.

This is, in a way, a book about the future. My children have taught me much more about the mechanics and the puzzles of guesswork and prediction than I could have possibly foreseen.

My first and foremost debt is reflected in the dedication.

Abbreviations

Abbreviations for ancient authors and works follow those of the *Oxford Classical Dictionary*; those for periodicals follow those of *L'Année Philologique*. In addition the following abbreviations are used throughout:

ANRW	*Aufstieg und Niedergang der römischen Welt*. Berlin and New York 1972–
BEFAR	*Bibliothèque des Écoles françaises d'Athènes et de Rome*
CEFR	*Collection de l'École française de Rome*
CIL	*Corpus Inscriptionum Latinarum*. Berlin 1863–
HABES	Heidelberger althistorische Beiträge und epigraphische Studien
LTUR	*Lexicon topographicum urbis Romae*, ed. E. M. Steinby. Rome 1993–2000
PAwB	*Potsdamer altertumswissenschaftliche Beiträge*
RE	*Paulys Real-Encyclopädie der classischen Altertumswissenschaft*. Stuttgart 1893–
RGRW	*Religions in the Graeco-Roman World*
RIC	*The Roman Imperial Coinage*. London 1923–94
RRC	M. H. Crawford, *Roman Republican Coinage*. Cambridge 1974

The power of signs

Let us begin with four vignettes. In 88 BC the sound of a trumpet was heard in the city of Rome. It was a loud, prolonged and shrill note, and no one could tell from whence it came, even though it was a cloudless day. It was regarded as a prodigy, an extraordinary event that was collectively understood as a sign of divine concern or hostility. Its interpretation and ritual expiation were necessary and a well-established process was followed. The Senate entrusted this to a body of expert diviners. The haruspices, a group of Etruscan seers who routinely advised the Roman government on the interpretation and expiation of prodigies, provided an explanation that went beyond a recommendation on matters of ritual. They argued that the prodigy announced the beginning of a new age. They also stated that history was not open-ended, as there were eight ages in the world, each one differing from a cultural point of view. The end of an age was marked by a sign such as the one that had just been reported: a new age was about to begin.[1] The interpretation of the prophecy is problematic, but it is clear that it established a link between political and intellectual developments. It also had a strong diagnostic value. The year 88 was a turning point in late Republican history, with the controversy between Marius and Sulla over the command in the war against King Mithridates and Sulla's decision to end the crisis and reassert his entitlement by marching on Rome with his army and driving his political opponents away. In the same year, just a few months before Sulla's *coup d'état*, a cohort of Etruscan diviners gave a complex prediction on the future course of Roman history to the Senate.

In 57 the king of Egypt Ptolemy XII Auletes fled to Rome after being toppled by a revolt. He was an ally of the Roman people and the Senate considered taking steps to restore him to the throne. There was no consensus, however, on who should be entrusted with the mission. While the

---

[1] Plut. *Sull.* 7.6–13. See the discussion of this passage in Chapter 4. The fundamental discussion of haruspicy remains Thulin 1905a, 1906a and 1909. See also North 1967: 548–95; Capdeville 1997; Jannot 1998: 20–49; Haack 2003; Martínez-Pinna 2007; Corbeill 2012.

debate was ongoing, at the beginning of 56, a thunderbolt struck the statue of Jupiter on the Alban Mount.[2] The event was regarded as a prodigy. The Senate instructed a college of priests, the *quindecemuiri sacris faciundis*, to consult the Sibylline Books, a collection of prophetic texts that were preserved on the Capitol.[3] The priests singled out a portion of the responses which seemed to bear special relevance to the crisis: if the king of Egypt should come asking for help, he was not to be refused friendship, but he was also not to receive military support. They were struck by the correspondence between the wording of the response and the events of contemporary politics, and the tribune C. Porcius Cato, who was also a *quindecemuir*, used this very argument to persuade the other members of the college not to take any further action. Under normal circumstances, the expectation was that the Senate would authorise the publication of a summary of the response. Cato, however, took an extraordinary step and made it public without seeking permission: he compelled the priests to read out a Latin version of the oracle to the populace. The Senate debated the matter, but no conclusion was reached on who was to be assigned the command. The outcome, after much deliberation, was inaction. Interestingly, none of the options that were discussed at the time included a rejection of the oracles and their authenticity.

In 44 Mark Antony and Julius Caesar held the consulship. When he entered office Caesar, who also held the perpetual dictatorship, expressed the intention to step down from the consulship later in the year in order to launch a campaign against the Parthians. He designated P. Cornelius Dolabella as *consul suffectus*, i.e. his replacement to the consulship. Dolabella happened to be a personal enemy of Antony, who promptly announced that he would do whatever was in his power to prevent his election.[4] Antony was both a consul and a member of the augural college, one of the senior priesthoods of Rome, which was entrusted with the interpretation of divine signs before all important public acts.[5] He had the prerogative to stop a voting assembly by declaring that he had detected a sign of divine opposition, and he had two options available. As a consul, he could prevent the assembly from taking place; in his capacity as augur, he could stop the assembly at any point after its inception. He chose the latter option and

---

[2] Dio 39.15–16.
[3] Diels 1890: 1–108; Hoffmann 1933; Parke 1988: 136–42, 148–50, 190–220; Caerols 1989; Orlin 1997: 76–115; Scheid 1998b; Buitenwerf 2003: 99–106; Monaca 2005; Takács 2003: 19–24 (= 2008: 64–70, 159–61); Guittard 2007b: 239–75; Satterfield 2008.
[4] Cic. *Phil.* 1.31; 2.79–84. See Appendix.
[5] Linderski 1986a is the reference modern discussion; collection and discussion of the primary sources in Regell 1881, 1882: 12–19 and 1893. See also Humm 2012a: 65–84 and 2012b.

declared his opposition when the election of Dolabella was about to be finalised. By adopting that solution Antony brought the political process to a halt and compelled Dolabella (and indirectly Caesar) to seek his support for the ratification of the election. The events that unfolded a few weeks later, after the Ides of March, confirmed the value of Antony's use of his augural prerogatives. When Dolabella and Antony decided to mend fences and co-operate in the aftermath of Caesar's assassination, Antony's willingness to accept Dolabella's election and set aside his opposition was a central part of the deal. The tactical advantage that he had earned with his handling of Dolabella's election was rooted in his expert knowledge of the complex rules that governed the interaction between politics and religion in the late Republic.

The advent of monarchy led to a narrowing of the range of options available for the exploitation of signs. Augustus' approach to the Sibylline Books is very instructive. In 18 he ordered that the *quindecemuiri* should themselves copy the books by hand, so that 'no one else could read them'.[6] In 12, shortly after his accession to the office of *pontifex maximus*, he took a decision of religious policing: he ordered an end to the circulation of a number of Latin and Greek prophecies that were available in Rome at the time and restated that the Sibylline Books were the only acceptable form of prophecy.[7] The operation was completed by the relocation of the books from the Capitol to the temple of Apollo on the Palatine, in the vicinity of the emperor's residence and under his direct patronage. The temple was also home to the collection of the Etruscan books that dealt with lightning and were part of the haruspical tradition.[8]

These four examples – which we will discuss in greater detail elsewhere in this book – show, in different ways, how divination was an essential feature of the religious landscape of the city of Rome in the last century of the Republic. The haruspical prophecy of 88 shows a group of foreign diviners being consulted by the Senate at a time of great political tension and producing a prophetic response that was based on a wide-ranging interpretation of Roman history. The crisis of 56 shows the disruptive potential of divinatory texts that were used and circulated outside the usual institutional framework. The events of 44 are an example of the unusual situations which the interaction between the contingency of the political situation and the complex rules that governed the workings of Roman public religion could bring about. Augustus' attention to and systematic review of the corpus of the Sibylline Books was a powerful illustration of

[6] Dio 54.17.2. [7] Suet. *Aug.* 31.1. [8] Serv. *ad Aen.* 6.72.

the major shift in the practice of divination with the advent of monarchy. Taken together, these four examples illustrate some of the key concepts of the discussion that will follow in this volume: the plurality and diversity of the forms of divination that were available, on both the public and private levels, in late Republican Rome; the tight integration of the political and the religious dimensions; the political and intellectual issues raised by the control of the sources of divination in Rome and the competition for it.

Divination must be understood not just as a set of techniques for the prediction of the future, but more widely as a strategy for interpreting the signs that the gods send to mankind.[9] It is widely attested throughout the ancient world, well beyond the Mediterranean, at both public and private levels, and it retains considerable (and to some surprising) relevance in our own time.[10] In the Roman world, however, divination had some unique features, which were especially strong under the Republic. It was central in the decision-making strategies of the Roman government: any serious political deliberation, any political process of some consequence was accompanied by the use of divinatory procedures.[11] Divinatory expertise was concentrated and readily available in the city of Rome; oracles from far afield were usually not consulted. It was also spread across several discrete centres, which often worked along with each other, and could enter into competition with one another. The history of these bodies of experts and their gradual inclusion is testimony to their complex and enduring importance.

Divination in Rome was based on some fundamental assumptions: that a relationship between the gods and the community could be secured by the performance of appropriate rituals; that rituals could also enable the exploration of the will of the gods; and that divine anger could be expressed through signs that required interpretation and appropriate action, in order to prevent further difficulties. It was therefore at the centre of religious practice and discourse, and applied to many different contexts. In Republican Rome and Italy it was used and practised by people from all walks of

---

[9] Koch 2010: 44. Divination, however, does involve the mastery of complex and teachable techniques: Evans-Pritchard 1937: 285; Fortes 1966: 414–15, 421.

[10] Curry 2010a: 6; cf. e.g. the use of a game of chance to decide a tied council election in Cave Creek, Arizona in 2009 (Heimlich 2010: 143). There was no culture of divination in ancient Egypt (Assmann 1992: 237–8, 250–1, with the important qualifications of Jambon 2012).

[11] This is a clear difference with the practice of the Greek *poleis* in the classical period, which hardly ever resorted to divination on matters of internal politics and legislation (Parker 1985: 310–11). Cf. Bowden 2005, who argues that establishing and enforcing the will of the gods was a central concern to the Athenian democracy in the classical period. A recent, comprehensive overview of Roman divination in Rüpke and Belayche 2005. Johnston 2005: 1–10 and 2008: 17–27 give splendid surveys of recent work on ancient divination. Bouché-Leclerq 1879–82 remains a fundamental reference tool, brilliantly epitomised in Bouché-Leclerq 1892.

life and it was employed by the Roman government in handling a range of important matters, especially through the taking of the auspices and the interpretation of prodigies.[12] However, it took on a particular relevance at a time of political turmoil, when it could be used both to allay deep-seated concerns and as a tool of political control.[13] The pervasiveness of Roman divination is another of its original features. B. Gladigow evocatively spoke of 'collectivisation of fear' (*Kollektivierung der Angst*) to describe the role that divination plays in securing and promoting civic cohesion.[14] Building on some recent work on Greek cultures of prediction, one could also argue, in more neutral terms, for a social distribution of risk.[15] A helpful working hypothesis is that divination – i.e. the consultation of the gods with a view to establishing their will and their position on an envisaged action – is a process that removes tensions and can make the human decision-making process possible. This may be described as the rule, but there are exceptions, or indeed enactments of different rules; moments in which divination is used in order to delegitimise a decision and stop a political process. It is by now a commonplace in religious anthropology that an oracle does not stand in the way of political decisions;[16] as we will see, in Republican Rome divinatory utterances could be used against decisions that had been made or were about to be taken. This book sets out to show that in the disrupted world of the late Republic the uses of divination were strongly contested, and its remit was reshaped and redefined.

[12] The literature on prodigies in the Republic is extensive: Bouché-Leclerq 1882: IV, 15–115, 175–317; Wülker 1903: 6–50; Luterbacher 1904: 18–43; Thulin 1909: 76–130; Wissowa 1912: 390–6, 538–49; Latte 1960: 157–61; Bloch 1963: 112–46; Günther 1964: 209–36; MacBain 1982; Guillaumont 1996; Rosenberger 1998 and 2007: 293–8; North 2000b: 27–9, 38–40; Rasmussen 2003: esp. 35–168; Engels 2007: esp. 724–97 (the catalogue of prodigies is an essential reference tool); Lisdorf 2007: 204–20, 242–76; Février 2009: 125–91; Orlin 2010: 111–36; Pina Polo 2011: 23–30, 251–4; cf. the note of caution in Beard 2012: 25. On how prodigies from outside Rome were reported under the Republic compare and contrast Mommsen 1853 (= 1909: 168–74); Rawson 1971; MacBain 1982: 25–33; Rosenberger 2005; Dart 2012. Cf. the classic discussion of ritual redress in Turner 1968: esp. 1–24, 89–127; cf. also Turner 1967: 361 on divination as a 'form of social analysis'.

[13] Reassurance and manipulation are central themes in several modern discussions of Republican religion: Liebeschuetz 1979: 7–17; Wardman 1982: 42–52, 182–3; Scheid 2001a: 137–40. Meyer 2002: 176, 180–1; Rüpke 2005a: 1448 (= 2005b: 224); and M. Flower 2008: 192–3 persuasively argue that manipulation is not a helpful category for the understanding of divination. Evans-Pritchard 1937: 313–51 remains a classic discussion; Bell 1992: 181 stresses that 'the social control wielded by ritual is more complex than the manipulation of affective states or cognitive categories'.

[14] Gladigow 1979: esp. 70–7. See also Bayet 1969: 51–6; Rosenberger 1998: 91–126; Rüpke 2005a: 1443 ('eine rationale, psychisch stabilisierende Form des Verhaltens bei herrschender Unsicherheit'; cf. 2005b: 219); M. Flower 2008: 74. *Contra* cf. Rasmussen 2003: 29 and Lisdorf 2007: 131–5. Fear in the late Republic: Kneppe 1994: 57–76, 218–29; Osgood 2006. Cf. Maul 1994 on divinatory rituals as stabilising factors in Assyrian society.

[15] Eidinow 2007 and 2011. Cf. the excellent interdisciplinary discussion of risk in Skinns, Scott and Cox 2011.

[16] Parker 1985: 301–2, 324.

This is a symptom of its enduring vitality. An influential strand of scholarship argued that Roman religion went through a steady decline in the last century of the Republic, caused by political manipulation on the part of the ruling elite and by widespread disregard for religious concerns by the Roman populace in general.[17] This reductionist view of Roman religion has been robustly challenged in the last three decades.[18] It is now widely accepted that divination retained a very important place in the political and intellectual landscape of the late Republic, even at a time of considerable instability. Religious change is not to be interpreted as a symptom of decline.

This book is a study of the role that divination played in the last two centuries of the Roman Republic and in the early Principate. Its central working hypothesis is that divination must be studied in association with the broader problem of how prediction was culturally constructed. In the late Republic, divination and prediction are excellent vantage points for the study of wider cultural developments. The focus of the study lies at the crossroads of political, religious and intellectual history. In Rome none of these categories was understood as independent; on the contrary, they were intimately intertwined. Much of the most thought-provoking recent work on the late Republic focuses on the cultural development of this period and on the paradox of an age in which traumatic political change coexisted with a profound change in the cultural domain. The term 'revolution' has been used, with an implicit reference to the time-honoured concept of 'Roman Revolution', a deep change of a political and constitutional nature.[19] Other studies have referred to the emergence of a new rationalistic trend in Roman culture, which was chiefly – though not exclusively – brought about by the influence of Greek models.[20] The late Republican debate on divination is not part of a wider movement that can be schematically reduced to a

---

[17] This idea has been dominant for a long time, especially (but not exclusively) in the scholarship on Republican *Prodigienwesen*: e.g. Wülker 1903: 71–5; Luterbacher 1904: 17; Warde Fowler 1911: 304–7, 428–9; Wissowa 1912: 70–2; Taylor 1949: 76–97, 212–16; Latte 1960: 264–93; Bloch 1963: 145–6 and 1968: 226–31; Günther 1964; Bayet 1969: 144–68; MacBain 1982; Burckhardt 1988: 178–209; Novak 1991; Bergemann 1992: 146–7; Fontanella 1997: 499–500, 527; Rosenberger 1998: 210–40; Montero 2006: 13–29.

[18] A selective bibliography: Liebeschuetz 1979: 7–29; Jocelyn 1982–3: 158–61; Wardman 1982: 22–62, 179–84; Troiani 1984: 936–8; North 1990; Scheid 1997, 2001a: 19–22, 119–42 and 2012; Bendlin 1998; Tatum 1999b; Linke 2000; Belayche and Rüpke 2007; Pina Polo 2011: 252–3; Lacam 2012: 19–167.

[19] Wallace-Hadrill 1989 and 2008; Habinek and Schiesaro 1997.

[20] Rawson 1985; Moatti 1997; Rüpke 2007a: 129–33, 2010b; 2012a. Cf., from different angles, Rawson 1978b (= 1991: 324–51); Fuhrmann 1987; Frank 1992. See Rüpke 2012a: 145 on how 'rationality' must be understood in this context: '[t]he validity of religious assumptions is examined on the basis of nonreligious premises and evidence' (cf. also Rüpke 2002: 256, 2007a: 130, 2009b: 139 and 2010b: 41). Cf. Harrison 2006 for the view that rationality is an important category for the understanding of Greek religion. On rationality as a culturally situated concept cf. Geertz 2000: 23–5.

dualism between the concepts of 'rational' and 'irrational'. One can speak, with J. Rüpke, of a process of 'rationalisation' as ordering, systematisation and increasing complexity of the late Republican intellectual life; as the emergence of a set of new *rationes* in a number of different domains.[21] Its outcome is not a process in which divination declines and other, more 'rational', strategies for the prediction of the future emerge, as, for example, in the case of the decline of magic in early modern Britain which has been memorably explored by K. Thomas.[22] On the contrary, the deep structures underlying the Roman approach to divination and the prediction of the future did not change in the period under discussion in this book. In some quarters, however, a more systematic reflection upon the foundations of divination and its practice emerged. It was part of a wider reflection on the role of foresight and the viability of prediction. One of the main factors that prompted such reflection was the very significant and ever-changing role that divination played in Roman society, especially in the political domain, where there was a wide range of different sources of divination and prediction, often in competition with each other.

Just as it would be misguided to speak of a struggle between rational and irrational approaches to divination in late Republican culture, it would also be misleading to depict a neat dualism between a disenchanted, cynical and sophisticated elite, and a credulous and superstitious populace.[23] On the contrary, pluralism and complexity were the rules of the game. A range of different attitudes must have coexisted at all levels; the same people will have had different approaches to the same aspects of divination at different times in different contexts and situations. The concept of 'brain-balkanisation' has been aptly evoked. To use D. Feeney's elegant formulation, the 'educated Greeks and Romans of the post-classical era' were capable of entertaining 'different kinds of assent and criteria of judgement in different contexts, in ways that strike the modern observer as mutually contradictory'; arguably this does not apply only to the educated.[24] Moreover, a range of different experiences and opportunities will have been available, in both public and private contexts. The 'market model' outlined for Republican religion by A. Bendlin becomes especially appropriate when we turn our attention to the practitioners of divination and prediction that were available in Republican Rome, especially because it urges us to look

---

[21] Rüpke 2012a.   [22] Thomas 1971. Cf. Bremmer 1993: 169–72.
[23] It is doubtful that this model can be helpful to the understanding of any aspect of religious (or indeed intellectual) history: see the masterful discussion in Brown 1981: 12–22, 136–9.
[24] Feeney 1998: 14; cf. Veyne 1983: 52–69. *Contra* see Rüpke 2012a: 3. Religious behaviour is never monolithic (Paden 2000: 194–5).

beyond the boundaries of civic religion.[25] Such pluralism is the fundamental rule of the game and that competition was a fundamental part of it is by now uncontroversial. The problem – to pursue Bendlin's metaphor – is to what extent was deregulation essential to the religious pluralism of the middle and late Republic.[26] The extent of such pluralism was considerable and the main concern emerging from the late Republican debate, especially from Cicero's works, was the devising of methods of control and restraint of the range of divinatory experiences that were available, especially those with a prophetic remit. With the fall of the Republic and the advent of monarchy a check was placed on this situation, albeit in ways of which Cicero would not have approved. Augustus' main concern was not to revive piety, despite the claims of his propaganda, nor to repress what did not fall into the fold of traditional divination. His aim was to devise a new model of religious participation that revolved around imperial authority.[27] In this framework, the point was not to organise a repression of what did not comply with the agenda of the *princeps*. In fact, Augustus appears to have been less hostile to cults that did not belong in the framework of public religion than the Senate had been for most of the Republican period.[28] The aim of his interventions on this front was to make sure that all forms of religious experience were placed under the control of the emperor. Within the space of a generation, this aim was attained, although there remained voices that expressed reservations, in more or less open terms, as to the desirability of the Augustan settlement.

Any form of divination engages with a set of signs.[29] The notion of the 'power of signs' has been employed in a recent discussion of the use

[25] Bendlin 2000: esp. 130–5; cf. Bendlin 1998; see also, independently, Slater 2000. Cf. the sympathetic objections in Steuernagel 2007. The concept of 'market' was already evoked in North 1979: 98. Arena 2011: 147–59 rightly notes that the coexistence of different cults in the late Republic is not a symptom of religious liberty. In a convincing critique of the account of the rise of Christianity sketched in Stark 1996 (esp. 191–208), Beck 2006: 242–4 has contested the validity of the concept of 'market' to the study of ancient paganism and has argued that 'exchange' may be a more appropriate category; surely, however, it is appropriate to speak of a 'market' even for contexts to which the laws of classical or neoclassical economics do not apply.

[26] Nice forthcoming. Beck 2006: 242 notes that in ancient paganism the state is not 'the market regulator', because it is 'directly engaged in the business of religion'; the experience of several modern states shows that the two positions are not incompatible. Modern economic terminology (e.g. 'religious firms', 'religious consumers', 'religious goods', etc.) is recurrent in recent debate on the rise of Christianity: Stark 1996 and Beck 2006.

[27] Scheid 2001b: esp. 87–8. Jocelyn 1966: 96 argues that Augustus encouraged the belief that neglect of the gods was a serious political issue of his time; Beck 2006: 251 n. 4 claims that the view was widely shared; *contra* see Galinsky 1996: 290.

[28] Orlin 2008 and 2010: 208–14.

[29] Vernant 1948: 320–5; Manetti 1987: 9–56, 243–7 (= 1993: 1–35, 169–71); Burkert 1996: 156–63. A clarification of the use of the word 'sign' is in order: Cicero uses the word 'sign' (*signum* or *nota*) only when he refers to artificial divination, while he avoids it for natural divination (Allen 2008: 169

of divination by Augustus; the temptation to extend the association suggested by the title of P. Zanker's seminal book, *The Power of Images in the Age of Augustus*, to such an important domain as Roman religion is indeed strong.[30] However, signs had been deeply powerful in Rome for several centuries before the advent of the Principate. Their presence was ubiquitous; attempts to use and interpret them were manifold and pervasive. While his approach to the use of iconographic themes was undoubtedly revolutionary, in divinatory matters Augustus normalised and exercised greater control over a set of practices and discourses that was already in existence. This book sets out to explore this hinterland: to study how divination was practised in the last two centuries of the Republic; to account for its success and diversity; to explore the discourses about and around it; and to show in what respects the advent of the Principate marked a discontinuity with the Republican past.

We will be analysing a range of material that testifies to the complexity of the practice of, and of the views about, divination in this period. Of exceptional importance is Cicero's *De diuinatione*, which both testifies to the rich diversity of views and approaches and is a major (arguably the major) contribution in its own right to the debate. The first chapter of this book sets out to offer a reassessment of this work and of its historical significance.

n. 28). Although this study will be predominantly concerned with 'artificial' forms of divination (those most commonly practised in Roman state religion), the focus will be broader, and will be dealing with 'signs' that the Romans would not have necessarily called *signa*, such as dreams. Turner 1968: 5 prefers to use 'symbol' in divinatory contexts instead of 'sign': 'symbols are never simple; only signs, which by convention are restricted to a single referent, are simple'. As it will soon be apparent, the signs that will be discussed in the present study do not quite fit this definition. On the concept of symbol in antiquity see Struck 2004; esp. 90–6 on symbols and omens.

[30] Rosenberger 1998: 233–40. Cf. also Schmid 2005.

CHAPTER I

The De diuinatione *in context*

In 45 BC Cicero started working on a trilogy of treatises devoted to religious and theological matters.[1] All three took the form of a philosophical dialogue.[2] The first work was the *De natura deorum* ('On the nature of the gods'), in which three characters set out competing approaches to the definition of what the gods do, their attitude to mankind, and how their cult should be understood and practised. The second dialogue, the *De diuinatione* ('On divination'), was devoted to divination, its remit and its reliability, and the third, the *De fato* ('On fate'), which survives only in part, was a discussion on fate and its role in human affairs. That Cicero decided to devote an entire work of this trilogy to divination is a remarkable enough testimony to the importance of this aspect of Roman religion and prompts detailed discussion of its place in late Republican Rome. The framework in which this belonged is telling. Cicero's discussion on the gods and their cult was closely related to the prediction of and control over the future. An important factor that led Cicero to establish this connection was his familiarity with Hellenistic philosophy, in which the debate on divination and fate also had a theological dimension.[3] There was, however, another set of concerns that drove him. Divination consistently played an important role in the decision-making process at the core of Roman government. Precisely for this reason Cicero knew from personal experience that in Rome divination was in many ways intertwined with political foresight.[4]

The agenda of the dialogue

The *De diuinatione* was written between 45 and 44 and was finished only after the death of Caesar. On the surface, the structure of the dialogue is

---

[1] Cic. *Att.* 13.38.1 (15 August); 13.39.2 (16 August).
[2] MacKendrick 1989: 25 and Schofield 2008: 67 speak of 'dialogue-treatises'.
[3] Magris 1995; Bobzien 1998: 45–7, 87–96, 173–5, 346–9.   [4] Cf. Bernett 1995.

straightforward. In the first book, after a brief prologue, Cicero's brother Quintus makes the case for the existence of divination, while in the second book, after another introduction, Marcus Tullius Cicero himself responds to the views expressed by his brother and makes the case against the existence of divination.[5] The dialogue is rounded off by a conciliatory remark on the provisional nature of any philosophical conclusion and the importance of leaving the judgement of the enquirer free. Even if one were not to embrace J. Linderski's powerfully argued view that the *De diuinatione* was written in response to Caesar's increasingly tight stranglehold on religion, the position of the dictator (and probably god-in-the-making) was certainly a deep concern to Cicero as he was writing a work on the prediction of the future.[6] More importantly, the *De diuinatione* is part of a trilogy: it is an element of a broader investigation into religious matters, which is opened by a debate on the nature of the gods and concluded by a discussion of fate. Cicero carefully explains the connections between these works and the place of this project within his literary production in two introductions at the beginning of each book of the dialogue. The voice that speaks in these introductory chapters is distinct from that of the character 'Marcus' who makes the case against divination in book 2.[7]

Cicero took special care to put the *De diuinatione* in context, and not just because the treatise was written at a time that happened to be a critical juncture in Roman history; he also singled it out as a pivotal moment in his intellectual biography.[8] It is in this framework that the work must be understood. As the *catalogue raisonné* that opens the second book makes clear, the central concerns of the *De diuinatione* are the same as those of the *De natura deorum*, and indeed of the rest of Cicero's philosophical production, at least since the *Tusculanae*: writing a literature in Latin that would make the perusal of Greek texts unnecessary, and offering the most intellectually ambitious sectors of the Roman youth an education that would contrast and offset the ongoing moral decline and the grave

[5] In the following discussion the character that makes the case against divination in the *De diuinatione* will be called 'Marcus', rather than Cicero, as is by now customary in current scholarship. I shall argue, however, that the voice of Marcus and that of Cicero overlap at the end of the dialogue.
[6] Linderski 1982: 34–8 (= 1995a: 480–4); the *De diuinatione* receives hardly any discussion in Strasburger 1999. On the impact of Caesar on Cicero's philosophy cf. Krostenko 2000: 385–9; Gildenhard 2007a; Baraz 2012: 187–223. Lintott 2008: 358 argues that the Ides of March will have made Cicero wonder whether divine providence existed.
[7] Cic. *Div.* 1.7 and 2.3. On the strong integration of the three works cf. Begemann 2012: 19–22 ('theologische Trias'), 94.
[8] On the prefaces of Cicero's philosophical works see Ruch 1958: esp. 295–7; Schmidt 1978–9; Habinek 1994; Gildenhard 2007a: 89–206; Schofield 2008: 76–80; Baraz 2012: 150–86.

threat posed by the present historical circumstances.[9] This mission had a
strong political dimension, and it is telling that Cicero chose to set it out in
full just after the death of Caesar, when the need to reposition himself on
the political map was more urgent than ever; we do not find a statement of
comparable significance in the *De natura deorum*. Divination was a topic
that enabled Cicero to engage with two worlds in which he felt at home.
On the one hand, it was a fundamental feature of the Roman political
experience; a point which may also be found in the *De natura deorum*.[10]
On the other hand, it was intensely discussed by Hellenistic philosophers,
both in the highly technical debate about signs and in wider theological
disputes.[11] Similarly, the choice of dealing with divination was not just
a tribute to an intellectual tradition that Cicero studied with great care,
but also an earnest contribution to the Roman political debate.[12] In the
first lines of the *De natura deorum* Cicero specifies that the exploration of
theological matters is not just relevant to the development of philosophical
knowledge, but is also crucial for the regulation of religion (*ad moderandam
religionem*).[13]

The method that Cicero adopts in his discussion, namely the confrontation of different points of view, is typically Academic (*Div.* 2.8):

[9] Gildenhard 2007a: 80–3; the whole volume is an invaluable exploration of the political dimension
underlying any attempt to write about philosophy *à la grecque* in late Republican Rome. See
also Gotter 2001: 36–62, 277–83; Peppel 2007: 19; Baraz 2012: 96–127. Bringmann 1971: 90–110
ingeniously attempts to deconstruct the list in *Div.* 2.1, based on the view that Cicero spelled
out his ambition to provide his readers with a political education only after Caesar's death, subtly
misrepresenting the agenda he had when he wrote his earlier philosophical works; it is doubtful that
such a clear watershed may be identified. Cf. also the brief discussion of *Div.* 2.1 in Schäublin 1991:
343. *Catalogue raisonné*: Schofield 1986: 48.
[10] Cic. *Nat. D.* 3.5; the speaker here is the pontiff C. Aurelius Cotta. Ando 2008: 105–6; Rosenblitt
2011: 421–2.
[11] Pfeffer 1976: 43–112; GoldSchmidt 1978; Sedley 1982; Manetti 1987: 135–200 (= 1993: 53–138);
Hankinson 1988; Kany-Turpin (2005).
[12] Rüpke 2005a: 1455 (= 2005b: 232) argues that the negative case in *Div.* is based on an interpretative
model derived from Greek philosophy, which sits oddly with Roman social practice. Cf. Liebeschuetz
1995: 315 ('[i]t is likely that sophisticated scepticism with regard to purported divine signs was an
integral part of Roman *mos maiorum*, at least as understood by the political elite'); Beard 2012:
38–9. Toner 2009: 40–1 convincingly argues that the non-elite population was perfectly capable
of being sceptical or critical about individual diviners; cf. Evans-Pritchard 1937: 183–4 on the
extent of scepticism on witch-doctors among the Azande and its significance in their divinatory
system.
[13] Cic. *Nat D.* 1.1: *perobscura quaestio est de natura deorum, quae et ad cognitionem animi pulcherrima
est et ad moderandam religionem necessaria* ('the enquiry on the nature of the gods is very arduous,
and it is eminently appropriate for the exploration of the mind and essential to the regulation of
religion'). I understand *religio* as 'religious practice', rather than 'religious sentiment' (*contra* Ando
2010: 66). We shall come back to the central concept of *religio* in Chapter 2.

dicendum est mihi igitur ad ea quae sunt a te dicta, sed ita nihil ut adfirmem, quaeram omnia, dubitans plerumque et mihi ipse diffidens. si enim aliquid certi haberem quod dicerem, ego ipse diuinarem, qui esse diuinationem nego.

So I must talk about the things that you have said, but in order not to assert things dogmatically, I will question everything, mostly expressing doubts and mistrusting even myself. For if I were to say something certain, even I, who deny the existence of divination, would be divining.[14]

However, the point of the work is more than to provide people with the means to understand a problem and make up their minds. The agenda is that set out in the *De natura deorum*, to think about religion (*religio*) and, as it becomes apparent at the end of the second book of the *De diuinatione*, to defeat superstition (*superstitio*).[15] This is made clear by the final intervention of Marcus, with its emphasis on the importance of fighting *superstitio* – an aspect in which the voice of Marcus and that of Cicero coincide.[16] On the other hand, the recent suggestion that the main point of Cicero's *Div.* 2 was to question the viability of any form of prediction, and to argue that the links between past, present and future are random, is unconvincing.[17] One of the central concerns of *Div.* 2 (and indeed of the whole dialogue) is to establish a framework within which informed and reliable predictions can be made and a closer control over the future can be gained. It would also be misguided to envisage a Ciceronian *Kulturkampf*, in which Cicero takes on ancestral superstition and acts as a champion of reason and free thinking.[18] Cicero had a loaded cultural agenda to convey when he chose to write about religious and theological matters and the structure of the theological trilogy that he put together was expected to convey a cultural

---

[14] Schultz 2009: 199 argues that Marcus is here stating his own 'uncertainty' about the arguments that he is about to put forward (cf. her translation: 'And so I must speak to these arguments you have made, but so that I do so in such a way as to assert nothing positively, I, generally in doubt and unsure of myself, will call everything into question. For if I were to accept anything I am saying as certain, I, who am denying divination exists, would be prophesying'); see also Leonhardt 1999: 43. On my reading, this statement says more about the method which Cicero is going to use in putting forward his views than about his commitment to them (cf. also Timpanaro 1988: 332 n. 14).

[15] There will be a detailed discussion of *superstitio* and *religio* in Chapter 2: for the purposes of the present discussion I use the established English translation of each word, even if this is not necessarily an accurate rendition of a complex term.

[16] Cic. *Div.* 2.148.

[17] Fox 2007: 211. The view that the dialogue ends with a 'völlig skeptische ἐποχή' (Leonhardt 1999: 48) is equally unconvincing.

[18] Opsomer 1996: 165–7 shows that it is unhelpful to understand Hellenistic philosophy in light of a struggle between scepticism and dogmatism.

project. A radical scrutiny and critique of divination as it was practised in mid first-century BC Rome and some innovative thinking about the limits of prediction were part of the brief.

The word *diuinatio*, which Cicero used throughout the dialogue, did not coincide with the boundaries of Roman public divination, but enabled Cicero to discuss a wide range of problems and materials. There was no formally defined category of 'divination'; precisely because *diuinatio* afforded so much creativity, Cicero's overview of divination is also an invaluable guide to the historical practice of divination in Republican Rome. The construction of divination outlined in the dialogue, however, poses some problems of great significance, which can hamper our historical investigation unless they are clarified at the outset. First of all, it risks creating a sort of 'tunnel vision': late Republican reflection on divination is very important and prominent, but it has deep roots. The discussion of divination that is developed in the dialogue, and notably the critique in book 2, was directly shaped by the concerns that a member of the political elite like Cicero developed in the mid first century BC and was the product of a specific intellectual climate. However, critical reflection on divination and on Roman religion in general had begun already several generations before. The developments of the last years of the Republic must be understood in a longer-term perspective, which arguably begins as early as Plautus.[19] Secondly, it is unhelpful to use the disenchanted critique of divination that is offered in *Div.* 2 as an argument in favour of the view that Roman religion went through a steady decline in the last century of the Republic. Divination was ubiquitous in the world of the late Roman Republic and it was taken very seriously by many, including Cicero.[20] The *De diuinatione* is the most powerful example of such interest and of the liveliness of the debate on this problem. The third problem that must be spelled out is the *De diuinatione*'s heavy, and perhaps inevitable, bias towards elite perceptions and experiences of Roman religion. In fact, most of the evidence for the practice of divination in Rome and Italy tends to be focused on the elite, not least because most of the surviving evidence is literary. There is not, for instance, a body of evidence for non-elite approaches to, and uses of divination comparable to the corpus of

---

[19] Bendlin 1998: 153 and 2009: 7–10; Rüpke 2009b: 137–43, 2011d, 2012a: 51–125 and 2012b, reacting to (and expanding upon) Moatti 1997. On the intellectual and religious developments of the second century BC cf. also, from a different angle, Rawson 1973 (= 1991: 80–101) and 1974 (= 1991: 149–68); Beard, North and Price 1998: 1.108–13.

[20] Cf. Struck 2007: 3–6 on the ubiquitousness and intellectual significance of divination throughout the ancient world.

the Dodona oracle consultations recently studied by E. Eidinow.[21] In this context of 'top-heavy' evidence, the *De diuinatione* is arguably the source that gives the fullest account of the diversity and complexity of divination in the last century of the Roman Republic – whatever line of interpretation one may choose for its overall scope and agenda.[22]

This leads to a fourth problem. In Cicero's plans the *De diuinatione* was part of a broader effort to explore the foundations of Roman religion, which was, however, confined to the boundaries of some quarters of the political and intellectual elite; its impact on the rest of the Roman society is difficult to assess. Arguably, this impact was far from deep. It is important, however, to explore the factors that made that critical effort possible and indeed necessary. Roman divination survived the *De diuinatione* and even the other examples of criticism or mistrust that can be found in the literature of the Augustan period. The evidence for divinatory activity under the Principate is rich, widespread and diverse at both the public and the private levels: imperial attempts to repress and curtail it are testimony to its vitality. There was no long wave of scepticism. Moreover, no comparable attempt to probe the foundations and remit of divination appears to have been made in Roman culture after Cicero.[23]

Structure and argument

The relationship of the *De diuinatione* to its historical context is complex and somewhat enigmatic. Recent scholarship has stressed the elusiveness of this work and of its conclusions.[24] No consensus appears to have been

---

[21] Eidinow 2007. The *sortes Astrampsychi*, a second- or third-century AD collection of oracular questions and answers known through several Greek papyri and attested well beyond antiquity, give a valuable glimpse into the concerns of the enquirers: Toner 2009: 46–52, 206–7; Naether 2010; Beard 2011: 101–4.

[22] North 1990: 52 evocatively speaks of a 'picture of diffusion'. On the elite bias of the evidence cf. Tatum 1999b: 276–8; imperial astrological literature is a possible exception (MacMullen 1971 = 1990: 218–24, 364–8).

[23] Cf. Altheim 1938: 375; Briquel 1997a: 40–1. Seneca never embarked on a full-scale discussion of divination, although he was interested in haruspicy (*NQ* 2.32–50): Armisen-Marchetti 2000; Gigandet 2005: 86–9. He also wrote a *De superstitione*, now lost: fragments and discussion in Lausberg 1970: 197–225; see also Bendlin 1998: 335–8; Tatum 1999b: 273–4; Setaioli 2007: 333–4, 357. Plutarch's reflection on divination and prediction is heavily indebted to the Hellenistic philosophical tradition, but does not engage with the role of divination in the Roman world: excellent treatments in Opsomer 1996: 172–94 and Veyne 1999. Van Nuffelen 2011: 16–17 argues that the 'academic tendencies' that prevail in Cicero were mostly absent from the reflection on religion in the early empire.

[24] Beard 1986, Schofield 1986 and, from a different angle, Denyer 1985. See also Schofield 2008: 71 and Beard 2012: 37 n. 68. Cf. Heibges 1969: 305, who cautioned against using Cicero's work to deduce his own views on religion. The views of Beard, Schofield and Denyer have found considerable

reached about the scope and purpose of the treatise. The central contention of the present discussion is that the argument and scope of the *De diuinatione* may best be understood in the light of its historical and intellectual context and by considering its place in Cicero's intellectual programme.[25]

Clarification about the significance of the dialogue as a historical source is necessary. It has recently been argued that the *De diuinatione*, like the philosophical treatises of Cicero, should not be included in a historical account of Roman religion; the history of Roman religion is about ritual and performance, not about theology.[26] The discussion that follows is based on different premises. Theological developments are a crucial aspect for the study of the history of any religion and they are also essential to the study of rituals and performance. Of course Cicero's attitude to religion, or indeed divination, was not representative of the views of most of his contemporaries. However, the very existence of a treatise like the *De diuinatione* shows that the topic was a worthy matter of debate, both political and intellectual, in some quarters of the Roman elite. Cicero knew that his work would circulate within a relatively small constituency.[27] It is difficult to reconstruct how this debate and the intellectual developments that it made possible influenced religious practice. In fact, the problem may be more convincingly approached the other way round: the late Republican debate on religion was prompted by developments in the sphere of religious practice and ritual. The *De diuinatione* is one of the best ancient sources for the study of these developments. It is also an invaluable source of events and *Realien* pertaining to Roman religion.[28] A proper understanding of the argumentative and ideological framework in which that evidence belongs

support: Scheid 1987–9: 128–9; Rosenberger 1998: 79–80; Leonhardt 1999: 39, 66–73; North 2000b: 79; Rasmussen 2000: 17–18, 23–4 and 2003: 183–98; Fox 2007: 209–40; Lisdorf 2007: 25; Samotta 2009: 251–2; Schultz 2009; Arena 2011: 155; Baraz 2012: 189–90. Krostenko 2000 argues that the dialogue is intended to showcase the flaws of both the fideistic and sceptical approaches; cf. also Begemann 2012: 72–6, 100–2. Rüpke 2012a: 186–7 stresses the importance of the Roman antecedents to Cicero's reflection and its embeddedness in an 'encyclopaedic' project.

[25] For a robust response to Beard, Denyer and Schofield see Timpanaro 1994. See also Brunt 1989: 194 n. 33; Blänsdorf 1991; Lévy 1992: 581–8; Repici 1995; Moatti 1997: 173–9; Escobar 2002: 54; Harris 2003: 27 (cf. Harris 2009: 182–3); Kany-Turpin 2004: 52, 69–86; Setaioli 2005: 243–9; Guillaumont 2006: 325–54. Schäublin 1991: 343–6, 352–3, 394–7, 400–18, Wardle 2006: 8–28 and Lehoux 2012: 23, 35 take nuanced stances.

[26] Gradel 2002: 3–4: 'interpretation should be based on a study of ritual, not merely as a reflection of an underlying theology, but in its own right, as what traditional Roman religion was all about: rituals constructing, and not merely reflecting, the theology, the world and its social order'. Cf. also Jocelyn 1966: 103–4 and North 2000b: 79: 'these philosophical tracts should be left on one side as evidence of religious activities and views'.

[27] Cic. *Div.* 2.5: *pauci utinam*!

[28] Schultz 2009: 201–2 notes that the 'Romanness of the discussion' must be regarded as an essential feature of Cicero's intellectual agenda.

and a reconsideration of the argument of the work are essential, if we are to use them as historical sources.

In recent studies of the *De diuinatione*, much has been made of the alleged inconclusiveness of the debate in the dialogue and of the mismatch between the views of Cicero, the prominent historical figure who speaks in the authorial voice, and the voices of the characters Quintus and Marcus, who should not be seen as mere reflections of the personal views of the historical Quintus and Marcus Tullius Cicero. This approach has the merit of showing how sophisticated the structure of the *De diuinatione* is, but fails to address some pressing questions. The place of the dialogue within the religious trilogy written by Cicero in the mid forties is one of them.[29] The *De fato* may have reached us in a mutilated form, but surely it deserves to be taken into account in a study of the *De diuinatione*. What survives of the treatise is a lengthy, continuous exposé addressed by Cicero to Hirtius; in one of the lacunae in the text, however, Hirtius set out the Stoic theory of Fate, which Cicero extensively criticises in the following chapters.[30] Cicero himself states that he lacked the time to give the work the same dialogic form as the previous two parts of the trilogy.[31] There is wide scholarly consensus that the treatise expressed a clear preference against determinism: indeed, what survives of the *De fato* is essentially a sustained critique of the Stoic approach (5–20, 28–45) and an attack on the Epicurean theory on causation (20–8, 46–8).[32] The scholars who maintain that the *De diuinatione* is not an attack on divination because it is argued *in utramque partem* (i.e. on both sides) do not account for Cicero's change of strategy in the work that he wrote immediately afterwards, and do not explain how this may fit within the framework of the trilogy.[33] It is conceivable that the finale of the *De fato* definitively clarified the scope of the whole trilogy. In what follows I shall argue that this is probably clear enough from what survives. On the other hand, great emphasis has been placed on the

[29] Cf. however Beard 1986: 34, 36; Schultz 2009: 197; Begemann 2012: 69.
[30] Lacuna B, with Sharples 1991: 18–19. Gildenhard 2007a: 83–6 and Schallenberg 2008: 92–3 explore the implications on the relationship between politics, rhetoric and philosophy suggested by the conversation between Cicero and Hirtius that precedes the beginning of Cicero's exposé (*Fat.* 3–5). Strasburger 1999: 47–8 and Schallenberg 2008: 34–8 explain the choice of Hirtius as a character of the dialogue with Cicero's wish to strengthen his political association with the consul of 43.
[31] Cic. *Fat.* 1.1. Sharples 1991: 3–6 and 1995: 246, 269–71; Bernett 1995: 66–83. The haste in which it was written does not prevent the *De fato* from being arguably 'the most terse and logically complex of any of Cicero's philosophical works' (Sharples 1995: 271); cf. also Begemann 2012: 66. Blänsdorf 1991: 63–4 offers some guesswork on the connections between *Div.* 2 and the *De fato*.
[32] Sharples 1991: 16–24 (cf. the notes of caution at iv and 23); Gildenhard 2007c: 99–100 ('he might as well have entitled [it] *In fatum*'); Schallenberg 2008: 72–81, 298–305; Begemann 2012: 22–69, 130–4.
[33] On Cicero's use of *disputatio in utramque partem* in his philosophical work see Leonhardt 1999: 13–25.

apparent contradiction between the finale of the *De natura deorum* and the
finale of the *De diuinatione*, which is supposed to reflect the absence of a
clear authorial voice in the theological works and the open, non-dogmatic
nature of that intellectual project.[34] Different readings are possible. The
first dialogue is set in a specific historical context, namely during Cicero's
youth, at some point between 77 and 75. The conciliatory remarks that
Cicero makes at the end of the dialogue may well be a reference to his
early views on theology, which were influenced by Stoicism. His transition
to the Academy is a later development and it is reflected, inter alia, by
the structure of the *De diuinatione*.[35] Alternatively, the finale of the *De
natura deorum* can be read as the cautious assessment of a man who holds
different views on different subjects, and subscribes to Stoic theology while
questioning divination.

Surprisingly little interest has been roused by the presence of Cicero's
brother, Quintus, as one of the main characters of the *De diuinatione*. It
has been argued that the two characters are put on the same level, that
they have the same prestige and that therefore their arguments must have
the same weight; even the roughly identical length of the two exposés
has been viewed as a clue to the philosophical agenda of the work.[36]
Some important aspects, however, must be considered. Cicero's choice to
personify the supporter of the negative case is a very strong statement, which
cannot be lightly dismissed.[37] Indeed, far from undermining the project,
the conclusion of the dialogue should not be read, for all its Academic
courteousness, as evidence that the discussion ends with no winners. In
the finale of the dialogue the voice of Marcus becomes indistinguishable
from that of Cicero the author that we hear in the prologues of books 1

---

[34] See e.g. Beard 1986: 35; Lévy 1992: 545.

[35] This hypothesis is not canvassed in the interesting overview of the possible interpretations of *Nat. D.*
3.95 in Tarán 1987 (= 2001: 455–77). DeFilippo 2000 reads this passage as evidence for a 'dogmatic
element in Cicero scepticism' (186); cf. Rüpke 2012a: 199–200. Dyck 2003: 7 argues that Cicero
wanted to portray an 'evenly divided court', with Velleius and Cotta on the one side, Balbus and
himself on the other; Schofield 2008: 73 emphasises that even in this case the choice is left to the
reader.

[36] Beard 1986: 44–5 stresses the 'parity of status' of Quintus and Marcus and draws a contrast with the
Tusculanae; *contra* cf. Begemann 2012: 73–5. Length: Leonhardt 1999: 38–9, 44–5. Pease 1920: 15–16
argues that the dialogue is 'by implication' dedicated to Quintus, since he is the only character along
with Marcus himself; *contra* cf. Baraz 2012: 209–10. Rüpke 2012a: 202 argues that the social position
of Marcus the augur is not without importance, as it conveys further authority to his statements.

[37] Harris 2003: 27 (= 2009: 182) also argues that the choice of presenting the case against divination
in the second book is significant: it is 'the standard capping position which ancient rhetoric gave
to what was viewed as the stronger argument'. This is certainly the case in historiography; it is
doubtful, however, that the principle may also apply to philosophical dialogues. I have not been
able to find any evidence that it was ever codified as such in ancient rhetoric.

and 2. We find Marcus establishing a link between the *De diuinatione* and the *De natura deorum* in the same terms which Cicero uses at the outset of book 2.[38]

Biography cannot always explain complex intellectual choices. However, Cicero's choice of having his brother as his counterpart in a philosophical dialogue deserves some discussion. Despite the gentleman-like tone of the conversation, it is doubtful that Cicero intended his brother's views to carry the same weight as his own. Something more subtle, and less flattering to Quintus, may be at work. The relationship between the two brothers had gone through difficult times in the fifties and it improved only shortly before the inception of the treatise.[39] In fact, Cicero's correspondence shows that the worst strain between the two men existed between 48 and 47. Quintus apparently tried to place his brother in a bad light with Caesar, probably in order to earn the pardon of the winner of the civil war. The terms of the controversy are largely unknown, because the letters in which Quintus laid down his grievances were not included in the corpus of Cicero's correspondence. Even when the two brothers were back on speaking terms, apparently thanks to Caesar's indifference to Quintus' allegations and to Atticus' patient mediation, they never became as close as they had been; not even the death of Tullia, Cicero's beloved daughter, in February 45 changed things. There is a case to argue that there is a private subtext to the *De diuinatione* and that the dissent between the two characters did not have a purely literary or philosophical dimension.[40]

An objection to this reconstruction is that featuring as a character of one of Cicero's dialogues was regarded as a great honour by many members of the Roman intellectual elite. Cicero's correspondence includes several friendly requests to the great man from people who wished to appear in his dialogues: even Varro expressed a desire to be included in one of Cicero's works and he was indeed portrayed as Cicero's interlocutor in Cicero's *Academica posteriora*.[41] The role of a character like Varro, however, was arguably different from that of Quintus in *De diuinatione*. The role of

---

[38] Cf. *Div.* 2.148 and 2.3.

[39] The evidence for the tensions between Marcus and Quintus is gathered and discussed in Shackleton Bailey 1971: 179–85. Mitchell 1991: 264–5 is rather more cautious.

[40] Quintus had already been pictured as a character in a Ciceronian dialogue: his role in the *De oratore*, for instance, is quite flattering (Wiseman 1966: 110). See the invaluable directory of the participants in Cicero's philosophical dialogues in Linderski 1989: 108–9 (= 1995a: 47–8).

[41] See esp. *Att.* 13.25.3: *uolo Varronem, praesertim cum ille desideret* ('I want Varro, and the more so because he wishes it'). See Kumaniecki 1962: 236–7; Glucker 1978: 409–15; Linderski 1989: 112–13 (= 1995a: 51–2); Baier 1997: 27; Schofield 2008: 80–1; Clark 2010: 191; Baraz 2012: 209. Cf. Shackleton Bailey 1971: 217: 'Varro, of whom Cicero always stood somewhat in awe'. The intellectual exchange between the two men was intense, especially in the forties: André 1975: 14–21; Momigliano 1984:

Quintus in the dialogue is merely to lay out the case in favour of divination (how accurately and competently he does that is a different matter). He plays no part in shaping the overall argument and scope of the dialogue, which is defined by the framework provided in the prologues to each book and in the conclusions, nor does he make any substantial contribution to the development of the argument.[42] In the last two chapters of book 2, the outcome of the discussion is summarised by Marcus, whose voice blends with that of Cicero the author.[43] Different people will no doubt have viewed their presence as characters in Cicero's dialogues in different ways, but it seems unlikely that Quintus' role in the *De diuinatione*, while prominent and ostensibly significant, will have been regarded as flattering, even by Cicero's contemporaries.

Cicero's decision to style himself as the central character of the dialogue on divination can be better understood in light of a passage of his correspondence that summarised his discussion with Sallustius on the composition of the *De re publica*. In a letter to Quintus, Cicero recalls that the original version of the dialogue was set in 129 and featured Scipio Aemilianus, Laelius and other prominent figures of that period, all discussing the organisation of the State and the ideal citizen.[44] When Sallustius attended a private reading of the first part of the work, he urged his friend Cicero to change strategy radically: the dialogue would have carried more conviction if it had been set in the contemporary period, and with Cicero as its main figure. Sallustius used an intriguing analogy to support his case. Cicero was a former consul, not Heraclides Ponticus, the fourth-century BC philosopher and cosmologist from Asia Minor who played a crucial role in the definition of the dialogue as literary genre.[45] Therefore, his duty was to set his dialogue in his own time and to take the lead in the discussion by staging himself as a character. Cicero claims to have been deeply struck by his friend's words. After that conversation, Cicero appears to have revisited his original project; instead of writing a dialogue in nine books, he wrote six books *De re publica*, which were still set in the second century as originally planned, and wrote three books *De legibus* in which he and his brother Quintus were the characters – a 'contemporary pendant'.[46] Cicero stressed his debt to and interest in the work of Heraclides on various occasions and

---

204–9 (= 1987: 268–75); Baier 1997: 15–70; Tarver 1997: 142–5, 154–5, 161–4; Baraz 2012: 80–6, 207–9. Wiseman 2009a: 107–29 draws attention to the areas of disagreement.

[42] *Contra* Schultz 2009: 202–5, with special emphasis on Quintus' choice of *exempla*.

[43] Cic. *Div.* 2.148–50. Cf. Schäublin 1991: 413: 'Paradoxerweise ist es der Gegner der *divinatio*, der nun wirklich Ordnung schafft.'

[44] Cic. *Q fr.* 3.5.1–2.   [45] On Heraclides see Fortenbaugh and Pender 2009.   [46] Dyck 2004: 10.

there is no doubt that his philosophical dialogues were influenced by the model of Heraclides' work. The passage discussed above has recently been read as further evidence for Cicero's strategy of distancing himself from the characters and effacing his authorial voice.[47] An opposite interpretation can be suggested. Sallustius persuaded Cicero that the philosophical treatises in which he focused on problems of specific political significance should have him as a leading character. He was a man with a great political past and a prestigious position within the State, and his predicament could not be compared to that of a Greek intellectual, let alone one who had lived centuries earlier. Refraining from speaking in the first person would have meant not doing justice to the potential of his philosophical message. Heraclides may well be a model for Cicero's philosophical prose, but the emphasis of this passage is on the contrast between the two men, their positions and their aims. If this reading is correct, it is not surprising to see Cicero as a character in the *De legibus*, where he outlines the laws of the ideal state, and in the *De diuinatione*, where he engages with a problem that was of great political importance and on which he, as an augur, could claim to have special expertise. These works may have offered plenty of room for future debate and disagreement, but Cicero had a clear message to convey in both cases.

A further problem needs discussing, namely the ineffectiveness of some of Marcus' objections to Quintus, argued by N. Denyer and often evoked by the supporters of the 'open work' case. Denyer argued that Cicero substantially misunderstood the basics of the Stoic theory of divination, which is based on the assumption that divination is about reading the messages that the gods address to mankind.[48] The core of Denyer's objections is that Marcus treats divination as a science, while the Stoics carefully distinguish between science and divination, although they see no contradiction or even competition between the two.[49] At the same time, they do

---

[47] Fox 2007: 86–8 and 2009: 52–60. Cf. also Dyck 1998: 153–5, who argues that Cicero's willingness to consider Sallustius' objection is a clear sign that the content of the philosophical dialogues set before Cicero's lifetime is not geared to the speaker; it is impossible to establish, however, what changes Cicero would have actually made to the dialogue, had he decided to follow Sallustius' suggestion.

[48] Denyer 1985; see also Hankinson 1988: 151; Krostenko 2000: 357 n. 12. Cf. the responses of Timpanaro 1994: 241–57; Setaioli 2005: 250–1. Schmitz 1993: 178–86 makes the case – without engaging with Denyer's work – for the originality of Cicero's engagement with the Stoic theories on divination.

[49] Cf. Sext. Emp. *Math.* 9.132, where divination (μαντική) is defined as a science (ἐπιστήμη). See Hankinson 1988: 125–35; Obbink 1992: 211–14; Barton 1994a: 16, 188–9 n. 56; Allen 2008: 161–5; Gourinat 2012: 558. Cf. also, from a different angle, Rasmussen 2003: 199–211. The distinction between natural and artificial divination goes back to Plato (*Phdr.* 244c–d and *Ti.* 71e–72a) and was taken up by Cicero: Manetti 1987: 34–9, 216–19 (= 1993: 19–23, 149–50). Chirassi Colombo 2012: 221 finds it 'très pertinente', while M. Flower 2008: 90 and Johnston 2008: 9 point out that it does

not argue that the things which science cannot predict are fortuitous and therefore unpredictable; on the contrary, they are intelligible to the wise man. Indeed, Marcus seems to miss this point (*Div.* 2.15) and he makes the more significant mistake of not regarding divination as a practice that deciphers the messages coming from the gods. Omens and portents are, according to the Stoics, one of the forms of the language of the gods and a means of communication with mankind.[50]

Many of the Stoic sources that Cicero used while he was writing the *De diuinatione* are lost.[51] However, the main reason why Cicero insisted on depicting divination as an art may be found in the Roman context. The form of prophetic divination he was most accustomed to, that of the haruspices – the Etruscan diviners who were routinely consulted by the Roman State for the interpretation and expiation of prodigies – presented itself as a discipline, or indeed as an art. The college of the augurs acted on the fringe of divination, and had a complex set of rituals and codified practices.[52] It was the whole Roman experience, based on the primacy of ritual and priestly intermediation, that encouraged Cicero to view divination as an art and to overlook – deliberately or not – the Stoic model of a direct interaction between gods and mankind. The *De diuinatione* is part of an attempt to produce a Roman discourse on religion; against this background, it is not surprising that Cicero used an approach to the Stoic theory of divination that was not suitable from a technical standpoint. Moreover, the philosophical flaws of Marcus' reply do not necessarily imply that Cicero was aware of them and that he was not genuinely interested in showing the strength of the negative argument. The shortcomings of both cases presented in the *De diuinatione* should not be seen as evidence that the dialogue ends without conveying a view that is meant to be prevailing.[53]

Cicero's religious trilogy conveys a forceful political message, although it cannot be read as a political manifesto. Its intended audience was the

---

    not do justice to the range and complexity of divinatory activities in the Greek world: the μάντις is not inspired in the same way as the Pythia; diviners who serve on military campaigns could claim divine inspiration; cf. also Rubino 1839: 44 n. 1.

[50] Hankinson 1988: 139 rightly warns that there was not one Stoic position on divination, but that there was a broad spectrum of views, which tended to recognise divination as a useful, if not entirely intelligible, contribution to human understanding. See also Lévy 1997: 325–43; Struck 2007: 6–16. Opposite approach in Gourinat 2012.

[51] Cf. Repici 1996 on the possible Socratic precedents of the model of the 'Stoic diviner'. Guillaumont 2006 provides a thorough overview of the problem of the sources of the *De diuinatione*; see also Pease 1920: 20–8; Finger 1929; Kany-Turpin 2004: 28–52; Wardle 2006: 28–36.

[52] Cf. Bloch 1989: 80–1 on ritualisation, transmission of traditional authority, and 'removal of authority from the person of power-holders'.

[53] A different reading in Krostenko 2000, although I agree that the ambition of the dialogue – to use Krostenko's own words (at 385) – is to set out 'the theory and practice of a limited, formal and symbolic divination' (*contra*, cf. Lehoux 2012: 37).

most intellectually lively sectors of the Roman and Italian elites. The aim was to encourage a new approach to religion, the message was complex, sophisticated and ambitious. Its novelty lay in its systematic approach, as much as in Cicero's personal (and indeed expert) involvement in Roman public religion. Although this discussion has taken issue with the general interpretation of the *De diuinatione* given by Beard and Schofield, their emphasis on the experimental character of the trilogy (especially of the *De diuinatione* and *De fato*) and on the effort of the *De diuinatione* to leave the door open to alternative approaches is certainly appropriate.[54] Cicero, however, expressed his views on divination very clearly; the negative case made by Marcus largely coincided with his own views.

The *De diuinatione* and divinatory practice: between augury and haruspicy

Divination is akin to grammar and philology.[55] The point is made by Cicero in two passages of the *De diuinatione*, where he establishes an analogy between the divinatory ability of the seers and the clairvoyance of the *grammatici* who set out to interpret a literary text; the analogy was already noticed by Panaetius, who used it to celebrate the skills of Aristarchus.[56] The affinity between the riddles faced by the reader of literary texts and the riddles presented by oracles is often pointed out in the ancient evidence, as the history of the word *ainigma* shows.[57] Both kinds of knowledge are specialised, are based on the scrutiny of a certain set of signs (or, to put it in different terms, of data), and are used in order to produce informed responses.[58] It is not fortuitous that a critical reflection on divination, its viability and its limits took shape in Rome at about the same time as a

---

[54] Cf. Schofield 2008: 82: 'it seems reasonable to infer that the author shares the interlocutor's scepticism – even though the dialogue is not written to tell us that'.

[55] Ginzburg 1986: 166–70.

[56] Cic. *Div.* 1.34 and 116. Panaetius: Ath. 14.634c–d. See Repici 1996: 51–2; Kany-Turpin 2003b: 71 ('les signes auguraux doivent être énoncés et, tout comme les signes linguistiques, ils n'ont de valeur que les uns par rapport aux autres'; cf. also Kany-Turpin 2004: 61); Wardle 2006: 198. Glassner 2012: 36–52 shows how the analogy with semiology applies eminently well to Mesopotamian divination.

[57] Manetti 1987: 41–7, 244–5 n. 10 (= 1993: 29–31, 170 n. 10); Schmitz 1993; Sluiter 1997: 163–5; Struck 2004: 90–6, 167–87 (171–9 on αἴνιγμα), 2005 and 2010: 63–4 (connection between divinatory interpretation and allegorical reading); Johnston 2008: 51–6.

[58] Cf. Bottéro 1974: 161–8. Divination as science: Bottéro 1974: 171–8; Rasmussen 2003: 199–211. 'Religious specialists': Rüpke 1996a; Lundgreen 2011: 138–46. Purcell 1995: 28–34 deals with the link between alea, the alphabet, numeracy, literacy and ordering in Greek and Roman culture; Beard 2011: 92 fascinatingly argues that 'the ancients' inhabited an 'aleatory society'. Cf. Vandermeersch 1974: 44–51 on the use of numbers as divinatory symbols in ancient China and the discussion of 'mantology' (i.e. 'the study of material which is ominous or oracular in scope and content') as a special kind of semiotics in Heimlich 2010: 175.

critical reflection on grammar. In at least one case the two intellectual pursuits were closely related: the grammarian Ennius wrote two books *De litteris syllabisque*, a work *De metris* and a treatise *De augurandi disciplina*.[59] Men like Varro, Caesar and Cicero were concerned with the debate on both sides.

Despite being aware of its affinity with literary criticism, Cicero deals with divination using the standards of natural science. N. Denyer argued that the only serious challenge to the Stoic theory of divination could come from an attack on its theological framework, which Cicero failed to make and which was not made until the rise of Christianity.[60] Cicero, however, does make an attempt to clarify his theological views. The finale of *Div.* 2 may offer some interesting clues. Marcus' exposé ends with a reference to the importance of preserving ancestral institutions on the one hand and, on the other hand, to the importance of paying tribute to the might and beauty of nature, which deserves the admiration of the whole of mankind. It may not be a very original arrangement, with its combination of Platonic and Stoic elements, but it is an effort to define a divine power that does not communicate with mankind through signs and the harmony of which should be comprehended through the study of nature (*Div.* 2.148–9):

> nec uero (id enim diligenter intellegi uolo) superstitione tollenda religio tollitur. nam et maiorum instituta tueri sacris caerimoniisque retinendis sapientis est, et esse praestantem aliquam aeternamque naturam, et eam suspiciendam admirandamque hominum generi pulchritudo mundi ordoque rerum caelestium cogit confiteri. quam ob rem, ut religio propaganda etiam est quae est iuncta cum cognitione naturae, sic superstitionis stirpes omnes eligendae.

> But I want to make clear that the elimination of superstition does not entail the elimination of religion. For I consider it the part of the wise man to preserve the institutions of our ancestors by retaining their sacred rites and ceremonies. Furthermore, the celestial order and the beauty of the universe compel me to confess that there is some excellent and eternal being that deserves the respect and admiration of men. For this reason, just as it is a duty to extend the influence of true religion, which is closely associated with the knowledge of nature, so it is a duty to weed out every root of superstition.[61]

---

[59] Suet. *Gram.* 1. It is unlikely that this Ennius and the poet were the same person (Timpanaro 1978: 84–5 n. 1; Rawson 1985: 130, 302); a late second- or early first-century BC context seems plausible. Rüpke 2012a: 6 draws a parallel between the discursive tradition on rhetoric and that on divination.

[60] Denyer 1985: 9–10.

[61] This definition of nature may be seen as a sign of continuity with the statement of sympathy to the Stoic theology at the end of the *De natura deorum*. There is clear evidence of Platonic influences in the *De diuinatione*, esp. 1.115: Glucker 1999 and Tarrant 2000. On the Aristotelian influences on

The definition of such divine power is the object of a serious inquest into *religio*, which can lead to the demise of *superstitio*. It may not be very impressive, but it may be viewed as an earnest attempt to rethink the theological dimension of the problem. One of the arguments most frequently used by those who view the *De diuinatione* as an open work, that has no clear philosophical conclusion, is the claim that Cicero's attitude to divination was not consistently critical and that on many occasions he publicly declared his support for it. This argument is, after all, a revised version of the old distinction between Cicero as a philosopher and Cicero as a politician, which was popular with positivistic *Altertumswissenschaft* and which must be overcome if we are to understand the political dimension of Cicero's philosophy.[62] It is Quintus who reminds Marcus of his inconsistencies and urges him to come to terms with them, with a punctiliousness that may partly be explained in the light of an uneasy personal relationship.[63] It is worth looking at these cases in some detail. In 1.59 Quintus mentions a dream that Marcus had some years before, during his exile, in which he received a visit from Marius, who encouraged him to keep hoping and foretold his return to Rome; Marcus replies that the dream is not evidence for the power of divination, but a symptom of the prominence of Marius in Cicero's imagination at the time.[64] Elsewhere Quintus mentions a bad omen of the imminent defeat of Pompey at Pharsalus that Marcus had witnessed.[65] Moreover, he later says that in his poem *Marius* Marcus had portrayed a prodigy involving a snake and an eagle, which Marius read as a sign of his future glory, thanks to his augural expertise.[66] Marcus' responses are consistently dismissive. Only on one occasion does Marcus seem to falter and not to find a convincing reply to Quintus – but the way he overcomes the hesitation is revealing. Again, Marcus' earlier poetic efforts are brought to the fore: Quintus does not fail to note that in the *Consulatus suus* there was a long section about the

the discussions of dreams in the dialogue see Kany-Turpin and Pellegrin 1989: esp. 236–41; Repici 1991: 167–71, 177–203; van der Eijk 1993. Lehoux 2012: 37–46 views Marcus' attempt to understand nature within a theological context as a powerful challenge to Quintus' enumerative argument in favour of divination.

[62] See e.g. Kroymann 1975. Cf. Beard's recent acknowledgment of the importance of exploring 'the important intellectual links between the *De divinatione* and the speeches' (2012: 18 n. 68).

[63] Cf. Haury 1955: 200: in the first book 'l'interrogation agressive remplace ironie et humour'.

[64] Cic. *Div.* 1.59 and 2.67. On Cicero's decision to publish this dream see Rosenberger 2007: 302. Stok 2010 draws attention to the analogies between this dream and that of Scipio in *Rep.* 6.10–29.

[65] Cic. *Div.* 1.68.

[66] Cic. *Div.* 1.106 (= F 17 Courtney). See Courtney 1993: 175–6 and Goldberg 1995: 141–4; on Cicero's recontextualising of his poetry in the *De diuinatione* see Krostenko 2000: 380–5 and Spahlinger 2005: 111–13. Marius was co-opted into the augural college only in 98–97, after he had been consul six times (Rüpke 2005a: 1140–1, no. 2389).

prodigies that accompanied the conspiracy of Catiline.[67] When he is
reminded of how he handled prodigies during the Catilinarian crisis, Marcus gives a very elusive reply, which sounds almost like an admission: 'I
am your brother, so I respect you.'[68] The tone of the answer is seemingly
polite, but may be read less favourably: perhaps it conceals a not so positive
judgement of Quintus' credulity (something along the lines of: 'I am your
brother and I have to respect you – but how could you possibly take that
argument seriously in the first place?').[69] Again, the reasons for Cicero's
choice of Quintus as one of the characters of the dialogue become significant. Cicero probably wanted to indicate that the traditional approach to
divination with which Marcus takes issue in book 2 was deeply engrained
in his education. The decision to emancipate himself from that traditional
model was a recent outcome of his intellectual itinerary; it was, indeed, one
of the factors that had prompted him to pursue the whole endeavour of the
trilogy.

Quintus' most powerful point is that Cicero is a member of the augural
college and cannot credibly make the case against divination. Quite the
contrary, he should take over the case in defence of the *auspicia*.[70] Marcus
replies that augury is not a form of divination; he is a Roman augur, not a
Marsian one, and divination is not part of his brief.[71] He does not predict
the future by looking at the flight of birds, or 'with the observation of other
signs'. The task of the augur is the performance of a ritual and to look
for signs of divine non-hostility. Marcus argues that Romulus believed

---

[67] Cic. *Div.* 1.17–22 (= F 10 Courtney). See André 1991: 116–17; Courtney 1993: 162–71; Köves-
Zulauf 1997 (esp. on the relationship with *Cat.* 3.18); Wardle 2006: 144–60; Kurczyk 2006: 93–103;
Gildenhard 2011: 294–8. Goldberg 1995: 148–51 offers a positive assessment of the *Consulatus suus*
and the whole of Cicero's poetic production; Hose 1995 stresses Cicero's debt to Hellenistic epic.

[68] Cic. *Div.* 2.46: *frater es; eo uereor*.

[69] Krostenko 2000: 380–3; see also Schiesaro 1997: 78. Cf. the different reading in Schultz 2009: 203:
'Marcus merely waves his hand . . . and moves on.'

[70] Cic. *Div.* 1.105: *auspiciorum patrocinium*. Schofield 1986: 54–5 stresses that some features of the *De
diuinatione* might recall forensic oratory; the use of the word *quaestio* in *Nat. D.* 1.1 and *Div.* 2.3 may
be significant in this respect. Cicero's augurate: Guillaumont 1984: 81–6 and Rüpke 2005a: 1328,
no. 3290.

[71] Cic. *Div.* 2.70: *non enim sumus ii nos augures, qui auium reliquorumue signorum obseruatione futura
dicamus* ('For we are not the sort of augurs who foretell the future by observing the birds and
other signs'); cf. 1.132. Santangelo 2012: 37–9. The Marsi had a reputation for having a special (and
partly disturbing) connection with the supernatural: Piccaluga 1976: 207–10; Habinek 2005: 249–52;
Farney 2007: 198. Cf. also the story of the augur of Patavium C. Cornelius, who prophesied Caesar's
victory at Pharsalus on the day of the battle by watching the flight of birds (Luc. 7.192–6; Plut. *Caes.*
47.3–6; Gell. *NA* 15.18; Dio 41.61.4–5; Obs. 65a, with Nice 1999: 198–9; Montero 2006: 54–6; Pelling
2011: 375–6). Greek ornithomancy: Pollard 1977: 116–29; Johnston 2008: 128–32. Ornithomancy in
Etruscan and Italic contexts: Catalano 1960: 130–2 n. 64; García de la Fuente 1973: 144–6; Briquel
1995b: 21–2, 25–6.

that augury could be used to predict the future, but he was mistaken; antiquity got it wrong in many respects.[72] There has also been a clear shift in practice by Cicero's time: rather than inspecting the flight of birds in the sky, serving magistrates tend to perform a ritual, the *tripudium*, with the assistance of a *pullarius*, that consisted of feeding a bird (usually a chicken, *pullus*) in a cage; the very fact that the bird would eat and that some crumbs would touch the ground was deemed a sign of divine favour, as was customary in augural lore.[73] Marcus contests the value and reliability of this ritual, which was strictly formalised and had a virtually forced outcome, determined under artificial conditions.

The background of this discussion is the development of public divination in Rome during the second and first centuries BC. The rise of the haruspices and their increasing influence in the handling of public prodigies had also resulted in more detailed and explicit predictions.[74] Augury, on the contrary, interpreted specific signs, and established whether they were warnings or indications that an envisaged action was allowed by the gods. The aim was not to predict its outcome, nor to disclose the plans of fate. Marcus promises to discuss the topic at greater length on a future occasion. Indeed, Cicero discussed the topic in greater detail in a lost treatise, the *De auguriis*, which was probably still unfinished when the *De diuinatione* was written.[75] He was gathering information on the topic as early as 50, when he asked his fellow augur Appius Claudius Pulcher to send him a copy of his work on augury.[76] It is likely that this background research was directly relevant to the *De legibus*, where Atticus states that some members of the augural college hold the view that the auspices exist just for the sake of the Republic, while others view them as a practice that has some affinity

[72] Cic. *Div.* 2.70: *errabat enim multis in rebus antiquitas.* Cf. North 1990: 54 and Lehmann 1999: 249–52.

[73] Cic. *Div.* 2.72–4; cf. 1.27–8. On the *tripudium* see Regell 1882: 8–9 and 1893: 16–17; Rüpke 1990: 148–51; Wardle 2006: 169–70, 173–8; Scheid 2012: 113–19. On the *pullarii* see Foti 2011. On Romulus' augural skills cf. Cic. *Div.* 1.3. This ritual is a partial exception to the principle set out in Fortes 1966: 414 whereby 'legitimate ("white") divination must be public and formal'.

[74] Montero 2006: 22–9 argues for a direct link between the alleged decline of augury and the increasing prominence of haruspicy in the late Republic.

[75] Charisius pp. 133.23, 156.23, 176.15–16 Barwick; cf. Serv. *ad Aen.* 5.738, who mentions *Cicero in auguralibus.* Guillaumont 1984: 85–6. Krostenko 2000: 375 argues for a deliberate omission.

[76] Cic. *Div.* 2.74–5; *Fam.* 3.9.3 (written from Laodicea in 50). Cicero had already received what seems to be the first part of the work in June 51 (*illo libro augurali*), which bore a dedication to him: *Fam.* 3.4.1. Regell 1878: 5–6; C. W. Tucker 1976: 174; Pavis d'Escurac 1981: 32; Guillaumont 1984: 46–8; Rawson 1985: 302–3; Lehoux 2012: 35–7. Scheid 2005: 278 argues that Appius had a 'warm' approach to the issue that contrasted with the 'cold ritualism' of his peers; Champeaux 2005: 213 suggests that he 's'est laissé contaminer par l'aire de son temps'. On the complex relationship between Appius and Cicero see Hall 2009: 139–53.

with divination.[77] On the surface, Cicero's reply contradicts the view put forward in *Div.* 2: divination exists, and watching the flight of birds is one of its components, as well as one of the tenets of augury. However, he claims that the augural lore went through a steady decline over the centuries, partly because of negligence.[78] Augury no longer has divinatory value, despite what Appius Claudius argued in his treatise; but it used to have it in times gone by, despite what C. Claudius Marcellus, another member of the college, thought.[79] The apparent tension with the views expressed in the *De diuinatione* is not unsolvable. In both instances Cicero denies that his role as augur entails an involvement in divination; the claim that augury used to be a form of divination is of relative significance and fits well in the idealised portrait of early Rome that is sketched in the *De diuinatione*. Moreover, the *De legibus* is a work that sets out rules and institutions for an ideal community. Cicero regarded augury as a valuable institution and justified its existence with more positive arguments than those he used in the *De diuinatione*. In the *De legibus* consensus and civic concord are central themes. It is not surprising that Cicero chose not to pursue a divisive issue in that context and provided a generally favourable assessment of divination.[80] It may also be argued, on a different line, that Cicero's approach to a complex problem like divination changed in the few, intense years that separated the composition of the *De legibus* from that of *De diuinatione*.[81] Moreover, what many modern readers have viewed as a contradiction in Cicero's assessment of augury was not perceived as such by his contemporary readers: there is no evidence that the *De legibus* was published during Cicero's lifetime, while the *De diuinatione* certainly was.[82]

---

[77] Cic. *Leg.* 2.32–3, esp. 32.2: *disciplina uestra quasi diuinare uideatur posse* ('it seems that your discipline almost has the ability to divine'). Fontanella 1997: 527–30; Dyck 2004: 344–50; Santangelo 2012: 39–41.

[78] Late Republican references to religious *neglegentia*: Cic. *Leg.* 2.29 and 33; Varro *ARD* f 2a (= August. *De civ. D.* 6.3); Livy 43.13.1. Develin 1978: 4–5; Romano 2009–10: 16–18 and ch. 10.

[79] Late Republican literature on augural matters: Jocelyn 1982–3: 188; C. W. Tucker 1976: 171–4; Harries 2006: 164–6; Rüpke 2012b: 491–5. Regell 1881: 595 and 1904: 9–10 argued that there was a substantial difference between the works *de auguriis* (on augural law) and those *de auspiciis* (on 'augural public law'). This debate is not evidence for, or a cause of, the decline of augury; *contra* cf. Montero 2006: 17–22.

[80] Goar 1968. Cf. also Setaioli 2005: 246–7.

[81] Fontanella 1997: 530 n. 203; Leonhardt 1999: 68–73. Mora 2003: 3–14 argues that Varro's work on religious and theological matters prompted Cicero to revisit his positions.

[82] On the apparent tension between the discussions of augury in the *De legibus* and the *De diuinatione*, see Goar 1972: 96–104; Pavis d'Escurac 1981: 34; Guillaumont 1984: 136–40; Dyck 2004: 347–8. On the publication of the *De diuinatione*, see Cic. *Fat.* 1.1: *in iis quod de diuinatione edidi*.

In the *De diuinatione* (and to some extent in the *De legibus*) Cicero defends the augural lore and its intellectual coherence, but also stresses that it was preserved mainly for its great political expediency. A similar line is taken towards haruspicy. In book 2 Marcus develops a radical critique of its foundations, and points out that there is no reason to accept its intellectual and divinatory credentials. However, he introduces his discussion with the cautionary remark that haruspicy must be preserved, for the sake of the State and of *communis religio*. A clear distinction is drawn between the political dimension and the intellectual agenda of the dialogue, which is to teach the reader how to rethink his attitude to religion and to set himself free from *superstitio*. It is not that of conveying specific proposals for the reorganisation of public religion. It is surely in this light that the ironic cautionary remark about the private nature of the dialogue between Quintus and Marcus should be interpreted.[83]

Moreover, the view that it was politically desirable for the elite to allow the survival of religious practices and beliefs that were popular with the lower classes for that reasons had authoritative precedents in fifth-century Athens.[84] In first-century BC Rome this reflection tied in with ongoing thinking about theology and its complexity. The necessity of deceiving the masses in matters of religion was also stressed by Varro.[85] This view has some connection with the theory that there exist three kinds of theology (*genera theologiae*): one for the poets, one for the philosophers and one for the political communities.[86] Such an approach was not unprecedented in the Roman intellectual debate. A slightly different tripartition was suggested by Q. Mucius Scaevola (*cos.* 95), the *pontifex maximus* and jurist, who presented a neat classification of the known categories of gods (*tria genera tradita deorum*), which mirrors conceptual schemes followed elsewhere in

---

[83] Cic. *Div.* 2.28: *sed soli sumus; licet uerum exquirere sine inuidia, mihi praesertim de plerisque dubitanti* ('But we are alone and we may, without causing bad feelings, pursue the truth; I, in particular, may do so, since I have doubts in most respects').

[84] Critias F 1 Nauck is the earliest surviving text advocating such approach; more sources and excellent discussions in Jocelyn 1966: 98–9 and Linderski 1982: 19–21 (= 1995a: 465–7); Krostenko 2000: 374–80. Fögen 1993: 254 explores the similarities between the approaches of Cicero and Constantine to the political significance of haruspicy. Lehoux 2012: 37 argues (against Krostenko 2000) that Cicero's assessment of divination may not be reduced to an endorsement of the 'noble lie' approach.

[85] August. *De civ. D.* 4.27: *expedire igitur existimat falli in religione ciuitates, quod dicere etiam in libris rerum diuinarum Varro ipse non dubitat* ('He thinks it appropriate, therefore, that states should be deceived in matters of religion; which Varro himself does not even hesitate to say in his books on divine matters'). Cf. also August. *De uer. rel.* 1.1.

[86] Varro *ARD* F 7 Cardauns = August. *De civ. D.* 6.5. The bibliography is extensive: Cardauns 1976: 139–43; Dihle 1996; Baier 1997: 46–56; Peglau 2003: 141–8; Wifstrand Schiebe 2006: 191–203; Rüpke 2009a: 76–84; Ando 2010: 76–8.

his work.[87] He identified three different strands in the tradition about the gods: the poetic one does not even deserve to be discussed, because it demeans the role of the gods; the approach of the philosophers is a combination of idle speculation and inconvenient truths, which must not be circulated or taught because they may harm social coexistence. The only form of tradition that is acceptable and worth promoting is that constructed by those who have political authority – the *principes ciuitatis*. According to Augustine, Scaevola was inclined to reject divine anthropomorphism outright, but was not prepared to question it openly for the sake of *religio*. Varro was certainly aware of Scaevola's reflection, but developed his *genera theologiae* independently: there is a significant difference in terminology, as Varro speaks of a *genus ciuile* that concerns the people, rather than just the political elite.[88]

An argument deployed by Marcus commands attention in this connection: the view that haruspicy should be 'practised for the sake of the state and of our common religion'.[89] The emphasis on the interest of the State may not be remarkable, but the reference to a *communis religio* is. It is not far-fetched to see an Italian background to this reference to the 'common religion'.[90] By the mid first century BC the horizon of Roman religion was the whole of Italy up to the Po Valley, and the involvement of the Etruscan haruspices at the very core of the Roman public religion had

---

[87] Varro *Logistoricus Curio de cultu deorum* 5 Cardauns = *ARD* lib. 1 app. 5 Cardauns = August. *De civ. D.* 4.27: *relatum est in litteras doctissimum pontificem Scaeuolam disputasse tria genera tradita deorum: unum a poetis, alterum a philosophis, tertium a principibus ciuitatis* ('It is recorded that the very learned pontiff Scaevola had discussed three kinds of gods that are handed down to us: one introduced by the poets, another by the philosophers, another by the statesmen'). See Fortin 1980: 238–50; Bauman 1983: 351–61; Rosenberger 1998: 83–90; Bendlin 1998: 74–85; Scheid 2001a: 129–37; Schiavone 2005: 198–213, 443–8; Rüpke 2005c and 2012a: 172–85, 252–6; Van Nuffelen 2010: 34–6. Importance of divisions into *genera* in Mucius' legal work: Pomponius in *Dig.* 1.2.2.41, with Talamanca 1987: 779–87 (who stresses the importance of this method to the control of the process that led to the production of responses) and Schiavone 2005: 160–3, 432–3. Cardauns 1960: 33–40 argued that Scaevola was a character of Varro's *Curio de cultu deorum* and that these views on theology were somewhat arbitrarily attributed to him by Varro; tentatively followed by Beard 1994: 757.
[88] August. *De civ. D.* 6.5 (= Varro *ARD* F 7–9 Cardauns): *tria genera theologiae dicit esse, id est rationis quae de diis explicatur, eorumque unum mythicon appellari, alterum physicon, tertium ciuile* ('He says that there are three kinds of theology, that is, of the account which is given of the gods; and of these, the one is called mythical, the other physical, and the third civil'). See also Tert. *Ad nat.* 2.1.9 and 2.8: *tertium gentile.* Varro and divine anthropomorphism: Boyancé 1976: 158–60; Van Nuffelen 2011: 30–2.
[89] Cic. *Div.* 2.28: *quam ego rei publicae causa communisque religionis colendam censeo.*
[90] Cf. the reference to *communis omnium gentium religio* in Cic. *Verr.* 2.4.115, in a discussion of the cult of Ceres at Henna. See Briquel 1995a: 21–2. Rüpke 2012a: 215 points out that in the first century BC the municipal elites are important addressees of literary communication; on the limits of religious integration cf. Bendlin 1998: 251–9 and Cancik 1999b.

become well established; it was an obvious, irreversible political necessity.[91] Cicero's long-standing political ties with sectors of the Etruscan elites should also be borne in mind. He acted as a patron of the city of Volaterra as late as in 44; in 69 he defended the Volaterran noble Aulus Caecina; the latter's homonymous son was a personal friend and correspondent of Cicero (see Chapter 2), and wrote an important work on haruspicy and specifically on the interpretation of lightning.[92]

Such appreciation of the political importance of haruspicy is not incompatible with a firm rejection of the value of specific haruspical responses. As in other passages of the *De diuinatione*, Cicero corroborates his arguments by making specific reference to contemporary politics. He gives, for instance, an explicit and damning critique of the responses issued by the haruspices during the Civil War: some joined Pompey and his troops in Greece and gave a number of misguided responses, which Pompey tended to take seriously. Cicero does not give any details, and seems to imply that the events are too painful to be recounted, but he makes it clear that the responses were 'almost' invariably disproved by the events.[93] The haruspices that the other faction used, however, were not necessarily more capable. Caesar's crossing to Africa would have never taken place if he had followed the advice of a haruspex whom he had consulted. However, Caesar acted on the basis of different considerations and used his political foresight.[94] The *De diuinatione* does not aim to question the possibility of predicting the future. Marcus' polemic is targeted at prophecies, rather than predictions based on rational inference. In this passage the attack is especially direct, although it is vague in an important respect. It appears to refer only to the responses given by the haruspices in a private capacity or in the context of factional conflicts, but does not discuss the interventions of the haruspices in the public domain, and their dealings with Senate and magistrates – arguably the most important area in which the haruspices were involved, and in which the political implications of their actions were deepest.

---

[91] Briquel 2008; Sordi 2008: 95. It is conceivable that the Etruscan elites were part of the intended audience of Cicero's philosophical works, as well as the Italian ones in general: the possibility is dismissed too hastily by Murphy 1998: 497–8. Guillaumont 1986 provides a thorough assessment of Cicero's knowledge of haruspicy: it was sound, but not detailed.

[92] Cf. the discussion of *Fam.* 6.6 below. On balance it seems likelier that the correspondent of Cicero was not the same person as his client: Rawson 1978a: 137 n. 43 (= 1991: 297 n. 43); Guillaumont 2000: 108. *Contra*, see Hohti 1975: 418–19. Not included in Haack 2006. Caecina in the Civil War: Hohti 1975: 429–32. Prosopography of the Caecinae: Ramelli 2003: 196–8.

[93] Cic. *Div.* 2.53: *uides tamen omnia fere contra ac dicta sint euenisse* ('still, you can see that the outcomes were nearly always contrary to what was said').

[94] Cic. *Div.* 2.52.

Cicero's discussion of divination is not an outright rejection of divination as was commonly understood in the Roman world. Moreover, the meaning of Latin *diuinatio* does not coincide with that of the English word 'divination'. The *De diuinatione* rules out the possibility of consulting the gods in order to predict that which is deemed fortuitous, whilst not dismissing the possibility of a dialogue between men and gods. Quite the contrary, it argues that the worship of the gods must be carried out through the performance of appropriate rituals and a tight public control. The craft of the augurs retains a substantial importance, because it enables the community to establish the position of the gods on an envisaged action. The expiation of prodigies receives hardly any attention, but the preservation of haruspicy, which revolves around prodigies, is firmly argued for on the grounds of its political desirability. What is left out of the account is prophetic divination. *Religio* is about a controlled, reflective process of engagement with the gods; *diuinatio* does not fall within its remit, and it risks turning into *superstitio* unless it is kept in check.[95]

The *De diuinatione* after the Ides of March

Cicero's critique of divination was not accompanied by a rejection of religion and of its philosophical foundations. A. Momigliano, who put forward the contrary view most authoritatively, gave too pessimistic an interpretation of the last chapters of the *De diuinatione* and of the celebration of the political importance of religion that they provide.[96] The *De diuinatione* appeared at a time of intense intellectual debate on religious matters in Rome. The names of M. Terentius Varro and P. Nigidius Figulus are the obvious reference points. However, the dialogue also appeared soon after the end of a Civil War that was marked by a plethora of premonitory signs: Cicero remarks upon Pompey's interest in extispicy and Caesar's detached attitude to haruspical responses.[97] More significantly, it was planned in a period of deep religious change, during the dictatorship of Caesar. Whatever one may make of S. Weinstock's reconstruction of Caesar's religious strategy, it is uncontroversial that in the forties a new relationship between political leaders and religion took shape, and the numerous changes that had occurred in the previous decades in the relationship between religion

---

[95] Useful working definitions of reflective and non-reflective beliefs in Barrett 2007: 180–5; cf. Laidlaw 2007: 227–9 for the interesting suggestion that the cognitive science of religion, being uninterested in self-conscious practices and traditions, is in fact a study of superstition.

[96] Momigliano 1984: 208–9 (= 1987: 273–4).

[97] Cic. *Div.* 2.53 (Pompey); 1.119, 2.52 (Caesar). Pompey in *Div.*: Schultz 2009: 204–5.

and politics became entrenched.[98] Caesar was killed as the *De diuinatione* was being written, and Cicero could afford to assess his rule much more explicitly in the *De diuinatione* than he was able to do in the *De natura deorum*. It would be reductive to say that the treatise was written in response to the rise of Caesar, but it is beyond dispute that the composition of the work and the choice of the topic were deeply influenced by political circumstances. The attempt to regulate religion (*moderare religionem*) set out in the *De natura deorum* was – inter alia – a response to the new construction of power devised by Caesar and to the long-term crisis which had made that revolutionary outcome possible.

This leads us back to the problem of the readership of the *De diuinatione* and of its political dimension. The treatise was explicitly addressed to the most receptive circles of the Roman elite and was intended to provide a comprehensive discussion of a problem of public significance.[99] This reference to the alleged private character of the conversation that Marcus and Quintus are having (2.48) is hardly more than a tongue-in-cheek understatement, and the fact that the two men are by themselves in Cicero's country house does not entail any serious interpretative consequence.[100] Cicero no doubt intended to provide his readers with a debate *in utramque partem* that would enable them to make an informed choice, but he certainly did not forgo the opportunity to make his own views very clear and to suggest strongly, with a recognisable authorial voice, what his preferences were. He wanted the jury of the readers to complete their *quaestio*; as a good lawyer, he tried to make his case as strongly as possible.[101] As W. Burkert noted, Cicero's Academism was a framework that afforded him the option to exercise critical judgement and not to commit to a specific philosophical school. It was also a choice that enabled him to stress the Roman-ness of his intellectual inquiry.[102] As argued above, by writing his religious trilogy Cicero embarked on a project of great political

---

[98] Weinstock 1971.

[99] Cicero's correspondence offers valuable evidence for how Cicero's works (and ideas) circulated within the educated Roman elite: Murphy 1998.

[100] Beard 1986: 35 uses *Nat. D.* 1.10 as evidence that Cicero did not want his own opinions to be identified from his philosophical writing; it may be argued that *Nat. D.* 3.95 contradicts that early statement of intents; moreover, in *Nat. D.* the character of Cicero does not take part in the philosophical discussion, while this is the case in *Div.*; at any rate, despite the link between the two works, what might apply to a treaty on the nature of the gods does not necessarily apply to a discussion of divination, a topic that has more obvious political implications. Dyck 2003: 67 argues that this attitude is 'typical of Skeptics'.

[101] Schäublin 1991: 395–6, 417–18. On the *De diuinatione* as *quaestio* cf. Scheid 1987–9: 127–8. Excellent semantic study of *quaestio* in Mantovani 2009 (esp. 66: '"inchiesta" mirante a un giudizio').

[102] Burkert 1965; see also Gigon 1978: 240–57 and Lévy 1992: 73. In this respect Quintus' attitude is not entirely dissimilar: at 2.100, after listening to Marcus' arguments, he acknowledges that the

significance. *Religio* will benefit from the undermining of *superstitio*. The gods remain an important part of the picture; so does public divination. The main target is divination as prediction of the future, especially in its prophetic form. Augury and haruspicy are part of the picture, because they are important features of public religion. The first does not have a prophetic dimension; the latter does, but can be confined to its diagnostic value. No overhaul of the public prodigy system is envisaged. Even if one assumed that Cicero himself did not subscribe to all the arguments put forward by Marcus in the second book, his preference for the negative case emerges forcefully, especially because it is so strongly affirmed at the end of the treatise.

The impact of Cicero's cultural project on his contemporaries is hard to assess. The making and the immediate reception of the *De diuinatione* are, after all, squeezed between two deaths, that of Caesar, whose rise and fall prompted questions that were central to Cicero's discussion, and that of Cicero, who left the scene too suddenly and too soon to be able to develop the arguments that he had put forward in his trilogy, and to plan and organise their contemporary reception.[103] It should also be borne in mind that Caesar's death prompted Cicero's return to a frenetically active political life. This may have hastened the completion of the trilogy and possibly affected the effectiveness and accuracy of Cicero's discussion. The *De fato* was written very quickly in spring 44: Cicero says that he lacked the time to compose and revise it thoroughly, although this dialogue is arguably the most technically sophisticated philosophical work that he ever wrote.[104] It is also unclear how widely the *De diuinatione* was read and debated, and how it influenced its intended readership: Virgil was certainly familiar with it, as were Valerius Maximus, Plutarch and Gellius.[105] Its very existence and the numerous references to contemporary events, however, show that the topic had a clear contemporary relevance, and it is a safe guess that the theses put forward by Quintus and Marcus both had their cohorts of followers

---

Stoic doctrine on divination is not satisfactory and that the approach of the Peripatetics to the problem is more sophisticated (Schultz 2009: 200 reads this passage as evidence that Quintus is not fully committed to the Stoic argument). Cf. Cuny-Le Callet 2005a: 133–7 on the differences between Stoic and Roman attitudes to fate and divination.

[103] Cf. Rosenblitt 2011: 417–25, who plausibly argues that the depiction of Cotta in Sall. *Hist.* 2.47 Maurenbrecher = 2.44 McGushin is a response to the portrait of Cotta in the *De natura deorum*.

[104] Schofield 1986: 50. Cf. Lévy 1997: 323 on the 'accidental' structure of the *De fato*.

[105] On Virgil's engagement with the *De diuinatione* see Chapter 11. See also Val. Max. 1.1.1, with Wardle 1998: 16–18 and Mueller 2002: 117–18; Plut. *C. Gracch.* 1.6; Gell. *NA* 4.11.3 and 15.13.7, with Guillaumont 1992. Langlands 2011 argues that Valerius Maximus owed a strong debt to the *De officiis*.

at that time.[106] Cicero's discussion undoubtedly catered for the elite, but its significance pertains to matters of much wider historical importance. Studying this work may not reveal much about the ritual dimension to Roman religion, but it certainly tells us a lot about those who controlled the rituals that were such an important part of Roman religious life and about how those practices were debated within that section of the elite.

This is not, however, the only aspect of the *De diuinatione* that makes it a fundamental historical source, and a suitable starting point. The philosophical dialogue is not a historical treatment of the topic, but it is a sustained, serious effort to address the complexity and pervasiveness of divination in the Roman world. This is carefully laid out in book 1 by Quintus and it is seriously engaged with by Marcus in his riposte. The clear interpretative option set out in the dialogue does not preclude an earnest discussion of the wide significance of divination. Indeed, the very existence of the dialogue is testimony to the efforts made to explain its substance and importance. Cicero's approach is critical, but is not deforming. More generally, there is no reason to regard Cicero as an unreliable witness on divination, whether in the *De diuinatione* or elsewhere. Divination is central in the Roman historical experience, and one of the dimensions of its significance is that it is constantly debated and contested. Cicero does so, in the *De diuinatione*, in other philosophical works and in his speeches. He must not be regarded as an unreliable witeness; he was a complex man, with complex agendas, but he was a competent and intelligent witness of Roman divination.

The following three chapters of this book will all engage, in different ways, with different aspects of the *De diuinatione*. The *De diuinatione* is an invaluable source for the vocabulary pertaining to the sphere of divination and prediction, and more generally to religion as a whole. There was no *patrii sermonis egestas*, no dearth of suitable vocabulary already before Cicero, but he did make a powerful contribution to refining and consolidating it.[107] The inventory of the sources of divination and inspired prediction that were available to any resident of the city of Rome and Roman Italy will be the main guide in the discussion in Chapters 3–7, which will provide an overview of how various forms of divination were practised, in both public and private contexts. In Chapters 8–12, which are devoted to the discussion of divination and foresight in a number of late first-century BC writers, we will see that the legacy of Cicero's reflection

---

[106] On the importance of anecdotes in *Div*. cf. Schofield 1986: 51–3; Leonhardt 1999: 92; Lehoux 2012: 24–5, 42–5.
[107] Lucr. 1.832. Cicero's reflection upon writing philosophical prose in Latin: Fögen 2000: 79–105.

on this point was clear to some authors, and that the issues that he raised and discussed played a role in contemporary reflection on the decline and possible fall of Rome. Even when, in the last chapter, we shall discuss the impact that the rise of Augustus had on how divination was practised and debated, we shall return to some of the central issues raised in Cicero's dialogue, and we shall see how the *princeps* acknowledged and addressed them.

CHAPTER 2

The terms of the debate

In the first chapter of this book we have explored some crucial aspects of Cicero's complex reflection on divination and we have discussed how it related to the historical development of political and religious life in that period. Like many aspects of intellectual life in this period, reflection on religion and specifically on divination was accompanied by a greater attention to logical organisation, the attempt to define concepts and problems by dividing them into specific headings, and increasing terminological diversity, which often led to greater accuracy.

Interest in and reflection on divination, however, did not necessarily bring about a clear differentiation in the use of the words that were employed to refer to supernatural occurrences: *prodigium, portentum, ostentum, monstrum* and *omen.* Close scrutiny of their occurrences shows that they often overlap in meaning and are used almost interchangeably. There were attempts to define them more precisely, but the debate never led to a consensus, as a passage of Verrius Flaccus shows (*ap.* Fest. 284 L):

> *portenta existimarunt quidam grauia esse, ostenta bona: alii portenta quaedam bona, ostenta quaedam tristia appellari. portenta, quae quid porro tendatur indicent; ostenta, quae tantum modo ostendant; monstra quae praecipiant quoque remedia.*

> Some have thought that *portenta* are unfavourable, while *ostenta* are favourable; others have thought that some *portenta* are called good, and some *ostenta* are called bad. *Portenta* point out what is headed forward (*porro*); *ostenta* are things that show (*ostendant*) what is to come; *monstra* the events that also set out the remedies.[1]

Cicero suggests different etymologies in the *De diuinatione*, where Quintus establishes clear links between nouns and verbs, and the emphasis is put on the predictive value of portents (1.94):

---

[1] Grandazzi 1993: 60–1; Montero 2006: 15.

quia enim ostendunt, portendunt, monstrant, praedicunt, ostenta, portenta, monstra, prodigia dicuntur.

Because they demonstrate (*ostendunt*), portend (*portendunt*), show (*monstrant*) and predict (*praedicunt*) they are called miraculous apparitions (*ostenta*), portents (*portenta*), divine warnings (*monstra*) and prodigies (*prodigia*).[2]

Despite efforts to establish the etymology and the accurate meanings of those words, in practice the usage of these terms was rather fluid.[3] More fruitful conclusions may be reached if one turns to the concepts that underpinned the late Republican debate on religion, and specifically on divination. The discussion of abstract concepts can show that a clearer terminological differentiation took shape, and that this can enable a better appreciation of their place in the wider historical context. It is therefore necessary to start from the fundamental opposition which Cicero establishes at the outset of his reflection on divination and which is the fundamental theme of the religious trilogy: that between *superstitio* and *religio*. In light of this opposition we will then be in a position to approach another fundamental dichotomy in the late Republican debate on divination and prediction: that between *diuinatio* and *prudentia*.

Superstitio and *religio*

As we saw in the previous chapter, Cicero points out that *superstitio* must be eradicated. Since this notion is so important to Cicero's reflection on religion, it is necessary to explore it in some detail.[4] On existing evidence, the adjective *superstitiosus* seems to have appeared before the noun *superstitio*. The original meaning of the adjective appears to have been 'divinely inspired' or 'prophetic'. It is most clear from the references we encounter in Plautus: in the *Amphitruo* (323: *illic homo superstitiosust*), in the *Rudens*

---

[2] The same etymologies are set out in *Nat. D.* 2.7; Wardle 2006: 330–1. Cf. also Fest. 254 L: *prodigia – quod prodicunt futura, permutatione g litterae; nam quae nunc c appellatur, ab antiquis g uocabatur.* ('prodigies – because they foretell future events, on account of the alteration of the letter 'g'; for the letter that is now called 'c' was called 'g' by the ancients'). The predictive value of prodigies is also acknowledged in Cic. *Phil.* 4.10: *siue enim prodigiis atque portentis di immortales nobis futura praedicunt* ('if indeed the immortal gods predict the future for us by prodigies and portents'). Manuwald 2007: 517–18; Gildenhard 2011: 371–2. It is noteworthy that this speech was written only months after the completion of the *De diuinatione*. Cic. *Har. resp.* 29 might suggest that prodigies may also serve as retrospective prophecies (Beard 2012: 33–4); however, the emendation suggested in Courtney 1960: 97 (*praedicatum* instead of *praedictum*) seems preferable to me.

[3] Thulin 1905b. Good overviews in Luterbacher 1904: 43–60; Moussy 1977; Guillaumont 1996: 50–2; Cuny-Le Callet 2005a: 43–50; Engels 2007: 258–82.

[4] On the importance of focusing on terminology in religious debate cf. Bell 2000: 13–14.

(1139–40: *si ista aut superstitiosa aut hariolast atque omnia / quidquid inerit uera dicet? anne habebit hariola?*, 'What if she is a prophetess or a diviner, and names everything in it correctly? Is a diviner going to get it?') and especially in the *Curculio* (*superstitiosus hicquidemst: uera praedicat*, 'this one is a prophet; he speaks the truth').[5]

In a fragment of a tragedy of Ennius, Cassandra refers to her prophetic frenzy: *missa sum superstitiosis hariolationibus* ('I have been overcome by inspired prophecies').[6] The adjective *superstitiosus* has a neutral connotation in this context, as is the case with other occurrences in second-century BC Latin. Nonetheless, the passage sets in a bleak light the prophetic talent of the Trojan princess: Cassandra makes clear that the force that drives her into an ecstatic state is unwelcome and violent (*meque Apollo fatis fandis dementem inuitam ciet*, 'Apollo, against my will, spurs me to frenzy to speak the future'). Having a divinatory ability is not a comfortable position to be in, and prophetic frenzy is an obscure and disquieting force. Prophets and individuals possessed by divine inspiration often feature in tragic plots and it is not surprising also to find an occurrence of *superstitiosa* in Pacuvius' *Iliona*.[7] The fragment of a tragedy of unknown authorship with which Marcus introduces his discussion of oracles calls the prophetic response of the god *superstitiosa* (*Div.* 2.115: *superstitiosa primum saeua euasit uox fera*, 'at first a prophetic, furious voice came out'); again, *superstitiosa* has the neutral meaning of 'prophetic', but it is associated with *saeua* and *fera*.[8] The semantic development from 'prophetic' to 'superstitious' (the prevailing meaning in late Republican texts) had not yet occurred, but prophecy had already attracted associations and resonances that were not uncontroversially positive. No doubt it is for this reason that Cicero readily (and ironically) exploited them in the polemical context of book 2 of the *De diuinatione*.

The earliest surviving occurrence of the noun *superstitio* is in Cicero's *De inuentione*, in a very instructive context: in a list of virtues and flaws that are quite close to each other: *audacia* is similar to *fidentia*, *pertinacia* is close to *perseuerantia* and *superstitio* is close (*propinqua*) to *religio*.[9] No further specification is given, but *superstitio* is clearly defined as an undesirable

---

[5] Plaut. *Curc.* 397.

[6] Enn. *Tr.* F XVII (c) Jocelyn (= Cic. *Div.* 1.66). Pease 1920: 211 notes that *superstitiosus* means 'prophetic', but has no negative connotations; followed by Jocelyn 1967: 212–13 (who draws attention to Gell. *NA* 15.18.3 and the rare noun *hariolatio*); Calderone 1972: 388–9; Timpanaro 1988: 283; Montero 1994a: 106–7, 127; Wardle 2006: 272. According to Jocelyn, *missa est* suggests that the image has a sexual connotation.

[7] F 216 Ribbeck: *paelici superstitiosae cum uecordi coniuge.*

[8] Benveniste 1969: 277–8; Timpanaro 1988: 395.   [9] Cic. *Inv. rhet.* 2.165; cf. *Part. or.* 81.

practice. It is clear from the context that the new meaning of the noun was not an innovation introduced by Cicero.[10] We do not know at what point in the second century BC it entered common use. The occurrences of *superstitio* in Cicero are not consistently negative. In a passage of the *Verrines* in which a religious crime of Verres is mentioned, *superstitio* is used to refer to an upsurge of religious fear among the people of Sicily.[11] The word sometimes requires a negative adjective to clarify its meaning in a specific context: when Cicero depicts the 'nighttime sacrifices' (*nocturna sacrificia*) that Sassia allegedly performs to further her horrible crimes, he accuses her of indulging in a *contaminata superstitio* which is in open breach of rightful and licit cultic practice.[12] Most interestingly, *superstitio* is here associated with sacrifices intended to make a crime possible and is sharply opposed to *pietas*, *religio* and *iustae preces*. *Superstitio* may also apply to foreign practices that are deemed unacceptable. For example, it can be used of the practice of collecting gold every year and of shipping it to Jerusalem, which Flaccus prohibited during his governorship of Asia in the sixties: Cicero calls it a *barbara superstitio* and praises Flaccus' firmness (*seueritas*), which led him to overlook (*contemnere*) the will of the Jews.[13] The foundations of the conceptual repertoire that will soon turn *superstitio* into an enemy of 'true religion' are already fully in place.

The range of the meanings of *superstitio* that we encounter in Cicero's work is remarkable. In the *De domo* Clodius' decision to take part in the celebration of the festival of Bona Dea in the house of the *pontifex maximus* Caesar is depicted as an act of unbridled curiosity, which is due to a form of uncontrolled superstition, more appropriate to an old woman (*anili superstitione*) than to a man in Clodius' position.[14] Cicero invites the pontiffs – to whom he is addressing his speech – to warn Clodius that there is a limit to *religio*, which all pious men must respect: *religio* is guaranteed only as long as one does not become exceedingly superstitious (*nimium esse superstitiosus non oportere*). This may seem almost a tautology,

---

[10] Gordon 2008: 81.

[11] Cic. *Ver.* 2.4.113: *tanta religione obstricta tota prouincia est, tanta superstitio ex istius facto mentis omnium Siculorum occupauit ut quaecumque accidant publice priuatimque incommoda propter eam causam sceleris istius euenire uideantur* ('the whole province is in the grip of such a great religious scruple (*religio*), such a great fear (*superstitio*) has taken hold of the mind of all the inhabitants of Sicily because of the deed of this man, that every public or private misfortune that may happen to them is thought to have happened because of his crime'). Gordon 2008: 79 interestingly argues that Cicero was translating the Greek δεισιδαιμονία that he found in a witness statement; this is still compatible with the view that this meaning of the word *superstitio* was well established by the late seventies. On δεισιδαιμονία see Martin 2004: 21–108, 249–62.

[12] Cic. *Clu.* 194, with Martin 2004: 128 and Gordon 2008: 79–80.

[13] Cic. *Flacc.* 67.   [14] Cic. *Dom.* 105.

a definition that explains nothing. It becomes clearer in light of the context, in which Cicero accuses Clodius of having set no limits to his curiosity and of having interfered in a ritual in which he was not allowed to take part. Cicero ironically suggests that Clodius violated the Bona Dea festival because he assumed that only his presence would have made the ritual effective; this may be an allusion to the original meaning of *superstitiosus*, that of 'prophetically inspired'. The general point of the speech, however, is clear and very serious: Clodius claims to be pious and honest and bases his personal revenge on Cicero on this claim, while Cicero argues that he is not, and insists at length on the difference between himself and Clodius on the one hand and between Clodius and the pontiffs on the other.[15] The sharp opposition that is outlined here between *religio* and *superstitio* serves this purpose well.

The only occurrence of *superstitio* in the *De haruspicum responso*, which is another moment in the long-standing confrontation between Cicero and Clodius, gives a different perspective on *superstitio*. As Cicero praises the religious knowledge of P. Servilius and M. Lucullus, he argues that their opinion can provide a solution to any doubt and any religious fear one may have: *in nostris dubitationibus atque in maximis superstitionibus.*[16] *Superstitio* is rooted in fear and ignorance: the duty of a priest is to impart knowledge and put it to the service of the community. Arguably the main difference in scope between *superstitio* and *religio*, which is further developed in the religious trilogy of the forties, lies here. *Superstitio* appears to be negatively connotated. In Cicero's philosophical works *superstitio* is an intellectual state from which one must try to break free.[17] The original link with divination and prophecy is lost. What Cicero presents us with is an important category in the late Republican intellectual debate.

Cicero was not the only one to discuss the relationship between *superstitio* and *religio* in the mid first century BC. According to Gellius, Nigidius Figulus explored the problem in a grammatical treatise and quoted the saying of a poet, whose name he did not record (Gell. 4.9.2):

> *Nigidius Figulus, homo, ut ego arbitror, iuxta M. Varronem doctissimus, in undecimo commentariorum grammaticorum uersum ex antiquo carmine refert memoria hercle dignum: 'religentem esse oportet, religiosus ne fuas,' cuius autem id carmen sit, non scribit. atque in eodem loco Nigidius: 'hoc' inquit 'inclinamentum semper huiuscemodi uerborum, ut 'uinosus', 'mulierosus', 'religiosus',*

[15] Tatum 1993: 16–20 convincingly stresses that Cicero's response to Clodius' claim to ritual correctness rested heavily on the critique of the character and intentions of his opponent.
[16] Cic. *Har. resp.* 12: 'in our greatest doubts and most serious religious scruples'.
[17] See e.g. Cic. *Fin.* 1.63; *Nat. D.* 1.45.

significat copiam quandam inmodicam rei, super qua dicitur. quocirca 'religio-
sus' is appellabatur, qui nimia et superstitiosa religione sese alligauerat, eaque
res uitio assignabatur.

Nigidius Figulus, in my opinion the most learned of men next to Marcus
Varro, in the eleventh book of his *Grammatical Commentaries*, quotes a
truly remarkable line from an old *carmen*: 'Best it is to be *religens*, lest
one *religiosus* be', but he does not name the author of the poem. And in
the same passage Nigidius adds: 'This suffix in words of this kind, such as
uinosus, mulierosus, religiosus, indicates an excessive amount of the quality
in question. Therefore *religiosus* is applied to one who has involved himself
in an extreme and superstitious *religio*, which was regarded as a fault.[18]

The anonymous poet drew a difference between *religens*, which carried
a positive sense, and *religiosus*, which had a negative resonance; Nigidius
clarified the problem by explaining that the suffix *–osus* always carries a
negative slant and by adding that the *religiosus* is someone who is bound
superstitiosa religione, by a 'superstitious' form of religious zeal.[19] The point
was made in the context of a grammatical and linguistic discussion, but
it is clear that Nigidius, like Cicero, relegated *superstitiosus* to a negative
sphere of meaning. It is likely that the same applied to *superstitio*.

Nigidius' discussion of *religiosus* leads us to the problem of the origin
of the vocabulary of piety in Latin. This is an issue in which etymology
becomes a matter of historical significance.[20] Nigidius appears to believe
that *religio* derives from *re-ligere*, although a few lines below he also associates it with *ad-ligare*. The problem is discussed more fully in a crucial
passage of Cicero's *De natura deorum* (2.72), where the Stoic Lucilius Balbus strongly states that *religio* must be firmly separated from *superstitio*
and adds that this separation was clearly set by the ancestors, not by the
philosophers. The etymology of the two terms explains the reasons for this
separation most clearly. Those who used to pray to the gods to make sure
that their children survived them were called *superstitiosi*, from *superstes*
('survivor'), and the word later took on a more general meaning. Those
who thought about the religious practices in which they were involved

[18] On the *sententia* quoted by Nigidius and its possible source see Mayer 1975; cf. also Scheid 2001a:
168–9.
[19] Cf. the distinction drawn by Varro *ARD* F 47 Cardauns (= August. *Civ. D.* 6.9): *quale autem illud*
est, quod cum religiosum a superstitioso ea distinctione discernat, ut a superstitioso dicat timeri deos, a
religioso autem tantum uereri ut parentes, non ut hostes timeri ('But what kind of distinction is this
which he makes between the religious and the superstitious man, saying that the gods are feared by
the superstitious man, but are only revered as parents by the religious man, not feared as enemies?').
Cf. Sen. *Ep.* 123.16 (Setaioli 2007: 349).
[20] *Contra*, cf. Gordon 2008: 80.

and made the effort to organise them in a systematic fashion were called *religiosi*, from the verb *relegere* – 'to review'. Cicero makes clear that the link between *religere* and *religiosus* is the same that exists between *elegans* and *eligere*. He also states that the meaning of *religiosus* was from the very beginning an absolutely positive one, because it referred to the concept of choosing and selecting, while *superstitio* indicated a flawed approach to religion. *Religio* is about knowledge (*Nat. D.* 2.71–2):

> *non enim philosophi solum uerum etiam maiores nostri superstitionem a religione separauerunt. nam qui totos dies precabantur et immolabant, ut sibi sui liberi superstites essent, superstitiosi sunt appellati, quod nomen patuit postea latius; qui autem omnia quae ad cultum deorum pertinerent diligenter retractarent et tamquam relegerent, <i> sunt dicti religiosi ex relegendo, <tamquam> elegantes ex eligendo, [tamquam] <ex> diligendo diligentes, ex intellegendo intellegentes; his enim in uerbis omnibus inest uis legendi eadem quae in religioso. ita factum est in superstitioso et religioso alterum uitii nomen alterum laudis.*

> Not just the philosophers, but our ancestors too have distinguished religion from superstition. People who spent whole days in prayer and sacrifice to ensure that their children should outlive them (*superstites*) were termed superstitious (*superstitiosi*) and the word later acquired a wider use. On the other hand, those who carefully reviewed and so to speak retraced all the things that pertain to the cult of the gods were called religious (*religiosi*) from *relegere* (to retrace or to re-read), like *elegans* (elegant) from *eligere* (to select), *diligens* (diligent) from *diligere* (to care for), *intellegens* (intelligent) from *intellegere* (to understand); for all these words contain the same sense of 'picking out' (*legere*) that is present in *religiosus*. Hence *superstitiosus* and *religiosus* came to be terms of censure and approval respectively.[21]

Whatever the etymology may be (whether from *religare* or from *relegere/*religere), *religio* is associated with concepts like 'gathering', 'collecting', 'checking': it conveys the idea of an orderly collection, an intelligently arranged system.[22] *Religare* also conveys the sense of binding

---

[21] I follow the text of Plasberg and Ax 1933. Warde Fowler 1920: 9–10; Pease 1958: 738–40; Sachot 1991: 364–6; Tatum 1999b: 279; Linke 2000: 273–93; Struck 2004: 117–18. The contrast between *relegere* and *neglegere* is noteworthy: Sachot 1991: 389. Cf. the alternative etymology of *religiosus* (from *relinquere*) suggested in Gell. *NA* 4.9.8–9 (Prescendi 2007: 76–8). Benveniste 1969: 267–73 takes a stance in favour of *religere, while Schilling 1971: 39–42 (= 1979: 40–3) makes the case for *religare*. Ronca 1992: 52–3 argues that the matter should be left open.

[22] Rüpke 2010a: 754: 'a reflected belief, an intellectual stance towards the deities addressed by the cult'. The most comprehensive discussion of the occurrences of *religio* in Latin literature is Michels 1976. See also Otto 1909: 533–48; Warde Fowler 1920: 7–15; Schilling 1971: 37–43 (= 1979: 38–44) and 1972: 540–5 (= 1979: 71–6); Wagenvoort 1972: 350–4; Muth 1978: 342–51; Feil 1986: 39–49 (stressing the distance between *religio* and 'religion'); Sachot 1991: 364–72; Bendlin 1998: 3–11; Rüpke 2007b; Ando 2008: 1–15, 105–6; Rüpke 2011b: 158–64. On the plural *religiones*, esp. in Cic. *Nat. D.* 3.5, see Rüpke 2007b: 68 and 2011b: 159; Ando 2008: 2–3.

rules and principles and at the same time the psychological implications of the awe and restraint that *religio* creates.[23] It is clear that both *religare* and *relegere/*religere* would have been connected with *religio* to a Roman mind. The etymology of *superstitio* and *superstitiosus* has also been intensely debated in modern scholarship.[24] It was already a matter of controversy in antiquity. Donatus, Servius and Isidore all agreed on the link between *superstitio* and the religious fear of old people and especially old women; we have already encountered a similar connection in Cicero.[25] The line of thinking of those authors was peculiar, but no doubt ingenious: *superstitio* can be thought to derive from *superstes*, because old people, who are proverbially superstitious, have survived until old age. The link between the two words is also established in Cicero's *De natura deorum*, albeit with a different (pseudo-)etymological argument: those who pray for the survival of their children (i.e. so that they can be *superstes*) were called *superstitiosi* and the word later applied more extensively to all pious people.[26]

The etymological link between *superstitio(sus)* and *superstes* was explored in great detail by L. F. Janssen, who argued for a strong conceptual link between the two words. According to his theory, which develops an insight of E. Benveniste, *superstitio* derives from *superstes*, whose primary meaning is 'present, witness': someone who can speak of the past as if he had witnessed it.[27] This ability to cross the boundaries of the past and the present is extended to the diviner, who can speak of the future as if he lived in it. The negative development of the meaning was generated by its association with foreign practices, which are allegedly driven by individualistic concerns, rather than by the ambition to secure the welfare of the whole community.[28] The argument is ingenious, but speculative. It may be more

[23] Sachot 1991: 364–7.
[24] Selected bibliography on *superstitio*: Pease 1923: 580–1; Solmsen 1944; Benveniste 1969: 273–9; Ross 1969; Calderone 1972; Wagenvoort 1972: 359–60; Janssen 1975; Belardi 1976; Scheid 1985a: 21; Sachot 1991: 372–8; Ronca 1992; Rasmussen 2003: 211–17; Martin 2004: 125–39, 265–6; Rüpke 2011c: 321–2.
[25] Don. *in Ter. Andr.* 3.2.7.487; Serv. *ad Aen.* 8.187; Isid. *Etym.* 8.3.6. *Anilis superstitio*: Cic. *Dom.* 105; *Nat. D.* 2.70, 3.92. *Superstitio muliebris*: Cic. *Tusc.* 3.29. See Massaro 1977: 108–9; Jakobi 1990; Gordon 2008: 87–9; Lehoux 2012: 26.
[26] Cic. *Nat. D.* 2.72.
[27] Benveniste 1969: 276–8 (esp. 277: '*superstitio*, la qualité de *superstes*'); Janssen 1975; Belardi 1976: 45–71; Sachot 1991: 373. The link between divination and the interpretation of the past was already clear to Epimenides of Crete, a contemporary of Solon, in the late seventh and early sixth century BC: Arist. *Rh.* 1418a, 21–6 mentions his prophecies 'on the obscurities of the past'. See Mazzarino 1966: 29–31, 540 n. 68 and Wardle 2006: 197; Cic. *Div.* 1.34 refers to Epimenides as an inspired prophet. Cf. Beard 2012: 34 for the suggestion (partly based on Cic. *Har. resp.* 29) that prodigy interpretation can amount to a prediction of the past.
[28] Janssen 1975: 187.

fruitful to pursue a different angle and to go back to an insight of Servius, who read between the lines of a well-known passage of Lucretius (1.62–5):

> *humana ante oculos foede cum uita iaceret*
> *in terris oppressa graui sub religione,*
> *quae caput a caeli regionibus ostendebat*
> *horribili super aspectu mortalibus instans . . .*

When human life lay grovelling in all men's sight, crushed to the earth under the heavy burden of *religio*, whose grim features loured menacingly upon mortals from the regions of the sky . . . (trans. R. E. Latham, modified)

Servius, followed by Isidore of Seville, read *horribili super aspectu mortalibus instans* as a coded, if poignant reference to *superstitio*.[29] On this reading, Lucretius thought that the etymology of the word was the fear of 'things above' (*superstantium rerum*): the sky against which Epicurus had the courage to raise his sight. This may well be the case; it is also conceivable that Lucretius is just playing on the assonance between *superstitio* and *super aspectu . . . instans*. It is also possible that, even if Lucretius did not accept this etymology, others did at that time. Moreover, a reference to *superstitio* here would create an interesting contrast with *religio*. Caution is in order, though: Lucretius never uses the word *superstitio* and this etymology does not account for the previous uses of the word in contexts where it does not have a negative meaning. Moreover, as we have seen, the original meaning of *superstitiosus* has nothing to do with the concept of fear, nor does it have any derogatory implication; it was probably linked with the concept of ecstasy, of separation from the material dimension.[30]

Modern speculation on the etymology of *superstitio* is often accompanied by attempts to establish when the various meanings of the word emerged. In an influential study, F. Otto argued that the original meaning of *superstitio* is that of 'darüberstehen' and 'hinauftreten', from which the meaning of 'wahrsagen' derived; the word is a close Latin equivalent of the Greek *ekstasis*. *Superstitio*, therefore, was originally associated with the frenzy of the diviner, and only a later development attached the word to the sphere of *Aberglaube*, superstition.[31] The second part of the argument is probably correct, although the etymological association that underpins it – *superstitio* as *ekstasis* – is less convincing. While a conceptual affinity between the two terms may be argued, there is no linguistic or etymological correspondence:

---

[29] Serv. *ad Aen.* 8.187; Isid. *Etym.* 8.3.7.   [30] Sachot 1991: 373–8.

[31] Otto 1909: 548–54: an influential view (cf. Janssen 1975: 137–9). Semantic ranges of *superstitio* and *Aberglaube*: Gordon 2008: 72–3.

it would be unwise to argue for such close and clearcut correspondences.[32] The suggestion of W. Belardi and I. Ronca is more attractive: *superstes* (in the sense of 'eye-witness') and *superstitiosus* (in the sense of 'diviner') share an archaic Indo-European meaning of 'knowing something hidden to others', and have a precise parallel in the Greek *epistenai*, 'to stand upon'.[33]

The question of the etymology of *superstitio(sus)* is probably unsolvable. Some other points, however, can be made on the meanings and usages of these words. First of all, the noun *superstitio* appears for the first time in the generation of Cicero: it has a variety of meanings, the prevailing one mainly negative, and refers to a set of behaviours especially in opposition to *religio*.[34] Secondly, the adjective *superstitiosus* appears earlier than the noun *superstitio* and has a variety of meanings: it can mean 'prophetic' and it can also mean 'superstitious' in a more negative sense. The range of meanings of *superstitio* is narrower than that of *superstitiosus*. It is conceivable that the noun derived from the adjective. At any rate, *superstitio* soon became a heavily loaded term, which formed part of a vigorous intellectual debate. R. Gordon has recently shown how central the concept of *superstitio* was in the construction of a mainstream version of Roman religion, which emphasised the elements of cohesion, tradition and consensus. *Superstitio* enabled the setting of boundaries – also in negative and exclusionary terms – and secured the cohesion of the religious community; at the same time, it enabled the recognition of an authority and the identification of the speaker with that authority.[35]

The main areas of the use of *superstitio* in the late Republic illustrate these implications: it is used, for instance, to refer to extravagant practices that do not fit in the *patrius cultus*, or to some foreign cults.[36] Unsurprisingly, this connotation of the term would feature in the later polemic between pagans and Christians: *superstitio* is a concept that applies eminently well to debates on exclusion and inclusion within a religious community.[37]

[32] Cf. the useful discussion of Calderone 1972: 389–90, who falls into the same pitfall as Otto and argues for a correspondence between *superstitiosus* and *anathematikos*, which is even less convincing than Otto's suggestion. From an etymological standpoint, *epistasis* is the obvious Greek correspondent of *superstitio*, but there is no semantic overlap between the two words.

[33] Belardi 1976: 79–80; Ronca 1992: 54–5.

[34] Belardi 1976: 27 uses Cic. *Nat. D.* 2.71 as evidence that the differentiation between *religio* and *superstitio* emerged before Cicero (*non enim philosophi solum uerum etiam maiores nostri superstitionem a religione separauerunt*, 'Not just the philosophers, but our ancestors too have distinguished religion from superstition'). This is doubtful.

[35] Gordon 2008: esp. 75–6.   [36] Martin 2004: 130–5; Gordon 2008: 83–6.

[37] Negative constructions of *superstitio*, especially in anti-Christian polemic: Sachot 1991: 382–94; Rives 1995: 77–80; Scheid 2001a: 167–74; Vigourt 2001a: 231–52; Nagy 2002; Martin 2004: 135–59, 266–8; de Ste. Croix 2006: 147–52; Gordon 2008: 92–4; Clauss 2011: 432–42; Girardet 2012: 304–11 (the latter two on *CIL* 11.5265).

The increasing interest in defining the boundaries of *superstitio* that is attested for the first century BC is an important aspect of our central problem. It was part of a wider attempt to define and regulate religious practices, including that essential constituency of Roman religion that was divination. The opposition between *religio* and *superstitio* was developed most clearly and coherently by Cicero and it was also clear to an intellectual like Nigidius. It penetrated more widely into the intellectual landscapes of the late Republican educated circles. One of the many virtues celebrated in the so-called *laudatio Turiae*, an inscribed funerary eulogy dating to the late first century BC, is the *studium religionis sine superstitione* – the pursuit of *religio* without *superstitio*.[38]

Diuinatio

The other fundamental opposition that underpins the *De diuinatione*, especially in the second book, is that between divination and foresight: two different practices and two different approaches to the prediction of the future. As is the case with the opposition between *superstitio* and *religio*, the terminology that defines this area of meaning becomes clearer in the late Republican authors, although it emerges already in the early second century *BC*. The key terms in this context are *diuinatio* and *prudentia*. Their close analysis, along with the discussion of the derivate of *prudentia*, *prudens*, will enable us to detect the lines of contact between these two conceptual areas.[39]

We have an important working definition of *diuinatio*. Cicero provides it at the very beginning of the *De diuinatione*, where he speaks in the authorial voice that is neither Quintus nor Marcus: *diuinationem, quam Graeci mantiken appellant, id est praesensionem et scientiam rerum futurarum*.[40] This definition puts to the forefront a clear, but far from obvious Greek parallel: *mantike*, the craft of the Greek diviners (*manteis*). Μαντική does not convey a fundamental level of meaning of *diuinatio*, the etymological and conceptual link between divination and gods, which Cicero himself stresses by pointing out that 'our ancestors derived the term for this most

---

[38] *CIL* 6.1527, a.30–1: *stud [ii religionis] / sine superstitione*. The text is corrupt, but the integration seems safe. Gordon 2008: 81 argues that Turia's 'religious observance' is 'free of that excess – or emotionality – associated with female religiosity'. On the political implications of the *Laudatio* see Osgood 2006: 67–74; see Horsfall 1983: 92 on its 'conservative' outlook on marriage and the role of women.

[39] Schaefer 1977: 190–216 and Milani 1993: 31–2.

[40] Cic. *Div.* 1.1: 'divination, which the Greeks call *mantike*, that is presentment and knowledge of future things'. Cf. *Div.* 2.13. *Diuinatio* in Cicero: Guillaumont 1984: 181–3.

excellent faculty from the gods'.[41] This reference to the ancestors appears
to rule out that *diuinatio* was coined by Cicero. However, as J. North has
pointed out, the word *diuinatio* is not attested before Cicero's time and it
is here used in a philosophical debate: it is the Roman version of a Greek
philosophical term, in a Roman version of a Greek philosophical treatise.
It is not a word that Cicero employs in order to define the mainstream
Roman practice of divination. *Diuinatio* is not a traditional category; quite
the contrary. One should also be cautious in establishing an equivalence
between Roman divinatory practice, be it public or private, and the concept
of *diuinatio* as Cicero presents it.[42] *Diuinatio* is an activity that enables
foreknowledge of the future, and notably of the aspects of the future that
fall outside the remit of human control. It carries a fundamental ambiguity.
It involves *praesensio* (presentiment), a process that does not entail the use
of logical categories. Yet, it is also a structured form of knowledge: it is a
scientia.[43]

The complexity of the meanings that the word *diuinatio* had acquired by
the time Cicero set out to write his treatise may be viewed as a symptom of
the significance that divination had in this period. Cicero was not isolated
in his effort to define *diuinatio* and to what domains it applied. A fragment
of Varro quoted by Servius and of uncertain provenance outlines a division
of *diuinatio* according to the elements that are used by the diviners: *Varro
autem quattuor genera diuinationum dicit: terram, aerem, aquam, ignem –
geomantis, aeromantis, hydromantis, pyromantis* ('But Varro says that there
are four kinds of divination: earth, air, water, fire – geomancy, aeromancy,
hydromancy, pyromancy').[44] The terms of the problem are clarified by the
following sentence in the passage of Servius in which the fragment of Varro
is preserved, when the commentator turns to Virgil's view on divination:
*Vergilius tria genera complexus est: per lauros geomantis, per sidera pyromantis,
per praepetes aeromantis* ('Vergil encompassed three kinds [of divination]:

---

[41] Cic. *Div.* 1.1: *huic praestantissimae rei nomen nostri a diuis... duxerunt.* Maltby 1991: 192; Fögen
2000: 103; Wardle 2006: 94. Burkert 1996: 158 translates *diuinatio* with 'divine activity'.

[42] North 1990: 57–8; Wardle 2006: 92–3; Santangelo 2012: 41. Cf. also Bouché-Leclerq 1892: 292 n. 3:
'définition... tout à fait insuffisante'.

[43] *Contra*, cf. Kany-Turpin 2003b: 63 ('Quintus qualifie indifféremment la divination d'art ou de
science et lorsqu'il emploie *scientia* il n'en propose aucune légitimation théorique'). On divination
as intellectual activity cf. Cryer 1994: 187–94; Meyer 2002: 180–2; Tedlock 2010: 17–18. A general
discussion of the status of ancient science, with a bibliographical overview, in Barton 1994b: 1–33,
185–90. In his discussion of contemporary meteorology Fine 2007: 101 singles out four elements
that are necessary for a public prediction: data, theory, experience and legitimation; cf. 133–4 on the
limited set of data that fortune-tellers have to come to terms with.

[44] Varro *ARD* App. ad lib. III a) Cardauns = Serv. *auct. ad Aen.* 3.359. Also quoted at Isid. *Etym.* 8.9.13.
See Cardauns 1960: 41–5; Nice 1999: 74; Dyck 2004: 347.

geomancy, with laurels; pyromancy, with the stars; and aeromancy, with birds'). Varro, as well as the authors who read and quoted him centuries later, was not interested in defining *diuinatio* along the lines of Cicero, in theoretical terms – at least, not in the *Antiquitates rerum diuinarum*. His concern was to identify the remits to which *diuinatio* could be applied and in doing so he used a familiar philosophical framework, that of the four elements. *Aeromantis* corresponds to augury, the relevance of which to *diuinatio* Cicero examines in the *De legibus* and the *De diuinatione*;[45] what survives of Varro's text prevents us from establishing how this definition and discussion of *diuinatio* were developed further by Varro and in what other respects they differed from Cicero's.

The word *diuinatio*, however, is intertwined with political prediction. An interesting, if often overlooked, insight into Cicero's approach to divination and his employment of the vocabulary connected to divination is provided by a letter that he addressed to one of his friends from Etruria, Aulus Caecina (*Fam.* 6.6).[46] Caecina was probably the son of the defendant in the cause célèbre of 69 on the citizenship rights of the Volaterrani, which Sulla had withdrawn at the end of the Civil War. That case had shaped a special relationship between Cicero and the city of Volaterrae, which lasted until the age of Caesar and upon which Cicero's correspondence often sheds light. Volaterrae was not the only Etruscan community that had a special relationship with Cicero: he also took action to prevent land assignments in the territory of Arretium.[47] Against this background, it is inevitable that Cicero's attitude to the haruspices and their *disciplina* had to be a complex and nuanced one. This emerges in the *De diuinatione* and, even more explicitly, in the letter to Caecina of October 46. This is about a year before the beginning of the composition of the *De diuinatione* and not long before the inception of the religious trilogy. The traces of an ongoing reflection on divination and its limits are apparent (§§ 3–4):

> si te ratio quaedam <m>ira Tuscae disciplinae, quam a patre, nobilissimo atque optimo uiro, acceperas, non fefellit, ne nos quidem nostra diuinatio fallet, quam cum sapientissimorum uirorum moni[men]tis atque praeceptis plurimoque, ut tu scis, doctrinae studio tum magno etiam usu tractandae rei publicae magnaque nostrorum temporum uarietate consecuti sumus; cui quidem

---

[45] Romano 2009–10: 33.

[46] Cic. *Fam.* 6.6. Haury 1966: 1627–8; C. W. Tucker 1976: 173–4; Schaefer 1977: 205–7; Linderski 1982: 13–14 (= 1995a: 459–60); Guillaumont 1984: 113–16 and 2000: 108–13; Briquel 1995a: 27; Walter 2004: 16–17; Cuny-Le Callet 2005b; Lintott 2008: 321–2; Gildenhard 2009: 108–9; Corbeill 2012: 254–5. Schneider 2004: esp. 12–14 argues that the foresight of Cicero may be compared to that of a haruspex: *Fam.* 6.6 is the most striking demonstration that the metaphor is unhelpful.

[47] Volaterrae: Cic. *Att.* 1.19.4; *Dom.* 79; *Fam.* 13.4.1 and 2. Arretium: Cic. *Att.* 1.19.4.

diuinationi hoc plus confidimus quod ea nos nihil in his tam obscuris rebus
tamque perturbatis umquam omnino fefellit.

If the admirable set of rules (*ratio*) of the Etruscan discipline, bequeathed
to you by your very distinguished and excellent father, has not misled
you, neither will my own divinatory skill (*diuinatio*) mislead me; I have
derived it not only from the writings and precepts of the wisest men, and
by the keenest pursuit of knowledge, as you know, but also from a great
experience in dealing with public affairs and by the great variety of my
own experience; and I have all the greater confidence in this divinatory skill,
because it has never once misled me in these so greatly obscure and disrupted
times.

The political agenda of the letter is clear: a general discussion of recent and
imminent political developments that Cicero offers to a friend, trying to
give him some consolation for the unfortunate events of recent times. The
issue of political prediction is at the forefront and Cicero discusses it in the
awareness that Caecina, like his father, is an expert and a practitioner of
haruspicy. Cicero has respectful words for such a remarkable legacy (*ratio
quaedam mira Tuscae disciplinae*), but makes it clear from the start that the
sort of prediction he attempts is very different.[48] It is based on the writings
and the teachings of the great men (*sapientissimorum uirorum monumentis
atque praeceptis*) and on learning (*plurimoque, ut tu scis, doctrinae studio*)
and, even more than that, on experience and the habit of dealing with the
complexity of his own time (*magnaque nostrorum temporum uarietate*).[49]
Cicero calls this form of prediction *diuinatio* and explicitly states that he
trusts it more than haruspicy (*hoc plus confidimus*). He then leaves the
domain of divination and seamlessly enters that of political prediction.
Cicero develops his argument by listing all the circumstances which he
had predicted correctly: he advised Pompey on his alliance with Caesar, he
understood before others the threat to the authority of the Senate in the age
of the first triumvirate, and he attempted to stop the outbreak of the Civil
War. He was equally accurate when it came to predicting the development
of the conflict.[50]

Cicero's summary of his earlier predictions leads to a further one, which
he introduces by an ironic comparison between himself and 'diviners and
astrologers' (§§ 7–8):

---

[48] Guillaumont 2000: 110 draws attention to the fact that *ratio* is used in association with the Etruscan
disciplina, and not with the kind of prediction that Cicero is able to produce. Frank 1992: 287
translates *ratio* as 'Lehre'.

[49] *Monumentis* should be preferred to *monitis* (Guillaumont 2000: 110).

[50] Bringmann 1971: 18–20; Bernett 1995: 209–21.

quare, quoniam, ut augures et astrologi solent, ego quoque augur publicus ex meis superioribus praedictis constitui apud te auctoritatem augurii et diuinationis meae, debebit habere fidem nostra praedictio. non igitur ex alitis uolatu nec e cantu sinistro oscinis, ut in nostra disciplina est, nec ex tripudiis solistimis aut soniuiis tibi auguror, sed habeo alia signa, quae obseruem; quae etsi non sunt certiora illis, minus tamen habent uel obscuritatis uel erroris. notantur autem mihi ad diuinandum signa duplici quadam uia, quarum alteram duco e Caesare ipso, alteram e temporum ciuilium natura atque ratione.

And therefore now that, as is the custom of diviners (*augures*) and astrologers, with my previous predictions, I have established, as a public augur, the authoritativeness of my augury and divination to your eyes, my prediction is bound to have some reliability. I do not offer you a prognostication based on the flight of a fowl in the air or on the omen-cry of a bird coming from the left, as is the case in our doctrine (*disciplina*), nor from the *tripudia solistima* or *soniuia*; but I have other signs to give attention to: even if they are not more certain than the other ones, they are less obscure and have a smaller margin of error. I detect the signs that I need in order to express my divinatory prediction by drawing a sort of double line: one of which I draw from Caesar himself, and the other from the nature and the logic of the political situation.

At the same time, he specifies that he is a 'public augur' himself and that his *diuinatio* is accompanied by an *augurium*, a predictive exercise that makes it possible.[51] However, Cicero promptly specifies that his divinatory technique is remarkably different from that which he uses with the other members of the augural college. His response is based on different signs: perhaps not intrinsically more 'certain' than those prescribed by augural lore, but definitely less obscure and less difficult to misinterpret (*minus tamen habent uel obscuritatis uel erroris*). The signs that are relevant to the divination of future political developments may be gathered by looking at two fronts: Caesar, on the one hand, and the nature of the political struggle on the other.[52] The combination of the two factors permits the formation of a reliable prediction, which, in the case in question, foretells the return of the exiles punished by Caesar.

[51] *Augurium* in Cicero: Guillaumont 1984: 175; Morani 1984: 70. The technical difference between *augurium* and *auspicium* is however profound, as is masterfully shown in Linderski 1986a: 2291–6, esp. 2296: '[t]he distinction between *auspicium* and *augurium* stands out: the former concerned an action to be undertaken by the subject (the auspicant) of the ceremony; the latter concerned the status of an object of the ceremony. When the magistrate accepted a propitious sign, he still had to carry out his action. When the augur accepted a propitious sign, he by this very fact carried out his action of *augurium* and transferred its object into the permanent status of *res* or *persona inaugurata*.' See also Regell 1904: 3–9.

[52] As Gildenhard 2009: 109 points out, the interpretation of the signs given by Caesar is central to Cicero's concerns in this period: see *Fam.* 6.14.2, a letter written to another exile, Q. Ligarius.

Despite its political connotation, this letter is, first of all, a *consolatio*: a message addressed by Cicero to a friend to give him some relief from his condition and to reassure him about the prospect of his return to Italy.[53] Irony is part of the strategy that Cicero uses to console his friend. Since Cicero has to offer a view on what is likely to happen in the future, he takes up the theme of prediction and divination and develops it with a tongue-in-cheek analogy between Cicero's augural lore and Caecina's haruspical expertise. To be sure, we are dealing with a variant of the philosophically loaded teasing that is so often at work in Cicero's correspondence with Atticus and his friends.[54] Just as the irony on philosophical issues reveals something about Cicero's thought, so the ironical device in this letter can shed light on some important aspects of Cicero's views on divination and prediction. The letter contains a clear discussion of the centrality of political prediction in this context and of its independence from divination. The use of the word *diuinatio* is ironic, in the etymological sense of the word: it is intended to prompt further reflection on what *diuinatio* might mean. The letter may be read as an extended metaphor, but it certainly was not an innocent one, especially if we consider who the author and the addressee of this letter were. It is interesting to see that the references to the augurate and augury mainly serve to stress an opposition between the 'Etruscan' divination practised by Caecina and the 'Roman' interpretation of the future carried out by Cicero.[55] However, in this context Cicero seems prepared to acknowledge the divinatory power of augury – something that Marcus refrains from doing in *Div.* 2. He claims that the signs observed by augurs can be used to predict the future and seems to employ the vocabulary of augury and divination almost interchangeably. At one point, he speaks of the *auctoritas augurii et diuinationis meae*; he then brands his prediction of the future as a *praedictio* and claims that he uses various signs 'to divine' (*ad diuinandum*). At the end of the letter, though, the long digression on the future of Roman politics is called an *augurium*. The irony that pervades the letter brings Cicero and Caecina closer in one way, as it brings out the affinity between the two men, who are not just friends and political associates, but are also both involved in divination. At the same time, it stresses the differences between their personal circumstances – Cicero is in Italy, while Caecina is not – by developing the differences in their divinatory methods.[56]

---

[53] Cic. *Fam.* 6.6.2: *nec iis quidem uerbis quibus te consoler* ('and not in the words that I should use to console you').
[54] Griffin 1995.   [55] *Contra* Cuny-Le Callet 2005b: 233–4, who speaks of a 'lettre de connivence'.
[56] On irony as a means to create common ground between Cicero and his correspondents see Griffin 1995: 329–30.

There is little trace here of the debate on the role of augury and its divinatory remit that can be found in the *De legibus* and in the *De diuinatione*. There is also very little discussion of the prerogatives of augury. Cicero just says that the signs interpreted by the augurs are not less certain than those that he is setting out to interpret by looking at the political situation. This is a rather cautious approach, it seems, but Cicero makes it clear that augural lore is not the sort of prediction he is interested in pursuing.[57] The same applies to haruspicy, which Cicero barely discusses, acknowledging its role in the culture and education of Caecina. Of course, we should not expect Cicero to provide a detailed theoretical discussion of this problem in this context, as he addresses Caecina, a prominent practitioner of haruspicy.

Cicero found the opportunity to dismiss the relevance and usefulness of any form of divination and divinatory signs at the challenging time of the Civil War between Caesar and Pompey in one of the passages of the *De diuinatione* that he wrote after the death of the dictator. According to Quintus, the Galatian king Deiotarus claimed that the auspices that had encouraged him to fight on Pompey's side were not misleading, because they led him to side with the cause of liberty. Marcus' reply is customarily abrasive, as it provides a list of all the evils that came Deiotarus' way after Pharsalus, including the loss of his kingdom: there was nothing favourable about that turn of events, and whatever premonition he received it must have been a misleading one. It is true that Deiotarus fulfilled his duty (*functus sit officio*) when he joined Pompey, but he was led to that decision by his manly courage (*a uirtute*), not by the auspices.[58]

Another letter written in this very period shows that the importance of forming reliable predictions was central to Cicero's concerns in this period. When he wrote to Varro in June 46, Cicero affectionately urged his friend to make up his mind about when to visit him. He knew that Varro was in great doubt as to what to do in the imminence of Caesar's arrival in Italy and he teased him, urging him to put his indecision aside at least as far as the visits to his friend were concerned. The shortest letter of the series starts with a brief reference to a philosophical theory on predestination and

---

[57] Cf. *uerissima auguria rerum futurarum* ('the truest auguries of things to come') in *Phil.* 2.89, where Cicero refers to his predictions of Antony's moves in the aftermath of Caesar's death. Interestingly, the expression appears after the allegation that Antony made a false statement about the auspices (see Appendix).

[58] Cic. *Div.* 1.27; 2.78–9. Struck 2003: 167 stresses the opposition between *uirtus* and divination in this context. As Wardle 2006: 172 notes, the references to the auspices are rather puzzling: the auspices only state the gods' view on whether an action can be undertaken on a particular day, but do not entail a statement on its merits or a prediction of its success.

specifically to a disagreement between Diodotus and Chrysippus.[59] Cicero claims that Varro and himself will soon debate this problem in person. Despite the irony of the letter and the fact that he does not know Varro's response to his own irony, it is undeniable that the topic must have been one of common interest. If the letter to Caecina can be seen as a reflection on problems that would soon be discussed in the *De diuinatione*, the one to Varro anticipates an interest in theories of predestination that found a fuller discussion in the *De fato*.

This letter is not about divination, but proves an excellent opportunity for Cicero to think about the nature and limits of divination and to present his take on the problem in a non-philosophical context. Despite paying lip-service to the great tradition of haruspicy and to augural lore, Cicero clearly places himself outside that legacy. The scope of his intellectual activity is not divination, but political prediction. It is an encounter between Roman pragmatism and Greek *paideia*, as he makes clear himself, which is based on logical inferences, and engages with non-religious premises and evidences. The Etruscan *disciplina* is not part of this horizon. The correspondence between the emphasis of the importance of reflective prediction in political matters outlined in this letter and the discussion of logical prediction developed by Marcus in *De diuinatione* 2 is very significant. This letter must be read as evidence for the period of the preparation of the religious trilogy and must be regarded as evidence for Cicero's growing concern about this problem. The recourse to irony and the thoughtful badinage did not prevent him from exploring serious issues and taking a serious stand on them.

Cicero's letter to Caecina is also an instructive example of the evocative power of the word *diuinatio*. As stated above, this noun does not appear before Cicero and it appears only sporadically in later authors. The verb *diuinare*, however, appears as early as in Plautus, and from the outset it appears to have a twofold meaning.[60] It can be used to refer to a divinely inspired guess, which may also be predictive, or it can just refer to a very clever guess. In a legal context *diuinare* could have openly negative connotations. In the *Pro Plancio* Cicero blames his opponent Laterensis for refusing to hold a trial before a panel of judges who could express an informed opinion on the case. The judges before whom the case is heard are not aware of the background and they will have to proceed by a divinatory

<hr/>

[59] Cic. *Fam.* 9.4. Manzo 1969: 86, 136; Griffin 1995: 339–41; Adams 2003: 316–17. Guillaumont 2002 offers a useful overview of the philosophical references and allusions in Cicero's correspondence (on Diodotus, see 63).

[60] Plaut. *Mil.* 1255–7; note also *hariolari* in 1256. Slater 2000: 359–60; Santangelo 2012: 41–2.

method, rather than using the information that men of their standing would need in order to reach an informed decision. The opposition is presented in clear-cut terms: 'why do you prefer having them to divine, rather than those men to decide who had means of establishing the facts?'[61] In a judiciary context the ability to 'divine' was apparently considered an unreasonable expectation.

There is, however, a level of affinity between divination and law, which even the Latin language recognises: the word *diuinatio* was also a legal term.[62] It defined a particular kind of judiciary speech, which was given by a prospective prosecutor before the jury, in order to prove his credentials and so be entrusted with the task of prosecuting the defendant.[63] The only surviving *diuinatio* is the *diuinatio in Q. Caecilium*, the speech that Cicero gave in 70 in order to be assigned the prosecution case against Verres.[64] Various attempts were made in antiquity to explain the origin of this meaning of *diuinatio*.[65] According to Gavius Bassus and Quintilian, it was the jury who had to divine who would be the best prosecutor; according to Gellius, the *diuinatio* was a mock trial, in which the figure of the prosecutor has to be supplied by divination – by imagining that a prosecutor has actually been entrusted with the case.[66] More theories may be found in a scholion to Cicero by pseudo-Asconius; they all revolve around the fact that the *diuinatio* is a speech that requires speaker and audience to make bold predictive efforts.[67] The similarities between the task of the diviner and that of the judge have been detected and explicitly developed in a number of cultures.[68] We have no evidence that it was ever explicitly pointed out in Republican Rome, but these definitions of

---

[61] Cic. *Planc.* 46.1: *cur denique se diuinare malueris quam eos qui scirent iudicare?* ('why do you prefer having them to divine, rather than those men to decide who had means of knowing the truth?'). Other uses of *diuinare* in legal contexts: Cic. *Rab. Post.* 1; *Inv. rhet.* 2.153. *Diuinatio* as guesswork in judiciary speeches: Cic. *Rosc. Am.* 96; *Clu.* 97; *Tul.* 50. We are a far cry from the working definition of *diuinatio* as *scientia* in *Div.* 1.1 (Santangelo 2012: 46–7).

[62] Cf. the analogy between Apollo and the jurist Q. Mucius Scaevola in Cic. *De or.* 1.199–200; see Leeman, Pinkster and Nelson 1985: 113–14; Romano 2008. Cf. also Meyer 2004: 44–72 on the relevance of the concept of *carmen* to the legal domain. Divination and law: Luhmann 2004: 234–7.

[63] Schaefer 1977: 209–16; Santangelo 2012: 43–7. Cf. also Manetti 1987: 203 (= 1993: 140: 'the consideration of signs rests at the heart of *inventio*, that is, when proofs must be 'found' to convince the court of the guilt or innocence of the accused').

[64] Kurczyk 2006: 143–9; Lintott 2008: 82–6; Tempest 2011. Suet. *Iul.* 55.3 mentions a *diuinatio* pronounced by Caesar in 77 in order to obtain the prosecution of Cn. Cornelius Dolabella (*cos.* 81).

[65] Maltby 1991: 192–3.   [66] Quint. *Inst.* 7.4.83; Gell. *NA* 2.4.1.

[67] Ps.-Asc. *In div.*, *Argumentum diuinationis* (= 186.4–8 Stangl).

[68] See e.g. Turner 1968: 25, 45 on the rituals of the Ndembu in Zambia or the discussion of Mesopotamian extispicy, in which the divinatory ritual was often described as a judgement, in Koch 2010: 51–3.

diuinatio show that an effort to think about the overlaps between divination and law was made in some quarters.[69]

By the mid first century BC the word *diuinatio* had developed a range of meanings which all provide insights into the meaning of divination itself. The main analogy was that between divination and guesswork; guesswork could be relevant for the interpretation of the present situation and for the understanding of the future. Cicero's correspondence shows similar shifts;[70] Livy's occasional explicit references to *diuinatio* show a comparable diversity. There is, for instance, an interesting reference to Scipio Africanus' impressive foresight and the reputation he had earned for it amongst friends of the allies: *nihilo minor fama apud hostis Scipionis erat quam apud ciuis sociosque, et diuinatio quaedam futuri, quo minus ratio timoris reddi poterat oborti temere, maiorem inferens metum.*[71] In light of the tradition that existed on the divine qualities of Scipio (on which see Chapter 10), this language can hardly be innocent. We find an even more intriguing reference in the description of the moments following a defeat on the Spanish front during the Hannibalic War: the Romans are subdued and in a gloomy mood, even before hearing about the outcome of the battle, as if they already knew that bad news was forthcoming. 'There was an afflicted silence and a silent *diuinatio*': almost a contradiction in terms, in a world where all kinds of prophecies and predictions were produced and circulated.[72]

Prudentia

Several occurrences of *diuinatio* raise the problem of the expertise of those who give predictions. This is hardly surprising. The issue of expertise is central to any discussion of divination and prediction and it was all the more significant in a period of Roman intellectual history in which the emphasis on ability, expertise and accuracy was increasingly strong. The diviner typically spoke through brief and well-targeted responses, which shed light on specific problems and were based on a body of specialised knowledge. The affinities of divination to some of the new fields of intellectual activity

---

[69] Santangelo 2012: 41–6.   [70] Cic. *Fam.* 3.13; 6.3; 15.15.

[71] Livy 26.20.5: 'His reputation was as strong among the enemy as among his own fellow-citizens and allies, and there was some kind of divination of what was to come; somehow a reason could not be found for the apprehension that had arisen, and this brought about even greater fear.' Rossi 2004b explores the complexity of Livy's portrait of Scipio and its analogies with the depiction of Hannibal.

[72] Livy 25.35.3: *maestum quoddam silentium erat et tacita diuinatio, qualis iam presagientibus animis inminentis mali esse solet* ('There was an afflicted silence and a silent divination, as is usually the case when people's minds can already perceive beforehand an impending evil').

that emerged at Rome in the second century BC – most notably law, grammar and literary criticism – are apparent.

Prudentia occurs more frequently than *diuinatio*, and this is mainly because *prudentia* is a philosophical concept, a virtue which has a strong political dimension: good sense, intelligence, wisdom.[73] With his usual keenness on identifying Greek parallels, Cicero argued that *prudentia* was the Latin equivalent of *phronesis*.[74] This is a good translation, but it does not reflect the etymology of the word: *prudentia* derives from *pro-uidere*, 'seeing before, seeing ahead'. Some occurrences of *prudentia* show that this association was still recognised and understood in the first century BC. Cicero is, again, the most instructive source, as he provides several definitions of what *prudentia* may be. In a fragment of the *Hortensius* he argued that *prouidere* is a faculty of the wise man, and for this reason *sapientia* is also called *prudentia*; a similar point is made in a fragment of the *De re publica*.[75] The fullest and most formalised definition, however, is in the *De inuentione* (2.160):

> *prudentia est rerum bonarum et malarum neutrarumque scientia. partes eius: memoria, intellegentia, prouidentia. memoria est, per quam animus repetit illa, quae fuerunt; intellegentia, per quam ea perspicit, quae sunt; prouidentia, per quam futurum aliquid uidetur ante quam factum est.*

> *Prudentia* is the knowledge of what is good, what is bad, and what is neither good nor bad. Its parts are memory, intelligence and *prouidentia*. Memory is the faculty by which the mind recalls what has happened. Intelligence is the faculty by which it ascertains what is happening. *Prouidentia* is the faculty by which it is seen that something is going to occur before it occurs.

As is so often the case in the *De inuentione*, the concept under discussion is divided into more specific ones. The constituents of *prudentia* are identified as *memoria*, *intellegentia* and *prouidentia*. Memory concerns the past, intelligence pertains to the understanding of the present, while *prouidentia* enables one to see something that is about to happen before it actually happens. In this definition, *prudentia* is more than foresight, and applies to all areas of understanding, including the prediction of the future.

Some later texts show a shift in this reflection. The definition of *prudentia* in the *De legibus* is both clear and complex. It is a virtue that derives its name from the ability to see in advance (*ex prouidendo*) and it may be

---

[73] Kirov 2010: 308 argues that the temporal connotation of *prudentia* is a symptom of the centrality of time and its control in the political culture of the Republic. *Prudentia* as a virtue: Hellegouarc'h 1963: 258–74.

[74] Cic. *Off.* 1.43.   [75] Cic. *Hortensius* F 33 Müller (*ap.* Nonius 41); *Rep.* 6.1. Maltby 1991: 504.

compared to the ability of the eyes to see clearly: it enables one to see what is good and to avoid what is bad.[76] Cicero argues that it may be developed as the consequence of a complex process: defeating the basest bodily instincts, overcoming the fear of death and embracing the cult of the gods in its purest and most appropriate form (*cultumque deorum et puram religionem susceperit*). There is, therefore, a relationship between the ability to foresee and predict the future and suitable religious choices; recognising the role of the gods without indulging in *superstitio* or, even worse, in unsanctioned foreign practices.[77] Unsurprisingly, Cicero is very interested in the intellectual dimension of *prudentia* and in exploring its importance as a political virtue. In this context, *prudentia* features quite prominently in the first book of the *De officiis*, where Cicero offers a working definition that contrasts it with *sapientia*. *Prudentia* is a form of practical knowledge, which tells us what must be pursued and what must be avoided.[78] The form of philosophical knowledge that Cicero advocates as most desirable is wisdom, *sapientia – sophia*.[79] It is a form of superior knowledge, which must be practised with the aim of benefiting the community: mere intellectual speculation will not suffice. For this reason, those who devote their energy to the study of wisdom often choose to put their understanding and intelligence to the service of fellow human beings, and their eloquence to the service of learning. Using one's own *prudentia* is a symptom of one's wisdom. In book 2, Cicero comes back to the scope that *prudentia* must have, emphasising the importance of ensuring that it is always accompanied by a sense of justice. Incidentally, Cicero offers another remarkable definition of *prudentia*, in which the link with the prediction of the future is evoked even more explicitly (*Off.* 2.33):

> nam et iis fidem habemus, quos plus intellegere quam nos arbitramur quosque et futura prospicere credimus et cum res agatur in discrimenque uentum sit, expedire rem et consilium ex tempore capere posse; hanc enim utilem homines existimant ueramque prudentiam.

> For we have confidence in those who we think have more understanding than ourselves, who, we believe, also have insight into the future and, when an emergency arises and a crisis comes, can clear away the difficulties and reach an intelligent decision according to the exigencies of the occasion; for that kind of wisdom men consider genuine and practical.

---

[76] Cic. *Leg.* 1.60.   [77] This is the likely meaning of *pura religio* in this context: Dyck 2004: 230.

[78] Cic. *Leg.* 1.43.

[79] The same concept is conveyed in the fragment of the *Hortensius* (F 33 Müller) mentioned above: *id est enim sapientis, prouidere; ex quo sapientia est appellata prudentia.* Cf. Hdt. 1.86.3 and 7.234.1 on the prophetic role of human wisdom; see Harrison 2000: 129–30.

In this definition *prudentia* is about predicting the future and having a clear understanding of the present. It is therefore a political virtue *par excellence*.[80] Against this background, it is not surprising that the references to *prudentia* in the *De re publica* 2 have an even more explicitly political slant. At the beginning of his account of the fall of the monarchy at Rome, Scipio invokes the concept of political *prudentia* and argues that the whole point of his work is precisely that of exploring it. *Prudentia* entails the ability to account for the development and the decline of states, so that the mechanics of decline can be properly understood and, whenever possible, stopped and prevented. It is regrettable that the context of this passage is fragmentary. We are quite clearly in a Polybian mood, as has often been noticed; the issue of the decline of political bodies has an obvious importance throughout the work.[81]

It would be irrelevant to the purposes of this inquiry to go through the many other briefer references to *prudentia* that may be found in Cicero's philosophical works, not least because in most of them *prudentia* appears to be mentioned generically as a form of practical wisdom, often in association with other virtues like *fortitudo* or *iustitia*. It is more rewarding to focus on the occasions in which Cicero explores and exploits the semantic complexity of the concept of *prudentia* and insists on the interaction between foresight and practical knowledge. The *Catilinarians* are – as is well known – a powerful celebration of Cicero's political intelligence and his ability to face the conspiracy and address the threat that it presented to the survival of the State. Strikingly, they feature only one reference to Cicero's *prudentia*, at the very end of the second speech, when Cicero promises his fellow-citizens that the conspiracy will be defeated.[82] He immediately makes clear that his promise is not based on his own *prudentia* or on any other human factor. It is based on clear signs sent by the gods, which Cicero has been able to read in order to devise his plan. The gods will ensure their protection of the city, as they ensured that it maintained its internal order in the past and they made possible the defeat of many external enemies. In the future they will also secure the defeat of internal enemies, provided that the citizens keep worshipping them. The role of *prudentia* is ostensibly marginal in this context, but Cicero's rhetorical strategy is quite clear. It is precisely because of his *prudentia* that Cicero could understand the role

---

[80] Martin 1982: 47–8.

[81] The expression *prudentia ciuilis* had considerable impact on Cicero's readers in the early modern period: most notably Justus Lipsius, in the third book of the *Politicorum sive civilis doctrinae libri sex*, published at Leiden in 1589.

[82] Cic. *Cat.* 2.29. Cf. *Att.* 1.16.6 (late June or July 61).

of the gods in protecting the city and securing its prosperity and share his predictions with his fellow-citizens. Recognising this bond between the city and the gods is both a demonstration of practical understanding and political intelligence and a method to predict the course of future events. This theme also emerges in the third *Catilinarian*, where *prouidentia* – a variant of *prudentia* that appears rarely in Republican literature – features among the qualities with which Cicero claims to have saved the State: his courage, counsel and foresight (*uirtute, consilio, prouidentia mea*).[83]

We encounter similar resonances in a number of other references to *prudentia* in Cicero's correspondence. The famous response to Lucceius' *consolatio* after Tullia's death opens with praise of Lucceius' *beneuolentia* and *prudentia*; it is surely because of the latter quality that Lucceius appears so thoroughly armed and equipped against *fortuna*.[84] The letter continues with long-winded praise of Lucceius' letter and of his personal qualities, and it soon moves on to depict the disastrous state the Republic is in. What is most remarkable here is the analogy between the private tragedy of an individual and the collective destruction that the State is heading for, already memorably explored in the letter of Servius Sulpicius Rufus that we will discuss in Chapter 8. There is no better illustration of the relevance of *prudentia* as both a philosophical virtue and a political skill.

A letter written to A. Manlius Torquatus, a supporter of Pompey, in January 45, is again dominated by the need to attempt to predict future political developments (*Fam.* 6.4). Torquatus' most pressing worry was to obtain Caesar's pardon and be allowed to go back to Italy. Cicero was apparently advocating his return, as he did for other Pompeiani. When he replied to this letter he was back in Rome and he tried to console his friend by arguing that his situation was in no way preferable to his own. Cicero claimed that he could offer his friend only two reasons to feel consoled. On the one hand, he had predicted the outcome of the civil war and had

---

[83] Cic. *Cat.* 3.14: *primum mihi gratiae uerbis amplissimis aguntur, quod uirtute, consilio, prouidentia mea res publica maximis periculis sit liberata* ('First, I am thanked with the most generous words, that thanks to my courage, wisdom and foresight the country has been freed from the most severe danger'). On *prouidentia* in this context see Dyck 2008: 151; Gildenhard 2009: 96 and 2011: 278–9, 292. *Prouidentia* is not widely attested in the late Republic: cf. however Cic. *Inv. rhet.* 2.160 (*prouidentia, per quam futurum aliquid uidetur ante quam factum est*, '*prouidentia*, through which something that will happen is seen before it takes place'); *Nat. D.* 2.58 and 89. See Martin 1982: 31–65; Luciani 2010: 260–2. Hellegouarc'h 1963: 256 argues that *prouidentia* is a quality that pertains to the gods' ability to predict the future, but does not apply to the political domain, to which the statesman's *prudentia* applied. It is possible that, in a speech addressed to the people, Cicero chose a term that – unlike *prudentia* – unmistakeably stressed his ability to 'see ahead' and had a transparent etymology. *Prouidentia* as an imperial virtue: Noreña 2011: 92–9.

[84] Cic. *Fam.* 5.13.1: *optime contra fortunam paratum armatumque.*

done his utmost to prevent it from starting; on the other hand, he did not have to fear death, because he would not be leaving behind a republic to treasure and defend. Cicero concedes that the whole series of events may have been fortuitous and have nothing to do with his quasi-divine ability to predict the future (*quod etsi casu, non diuinatione mea, factum est*); still, he is pleased to see that there is hollow praise for his foresight (*tamen in hac inani prudentiae laude delector*).[85] This passage shows how slight the distinction between *prudentia* and *diuinatio* can be in some contexts. It was Cicero's *prudentia* that could have given him the ability to produce an accurate *diuinatio* – even if the whole exercise was probably useless, because the dominant factor in the build-up to the war and its development was *casus*.[86] Again, we should not expect to find too fixed a terminology in Cicero's correspondence, which is a formidable laboratory of linguistic and lexical creativity.

Atticus is often praised for his *prudentia*;[87] on one occasion, however, the acknowledgment of his friend's foresight takes a bitter turn, when Cicero blames his friend for not having offered him his advice.[88] In 7.1 Cicero urges Atticus to advise him on his personal position at a time of great political crisis: the letter in question was written from Athens in 50 and Cicero admitted very candidly that he foresaw turmoil (*dimicatio*) of unprecedented scale in Rome and Italy: only a god could avert that grim destiny. He does not ask Atticus for advice, or for a prediction on the outbreak of war, which was by then inevitable; on the contrary, he urges him to use his unrivalled foresight to advise him as to what side he should take – Caesar's or Pompey's. The letter has a light-hearted touch that is all the more surprising in light of the context in which it was written. Cicero ironically defines his personal dilemma with the Greek word *pròblēma*; and the request for advice to Atticus is made in the name of *fortuna* (*per fortunas*). We should not make too much of the use of *prudentia* in this context: surely there is a philosophical joke in Cicero's request to his Epicurean friend to predict the future.[89] It is nonetheless interesting to see that while *prudentia* is not deemed useful to avoid great catastrophes, it is still considered a valuable tool to help individuals to make decisions about their own future.

[85] Cf. the unfaithful but perceptive translation in Thomas 2002: 277–8 n. 74: 'je me rejouis cependant de cette considération même imméritée pour ma prévoyance'.
[86] Cicero on chance: Bernett 1995: 236–49.   [87] See e.g. Cic. *Att.* 5.18.3; 6.9.1; 7.2.2; 11.6.1; 16.11.2.
[88] Cic. *Att.* 3.15.7. White 2010: 129 stresses the polemical tone of this letter.
[89] Epicureanism argued that, if there are gods, they do not put men in a position to predict the future; the argument is implicitly attacked by Quintus in Cic. *Div.* 1.81–3. As Griffin 1995: 328 notes, there is 'a lot of philosophical teasing' in the correspondence with Atticus.

Atticus' *prudentia* is again briefly evoked in association with his *temperantia* in the following letter, written from Brundisium in November 49 (7.2), and, implicitly, at the end of a letter written from Minturnae in January 49 (7.13), as Caesar was beginning his march into Italy and Pompey and his supporters were planning to leave Rome. Cicero's attention is rather touchingly focused on his family, especially his wife and daughter, and on whether it would be safe for them to remain in Rome with Caesar's arrival imminent. Atticus is asked to find out as much as he can about the political and military situation in Rome and not to limit himself to describing it.[90] As so often in their letters, Cicero and Atticus communicated through a literary quotation, even an incomplete one, as in this case: a *sententia* from Euripides, which goes 'as the best diviner I maintain to be the man who guesses or conjectures best'.[91] Surely it is not coincidental that this is the first poetic quote to be found in the second book of the *De diuinatione* – the Ciceronian text where a contrast between *diuinatio* and *prudentia* is developed most fully and coherently. Marcus quotes a Latin translation of this dictum, without even referring it to Euripides: *bene qui coniciet, uatem hunc perhibebo optumum*. In fact, he refers to it as a *Graecus uulgaris uersus* and it has rightly been argued that the line may be reflecting a proverbial saying, rather than a literary quote.[92] Marcus uses this famous line as an ironic critique of divination: its meaning is that anyone who may be able to make a good prediction should be regarded as a *uates*, as a good diviner. He uses it as a helpful device in a longer discussion on the limits, or indeed on the complete uselessness, of divination. It is preceded by an explicit statement, which, despite its cautious wording, summarises the whole point of book 2 (*uide igitur, ne nulla sit diuinatio*) and it is followed by a discussion which completes the introductory section of the book and uses the concept of *prudentia* as an alternative to *diuinatio*. Marcus argues, again ironically, that a *uates*, a diviner, may not be considered a more suitable weather forecaster than a sailor, or a better diagnostician than a doctor. Neither can a *uates* be expected to arrange the management

---

[90] Cic. *Att.* 7.13.4: *reliquum est ut et quid agatur quoad poteris explores scribasque ad me et quid ipse coniectura adsequare; quod etiam a te magis exspecto. nam acta omnibus nuntiantibus a te exspecto futura.* 'μάντις δ' ἄριστος'. *loquacitati ignosces, quae et me leuat ad te quidem scribentem et elicit tuas litteras* ('It remains for you to explore what is going on as best as you can and write it to me, and what you are able to understand by means of a conjecture; I expect the latter from you even more than the former. For everyone reports to me what has been done; from you I expect the things to come. '*Le meilleur devin . . .*' You will forgive my talkativeness; it gives me relief, as I write to you, and elicits letters from you').

[91] Guillaumont 2000: 104–6 and Schneider 2004: 11. On the Euripides quote (F 973 Nauck) cf. Gieseler Greenbaum 2010: 209.

[92] Cic. *Div.* 2.12. Timpanaro 1988: 335–6.

of a war in advance (*coniectura*) more capably (*prudentius*) than a military commander.[93]

Marcus is trying to give an answer to the problem with which he started his critique of divination, i.e. the limits of prediction and the definition of what may be an object of divination. According to his summary of the first book, Quintus has defined divination as a practice confined to the things that are deemed fortuitous and has drawn a distinction between these and the predictions that are based either on the senses (*sensibus*), on techniques (*aut artificiis*), or indeed on some specific ability and understanding (*ab iis coniecturis quae haberent artem atque prudentiam*).[94] In this context, *prudentia* is deeply connected to *ars*; it is a technique that derives from and depends upon a specific set of knowledge. In this respect, there is agreement between Quintus and Marcus. However, Marcus believes that the field of what is fortuitous should be extended and that *ars* and *prudentia* may be useful for the prediction of fortuitous events: sailors, doctors and generals face these kinds of events at all times and use their knowledge to anticipate, or face them. Predicting someone's death is tantamount to reading what is 'in the domain of *fortuna*' (*quae in fortuna positae sunt*); such prediction is not based on any practice (*ars*) or knowledge (*sapientia*). After cornering divination into this partial and reductive definition, Marcus then embarks upon a critique of the concepts themselves of *fortuna* and *fatum*, or at least of their Stoic incarnations. It is not possible to predict anything unless there are signs or symptoms for it; at any rate, if fate truly is so powerful and cannot be altered, there would be no point in exploring it through divinatory practices.

The role of *prudentia* in the *De diuinatione* is carefully framed. The word indicates a form of technical knowledge, firmly separate from, or indeed opposed to any form of divination. It is probably for this reason that it features infrequently in the rest of the book.[95] Things are not much different in the first book, where there is only one reference to *prudentia*, this time in association with *ratio*.[96] There is, however, an interesting occurrence

---

[93] *Coniectura*: Guillaumont 2000: 105–6; Kany-Turpin 2003b; Gieseler Greenbaum 2010: 183. Epistemological importance of conjecture: Ginzburg 1986: 170–1; Manetti 1987: 55–6 (= 1993: 35: the 'adoption of conjecture' was central to the emergence of forms of divination that were not based on 'vision'). Augury, however, is based neither on vision nor on conjecture, but on observation: Regell 1878: 4–5.
[94] Cic. *Div.* 2.13: 'from conjectures based upon skill and experience in public affairs'.
[95] Cic. *Div.* 2.150. It appears on a couple of occasions with its meaning of 'wisdom, good sense' (2.50, 2.130); cf. also the use of *prudens* (2.113).
[96] Cic. *Div.* 1.24.

of *prudens* elsewhere in the same book.[97] Quintus speaks of the wise men
who are able to make informed predictions, about either meteorological
phenomena or political developments: a rare breed of individuals, to which
the Greek wise men Solon and Thales belonged.[98] The former predicted
the advent of tyranny in Athens: the latter purchased all the olive trees
in the territory of Miletus before they flourished, since he had foreseen,
unlike anyone else, that there would be an excellent harvest. These people
may not be called diviners (*diuini*), but they deserve the label of *prudentes*,
id est prouidentes. It is the only case in the dialogue when the etymology
of *prudens* and *prudentia* is discussed. This is all the more striking, since
there are numerous occurrences of *prouidere* in the dialogue. The meaning
of the verb may be that of 'foresee', but it can also mean 'to take appropriate action before something happens', as in 1.29, when the purpose of
unfavourable predictions is defined precisely in urging people to act, as
something bad will happen unless they make arrangements (*non causas
adferunt, cur quid eueniat, sed nuntiant euentura, si prouideris* – 'are not the
cause of anything happening, but announce what will happen unless measures are taken').[99] In most cases, however, *prouidere* occurs in its meaning
of 'foreseeing', with reference to the soul during dreams.[100] It is also used,
perhaps most notably, in the passage where the divinatory scope of augury
is discussed and ultimately denied.[101] *Prouidere* appears fairly often in the
De diuinatione, although not quite as frequently as *praedicere*.[102] However,
it is not necessarily related to the remit of divination. In fact, both Quintus
and Marcus appear to use the verb in a broad sense; at the same time,
they both agree that *prudentia* and *diuinatio* belong to different levels.
Their disagreement is mainly on the definition of what may be considered

[97] Cic. *Div.* 1.111, with Guillaumont 1984: 109–10. The distinction of political wisdom from divination
    was not an original idea. Wardle 2006: 374–5 argues that this passage is based on Cratippus, like
    the whole section of the book on natural divination and rational prediction (*Div.* 1.109–31; see also
    Wardle 2006: 32–6).

[98] The affinity between meteorology and prediction is also developed by Marcus in 2.33–4, 44: Taub
    2001: 60–3; Kany-Turpin 2003a. For a thought-provoking modern appraisal cf. Fine 2007.

[99] Cf. Cic. *Div.* 2. 69: *audita uox est monentis ut prouiderent ne a Gallis Roma caperetur* ('a voice was
    heard warning the people to act in order to prevent the capture of Rome by the Gauls').

[100] Cic. *Div.* 1.63: *meminit praeteritorum, praesentia cernit, futura prouidet* ('it remembers the past, sees
    the present, and foresees the future'); cf. 1.64 (the soul of the dying) and 2.16 (predictions of sailors,
    doctors and generals). Cf. also 2.25 and 27.

[101] Cic. *Div.* 2.70. Cf. also 2.124 and 126.

[102] *Prouidere* in Cic. *Div.*: 1.29 (Linderski 1986a: 2201–2 links it to Cic. *Leg.* 2.21, where it refers to the
    priests' duty to foresee divine anger), 1.63, 1.64, 1.81, 1.111; 2.14, 2.16, 2.17, 2.25, 2.27, 2.69, 2.70,
    2.124, 2.126. *Praedicere*: 1.2 (twice), 1.24, 1.35, 1.48, 1.58, 1.78, 1.93, 1.114, 1.124, 1.125 (twice), 1.128,
    1.132; 2.17 (twice), 2.19, 2.26, 2.48, 2.52, 2.54, 2.66, 2.88, 2.90, 2.109. Although *fari* can be referred
    to divinatory utterances, *praefari* is not a synonym for *praedicere*: its meaning is 'to say before', or
    'to say something in a position of importance' (Bettini 2008: 332–4).

fortuitous or not; and therefore on what may be considered the domain of divination and what may not.

Although *prudentia* and *diuinatio* have different spheres of action, there may be an important area of contact between the two – or, at least, they may be meaningfully related to one another. In the *De haruspicum responso*, Cicero gives an emphatic statement of loyalty to public divination and to the place of tradition in Roman religious life.[103] The teachings of the ancestors are the necessary reference point; the ancestors were *prudentes*, because they put in place public divination. It is tempting to see a play on the etymology of *prudentia* in this discussion of divination. However, the praise for divination is not unqualified. The foresight of the ancestors is all the more noteworthy because they set limits on the potential options of divinatory practices. Augury sets limits to the use of magistratual power, the Sibylline Books provide a framework for the handling of ancient prophetic utterances, and the Etruscan *disciplina* establishes rules for the expiation of prodigies. *Prudentia* therefore becomes essential in completing and qualifying Cicero's assessment of Roman public divination.

Prudens

Those who have *prudentia*, the *prudens* and the *prudentes*, deserve as much attention as the concept of *prudentia* itself. *Prudens* is a contraction of *prouidens*, and in some of its many meanings it shows traces of this etymology.[104] Its earliest attested meaning can be defined as 'well aware of what one does, or of the consequences of what one is doing': the expression *prudens boni*, for instance, is used in opposition to *insciens boni* (Plaut. *Capt.* 45) and it is used precisely to convey the sense of a form of wisdom that is based on the awareness of what is good and of how it can be achieved. The affinity between *prudens* and *sciens* is repeatedly stressed in Latin literature. The two words are used together on a number of occasions, in authors as different as Terence, Cicero, Apuleius or Ulpian, and their association sometimes sounds even pleonastic. Many occurrences of *prudens*, however, mirror the most common meaning of *prudentia* that we have explored above – that of 'wisdom', indeed of 'practical wisdom'. *Prudens* usually features as an adjective and often means 'sensible', 'acting

---

[103] Cic. *Har. resp.* 18. Santangelo 2012: 47–8.
[104] Cf. Varro *Ling.* 8.15 (*a prudentia prudens*) and Isid. *Etym.* 10.201 (*prudens, quasi porro uidens, praespicax enim et incertorum praeuidet casus*).

intelligently'.[105] Cicero qualifies his protégé Deiotarus as *consideratus, tectus* and *prudens* ('careful', 'guarded', 'sensible'); he defines the letters of his friend M. Caelius as *suaues* and *prudentes, multi et offici et consili* ('charming' and 'shrewd', 'full of kindness and good advice'); and he uses the adjective *prudens* to refer to the consolation sent by his son-in-law P. Cornelius Dolabella in 44, shortly after the death of his daughter Tullia.[106] The list could continue and would include a number of authors after Cicero, an Augustan poet like Ovid, or Gellius, who refers to Sophocles as *prudentissimus poetarum*, 'the wisest of poets'.[107] In this respect, the history of the adjective *prudens* is similar to that of the noun *prudentia*. Only occasionally do we see an intentional reminiscence of the etymology of the word. In a letter he wrote to Plancius in October 45, Cicero claims that in his attempt to avoid the civil war he was far from fearful; on the contrary, he was *prudens* and was able to predict (*praedicere*) the grim consequences of the conflict.[108]

The adjective *prudens* also has an important application within the legal domain. When Q. Mucius Scaevola (*cos.* 95) set out to establish whether the praetor who carried out business on a *dies nefastus* should be deemed guilty of a religious crime, he concluded that the religious breach could not be expiated only if the praetor had committed it intentionally (*si prudens dixit*).[109] *Prudens* is eminently suited to convey the concept of a deliberate initiative; the *prudens* knows the implications of his action and can foresee its consequences.[110] Scaevola uses it to define and apply a general principle which plays an important role in the formation of a systematic discourse on law and jurisprudence.[111]

---

[105] Moatti 2003: 305–7 establishes an interesting link between *prudens* and *peritus*. The knowledge of the *peritus* applies to fields 'étroitement associées à la définition de l'activité et à la vertu politique', such as law, rhetoric, history and military leadership; that of the *prudens* is a 'connaissance approfondie . . . qui permet . . . de prévoir, de savoir "avant"'; they both have a strong political connotation.

[106] See respectively Cic. *Deiot.* 16; *Fam.* 2.13.1; 9.11.1.

[107] Ovid called himself *Naso parum prudens*, alluding to his misguided choice to write the *Ars amatoria*: Ov. *Pont.* 2.10.15. Gellius: 12.11.6.

[108] Cic. *Fam.* 4.14.3.

[109] Varro *Ling.* 6.30: *praetor qui tum fatus est, si imprudens fecit, piaculari hostia facta piatur; si prudens dixit, Quintus Mucius aiebat eum expiari ut impium non posse* ('the praetor who has made a legal decision at such a time is freed of his wrongdoing by the sacrifice of an expiatory victim if he did it unintentionally; if he made the pronouncement with a realisation of what he was doing, Quintus Mucius said that he could not in any way expiate his wrongdoing, as someone who was *impius*'). Cf. also Macrob. *Sat.* 1.16.9–10.

[110] Cf. the use of *prudens* with reference to intentional criminal behaviour in Gell. *NA* 20.1.17.

[111] Tromp 1921: 82–7; Cornell 1981: 35–7; Scheid 1999b and 2006a: 20–32; Santangelo 2012: 49–50. Quintus Mucius' place in Roman legal and intellectual history: Bauman 1983: 340–423; Schiavone 2005: 155–213.

Prudens may also indicate a specific expertise and a form of knowledge that has a practical dimension.[112] Moreover, since Cicero's time at the latest, the adjective *prudens* was often used as a noun. The *prudens* is, first and foremost, a person who has a special knowledge on a specific issue.[113] This word is eminently suited to the legal field, where *prudens* labels the expert practitioner who is able to talk about legal matters and to give informed and binding opinions about it. In Gaius' *Institutiones* the *responsa prudentium* are a fundamental constituency of Roman law.[114] Gaius' work is deeply embedded in the political and social context of the second century AD, but the effort to define the constituents of law (the *partes iuris*) belongs within an intellectual tradition that began in the early first century BC, and is well attested in the *Rhetorica ad Herennium* and in Cicero's *De inuentione* and *Topica*.[115] As far as we can tell from the *Digest*, the emergence of this meaning of *prudens* dates to the early Principate. It is not found in the late Republican jurists like Scaevola, Sulpicius or even Labeo, but its non-existence cannot be inferred, as so many texts do not survive, in this as in other literary genres. Its appearance in this context shows the endpoint of a remarkable semantic development. *Prudens* evolves from adjective to noun; it used to be applied to good sense, wisdom or expertise, while it is now applied to jurisprudence, one of the new disciplines that changed the Roman intellectual landscape between the second and first centuries BC. The *responsa prudentium* show us the jurists at work; and it is through *responsa* that law and divination alike are practised, in Rome and elsewhere, producing a series of expert utterances, devoted to a specific problem and based on a set of specific observations.[116]

This overview has drawn attention to two fundamental oppositions: *superstitio* and *religio*, and *diuinatio* and *prudentia*. The terms of the first opposition are rather clear: *religio* is a form of worship that takes place in an organised context, mediated through several filters; public religion goes under this label, although *religio* and public religion do not quite coincide.[117] *Superstitio*, on the contrary, is a product of exclusionary rhetoric: it is a term that applies to a vast array of unofficial and unsanctioned forms of religious participation. Both terms are rooted in the late

---

[112] Nep. *Con.* 2.1; Hyg. *Fab.* 14.11.
[113] Cic. *Or.* 1: *reprehensionem doctorum atque prudentium* ('the criticism of learned and knowledgeable men'). Cf. also Tac. *Agr.* 25.5 (*ignaui specie prudentium admonebant*); *Ann.* 1.9.3 (*apud prudentes*).
[114] Gai. *Inst.* 1.2, 1.7. Schiavone 2005: 328–32; Santangelo 2012: 51–2.   [115] Ferrary 2007.
[116] Santangelo 2012: 53–4. *Responsum*: Milani 1993: 40; Moatti 1997: 137–41, 363–5; Schiesaro 2003: 62–9 and 2011: 157–8; Romano 2008.
[117] A different reading in Scheid 1998a: 23 and 2001a: 48, 133. Cf. a more nuanced discussion of public and private *religio* (and *religiones*) in Rüpke 2007b: 73–7.

Republican debate on religion and in the contemporary attempts to provide more accurate definitions and categories. They apply to the historical
understanding of divination, and not just because *superstitio* is related to
the adjective *superstitiosus*, the original meaning of which is 'prophetic'.

The other tension, that between *diuinatio* and *prudentia*, is less clearly set
out in the ancient evidence, but is nonetheless important for our purposes.
In the late Republic we find evidence for attempts to define the vocabulary
of prediction and foresight. Again, it is only in the age of Cicero that we can
make informed judgements. *Diuinatio* does not coincide with 'divination',
or with Roman public divination. It applies to the prediction of things that
are deemed fortuitous; *prudentia*, on the contrary, refers to specific forms
of expertise, which are clearly codified and may be taught. It is also used to
refer to wisdom. While the areas of these meanings are clear for the nouns,
the meanings of the verbs are less clearly defined. At any rate, the debate on
the boundaries of prediction and divination became more intense in the
first century BC. The emergence of the relevant terminology and its fluidity
is a symptom of its importance and pervasiveness. It also draws attention
to the emergence of a strong trend in late Republican culture.

Most of our understanding of *diuinatio* relies on Cicero's construction
of it. The fundamental distinction drawn that Cicero drew is that between
besought (*impetratiua*) and unsolicited (*oblatiua*) signs on which so much
of Roman divination relied.[118] In the following chapters the survey sketched
by Cicero will be a constant reference point. We will start from two forms
of divination that Cicero placed on the margins of the picture.

---

[118] Rüpke 2005a: 1442 (= 2005b: 218–19). Bottéro 1974: 87–9 bases his account of Near Eastern
divination on this very distinction. Parker 1985: 298 notes that besought signs carry more authority
precisely because of the decision to seek them. Cf. the categories into which Trampedach 2011: 29
divides unsolicited signs: physical signs (e.g. fire or lightning), pragmatic signs (e.g. an accident
to a person or an animal), and 'Wunderzeichen' (e.g. the opening of the door of a temple for
no apparent reason). Lisdorf 2007: 47–52 discusses the cognitive differences between oblative and
impetrative divination.

CHAPTER 3

Fringe divination?

In the first chapter we took issue with the view that the *De diuinatione* is uninformative on matters of ritual or religious practice. In the second chapter we drew attention to the fact that, while Roman divination should not be confused with *diuinatio* as Cicero understood and constructed it in the *De diuinatione*, this work provides the most comprehensive picture of divination in Republican Rome. A positivistic or merely 'old-fashioned' reader would no doubt appreciate the treatise because of the wealth of information that it provides on many aspects of Roman religion and culture. Cicero's consistent use of specific examples in the unfolding of his philosophical discussion gives his readers access to an impressive array of *Realien*. Whatever view one may have of the general interpretation of the dialogue, it is uncontroversial that the dialogue offers a sense of how impressively diverse and wide-ranging the historical experience of divination at Rome was. In the mid first century BC Rome offered access to a number of possible sources of divination, which people from the most diverse quarters of society sought after and engaged with. The *De diuinatione* is the best surviving inventory of the 'market of sooth' that inhabited late Republican Rome.[1] Even a cavalier reading of the dialogue conveys a sense of this complexity, and an overview of the forms of divination discussed by Cicero can serve the purpose of this study well. While the *De diuinatione* poses a number of interpretative problems, it is nonetheless the most comprehensive map that we possess of divination in late Republican Rome, in its diversity and complexity. The discussion to be developed here will be heavily indebted to Cicero's account, even when it will part company from it. The topic of the following chapter is an instance of how Cicero's evidence should be taken critically.

---

[1] Slater 2000.

Dreams

Unsurprisingly, the most prominent and influential centres of divinatory expertise in the world that the *De diuinatione* tells us about are the organised bodies of experts at the service of the Roman State: the haruspices, the *decemuiri* (later *quindecemuiri*, probably after Sulla) who were in charge of the Sibylline Books, and the augurs.[2] The role of the latter body was especially important and controversial at the same time. As we saw above, the dialogue reflects the complex debate on the scope of the augural doctrine and its relevance to divination. It is also concerned with the exceptional character of Roman augural lore in contrast with foreign practices that are called 'augury': there are occasional sarcastic references to the augury of the Marsians, of the Umbrians or of Sora, but the label 'augury' is used also in reference to non-Italian contexts, like Asia Minor and Arabia.[3]

The auspices (*auspicia*), i.e. the observation and interpretation of the flight of birds, are another key feature of Roman public religion, closely related to augury; like augury, they have a complex divinatory status.[4] Their main aim is to secure the human understanding of the gods' will, but not necessarily to predict the future. In the *De diuinatione* they are one of the main points of dissent between Quintus and Marcus, with Quintus who celebrates the auspices as a great symptom of the importance of divination and complains about the increasing disregard for this institution in the late Republic, and Marcus who regards them as a tool for an effective relationship with the gods that does not have any divinatory significance and is however invaluable from a political standpoint.[5]

The *De diuinatione*, however, sheds light on forms of divination that were not included in public religion. At the most private and intimate level, there were dreams.[6] In the dedication of his memoirs, which he addressed to Lucullus, Sulla famously argued that the orders imparted by the gods

---

[2] Cf. also the reference to *haruspices* in non-Etruscan contexts in *Div.* 1.91 (Telmessus in Caria and Elis in the Peloponnesus: the term must be intended as a generic reference to 'diviners', according to Wardle 2006: 324).

[3] See esp. 1.92 (Umbria, Phrygia, Pisidia, Cilicia, Arabia); 1.105 (Pisidia and Sora; on the mention of Sora see Nice 2001: 158–9; Otto 1913: 1934 sees a reference to Mount Soracte); 1.132 (Marsi). Foreign examples in *Div.*: Krostenko 2000: 361–5. There was, however, a tradition that claimed that augury was brought to Rome from Tarquinia by Tarquinius Priscus: Strabo 5.2.2 (c 220), with Briquel 1986b: esp. 68–71, 83–6. The existence of auspication and ornithomancy in Umbria is attested by the Iguvine Tables, on which Pfiffig 1964: 109–15; Prosdocimi 1972: 624–35; Wilkins 1994 (see 171–2 for the suggestion that the Tables may belong in the context of Augustan monumentalisation); Bradley 2000: 74–7, 178–83; Lacam 2012: 193–9.

[4] Linderski 1986a: 2148.   [5] See esp. Cic. *Div.* 1.105 and 2.70–1.

[6] Krauss 1930: 139–53; Cancik 1999a: 169–73, 185–6; Kragelund 2001; Harris 2003 (cf. Harris 2009: 129–41, 174–85).

(*daimonion*) in dreams are the most reliable form of advice;[7] his narrative was interspersed with accounts of dreams in which he received divine guidance or could foresee events that would happen in the near future.[8] Whatever their contemporary reception may have been, Sulla's dreams were not dealt with through the channels of Roman public religion.[9] Other dreams were, or at least were believed to have been. A defining moment of Roman piety, the *deuotio* (consecration) of P. Decius Mus, which the tradition places in 340, was preceded and foretold by the combination of a prophetic dream and a haruspical response. According to Livy, the two consuls, Decius Mus and T. Manlius Torquatus, who were in charge of the war against the Latins, had the same vision at night: a man of greater size than a human being – certainly a god – instructed them to devote to the Manes and Mother Earth (*Mater Terra*) the commander on one side and the army on the other; a general would have to offer his death for his army to win. The reaction of the consuls was to perform sacrifices in order to avert the wrath of the gods; they also agreed that, should the readings of the entrails confirm the message of the dreams, one of them would face death. The responses of the haruspices confirmed it.[10] Before leading the army to the battlefield, the consuls performed another round of sacrifices with the haruspices. A haruspex told Decius that the lobe of the liver of his victim was wounded on the *pars familiaris* (the portion of the organ in which the omen would affect the sacrificer); Manlius' victim, on the contrary, achieved *litatio*, that is it was accepted by the gods. Decius understood the meaning of the sign: he had to perform his *deuotio* and lose his life, and declared that it was sufficient if his colleague's sacrifice was successful.[11] He then performed his *deuotio* during the battle, which took place at Veseris near Vesuvius, by riding headlong into the enemy ranks. The Romans obtained the victory. The dreams of the consuls were not handled as public prodigies, but they did shape the private concerns and the public actions of the senior magistrates, and they found striking confirmation in public sacrifices performed by the consuls with the assistance of the haruspices.

[7] Plut. *Sull.* 6.10 (παραινεῖ μηδὲν οὕτως ἡγεῖσθαι βέβαιον ὡς ὅ τι ἂν αὐτῷ προστάξῃ νύκτωρ τὸ δαιμόνιον), cf. *Luc.* 23.6.
[8] Plut. *Sull.* 9.7–8 (Bellona), with Giardina 2008; App. *B Civ.* 1.97 (Aphrodite). Premonitory dreams: Plut. *Sull.* 28.7–8 and 37.3; App. *B Civ.* 1.105.
[9] Harris 2009: 180 states that the members of the social elite are very unlikely to have taken Sulla's dreams seriously.
[10] Livy 8.6.11–12.
[11] Livy 8.9.1. Cf. Cic. *Div.* 1.51 (Wardle 2006: 235–6); Val. Max. 1.7.3 (Wardle 1998: 221–3); Plut. *Par. Min.* 18; *De vir. ill.* 26; Zonar. 7.26. Stübler 1941: 181–6; Guittard 1986b; North 1989: 593–4; Oakley 1998: 487; Kragelund 2001: 79–80. Guittard 1988 surveys the tradition on the Decii beyond Livy.

If we move into the late Republican period, the best-known case of a dream that was handled as a public matter is that of the dream of Metella, the daughter of Q. Caecilius Metellus Balearicus. Her dream was reported to the Senate in 90 and prompted the voting of a senatorial decree for the refurbishment of a temple of Juno Sospita, either at Rome or at Lanuvium.[12] Dreams could therefore be treated as portents and referred by the Senate to at least one priestly college.[13] On most occasions, however, a dream that was deemed to carry some significance did not enter the public discourse, but was handled privately.[14] As he quotes a lengthy passage from the *Brutus* of Accius (170ca.–86ca.), Quintus mentions the intervention of *coniectores* who gave their interpretative advice on a dream of Tarquinius.[15] It is impossible to establish more detail about the activity of these figures in this context or even about their background. No doubt in late Republican Rome there were dream interpreters from various backgrounds and different origins; the word *coniector* can apply to different kinds of religious practitioners.[16] The haruspices could be entrusted with the interpretation of a dream, but Quintus candidly admits consulting some experts (*periti*) about a dream he had during his governorship of the province of Asia in 61.[17] Possibly these experts were Greek, and this would be by no means surprising; nor should Quintus' decision to seek their advice be surprising either. They were probably the closest source of expertise that he could find in the province, and even if he had had a haruspex on his staff – as was often the case for a Roman promagistrate overseas – he may have wanted to seek a second opinion and possibly show his respect for local traditions and practices.

The dialogue touches upon other forms of divination that did not belong in the public sphere, but cannot be dismissed as insignificant.

[12] Cic. *Div.* 1.4, 99; Obs. 55. Luterbacher 1904: 31; Kragelund 2001: 54–75; Wardle 2006: 104–6; Schultz 2006a: 26–8, 160–2 and 2006b; Corbeill 2010b: 92–5. Sisenna may be the source of this passage (Wardle 2006: 339); he apparently had reservations on the value of prophetic dreams, even if he reported the Metella episode, but he did not dispute the significance of prodigies (cf. *Div.* 1.99): La Penna 1978: 114–15; Montero 1998: 381–2; Wardle 2006: 344. Religious tradition of the Caecilii: Paladino 1989: 31–6.

[13] Corbeill 2010b. Cf. *Div.* 1.55, where the dreams of a Roman peasant (*rusticus Romanus*) are read by the Senate as a divine admonishment that prompts the repetition of the *ludi Romani* at the beginning of the fifth century (Timpanaro 1988: 274–5; Wardle 2006: 244–8).

[14] Cancik 1999a: 173–87.

[15] Cic. *Div.* 1.44 (= 651–72 Dangel). Fauth 1976; Guittard 1986a; Walde 2001: 230–8; Rüpke 2012a: 58–60.

[16] It appears already in Plautus (e.g. *Amph.* 1128 of Tiresias and *Poen.* 443 of Oedipus); several occurrences in Cicero show that it could refer to groups of diviners that were neither augurs nor haruspices (e.g. *Div.* 1.72; *Nat. D.* 1.55; *Part. or.* 6). Republican *coniectores*: Nice 2001: 157–8, 162; Harris 2009: 136.

[17] Cic. *Div.* 1.58. Cf. Wardle 2006: 252 on the link of this episode with Clodius' threat to Cicero.

Quintus mentions astrology on several occasions and discusses cleromancy (i.e. divination based on the casting of lots and sortition), with special emphasis on the sanctuary of Fortuna Primigenia at Praeneste.[18] Finally, there are several references to divinatory activity outside Rome, such as the prophetic books of the city of Veii, and even outside Italy, such as the oracles of Delphi and Lebadea.[19]

The traditional idea of the decline of Roman religion in the late Republic derives, to an extent at least, from the rhetoric of decline in which several ancient authors indulged: the State is decaying fast, and religious institutions are no exception.[20] Cicero undoubtedly played a part in the development of this rhetoric, but in the *De diuinatione* he chose a different strategy and showed a positive interest in religious change, which is not necessarily constructed in terms of decline.[21] An interesting example is provided by his discussion of augural lore and its development, which was reshaped by centuries of practice, by the emergence of new doctrines, and by the long lapse of time (*uel usu iam uel doctrina uel uetustate*).[22] The picture is not free from problems. It becomes even less tenable when one turns to forms of religious activity that did not involve the elites or were not primarily intended to cater for the elites.

Cleromancy

Cicero's discussion of the history of the oracle of Praeneste is instructive too. Marcus' denial of the effectiveness of cleromancy is centred on the case of the temple of Fortuna Primigenia, which was well known in Rome.[23] The sanctuary was home to an oracle which produced responses on the basis of the consultation of lots. The consultation would take place in a cave within the sanctuary of Fortuna Primigenia, now known as the Antro delle Sorti. The consultant would address the question to the oracle, and a blindfolded boy would draw a lot, made of oak wood, from an urn (*cista*). The lot would then be passed to an expert diviner, the *sortilegus*, who would interpret the brief text carved on the lot and produce a response.[24] Cicero summarised the foundation myth of the sanctuary as he found it in the

---

[18] Astrology: 1.85, 1.91 (*Chaldaei*); 2.88–90. Cleromancy: 2.85–7.
[19] Veii: 1.100; Delphi: 1.38; Lebadea: 2.56.   [20] Lintott 1972; Levick 1982; Engels 2009.
[21] Cf. however Cic. *Div.* 2.36–7 on haruspicy and 2.70–4 on augury. Cicero's references to religious decline: *Leg.* 2.29 and 33; *Nat. D.* 2.9. Cf. also Dion. Hal. *Ant. Rom.* 2.6.2–4 on augury.
[22] Cic. *Div.* 2.70.
[23] General discussions of the sanctuary: Champeaux 1982: 55–148; Coarelli 1987: 35–84.
[24] It is not clear what was engraved on the *sortes* of Praeneste; possibly there was no more than a 'yes' or a 'no', but the likeliest view is that they had short and generic texts, which could be applied to

historical records of the city and dismissed the whole cult apparatus as patently unreliable and even fraudulent.[25] The verdict that closes the discussion is extraordinary. Marcus claims that most people have lost interest in that form of divination and that only the *uolgus* takes any notice of it. He then rhetorically asks what magistrate or man of any consequence would still bother to consult it. The denunciation of the oracle is so firm that it leads to the suspicion that Cicero may be overstating his case. Indeed, the archaeological evidence from the sanctuary suggests a more complex picture, and certainly not one of decline. Between the late second and the first century BC the shrine went through a phase of impressive development that would have hardly been possible without some involvement by the local elites. The sack of Praeneste and the foundation of a Sullan veteran colony do not appear to have affected the sanctuary, which even benefited from the dictator's generosity.[26] Even Marcus pays tribute to the beauty of the shrine, if only to say that it is the only factor that still preserves the prestige of the oracle. Things are complicated by the scarcity of the evidence for the practicalities of oracular consultation at Praeneste. No *sortes* (inscribed lots) have been discovered in the sanctuary and Cicero's account on how the lots were drawn lacks detail (*Div.* 2.86):

> *eodemque tempore in eo loco, ubi Fortunae nunc sita est aedes, mel ex olea fluxisse dicunt, haruspicesque dixisse summa nobilitate illas sortis futuras, eorumque iussu ex illa olea arcam esse factam, eoque conditas sortis, quae hodie Fortunae monitu tolluntur.*

They say that, concurrently with the finding of the lots and in the spot where the temple of Fortuna now stands, honey flowed from an olive-tree. The haruspices, who had declared that those lots would enjoy an unrivalled reputation, gave orders that a chest should be made from the tree and the lots placed in the chest, from which at the present time the lots are taken under the guidance of Fortuna.[27]

---

a range of different situations, like those on the *sortes* found elsewhere in Italy (Champeaux 1982: 74–5).

[25] Cic. *Div.* 2.85–7. As Sabbatucci 1989: 143–4 noted, several forms of divination, including haruspicy, feature in the tale of the discovery of the *sortes* by Numerius Suffustius (2.85–6); this is no doubt intended to emphasise the authoritativess of the oracle.

[26] Plin. *HN* 36.189 mentions the donation of a *lithostroton* (a mosaic). History of the sanctuary in the late Republic: Champeaux 1987: 224–33; Coarelli 1987: 62–6, 110; Santangelo 2007a: 137–41.

[27] An outline of the ritual that was performed in the sanctuary in Coarelli 1987: 67–72. Zevi 1982: 606–8 offers some guesswork on the shape of the Praenestine *sortes* and shows that no safe conclusion is within reach. On the lack of attention to detail in Roman prose cf. Horsfall 2003: 21. The lid of a *cista* from Praeneste dating to the first half of the third century BC (Villa Giulia 13133: photograph in Kuttner 1991, pl. 38.1; drawing in *ibid.*: 148) may provide a visual representation of the casting of the lots, possibly in a military context: see Zevi 1992: 356–60, with an extensive overview of the

Praeneste was not the only centre in Italy where lot divination was practised. Tibur was home to an important and widely respected oracle, which had a similar foundation myth to that of Praeneste.[28] The oracle at Ostia appears to have emerged and gained prominence only in the late second century BC. This is not an isolated anomaly, as other oracles by lot emerged even at later times: the evidence suggests that an oracle at the sanctuary of Fortuna in Antium rose to prominence no earlier than during Caligula's reign.[29] Other sanctuaries, however, were very prominent in the Republican period and their reputation spread to Rome. When in 218 and in 217 some alteration of the *sortes* at the shrines of Caere and Falerii was reported to Rome, the episode was handled as a prodigy by the Senate.[30] The picture of the diffusion of lot divination in Italy is rather sketchy, but it is sufficiently diverse and rich to support the conclusion that it was of great importance, and not just because the Latin word *sors* was used to refer to any kind of oracle. It is likely, as suggested by J. Champeaux, that the centres where lot divination was practised were concentrated in two geographical areas: in central Italy – Latium, southern and central Etruria, Umbria – and in the north-east, notably among the Veneti.[31] The archaeological evidence is fairly rich. *Sortes* inscribed in Latin, Etruscan and Oscan have been discovered; informed guesses can be made on the various types of *sortes* that were available in the sanctuaries where lot divination was practised.[32] Such a considerable geographical spread should lead us to take lot divination seriously and invite caution on embracing the theory that by the late Republic it was confined to the private domain. The fact that the Roman government did not use it and did not include it into the system for the interpretation and expiation of public prodigies does not

---

scholarly debate. Kuttner 1991 has argued for a radically different interpretation, whereby the scene is not an oracular consultation, but a military census operation.

[28] Coarelli 1987: 85–112. Coarelli 1987: 105–11 (tentatively followed by Buchet 2012: 361–2) argues that the prophetic material of the Tiburtine oracle was moved to Rome when the Sibylline corpus was restored in 76 in belated retaliation for the city's support of the cause of Sulla's enemies; however, the evidence of Tib. 2.5.69–70 is problematic and it is not quite clear how material that was used in cleromantic rituals could be included in the Books.

[29] Champeaux 1990b: 810. Brendel 1960 discusses the ties between the cult of Antium and that of Praeneste: the Fortuna Primigenia was an individual goddess, while at Antium two *Sorores* were worshipped. Cf. also Suet. *Tib.* 63.3. on Tiberius' interest in the Praenestine oracle, and *Dom.* 15.2 on Domitian's.

[30] Livy 21.62.5 and 8; 22.1.11. Livy speaks of *sortes extenuatae* and *adtenuatae*: see Champeaux 1988 on the possible interpretation of these terms (66: 's'amincir, perdre son épaisseur?'); Bagnasco Gianni 2001: 217–18 points out that the alteration of the *sortes* affected the randomness of the procedure.

[31] Champeaux 1986: 91–3; 1990a: esp. 300–1; 1990c. See also Bouché-Leclerq 1882: IV, 145–59; Purcell 1995: 22–3 n. 82; Maggiani 2005: 66–8, 75–8; Guittard 2007a: 233–8.

[32] Champeaux 1986: 96–8 and 1990b: 801–3; Poccetti 1998: 97–105; Grottanelli 2005: 138–41. On the Etruscan material see Bagnasco Gianni 2001.

rule out that this system may have been used by a number of municipal communities, including, no doubt, the colony of Praeneste itself.

In the first book of the *De diuinatione* Quintus takes a somewhat awkward detour from his discussion of inspired divination to express his esteem for the sanctuaries where the *sortes* are consulted, either on account of their antiquity or because the *sortes* actually offer predictions that make sense. He also makes an implicit but clear reference to Praeneste as an example of an oracle that deserves respect, because its lots are said to have sprung from the earth, and this points towards a genuine divine connection (*Div.* 1.34):

> *etsi ipsa sors contemnenda non est, si et auctoritatem habet uetustatis, ut eae sunt sortes, quas e terra editas accepimus; quae tamen ductae ut in rem apte cadant fieri credo posse diuinitus.*

> The lot itself is not to be despised, if it also has the sanction of antiquity, as in the case of those lots which we are told sprang from the earth. I believe, however, that under divine influence it may happen that they can be drawn so as to fall appropriately. (trans. D. Wardle)

However, Quintus also seems to issue a warning against those oracles where the *sortes* are 'equalised' (*aequatis sortibus*). The interpretation of this expression is not straightforward: it may refer to lots that have equal weight and size, or may mean that the urn contained an equal number of 'yes' and 'no' lots. It is not entirely clear, though, why this would have to be emphasised: were there sanctuaries where the *sortes* were not 'equalised'? If so, why was that the case?[33] Quintus appears to imply that this system usually limited the incidence of divine inspiration, that it was based on an excessive degree of human interference, and perhaps even that it was fraudulent. This criticism could easily be overturned: using a set of identical or closely similar lots enhances the randomness of the cleromantic process, and may be read as a way of allowing more space for the expression of divine will. This was not the only form of divination by lot about which Quintus had reservations, for in the closing stages of his plea in favour of divination, he makes it clear that his endorsement does not extend to certain practices that took place in private contexts. The list begins with the *sortilegi*, who must be identified with people who practised lot divination for money (*Div.* 1.132):

---

[33] I share the doubts of Timpanaro 1988: 259–60; Wardle 2006: 197 translates 'equalized lots' and appropriately refers to examples of equalised lots used for the selection of jury members and for assemblies. Johnston 2003: 152 argues that the lots were physically identical. Cf. Asc. *Mil.* 39 and *Corn.* 71 Clark and the epigraphical parallels discussed in Crawford 1996: 189–91.

nunc illa testabor, non me sortilegos neque eos, qui quaestus causa hariolentur, ne psychomantia quidem, quibus Appius, amicus tuus, uti solebat, agnoscere; non habeo denique nauci Marsum augurem, non uicanos haruspices, non de circo astrologos, non Isiacos coniectores, non interpretes somniorum. non enim sunt ii aut scientia aut arte diuini, sed 'superstitiosi uates impudentesque harioli . . .'

At this point I will affirm that I do not recognize the drawers of lots, nor those who divine for the sake of money, nor the necromancers whom your friend Appius used to consult; in short I do not care about the Marsian augur, the village haruspices or the astrologers from the Circus, nor Isiac prophets or interpreters of dreams. They are not diviners either by science or technique. But 'are superstitious seers and shameless prophets . . .' (trans. D. Wardle)[34]

It is a safe guess that these individuals were active in the first century BC, along with other categories of private diviners; the absence of a temple where lot divination was practised in the city will have made their trade especially attractive at Rome. With good reason W. E. Klingshirn has gone as far as to say that *sortilegus* is a 'professional title'.[35] It is beyond doubt that the word was used to refer to a specific group of diviners, who did not practise within the context of a sanctuary. It is unclear if the label was imposed by insiders or outsiders, and not all the people who may be called *sortilegi* will have been involved exclusively in lot divination.

The distinction between *sortes* and *sortilegi* was already clear to Quintus, as we have seen, and it must have been all too clear to the *sortilegi* themselves, who surrounded themselves with ritual paraphernalia that could be comparable to those available to the diviners who operated in temples. The handling of written material was an important feature of this process, as has been convincingly argued. *Sortilegi* were aware that, unlike the haruspices and the astrologers, they lacked a *disciplina* and made efforts to demonstrate their authoritativeness: the use of inscribed *sortes* was probably part of this strategy.[36] Quintus' attack on the *sortilegi* is only one of the pointers to the enduring significance of lot divination in the first century BC, which was not just restricted to the gullible populace as Marcus would like us to believe. A *denarius* struck by the moneyer M. Plaetorius Cestianus in

---

[34] On this list of diviners see Nice 2001: 155–63; Klingshirn 2006: 147–53. For another occurrence of the word *sortilegus* see *Div.* 2.109. Cf. the reference to the *fallax circus* and the *diuini* in Hor. *Sat.* 1.6.113–14.

[35] Klingshirn 2006: 139.

[36] Zevi 1982: 605–9; Champeaux 1990c: 109 and 1997: 409–17; Klingshirn 2006: 153–8. The equipment used by a diviner is intrinsically relevant to the expertise that he intends to share with those who seek his advice: cf. Pentikäinen 2010: 53–4 on shamans. Cf. Belayche 2007: 187 on the use of writing in oracular divination in Asia Minor ('volonté d'auto-illustration'); and Bottéro 1974: 154–7 on the use of cuneiform writing as an exclusionary strategy in Near Eastern divination.

Figure 3.1 Relief of the haruspex C. Fulvius Salvis, from Ostia. Ostia, Museo Ostiense, inv. 157. Schwanke © Neg. D-DAI-ROM 81.4534.

68 displays a boy holding a tablet with the legend *SORS* on the reverse and a bust that is almost certainly that of Fortuna Primigenia on the obverse. No doubt Plaetorius wanted to draw attention to the fact that he originally belonged to the Praenestine family of the Cestii, although he was later adopted into the family of the Plaetorii from Tusculum.[37] It was a statement of municipal belonging and a declaration of piety and allegiance to a goddess who was worshipped both at Rome and at Praeneste. A couple of decades earlier, around 90, the notable of Ostia C. Fulvius Salvis commissioned a relief portraying Hercules handing over a lot to a boy; the lot carries an inscription that reads *ORT H*, which should probably be understood as (*s*)*ort*(*is*) *H*(*erculis*) (Figure 3.1).[38]

The relief refers to the cult of Hercules at Ostia, where lot divination was practised; the most interesting feature, though, is that Fulvius Salvius was a

[37] *RRC* 405/2. Wiseman 1971: 251, no. 320.
[38] *CIL* 1.3027. Becatti 1939 and 1942; Klingshirn 2006: 144–5; Haack 2006: 54–8, no. 3; Cébeillac-Gervasoni, Caldelli and Zevi, 2010: 115–17, with bibliography.

haruspex, and that he had no reservations in appearing closely associated with a different form of divination on a monument that he had commissioned.[39] The list of satisfied consumers of lot divination might also include Tibullus' beloved Delia, who is said to have consulted the sacred lots on three occasions.[40]

What are we to make, then, of Marcus' statement on the decline of lot divination? J. Champeaux argued that Cicero was confusing his desires with reality, being the sceptic that he was.[41] Klingshirn has suggested that the decline of lot divination in sanctuaries was real and was caused by the rise of the *sortilegi*, who were not attached to any institution.[42] This hypothesis is tempting, but the evidence is too patchy to allow a safe conclusion. It is surely preferable to err on the side of caution and regard Marcus' depiction of the decline of lot divination as an instance in which he slightly distorts reality in order to state his case more forcefully. The focus of Marcus' discussion is on what the educated and powerful are supposed to make of divination; non-elite approaches to, and uses of, divination receive only tangential discussion. A chief concern (not just in the second book) is on how to control and contain divination. The divination practised by the *sortilegi*, therefore, can be singlehandedly dismissed as a lowly practice, because it does not interfere with the political domain. The lot divination of Italic sanctuaries like Praeneste can be depicted in sketchy and almost caricatural terms, because its reasonable distance from Rome enables Cicero to do so. This reference to the dictum of the Academic master Carneades, who – no doubt ironically – remarked that the Fortuna of Praeneste was the most fortunate of all, provided a further opportunity to challenge the credibility of that practice.

The attempt to marginalise lot divination was corroborated by a number of historical factors. Lot divination must have had a municipal flavour for many Romans. There were no centres of lot divination in the city, and it is conceivable that most of its practitioners were of municipal origin and settled in Rome attracted by the prospect of finding a large market; this fits well with the pattern of mobility from Italy to Rome that is

---

[39] Cf. the involvement of the haruspices before the discovery of the Praenestine *sortes* (Cic. *Div.* 2.86).
[40] Tib. 1.3.11. Cf. Champeaux 1982: 63.
[41] Champeaux 1987: 81. Tatum 1999b: 277 reads this passage as evidence for the vitality and autonomy of non-elite religion. Cf. the abundant evidence for oracular divination in the Greek world under the Principate, despite Plutarch's claims to the contrary in the treatise *On the disappearance of oracles* (Belayche 2007: 172).
[42] Klingshirn 2006: 149–50.

well attested in the last century of the Republic.[43] There is only one
attested case in which the possibility of consulting the oracle of Fortuna
Primigenia was raised in a public context. In 241 the consul Lutatius Cerco
intended to consult the oracle, but he was prevented from doing so by
the Senate, which was not prepared to cede to the oracle of Praeneste a
share in the Roman decision-making process.[44] The argument was that
the State had to be ruled by ancestral auspices (*auspicia patria*), rather
than by foreign (*alienigena*) ones.[45] The analogy with haruspicy, which
was also *alienigena*, practised by outsiders and based on a set of doctrines
established outside Rome, comes to mind, but there is also a very important
difference.[46] No systematic strategy was ever envisaged for the integration
of cleromancy into the machinery of Roman government, and there is
no evidence that cleromancy was used in public contexts. On the other
hand, apart from the obvious differences in their epistemological statuses,
there are striking similarities between cleromancy and astrology, which was
kept at the margins of public discourse until the late Republic, only to be
spectacularly brought to the fore by Octavian. This was never the case with
lot divination.

Public lot

A related point must be discussed against this background. The drawing of
the lot is significant for the student of Roman culture for another reason,
which has not much to do with divination, but nonetheless pertains to
the sphere of the scrutiny of divine will and the control over the future
that may derive from it.[47] In the Roman Republic the lot was routinely
used for the handling of a number of political and administrative issues,
such as the assignment of the provinces to two magistrates serving in the

---

[43] The analogy with the diviners that crowded Rome during the Hannibalic War (Livy 25.1.8) is
appropriate (Klingshirn 2006: 145–6).

[44] Cf. Parker 1985: 298.

[45] Val. Max. 1.3.2, known through the epitomes of Julius Paris and Nepotianus. Wardle 1998: 146–8
and 2005a. Ando 2008: 107 argues that the decision of the Senate implied no negative judgement
on the value of the oracle. Orlin 2002: 2 stresses how exceptional this emphasis on the foreignness of
the Fortuna cult is; *pace* Sandberg 2009: 158, this passage cannot be used as evidence that the temple
of Fortuna Primigenia at Rome was outside the *pomerium*. Champeaux 1982: 78–80 argues that the
Senate's hostility to the oracle of Praeneste was caused by the dealings between the city and Pyrrhus
a few decades earlier; see also Zonar. 8.3, with Briquel 1986a. Lutatius Cerco had Praenestine origins
(Wardle 2005a: 383). Roman prejudices towards the Praenestines: Farney 2007: 75–6.

[46] Note, however, the striking contrast with Greek divination, where the most authoritative and
influential prophecies tend to come from afar (Parker 1985: 300).

[47] *Contra*, Jaillard and Prescendi 2008: 83–4 argue that the Romans were interested not in establishing
divine will, but in asserting and attesting divine support for the actions they envisaged.

same year. This prompts questions on the wider cultural significance of this practice and the religious meanings and implications that were attached to it. In an invaluable study N. Rosenstein carefully explored the evidence and concluded that the widespread use of the lot in these contexts should not be used as evidence for a belief that the gods were involved in the process and that the outcome was determined by their intervention.[48] On the contrary, the use of the lot is just determined by the need to identify a 'neutral' method for the solution of a potentially divisive dilemma. In Rosenstein's view, the role of lot divination must be understood against the background of the *pax deorum*, the relationship between gods and men that was supposed to secure the prosperity of Rome: since the *pax* is an understanding between men and gods, it also entails specific duties for both parties. The gods should not necessarily be expected to interfere with human affairs.[49]

This intelligent solution is not immune from serious difficulties. As R. Stewart has shown, in Republican Rome the religious implications of allotment are wide-ranging: it is closely associated to the patronage of Jupiter and it is best understood as a ritual that fell within the remit of the auspices.[50] Moreover, a rigidly legalistic understanding of the *pax deorum* is hardly helpful. The *pax deorum* is not a strictly defined theological category. It is a concept that must be understood as a dynamic process, a bargain between men and gods that must be constantly renewed and should not be regarded as the rule. The evidence never refers to the limits of the *pax deorum* or to the boundaries of the sphere of the gods once the *pax deorum* is secured.[51]

A more nuanced approach to the status of cleromancy is necessary. Arguing that the whole Roman elite shared the same views on the drawing of the lot, its foundations and its effectiveness is as rash as claiming that there was a consensus on the remit of augury or haruspicy. The fact that a practice is widely attested can be fully compatible with sharp disagreement on its remit within a political community; indeed, its success may be determined by the ability of people to construct it in many different ways. It is possible, therefore, that some people, in certain periods, thought that

---

[48] Rosenstein 1995. A convenient list of relevant cases in Lundgreen 2011: 122–7.
[49] A similar approach in Ehrenberg 1927: 1465–6; see also Bunse 2002: 428–9 and Lundgreen 2011: 131–6 (with more bibliography). Cf. Maffi 2001: 138 on the use of the lot for the choice of the ambassadors of a city in ch. 44 of the Flavian *lex Irnitana*: 'un sistema di equa ripartizione degli oneri senza alcun riferimento alla volontà divina'.
[50] Stewart 1998: 12–51. See also Linderski 1986a: 2173–5 and 1996: 176–7 (= 2007: 165–6) on the augural dimension of *sortitio*, which took place in an inaugurated spot, a *templum*.
[51] Santangelo 2011.

there was a connection between the outcome of the lot in political contexts and the will of the gods; others will have had a more critical approach; many, possibly most, will have not asked themselves many questions on the foundations of this practice.[52] Moreover, positing a straightforward dualism whereby the lots have a religious value in private contexts and a purely functional one in public ones seems too rigid a distinction. Arguably, there is no public act in Republican Rome that could not (and should not) be constructed as religious. It is also debatable that such a neat divide may be traced between public and private behaviour.

At any rate, the religious implications of the drawing of the lot are confirmed by some literary sources, and most impressively by Livy's narrative of a controversy between the censors of 209 over the designation of the *princeps senatus*: P. Sempronius Tuditanus was chosen by lot as the censor in charge of the decision. Although previous practice prescribed that T. Manlius Torquatus, who was the oldest of his surviving contemporaries to have been elected to the censorship, should have been chosen as *princeps senatus*, Tuditanus refused to give way and declared that, by causing his victory in the lot, the gods had given him the right to make an unrestricted choice; he then designated, against the opinion of his colleague, Q. Fabius Maximus.[53] This passage is explicit enough evidence that religious implications could be attached to the use of the lots; whether Tuditanus was right is a different matter. This element forcefully emerges from some passages of Cicero, where the divine nature of the lots is used to create a sharp contrast with the evil and impious conduct of the opponent under attack, be it Verres or Mark Antony.[54] Instead of dismissing these instances as symptoms of the intention to create confusion on the religious and intellectual foundations the use of the lots was based upon, they must be taken seriously as evidence that, in some quarters and on some occasions, the divine connection of the lots could be legitimately invoked.

Rosenstein argued that the inconsistency with which the drawing of the lot was used in Rome and its outcomes were respected is further testimony to the fact that it was used as a mere political expedient: after all, provinces could be allocated by mutual agreement between the consuls, and the results of the lots on provincial assignments were frequently altered. Again, this argument could apply to other aspects of Roman political and religious life. Inconsistencies and exceptions can usually be explained as instances

---

[52] Johnston 2003: 153: 'there was no single explanation, just as there was no single Roman mentality'. On the importance of recognising different expectations among various individuals in religious matters see Tatum 1999b: 282–4.

[53] Livy 27.11.9–11. Cf. Rosenstein 1995: 62; Johnston 2003: 151.   [54] Cic. *Phil.* 3.24 and 26.

of different, competing rules, and the overriding of what may appear as previous established practice was often the outcome of a carefully planned and elaborate process, which could be fully justified.[55] The central point remains: some people claimed the use of lots in political contexts was based on an explicit divine endorsement and that the lots were a reflection of divine will. Others will have disagreed, but that was not exceptional.

[55] North 1976.

CHAPTER 4

The haruspices and the rise of prophecy

The discussion of the lot and its role in Roman politics and society has taken us back to the domain of Roman public divination. As we saw in Chapter 1, one of Cicero's crucial concerns was to practise and use divination in a way that was suitable to the context of Republican Rome, and could be constructed as compatible, and indeed consistent, with Roman traditions.[1] This strategy was not immune from problems: a very important role in the divinatory practice of this period was played by a non-Roman priestly body, the Etruscan haruspices. It is now necessary to focus in greater detail on their role in the religious scene of the late Republic. The emergence of prophecy as a substantial presence in the landscape of Roman public religion coincides with the increasing prominence and influence of the haruspices, especially in the domain of the interpretation of prodigies. The historical record is rather patchy, especially because a considerable portion of Livy does not survive; however, a pattern emerges with sufficient clarity from the extant evidence.[2] The earliest securely attested evidence for an intervention by the haruspices as a corporate body advising the Roman government on the interpretation of a prodigy is in 278, when a bolt of lightning hit a statue of Summanus on the top of the temple of Jupiter Optimus Maximus; the episode is connected to the imminent arrival of Pyrrhus in southern Italy.[3] It is only a century later, however, that we find the haruspices producing a prophecy instead of a ritual prescription after a prodigy. In 172 the *columna rostrata* on the Capitol was completely

---

[1] Difficulty (and undesirability) of singling out the 'truly Roman' elements of Roman religion: Perfigli 2004: 183–217; Clark 2007: 21–8.
[2] North 1989: 618 speculatively wonders whether the tradition conceals the complexity of religious life in early Rome.
[3] Cic. *Div.* 1.16; 2.45; Livy *Per.* 14 (who speaks of a statue of Jupiter; cf. Pease 1920: 98 on Summanus as an epithet of Jupiter); see Ov. *Fast.* 6.731 on the link with Pyrrhus' arrival and the dedication of a temple of Summanus. Wardle 2006: 143–4; Engels 2007: 403; Orlin 2010: 88–9. MacBain 1982: 46–7 argues that the haruspices were active in Rome from the sixth century BC, under the Tarquins, and that their presence was fully stabilised when *foedera* were sealed between Rome and the Etruscans in 280–278.

destroyed by lightning during a storm at night and both the *decemuiri* and the haruspices were consulted.[4] The difference in their approaches was striking. The *decemuiri* suggested expiation, while the haruspices shifted the focus of the debate and argued that the prodigy would lead to a positive development. In their view, it was a premonition of the extension of the boundaries of the empire, since the storm had damaged a monument that displayed the *spolia* of the enemies.[5] That was an unusual reaction: prodigies were usually understood to have negative implications. However, it was not the first time that the haruspices predicted the extension of the boundaries of the empire (*prolatio finium*). It had been the case in 200, on the eve of the Second Macedonian War (and the parallel in the wording of this prophecy with that of 172 is striking); similar predictions, albeit worded slightly differently, were made in 191 and in 171.[6] The haruspices' intervention of 172, however, stands out in an important respect: the earlier predictions on the expansion of the empire were not given in response to a prodigy. The haruspices were beginning to adopt a distinctive profile in their handling of prodigies, focused more on prophecy than on expiation, and more interested in foretelling the future than in prescribing or rectifying the performance of a ritual.[7]

There is a striking concentration of haruspical responses in the build-up to several Eastern campaigns in the second century BC, which is all the more impressive in light of the intermittent presence of the haruspices in

[4] Livy 42.20.2–4, with Palombi 1993. Gell. *NA* 4.5 records another haruspical intervention on a similar occasion, after the statue of Horatius Cocles in the Comitium was hit by lightning, stressing that the haruspices deliberately gave the Romans misleading advice; good discussion in Sacchetti 1996: 232–3. The chronology is uncertain (Roller 2004: 21 n. 47; Engels 2007: 714–16 places it in the fifth century).

[5] Bloch 1963: 135–6; North 1967: 570–5; Blänsdorf 1991: 49–50; Engels 2007: 515–16; Satterfield 2008: 70; Lacam 2012: 71. According to Wülker 1903: 1 n. 1 the prodigy could be interpreted favourably by the haruspices only because it had already been expiated.

[6] See respectively Livy 31.5.7; 36.1.3; 42.30.9. See Harris 1979: 122 (these responses are strikingly at odds with Livy's account of the motives of the wars in question); North 1990: 62–4; Guittard 2006: 72–3. On the episode of 191 and the role of the haruspices in corroborating a decision of the Senate see North 1990: 62–4. Cf. also the story of the *caput Oli* (Livy 1.55.5–6 and Dion. Hal. *Ant. Rom.* 4.59–61): when a man's head was unearthed during the building of the temple of Jupiter Capitolinus during the reign of Tarquinius Superbus, the haruspices (or, according to Dionysius, a haruspex) argued that it was a sign of the future greatness of Rome (cf. Plin. *HN* 28.15; Serv. *auct. ad Aen.* 8.345; Arn. *Adv. nat.* 6.7). Bloch 1965b: 66–7; Borgeaud 1987; Thein forthcoming.

[7] Cf. a portent recorded in Zonar. 8.1 for the year 296, when a statue of Victoria on a pedestal in the Forum was found standing on the ground below, pointing in the direction from which the Gauls were approaching, and blood issued from the altar of Jupiter for three days, milk for one day and honey for another. There was disagreement on the meaning of the portents between some unnamed prophets, who argued for an unspecified terrifying expiation, and an Etruscan called Manius, who gave a more encouraging interpretation, but warned that the milk portended famine and the honey disease; the following years proved Manius right. See Wiseman 1995: 118–20, 205–6.

the evidence for the following years. In fact, there is no clear pattern as to the matters on which the haruspices were consulted in this period.[8] There is, however, good evidence that prophetic elements became increasingly prominent in the responses of the haruspices, and that they made considerable impact. In 152 the column in front of the temple of Jupiter in the Campus Martius was overthrown, along with the golden statue that was at its top.[9] The haruspices ruled that it warned of the imminent death of magistrates and priests; the magistrates reacted by resigning en masse. However, the consular *fasti* of the year do not provide any evidence for these resignations; we do not know what happened to the priests. The episode is reported only by Obsequens, but there is no reason to dismiss the evidence of this author, who usually appears to use Livy competently.[10]

Obsequens records another prophetic intervention of the haruspices in this period. In 130, a statue of Apollo Cumanus, brought to Rome from Greece, started weeping and the haruspices, in awe (*territi*), immediately ruled that the statue had to be thrown into the sea.[11] Some wise old men from Cumae became involved in the dispute and tried to prevent the loss of the statue by pointing out that it had already wept in the past on the eve of wars that turned out to be favourable to the Romans, such as those against Antiochus and Perseus. This prompted second thoughts in Rome and the intervention of a second group of haruspices, who ruled that the tears of the god were in fact an implicit sign of favour to the Romans. Apollo Cumanus hailed from the Greek colony of Cumae and it was no surprise that he mourned the imminent defeat of the Greeks. The political relevance of the incident is remarkable, and not just because we see two groups of haruspices in action, perhaps in competition with each other. The haruspices were compelled to reconsider their response under pressure from the elite of an Italian community that was not prepared to see a statue of their poliad deity being destroyed because of the advice that a body of foreign advisors had given to the Roman government. This episode is

---

[8] MacBain 1982: 118–20. A different emphasis in Lacam 2012: 70–1.

[9] Obs. 18: *turbinis ui in campo columna ante aedem Iouis decussa cum signo aurato; cumque aruspices respondissent magistratuum et sacerdotum interitum fore, omnes magistratus se protinus abdicauerunt* ('In the Campus Martius the column in front of the temple of Jupiter was overturned by the force of a whirlwind with its golden statue; and when the haruspices responded that there would be deaths of magistrates and priests, all the magistrates resigned immediately'). North 1967: 575–6; Engels 2007: 534. On the verb *decutere* ('to shake off') see Lorsch Wildfang 2000b: 76.

[10] Reliability of Obsequens' working method: North 1967: 585–6; Schmidt 1968: 161–217; Nice 1999: 192–200. Style: Santini 1988. Günther 1964: 212–32, 275–81 has an extended commentary on Obsequens' evidence for late Republican prodigies.

[11] Obs. 28 (note the use of *uates*); August. *De civ. D.* 3.11.1–3; cf. Dio 24 fr. 84.2. Gagé 1955: 39–41; North 1967: 576–7; Rosenberger 1998: 119; Corbeill 2009: 299–300, 302–4.

a reminder that the haruspices offered the Etruscan elites an unparalleled position in the Italian context long before the enfranchisement of the Allies that followed the Social War. Their role, however, had to be negotiated with the agendas and concerns of other sectors of the Italian world and could at times create some tensions. The recantation of the haruspices and Rome's eventual victory in the war against Aristonicus a few months later must have settled the matter.

Consultations of the haruspices could take place in private contexts too, and the earliest attested instances date to the mid second century BC.[12] A famous portent that allegedly occurred in the house of T. Sempronius Gracchus (*cos.* 177 and 163), the father of the tribunes, and the following consultation of the haruspices can be dated to the mid 150s, probably to 154. When two snakes were found under a bed, the haruspices who were summoned to interpret the prodigy (it is unclear how they were chosen) presented Gracchus with a dilemma: if he let the male snake go, his wife was to die in a short time and if he released the female snake his death must soon occur.[13] Again, the interpretation of a prodigy – albeit one reported in a private context – revolved around a fully fledged prophecy, which was accompanied by a clear strategy on how to react to the incident. The haruspices did not contemplate inaction: one of the snakes had to be killed and only two possible outcomes were available.[14] This is an interesting divergence from the responses given by the haruspices in public contexts at roughly the same period. Responses given in private contexts perhaps allowed for more creativity. We do not find this combination of choice and predestination in other contemporary cases, not even in the episode in 129, reported by Obsequens, in which snakes feature prominently: their appearance in the *cella* of the temple of Minerva on the Capitol was readily viewed as a premonition of impending political disaster.[15] Three

---

[12] Cf. Haack 2002 on the difficulty of distinguishing between public and private haruspices on the basis of the available evidence.

[13] Cic. *Div.* 1.36; 2.62; Val. Max. 4.6.1; Plut. *Ti. Gracch.* 1.4–5; Plin. *HN* 7.122; *De vir. ill.* 57.4. See Santangelo 2005a and Citroni Marchetti 2008 (= 2011: 203–27).

[14] The annalistic tradition records other strikingly similar haruspical interventions. See especially the story of the praetor Aelius, which should probably be dated between the end of the third century BC and the beginning of the second (Varro, *De uita populi Romani* F 94 Riposati; Val. Max. 5.6.4; Plin. *HN* 10.41; Frontin. *Str.* 4.5.14): a woodpecker perched on his head; the haruspices ruled that if he killed the bird it would be disastrous for himself and his family, but beneficial for the Republic; sparing it would have had opposite consequences; Aelius killed the bird (this response appears to have been given in a public context). Cf. also the case of Genucius Cipus, who in 362 discovered just outside the city gates that he had grown horns and decided never to return home after consulting a haruspex and being told that he would be king if he entered the city (Ov. *Met.* 15.565–621; Val. Max. 5.6.3). On both episodes see Wiseman 1995: 108–9, 201–2.

[15] Obs. 28a.

years later, a series of natural events, which culminated in the eruption of Mount Etna, was read in the same way.[16] We are not better informed about the involvement of the haruspices in the political crisis that followed the foundation of the Gracchan colony of Junonia, near the site of Carthage. Unfavourable prodigies were reported to the Senate and it is likely that the haruspices were involved in their interpretation – but it is unclear how and where they acted.[17]

Divinatory advice is often sought when the consultant has a clear idea of the outcome of the events and of how the ensuing response may be fulfilled; stating this entails no concession to modern(ising) rationalism.[18] A detailed prophecy was produced in the build-up to the scandal of the Vestal Virgins in 114. The unusual prodigy reported from the *ager Stellas* – where the virgin Helvia, the daughter of the Roman *eques* P. Helvius, was hit by lightning – was read in connection to the incest of the Vestal Virgins with three members of the equestrian order. The involvement of the haruspices is recorded by Plutarch, who calls them *manteis*: they read the episode as a sign of the disrepute that threatened both groups, the Virgins and the *equites*.[19] Chronology is not easy to determine; the likeliest reconstruction places the response of the haruspices in September 114, shortly before the prosecution of the Vestals. The procedure was exceptional and no doubt politically motivated. The involvement of the Senate and the response of the haruspices were exactly what was needed to prompt the intervention of the pontiffs, who started hearing the case against the priestesses in December 114.[20] There are other cases of detailed prophecies in this period, especially at the very beginning of the first century BC. Prophecies apparently became more frequent in that period; they did not come exclusively from the haruspices. There is evidence that, at least on one occasion, the Sibylline Books were opened on the same matter on which the haruspices were consulted. In a year that is not specified in the ancient sources, but which could reasonably be thought to be 87, haruspices and *decemuiri* agreed that a subsidence reported at Privernum and the earthquakes that took place in Apulia were premonitions of seditions and wars.[21] Whatever its correct dating may be, the episode is yet another symptom of a growing interest in prophecy

---

[16] Obs. 29.
[17] App. *B Civ.* 1.24: Appian speaks of μάντεις. Gargola 1995: 166–7, 243–4 n. 79 suggests that the priests mentioned by Appian were in fact augurs; Wells 2004: 38–43 shows why this is unlikely.
[18] Eidinow 2007: 132–9; Eidinow and Taylor 2010: 47.   [19] Plut. *Quaest. Rom.* 83.
[20] North 1967: 334–40, 578–9; Rosenberger 1998: 172–4. On the trial of the Vestals see Richardson 2011: the loss of the virginity of a Vestal Virgin was regarded not as a prodigy to be expiated, but as a horrific event that had to be obliterated by the entombing of the unchaste Vestal.
[21] Cic. *Div.* 1.97; Granius Licinianus 35.1–2. Santangelo 2005b.

and of the potential for competition (which did not preclude agreement) between different centres of religious and divinatory expertise.

Haruspices and late Republican politics

In 91 the outbreak of the Social War was foretold by several prodigies, which Cicero carefully relates, no doubt following Sisenna: some mice reportedly ate some shields preserved at Lanuvium, and the haruspices read that as a sign of imminent disaster.[22] In 88 mice were also involved in one of the prodigies that foretold the outbreak of the Civil War between Marius and Sulla, carefully reported by Plutarch in the *Life of Sulla*. Some mice gnawed consecrated gold in a temple; one of them was captured, gave birth to five young ones, and ate three of them. This disturbing scene was only one of a series of prodigies that marked the days preceding the clash over the Mithridatic command. They all pointed to a scenario of internal discord and disorder: ravens ate their young and brought their remains back to their nest, and fire broke out from the staves that supported the ensigns.[23]

The most striking sign that occurred in that year was, however, of a different kind. The sound of a trumpet, coming from no obvious place, was heard in the city of Rome.[24] This prompted the Senate to consult the haruspices, who claimed that the prodigy marked the end of one age and the beginning of a new one:[25]

> Τυρρηνῶν δὲ οἱ λόγιοι μεταβολὴν ἑτέρου γένους ἀπεφαίνοντο καὶ
> μετακόσμησιν ἀποσημαίνειν τὸ τέρας. εἶναι μὲν γὰρ ὀκτὼ τὰ σύμ-
> παντα γένη, διαφέροντα τοῖς βίοις καὶ τοῖς ἤθεσιν ἀλλήλων, ἑκάστῳ
> δὲ ἀφωρίσθαι χρόνων ἀριθμὸν ὑπὸ τοῦ θεοῦ συμπεραινόμενον ἐνιαυ-
> τοῦ μεγάλου περιόδῳ. καὶ ὅταν αὕτη σχῇ τέλος, ἑτέρας ἐνισταμένης
> κινεῖσθαί τι σημεῖον ἐκ γῆς ἢ οὐρανοῦ θαυμάσιον, ὡς δῆλον εἶναι τοῖς
> πεφροντικόσι τὰ τοιαῦτα καὶ μεμαθηκόσιν εὐθὺς ὅτι καὶ τρόποις ἄλλοις
> καὶ βίοις ἄνθρωποι χρώμενοι γεγόνασι, καὶ θεοῖς ἧττον ἢ μᾶλλον τῶν
> προτέρων μέλοντες. τά τε γὰρ ἄλλα φασὶν ἐν τῇ τῶν γενῶν ἀμείψει

---

[22] Cic. *Div.* 1.99; Plin. *HN* 8.221; more prodigies in Obs. 54. Lanuvium featured prominently in Roman concerns at the eve of the Social War: cf. the presence of Juno Sospita in Metella's dream reported to the Senate in 90 (Schultz 2006b: 221–2).

[23] Plut. *Sull.* 7.4–5. Mice in Roman prodigies: Pease 1920: 276. Ravens: Krauss 1930: 103–5; cf. Patera 2012 on their significance in Greek divination.

[24] Plut. *Sull.* 7.6.

[25] Plut. *Sull.* 7.7–10. Cf. also Serv. *auct. ad Aen.* 8.526: *Varro de saeculis auditum sonum tubae de caelo dicit* ('Varro in the work *On ages* says that the sound of a trumpet from the sky was heard'; this is probably a reference to a section of the *Antiquitates rerum humanarum*). This episode is told also by John of Antioch (Walton 1965: 241); this account closely follows Plutarch's wording and almost certainly derives from the *Life of Sulla*.

λαμβάνειν μεγάλας καινοτομίας, καὶ τὴν μαντικὴν ποτὲ μὲν αὔξεσθαι τῇ τιμῇ καὶ κατατυγχάνειν ταῖς προαγορεύσεσι, καθαρὰ καὶ φανερὰ σημεῖα τοῦ δαιμονίου προπέμποντος, αὖθις δ᾽ ἐν ἑτέρῳ γένει ταπεινὰ πράττειν, αὐτοσχέδιον οὖσαν τὰ πολλὰ καὶ δι᾽ ἀμυδρῶν καὶ σκοτεινῶν ὀργάνων τοῦ μέλλοντος ἁπτομένην.

The Tyrrhenian wise men ruled that the prodigy foretold the advent of a new breed (*genos*) and a cosmic renewal (*metakosmesis*). For in their view there are eight human breeds, differing from each other in ways of life and habits, and to each of them the god has allocated a time span, marked by the time period of a great year. When a cycle comes to an end and another one begins, a prodigious sign manifests itself from the earth or the sky, and through that it becomes evident to those who have studied this topic and have learnt about it that new men with a different disposition and different habits have come to exist, and that these are more or less dear to the gods than those that preceded them. They say that in the moment in which the races succeed one another profound changes take place, and that divination at times increases its standing in general reputation and is successful in its predictions, because the deity sends pure and manifest signs, while at other times it becomes less effective under another breed of men, because it is largely improvised and investigates the future with dim and obscure tools.

The intervention of the haruspices is further testimony to the prominence they had reached by the early first century BC. However, what is most remarkable is their response, which fitted impressively well in a context marked by prodigies that had so much to do with themes of birth, death and regeneration.[26] It also established a link between Etruscan doctrines on the organisation of time and the anxiety and despair that marked several phases of the last century of the Republic. According to the prevailing interpretation of this passage, the haruspices told (or possibly reminded) their Roman audience about an Etruscan doctrine which claimed that there had been eight ages up to that moment; the ninth and last age was about to start.[27] Each era was marked by different men and different customs

---

[26] 'Liminality' in Roman prodigies: Rosenberger 1998: 107–26 and 2007: 295–6; Cuny-Le Callet 2005a: 58–62. Liminality in religious anthropology: Douglas 1966: 115–29; Turner 1967: 93–111 and 1995: 94–130, 66–203.

[27] Thulin 1909: 65, 67–8; Diehl 1934: 260; North 1967: 556–61; Gladigow 1989: 263–4; Sordi 2002a: 719–21; more cautiously Briquel 1990a: 64–5; Champeaux 1996b: 58–62; Angeli Bertinelli *et al.* 1997: 324–5; North 2000a: 99; Briquel 2001: 272–4. *Contra*, see Mommsen 1859: 189–90 n. 372; Clemen 1928: 236; Mazzarino 1957: 112 (= 1980: 279–80); Alföldi 1975: 177–8 (= 1997: 79–80), who argue that the eighth age *began* in 88. According to Turcan 1976: 1012–13 and Massa-Pairault 1991: 7, 23, the *gene* mentioned by Plutarch are not eras, but 'human races' (cf. also Bouché-Leclerq 1882: IV, 881–2 n. 247); this view, however, sits oddly with what is known about the lore of the haruspices. See the overview of the problem, with extensive bibliography, in Firpo 1998: 263–9. On the meaning of *saeculum* as 'generation' see Diehl 1934: 255–6. Cf. the astrological doctrine mentioned by Varro in

and consisted of a definite number of seasons.[28] The end of each age was characteristically marked by a divine sign that advised mankind of the advent of a new generation. Only diviners were equipped to notice and understand such signs, but their skill was bound to be a short-lived one, because the advent of the new age would bring divination back into disrepute and diviners back to the ignorance that their predecessors had at the beginning of the previous age – a model of decline that seems to anticipate some modern accounts of late Republican religion.[29] The prophecy was both remarkably explicit and suitably elusive; no other divinatory response produced in the late Republic establishes such a clear link between political change and intellectual developments.[30] Its timing is noteworthy. The controversy over the Mithridatic command was a watershed in Republican history, which eventually led to a Civil War and to the victory of Sulla. A new epoch was truly about to start for the *res publica* and many of those who experienced it struggled to find the intellectual instruments to comprehend it.

The prophecy of the coming of the new age was soon supplemented by another one, when a sparrow flew into the temple of Bellona, where the Senate was meeting. The bird was holding a grasshopper in its beak and let an end of it fall, while holding another end in its beak. The haruspices understood the incident as the sign of an imminent controversy between landowners and populace: the sparrow hunts in the fields, while the populace is as loud and vociferous as a grasshopper.[31] The Mithridatic crisis did not have an agrarian aspect, although the reward of the veterans at the end of the ensuing Civil War certainly did affect the agrarian situation in the peninsula. However, the problem of the use and distribution of land in Italy had been on the political map for at least five decades.

Interventions of the haruspices in agrarian matters were not a novelty. In 122 unfavourable omens were reported to Rome from the colony of Junonia, near the site of Carthage, which Gaius Gracchus had just founded. Although Gracchus and his associate M. Fulvius Flaccus denied the truthfulness of the prodigies, the haruspices readily interpreted them as

the *De gente populi Romani* (F 2 Fraccaro = August. *De civ. D.* 22.28.6–9), according to which after 440 years the same body and soul which were joined in a man come back to be joined once again. Martínez-Pinna 2001: 89–92 tentatively links the prodigy to Sullan propaganda.

[28] Thulin 1909: 63–75; Martínez-Pinna 2001.

[29] An interesting overlap of cognitive and social memory, to use the terms put forward by Connerton 1989: 22–40.

[30] Cf., however, the reference to the imminent death of the haruspices and their children in the prophecy of Aemilius Potensis of 102 (Obs. 44).

[31] Plut. *Sull.* 7.12–13; note the use of *teratoskopoi* instead of the *manteis*. Harris 1971: 37–40; Lantella 1984: 2159–73; Valvo 1988: 137–51; Angeli Bertinelli *et al.* 1997: 325–6; Farney 2007: 162–4.

ill omens for the new colony. It is unclear what expiation they suggested. The portents were seen as a decisive argument in favour of the repeal of the colony, which was voted by the *comitia* in a process that culminated with the riots in which Gracchus and many of his supporters lost their lives.[32] A notice in Julius Obsequens mentions an agrarian bill put forward by the tribune Sex. Titius in 99: two ravens were seen flying and fighting above the *contio* in which the bill was being presented. The haruspices ruled that a sacrifice to Apollo had to be performed and that the bill had to be abandoned.[33] Cicero gives a different account, whereby the law was blocked by a decree of the augural college.[34] It is likely that the haruspices and the augurs expressed their hostility to the bill and that they urged the Senate to oppose it.[35] Whatever the specific details of this crisis may have been, it can safely be viewed as an instance of hostility to agrarian reform among the Etruscan elite to which the haruspices that advised the Roman government belonged, and as an indication that by the early first century BC the haruspices did not refrain from taking public stances on controversial political matters in Rome.

A scenario of agrarian conflict is sketched in a famous and elusive prophetic text, the so-called prophecy of Vegoia. The Latin version of the prophecy that the nymph Vegoia purportedly gave to Arruns Veltumnus as she taught him the doctrine of the haruspices mentions boundary stones; for this reason it was included in the *Libri agrimensorum*.[36] In an influential study J. Heurgon linked the text to the crisis of 91 and the initiatives of Livius Drusus.[37] The main argument in support of this thesis is the interpretation of the clause which marks the accomplishment of the prophecy *prope nouissimi octaui saeculi*, which may be translated as 'almost at the end of the eighth age'.[38] This is an elegant hypothesis, but

---

[32] App. *B Civ.* 1.24; cf. Plut. *C. Gracch.* 11.   [33] Obs. 46.   [34] Cic. *Leg.* 2.31. Weinrib 1970: 398–9.

[35] Linderski 1986a: 2167 n. 1 argues that the haruspices got involved first and suggested a *procuratio* to the prodigy of the ravens; the augurs were consulted later and corroborated that interpretation; Dyck 2004: 344 rightly notes that the augural college did not have the power to stop legislation, but could refer the matter to the Senate for action.

[36] Text and English translation in Campbell 2000: 256.33–258.10. Valvo 1988: 19–57; Guittard 2007a: 289–305; Martínez-Pinna 2007: 61–3. Palmer 1970: 111–12 stresses Vegoia's 'reputation as an authority on systematizing territory'. Her iconography may point towards further connections with the agrarian dimension: Domenici 2009: 105–8. Briquel 1990b and 1997b stresses the marginal, but not irrelevant, role of inspired divination in Etruscan religion, where 'le livre' usually prevails upon the 'parole révélée'; cf. however the *libri Begoes nymphae* in Serv. *ad Aen.* 6.72.

[37] Heurgon 1959; followed by Jal 1963: 247–8; Harris 1971: 36–8; Valvo 1988: 103–36; Campbell 2000: 445–6 n. 13; Mastrocinque 2005: 138–40. *Contra*, Turcan 1976: esp. 1011–12; North 2000a: 99. Cf. also Pfiffig 1961, who speculatively links the prophecy to the Social War.

[38] Heurgon 1959: 42–4; followed by Pfiffig 1961: 62; Novara 1982: 190; Briquel 1990a: 69. Different translations in Zancan 1939: 210: 'dell'ottavo secolo, che è quasi l'ultimo' and Mazzarino 1957: 112 (= 1980: 279): 'dell'ottavo, ed ultimo, secolo che si avvicina'. Guittard 2007a: 303–4 suspends judgement.

possibly an overconfident one, as the age between the Gracchi and Sulla was not short of phases in which critical events could be deemed to be bearers of traumatic events. Moreover, the end of a *saeculum* (age) could hardly be predicted far in advance, as the Etruscan ages did not have a fixed length.[39] It is safer to infer that the prophecy contained a generic reference to the end of the eighth age, which would fall some time in the early first century BC.

There are also substantial problems with the language of this text. J. N. Adams has persuasively argued that the Latin of the prophecy is quite stylish and not devoid of literary ambitions. The vocabulary strongly suggests an imperial dating. There is no compelling reason to view it as a clumsy translation of an Etruscan original, and indeed to believe that there is an Etruscal original behind the Latin text at all.[40] Whatever the dating and context of the prophecy may be, it is a document that provides significant information in several respects. Even forgeries can be instructive. First, Vegoia's prophecy gives a flavour of what Etruscan prophetic texts must have been like, or rather of how they were perceived by an intelligent Latin-speaking reader. Secondly, it confirms the importance of the theme of the Etruscan *saecula* within the broader context of reflections on the crisis of the Republic. Thirdly, it suggests that a link between the prophetic dimension of the *Etrusca disciplina* and the agrarian debate in the late Republic was at least deemed credible by some ancient readers.[41] A further factor must be taken into account: as various sources show, the haruspices were directly involved in the rituals that pertained to land-surveying. A tradition that went back to Varro established a direct analogy between the division of the land and the Etruscan doctrine that divided the earth into two regions.[42] This tradition was not unchallenged, as other ancient authors argued that centuriation was modelled on the augural ritual. Indeed, the ties between centuriation and augury are far-reaching and the involvement of the haruspices in centuriation attested by the gromatic sources should be regarded as a late development of earlier practices. Unfortunately, the antiquarian scope of the evidence makes it hard to establish when a significant change of practice took place, and how the haruspices put their expertise at the disposal of centuriation rituals.[43]

[39] Cens. *DN* 17.6. On the late Republican debate on the *saecula* see Chapter 5.
[40] Adams 2003: 179–82.
[41] Cf. North 2000a: 99: 'there is nothing in the content that is incompatible with its having been written centuries before the 90s BC'.
[42] Frontinus, *De controversiis*, 8.23–9 Campbell. Gargola 2004: 123–8; Wiseman forthcoming. Cf. Campbell 2000: xlv: '[b]ut Varro was not necessarily right'.
[43] Mazzarino 1957: 101–3 (= 1980: 263–66); Alexandratos 2009. The Etruscan *disciplina* also laid out rules on the orientation of temples: Vitr. *De arch.* 1.7 (Mansuelli 1998: 117).

Whatever the answer to this question may be and whatever interpretation of the events of 91/90 one may choose, the involvement of the haruspices in rituals that pertained to the use and organisation of land is well
attested and is yet another pointer to the complexity and importance of
their craft. The lore of the haruspices was not a doctrine that perpet-
uated itself across the generations in isolation from political and social
developments, nor was it an exclusively Etruscan discipline that had no
debts to other cultures. The doctrine on lightning that was contained in
the *libri fulgurales*, for instance, has a demonstrable link with Hellenistic astrology and ultimately with Babylonian doctrines, mediated to the
Greek-speaking intellectuals by the work of the late fourth- to early third-
century BC astrologer Berossus.[44] Moreover, the engagement with Roman
politics undoubtedly caused further developments in the Etruscan *disciplina*. The participation of the haruspices in late Republican politics, at
both the individual and the collective level, was undoubtledly very significant, but generalisations, while tempting, must be avoided. Close scrutiny
of the evidence for haruspical activity suggests that in the late Republic the
haruspices were a divided constituency on matters of politics and doctrine
(the evidence for earlier periods is insufficient). The increasing political
significance of their craft was not matched by an effort to rally together
behind an Etruscan cause, or even a Roman political faction.[45]

Moreover, determining the political background and loyalties of some
individual haruspices is often a hopeless undertaking. The evidence for the
Gracchan period is a case in point: while we know that some haruspices
based in Rome were prepared to interpret a number of prodigies against
the foundation of the Gracchan colony at Carthage, we also know that
Gaius Gracchus relied on the services of a haruspex, C. Herennius Siculus,
who was a committed political supporter of the tribune and died in the
repression launched by the Senate against him.[46] The same problem applies
to the Sullan period: Sulla had many enemies in Etruria, but also used the
services of the haruspex Postumius.[47] Working for a powerful individual,
however, was not the only opportunity for a haruspex to establish his reputation. Obsequens has a remarkable notice recording the intervention of a

[44] Weinstock 1951; cf. also Thulin 1905a: x–xv; Vigourt 2001a: 228–31; Bakhouche 2002: 20–2; Liébert
   2006: 137–8. Cf. Valvo 1988: 58–101 for a discussion of the links between the prophecy of Vegoia
   and other prophecies that were produced and circulated in the Hellenistic world.
[45] Rawson 1978a (= 1991: 290–323); Briquel 1999; Aigner-Foresti 2000: 11–18; Haack 2003: 52–83;
   Torelli 2011: 139–43.
[46] Santangelo 2005a: 213 n. 54; Haack 2006: 61–3, no. 88.
[47] Cic. *Div.* 1.72; 2.65; Val. Max. 1.6.4 (directly based on Cicero, according to Wardle 1998: 189); Plut.
   Sull. 9.6; cf. also 27.7; August. *De civ. D.* 2.24. See Haack 2006: 99–101, no. 75; Marastoni 2008.

haruspex called Aemilius Potensis in 102.[48] A temple of Jupiter (it is unclear whether it was in Rome or elsewhere) was hit by lightning and the only haruspex who had the courage to suggest the appropriate expiation was Aemilius Potensis. All his peers, according to Obsequens' brief summary, refused to speak out, because they regarded the prodigy as a sign of imminent destruction for themselves and their children. Aemilius' courage was rewarded by the Romans. It remains unclear in what framework Aemilius operated, in what context he gave his prophetic response, and how it was received by the Roman Senate and magistrates, in the tense period of the wars against the Cimbrians and the Teutons. It would be unhelpful to make general statements on the political positions taken by the haruspices as a whole in the late Republic. The evidence is too scarce and elusive to allow safe conclusions: only the names of a few individuals are recorded for the Republican period.[49]

A broad range of groups are covered by the label of 'haruspices': diviners who are consulted by the State, diviners consulted by a community, and diviners who are privately employed, usually by a prominent individual. Most of these diviners were of Etruscan origin; others were not, but they all used Etruscan doctrines. This internal differentiation became even stronger under the Principate, a period in which the evidence for individual haruspices becomes much richer. The late Republican evidence enables us to trace just the beginnings of this differentiation process. One of the major problems is that the evidence for this period does not answer the question of how the haruspices were organised as a corporate body. We have reasonably safe evidence that by the Augustan age (at the very latest) there was an *ordo* of sixty haruspices; in AD 47 Claudius promoted a *senatusconsultum* that set out rules for its reorganisation.[50] It is likely that

---

[48] Obs. 44: *aedes Iouis clusa fulmine icta. cuius expiationem quia primus monstrauerat Aemilius Potensis aruspex, praemium tulit, ceteris celantibus, quod ipsis liberisque exitium portenderetur* ('A temple of Jupiter, when it was closed, was struck by lightning. Since the haruspex Aemilius Potensis had been the first to prescribe the expiation for that, he obtained a prize, as the other haruspices had not disclosed it, because it portended death for them and their children'). Torelli 1975: 122 n. 2 argues that the *cognomen* of the haruspex is 'certainly corrupt' and the gentilician name is also doubtful; Haack 2006: 150 leaves Aemilius out of her prosopography of known haruspices.

[49] List in Torelli 1975: 122. Hano 1986: 108 notes that in Livy the word *haruspex* appears in the singular only six times out of twenty-seven occurrences. North 1990: 53 suggests that the haruspices who read the entrails at sacrifices were of lower rank than those who were consulted on the interpretation of prodigies; the evidence is inconclusive. On haruspical anonymity cf. Corbeill 2012: 257–8.

[50] Augustan (or late Republican?) period: *CIL* 6.32439, from Rome, with the cautious discussion of Thulin 1909: 146–7, 150. AD 47: Tac. *Ann.* 11.15. See also the fragments of a list of haruspices from Tarquinia, published and discussed in Torelli 1975: 105–35, which may have been a list of all the citizens of Tarquinia who had been members of the *ordo*; North 1990: 67–8 is more cautious, although he concedes that these texts are 'a local Etruscan record of individual priests'.

a similar form of organisation existed in the previous decades, especially in light of the considerable involvement of the haruspices in public affairs, but there is no firm evidence that this was the case.[51] On the other hand, the decision not to create a permanent *ordo* of haruspices until the Augustan age may be a symptom of the problems and the controversy entailed in the involvement of a part of the Etruscan elites in the very core of the political process. Establishing an *ordo* meant that the process was irreversible; that the haruspices were there to stay, along with the senior priestly colleges of the Republic.[52]

On balance, the view that Rome developed a framework for the haruspices already during the Republic should be accepted. This is suggested by a famous passage of the *De diuinatione*, which sheds light on the decisions taken by Rome on the organisation of the haruspicy in Etruria. According to Cicero, the Roman Senate had set rules concerning the training of the haruspices-to-be, which entailed collaboration between Rome and the Etruscan communities (*Div.* 1.92):

> *Etruria autem de caelo tacta scientissume animaduertit, eademque interpretatur quid quibusque ostendatur monstris atque portentis. quocirca bene apud maiores nostros senatus, tum cum florebat imperium, decreuit ut de principum filiis X singulis Etruriae populis in disciplinam traderentur, ne ars tanta propter tenuitatem hominum a religionis auctoritate abduceretur ad mercedem atque quaestum.*

> Etruria has the deepest knowledge of things struck by lightning and also interprets what is signified by each prodigy and portent. For this reason, in the time of our forebears, the Senate, at a time when our empire was thriving, decreed that of the sons of the leading citizens groups of ten should be handed over to the individual Etruscan peoples to be instructed in the discipline so that an art of such great importance should not, because

---

[51] Torelli 1975: 120–1, Haack 2002: 126 and Farney 2007: 154–5 argue that the *ordo* already existed in the late Republic. Capdeville 1998: 392 n. 36, Turfa 2006: 62 and Briquel 2008: 121 suggest that it existed even before the first century BC. The need for a formal organisation of the haruspices in the Republic is recognised by Latte 1960: 397 and MacBain 1982: 49–50. *Contra*, Rawson 1978a: 140, 147–8 (= 1991: 302–3, 315), who favours an Augustan date.

[52] Torelli 1975: 133–4 argues that the haruspices and their *disciplina* were under the direct control of the (*quin*)*decemuiri s.f.*: the argument rests on the evidence of a fragmentary *elogium* from Tarquinia: *post o[bitum huius]* / *sub (decem)uiros ea disciplina[a relata est]*. The inscription must be dated before Sulla, because it speaks of *decemuiri*. Torelli's view is accepted by Massa-Pairault 1985: 18; Farney 2007: 154–5. MacBain 1982: 59 n. 157 and Orlin 2010: 97–8 view the inscription as evidence for institutional ties between the two priestly colleges. However, the inscription is heavily integrated and there is no parallel evidence for the subordination of the haruspices to the (*quin*)*decemuiri*. Moreover, North 2000a: 95–8 convincingly argues that in this context the word *discipulina* is best understood as a reference to the teachings and writings of an individual haruspex, rather than to the Etruscan discipline in general.

of a lack of manpower, lose its religious authority to become an object of commerce and profit. (trans. D. Wardle, modified)[53]

The main concern underlying this measure was that the knowledge of the haruspices be protected from any risk of corruption. There is a direct, if rather vague reference to the possibility of the haruspices being bribed, with a reference to a decline of the discipline *ad mercedem atque quaestum* ('becoming object of commerce and profit'). Even divination is corruptible, and the risk was openly acknowledged.[54] The text of this passage is uncertain and various attempts have been made to emend it. It seems certain that the haruspices in question were Etruscan, not Roman, and that the would-be haruspices were recruited from each Etruscan city; however, not all the young Etruscans involved in the exercise were automatically recruited as haruspices. The dating of this measure is a matter of speculation: the generic reference to the period of prosperity for the empire could suggest any time between the Hannibalic War and the Gracchan crisis. J. North rightly argued that the chronological spectrum must be narrowed to the period between 167 and 133, since the extant books of Livy do not mention any such decision.[55]

One of the most striking aspects of this passage is that a senatorial decree could set rules on the religious life of the Etruscan communities, even well before the Social War.[56] It conveys a picture of ties between Rome and Etruria which cannot be underestimated. Its most significant implication,

[53] The manuscripts have *sex* (six), which is usually emendated to *X* (ten); the emendation of the numeral is suggested by Val. Max. 1.1.1, which is closely based on Cicero: *tantum autem studium antiquis non solum seruandae sed etiam amplificandae religionis fuit, ut florentissima tum et opulentissima ciuitate decem principum filii senatus consulto singulis Etruriae populis percipiendae sacrorum disciplinae gratia traderentur* ('Among the ancients the desire for not only preserving but also increasing worship was so great that, when the state was very flourishing and very wealthy, by a decree of the Senate the sons of ten leading citizens were entrusted to the individual peoples of Etruria in order to learn the lore of the sacred rites', trans. D. Wardle). Pease and Timpanaro, however, prefer *X ex singulis Etruriae populi* and translate the text on the following lines: 'the Senate . . . decreed that ten sons of the leading citizens of each of the Etruscan peoples should be handed over to be instructed in the discipline' (also accepted by Corbeill 2012: 248 n. 14). Pease 1920: 259–60, Timpanaro 1988: 300–1 and Wardle 1998: 80–1 and 2006: 326 provide a full discussion of Cicero's passage and the textual and historical problems it raises. Torelli 1975: 121 concludes that they are unsolvable.

[54] The greed of seers is a commonplace in Greek discourses on divination: M. Flower 2008: 135–47; cf. the recurrent allegations of greed against dice players (Purcell 1995: 8). Bowden 2003 deconstructs the category of the *chresmologoi*, the 'collectors' (and sellers) of oracles that are often mentioned in the evidence for the Classical period.

[55] North 1967: 572–3. Timpanaro 1988: 300–1 and Ampolo 1990–1991: 195 argue for a date between 241 and 133; Haack 2003: 41 for the third century BC. More suggestions in Wardle 2006: 325.

[56] The *senatusconsultum de Bacchanalibus* of 186 is another instance of Roman intervention in the religious affairs of the Italian communities: Pailler 1988: 275–324; Rasmussen 2003: 233–7. A different reading in Lacam 2012: 274–5.

however, is that the Roman elite, while recognising the importance of the haruspices and their doctrine, decided to regulate their activities and to interfere in a very significant respect, namely the process through which the discipline was taught and transmitted from one generation to another. The number of young Etruscans who were involved in the recruitment operation is another important factor, which suggests that Rome intended to bring about a structural, long-term reorganisation. The significance of this measure is such that it makes the problem of the existence of an *ordo* of the haruspices under the Republic almost irrelevant. Whatever the organisation of the haruspices that advised the Senate and the magistrates was called, it is hard to escape the conclusion that Rome set rules for the training of the haruspices and that all the haruspices who were admitted to advise the Roman government had to be educated within that framework. Nonetheless, as we have seen, the history of the last two centuries of the Republic shows that there were considerable margins of freedom and change in haruspical practice and lore.

Letting the haruspices speak (for themselves?)

We know that there existed traditions in Roman Republican culture that were hostile to haruspicy and that its foreignness was never forgotten or overlooked, even when it was successfully included into the fabric of public religion.[57] We have hardly any evidence for the attitude of the Roman populace to the haruspices and their doctrine, but we know that the senatorial elite was prepared to listen to them, if for no other reason than to exploit their responses for the sake of the conflicting political agendas of its factions. We need to make allowances for the fact that all we know about the responses of the haruspices (or indeed the haruspices themselves) in this period comes from Roman sources and is presented in Roman terms. In Cicero's *De haruspicum responso*, the fragmentary quotations from the response given by the haruspices in 56 are conveyed through Cicero's critical representation, which is primarily aimed at countering Clodius' reading of the responses. Recognising the paramount importance of haruspical activity in late Republican Rome does not change the fact that our record is largely incomplete and that we should allow for a great level of diversity within the range of haruspical interventions.

The response of the haruspices to the prodigies that were reported in 65 shows that prophecy was not necessarily their only response and

[57] Orlin 2010: 96–100.

that traditional and innovative responses to prodigies could at times be reconciled.[58] When the Capitol was struck with lightning, haruspices were summoned to Rome *ex tota Etruria*; again, it is unclear how they were chosen, although the involvement of the haruspices in a prodigy involving lightning is not surprising, given their consolidated expertise in the field.[59] They predicted that horrible evils were about to fall upon Rome and her empire, unless action was taken to avert them. The measures to be taken were quite vague: gods had to be pacified by every method (*omni ratione placari*). The State responded with the organisation of a ten-day festival and with the dedication of a new statue of Jupiter on the Capitol.[60] Its completion took some time and the dedication took place only in 63, under Cicero's consulship, and indeed on 3 December, the day when the conspirators were brought before the Senate. Cicero did not hesitate to view this coincidence as a sign of the direct support of Jupiter Optimus Maximus for the repression of the conspiracy. The response given in 65 provides an interesting and possibly innovative solution. On that solemn occasion a prophecy was given, but a whole set of ritual remedies that could have averted disaster was also suggested:

> *quo quidem tempore cum haruspices ex tota Etruria conuenissent, caedes atque incendia et legum interitum et bellum ciuile ac domesticum et totius urbis atque imperii occasum adpropinquare dixerunt, nisi di inmortales omni ratione placati suo numine prope fata ipsa flexissent.*

> At that time the haruspices, who had convened from the whole of Etruria, said that slaughter and arson, the death of the laws, civil and internal war, and the downfall of the whole city and the empire were approaching, unless the immortal gods, placated by every possible means, averted with their might what was nearly destiny itself.[61]

It seems beyond doubt that similar responses were given in this period, although they are not explicitly recorded elsewhere. Cicero indirectly

---

[58] Cic. *Cat.* 3.19–21.

[59] Lightning in haruspicy: Thulin 1905a: 3–8, 13–128; see esp. 111–17 on public prodigies involving lightning. It is noteworthy that not even Marcus denies the haruspices' ability to establish where lightning originates and what it hits (Cic. *Div.* 2.45).

[60] Köves-Zulauf 1997: 223–5 draws attention to the important detail that the orientation of the statue was changed from west to east (*Cat.* 3.20); Cicero points out that the rationale of the choice was to ensure that light be shed on future plots against the Republic (*inlustrarentur*), so that the Senate and the people could see them (*perspici*). Dyck 2008: 196 sees a wordplay with the haruspices' warning of *urbis atque imperi occasus* (3.19).

[61] Cic. *Cat.* 3.19. Bloch 1963: 54–5, 1965b: 65–6 and 1966: 163; Weinstock 1971: 192; Begemann 2012: 151–4. North 1967: 583 plausibly suggests that this is 'an ingenious reconciliation of Roman and Etruscan ideas'. *Omni ratione*: Frank 1992: 115–16.

points to their existence in Marcus' attack on the philosophical basis of divination, when he says that, if one is to take fate seriously, there is no point in prescribing expiatory rituals as the haruspices usually did.[62]

More evidence gives further depth to a scenario of pluralism and diversity. The lives of several prominent Etruscans in this period tell us that the form of divination practised in Etruria and in Rome was a set of doctrines, a *disciplina*, but it was not an immutable practice.[63] It was the object of study and reflection and that very process of critique and enquiry took place within the Etruscan elites – although, again, we know about it through the filter of Roman sources. Nigidius Figulus himself may have had Etruscan origins.[64] At any rate, he certainly wrote on haruspical matters and was regarded as an authority by posterity.[65] He was, for example, the source for the 'brontoscopic calendar' (i.e. a calendar based on the observation of thunder) that John Lydus, a Byzantine antiquarian, included in his work on prodigies.[66] This exceptional document is based on the principle that claps of thunder have prophetic meanings, which change according to the day on which thunder is heard. The calendar provides a detailed overview of these different possible meanings, which are organised into daily entries and introduced by a recurrent formula ('if there is a clap of thunder, then . . . ').[67] Despite this formulaic structure, the meanings vary considerably in scope, ranging from agricultural to political and social matters. John Lydus states that he derived the text of this lunar calendar from Nigidius, who had in turn derived it from the Etruscan seer Tages: we are apparently faced, then, with a Greek translation of the Latin version of an Etruscan original. A postscript makes clear that the calendar applied only

---

[62] Cic. *Div.* 2.20–5. Cf. esp. 2.24–5: *cum res tristissumas portendi dixerunt, addunt ad extremum omnia leuius casura rebus diuinis procuratis* ('having said that the greatest misfortunes loom upon me, they add in the end that everything will go better if expiatory rituals will be performed').

[63] *Disciplina*: Vigourt 2001a: 227; Rüpke 2007b: 72–3, 2010a: 755–6 and 2011c: 318–19.

[64] Della Casa 1962: 14 n. 13; Hadas-Lebel 2004: 37.

[65] He wrote a treatise on extispicy, the *De extis*: F LXXXI Swoboda. Some speculation on Nigidius' connection to Etruscan culture in Aigner-Foresti 2000: 21–6. Nigidius' interests encompassed other forms of divination and premonition: he wrote a *De somniis*, the only Latin work on dreams attested for the classical period (Lyd. *Ost.* 45 Wachsmuth = Nigidius F LXXXII Swoboda, with Harris 2009: 183–4).

[66] Lyd. *Ost.* 62–88 Wachsmuth = Nigidius fr. LXXIII Swoboda. English translation and extensive discussion in Turfa 2012 (*adhuc non uidi*). This text has attracted considerable attention: Piganiol 1951; Dumézil 1966: 605–9; Liuzzi 1983: 84–93; Rawson 1985: 310–11; Ampolo 1990–1; Montero 1994a: 92–3; Guittard 2003; Turfa 2007. John Lydus and the *De ostentis*: Mastandrea 1979: 74–95; Maas 1992: 105–13, 179–81; Domenici 2007: 7–43.

[67] Cf. the use of the same structure in the evidence for 'deductive divination' in the ancient Near East (Bottéro 1974: 99–124).

to the city of Rome.[68] Nonetheless, it is plausible that the text preserved by Lydus is a genuine reflection of Nigidius' work on these problems, rather than a Byzantine forgery.[69] The text shows the influence of several different traditions. There are elements that can be explained with Babylonian influences, from the structure of the calendar to the very idea that thunder can be used to predict the future to the frequent references to cardinal points.[70] Moreover, various sections refer to a context of social conflict and traumatic political change, including allusions to the imminent rise of one man to supreme power and to the tension between the rich and the poor. The entry for 19 August even points to an alliance of women and slaves to subvert the city.[71] Some of these elements point to the troubled context of the late Republic, the age when Nigidius Figulus lived and wrote, but others are undoubtedly earlier and could be read as references to social tensions in Etruscan society going as far back as to the fourth and third centuries BC.[72] Disentangling these two levels and establishing the extent of Nigidius' reworking of the material that he found in his Etruscan sources is impossible. However, an important historical fact is clear: a highly educated member of the Roman political elite set out to make an Etruscan divinatory text accessible to a Roman audience.

Nigidius was not alone in this undertaking. John Lydus used another brontoscopic calendar compiled by C. Fonteius Capito, a friend of Mark Antony who was also a member of the pontifical college.[73] Pursuing an interest in the Etruscan *disciplina* was by no means in contradiction with the duty of piety that a member of the Roman elite was expected to fulfil. In fact, it could be conducive to a better understanding of the workings of Roman *religio*. The response of the haruspices given in 56 and reported in Cicero's *De haruspicum responso* was ultimately based on the same blueprint as some entries of the calendar. After a rumbling sound was heard in the *ager Latiniensis*, the haruspices warned that unless the concord among the

---

[68] Nigidius' translation (or reworking) of Etruscan texts was not isolated, as the case of his contemporary Tarquitius Priscus shows (*CIL* 11.3370, 7566; Plin. *HN index* 2, 3; Amm. Marc. 25.2.7; Macrob. *Sat.* 3.7.3, 3.20.3). On the circulation of the *Etrusca disciplina* among Roman audiences see Rawson 1985: 303–6; Capdeville 1993, 1997: 471–508 and 1998: 395–403; Hadas-Lebel 2004: 37–41, 45–9. Translation of Etruscan technical terms into Latin: Capdeville 1994.

[69] Piganiol 1951: 81–2 = 1973: 50–1; Harris 1971: 6–8; Ampolo 1990–1: 185–8.

[70] Ampolo 1990–1: 188–9.   [71] Montero 1993b: 654–7 and 1995b: 149.

[72] Cornell 1978: 172; Ampolo 1990–1: 192–5. Turfa 2007 argues (somewhat overconfidently) that the Etruscan original of the calendar dated back to the Iron Age. Reconstructing the development of haruspicy in the fourth century BC and in general before Rome began to use it systematically is an impossible undertaking. Massa-Pairault 1985 presents some potentially relevant iconographic evidence.

[73] Weinstock 1950; Briquel 1999: 192–3; Rüpke 2005a: 1001, no. 1734.

optimates was restored there would be great detriment to the senators and the most illustrious citizens, the city would lose the support of the gods, and the rule of one individual would soon emerge.[74] The concerns of Nigidius, the Roman student of the Etruscan *disciplina*, overlapped to some extent with those of the haruspices who served the Roman government in his own day.

The *De diuinatione* powerfully illustrates the extent of disagreement that could exist on matters of religion and divination in late Republican Rome. Cicero is certainly interested in providing a rigorous and searching discussion of divination, but he also insists on the importance that divination can have as a factor in political and social cohesion. The discussion of haruspicy in *Div.* 2, with the emphasis on the importance of this misguided doctrine for the *communis religio*, is very instructive. Yet, the work of the haruspices and its interpretation could introduce very divisive political issues, as is powerfully shown by Cicero's speech on the responses of the haruspices (*De haruspicum responso*) delivered before the Senate in 56.[75] This speech is remarkable for a number of reasons, not just because it is an invaluable document of the clash between Cicero and his arch-enemy, P. Clodius Pulcher. Most significantly for our purposes, it provides a clear example of how Cicero depicted and used public divination in his political activity, and substantial extracts from a late Republican haruspical response.

The background of the speech is Cicero's return from exile and Clodius' attempt to secure the confiscation of his house. The Senate had recently voted against his proposal to this effect, but Clodius claimed in a *contio* that some recent responses of the haruspices referred to Cicero's home as a contaminated site which had to be purified.[76] The haruspices were consulted by the Senate for an apparently unrelated reason, according to a procedure that was common in Republican history: rumbling and clattering (*strepitus cum fremitu*) had been heard in the *ager Latiniensis*, in the vicinity of Rome.[77] The haruspices were consulted on how to interpret this message and came up with a series of responses that were more a

---

[74] Cic. *Har. resp.* 40. Ampolo 1990–1: 186–7.

[75] Introductions to the speech: Lenaghan 1969: 22–31 and Beard, North and Price 1998 1.137–40. Chronology: Beard 2012: 23–4. Kumaniecki 1959 and Tatum 1999a: 216–19, 320–1 offer reliable discussions of the political background. Clodius' priesthood: Rüpke 2005a: 897, no. 1265. Corbeill 2010a: 145–6 and 2012: 259–60 stresses that Clodius was a *quindecemuir* and his potential conflict of interest may have been the reason for the Senate's decision to get the haruspices involved in the interpretation of the prodigy.

[76] Cic. *Har. resp.* 9. Religious aspects: Bloch 1963: 49–54; North 1967: 582–5; Goar 1972: 56–72; Guillaumont 1984: 32–6; Guittard 2007a: 331–41; Corbeill 2010a and 2012: 257–64; Gildenhard 2011: 326–43; Beard 2012.

[77] Beard 2012: 20 n. 1, 27–31 on the origin and nature of this sound.

diagnostic overview of the recent past than a string of predictions: arrears of sacrifices (*postiliones*) were due to Jupiter, Saturnus, Neptune, Tellus and the Celestial Gods; and the 'games' (*ludi*) had been celebrated with less scruple than usual and were desecrated (*polluti*).[78] It is likely that some specific ritual prescriptions were set out in the same context, although they are not explicitly mentioned in the speech.[79] The polysemy of the responses enabled Clodius to use them against Cicero (whether or not the haruspices intended them to be exploited in this way it is hard to say).[80] In his speech to the Senate, Cicero gave a completely different interpretation from that of his opponent.

To our purposes, what is most interesting about the speech is not the panoply of arguments that Cicero uses to turn the responses of the haruspices against Clodius, but the theoretical and ideological position that he puts forward about the predictions of the haruspices. Of course, Cicero does not go anywhere near the negative stance expressed by Marcus in book 2 of *De diuinatione* about the Etruscan *disciplina*. On the contrary, he repeatedly expresses appreciation of, and support for, this practice.[81] It is very interesting, however, to look at the nuances of Cicero's appreciation of the haruspices and to consider how he deals with the interpretative problems that their responses posed. The key passage is *Har.* 18–19, a digression that falls between the summary of Cicero's own position after his return from exile (11–17) and the refutation of the interpretation provided by Clodius (20–41). At the outset Cicero stresses that he does not intend to challenge the response of the haruspices and that he does not underestimate the importance of the prodigy reported in the *ager Latiniensis*. This declaration of allegiance then turns into an *excusatio non petita*: although he is a man of letters (*uersari in studio litterarum*) more than most of his peers, his interests do not distract him from the importance of religion (*religio*).[82] The project of reconciling intellectual education and *religio* will be at the forefront of the religious trilogy ten years later. The arguments that Cicero brings in support of his allegiance to *religio*, however, may not be necessarily the ones he used in the forties. The main foundation of *religio*, he claims, is the practice of the ancestors, who are its champions and teachers. It is from the ancestral tradition that the centrality of the *pontifices* in all the constituencies of public cult derives, and it is from it that the use of the Sibylline Books and the consultation of the haruspices have derived. Ancestral tradition is also corroborated by experience, as the haruspices

---

[78] Cic. *Har. resp.* 20–3.   [79] North 1967: 583 n. 107.
[80] Cf. Beard 2012: 21 ('a classic combination of the specific and the vague').
[81] Cic. *Har. resp.* 20, 56, 60–1.   [82] Corbeill 2010a: 150–1; Gildenhard 2011: 331.

have shown their reliability by foreseeing the great civil disturbances of the first quarter of the century well in advance.[83]

The discussion then focuses on the need to connect and reconcile ancestral religion with philosophical practice. Many learned and wise men (*homines doctos sapientesque*) have written about the existence of the gods and their nature, in such a way that their writings themselves seem to be divinely inspired. According to Cicero, ancestral wisdom and philosophical speculation have taken shape independently; but their agreement is so strong that one may think that the philosophers have been taught by the ancestors. The elaborate argument is apparently supposed to elide the opposition between philosophy and traditional religion. As Cicero states a few lines below, the existence of the gods who order and rule the universe should be plainly obvious to anyone who just bothers to look at the sky.[84]

This divine order has significant political implications too. It is precisely to the support of the gods (*eorum numine*) that Rome owes the emergence of the empire and its survival.[85] After all, Rome's greatest virtue is precisely its piety towards the gods, as much as Spain is remarkable for its populousness and Gaul for its strength. It is this particular form of *sapientia* which makes Rome so successful and unique. In this context, respect for the gods is at the core of the problem. Heeding the response of the haruspices is just part of a broader commitment to piety. Indeed, no matter what their teachings may be about, the haruspices are far from central in Cicero's vision. His statement of loyalty to public divination and traditional religion ends with a statement of the Roman-ness of religion, which immediately turns into an opportunity to create some distance from the haruspices and their Etruscan lore. Cicero says that the nature of the portents reported to the Senate is unmistakeable: they are clearly prophesying and predicting an awful destiny for the Republic. In fact, there is no need for haruspices: 'cannot we ourselves be haruspices?' (*nos nonne haruspices esse possumus?*). Cicero is treading a very fine line: on one hand, he is vigorously asserting his loyalty to the State religion; on the other he is discreetly implying that the lore of the haruspices, which is part of public religion, can comfortably be renounced.[86] What is at stake is the interpretation of the prodigies, which

[83] The centrality of the ancestral tradition is emphatically restated at the beginning of Valerius Maximus' overview of Roman religion (1.1.1); the opening sentence of the chapter is directly based on *Har. resp.* 18 (Wardle 1998: 16–17, 75–6; Ando 2008: 1–3).

[84] Cic. *Har. resp* 19. Gildenhard 2011: 333–8.   [85] Begemann 2012: 175–9, 277–8.

[86] Beard 2012: 31–2.

the haruspices have presented in ambiguous enough terms for Clodius and his friends to build a narrative of the recent political developments entirely hostile to Cicero. To make his alternative reconstruction tenable, Cicero needs to probe the authority of the haruspices on the interpretation of the prodigies, or rather to state that the responses of the Etruscan priests are just not enough by themselves. They require an interpretative effort on the part of those who receive them.[87]

The central aim of the speech, as has been pointed out, is to provide an alternative reading of the prodigies to that produced by Clodius, through the loose net built by the response of the haruspices. In fact, the voice of the haruspices quickly becomes almost irrelevant: the focus shifts towards the real fundamental dispute, that between Cicero and his enemy. It cannot be overlooked that this is a political speech, where we should not expect to find wide-ranging, or explicit, views on the role of the haruspices and divination. In fact, Cicero uses this sort of argument very sparingly. The concluding section, however, offers a significant statement. After a speech that has been spent building on the gaps left by the responses of the haruspices, Cicero claims that his interpretation is the most genuine one, as it is most loyal to the spirit of the haruspices. Indeed, his argument issues from the final part of the response of the haruspices: to act 'so that the order of the State may not be changed' (*prouidete ne rei publicae status commutetur*). This is a political statement if ever there was one: the haruspices are keen to defend the status quo and to issue a warning to the citizen body on the importance of avoiding a revolutionary outcome.[88] It is worth restating that this is one of the few surviving verbatim quotations of the responses given by the haruspices in the late Republic, and by the far the most extensive one.[89] It is remarkable to see that a text of this kind could take such an explicit stance on the political agenda, or on the concerns and principles that underlay

---

[87] As Corbeill 2010a: 144 notes, 'it is not the text's truth value but its interpretation that requires discussion'. The image of Cicero as a 'public literary critic' (*ibid.*) is especially felicitous; cf. also Cancik 1995 and Chapter 1.

[88] The generic, but politically loaded wording of the haruspical response is vaguely reminiscent of the late Republican *senatusconsulta ultima*, such as that mentioned in Sall. *Cat.* 29.2: *senatus decreuit darent operam consules ne quid res publica detrimenti caperet* ('the Senate decreed that the consuls should do their utmost "to prevent the State from suffering any damage"'); Bloch 1965a: 286 notes a parallel with the response of the *duumuiri s.f.* in Livy 3.10.7. Lenaghan 1969: 196 speculates that 'some such clause' was part of every response of the haruspices. Similarities between the response and Etruscan brontoscopic calendars: Piganiol 1951: 84–5 = 1973: 53–4 and Ampolo 1990–1: 186–7.

[89] The response was made public in Latin, but it probably derived from an Etruscan original (Corbeill 2010a: 147–8). Beard 2012: 26–7 is sceptical on the possibility of reconstructing the text of the haruspical response on the basis of the quotes in Cicero's speech.

the political controversy.[90] Cicero does not have any objection to that.
Indeed, he appears to take the point of the haruspices, because it is directly
relevant to his own rhetorical and political point. The central issue, he
claims, is the precariousness of the State and the following paragraph is
devoted to a forceful contrast between the glorious past of the State and
its bleak present: the very fabric of the State is falling apart, the rule of law
itself is under question; the central problem is, of course, Clodius. Cicero
states very clearly that the prodigies discussed by the haruspices are, in fact,
divine warnings on the nature of the political life of the State and of the
threat that looms over it. The stated aim of the speech is to do justice to
the responses of the haruspices and therefore to serve the cause of public
religion.[91]

Cicero's speech must be read within the context of a wider political
operation against Clodius, who had advocated a different reading of the
prodigies and of the responses of the haruspices. In Cicero's view, Clodius'
strategy served the purpose of his own political agenda, but was founded
on a ruthless manipulation of the message conveyed by the gods. His
response is that it is not acceptable to deform and manipulate messages
sent by the gods; most importantly, it is not acceptable to depict them in
caricatural terms. The gods do interfere in human affairs and the political life of the Republic and they do send messages to mankind, making
sure that their voice is understood. However, there is no reason to represent the gods as is done in the theatre, as if they come down to earth
from the heavens and hold conversations with mortals.[92] The interpretation of their messages must be sensible and carefully thought through,
and must translate into appropriate ritual action. This applies to the
prodigy from the *ager Latiniensis* as well as to a prodigy from Potentia
Picena which had not yet been officially reported when the speech was
given:

> cogitate genus sonitus eius quem Latinienses nuntiarunt, recordamini illud etiam
> quod nondum est relatum, quod eodem fere tempore factus in agro Piceno Poten-
> tiae nuntiatur terrae motus horribilis cum quibusdam multis metuendisque
> rebus: haec eadem profecto quae prospicimus impendentia pertimescetis.

---

[90] Cic. *Har. resp.* 60. The verb *prouidere* does not appear in the response of the haruspices, but it is
used by Cicero: its presence in this context is telling.
[91] Cic. *Har. resp.* 61.
[92] Cic. *Har. resp.* 62.1–2. On the theological implications of this passage see Levene 2012: 67.

Reflect upon the kind of noise which the Latinienses have reported. Remember that prodigy too, which has not as yet been formally reported: at almost the same time a terrible earthquake is said to have taken place in the Picenum, at Potentia, along with many other frightening events.[93]

Cicero suggests that the response to these events must be the same, with or without an official endorsement. But again there is a significant proviso. Recognising the importance of prodigies and doing justice to the voice of the gods, however, is not enough. Prayers are as important as they are easy (*faciles*), but the engagement of the citizens against discord and political conflict is even more significant.

Even in a speech that is centred on a response of the haruspices and its role in a complex political crisis, it is striking to find two important provisos. The haruspices and their responses are not sufficient to secure the prosperity of the State, and expiation and piety are not enough either. Human intelligence and *industria* are equally significant. There is no opposition between them and religion. In fact, the appropriate way to experience religion is to practise it both intelligently and diligently. The project of the gods must be understood and thought through. Against this background, the agenda of the speech is much closer to that of the *De diuinatione* than it has often been recognised.[94] It reflects an idea of the use of prodigies and of their value that is part of a wider approach to religion. There is some continuity between the construction of divination outlined in the speech of 56 and the arguments of the treatise that Cicero wrote on divination towards the end of his life.

Caesar and the haruspices

A. Caecina, the Volaterran friend and correspondent of Cicero, was as busy thinking about haruspicy as Cicero and Nigidius Figulus were. His work on the interpretation of lightning was still used well into the first century AD.[95] He was not a senator, but he was a leading member of the elite of Volaterrae and a committed supporter of Cato; he fought at Utica and was pardoned

---

[93] Cic. *Har. resp.* 62.3; this notice is a reminder of how prodigies, even when they were (yet) unreported, could shape the political debate. Cf. Beard 2012: 23 n. 9 for the suggestion that these prodigies may be those mentioned in Dio 39.20.

[94] Beard 2012: 37–9.

[95] Plin. *HN index* 2; Sen. *Q Nat.* 2.39. Caecina's work on haruspicy: Hine 1981: 379–82; Rawson 1985: 304–5; Capdeville 1993: 13–25, 28–30 and 1998: 400–2.

by Caesar, whose clemency he later celebrated in writing.[96] We have no evidence that Caecina ever practised haruspicy in Rome, but we know that another Etruscan noble, Spurinna, member of a distinguished family of Tarquinia, did practise it in the age of Caesar and advised the dictator on several occasions.[97] In the first reference to Caesar's assassination in the *De diuinatione*, Cicero states that, when Caesar performed a sacrifice, sitting on a golden throne and wearing a purple dress, no doubt at the Lupercalia, the bull was found to have no heart. Spurinna was consulted and ruled that it was a bad omen and that Caesar would soon lose his mind and his life, which both proceed from the heart. The response is puzzling in many respects. We do not know in what capacity Spurinna gave it, what relationship he had to Caesar, who was assisting him in his duties, whether he had any interest in misreporting what he saw in the animal's entrails and what the implications of that prophecy were.[98] E. Rawson argued that it was a warning that Caesar's policy 'would lead to disaster'.[99] Not everybody agreed, though: Quintus, who reports the incident in his plea in favour of divination, remarks that Spurinna's response was just an interpretation of signs that the gods had sent to Caesar so that he could foresee his death; it was not meant to enable him to avoid it.

A variant of the episode is reported by Suetonius, who uses it as evidence for the mounting arrogance of Caesar in the final period of his life.[100] He does not give any details on the context in which it occurred, and just states that when a haruspex ruled that the entrails of an animal and the absence of the heart were signs of evil to come, Caesar replied that future sacrifices would be favourable because that was his wish and that, at any rate, the absence of the heart of the victim should not be regarded as a prodigy (*Iul.* 77.3):

> *eoque arrogantiae progressus est, ut haruspice tristia et sine corde exta quondam nuntiante futura diceret laetiora, cum uellet; nec pro ostento ducendum, si pecudi cor defuisset.*

---

[96] Cic. *Fam.* 6.6.8: the title of the work was *querelae*. Caecina had also written a *criminosissimus liber* against Caesar (Suet. *Iul.* 75.5, with Strasburger 1999: 28).

[97] Haack 2006: 110–12, no. 88; Montero 2006: 140–1. On the Spurinnae see Torelli 1975: 23–102; Morandi Tarabella 2004: 476–86. Spurinna and Caesar: Zecchini 2001: 72–5; Guittard 2002/3: 113–14. Cic. *Fam.* 6.6.3 and Tac. *Ann.* 11.15.1 suggest that the transmission of divinatory lore within the same family was common in Etruria (cf. the provisos in Linderski 2001: 518 = 2007: 431–3); this is also attested in the Greek world (M. Flower 2008: 37–50).

[98] Cic. *Div.* 1.119. Wardle 2006: 393–4 on the dating of this episode: the Senate meeting of 13 or 14 February 44 is the likeliest solution.

[99] Rawson 1978a: 143 (= 1991: 308).   [100] Gugel 1970.

He reached such a level of arrogance that, when a haruspex reported that the entrails were unfavourable and the heart was missing, he said that future sacrifices would be more favourable, since such was his wish, nor should it be deemed a sign of ill fortune (*ostentum*) if an animal had no heart.[101]

Suetonius' source was T. Ampius Balbus, who is known to have criticised Caesar in his lost work on contemporary history; he was, in fact, a committed supporter of Pompey.[102] The *Tendenz* that underpins this passage, which is echoed in Suetonius' moralising account, would be sufficient reason to invite caution, but there are other factors to be considered. The dialogue with the haruspex was not a public statement and it cannot be used as evidence for Caesar's handling of religious matters. Moreover, even if one assumes that Caesar said what Suetonius has him say, his statement would not be so extraordinary after all. When a sacrifice was performed, there was always the possibility that the entrails would reveal that the sacrifice was not accepted by the gods.[103] If this was the case, two options were available: to stop the sacrifice and declare that there was a religious crisis; or to slaughter more victims until the entrails made clear that the gods had accepted the sacrifice. The successful completion of the sacrifice was called *litatio*, from the verb *litare*, the main meaning of which is 'to sacrifice'; it was never to be taken for granted, and securing it was a divinatory exercise, which required the ability to read through the unpredictable and potentially disruptive choices of the gods.[104] Pursuing the *litatio* was a divinatory exercise, but not one of the prophetic kind: like an augural ritual, it was merely intended to verify whether the gods were in favour of or against an envisaged action. The *litatio* is a Roman practice that was gradually reshaped by the influence of Etruscan extispicy, which had a traditionally prophetic dimension.[105] At any rate, seeking *litatio* repeatedly, rather than conceding the impossibility to proceed and triggering a state of crisis, was

---

[101] Cf. Polyaen. 8.23.32. Blecher 1905: 57; Thulin 1906a: 44–5; Martínez-Pinna 2007: 73.
[102] Gascou 1984: 463–4; Morgan 1997: 23–5.
[103] Etruscan extispicy: Blecher 1905; Thulin 1906a; Pease 1920: 94–8; Rasmussen 2003: 117–48. Cf. Johnston 2008: 125–8 on extispicy in Greece and Bowden 2005: 5–6 on hepatoscopy.
[104] *Litatio*: Blecher 1905: 49–54; Thulin 1906a: 1–10; Schilling 1962 (= 1979: 183–90); Scheid 1987–9: 130–2; North 1989: 594–5; Rüpke 2001: 149–50; Kany-Turpin 2005: 212–13; Scheid 2012: 119–20. Key ancient sources: Cato *Agr.* 141.4; Fest. 351L; Serv. *ad Aen.* 2.104; Macrob. *Sat.* 3.5.4 (with Nasse 1999); Plut. *Aem.* 17.11 (twenty-one consecutive sacrifices were performed before *litatio* was obtained). Cf. Livy 41.8.3, 14–15; *ILS* 9522 (Acta of the Arval Brethren, from AD 240, lines 16–17.
[105] Blecher 1905: 52–3; Thulin 1906a: 5; Wissowa 1912: 418–19. The word *extispicina* is not attested in antiquity (Nasse 1999: 112), but this does not invalidate the use of 'extispicy' as a legitimate and useful historical category.

no doubt the option that was most commonly pursued, and that is what Caesar did on the occasion recorded by Ampius Balbus and Suetonius.[106]

The understanding of this episode is complicated by the nature of the tradition on the death of Caesar and the prophecies that announced it. The picture of an impious or fatalistic Caesar who readily overlooked all the premonitions of his death served both political propaganda and literary effect, and most of the tradition should be used very cautiously. Spurinna features in two versions of the famous anecdote in which Caesar is warned against a danger he would meet on the Ides of March. When the dictator met the haruspex on the day, he remarked that the Ides had come, only to receive the bitter reply that they had not passed yet.[107] Appian states that Caesar performed a sacrifice as he was about to enter the Senate house on the Ides: when an unnamed *mantis* warned him that the entrails were foretelling imminent death, he first laughed the warning off, claiming that he had received the same prophecy at the beginning of the campaign against the Pompeiani in Spain; however, he asked for more sacrifices to be performed; they all proved unfavourable.[108] Only at that point did Caesar decide to go to the Senate, partly because he wanted not to delay the proceedings, and partly because he was urged to do so by some of the conspirators.[109] Appian, however, claims that the ultimate cause was that fate had decided that he should meet his death.

Against this background, there is no reason to believe that Caesar was especially hostile to the haruspices, or indeed to any other form of divination. As to his personal views, one can only speculate;[110] in the public sphere, however, he was *pontifex maximus* from 63 and no doubt he had

---

[106] Wardle 2009: 109.

[107] Suet. *Iul.* 81.2–4; Val. Max. 8.11.2r; the same anecdote is told in Plut. *Caes.* 63.5–6, App. *B Civ.* 2.149 and Dio 44.18.4, who do not mention the name of the seer. Haruspical warnings to Caesar are also recorded in Vell. 2.57.2 (*haruspices praemonuerunt*). Ramsey 2000 shows that there is no evidence that the prophecy was based on an astrological prediction.

[108] App. *B Civ.* 2.116 and 153. Vaahtera 2001: 84–91. On the use of μάντις in Appian see Fromentin 1996: 87–90 (at 90 she argues without discussion that the sacrifice was performed by the haruspex Spurinna).

[109] Cf. Plut. *Caes.* 63.12–64.6 and Nic. Dam. *FGrHist* 90 F 130.84: the unfavourable response of the haruspices almost convinced Caesar to call off the Senate session, but the intervention of Decimus Brutus Albinus decisively persuaded him not to change his plans. Pelling 2011: 473–6.

[110] It is hard to make anything of Caesar's habit mentioned by Plin. *HN* 28.21: *Caesarem dictatorem post unum ancipitem uehiculi casum ferunt semper, ut primum consedisset, id quod plerosque nunc facere scimus, carmine ter repetito securitatem itinerum aucupari solitum* ('The dictator Caesar, after a serious accident to his carriage, is said always, as soon as he was seated, to have had the habit of repeating three times a prayer for a safe journey, something that we know most people do today'). It should certainly not be used to reconstruct his religious views; it could be used, if anything, as a reminder of how diverse and complex individual attitudes to risk could be. See Meyer 2004: 71–2 on the use of *carmen* in this context.

plenty of occasions to interact with the haruspices. There is also no evidence that the whole of Etruria was hostile to him and that he had a political interest in tackling haruspicy and posing as the champion of Roman religion against non-Roman practices. The evidence for his dealings with the haruspices is minimal and it does not suggest that he publicly expressed contempt for haruspicy. Cicero reports that in 47 he was warned by a *summus haruspex* not to cross to Africa before the winter solstice (*ante brumam*): had he followed the spirit of the response, his enemies would have gained a significant advantage.[111] Caesar decided to cross nonetheless, but using a stratagem that enabled him to respect the letter of the response and was made possible by his calendar reform: he crossed on 27 December, which was 7 October in the new Julian calendar.[112] Two years earlier, in 49, the bull that he intended to sacrifice to Fortuna before leaving Rome to continue the Civil War escaped, left the city of Rome, arrived at a lake and swam across it.[113] The escape of the sacrificial victim could have easily been read as a negative omen.[114] However, the haruspices (*manteis*) ruled that it was an exhortation for Caesar to leave the city and cross the sea: he would have met disaster only if he had stayed in Rome. This peculiar episode may be read as evidence that some haruspices were prepared to support Caesar's campaign against Pompey and that Caesar made sure that their support was put on record. Given Caesar's prominence and the well-established influence of the haruspices at Rome, this is hardly remarkable.

E. Rawson has shown that the claim that Caesar enjoyed widespread support in Etruria must be accepted with great caution. However, it is only with Caesar that an effort to include some members of the Etruscan elite into the Roman Senate appears to have been made.[115] Haruspicy is again a central part of the picture. In a letter to Q. Lepta in February 45, Cicero noted, with some irritation, that some practitioners of the Etruscan *disciplina* were sitting in the Senate, while a new municipal law passed by Caesar barred auctioneers from joining town councils.[116] Cicero apparently found it odd that practising haruspices were entitled to join the Senate, while practising auctioneers were not entitled to join less prominent

[111] Cic. *Div.* 2.52. The epithet *summus haruspex* might be read as evidence for the existence of an established *ordo* by the mid-forties, recognised and organised by the Roman State, but it may just refer to Spurinna's prestige and seniority among his peers (Pease 1923: 440). Under the Principate the most senior haruspex of the *ordo* was called *maximus* (*CIL* 6.2164 and 2165), not *summus* (cf. Thulin 1909: 149).
[112] Rawson 1978a: 142–3 (= 1991: 307); cf. Suet. *Iul.* 59. *Bell Afr.* 2.2–5.   [113] Dio 41.39.2.
[114] Cf. Val. Max. 1.6.7 and 12; Fest. 284L; Serv. *auct. Aen.* 10.541.
[115] Rawson 1978a (= 1991: 290–323). Aigner-Foresti 2000: 12–18 suggests some geographical patterns in the distribution of support for Caesar.
[116] Cic. *Fam.* 6.18.1–2. Zecchini 2001: 70–1; Corbeill 2012: 246–7.

assemblies. The reason for the exclusion ordered by Caesar must be found in the low social clout of the trade; Cicero's passing remark, which was significantly made to a friend who had no Etruscan connections, seems to imply that the haruspices do not deserve more respect than those who profited from the condition of debtors who are compelled to sell their properties. It is a brief and elusive reference, and one should not make too much of it. However, it fits well with the views that Cicero expresses on haruspicy elsewhere. He never expressed positive admiration for, or interest in, the Etruscan discipline – not even in the *De haruspicum responso*, where the leading argument is that haruspicy deserves the respect that is owed to ancestral practices, not that it is intrinsically valid.[117]

The fact that Caesar included some practising haruspices in the Senate is no evidence that he approved of their lore; at any rate, many members of the Etruscan elites must have been practising the *disciplina* in public and in private, whether in Rome or in their hometowns. His relationship with Spurinna was clearly important, even if there is no evidence that it was based on a personal intellectual interest in the workings of haruspicy, or that it was as close as that between Gaius Gracchus and Herennius, or Sulla and Postumius. He certainly had no exclusive claim on his services, assuming that anyone could have the exclusive claim on the services of any haruspex. The view that Caesar was a sceptic on religious matters appears to be based on two points: Caesar's interest in Epicureanism and the dearth of references to divination and augury in his *Commentarii*. Neither argument poses insurmountable obstacles.[118] The evidence for Caesar's familiarity with Epicureanism is reasonably safe, although it is not clear in what respects it involved an acceptance of Epicurean theology.[119] We may expect him to share Lucretius' contempt for the *uates* who terrified their audiences with their prophecies, but this was not an uncommon position within the Roman elite.[120] The impressive array of religious honours which were decreed for him in the forties, and which he no doubt planned and designed with great care, are clear evidence for his ability to think creatively and innovatively about religion – not just to exploit the existing frameworks.

The lack of references to prodigies and other related matters in the *Commentarii* cannot be explained as the symptom of a negative take on divination. It must be a literary and, by reflection, a political choice. The *De bello Gallico* is chiefly about Caesar's military and strategic prowess; the

---

[117] Cic. *Har. resp.* 18.　　　[118] Wardle 2009.
[119] Benferhat 2005: 285–302; Garbarino 2010 stresses Caesar's intellectual autonomy.
[120] Lucr. 1.102–11.

De bello ciuili is about Caesar's virtue and the political and constitutional legitimacy of his position. In Gaul Caesar certainly had priests on his staff; however, he chose not to use the system of reporting and expiating prodigies as one of the defining features of his account. Possibly he remembered the destiny of Gaius Gracchus, whose foundation of the colony of Junonia near Carthage in 122 was hampered and ultimately stopped by reports of unfavourable prodigies which hostile haruspices must have played a part in handling against the Gracchan agenda.[121] There is no evidence that at the time he used religious themes in his dealings with the troops, even to build up his charismatic credentials. It is hard to escape the impression that, in this as in other important respects, Caesar pointedly tried to distance himself from the precedent of Sulla: the supernatural played a very important role in the latter's self-representation, even before his victory in the Civil War.[122] There may have also been a purely political reason for the omission. Reporting prodigies in an account that was ultimately addressed to the Senate could have triggered debate on the response that Caesar had devised to the events and would have perhaps reopened the controversy on their expiation and Caesar's concern for the *pax deorum*.[123] In the aftermath of the Civil War, of course, there was no longer a risk of senatorial interference. Arguably this is one of the reasons why the only list of prodigies in Caesar's *Commentarii* appears towards the end of *De bello Gallico* 3, after the account of Caesar's arrival in Asia Minor. The victor of Pharsalus is welcomed by a series of favourable omens from a number of communities across an impressive geographical span: Elis, Antioch, Ptolemais, Pergamum and Tralles.[124] It is true that, as D. Feeney observed, this digression catches the reader by surprise, to the extent that it has been argued (implausibly, in my view) that it is a later interpolation.[125] However, there is also something familiar about it: it is not unlike the lists of prodigies that annalistic historians used to put together for each year. Caesar surely obtained the information on the prodigies from the official reports he

---

[121] App. *B Civ.* 1.24; Plut. *C. Gracch.* 11.   [122] Smith 2009: 79.

[123] Publication and public *recitationes* of the *De bello Gallico*: Wiseman 1998b.

[124] Caes. *B Civ.* 3.105.3–6. Rambaud 1966: 266–7; Feeney 1998: 19–20; Pelling 2011: 374–5.

[125] Reggi 2002, followed by Wardle 2009: 108. Reggi's assumption that Caesar refrained from using 'tratti del monarca ellenistico' (217) is incorrect; the linguistic arguments in favour of the transmitted text made by Barwick 1938: 218–19 remain valid; it is conceivable that the citizens of Tralles may have dedicated a statue of Caesar between Pharsalus and his arrival in the region; the view that there was a Hellenistic tradition on prodigies from the Civil War, which took shape independently from Caesar and influenced the literary tradition, including Livy, is impossible to prove. The prodigies are also mentioned in Val. Max. 1.6.12; Plut. *Caes.* 47.1–2; Obs. 65a (on which see Nice 1999: 198–9); Dio 41.61.3. A comprehensive overview of the tradition in Wardle 1998: 206–9; on Valerius' handling of the story see also Mueller 2002: 93.

received from the communities that were keen to declare their loyalty, just as the Senate derived the prodigy reports from the Italian communities that reported them. With this, a typical, isolated prodigy list, Caesar implies that he is the new central institution of the empire that can, whenever necessary, subsume the tasks once performed by the Senate; moreover, the favourable prodigies emphatically state his exceptional qualities and the central position he holds after the victory in Thessaly. The checks and balances of the Republican past no longer have a reason to exist. The appearance of prodigies in Caesar's *Commentarii* is a sign that the Roman Revolution is truly in the making.

CHAPTER 5

Etruscan ages and the end of the Republic

Periodisation does not interest just modern historians. It was a matter of debate in late Republican Rome too. It is striking (and to some even puzzling) that the ninth *saeculum*, which started in 88 as the Mithridatic crisis was unfolding, appears to have ended when the Republic was on the brink of collapse and Octavian was about to start his formidable rise.[1] The prodigies of the late forties shed light on other important aspects of the problem. Two sources show that the theme of the beginning of a new age was aired in the months following Caesar's death, although establishing the terms of the problem in any detail presents serious difficulties. According to Appian, the reconciliation between Octavian and Antony in 43 was accompanied by a series of disturbing prodigies, from dogs howling like wolves to wolves roaming in the Roman forum, and statues dripping sweat or blood. This series of omens was addressed with another consultation of the Etruscan seers. The most senior of them argued that an era was coming to an end and that monarchy was about to be restored: everybody would be enslaved, except for himself. After uttering these few words, the haruspex started to hold his breath, until he choked and died.[2] Soon after this episode, the run-up to the proscriptions began. Only a late Republican source may have cared to record the incident, in which the Etruscan discipline curiously blends with a vague reminiscence of the Polybian *anakuklosis*, whereby all political forms end up in ruin, neatly following a cyclical development. It is unclear how and why the haruspices devised this response at that particular time, but its central message was clear: an age, a *saeculum*, was ending and a new one was beginning, somehow leading to a return to the past.

A similar episode is related in different terms by pseudo-Probus in an additional note to Servius' commentary on Virgil's Ninth Eclogue. Servius mentions the appearance of a star in the middle of the sky in 44 when

---

[1] Sordi 1972: 782–4 (= 1995: 176–8); Rawson 1978a: 146–7 (= 1991: 312–14). A different reconstruction in Turcan 1976: 1011–14.

[2] App. *B Civ.* 4.4. Gowing 1992: 249, 251–2; Fromentin 1996: 86.

Octavian was celebrating the funeral games in honour of Caesar. The episode was narrated by the historian Baebius Macer, who related that it afforded Octavian the opportunity to label that day a sign of Caesar's divine status and to celebrate the event by putting up a statue of Caesar and placing a star around his head.[3] However, the haruspex Vulcatius explained the episode in public and gave a different interpretation:

> sed Vulcatius aruspex in contione dixit cometen esse, qui significaret exitum noni saeculi et ingressum decimi; sed quod inuitis dis secreta rerum pronuntiaret, statim se esse moriturum: et nondum finita oratione in ipsa contione concidit. hoc etiam Augustus in libro secundo de memoria uitae suae complexus est.

> But the haruspex Vulcatius said in a public meeting that it was a comet, signifying the end of the ninth age and the beginning of the tenth, but that, since he was revealing the secret against the will of the gods, he would immediately die; and he fell dead in that public meeting, without having finished his speech yet. Augustus included this too in the second book of the memoirs of his life.[4]

In his view, the comet was the sign of the beginning of a new *saeculum*: the ninth was drawing to a close and the tenth was about to start.[5] After uttering this response, Vulcatius said that revealing the truth would lead to his immediate death; indeed, he collapsed on the spot. According to Servius, the episode was related by Augustus himself in his autobiography (*in libro secundo de memoria uitae suae*). It has been interestingly suggested that the episode mentioned by Servius is merely a variant of the episode narrated by Appian, albeit presented in a way that could be deemed favourable to the Augustan agenda.[6] Moreover, in his memoirs (*De uita sua*) Augustus offset the impact of this traumatic event with the account of the augural ritual

---

[3] Weinstock 1971: 373–82.

[4] Serv. *auct. ad Ecl.* 9.46 = *HRR* II, F 5 = F 2 Smith. Haack 2006: 135–7, no. 108. Vulcatius is a safer option than the Volcatius or Vulcanius of the manuscript tradition of Servius: Massa-Pairault 1991: 10–11, 24; *contra*, cf. Haack 2006: 136, who chooses Volcatius, and Montero 2006: 315 (*Vulcanius*; see also F 2 Smith). Torelli 2011: 143–4 suggests that the *C. Volcacius haruspex* who put up a mosaic inscription in a shrine on the Tiberine Island (*CIL* I².990 = *ILLRP* 186) is the haruspex who gave the prophecy in 44; cf. Haack 2006: 133–5, no. 107. The response was given *in contione*, on an important public occasion; cf. Cic. *Har. resp.* 9. See Bendlin 1998: 298 and 2000: 127 on the *contio* as a venue in which 'religious information' is transmitted.

[5] The comet is mentioned by Obsequens in his extensive list of the prodigies for the year 44: Obs. 68; see also Verg. *Ecl.* 9.47–9. The same comet was seen in China in May 44: Ramsey and Licht 1997: 65–81. There is no evidence that the imminent end of the tenth age was ever announced by an Etruscan haruspex (Diehl 1934: 260).

[6] Hahn 1968: 243–6 (with some speculation on the background of Verg. *Ecl.* 4); Hahn 1983: 62 (stressing the ambiguity of Vulcatius' prophecy); Briquel 1990a: 65–6; Bechtold 2011: 214–15. *Contra*, see Weinstock 1971, 194–5; Massa-Pairault 1991: 9. Martínez-Pinna 2001: 92–5, 214–15 argues that Vulcatius' prophecy did not refer to the end of a *saeculum*.

that he performed after his election to the consulship on 19 August 43, when twelve vultures appeared in the sky.[7] The same number of vultures had appeared to Romulus, according to Ennius, and Vettius, an expert on augural matters consulted and quoted by Varro, regarded that as a sign that Rome had twelve *saecula*, not ten.[8] The catastrophe could be postponed, and young Caesar was the guarantor of that fresh lease of life for Rome.

The problem of the Etruscan ages is complex and its implications in the context of the late Republic are somewhat elusive. It is far from clear, for instance, why the problem was raised in the aftermath of Caesar's death, amidst prodigies that have no known parallel in Roman history, and why the disappearance of the Etruscans was foretold just when Octavian's effort to gather the consensus of *tota Italia* was taking shape. It is not surprising, therefore, to find other references to it in the antiquarian literature. Varro did not fail to give his own version of the problem, which he apparently derived from some *Tuscae historiae* and which we find summarised in Censorinus' *De die natali*, a learned work published in AD 238 that deals at length with matters of periodisation and chronography.[9] According to Varro, Etruscan wise men divided time into ten eras of varying length, the duration of which was determined according to a system based on the dates of birth and death of the most long-lived members of a community: the first *saeculum* of a city ended with the death of the last person who was born on the day of the city's foundation, at which point a new *saeculum* began that would end in the same fashion, leading to the beginning of another one.[10] There was no unified Etruscan system for establishing the length of an era, but each city had its own framework, starting with its foundation date. It is conceivable that the haruspices who were active in Rome in the last century of the Republic still used different chronological frameworks.[11] The beginning of a new age was usually announced by some

---

[7] Suet. *Aug.* 95.2; Obs. 69; App. *B Civ.* 3.94; Dio 46.46.2–3, with Gowing 1992: 77; Hurlet 2001: 156–62; Montero 2006: 70–7. There are slight discrepancies among the sources on the number of the vultures: twelve in Suetonius and Appian, six followed by six in Obsequens, six followed by twelve in Dio.

[8] Cens. *DN* 17.15, with Wiseman 2009b: 116–17. Romulus and the twelve vultures: Enn. *Ann.* 88–9 Skutsch (= Cic. *Div.* 1.108); see also Livy 1.8.3 on the link between the twelve vultures and the number of the lictors (La Penna 1978: 70). Cf. the twelve swans in the omen received by Aeneas in Verg. *Aen.* 1.393–400 (Hardie 1987: 149: 'a kind of foundation omen'; Habinek 2005: 163–4). Twelve vultures motif: Magotteaux 1956 and Hübner 1970: 113–17.

[9] Cens. *DN* 17.6. Clemen 1928; Lantella 1984: 2155–64; Briquel 2001: 268–74; Feeney 2007: 145–8, 276–7.

[10] According to Censorinus (17.6), Varro gave details of the length of the first seven *saecula*: the first four lasted 100 years, the fifth 123, the sixth and the seventh 119.

[11] Briquel 1990a: 61–2, 67–8; this would explain the relatively short gap between the end of the eighth *saeculum* (88) and that of the ninth (44), which seems hardly compatible with the doctrine of the

prodigies, as men were not aware of the beginning of a new *saeculum* and had to be alerted to it. Arguably for this reason the matter became a concern of the Etruscan haruspices and eventually part of the Etruscan *disciplina*. Censorinus states that Varro had access to Etruscan historical sources that were composed during the eighth *saeculum*, i.e. before 88, and predicted that the series of the *saecula* was supposed to end with the tenth age.[12] After its end, the whole 'Etruscan name' would disappear. Accidentally or not, therefore, the chronology of the Roman revolution coincided with that of the main tenet of Etruscan lore: the age of the second triumvirate, the proscriptions and the run-up to the Civil War marked the beginning of the last age of the Etruscan people (*finis nominis Etrusci*, 'the end of the Etruscan name').[13] The relevance and appeal of that theme were no doubt clear even to the many people who were not aware of the precedent of 88 and of the rules that governed the Etruscan system of periodisation. It is well known what a deep significance the theme of a new age had in the Augustan period.

The continuation of Censorinus' discussion of the *saecula* shows that the problem was acutely felt not only in Etruscan quarters. The Romans developed their own system of *saecula*, in which – according to some ancient traditions – the beginning of a new era was marked by the celebration of 'secular games', the *ludi saeculares*.[14] Several ancient authors offered more or less imaginative contributions to the debate. Censorinus records the existence of different traditions concerning the *ludi* and the dates when they were performed: he could find evidence that they were celebrated in 509, 456, 346 (or, alternatively, 344), 249 (or 236) and 149 (or 146, or 126).[15] The only point of agreement was that Augustus had led the celebration of the *ludi* in 17.[16] There was disagreement on individual dates: the date of the fourth *ludi*, for example, was set in 149 by Antias, Varro and Livy, while the second-century authors Cassius Hemina, Calpurnius Piso Frugi and Gnaeus Gellius gave the alternative date of 146, and the records of the

---

      saeculum as it is outlined by Censorinus (cf. Turcan 1976: 1014–15). There was no consensus on the length of a *saeculum* in Rome either (Havas 2000: 82–7).

[12]   Wiseman 2006: 525 (= 2008: 48) stresses that only an educated minority of the population was aware of what Etruscan ages were.

[13]   Jal 1963: 246–50. As Martínez-Pinna 2001: 87 stresses, the end of the *nomen Etruscum* must not be understood as the end of the world, or as the end of history; *contra* cf. Sordi 1972: 784 (= 1995: 178; cf. Sordi 2008: 93); Novara 1982: 190–1.

[14]   Pavis d'Escurac 1993: 79–85 is the best modern discussion; see also Schnegg-Köhler 2002: 156–64; Orlin 2010: 67–71, 213–14. Comprehensive bibliographies in Bernstein 1998: 131 n. 66 and Havas 2000: 83 n. 14.

[15]   Cens. *DN* 17.7–11.

[16]   The reference study of the *ludi* of 17 is Schnegg-Köhler 2002, which superseded Pighi 1965.

quindecemuiri s.f. stated that the *ludi* had taken place two decades later, in 126.[17]

Most importantly, there were different traditions on when and how the sequence of the *ludi saeculares* had come about. Not everybody shared the view that the *ludi* went all the way back to the time of the expulsion of the kings.[18] Varro, for instance, in his *De scaenicis originibus*, appears to place their origin in 249, when *ludi* in honour of Dis and Proserpina were instituted according to the instructions of the Sibylline Books, and were expected to take place every one hundred years (Cens. *DN* 17.8):

> *cum multa portenta fierent, et murus ac turris, quae sunt inter portam Collinam et Esquilinam, de caelo tacta essent, et ideo libros Sibyllinos XV uiri adissent, renuntiarunt, uti Diti patri et Proserpinae ludi Tarentini in campo Martio fierent tribus noctibus, et hostiae furuae immolarentur, utique ludi centesimo quoque anno fierent.*

> When many portents occurred, and the wall and tower which lay between the Colline Gate and the Esquiline were struck by lightning, and for that reason the quindecemviri consulted the Sibylline Books, they announced that the *ludi Tarentini* should be held in the Campus Martius to Father Dis and Proserpina for three nights, and black animals should be sacrificed, and that the Games should be held every hundred years.[19]

In fact, Varro does not call these *ludi saeculares*, but *Tarentini*. Later authors stated that they were named after a spot in the Campus Martius where a prodigy took place;[20] however, the festival may well have been related to the Greek city of Tarentum. Even if one leaves aside the problem of the Roman-ness of the games, Varro's *ludi Tarentini* appear to be quite different from the *ludi* celebrated by Augustus in 17. Their central message was not about the beginning of a new age and the need to secure the protection of the gods for the city in the new *saeculum*.[21] Rather than marking the beginning of a new age, they were a festival that was created in response to a number of prodigies, and the ceremony was dedicated to two gods of the

---

[17] Liberman 1998: 69–71. Written records of the decemviral college are attested in 173 (Livy 42.2.7).

[18] The debate continues in modern scholarship: cf. e.g. the sceptical take of Wagenvoort 1956: 196 and Orlin 2010: 68 with Coarelli 1993a: 217–19.

[19] A full discussion of the games of 249 in Bernstein 1998: 129–42. See also Caerols 1989: 208–15, Russo 2008: 120–32 and Orlin 2010: 69–71 on the Italian background of the *ludi*. Altheim 1938: 287–91 stresses the Greek influence; Hall 1986: 2567–80, 2586–8 argues that the *ludi saeculares* had a predominantly Etruscan background. Brind'Amour 1978 overemphasises the role of Apollo in the *ludi*; cf. Miller 2009: 247–52. On the *De scaenicis originibus* see Baier 1997: 82–3.

[20] Val. Max. 2.4.5, with Themann-Steinke 2008: 241–55; Zos. 2.4.1–2, with Paschoud 2000: 197–8 n. 5; Fest. 440 L. See Wagenvoort 1956: 198–204 and Coarelli 1993a: 229–30 on the *Terentum*.

[21] Cooley 2006: 229–37 has an excellent discussion of the 'imperialist tone' of the *ludi* of 17.

underworld. Modern scholars have even doubted whether the *ludi* were intended to be performed every hundred years since their inception.[22]

Censorinus' summary of the debate on the *ludi saeculares* is wide-ranging, but not exhaustive. Zosimus, a historian who wrote in the first quarter of the sixth century AD, also dealt with the topic because he was interested in emphasising the religious and moral decline of the age of Diocletian and Constantine, who failed to perform the *ludi* (2.1–7). The lengthy excursus on the history of the *ludi* at the beginning of the second book of his *New History* follows yet another tradition, whereby the games took place in 348, 249, 149 and 17.[23] The sequences provided by Censorinus and Zosimus show that the apparent lack of a clear pattern is in fact evidence for two competing patterns: one in which the games took place every hundred years, and another in which the interval was 110 years; Augustus used the latter.[24] This disparity was intertwined with the late Republican debate on the length of a *saeculum*. Varro, like others, argued that a *saeculum* was meant to have a fixed length of a hundred years.[25] The most logical conclusion to be drawn from this picture is that there was a difference between the 'natural' *saeculum*, which had an arbitrary and inconsistent length, and the 'civil' one, which lasted one hundred years.[26]

Again, Censorinus provides a brief, invaluable glimpse of the late Republican debate to which he had access. Varro and the astrologer Dioscorides speculated on the reason why a *saeculum* lasted one hundred years; most importantly for our purposes, Varro also offered some thoughts on the number of *saecula* that were allocated to Rome.[27] Vettius, a contemporary of his who was renowned for his expertise in augural matters, told him that, since twelve vultures had appeared in the sky during the foundation of the city, Rome could be expected to survive for 1,200 years – one century for each vulture.[28] We do not know in what context and for what reasons Varro discussed this problem in the seventeenth book of his *Antiquitates*

---

[22] Wagenvoort 1956: 232; Weiss 1973: 213–16; Orlin 2010: 68, 213.

[23] Zos. 2.1–7. Zosimus' account is garbled in places and the Greek is often unclear. Excellent discussion in Paschoud 2000: 192–9; cf. also Scheid 2000: 653–5.

[24] Coarelli 1993a: 213–15 argues that it was masterminded by Augustus himself, since it is not mentioned in any Republican source; Sudhaus 1901: 37–9 speculated that the tradition was invented by Caesar, with some expert help from Varro. Augustan codification of the *ludi*: Benoist 1999: 176–91.

[25] Cens. *DN* 17.7–13. Censorinus mentions the views of Valerius Antias, Livy and Varro. Mommsen 1859: 187–91 is still essential reading; Bouché-Leclerq 1882: IV, 301–3 provides an excellent summary of the tradition on the *ludi* and the problems and anachronisms that it entailed. Diehl 1934: 258 finds evidence for as many as five ancient definitions of what a *saeculum* may be; see also *ibid.* 263–4 on the Roman model.

[26] Cens. *DN* 17.12 and 15. Cf. L. Calpurnius Piso, *HRR* I², F 36 = Cens. *DN* 17.13; discussion in Baudou 1995.

[27] Cens. *DN* 17.14–15.   [28] Cens. *DN* 17.15. Wiseman 2006: 528–9 (= 2008: 50–1).

rerum diuinarum. Varro was interested in the Roman division and organisation of time, which he must have discussed along with (and possibly in
competition with) the Etruscan paradigm.[29] He consulted a man whom
he regarded as competent on the matter, and he probably presented his
version as the only authoritative one. If not, we could expect Censorinus to
have mentioned and discussed others. Moreover, he saw and developed the
connection between the organisation of time, the making of the calendar,
and the future of the city and the State: by giving time a framework it
was possible to make informed guesses on when the city would come to an
end.[30] In this framework, the evils of the Civil War may have been regarded
as a phase of a much longer and more complex history, which would soon
come to an end and would open the way for a new season of stability. The
preoccupations of some Etruscan haruspices with looming disaster could
be set aside.

Late Republican interest in, and reflection on, the *saecula* that were
allocated to Rome was part of a broader reflection on time that was deeply
indebted to Hellenistic debates on historical and chronographical matters.
Ennius played a path-breaking role in it, with the interest in *fasti* that
he shared with his prominent friend M. Fulvius Nobilior (*cos.* 189). This
reflection upon Roman time and the history of the city was accompanied
by an interest in the history of the world and its periodisation. Its most
spectacular example was no doubt Varro's *De gente populi Romani*, which
outlined a division of time into the obscure age (*adelon*: from the origins
of mankind to the first flood), the mythical period (*mythicon*: from the
flood to the first Olympiad), and the historical period (*historicon*).[31] It is
likely, although not firmly attested, that such reflection on the overarching
pattern of human and Roman history was combined with an attempt to
make predictions on its future course. The working hypothesis of Varro
and people like his friend and advisor Tarutius was that important events
are usually marked by celestial omens, and that establishing the dates of
important historical events can be done by using the dates of the omens that
are known to have taken place roughly in the same period. Establishing
a pattern in relation to the occurrence of omens in the past and their
link with important historical events could also have implications on the

---

[29] Weiss 1973: 212 draws attention to a central difference between the Etruscan and the Roman models:
the Etruscans had a 'Säkulartheorie' without *ludi*, while the Roman *ludi* had a 'Säkularcharakter'.

[30] Feeney 2007: esp. 147–9. Roman calendar: Rüpke 1995 and 2011a; see esp. 2011a: 124–34 on the
'power of dates' in the Augustan age. Imperial monopoly of time: Ker 2009.

[31] Cens. *DN* 20.12–21.2. Feeney 1999: 14–15 and 2007: 81–2, 246 n. 74 (with previous bibliography);
the flood to which Varro refers is that of Ogygus.

understanding of the future, and might indeed enable people to make informed predictions.[32]

Reflection on Roman time, its shape and direction, was not confined to intellectual circles that were not directly involved with the political arena. Caesar's calendar reform was accompanied by a sustained effort to provide a full intellectual justification for it.[33] According to Macrobius and a scholion on Lucan, Caesar wrote a treatise on calendrical matters, the *De astris*, which revealed considerable astronomical expertise, discussed the ordering of the calendar in light of a study of the movements of the celestial sphere, and relied heavily on Egyptian doctrines.[34] It is conceivable, perhaps even likely, that Caesar sought expert help in this endeavour, but his decision to back the reform with a full-scale discussion of astronomical and calendrical matters is telling of a wider intellectual climate.

Virgil was aware of this contemporary debate. *Eclogue* 4 is the earliest and most striking example of his interest (4–14):

> *ultima Cumaei uenit iam carminis aetas;*
> *magnus ab integro saeclorum nascitur ordo.*
> *iam redit et Uirgo, redeunt Saturnia regna,*
> *iam noua progenies caelo demittitur alto.*
> *tu modo nascenti puero, quo ferrea primum*
> *desinet ac toto surget gens aurea mundo,*
> *casta faue Lucina; tuus iam regnat Apollo.*
> *teque adeo decus hoc aeui, te consule, inibit,*
> *Pollio, et incipient magni procedere menses;*
> *te duce, si qua manent sceleris uestigia nostri,*
> *inrita perpetua soluent formidine terras.*

The last age of the Cumaean Sibyl's song has now come, a great sequence of ages is born anew. Now also the Virgin returns, the reign of Saturn returns; now a new offspring is despatched down from high heaven. Only do, chaste Lucina, smile on the birth of the child, under whom the iron brood shall first end, and a golden race spring up throughout the whole world; your Apollo now rules. In your consulship indeed, in yours, the glorious age will come in, Pollio, and the great months will begin their advance; with your leadership whatever traces of our sin remain will be blotted out and free the earth of its perpetual fear.

The poem opens with a reference to the fulfilment of the prophecy of a Sibyl from Cumae, the coming of the last age that she had foretold,

[32] Grafton and Swerdlow 1985: 460–1.   [33] Rüpke 2011a: 108–21.
[34] *ad Luc.* 10.187; Macrob. *Sat.* 1.16.39. Domenicucci 1996: 85–99; Gee 2000: 17–20.

and the beginning of a new sequence of ages.[35] The identification of the Sibylline prophecy to which Virgil is referring is uncertain, but it is clear that the beginning of the new *saeclorum ordo* is a break from the traditions of the cyclical time and from the well-established model of the Golden Age, which was usually depicted as a period from the remote past that was never attainable. It was also a markedly different development from the Etruscan theory of the *saecula*, which was centred on the process that would lead to the end of history. Virgil gives a clear indication on when the new age began: in 40, during the consulship of Cn. Domitius Calvinus and C. Asinius Pollio, who is also the dedicatee of this poem. He completes his prophecy by foretelling the birth of a child, a *puer* who will mark the beginning of the period and will eventually rise to rule a peaceful and prosperous world. However, as prophets so often do, Virgil fails to clarify the terms of his prediction and does not specify the identity of the young boy. The identification of this figure has been the object of intense speculation since antiquity and was especially fascinating to the Christian readers of Virgil in the Middle Ages, who regarded it as an anticipation of the advent of Christ. A more economical interpretation is suggested by contemporary politics. The Eclogue is dominated by the theme of concord and the prospect of peace, which the appeasement between Antony and Octavian at Brundisium in 40 seemed to make possible. The *puer* is arguably the son that would have been born from the union of Antony and Octavia, the sister of Octavian, which was a consequence of the renewal of the entente between the two triumvirs. The prophecy that lies at the heart of the Fourth Eclogue is an unfulfilled one. The restored harmony soon broke; renewed hostility and the beginning of a new Civil War followed. The *Eclogues* were probably published in 39. Their contemporary readers will have soon felt the bitter unintended irony underlying the poem that hailed the beginning of a new age under the consulship of Calvinus and Pollio.

There is no reason to believe that Virgil's prophetic enthusiasm for the beginning of the new age in the Fourth Eclogue was insincere. However, prophecies are a problematic feature of Virgil's work, especially when they engage with the historical development of Rome and the timeframe in which the history of the city develops. The prophecies of the *Aeneid* pose especially challenging interpretative problems, as we shall see in more detail in Chapter 11. The prophecy of Jupiter in the first book (1.257–96) and

---

[35] Novara 1983: 682–712. Nisbet 1978 (= 1995: 4775) and Clausen 1990 are invaluable introductions to the poem. Reference to Apollo's rule: Miller 2009: 254–60. Influence of contemporary prophetic traditions on Virgil: Wagenvoort 1956: 1–29; Osgood 2006: 195. Cf. Bakhouche 2012: 64–5 on the link between Capricorn and Saturn.

that of Anchises in book 6 (6.756–886) offer predictions on the future of Roman history: one thousand years will pass from the end of the poem to the birth of Romulus and Remus; the Golden Age will return under Augustus, and will be marked by the Secular Games. A coherent framework is provided to the interpretation of Roman time and Roman history; any attempt to question or subvert it – even within the poem itself – must engage with it. Yet, this model has some limitations. Firstly, the future outlined in the prophecies remains outside the framework of the primary narrative of the poem, which ends on the sombre note of the duel between Aeneas and Turnus and does not depict the moment of the unification of Latins and Trojans.[36] Moreover, as J. Zetzel has noted, Virgil never states that the Golden Age is irreversible, or that history finds a happy ending with Augustus. The direction of Roman history is ultimately never made clear. When Aeneas and Evander make their way through the site that will become Rome and go past the Capitol, Virgil reflects on the destiny of that place (*Aen.* 8.345–8):

> *hinc ad Tarpeiam sedem et Capitolia ducit*
> *aurea nunc, olim siluestribus horrida dumis.*
> *iam tum religio pauidos terrebat agrestis*
> *dira loci, iam tum siluam saxumque tremebant.*

> From there he [Evander] leads him [Aeneas] to the house of Tarpeia and the Capitol, which now is made of gold, but *olim* [then?] was bristling with rough scrub. Even then a dreadful awe [*dira religio*] of the place caused great fear among the peasants; even then they feared the wood and the rock.

The adverb *olim*, neatly opposed to *nunc*, is the elusive key: it may refer not just to the past, but to the future too. The thickets used to cover the Capitol, but they may well cover it again at some future time.[37]

In many respects Ovid followed a very different route from Virgil, but he was animated by similar concerns over the direction of time and of the history of Rome.[38] The *Metamorphoses* lack any interest in establishing synchronic links between different events; while there is a general awareness of the canonical periodisation of human history, there is a keen interest in blurring the boundaries between the different epochs, and a characteristic effort to overlook or break down the time patterns that are put forward by the chronographic tradition. There is room, especially in the first two books of the *Metamorphoses*, for 'forward references' to the future rise of

---

[36] Rossi 2004a: 161–8.   [37] Zetzel 1994: 20–1; Feeney 2007: 165.
[38] Feeney 1999: esp. 18–30.

Augustus and the coming of Roman domination, but they do not feature in the remaining portion of the work.[39] The fifteenth book betrays concerns with the problem of succession, which clearly reflect late Augustan worries and are put forward through the depiction of the aftermath of Romulus' death.[40] The finale of the poem spells out the difference between Augustus and Ovid. While even the time of the *princeps* is finite, the future of Ovid's poetry is qualified as *perennis*. This is an even bolder statement than Horace's famous *exegi monumentum aere perennius*.[41]

A similar agenda can be seen at work in Ovid's *Fasti*, where the reflection on the calendar may seem at first sight in line with the Augustan concern with traditions, aetiologies and time, but his interest is more in the individual episodes and problems than in producing a full narrative. Ovid is aware of the work of antiquarians such as Verrius Flaccus on calendrical matters. The way he styles his poetic persona is based on the recognition of the importance of antiquarian knowledge for the pursuit of the *Fasti* and on the inherent tension between inspiration and culture that is crucial to the concept of *uates*.[42] Moreover, each book has a reference to a major feature of the Augustan agenda, be it the restoration of the *res publica* in book 1 or the temple of Mars Ultor in book 5.[43] However, the overall tone of the poem, the gusto with which it pursues entertaining detail, makes it seem oddly incompatible with the austere touch that dominated the agenda of Augustus and his antiquarian collaborators.[44] Augustus becomes an aspect of Ovid's investigation on the Roman calendar: he is

[39] Ov. *Met.* 1.560–3; 2.259; 2.538–9; 2.642–54. 'Forward references': Feeney 1999: 27.
[40] Barchiesi 1997: 210–13; Feeney 1999: 28.
[41] Ov. *Met.* 15.871–9, esp. 875. Barchiesi 1994: 265 notes that Ovid leaves his readers the option to 'preparare, se vogliono, un futuro senza Augusto'. Cf. Hor. *Carm.* 3.30.1–5: *exegi monumentum aere perennius / regalique situ pyramidum altius, / quod non imber edax, non Aquilo inpotens / possit diruere aut innumerabilis / annorum series et fuga temporum* ('I have finished a monument more lasting than bronze, more lofty than the regal structure of the pyramids, one which neither corroding rain nor the ungovernable North Wind can ever destroy, not the countless series of the years, nor the flight of time', trans. N. Rudd).
[42] Pasco-Pranger 2000 stresses the importance of *uates operosus* at *Fast.* 1.102. Cf. the expression *uates mundi* with which Manilius styles himself as the bearer of cosmic knowledge: *Astr.* 2.141–2, with Volk 2009: 210–15; on *uates* in Manilius see also *Astr.* 1.23 and Habinek 2007: 231–2, 235.
[43] Restoration of the *res publica*: Ov. *Fast.* 1.587–616; restoration of peace: 1.709–24. Temple of Mars Ultor: 5.549–98. See Newlands 1995: 87–123 and Barchiesi 2002.
[44] Wallace-Hadrill 1987. Following a similar interpretative line, Beard 1987 argued how Ovid used the flexible form of the Roman calendar to explore aspects of the Roman identity. Fantham 1995: 367–71 offers a masterful overview of the debate prompted by these two studies. Newlands 1995 is the fullest exploration of Ovid's ambivalence towards the Augustan settlement; see also Cooley 2006: 240–3. Prescendi 2000 discusses the disenchanted representation of the past in the *Fasti*. The tension that pervades the *Fasti* was also explored, from a different angle, by Fauth 1978: esp. 167–73; Scheid 1985b: 43 stressed that piety and 'liberté de ton' are not incompatible in Ovid.

not an interlocutor of the poet, but a topic that must be discussed and understood.[45]

The same tension can be seen in the handling of astrological themes in the poem. As he goes through the Roman calendar, he has to engage constantly with the astronomical developments that underpin the passing of time and, indirectly, to engage with the contribution that astronomy can make to the control over time. In this pursuit Ovid relied heavily on the *Phaenomena* of Aratus, the third-century BC poem that had considerable success in late Republican Rome and was translated into Latin by Cicero, by Varro Atacinus, and apparently also by Ovid.[46] The astronomic lore of Aratus, however, is not fully taken up in the poem. Ovid does not accept the Stoic outlook of the *Phaenomena* and does not even embrace Aratus' use of astronomical themes to pinpoint the agenda of a Hellenistic ruler. The catasterism (i.e. rise to heaven) of Caesar is mentioned twice in the *Fasti*; it also plays a prominent role in the finale of the *Metamorphoses*, where the rise to heaven of Julius Caesar is framed into a prophecy of Jupiter on the rule of his adoptive son, and is followed in due course by that of Augustus and of the poet himself.[47] Moreover, the reliance on Aratus was heavy, but not exclusive: there is evidence that Ovid used other traditions on the rise of the stars, their different phases and their meteorological implications – notably the Hellenistic *parapegmata* (astronomical and metereological calendars) that had a wide circulation in first-century BC Rome.[48] The complexity of Ovid's intellectual project, which integrates different and competing forms of discourse (*fasti*, calendar, almanac), is matched by the openness of its outlook. Ovid had a keen eye for exploring the indeterminacy and unreliability of knowledge; this had an impact on his appreciation and use of technical expertise.[49]

It is unclear whether in the late Republic thinkers envisaged eternity as a time that does not have any end or boundaries. The adjective *aeternus* is etymologically related to *aetas* and may be translated as something that is supposed to last for a long period of time, but not for ever: that sphere of meaning is arguably covered by the adjective *sempiternus*, which is

[45] Barchiesi 1997: 69–73; Pfaff-Reydellet 2009: 163–4, 167–8. Habinek 2002: 55–9 urges that we look beyond the tension between Ovid and Augustus and explore Ovid's adhesion to the empire and its mission.

[46] Gee 2000. See also Newlands 1995: 27–50 and Barchiesi 1997: 177–80. On Ovid's *Phaenomena* see F 1–2 Courtney; the work is never mentioned in what survives of Ovid's production. Intellectual fashion of astrology in the late Republic: Le Glay 1976: 529–32; Barton 1994a: 47–50, 194–5.

[47] Ov. *Fast.* 3.155–67 and 697–708; *Met.* 15.839–79.

[48] Rüpke 1996b: 293–302. Taub 2001: 20–33, 193–9 and Lehoux 2007 provide comprehensive discussions of παραπήγματα.

[49] Schiesaro 2002.

constructed with the adverb *semper*, 'ever'.[50] Most people will have used the two adjectives interchangeably, but a passage of Cicero's *Pro Rabirio perduellionis reo* suggests that the difference in meaning could be felt and that it had implications on how the destiny of Rome was perceived: 'if you want this city to be immortal (*immortalem*), this empire to be lasting (*aeternum*), and our glory everlasting (*sempiternam*), we must be on our guard against our own passions, men of violence and desirous of political upheavals, evils from within, and plots devised at home'.[51] This may well be just an instance of variation; or perhaps here Cicero implies that the empire is bound to have an end, albeit in a very distant future, while the city can reasonably hope to survive for ever, as well as its renown and glory.[52] What is beyond dispute is that this passage refers to a very distant future; so distant that it blurred into an undifferentiated eternity. An even bolder confidence can be found in the famous passage of Horace's *Odes* 3.30, where the end of time seems to be identified with the end of Rome, powerfully summarised in the image of the Vestal Virgin making her way up the Capitol with the *pontifex maximus*.[53] As E. Fraenkel pointed out, we could not be further away from the mood of the conversation that allegedly took place on the ruins of Carthage in 146, when Scipio Aemilianus shared with his friend Polybius his concern that even Rome would have to fall one day.[54]

---

[50] Cf. the slight difference in meaning between αἰώνιος and ἀίδιος in Greek; according to *LSJ* (*s.u.*), 'ἀίδιος is distinct from αἰώνιος as *everlasting* from *timeless*'.

[51] Cic. *Rab. perd.* 33: *si immortalem hanc ciuitatem esse uoltis, si aeternum hoc imperium, si gloriam sempiternam manere, nobis a nostris cupiditatibus, a turbulentis hominibus atque nouarum rerum cupidis, ab intestinis malis, a domesticis consiliis est cauendum.*

[52] Bowersock 2006: 979. Cf. Luciani 2010: 134–8 on Cicero's choice to use *aeternitas* instead of *sempiternitas* in his philosophical work, and 173–82, 191–221 on the ambiguity of *aeternitas* as a philosophical concept (221: 'espoir d'immortalité' and 'omnitemporalité').

[53] Hor. *Carm.* 3.30.6–9: *non omnis moriar multaque pars mei / uitabit Libitinam; usque ego postera / crescam laude recens, dum Capitolium / scandet cum tacita uirgine pontifex* ('I shall not wholly die, and a large part of me will elude Libitina. I shall continue to grow, fresh with the praise of posterity, as long as the pontiff climbs the Capitol with the silent virgin', trans. N. Rudd, modified). On the presence of divinatory themes and vocabulary in Horace see Champeaux 1991.

[54] Polyb. 38.22 (= App. *Pun.* 132); Fraenkel 1957: 302–4 (cf. 303: '[t]he future life of Rome, with its unalterable ceremonies is taken for granted, if not to the end of all time, yet for so immense a period that no one needs to cast his thought beyond it'); Ando 2011: 67.

CHAPTER 6

Alien sooth: the Sibylline Books

The image of the Roman statesman sharing his concerns with his Greek mentor is an apt reminder of the depth of the cultural and intellectual ties between Rome and the Greek world.[1] Roman religion was filled with Greek gods and rituals; the Sibylline Books, one of the most prominent features of Roman public divination, are perhaps the most impressive instance. They were a collection of prophetic texts, written in Greek, which were consulted by a college of priests, the *decemuiri* (after Sulla, the *quindecemuiri*), following a prodigy. The consultation was ordered by the Senate, on the initiative of a magistrate; the priests were ordered to access (*adire*) or inspect (*inspicere*) the Books and to consult the relevant section behind closed doors. Once the relevant section was identified, an oracle was singled out and handed over to the Senate, which would then decide whether to accept the oracle or not and – if appropriate – would give instructions about the expiation of the prodigy.[2] The consultation of the Books is well attested throughout the early and the middle Republic. While there is no clear pattern regarding the kind of prodigies on which the consultation of the Books was required, they were certainly used on a regular basis, often in association with other divinatory practices, especially haruspicy.[3] They were a trace of the importance of the Greek element in Roman religion and divination.[4] Their frequent consultation is also a remarkable example of how complex and sophisticated the interaction between magistrates, Senate and priests could be. Moreover, the process that revolved around the consultation of the Books implied the existence of a

---

[1] Cf. Altheim 1938: 241–2.
[2] Good discussions on the procedure in North 1967: 482–4 and Scheid 1998b: 13.
[3] See the negative conclusion in North 1967: 489–90.
[4] On this background see Gagé 1955: 19–68; Bloch 1963: 93–111; North 2000b: 54–6. Bloch 1940, 1963 and 1965a argued for an Etruscan origin of the Sibylline Books; accepted by Champeaux 2005: 215; see also Takács 2003: 22–4 (= 2008: 68–70). Extensive *état de la question* in Caerols 1989: 27–36, 94–103, who also opts for a derivation from Etruria. Montero 1994a: 58 draws attention to the complexity of Sibylline divination: a board of men consults and interprets a text dictated by a woman, the Sibyl.

specific expertise in their use and interpretation. J. Scheid has aptly spoken of a 'divinatory jurisprudence', based on the knowledge of precedents which was made possible by the creation of an archive.[5] The importance of the Books was conveyed by the place where they were stored – the Capitoline Hill. They were locked in a stone chest, under the watch of the *decemuiri*; the mode of their preservation is the clearest testimony to the problems and risks that this sort of material could pose.[6] The contrast with the destiny of the so-called books of Numa is instructive. These texts, which included regulations that were not included in the public *sacra* set up by the king, were buried with him. When some texts written in Greek and Latin were fortuitously discovered in a tomb on the Janiculum in 181 and were taken to be writings of King Numa, the praetor Q. Petilius' decision – taken in consultation with the Senate – was to order their public destruction.[7] As J. North has argued, the most economical explanation for this extraordinary decision is that, since there was no obvious strategy available for their inclusion into public religion, their elimination was preferable to the risks posed by their use outside an established ritual and interpretative framework.[8] The success of the Sibylline Books was the outcome of a completely opposite process: the revelation of the responses of the Sibyls was placed under State control through a process of collection, codification and specialised interpretation.

The eighties of the first century BC are a crucial decade in the history of the Sibylline tradition in Rome, and beyond. As the appearance of the motif of the Etruscan *gene/saecula* suggests, the events of 88 were of great importance and their religious implications must be read against a wider background. In the Greek East the First Mithridatic War was accompanied

---

[5] Scheid 1998b: 18; see also Scheid 1987–9: 132 ('les prêtres savaient d'avance ce que l'oracle devait annoncer et prescrire'). See also Santangelo 2012: 52–3. Cf., however, Satterfield 2008: 38, stressing how little is known about the modes of consultation of the Books.

[6] Dion. Hal. *Ant. Rom.* 4.62.5 (= Varro *ARD* F 60 Cardauns): οὗτοι διέμειναν οἱ χρησμοὶ μέχρι τοῦ Μαρσικοῦ κληθέντος πολέμου κείμενοι κατὰ γῆς ἐν τῷ ναῷ τοῦ Καπιτωλίνου Διὸς ἐν λιθίνῃ λάρνακι, ὑπ' ἀνδρῶν δέκα φυλαττόμενοι ('These oracles, until the so-called Marsic War, were kept underground in the temple of Jupiter Capitolinus in a stone chest, under the guard of ten men').

[7] Livy 40.29.3–14; Val. Max. 1.1.12 (with Wardle 1998: 105); Plin. *HN* 13.84–7; Plut. *Num.* 22.2–5; Fest. p. 178, 19–22 L; Lactant. *Div inst.* 1.22.1–6; *De vir. ill.* 3.2; August. *De civ. D.* 7.34 (= Varro *ARD* App. ad lib. 1 F III Cardauns). Useful surveys of the literary tradition in Della Corte 1974: 7–20 (although the interpretation of the contents of the book is entirely speculative); Pailler 1988: 623–67; Storchi Marino 1992: 138–42 and 1999: 163–96; Willi 1998; Rosenberger 2003: 39–48. According to Livy and Plutarch, Numa's books were contained in a stone case – like the Sibylline Books preserved on the Capitol. According to Cassius Hemina (*HRR* I², F 37 = Plin. *HN* 13.84) the Books were discovered by the *scriba* Cn. Terentius in his allotment on the Janiculum: he was probably a priestly *apparitor* or a *pontifex minor* (Rüpke 2005a: 1315–16, no. 3222 and 2011a: 110–11).

[8] North 2008: 32–4; see also North 2000a: 105–7. On the importance of this episode in the history of Roman philhellenism cf. Rosen 1985; Gruen 1990: 163–70; Humm 2004.

by the emergence of several contrasting divinatory and prophetic traditions. The evidence presents a fragmentary picture, as is so often the case, but it is clear that activity was intense on both sides of the conflict. Mithridates encouraged a strong tradition concerning his birth and his association with the gods.[9] The beginning of his offensive against the Romans in 89 was marked by a surge of oracles that predicted the imminent defeat of Rome and the end of the empire, themes which featured very prominently in the propaganda of his supporters. When Athenion returned to Athens after a meeting with the King and warned his fellow-citizens of the necessity of joining him, he used the response of the oracles as one of the signs of the necessity of the action.[10] Against this background, it is not surprising that Sulla sought the support of an important oracle, almost certainly that of Delphi, in the immediate aftermath of the war. The response that he received recognised both his personal qualities and the more general connection between Rome and the Greek world, through Aphrodite.[11]

During the war, however, pro-Roman prophecies sometimes came from less established sources. At Tralles a boy was consulted about the outcome of the war; it must be assumed that his magical powers were already recognised, as the episode took place in the context of a magical consultation (Apul. *Apol.* 42.6):

> *memini me apud Varronem philosophum, uirum accuratissime doctum atque eruditum, cum alia eiusdem modi, tum hoc etiam legere: Trallibus de euentu Mithridatici belli magica percontatione consultantibus puerum in aqua simulacrum Mercuri contemplantem quae futura erant CLX uersibus cecinisse.*

> I remember that, when I was reading about other matters of the same kind in the works of the philosopher Varro, an exquisitely educated and learned man, I read the following too: in Tralles a boy, gazing at an image of Mercury in water, sang the things that were to happen in one hundred and sixty verses to those who asked him about the outcome of the Mithridatic War in a magical consultation.[12]

He gave his answer as he was looking at a statue of Mercury in a bowl of water; his response was impressively lengthy – 160 lines. It is not clear in what phase of the conflict the episode occurred – Tralles sided with Mithridates – and who asked the boy to give a response: a citizen of Tralles, a Roman resident, or even a Roman magistrate. Someone must have taken the trouble to transcribe it in full, if Varro was able to mention it a few decades later and even to give details on its length. We do

---

[9] Mayor 2010: 27–38, 386–8.   [10] Athen. 5.211d–215b = *FGrHist* 87 F 36.
[11] App. *B Civ.* 1.97.   [12] Cardauns 1960: 45–51; Potter 1994: 13; Ogden 2001: 196–7.

not know in what context he referred to this episode, although he probably used it to discuss the divinatory skills of young boys. Apuleius, who quoted Varro's account in his *Apologia,* followed the episode with a reference to a similar incident, possibly also derived from Varro, in which a certain Fabius asked Nigidius Figulus to establish how he had lost 500 denarii; Nigidius (who apparently features in this anecdote in his capacity of *magus,* 'sorcerer') instructed some young boys in a magic ritual, and they gave a precise and accurate response on where the coins were.[13] These episodes are very significant for a number of reasons. They are a reminder of the plurality and diversity of forms of divination in the late Republican period; they reveal in what complex and fortuitous ways traditions developed; at the same time, they show the analogies and connections between Greek and Roman approaches and practices, which cannot simply be explained by the intermediation of a learned individual like Nigidius.

The Sibylline tradition – a complex religious and intellectual development that encompassed Paganism, Judaism and Christianity – is the most important feature of this shared background.[14] Tralles was apparently a place where there was a strong interest in prophecies and divinatory utterances. A native of the city, Phlegon, became a slave of the emperor Hadrian and, after his manumission, wrote a compilation of bizarre and supernatural events, the *Peri thaumasion* ('Book on Wonders'), which records a number of prophecies and sheds light on the relationship between Rome and the Greek world. It is thanks to this work that we have one of the most important sources for the study of ancient divination: the only known text of a Sibylline oracle produced during the Republic. It is a lengthy Greek text that contains some ritual prescriptions for the expiation of a prodigy (notably the birth of a hermaphrodite child), which Phlegon dated to 125.[15] The surviving version of the oracle consists of seventy lines in hexameter, although there are some lacunae and about thirty lines are missing at the end. Its most striking feature is an acrostic: the first letters of the lines correspond to the first line of the oracle.[16] The scholarly debate on this

[13] Apul. *Apol.* 42.7–8. On Nigidius' interest in magic and his role in the establishment of magic as a worthy intellectual activity see (with some caution) Le Glay 1976: 542–4.

[14] Momigliano 1988 (= 1992: 725–44); Sfameni Gasparro 2002: 61–112; Buitenwerf 2003: 92–123; Lightfoot 2007: vii–x, 3–93; Suárez de la Torre 2007; Waßmuth 2011: 3–86, 466–512. Splendid collection of sources (in German translation) with extensive commentary in Kurfeß and Gauger 1998.

[15] *FGrHist* 257 F 36 x = Phlegon *Mir.* 10. English translations in Hansen 1996: 40–41 and Beard, North and Price 1998: II, 180. Guittard 1996: 127–30 and 2007a: 254–68.

[16] Pease 1923: 530 argues that the purpose of the acrostics was 'to prevent unauthorized insertions and excisions from impairing the integrity of the collection, and they were thus an evidence of

text has concentrated on its chronology, which also has implications for its composition. While it is possible that, as Phlegon reports, the oracle was made public in 125 and was used to interpret and expiate a prodigy that did occur in that year, it is perhaps likelier that it was written and included in the Books some time earlier. H. Diels argued that the text was in fact the combination of two different oracles, which blended two different agendas, although they referred to the same prodigy or to two prodigies of the same kind: while the focus of the first oracle deals with ritual matters, the second has a focus on prophecy. In Diels' view, the oracles could be dated precisely, to 207 and 200 respectively.[17] This was a ground-breaking approach, not least because it showed the Sibylline Books as a collection that developed over a considerable time span. While not all the conclusions of Diels' analysis command support, this methodological point remains central.

The date recorded by Phlegon is possible in principle: 125 was a year of great political tensions, when in the consulship of Fulvius Flaccus a bill to extend the citizenship to the Latins was repealed and the revolt of Fregellae broke out; the prodigy of the hermaphrodite birth followed by the consultation of the Sibylline Books is compatible with that scenario.[18] However, another hypothesis can be put forward. Most of the text of the two oracles is concerned with ritual prescriptions concerning the expiation of the prodigy, but the final lines of the second oracle also include a prophecy pointing to a time when new prodigies will occur and a 'Trojan' (Τρώς) will set Rome free from any evil and 'from Greece'. This passage is compatible with the atmosphere of the age of the First Mithridatic War, when the Roman rule in the East was briefly put to an end. Hellas could be read as Asia Minor, while the 'Trojan' might be Sulla, who won the war and made use of the myth of the kinship between Rome and Troy, especially in his dealings with the Greek world. If this interpretation is correct, Sulla and his entourage put together an oracle that was somehow related to an oracle produced in 125, probably in circles that were hostile to the reform plan of Fulvius Flaccus. The oracle will have probably been included in the new collection of the Sibylline Books that was gathered after the fire on the Capitol of 83.[19] This new collection must have also included the other Sibylline oracle that is known to us, recorded by both Phlegon and

---

genuineness'; Gagé 1955: 361–2 convincingly notes that the acrostic is the strongest indication that the oracle was a Hellenistic fabrication, composed some time before 125.

[17] Diels 1890: 90–1.   [18] Satterfield 2011: 119–22.

[19] Breglia Pulci Doria 1983: 224–309; Guittard 1996: 129. North 2000a: 104 also suggests a Sullan dating and argues that the text of the oracle has no obvious relevance to the events of 125.

Zosimus, which prescribes the celebration of the *ludi saeculares* that took place in 17.[20]

Phlegon is our source for other important episodes that take us back to the early second century and the wars which marked the beginning of the Roman hegemony in the Greek East. The third chapter of his work features two extraordinary stories, which Phlegon linked to one another, even if he probably derived them from two different sources.[21] In the first tale, a Syrian cavalry commander called Bouplagos, after being killed in the battle won by the Romans at Thermopylae in 191, reappears on the battlefield warning the Romans of the wrath of the gods against them; the oracle of Delphi is consulted, and corroborates the prophecy; the Romans decide to abandon plans for another campaign in the West and celebrate sacrifices at Naupactus in Aetolia. In the second tale, which is set immediately after the rituals performed at Naupactus, the Roman general Publius suddenly begins to rave in a state of divine possession and gives a prophecy, partly in prose and partly in verse: he predicts the invasion of Italy by an Eastern king, which would however be preceded by a Roman victory against Antiochus III in Asia Minor. He also predicts that a wolf would soon devour him; this indeed happens shortly afterwards; only Publius' head remains unscathed and utters another prophecy of the victory of Asia over Rome. This 'Publius' must no doubt be identified with Scipio Africanus, the *fatalis dux* whose reputation for a unique connection with the gods spread even to the Greek world.[22] Both prophecies were certainly fabricated and spread in Greek circles, probably in the immediate aftermath of the defeat of the Seleucids, but they have independent origins and were probably joined by one of Phlegon's sources (possibly Antisthenes of Rhodes), who gave them a new narrative framework and adapted some of their anachronisms. There is no evidence that these stories circulated in Rome, but it should not be ruled out: Varro's reference to the story of the boy from Tralles is unlikely to have been isolated. Moreover, these episodes were part of an anti-Roman discourse that featured in the political climate of the second and first centuries: they did require a response, or at any

---

[20] *FGrHist* 257 F 37 = Phlegon *Macr.* 99.4 = Zos. 2.6, with Paschoud 2000: 201–3; Schnegg-Köhler 2002: 221–8; Cooley 2006: 234–5; Guittard 2007a: 268–75. English translation in Hansen 1996: 56–7. The wording of the oracle is strikingly close to the prophecy of Anchises in Verg. *Aen.* 6.851–3 (*tu regere imperio populos, Romane, memento*). See Zetzel 1989: 277–9, also discussing earlier bibliography; it is impossible to establish who is alluding to whom.

[21] Phlegon *Mir.* 3.4–15. English translation in Hansen 1996: 32–7. See Ferrary 1988: 238–64, including a comprehensive review of the earlier scholarship; Hansen 1996: 101–12; Ogden 2001: 207–10, 232; Sordi 2006: 140–2.

[22] Ferrary 1988: 245–6; Hansen 1996: 107.

rate they had to be incorporated into the Roman political discourse and reckoned with.

The Third Sibylline Oracle, a lengthy prophetic text the bulk of which was probably produced in Greek-speaking Jewish circles in Asia Minor during the first century BC, referred to the punishment of Rome (3.324–36, 350–66) and the coming of an Eastern king (3.652–6).[23] These themes circulated widely in the Greek world and in Rome, and they served Mithridates' propaganda well, because they promoted the figure of an Eastern king, they denounced Roman violence and greed, and they challenged the myth of Roman piousness and the idea of a necessary bond between Rome and the gods.[24] We have seen how prominent the rhetoric of the decline and imminent fall of Rome was at various stages in the last decades of the Republic, and what role prophecies played in it. A similar picture can be sketched for the Greek East. There was an impressive body of prophecies, produced by public centres of divination and by independent diviners, which expressed views on the prospects of Roman rule and of Rome, and forged an alternative version of history that placed the winning side in the East, not in Rome.

The fire on the Capitol

Another major historical event makes the eighties of the first century BC a crucial stage in the history of the Sibylline tradition: the loss of the Sibylline Books in the fire on the Capitol on 6 July 83. The temple of Jupiter, where the Books were preserved, was almost completely destroyed.[25] The fire took place at a time of great political tension, at the very beginning of a civil war. Appian eloquently recalls the atmosphere at the time and mentions the fire at the end of a lengthy list of prodigies that took place throughout Italy and brought about panic: a mule foaled, a woman gave birth to a snake, earthquakes happened. Everything seemed to indicate that the imminent tragedy of civil war and a major, traumatic political

---

[23] Commentary in Buitenwerf 2003: 218–24, 272–5. Dating and historical context: Geraci 1983: 71–81; Buitenwerf 2003: 124–34; Lightfoot 2007: 95–6; Suárez de la Torre 2007: 68–72. The lines 1–96 of the Third Oracle are an Augustan addition (Buitenwerf 2003: 65–91; Lightfoot 2007: 95–6; Suárez de la Torre 2007: 68).

[24] McGing 1986: 102–6.

[25] Cic. *Verr.* 2.4.69; Dion. Hal. *Ant. Rom.* 4.62; App. *B Civ.* 1.83; Plut. *Sull.* 27.12–13; *Publ.* 15.2; Plin. *HN* 33.16; Tac. *Hist.* 3.72.8–10; *Ann.* 6.12.5; Obs. 57; Cassiod. *Chron.* 132.486 Mommsen. See H. Flower 2008; Thein forthcoming.

change was about to fall upon the city.[26] The narrative conveys the impression that the atmosphere was even more frenzied than a few years earlier, when the haruspices announced the end of an age and the *uates* Cornelius Culleolus was uttering his prophecies. Moreover, the destruction of the temple of Jupiter on the Capitol was not just a premonition of what was to come. It was an irretrievable loss; it was, in a sense, the end of the past. The fact that the causes of the fire, according to Appian, were never established must have created an even deeper sense of unescapable doom.[27]

Sulla was quick to connect the fire on the Capitol with the presence of his enemies in Rome. In his memoirs he wrote about the visit he received during the Civil War from a slave who announced to him, in a state of prophetic inspiration, the support of Bellona and the imminent destruction of the Capitol – which could have been averted by a quick victory that, however, Sulla was not able to achieve.[28] He handled the reconstruction of the temple of Jupiter as a matter of urgency, but did not live to see its completion: Tacitus ironically remarked that this was the one aspect in which his *felicitas* did not assist him.[29] The new temple was dedicated in 69 by Q. Lutatius Catulus. We have no explicit evidence that Sulla worked on the restoration of the corpus of the Sibylline Books, although his decision to add five members to the decemviral college must no doubt be understood against this background.[30] According to Lactantius, who derived his information from Fenestella and Varro, it was only in 76 that a sustained attempt was made to gather a new body of Sibylline prophecies, when the consul C. Curio recommended that the Senate send envoys to Erythrae in Asia Minor with the task of gathering the oracles of the Sibyl (Lactant. *Div. inst.* 1.6.14):

> *restituto Capitolio rettulisse ad senatum C. Curionem consulem, ut legati Erythras mitterentur, qui carmina Sibyllae conquisita Romam deportarent: itaque missos esse P. Gabinium M. Otacilium L. Valerium, qui descriptos a priuatis uersus circa mille Romam deportarunt.*

After the Capitol was restored, the consul Gaius Curio proposed to the Senate that legates should be sent to Erythrae to gather the verses of the

---

[26] App. *B Civ.* 1.83: Πάντα δ' ἔδοξεν . . . προσημῆναι.

[27] The disagreement among the extant sources on the cause of the fire is noteworthy: cf. Cic. *Verr.* 2.4.69 (lightning); Cassiod. *Chron.* 132.486 м (negligence of the custodians); Obs. 57 and Tac. *Hist.* 3.72 (arson); Dion. Hal. *Ant. Rom.* 4.62.6 (arson or accident).

[28] Plut. *Sull.* 27.12–13. See H. Flower 2008: 82–3.

[29] Tac. *Hist.* 3.72.5. This passage provides a thought-provoking history of the Capitol and the temple, on which see H. Flower 2008: 90–2. Cf. also Plin. *HN* 7.44.

[30] Serv. *ad Aen.* 6.73.

Sibyl and bring them back to Rome; and thus Publius Gabinius, Marcus
Otacilius and Lucius Valerius were sent out, and brought back to Rome
around 1,000 verses that were copied from private citizens.[31]

The workings of the process initiated by C. Curio are most remarkable.
The names of three envoys are recorded; others were involved with the
collection of other prophetic sayings from various cities of Italy and also
from Africa, Sicily and again from Samos and Ilium in Asia Minor.[32] The
quindecemuiri were then instructed to go through the material gathered
in that survey and establish which ones were to be deemed genuine and
could be included in the collection. According to the rather uninformative
accounts of Cicero and Dionysius, the selection was carried out on the
basis of the so-called acrostics: the priests would seek either the initial
letters of the verses or a string of words that, if taken together, would form
a word that might be relevant to the interpretation of the prodigy.[33] If the
reconstruction of Diels, subsequently developed by Scheid, is correct, only
the part of the oracle that was necessary for the interpretation of the prodigy
was intended to be made public. This contributed to the proverbial lack of
clarity of the Sibylline responses.[34]

The reconstruction of the corpus that was undertaken in 76 was a major
political operation, which revived old ties between Rome and a number
of *poleis* across the empire and no doubt initiated some new ones. Making
use of material drawn from other cities was a necessity, since there was not
enough available in Rome. However, it was also a political choice, which
afforded the creation or the consolidation of a number of religious and
cultural connections which could strengthen the cohesion of the empire.[35]
It is also important to consider the implications of the decision to gather
a new version of the corpus. Before 83 the Sibylline Books had been a
very prominent aspect of Roman public divination; over the previous

---

[31] Beard 1994: 737 argues that by 76 the temple must have been in sufficiently good condition to
house the oracles, even if the reconstruction was not quite complete. Satterfield 2008: 179–80 notes
that the decision to copy the oracles, rather than to take them away, made possible the emergence
of 'potentially competing versions'. Orlin 2010: 203 rightly stresses that the decision to use oracles
from a city of Asia Minor in the aftermath of the Mithridatic War was politically very significant.

[32] Discrepancies among the sources: Tac. *Ann.* 6.12.5 (Samos, Ilium, Erythrae and even in Africa, Sicily
and the Italian colonies); Dion. Hal. *Ant. Rom.* 4.62.6 (some cities of Italy, Erythrae and other
cities, transcribed by private persons); Lactant. *Div inst.* 1.6.13 ('all cities of Italy' and Erythrae).
On the mission of the three envoys see Gagé 1955: 446–61; Pina Polo 2011: 158 stresses the consular
involvement in the process. Coarelli 1987: 105–11 argues that some material was moved to Rome
from Tibur, which was home to an important oracle, but the evidence is inconclusive. Varro argued
that the original Sibylline Books were the work of the Sibyl of Erythrae (Varro *ARD* F 56c Cardauns
= Serv. *ad Aen.* 6.72); Hoffmann 1933: 6–15. Sibyl of Erythrae: Buitenwerf 2003: 118–21.

[33] Cic. *Div.* 2.110–11; Dion. Hal. *Ant. Rom.* 4.62.6.

[34] Diels 1890; Scheid 1998b: 13–17.   [35] Orlin 2010: 202–3.

decades they had been put under increasing pressure by other sources of divinatory and prophetic expertise, especially the haruspices. However, they retained a distinctive profile, as they enabled a sector of the Roman elite to produce its own divinatory responses without having to seek advice from foreign experts. Rewriting the corpus meant restoring a formidable political weapon, which still had much clout in the complex landscape of late Republican religious life.

We find a revealing confirmation of the importance of the Sibylline Books in one of the first decisions that Augustus took in 12, after taking up the office of *pontifex maximus*.[36] He did not just remove from circulation a number of Latin and Greek prophecies that were available in Rome at the time and restate that the Sibylline Books were the only acceptable form of prophecy. The operation was completed by the decision to relocate the books from the Capitol to the temple of Apollo on the Palatine, in the vicinity of the emperor's residence, under the patronage of the man who had revisited the books and redefined their place within Roman public religion (Suet. *Aug.* 31.1):

> *postquam uero pontificatum maximum, quem numquam uiuo Lepido auferre sustinuerat, mortuo demum suscepit, quidquid fatidicorum librorum Graeci Latinique generis nullis uel parum idoneis auctoribus uulgo ferebatur, supra duo milia contracta undique cremauit ac solos retinuit Sibyllinos, hos quoque dilectu habito; condiditque duobus forulis auratis sub Palatini Apollinis basi.*

> After the death of Lepidus, when he finally took on the office of *pontifex maximus*, which he had never taken upon himself to remove from Lepidus while he was alive, he collected whatever prophetic works of Greek and Latin origin were in circulation with no author's name or authors of insufficient worth, burning more than two thousand of them, and kept only those written by the Sibyl, making a selection even from these. He deposited them in two golden cases under the pedestal of Apollo Palatinus. (trans. D. Wardle)[37]

This was not Augustus' first intervention on the corpus of the Sibylline Books. In 18 he had decreed that the *quindecemuiri* should themselves copy the books by hand, so that 'no one else could read them'. Cassius Dio

[36] On Augustus' accession to the highest pontificate and its wider significance see Fraschetti 1990: 331–8; Strothmann 2010: 226–7.

[37] Wardle 2011a: 274–7 argues in favour of the accuracy of Suetonius' chronology; *contra* see Miller 2009: 240 n. 118. There is no reason to believe, with Kienast 1982: 196 n. 103, that the 'time-honoured' Sibylline Books were not affected by Augustus' selection and were not removed from the temple of Jupiter Capitolinus. Apollo's association with the Palatine: Gagé 1955: 522–81; Miller 2009: 185–252. Small 1982: 98–102 discusses the factors that made the association with Apollo attractive to Augustus.

reports this action in an overview of various administrative decisions taken by Augustus, including limitations on private expenditure (54.17.2):

τόν τε πολίαρχον τὸν ἐς τὰς ἀνοχὰς καθιστάμενον ἕνα ἀεὶ αἱρεῖσθαι, καὶ τὰ ἔπη τὰ Σιβύλλεια ἐξίτηλα ὑπὸ τοῦ χρόνου γεγονότα τοὺς ἱερέας αὐτοχειρίᾳ ἐκγράψασθαι ἐκέλευσεν, ἵνα μηδεὶς ἕτερος αὐτὰ ἀναλέξηται.

He also ordered that only one man should be elected to the office of the urban prefect that was appointed for the *feriae*, and that the priests should transcribe the Sibylline verses, which had lost their force because of the passing of time, by hand, so that no one else might read them.[38]

It is plausible that the decision belonged in the wider context of the preparations for the *ludi saeculares* that were held in 17.[39] The Books were certainly central to Augustus' plan, but their prominence was not unparalleled: the temple on the Palatine was also home to the collection of the prophecies of the Marcii and to the Etruscan books that dealt with lightning.[40] With this decision Augustus stressed that the haruspices and their lore were a fundamental feature of Roman public religion and that their significance was not inferior to that of the Sibylline Books. The practice of those two fundamental sources of divination and prophecy was now taking place under his own patronage and control.

The temple of Apollo on the Palatine was the ideal venue from which to assert such control. It was closely linked to the person of Octavian and it asserted most forcefully his own association with Apollo; yet, it did not belong in the tradition of the Republican temples that were intended to celebrate the deeds of a great man. It was not just home to the Greek prophecies of the Sibylline Books. It also hosted an impressive set of cult statues that were the work of great Greek masters: one of Apollo by Scopas,

---

[38] Rich 1990: 193–4. Cf. the survey of the Sibylline Books ordered by Tiberius in AD 19 after the publication of a response that foretold civil strife (Dio 57.18.4) and Tiberius' rejection of the attempt of the *quindecemuir* L. Caninius Gallus to add a new book to the Sibylline corpus in AD 32 (Tac. *Ann.* 6.12). On limitations on religious knowledge in the early Principate see Várhely 2010: 161–2.

[39] Scheid 1999a: 17–18 rightly stresses that the transfer of the Sibylline Books to the Palatine fell within the prerogatives of the *pontifex maximus*; Augustus was careful not to interfere with the prerogatives of this priesthood before he took it up in 12. On the other hand, the order to transcribe the Books fell within the remit of the *cura morum* and did not require the approval of the college of the pontiffs.

[40] Serv. *ad Aen.* 6.72: *libri ... Marciorum et Begoes nymphae, quae artem scripserat fulguritarum apud Tuscos* ('the books ... of the Marcii and of the nymph Begoe, who had written among the Etruscans about the art of the things struck by lightning'), with Hekster and Rich 2006: 160. There is no evidence that such collection was ever stored in a public venue during the Republic, unless some of the prophetic material mentioned in an *elogium* from Tarquinia was put under decemviral control after the death of a haruspex (cf. Torelli 1975: 133–4 and North 2000a: 95–8, and see above Chapter 4).

Figure 6.1 Diana, Apollo, Latona and the Sibyl. Sorrento, Museo Correale, inv. 3657.
Nachlass Hoffmann © Neg. D-DAI-ROM 31.2352.

one of Diana by Timotheos, and one of Latona by Cephisodotus.[41] There
was no precedent for the use of Greek originals as cult statues in the city
of Rome. A statue base, now in Sorrento, depicts these statues one next to
the other, and a Sibyil is added to the group: she sits at the feet of Latona,
exhausted and subdued, holding an urn that may be identified as one of
the cases in which the Sibylline prophecies were stored (Figure 6.1).

Whatever the original context of the Sorrento base may have been, and
whatever relationship one establishes between it and the cult statues on the
Palatine, the relief gives clear indication that the presence of the Sibyl and
her prophecies was readily identified in the contemporary discourse as a
central feature of the new cult of Apollo on the Palatine.[42]

The decision to build a temple on the Palatine was taken at a crucial
stage in Octavian's life, shortly after his return to Rome after the battle

[41] Plin. *HN* 36.24–5, 32; cf. Prop. 2.31.15–16. Sibyl in the Sorrento base: Rizzo 1932: 71–6 (who identifies
her with the Cumaean Sibyl); Zanker 1988: 240–1; Galinsky 1996: 216; Lange 2009: 179.
[42] The base was reused as a cornerstone at a crossroads near the Arcivescovado in Sorrento and the
circumstances of its discovery are unknown (Rizzo 1932: 7–15).

of Naulochus, in 36, but the choice of the exact location was determined by a prodigy: an area of the Palatine that he had purchased was struck by lightning and he consequently decided to make it public property and dedicate it to Apollo.[43] The dedication of the temple had, therefore, a clear divinatory dimension. Suetonius makes the picture more coherent by giving an essential detail: when a portion of the house on the Palatine was struck by lightning, the haruspices were consulted and ruled that the place was 'desired by a god'.[44] Octavian's response was the dedication to Apollo. The details of the consultation of the haruspices are unknown, as well as those of the response that Octavian received. It is unclear whether the consultation happened in a public or private framework and whether the advice to dedicate a temple to Apollo was given by the haruspices or was Octavian's idea.[45] Whatever the solution to these specific problems may be, the prodigy of the Palatine draws attention to several aspects of primary importance. First of all, an intense and fruitful relationship between Octavian and the haruspices took shape. Secondly, Octavian fully realised and exploited the range of knowledge of the Etruscan diviners in their ability, both to handle prodigies and to express responses of prophetic significance, and put it to the service of his design to gain control over the religious landscape of Rome. Thirdly, Octavian was able to use the established mechanisms for the handling of prodigies in Rome in order to bring about revolutionary outcomes: asserting a special connection with the gods and singling out cult places that, whilst carrying a more general significance for the whole community, were under his direct patronage.[46]

The development of the triumph in the early Principate, notably its monopolisation by the emperor and his family, provides an interesting analogy with the itinerary that is sketched here.[47] The advent of complete control by the imperial family over a crucial area of public religion is accompanied by two parallel developments: the creation of new domains

---

[43] Dio 49.15.5; cf. Vell. 2.81.3. The temple was dedicated on 9 October 28 (Dio 53.1.3; *InscrIt* 13.2, 37, 195, 209): overview of the site in Gros 1993.

[44] Suet. *Aug.* 29.3: *desiderari a deo*. See Hekster and Rich 2006: 150–2. Cf. Nisbet and Hubbard 1970: 348: 'As Octavian wanted the space (Vell. 2.81.3), it was useful that the god did too.' Champeaux 1995: 66, 80 n. 15 notes an interesting parallel with the divine *postilationes* ('arrears of sacrifice', but also 'claim to entitlement') mentioned in Cic. *Har. resp.* 20.

[45] A survey of the possible scenarios in Hekster and Rich 2006: 155–62.

[46] Hekster and Rich 2006: 156 stress that there is no evidence for an involvement of the Senate in the decisions to build the temple of Apollo Palatinus. The Senate was customarily responsible for the handling of prodigies and the dedication of new temples, and it would be extraordinary if Augustus had decided not to involve it in the process; but it is not uncommon that the involvement of the Senate in complex decision processes is overlooked in the literary sources for the early Principate (Brunt 1984: esp. 438–9 on religious matters).

[47] Hickson 1991: 127–30; Beard 2007: esp. 69–71; Itgenshorst 2008.

of ritual activity for other sectors of the elite, albeit always within limits and frameworks set by the monarch, and the emergence of a complex theoretical, antiquarian and historical reflection, not necessarily directed by the new regime, but definitely inspired by its ideological agenda. The question must be asked whether the activity of the (*quin*)*decemuiri* was prophetic or not. As we have seen, the most innovative aspect of the role played by the haruspices was their frequent production of prophecies, albeit usually in association with religious prescriptions. The activity of the (*quin*)*decemuiri* had some features in common with it, but there were also some important differences. The (*quin*)*decemuiri* were consulted by the Senate when a prodigy required interpretation and a set of expiatory remedies had to be devised. Unlike the haruspices, they were a priestly college that was fully embedded within the framework of Roman public religion. Moreover, their responses were always based on the reading of a text: the Sibylline Books. The consultation and interpretation of the relevant sections of the collection would enable them to identify the nature of the problem and to give ritual prescriptions, which would sometimes refer to the consequences of lack of action, and would therefore include a prophetic element. This general account of the action of the *decemuiri* is generally accepted; what requires further discussion is the scope of these prophetic utterances and how detailed they were. Things are complicated by the nature of the historical record. Most of our information derives from Livy, whose text is incomplete, and whom we should not expect to be providing a comprehensive overview of public religious activity or of the interventions of all the priestly colleges.[48] Some gaps in the historical record are, however, striking, and probably not fortuitous. During the Hannibalic War, for example, there was a series of three consultations in close sequence between 218 and 216, but the involvement of the *decemuiri* in the expiation of prodigies, and notably in supplications, is not recorded until 193.[49] This is difficult to account for: either there was a shift in practice, or Livy's narrative is marred by a series of major omissions. The problem is further complicated by the evidence for the intervention of the *decemuiri* in 205, when some showers of stones prompted the consultation of the Books and the Senate received a response that blended a prophecy with a significant religious prescription (Livy 29.10.4–8):

---

[48] A different view in Satterfield 2012b.

[49] Mazurek 2004: 151–4. Cf. also Février 2009: 133–9. The *decemuiri*, however, made important interventions on religious matters during this period, most notably in recommending the institution of the *ludi Apollinares* in 212 and the importation of the cult of Magna Mater in 205. Hoffmann 1933: 15–18 is still invaluable.

ciuitatem eo tempore repens religio inuaserat inuento carmine in libris Sibyllinis propter crebrius eo anno de caelo lapidatum inspectis, quandoque hostis alieni-gena terrae Italiae bellum intulisset eum pelli Italia uincique posse si mater Idaea a Pessinunte Romam aduecta foret. id carmen ab decemuiris inuentum eo magis patres mouit quod et legati qui donum Delphos portauerant referebant et sacrificantibus ipsis Pythio Apollini omnia laeta fuisse et responsum oraculo editum maiorem multo uictoriam quam cuius ex spoliis dona portarent adesse populo Romano.

At this time a religious concern had invaded the city, after the discovery of a prophecy in the Sibylline Books, which had been inspected after a shower of rain had fallen from the sky during that year. It stated that whenever a foreign enemy should bring war, he would be repelled from Italy and defeated, if the Mother Idaea were to be brought to Rome from Pessinus. This prophecy, discovered by the *decemuiri*, made all the more of an impression on the Senate, because the ambassadors who had taken an offering to Delphi had also reported that they had received happy signs when sacrificing to Apollo Pythius and that the oracle had given a response, whereby the Roman people would obtain a much greater victory than that from the spoils of which they were bringing presents.

Rome would be able to repel an enemy from Italy, if the cult of the Idaean Mother was to be imported to Rome from the sanctuary of Pessinus.[50] According to Livy, the prescription was corroborated (independently, or so we are told) by a Delphic response, and the Senate took a radical step: a new goddess was introduced to Rome with a lavish ceremony. The significance of the Sibylline Books was powerfully asserted by this episode. The response extracted by the *decemuiri* had a complex structure and, in a broad sense, a prophetic dimension. Like some haruspical responses, it set a religious requirement and offered a prediction on what would happen if the prescription was not acted upon.[51]

An innovation of practice apparently intervened in the following decades. There is sparse evidence for later episodes in which the Sibylline Books offered some specific prescriptions on how to address a critical situation. In 143 there was an intervention of the *decemuiri* on the route of

---

[50] Cf. also App. *Hann.* 56, where the *decemuiri* are said to have predicted the fall of a meteorite from the sky at Pessinus in Phrygia and prescribed bringing it to Rome. More references and discussion in Hoffmann 1933: 30–1; Orlin 2010: 76–85; Satterfield 2012a. On the use of *alienigena* in this context see Urso 1994; Russo 2012: 240–2.

[51] Mazurek 2004: 157–8; on the prophetic elements of the Books cf., from a different angle, Cancik 1989: 562–5; North 1990: 54–5; North 2000a: 104; Février 2004. A stronger emphasis on expiation in Gagé 1955: 32–3; Santi 2000; Montero 2003; Satterfield 2008: 62–72. Hoffmann 1933, Bloch 1940: 22–5 and Caerols 1989: 156, 598 argue for a gradual increase in the prophetic scope of the Books.

the aqueduct of the Aqua Marcia, which does not appear to have been caused by a prodigy, but was probably entailed by the consultation of the Books for a different reason.[52] Whatever the background of the episode, the prescription of the *decemuiri* was taken seriously and the issue was debated in the Senate. It is unclear how frequent these interventions were. It is conceivable that a change in practice occurred from the late third century BC, as the political allegiances of the members of the decemviral college will have at times shaped its concerns and the remit of its activity. A general point can be made: the boundary between ritual prescription and prophecy is not always neat, and possibly it was not understood in these terms by the members of the college themselves. Prophecies featured with increasing prominence in the public discourse, and Roman *decemuiri* and Etruscan haruspices contributed to this development in their own different ways. However, unlike the haruspices, the *decemuiri* had to work within the limits of the texts that they were expected to use and preserve. Whatever prophetic intervention they made, it had to be based on a specific interpretative exercise, which had almost a diagnostic dimension, as it had to be based on the understanding of a specific crisis.[53] Over the centuries, the interpretative tradition of the college developed along more sophisticated lines. There is no reason to believe that the fire of 83 affected this trove of expertise; rather, the later effort to recreate the body of the oracles will have in fact enhanced it. As Mazurek rightly notes, the Sibylline Books are sometimes referred to as *libri fatales*, a label that stresses the significance of their prophetic character.[54] Even if one regards the definition of the *decemuiri* as 'interpreters of the verses of the Sibyl and of the destiny' of the Roman people that we find in Livy as overemphatic, the interpretation of the Books on behalf of the State entailed the understanding of prophetic material and the ensuing production of informed views on the future of the city.[55] We are not in a position to follow the historical development in the use of this aspect of the Books under the Republic, although some significant episodes must be singled out.

However, the control of the *quindecemuiri* over the Books was not a monopoly, especially after 83. Two well-known incidents of late Republican

---

[52] Frontin. *Aq.* 1.7.5; cf. Livy *Ep. Ox.* 54. Mazurek 2004: 159–60.

[53] *Contra* MacBain 1982: 57–9, who denies any competition between haruspices and (*quin*)*decemuiri* and claims that the latter were in fact 'patrons and collaborators' of the Etruscan seers.

[54] Mazurek 2004: 164. Cf. also Guittard 2004: 30–1.

[55] Livy 10.8.2: *decemuiros sacris faciundis, carminum Sibyllae ac fatorum populi huius interpretes* ('the *decemuiri* for the performance of sacred duties, the interpreters of the songs of the Sibyl and of the destinies of this people').

politics showed what unpredictable consequences the use of the Sibylline oracles could have on political competition. In 63 the praetor P. Cornelius Lentulus Sura sought support for the cause of Catiline's conspiracy by telling potential allies about a Sibylline prophecy that was relevant both to his own destiny and to that of Rome. Cicero was given a summary of it from the envoys of the Allobroges, who were approached by Lentulus but eventually refused to join him:

> *Lentulum autem sibi confirmasse ex fatis Sibyllinis haruspicumque responsis se esse tertium illum Cornelium, ad quem regnum huius urbis atque imperium peruenire esset necesse; Cinnam ante se et Sullam fuisse. eundemque dixisse fatalem hunc annum esse ad interitum huius urbis atque imperii, qui esset annus decimus post uirginum absolutionem, post Capitoli autem incensionem uicesimus.*

> Lentulus had assured them that he was, according to Sibylline prophecies and the responses of haruspices, that third Cornelius to whom the kingship over this city and empire was destined to come; Cinna and Sulla were those before him. He also said that this year was destined for the demise of this city and the empire, it being the tenth year after the absolution of the virgins, and the twentieth after the fire of the Capitol.[56]

Lentulus was referring to prophecies that were produced in private contexts, and must have looked broadly comparable to the texts that were known to be part of the Sibylline corpus. It is unclear whether he also claimed that they were genuinely part of the corpus. Haruspical responses were used for this purpose too; again, they will have been produced by private practitioners. Plutarch states that Lentulus liked to surround himself with 'pseudo-prophets and charlatans' (*pseudomanteis tines kai goetes*) who produced these forged responses and urged him to take action and fulfil the destiny that was prophesied for him: in his account, Lentulus is the credulous victim of unscrupulous diviners, rather than the shrewd manipulator of popular gullibility.[57] The prophecies were not just about Lentulus' prospects of rule, but about the historical prospects of Rome more generally: the diviners established a link between the fire of the Capitol of 83 and the prosecution of the Vestal Virgins Fabia and Licinia, who were charged with *incestum* with Catiline and M. Licinius Crassus in 73; the prophecy engages with the same horizon of the haruspical prophecy of

---

[56] Cic. *Cat.* 3.9. See also App. *B Civ.* 2.4.
[57] Plut. *Cic.* 17.5. On ψευδομάντεις and γόητες in the literature of the Second Sophistic cf. Bendlin 2008: 193–203 (= 2011: 226–41).

the beginning of a new age in 88. Indeed, some haruspices were involved with this prophecy in a private capacity. Agreement between Sibylline and haruspical responses had occurred before in the history of Roman public divination and was usually viewed as a corroborating factor; this is also the case here. In most respects, however, the prophecy circulated by Lentulus runs against the established practice of Roman *religio*: as far as we know, it was not produced in response to a prodigy and did not contain a set of ritual recommendations or conditions. Quite the contrary, it offered an anticipation of the future and a teleological vision of Roman history.[58] It was an instance of the prophetic forms of divination that are the central target of the *De diuinatione*, and a powerful example of their political and social disruptiveness.[59]

In 57 the king of Egypt Ptolemy XII Auletes was toppled by a revolt and fled to Rome. In the summer the Senate passed a decree that entrusted the governor of Cilicia, P. Cornelius Lentulus Spinther (*cos.* 57), with the task of restoring the king – a trusted ally of Rome – to the throne. The choice was not unanimous; various members of the Senate advocated that Pompey was the best choice for the mission and Ptolemy shared that opinion. We get a sense of the complexity of the crisis from the correspondence between Cicero and Lentulus Spinther, in which Cicero confirmed his support for the cause of his friend, who had advocated his return from exile a few months earlier.[60] The impasse was solved by a divinatory interference, the political implications of which were vividly clear. At the beginning of 56 a thunderbolt struck the statue of Jupiter on the Alban Mount: Dio, who provides a full account of the event, says explicitly that the prodigy was a consequence of the wrath of the gods at the corruption created by Ptolemy's presence in Rome and the bribes that he had paid to a number of senators in order to prevent a senatorial hearing of the envoys of the people of Alexandria from taking place. The Senate prescribed the consultation of the Sibylline Books. The response that was singled out from the books was very specific and called for a change of policy: had the king of Egypt sought help from Rome, it would have been necessary to help him without gathering a large military force.[61] The circumstances that followed are

---

[58] Parke 1988: 140–1; Monaca 2005: 242; Dyck 2008: 179–80; Gildenhard 2011: 281–4.

[59] Cf. however the important qualification of Beard 1994: 741: forged (or allegedly forged) oracles appear wherever oracular divination is an important part of the religious system; they are not evidence of crisis or decline.

[60] Cic. *Fam.* 1.1–9. Steel 2001: 229–33.

[61] A full account of the affair in Dio 39.15–16; on the response see 39.15.2: Ἂν ὁ τῆς Αἰγύπτου βασιλεὺς βοηθείας τινὸς δεόμενος ἔλθῃ, τὴν μὲν φιλίαν οἱ μὴ ἀπαρνήσασθε, μὴ μέντοι καὶ πλήθει τινὶ

most extraordinary. The *quindecemuiri* were struck by the correspondence between the wording of the response and contemporary events, and they were persuaded by the tribune C. Porcius Cato not to take any further action. However, Cato decided to make it public, without waiting for the Senate's permission, which was normally necessary for divulging a Sibylline prophecy. According to Dio, Cato feared that an attempt would soon be made to conceal the response and neutralise its political implications. He therefore took the unprecedented step of compelling the priests to read out a Latin version of the oracle to the populace. Despite the opposition of some members of the college, the oracle was read out to an eager crowd. This breach of the established practice did not stop the eventual discussion of the oracle in the Senate, where different views were put forward on how to address the crisis.[62] Cicero took part in the debate, with a speech delivered in the session of 13 January, in which he supported the assignment of the command to Spinther.[63] Cato, however, put forward a proposal to revoke the command. The majority of the Senate opposed a command for Pompey. The final outcome was senatorial inaction. Even the proposal of Servilius Isauricus not to take any action was vetoed. When A. Gabinius, a year later, led a mission to Egypt and reinstated Ptolemy on the throne, he was prosecuted. Many argued that his conduct was sacrilegious as he had disregarded the response of the Sibylline Books; he was eventually convicted.[64]

The episode is of great importance for a number of reasons, some of which have been discussed in the introduction. It is an example of the increasing difficulty expressed by the Senate in playing a leading role in foreign policy; it is also a testimony to Cicero's limited influence on his peers. For our purposes, the political use of the Sibylline oracle is the most remarkable aspect. We do not just have a response that addresses a current political crisis very specifically and gives us a reminder of the political implications of divinatory material. There is also tribunician interference in the proceedings of one of the most important priestly colleges of the Republic: a tribune who happens to be a member of the quindecemviral college manages to stop its initiative and eventually compels his peers to breach their duty of secrecy and reveal the oracles to the populace before

ἐπικουρήσητε. Εἰ δὲ μή, καὶ πόνους καὶ κινδύνους ἕξετε ('If the king of Egypt shall come begging help, do not refuse him friendship, but also do not assist him with any multitude, or else you will have toils and dangers'). Parke 1988: 207–8; Wiseman 1994b: 391–3; Breglia Pulci Doria 1998: 285–7.
[62] Satterfield 2011: 117 notes that Cato does not appear to have been punished for this initiative.
[63] Cic. *Fam.* 1.2.1.
[64] Dio 39.61.4–63.5; Cic. *Rab. perd.* 8, 19, 33; Val. Max. 4.2.4. See Wiseman 1994b: 399–402.

divulging them to the Senate. The extraordinary nature of the event is completed by the translation of the response into Latin – an act that puts the prophecy fully into the public domain. Cato was a member of the college of the *quindecemuiri* and he exploited his position to interfere with, and ultimately reshape, the political process.[65] Dio's narrative also conveys a picture of coercion, which no doubt has a basis of truth: Cato spurs the interest of the crowd in the responses and exploits the pressure that the populace was exerting on the members of the college to make the response public.

After 83 the composition of the Books and the authenticity of the material that they contained were controversial issues. The final stages of Caesar's dictatorship were marked by the debate concerning the supposed Sibylline prophecy which stated that the Parthians would be defeated only by a king; the *quindecemuir* L. Aurelius Cotta used it to justify his proposal to bestow royal status upon Caesar.[66] According to Cicero, writing a few months after the event, the prophecy was recently (*nuper*) denounced as a forgery; this must have occurred after Caesar's death, which according to Suetonius was hastened by this incident.[67] The event is a powerful illustration of late Republican developments in the handling of public religion. Even the prestigious priestly college of the *quindecemuiri* was not immune from the control of the new strongman, and its proceedings were heavily shaped by his agenda. A member of the priestly college that was in charge of the Books produced a false interpretation, which was intended to be presented to the Senate and discussed in the open; Caesar's death pre-empted it. It is unclear what the role of the other members of the priestly college was in the promotion of this interpretation, which was both prophetic and prescriptive: as Cicero says, calling the new king 'a king' was necessary if the state was to be saved.[68] It seems likely, on the basis of Cicero's evidence, that Cotta did not present a forgery, but put forward a self-serving interpretation of a passage that was actually included in the Books. Suetonius makes clear that the response was produced by the whole quindecemviral college and suggests that it included a specific proposal to give Caesar royal status; Plutarch and Dio do not refer to this official context, but say that the response of the Books was widely spread among the populace by Caesar's agents; Dio also includes some discussion

[65] He apparently joined the college in 65 or 64, before holding the quaestorship: Plut. *Cat. Min.* 4.1, with Rüpke 2005a: 1230, no. 2808.
[66] Cic. *Div.* 2.110; Suet. *Iul.* 79.4; Plut. *Caes.* 60.2; Dio 44.15.3. Cf. Plin. *HN* 17.243. Pelling 2011: 446–7.
[67] Suet. *Iul.* 80.1.   [68] Cic. *Div.* 2.110: *si salui esse uellemus.*

on the possible role of the episode in prompting the decision of Brutus and Cassius to carry out the conspiracy. After Caesar's death the interpretation was deemed invalid and dismissed as one of the aspects of Caesar's *adfectatio regni*. However, the exploitation of the Books for partisan purposes was a trend that, in the disrupted climate of the last years of the Republic, could not be easily stopped.

CHAPTER 7

Wild prophecies

The overview that has been outlined in the last three chapters shows that in the last two centuries of the Republic divination was practised and produced by a wide range of experts, both in public and in private contexts. Cato's admonition that the *uilicus* should not consult the haruspex, the *hariolus* and the Chaldean seer is a clear illustration that there was a variety of sources of prediction available to a private citizen in the second century BC. It is also evidence that there were concerns relating to access to divination: Cato's emphasis is not on the unreliability of the diviners that he mentions, but on the importance of making sure that a mere *uilicus* did not have unrestricted access to them.[1] No doubt Scipio Aemilianus was driven by similar concerns when a few decades later, in 134, he took care to expel all the diviners from the Roman camp at Numantia as soon as he took over the command. According to Appian, the soldiers consulted the diviners because they were demoralised by the lack of success in the campaign and the responses were clearly seen as destabilising factors. Containing the use of these private, unsanctioned sources of sooth was especially important during a military crisis. No chances were taken: Aemilianus even prohibited bringing into the camp animals that were to be sacrificed for divinatory purposes.[2]

---

[1] Cato *Agr.* 7.4: [*uilicus*] *haruspicem, augurem, hariolum, Chaldaeum nequem consuluisse uelit* ('Let him [the overseer of the estate] not consult any haruspex, augur, seer, or Chaldaean [astrologer]'). Pavis d'Escurac 1981: 31; North 1990: 58–60. For 'wild prophecies' cf. Gildenhard 2011: 282.

[2] App. *Hisp.* 85.367: it is instructive to see that, along with μάντεις and θύται, Aemilianus expelled traders (ἔμποροι) and prostitutes (ἑταῖραι). Fromentin 1996: 87 notes that the juxtaposition of μάντεις and θύται is not easy to interpret in this context (cf. her literal translation: 'les devins et sacrificateurs') and that establishing the provenance of the diviners is impossible. Cf. Plut. *Mor.* 201b, who also mentions μάντεις, θύται and πορνοβοσκοί (brothel-keepers); cf. also the *sacrificuli* and *uates* in Livy 25.1.8, 35.48.13, 39.8.3–4, 39.16.8. A prophecy foretelling Scipio's rise to power was apparently produced at the sanctuary of Clunia around that time: Suet. *Galb.* 9.2, with Hillard 2005.

Harioli and *uates* between awe and mockery

The role of these competing constituencies of prophets was discussed and debated as early as the beginning of the second century BC. Plautus uses the word *diuinare*, and he also employs other words that refer to divinatory activities: he once refers to someone who seems able to predict the future as a *bonus uates* (*Mil.* 911) and he refers even more frequently to the actions of the *hariolus*.[3] In Plautus' work there are several occurrences of the nouns *hariolus* or *hariola*, referring to people who are able to make predictions; more strikingly, there are several occurrences of the verb *hariolari*, which can have the same meaning as *diuinare*, but may also mean 'to talk nonsense'. When it has a positive connotation, it is usually associated with self-evident prophecies that require little or no divinatory skills.[4] A passage of the *Rudens* is especially instructive on what *harioli* and *hariolae* may be expected to do. Young Palaestra bets that she will be able to guess the contents of a basket that was discovered at sea; the fisher Gripus doubts that this is possible and wonders if Palaestra has divinatory abilities (*superstitiosa aut hariolast, atque omnia quidquid insit uera dicet? an<u>e</u>habebit hariola?*).[5] *Superstitiosa* and *hariola* are used as synonyms in this context; there is no clear difference in meaning. *Miles* 692–4 lists a striking series of elusive female figures who are involved in divinatory practices: *da quod dem quinquatribus / praecantrici, coniectrici, hariolae atque haruspicae; / flagitiumst, si nil mittetur quae supercilio spicit.*[6] The list has a clear humorous purpose, like many other lists in Plautus; the joke here seems to be both on women and on diviners. The comic effect is created by the juxtaposition of categories that really existed in Roman society – the *praecantrix*, the *hariola*, possibly the *coniectrix* – with a non-existing figure, the *haruspica*.[7] Despite the comic

---

[3] *Hariolus* in Latin literature: Montero 1993a: 115–17.

[4] Slater 2000: 346. See Plaut. *Mostell.* 569–71; *Cas.* 356. References to divination in Plautus: Hoffmann 1985/8; Cuny-Le Callet 2005a: 82–93 (often confusing mockery with criticism of divination). Religion in Plautus: Dunsch 2009; Slater 2011.

[5] Plaut. *Rud.* 1139–40: 'is she a prophetess or a diviner, and names everything in there rightly? Is a diviner going to get it?'); Daemones replies that prophecy will not help her in that situation (*nequiquam hariolabitur*). Slater 2000: 357 sees a trace of worries about supernatural knowledge in this passage; cf. 344 on the significance of this play for the exploration of religious issues, and especially of the problem of 'divine justice'.

[6] Plaut. *Mil.* 972–4: 'give me some money to give to the sorceress at the *Quinquatrus* [a festival in honour of Minerva], to the dream interpreter, the seer, and the haruspex lady; and it's a shame if I don't hand anything to the woman who observes omens from your eyebrow'. The latter kind of diviner, also known as *metoposcopus/metoposcopa*, practised a form of physiognomy: Montero 1993c. On this list see Hoffmann 1985/8: 370–1.

[7] Montero 1994a: 50; Traill 2004. Association between women and *superstitio*: Gordon 2008: 87–9. *Coniectrix* is a hapax, but *coniector* is well attested, and probably its feminine would not have sounded

intention of the passage, two implications are clear: women could act as religious experts and in a divinatory capacity, and they could be paid for their services. A passage of Terence's *Phormio* has a brief summary of how a prodigy could be handled in a private context: a *hariolus* and a haruspex are summoned to interpret it and they give (independently, it seems) the same response.[8]

It is not entirely clear who a *hariolus* might be. With some degree of approximation, we could regard the word as a definition that applies to any diviner who is not a haruspex.[9] The fragments of Ennius' plays seem to include some scathing references to divinatory activity. The best-known one is probably the fragment of the *Telamon*, quoted by Cicero in the *De diuinatione*, which attacks *superstitiosi uates inpudentesque harioli*: they are either useless, or crazy, or driven by the need to fight poverty; they have no wisdom themselves, but claim to be able to show the way to others; they promise wealth, but they are always ready to ask for money from those to whom they give advice.[10] The polemic against diviners often features in Greek epic and tragedy and it is likely that Ennius found it in his source or model. However, the choice to echo it in his Latin version deserves attention in its own right.

Establishing the difference between *uates* and *harioli* in this context is far from straightforward. Interestingly, Ennius seems to note an important difference between the two groups: the *uates* are *superstitiosi* (and therefore in good faith, if misguided), while the *harioli* are shameless. But the impression that a set rule may apply would be incorrect. Another tragic fragment of Ennius features the interesting noun *hariolatio* – nearly a hapax, which reappears only in the quotation of this passage in the *De diuinatione* and in Gellius. The term defines the divinatory exercise of the *hariolus* and indeed his response and – at least in Gellius – it can be used in a neutral sense. Ennius used it in a passage of the *Alexander* quoted by Cicero, in which Hecuba asks Cassandra the reason for the frenzy she has fallen into and the seer explains how shameful it is for her to be falling prey

---

odd (*contra* Traill 2004: 123). The *praecantrix* is a woman who performs magical practices, sometimes in alternative to medical treatment: Varro, *Catus uel de liberis educandis* (F 15 Riese, *ap.* Nonius p. 494); cf. Varro *Sat. Men.* 152 and Ov. *Fast.* 2.572.

[8] Ter. *Phorm.* 705–10. Cuny-Le Callet 2005a: 84–5 sees evidence of 'critical distance' towards prodigies in this passage.

[9] Slater 2000: 359–61 convincingly argues that Plautus tends to portray haruspices rather favourably, which is not the case with the *harioli*.

[10] Enn. *Tr.* F CXXXIV (b) Jocelyn (= Cic. *Div.* 1.132); Jocelyn 1967: 399. Cf. Ross 1969: 355: 'clearly ... uttered with a sneer'; similarly Calderone 1972: 389; Nice 2001: 164–5; Wardle 2006: 424–5; Bettini 2008: 362. *Contra*, Grilli 1996: '[i] vati scrupolosi e gl'indovini impudenti'.

to *superstitiosae hariolationes*. In this context *superstitiosae* means 'prophet-ically inspired', and we are in a divinatory context.[11] A fragment of the *Iphigenia* refers to the practice of astrology in terms that appear to be crit-ical, and which Cicero quotes in the *De re publica* within a discussion of the tension between contemplative and practical lives: *astrologorum signa in caelo quid sit obseruationis? / cum Capra aut Nepa aut exoritur nomen aliquod beluarum, / quod est ante pedes nemo spectat, caeli scrutantur plagas* ('Why must astrologers look for signs in the sky? When the Goat or the Scorpion or some other animal's name rises, no one looks at what is before his feet: they look at the quarters of the sky').[12]

It is difficult to make much of these fragmentary texts. There are signifi-cant problems concerning their tradition, which further complicate the usual difficulties of using literary texts to discuss a historical problem. If anything, however, they confirm that discussing and criticising misguided forms of divination was deemed a viable pursuit in literary contexts. Plau-tus' references to *diuinare* and *hariolari* show that it was acceptable, or at least conceivable, to use these very serious concepts ironically; Ennius' references to the risk of divination degenerating into a misleading prac-tice show his awareness of how complex this activity was. They should be viewed against the wider background of Ennius' work, which included the *Euhemerus*, possibly the first work of prose ever written in Latin, with an agenda that introduced elements of religious critique. An isolated scathing reference to the *uates* and the *harioli* is just part of a bigger picture, the details of which are elusive. A passage quoted (amongst others) by Cicero in the *De diuinatione* may be evidence, for example, that Ennius was already engaging with the concept of the *uates* as poet-prophet: a brief reference to Naevius' poem on the First Punic War said that others had written about that topic 'with the verses which of old the Fauns and prophets chanted'.[13]

The passage is usually discussed because of the literary polemic it sheds light upon, but it is also significant for what it reveals about the role of prophecy in the archaic period, as some of the ancient authors that quoted it knew well.[14] Its interpretation was problematic even in antiquity, though. Varro thought that in this passage *uates* meant 'poet', while Cicero understood it as 'seer'.[15] The two meanings appear to be reconciled in

---

[11] Enn. *Tr.* F XVII (c) Jocelyn (= Cic. *Div.* 1.66).

[12] Enn. *Tr.* F XCV (a) Jocelyn (= Cic. *Rep.* 1.30.3). Jocelyn 1967: 324–7; Zetzel 1995: 121; Nice 2001: 165.

[13] Enn. *Ann.* 206–7 Sk.: *scripsere alii rem / uorsibus quos olim Faunei uatesque canebant*. According to Gildenhard 2007c: 88, 'this is our earliest evidence for a positive conception of *uates* as poet'.

[14] Skutsch 1985: 371–2; Wiseman 2006: esp. 516–20 (= 2008: 41–4).

[15] Varro *Ling.* 7.36 and Cic. *Div.* 1.114, with Skutsch 1985: 372 and Gildenhard 2007c: 87–8. Cf. also Enn. *Ann.* 374 Sk.: *satin uates uerant aetate in agunda* ('Do prophets in the course of their lives speak

the aetiology provided in the *Origo gentis Romanae*, where the Fauni are said to have been the inventors of the Saturnian meter.[16] Whatever the best interpretation may be, this passage and the ancient debate about it are further confirmation of the centrality of divination and prophecy in Roman intellectual debate. The link between poetry and prophecy was probably understood from the mid third century BC. The word *uates* provided the framework to convey the semantic complexity conjured up by the overlap of these two areas of the myth. Ennius' reference to the Fauni was significant for at least two reasons. First, they were divinities 'of the wild', who nonetheless enjoyed a close relationship with mankind and had a liminal status with civilisation; moreover, the etymology of their name was widely linked to *fari*, an archaic word that has a prominent place in Latin literature, is often related to the sphere of prophecy, and is connected to a semantic field of very loaded terms, such as *fama, facundus* and *fabula*.[17] As Wiseman rightly notes, this passage is a powerful pointer to the importance of oral prophecy in Rome, in Ennius' day and beyond.[18]

This passage of Ennius was at the centre of the ancient debate on the etymology of *uates*. Even if all the early occurrences of the word seem to have the meaning of 'prophet, diviner', Varro argued that the ancient meaning of the word was that of 'poet' and that *uates* derived *a uersibus uiendis*, 'from weaving verses'; he also implies that this was the meaning of the word in the passage of Ennius that mentions the verses of the Fauni.[19] Varro offered a fuller explanation of this theory in the *De poematis*, which has not survived. It is probably in that lost text that Varro put forward another etymology, which we know through Servius Auctus: *uates a ui mentis appellatos*.[20] This etymology emphasises the intimate nature of the knowledge controlled and practised by the *uates*: it is a form of inspiration which makes the *uates* so extraordinary. It is in this light that the affinity between divination and poetry becomes apparent. Servius focuses on the

---

the truth enough?') on which Skutsch 1985: 540 ('clearly disparaging in sense'); *contra*, Grilli 1996: 229–30.

[16] *Origo* 4.3–5.   [17] *Fari*: Bettini 2008.

[18] Wiseman 2006: 520–6 (= 2008: 44–8). For a less optimistic assessment of the importance of orality in Republican culture cf. Horsfall 2003: 96.

[19] Enn. *Ann.* 206–7 Sk. = Varro *Ling.* 7.36. Guittard 1985: 34–41, 48–54; Pasco-Pranger 2002: 306–10; Gildenhard 2007c: 87–9. Dahlmann 1948: 337–46 and 1963: 18 argued that Varro misunderstood Ennius and confused the Roman *uates* with the Greek ῥαψῳδός; *contra* cf. Bickel 1951: 257–65. Cf. the reading of divination as a movement 'from a boundless to a bounded realm of existence' in Tedlock 2010: 21.

[20] Serv. *auct. ad Aen.* 3.443; see also Isid. *Etym.* 8.7.3. On this etymology and its possible echoes in post-Virgilian poetry see Korenjak 1999. There may be an allusion in Verg. *G.* 4.450–2 (O'Hara 1996: 288).

word *uates* when he comments on *Aen.* 3.343 (*insanam uatem*) and states
that there are two kinds of divinatory efforts, the simple one, practised
by Helenus, and the one which happens 'through a frenzy' (*per furorem*),
like that of the Sibyl as depicted by Virgil. Both the diviner and the poet
have access to a specific form of inspiration, which makes the analogy
between their crafts meaningful and confers some authority upon them,
precisely because it puts them in a domain that most people do not have
access to. However, the craft of the diviner and the poet is also based on
the ability to harmonise different elements and bring them to the service
of a broader narrative by using a specific and specialised technique. The
two etymologies offered by Varro may be read as a pointer to the tension
between inspiration and artistry that is typical of the construction of the
uates in the Augustan authors.[21]

Ennius had already achieved a sophisticated encounter between tradition
and innovation. An appreciation of orality was compatible with a serious
effort to provide a comprehensive account of Roman history and an organisation of time based on a framework that is directly related to the written
form of the calendar. This is, briefly put, the agenda that lies at the core of
the project of the *Annales*, a project that was not conceived and carried out
in isolation.[22] As he emphatically admitted, Ennius – a man from Rudiae in
Messapia who had earned a prominent position in Rome – was at the crossroads of different cultural and intellectual traditions.[23] The influence of
Greek elements was certainly important, but it was not by any means
the only factor.[24] Engagement with foreign cults is central in the development of Roman religion, and its interaction with Greek practices and
models dates back to long before the age of Ennius.[25] I. Gildenhard has
pointed out that the sense of 'cultural heterogeneity' in the *Annales* is
clearest in the handling of religion.[26]

Ennius' project was also influential in some sectors of the Roman elite.
Although generalisations on the nature of Ennius' 'circle' of influential

---

[21] Pasco-Pranger 2000: 278–9. Gildenhard 2007c: 88 notes that the Augustan poets were fully confident
about their literary sophistication and had no hesitation in likening themselves to the *uates* as
'primitive poet'; Ennius was not, and felt the need to call himself a *poeta*.

[22] On religion in the *Annales* see Gildenhard 2007c: 82–4.

[23] Gell. *NA* 17.17.1: *Quintus Ennius tria corda habere sese dicebat, quod loqui Graece et Osce et Latine
sciret* ('Q. Ennius used to say that he had three hearts, because he could speak Greek, Oscan and
Latin'), with Adams 2003: 116–17; and cf. the *elogium* quoted in Cic. *Tusc.* 1.34, which was attached
to a bust or statue on public display (Morelli 2000: 41–2; Gildenhard 2007c: 76–7).

[24] Cf. the appearance of the word *sophia* along with *sapientia* in Enn. *Ann.* 211–12 Sk. (*nec quisquam
sophiam sapientia quae perhibetur / in somnis uidit prius quam sam discere coepit*, 'nor has anyone had
dreams of *sophia*, which is called *sapientia*, before he has begun to study it'), on which Habinek
2006.

[25] Feeney 1998: 2–8.   [26] Gildenhard 2007c: 82.

friends should be avoided, the connection between the *Annales* and the setting up of the Fasti of M. Fulvius Nobilior in the temple of Hercules Musarum is as clearly demonstrable as it is significant.[27] A new interest in time, its construction and its control, was emerging in Rome as the Mediterranean empire was taking shape; the political influence of prominent *euergetai* like M. Fulvius Nobilior, the rethinking of the function of sacred spaces, and the engagement with wider intellectual developments could be the catalyst for innovative outcomes. Poetry had a role to play in this context, and the critical reflection on prediction and prophecy that it provided was part of a process in which sectors of Roman society tried to appropriate for themselves new intellectual tools.

When Cato the Censor advised his son Marcus on the importance of distrusting the Greeks, and especially Greek medicine, he urged him to believe his words as if they came from a seer (*et hoc puta uatem dixisse*); the implication was that there was not a more authoritative source of advice.[28] However, evidence for polemic against, or at least sarcasm about, divination may be found in Latin literature well before Cicero's *De diuinatione*, and it should not surprise: as R. Parker pointed out, 'anthropology teaches that societies which depend on seers also regularly deride them'.[29] The context of those references, however, is hardly ever more informative than that of the passages of Ennius mentioned above or of Cato's brief throwaway remark in which he marvelled that a haruspex did not laugh when he saw another haruspex.[30] In Plautus' *Pseudolus* the protagonist eludes the questions of his master by pretending to be possessed by a god, and starts to speak in Greek, like a Sibyl: the adoption of a divinatory code conceals

---

[27] On Ennius and Nobilior cf. Chapter 6. Nobilior's project: Badian 1972: 183–95; Aberson 1994: 199–216; Gildenhard 2003: 94–7, 109–11 and 2007c: 84–6; Sciarrino 2004; Rüpke 2006, 2011a: 87–108 and 2012: 152–71, 249–52; Sehlmeyer 2009: 58–60.

[28] Plin. *HN* 39.14. See Cugusi and Sblendorio Cugusi 2001: 1.78–9, n. 377; Schiesaro 2007: 69; Sciarrino 2011: 4–5, 158–9.

[29] Parker 2012: 470; see also Parker 1985: 302. Cf. Bremmer 1993: 157–8; M. Flower 2008: 144–7. See also Liebeschuetz 1995: 315: 'In a society in which divination played as prominent a part in politics as it did in the politics of Rome, politicians must always have had at their disposal an armoury of sceptical arguments to discredit the divine signals claimed to have been received by opponents. The discrediting of inconvenient prodigies is likely to have been a routine activity of the Senate... It is likely that sophisticated scepticism with regard to purported divine signs was an integral part of Roman *mos maiorum*, at least as understood by the political elite.'

[30] Cic. *Div.* 2.24; see also *Nat. D.* 1.71. Burkert 2005: 45 reads the smiling not as a 'failure of belief', but as a sign of embarrassment towards anachronistic traditions ('I could not suppress smiling the one time I had to wear a dinner jacket'); cf. Fine 2007: 199 on the 'joking culture' of contemporary weather forecasters. See also the fragment of Varro's Menippean satire *Serranus* (F 451 Bücheler): *ait consulem mihi +pelum+ cedere. subsilio et hostias et extispices disputantis relinquo* ('He says that the consul gives me . . . [*crux*] I spring up and leave behind the sacrificial victims and the entrail-readers who are discussing among themselves'). It might refer to the preliminary of an election (Krenkel 2002: 839–41) or to a haruspical consultation ordered by the Senate (Cèbe 1996: 1836–8); it certainly should not be read as evidence for Varro's scepticism on extispicy, as in Blecher 1905: 41.

deception.[31] There are other sparse instances. L. Pomponius, the author of *fabulae Atellanae* who flourished in 89, wrote a comic play entitled *Aruspex uel pexor rusticus* – 'the haruspex, or country barber'.[32] The loss of this work is made all the more regrettable by the fact that he was from Bononia, a city that had a strong Etruscan background; his viewpoint on haruspicy and its practice may well have been an informed one. A play of the mimographer Decimus Laberius (*c.* 106–43), was entitled *Augur*: we have only one fragment of it, which intriguingly refers to the gain of a large sum of money.[33] Even the word *fatum* could become the object of intelligent wordplay. In the late third century BC the poet Naevius saluted the election of one of the Metelli (probably Q. Caecilius Metellus, *cos.* 206) with the line *fato Metelli Romae fiunt consules. Fato* could be understood in two ways: as a dative ('to Rome's misfortune the Metelli become consuls') or as an ablative ('by the workings of Fate the Metelli become consuls').[34]

A fragment of Accius' *Astyanax* has a tone very similar to that of Ennius' reference to the *harioli* who exploit credulity to enrich themselves: *nil credo auguribus, qui auris uerbis diuitant / alienas, suas ut auro locupletent domos* (264–5 Dangel: 'I do not believe augurs, who fill other people's ears with words, so that they can enrich their own homes with gold').[35] Another fragment of the *Astyanax* is an invitation to Calchas to change his prophecy and to lift his prohibition against the Greek army's fighting. The wording is strong: *nunc, Calcas, finem religionum fac: [ac] desiste exercitum / morari meque ab domuitione arce ex tuo obsceno omine* (281–2 D.: 'refrain from holding up the army and preventing me from returning home with your disgraceful prophecy').[36] Again, caution is in order, especially because the engagement with divination could take far less direct and less confrontational forms in Accius' writings. In a fragment of Accius' *Brutus* some

---

[31] Plaut. *Pseud.* 481–4. Fontaine 2010: 130–2 argues that there is a pun in Pseudolus' answer: *nai gar* ('yes indeed') sounds almost like *negare* ('to deny'); Goldberg 2011: 216 seems sceptical.

[32] Nonius 830 L = F 12 Frassinetti. It is not clear whether the haruspex and the barber are actually the same character (Frassinetti 1953: 138). On Pomponius see Frassinetti 1953: 95–120 and 1967: 8–11; Manuwald 2011: 267–70.

[33] Charisius 265.18 = F 7 Panayotakis: *largiter . . . feci lucri* ('I made a large amount of profit'); useful commentary at Panayotakis 2010: 135–8. Blecher 1905: 41 argues that Laberius' play *Tusca* (fr. 62 Panayotakis) mocked haruspicy; Panayotakis 2010: 383–5 rightly argues that the focus was probably on the reputation of Etruscan women for luxuriousness.

[34] Ps.-Asc. *Verr.* 1.10.29 (= 215.16–23 Stangl). Goldberg 1995: 33–5.

[35] Rüpke 2002: 264–5; 2012b: 484. Dangel 1995: 319 plausibly argues that these lines were pronounced by Agamemnon or Hecuba rejecting Calchas' prophecy that Astyanax must die if the Greeks are to return home; their opposition is doomed to fail.

[36] Rüpke 2002: 265; 2012b: 484. According to Dangel 1995: 319–20 this is merely a 'thème d'école'; it must also be noted that the lines are probably spoken by Agamemnon, who rejects Calchas' correct prophecy of his imminent death.

coniectores are called in to offer an interpretation of a dream of Tarquinius Superbus.[37] On the one hand, the episode may be read as a confirmation of the divinatory powers of dreams and for this reason the whole passage was probably included by Cicero in the first book of *De diuinatione*; on the other hand, the response of the interpreters is introduced by a general principle that set some limits. Dreams can be made of the things that happen to people when they are awake, or that they happen to think about, but some extraordinary dreams, like the one that Tarquinius had, must be explained otherwise. This is in itself an important consideration, which both limits and specifies the role of the supernatural in the making of dreams. Moreover, the interpretation of the dream is based on the use of a different technique: in the dream, the trajectory of the sun goes from right to left and that detail may be interpreted as evidence for positive developments for the State. One form of divination shows the way to another kind of divination: the divinatory context is confirmed by the use of terms that have a clear relevance to divination, such as *ostentum*, *signum* and *augurium*.[38]

Other fragments of Accius show a similar interest in divination and emphasise the necessity to provide competent predictions.[39] The verb *augurare* features in two fragments, respectively from the *Oenomaeus* and the *Amphitruo*, with the meaning of 'to conjecture': the latter reads *si satis recte aut uera ratione augurem* (643 D.), perhaps implying that augural exercises can sometimes be misguided and unhelpful.[40] In another fragment, from the *Telephus*, a character declares allegiance to cleromancy, oracles, augury and other forms of divination (91 D.: *pro certo arbitrabor sortis, oracula, adytus, auguria* – 'I will hold for certain lots, oracles, temples, prophecies').[41] It is quite clear that Accius repeatedly explored the realm of divination and, more generally, the prediction of the future. While his overall line of approach to the problem escapes us, it is clear that he did have something to say about the limits of divination and about how it should be practised. Not all forms of divination are helpful, or acceptable; on the other hand, when divination is based on a sound knowledge and expertise, it can be a

---

[37] Cic. *Div.* 1.44–5 (= 651–72 Dangel). On this episode see Guittard 1986a; Rüpke 2002: 265–8; Wardle 2006: 218–22. The word *coniectores* is used by Cicero, but does not feature in the text quoted from Accius (1.45: *eius igitur somnii a coniectoribus quae sit interpretatio facta uideamus*, 'so let us see what interpretation of that dream was given by the diviners'). On *coniectores* see Chapter 3.

[38] Rüpke 2002: 267–8; 2012b: 481–3. See also Guittard 1986a: 57; Crampon 2002: 114–18; Harris 2003: 26 (cf. Harris 2009: 178).

[39] Rüpke 2012a: 51–61; 2012b: 481–5 on Accius' reflection on religion.

[40] Note the use of the verb *auguro* – 'If I were to conjecture well enough or with true reasoning'. See also 5 D.

[41] Dangel 1995: 287 argues that this fragment derives from Sophocles.

fruitful method to read the future and to control it. The agenda of Quintus in *Div.* 1 was not very different.

The most famous piece of literary polemic in Latin against divination (with the obvious exception of *Div.* 2) is probably the attack against the *uates* in the first book of Lucretius' *De rerum natura*. Before we read it in more detail, though, it must be established who the *uates* could have been in that context. As we have seen above, the difference between *harioli* and *uates* is often hard to define in clear terms. In fact, the extant evidence does not convey any idea of what a *hariolus* actually did: it has been suggested that the *harioli* were diviners who operated in private contexts, in spite of and even against the Senate's control of religious affairs, and in open competition with the haruspices. It is remarkable, though, that the *harioli* almost disappear from the literary evidence from the late first century BC onwards.[42] This dearth of attestations is all the more striking if we think of the number of occurrences in second-century BC authors. It can hardly be fortuitous; its most economic explanation is that the form of divinatory expertise offered by the *harioli* declined at the end of the first century BC and was accompanied by the rise of other sources of prophecies.

Lucretius, whom we will discuss at the end of this chapter, was no isolated case. Poets were reflecting upon religious problems as early as in the second century BC and divination was inevitably part of their inquiry. The evidence of poetry is important for at least two reasons. First of all, it is a symptom of changing attitudes towards religion, which are an essential part of the background of this research and its central working hypothesis. If there was a change in the perception and understanding of divination in Roman culture over the last two centuries of the Republic, poetry is likely to be one of the contexts where the symptoms of this change may be found. The evidence is sparse, but nonetheless instructive. This leads to a second factor that makes this evidence so important. The views on religious problems that poets and playwrights put forward in their work are a powerful sign of the diversity and complexity of the approaches that were put forward and debated within Roman society. It would be reductive to view the references to divination in poetry as a mere reflection of what some sectors of the elite thought about it and therefore to exclude them from a historical discussion. Roman religious life cannot be regarded as a monolith or as a political construction dominated by manipulative elites, where no room was left for alternatives or variants to the dominant discourse.

---

[42] Phaedr. 3.3.1, 5; Gell. *NA* 3.3.15, 18.6.5; Apul. *Apol.* 41.3; Apul. *De deo Soc.* 7, 17, 18, 20. Cf. Montero 1993a on their reappearance in late antique sources.

The observation and preservation of the *sacra* was undoubtedly essential to the coherence and welfare of public life. At the same time, however, there was plenty of room for diversity, creativity and experimentation. The complexity of Roman religious life cannot be reduced to the public dimension; nor can it be postulated that the same set of views was held and debated among individual members of the Roman elite. Some of the best recent work on Roman Republican religion has been devoted to exploring the features of such diversity. Such a picture of liveliness and even conflict is not limited to the problem of the interaction between elite and non-elite perception; it applies to several different approaches within the elite itself.

The occurrences of the word *uates* in Republican literature conjure up a very complex picture. As is well known, the term has a striking semantic complexity, because it can be understood both as 'poet' and as 'diviner'.[43] The latter meaning prevails in the early attestations of the term, although confusion or overlaps are sometimes inevitable. They are reflected in the ancient debate on the etymology of the word, which we discussed above. There is a further important affinity between the *uates* who divine and the *uates* who compose poetry: they all sing *carmina*, which are usually performed in public and may be collected into books. The *uates* that feature in the mythical tradition share these attributes. The goddess Carmenta is an impressive case, recently studied by T. Habinek.[44] The mother of Evander, who accompanies his son on the way from Arcadia to Italy and guides him in choosing a site for a new city along the Tiber, is celebrated in the *Aeneid* (8.340) and, much more diffusely, in the *Fasti* (1.461–636). She is labelled a *uates* and credited with prophetic skills. The etymology of her name was associated with *carmen* (song) already in antiquity. There is a strong connection between song, prophecy and sacrifice; the knowledge of the *uates* is a song that restores mankind to nature, and revives the connection between prophecy and body.[45]

The relationship between prophecy and song is discussed more directly in the *De diuinatione*. Quintus states that many predictions were produced by *uaticinantes*, either in prose or in verse; the quote from Ennius, *uersibus quos olim Fauni uatesque canebant*, proves useful (even if its meaning in the

---

[43] Habinek 2005: 229, 239 draws attention to another level of semantic complexity and potential ambiguity: *uates* does not have a gender connotation.

[44] Habinek 2005: 221–30. Tels-de Jong 1959: 21–66 remains valuable; see also Montero 1994a: 15–18, 34–5 and Guittard 2007a: 224–33.

[45] Habinek 2005: 229. On the 'embodied, sexuate and ecological dimension' of any divinatory act cf. Curry 2010b: 113–17. Cf. Bloch 1989: 37 ('*you cannot argue with a song*', emphasis original).

original context was not necessarily positive).[46] Immediately afterwards, the example of two Roman *uates*, Marcius and Publicius, who lived probably at the time of the Hannibalic War, is touched upon.[47] These two diviners used to 'sing' their prophecies, in a way that was not different from the utterances of Apollo's oracles, or indeed from the premonitory visions that visit people in their dreams: the *uates* can see whilst awake what others can see only in their sleep. Indeed, according to Quintus, 'natural divination' is a prerogative of two constituencies of people: those who dream and the *uates*.[48] One may infer that, under the generic label of *uates*, Quintus is including anyone who has some kind of divinatory ability. Again, Cicero's *usus scribendi* is not unfailingly consistent: in 2.9 Marcus refers to *uates aut hariolos* and in 2.13 to *aut haruspex aut augur aut uates quis aut somnians* – in both cases the reference is sarcastic, and indeed rather polemical. We should not expect Cicero to be more specific than other authors in the use of *uates* or other similar terms, but it would be reasonable to expect to find more in the *De diuinatione* about what *uates* did and in what contexts they operated. However, the dialogue has only a few references to the *uates* and none to the context in which they acted.

We can find more specific information in Livy.[49] The first two mentions of *uates* in book 1 feature the syntagm *cecinere uates* ('the prophets sang'). In 1.45, the response itself of the *uates* is called *carmen*.[50] This agrees with the stance taken by Cicero: *uates* can and usually do give their responses in verse. Such passing references to the *uates* can hardly be used for a reconstruction of the role of divination in early Rome; if they can tell us anything, it is something about divinatory practices in Livy's day. In this context, 1.55 is interesting: a prodigy that announces the future might of Rome, under the reign of Tarquinius Superbus, is interpreted favourably both by the *uates* who were in the city and by those who were called from Etruria to interpret the prodigy.[51] The haruspices, therefore, are also *uates* in this context; qualification occurs in the following chapter (1.56) with reference to their exclusive involvement with public prodigies. Other *uates* are involved with private prodigies, or are consulted by private individuals

---

[46] Cic. *Div.* 1.114: 'in verse which Fauns and seers once used to sing'. See Skutsch 1985: 371: 'the contemptuous note'; cf. Novara 1982: 100–1, 146–7.

[47] Cic. *Div.* 1.115. See Timpanaro 1988: XXXII–XXXIII, LV: a form of 'natural divination'. Russo 2005: 8–11 discusses the prosopographical problems surrounding the identity of the Marcii and convincingly argues that there is no evidence that a Publicius belonged to the *gens* Marcia.

[48] On the choice of the word *naturalis* to define inspired divination see Kany-Turpin 2003b: 63.

[49] *Uates* in Livy: Hano 1986: 108–14, 118–21.   [50] Hano 1986: 109.

[51] Livy 1.55.6: *idque ita cecinere uates, quique in urbe erant quosque ad eam rem consultandam ex Etruria acciuerant* ('and the diviners spoke on those lines, those who were in Rome and those that were specially brought in from Etruria for consultation').

on the interpretation of prodigies. When a series of portents occurs in the aftermath of the crisis caused by Spurius Cassius' agrarian bill, in Rome and in the surrounding territory, the *uates* are consulted in public and in private contexts (*publice priuatimque*): some of them specialised in the consultation of animals' entrails, others in the observation of the flight of birds.[52] Livy's emphasis is on the fact that, despite their different methods, the diviners all came to the same conclusion (namely that the gods were punishing the Romans for overlooking their religious duties); he uses the verb *canere* to refer to the whole range of their responses.

Livy also uses the word *uates* in a more general sense, even with reference to an outsider. The Veientine prisoner who is captured in 398 and advises the Romans on the interpretation of some prodigies is called a *uates*, whose advice is sought because the hostility between Rome and the Etruscans has caused a dearth of haruspices in the *Urbs*.[53] Elsewhere Livy uses the word *uates* when he wants to stress, or question, someone's ability to make predictions.[54] It is difficult and indeed unwise to make general statements on the presence of any theme or motif across Livy's work, given the extent of it that has survived. However, it is clear that diviners, and specifically *uates*, gain a special importance in the account of the Hannibalic War. The famous opening chapter of book 25 insists on the negative influence that *sacrificuli ac uates* had on the urban populace at a crucial phase of the war, in 213 (25.1.8):

> *sacrificuli ac uates ceperant hominum mentes quorum numerum auxit rustica plebs, ex incultis diutino bello infestisque agris egestate et metu in urbem compulsa; et quaestus ex alieno errore facilis, quem uelut concessae artis usu exercebant.*

> Dealers in sacrifices and diviners had seized people's minds and their number was increased by the rural populace, which had been pushed into the city by poverty and fear from fields that were dangerous or uncultivated because of the long war; and there was the prospect of easy gain from others' ignorance, a trade that they followed with the assumed confidence of established professionals.[55]

Livy is arguably referring to private diviners and self-proclaimed priests who were acting outside any form of public control. His judgement on

---

[52] Livy 2.42.10.

[53] Livy 5.15.4–15; cf. Dion. Hal. *Ant. Rom.* 12.11–14; Cic. *Div.* 1.100, 2.69; Plut. *Cam.* 4. Ruch 1966 (see esp. 366: it is striking to hear an inspired prophecy from a haruspex); Briquel 1993 and 1998; Guittard 1998: 57–9; Martínez-Pinna 2001: 99–102, 216–17. Montero 2007: 69–70 interestingly links this episode to the flood of the Tiber in 27: in both cases the haruspices gave a favourable interpretation of a flood, which was usually regarded as an unfavourable prodigy.

[54] Cf. the expression *falsus uates* in 4.46.4 and 21.10.10.

[55] Caerols 2006: 98–132. Cf. Scheid 2011: 412–13 on the role that emotions play in these events.

their practices is clearly scathing; he even implies that the success with which these figures met was due to the increasing presence of elements of the rural plebs that emigrated to Rome after the outbreak of the conflict. The expression *sacrificulus et uates* reappears in the description of the anonymous Greek prophet who emigrated to Etruria, practised divination for money during the day, and led mystery rituals at night; these eventually spread to Rome and became an important feature of the build-up to the crisis of the Bacchanalia in 186 (39.8.3–4):

> *Graecus ignobilis in Etruriam primum uenit nulla cum arte earum, quas multas ad animorum corporumque cultum nobis eruditissima omnium gens inuexit, sacrificulus et uates; nec is qui aperta religione, propalam et quaestum et disciplinam profitendo, animos errore imbueret, sed occultorum et nocturnorum antistes sacrorum.*[56]

> First a Greek of humble origins, who possessed none of the accomplish-ments that the Greek people, the most highly educated and civilised of all, introduced among us for the cultivation of mind and body, came to Etruria; he was a dealer in sacrifices and a diviner; and he did not infect people's mind with error by practising his rites openly and advertising his trade and his doctrine publicly, but he was the leader of secret rituals performed at night.

So strong a dislike of such *uates* is based on a clear understanding of the dangers that they pose to the stability of society and to the State itself; the point is made quite directly in the speech of the consul in which the repression of the Bacchanalia is outlined: the decision of previous consuls to expel *sacrificuli* and *uates* from the city and to burn their books is explicitly praised (39.16.8):

> *quotiens hoc patrum auorumque aetate negotium est magistratibus datum, uti sacra externa fieri uetarent, sacrificulos uatesque foro circo urbe prohiberent, uaticinos libros conquirerent comburerentque, omnem disciplinam sacrificandi praeterquam more Romano abolerent.*

> How often in the time of our fathers and grandfathers have the magistrates been given the task of forbidding the performance of foreign ceremonies, of excluding the dealers in sacrifices and diviners from the forum, the circus, the city, of searching out and burning prophetic books, and of abolishing every system of sacrifice except the traditional Roman method?[57]

---

[56] On the expression *sacrificuli ac uates* see Caerols 2006: 100–3; on its use in this context see Pailler 1988: 242.
[57] Hano 1986: 113–14, 119.

Livy has a clear preference for the *uates* who operate on behalf of the State, within the safe framework of public religion. However, this attitude does not necessarily entail hostility to all the *uates* who operate in a private capacity. The role that the prophecies of the *uates* Marcius played in 212, at a crucial juncture of the Hannibalic War, takes up an important part in Livy's narrative.[58] In 213 the Senate ordered the urban praetor to carry out an inspection of books containing divinatory and ritual texts (*libros uaticinos precationesue aut artem sacrificandi conscriptam*), which had been produced and used by the seers who were active in the city.[59] Even diviners who acted in a private capacity, therefore, could produce written material and use it for their own purposes. The material requisitioned was carefully scrutinised by the urban praetor M. Aemilius. Before leaving office, Aemilius singled out two texts written in verses by Marcius and handed them over to his successor P. Cornelius Sulla, since they had obvious relevance to the Hannibalic War.[60] The publication of these texts – usually referred to by modern scholars as *carmina Marciana* – caused an immediate surge of religious interest in Rome (*religio deinde noua obiecta est*): a very strong expression, which is meant to convey the sense of a new beginning, a fresh start in the religious life of the city, although not an entirely reassuring one. One *carmen* was viewed retrospectively as a premonition of the battle of Cannae: it contained a reference to an *amnis Canna* and when the prophecy was read in public those who had taken part in the battle recognised similarities between the site of the battle and the places mentioned in the *carmen*.[61] The second prophecy was more obscure, especially because of the style in which it was written.[62] It referred to the necessity of driving an enemy out of Roman territory and recommended that the praetors take up the task of organising a new festival in honour of Apollo, the *ludi Apollinares* which had to be organised with public and private funds. The creation of a new festival would have the direct effect of enabling Rome to defeat the enemy. Livy uses an interesting expression to describe the reaction of the Senate: 'they devoted a whole day to expiating that

---

[58] Livy 25.12. Gagé 1955: 201–2, 270–9; North 2000a: 92–4, 100–2; Russo 2005; Schultz 2006a: 30–3; Farney 2007: 116–18; Orlin 2010: 154–6; Satterfield 2011: 122–4. In general on the religious climate in this period see Gagé 1955: 546 and Develin 1978 (esp. 7: 'the religious fever of 213').

[59] Livy 25.1.6–12. See Caerols 2006: 98–132. Gagé 1955: 271–2 speaks of an 'enquête de police religieuse'; Parke 1988: 199 of 'a put-up job'.

[60] Livy 25.12.2–3. On the prosodic and metric structure of the *carmina* cf. Herrmann 1960, who argues that the length of the lines was determined by the number of the syllables and not by vocalic quantity, and Guittard 1985: 42–7, 54–5, who concludes that they follow neither the hexameter nor the *saturnium* and labels them as a 'pre-Ennian literary form of metrical prose' (47).

[61] Livy 25.12.4–8. Guittard 2007a: 275–87.   [62] Livy 25.12.9–10; see also Macrob. *Sat.* 1.17.25.

prophecy'.[63] The *carmen* is regarded as something that must be expiated, as an event that compels the State to adopt extraordinary measures: like a prodigy, it warns that the gods have a hostile attitude towards the city and that action is required. What happened next is reminiscent of the familiar pattern of action that follows the reporting of a prodigy. The Senate consults a body of experts – the *decemuiri* in this case – which is asked to look into the matter and recommends a set of ritual expiations. The Sibylline Books recommended the institution of the *ludi Apollinares*, which was later carried out by the praetor, in accordance with Marcius' *carmen*.[64]

Marcius' position in this section of Livy's work is strikingly different from that of the *uates* who are mentioned at other stages of the narrative. He is first referred to as a distinguished diviner (*uates inlustris*) – unlike the independent seers that we encountered in the earlier narrative, he deserves praise. His background is remarkable: the *gens* Marcia had a close mythical connection with King Numa, who supposedly appointed Numa Marcius to the supreme pontificate; the latter was also related to Ancus Marcius.[65] The connection with Numa was repeatedly asserted in the numismatic evidence and is echoed in the literary evidence. The other *carmina* no doubt derived further authoritativeness from the connection with the king who had initiated the great religious institutions of the city. The operation may have been made more feasible by the fact that the position of *rex sacrorum* in the 210s was held, almost certainly, by M. Marcius.[66] It has been argued that the Marcii were at the centre of a prophetic tradition which dated back to the early third century BC.[67]

Such a loaded partisan agenda did not stop the *carmina Marciana* from making a great impact in Rome, and (if we are to believe Livy) from reinvigorating religious fervour at a critical time in the Hannibalic War. Livy uses the word *religio*, and not by chance: the wave of interest in Marcius' *carmina* is not an uncontrolled movement that could have potentially destabilising consequences. The *carmina* are discovered, divulged and interpreted by the praetor and the Senate; at a later stage, the *decemuiri* become involved and the Sibylline Books are used to clarify, and at the same time to corroborate, the suggestion made by Marcius' prophecy. The prediction of the *uates*

---

[63] Livy 25.12.11: *ad id carmen expiandum diem unum sumpserunt* ('they took one day for rituals of expiation after this prophecy').

[64] Livy 25.12.12–16. Orlin 2010: 154–6.   [65] Evidence gathered and discussed in Russo 2005: 13–24.

[66] M. Marcius died in 210: Livy 27.6.16. Rüpke 2005a: 1135–6, no. 2368, and Russo 2005: 21 (with previous bibliography).

[67] Palmer 1970: 146–50, building – rather speculatively – on Cic. *Div.* 1.89; cf. Wiseman 1994a: 59, 62–3 and Wardle 2006: 320.

is carefully channelled through the political and religious institutions of the Republic. It is this complex set of filters and procedures that makes possible a meaningful contribution to *religio*. The creation of a new festival in honour of Apollo is the lasting contribution of the *carmina* to Roman public religion and is also the aspect of the prophecy that has the most immediate political implications, as Apollo was closely connected with the city of Tarentum, which had recently defected to Hannibal: the aim of the new festival, according to this reconstruction, would have been to regain the god Apollo to the cause of Rome despite the defection of Tarentum.[68] The *carmen* made clear that the festival had to be celebrated 'according to the Greek ritual' (*Graeco ritu*). This corroborates the hypothesis of a ritual modelled on that of Tarentum and it fits well with the involvement of the *decemuiri*: unsurprisingly, the Sibylline Books endorsed the use of the Greek ritual in the new festival.[69]

The events of 212 are part of a wider development that took place in the age of the Hannibalic War, when new religious practices were introduced in order to enable the city to re-establish her relationship with the gods at a time of crisis.[70] Prodigies played a central role in the emergence of these rituals; it is during the Hannibalic War that we witness a steady increase in the number of prodigy reports from outside the city of Rome.[71] The events of 207, of which Livy gives a detailed account, require close scrutiny.[72] A series of prodigies was reported from a number of communities across Italy: a rain of stones fell at Veii, and a *nouemdiale sacrum* was decreed in order to expiate the prodigy; however, more portents were reported from other communities, notably two from Minturnae and one from Capua. Their expiation was dealt with by the pontiffs, who performed a *supplicatio* of a whole day.[73] However, another rain of stones was reported at the Armilustrum on the Aventine, and a *nouemdiale* was decreed.[74]

According to Livy, this sufficed to put the people's minds to rest; however, their tranquillity was soon put to an end by a new prodigy from Frusino,

[68] Russo 2005: 27–32.
[69] On the *ludi saeculares* see Chapter 5. Sibylline Books and *Graecus ritus*: Scheid 1995: 26.
[70] Wardman 1982: 33–41 has a good discussion of the religious atmosphere in Rome during the Hannibalic War.
[71] Rosenberger 2005: 242–7 and 2007: 296–7.
[72] Livy 27.37. Boyce 1937; Breglia Pulci Doria 1983: 111–66; Champeaux 1996a; Rosenberger 1998: 185–96; Engels 2007: 470–6; Orlin 2010: 129–36.
[73] Livy 27.37.1–4. Orlin 2010: 78 stresses the link between showers of stones and consultation of the Books.
[74] No priestly intervention is recorded in this instance; this is one of the instances in which Livy is unspecific about the details of the expiation (e.g. Livy 25.7.9 and 27.11.6). Berthelet 2011 implausibly argues that Livy's silence should be viewed as evidence for pontifical involvement.

where a hermaphrodite had been born. On this occasion the haruspices were involved and they advised that the creature had to be thrown into the sea. Most interestingly, though, that intervention was accompanied by a parallel initiative of the pontiffs, who decreed that a new ritual must be celebrated, in which three groups of nine maidens each had to proceed through the city singing a hymn.[75] The poet Livius, certainly to be identified with Livius Andronicus, was the author of that text.[76] This episode is a splendid example of the level of creativity that Roman public religion was capable of attaining. The competition with the haruspices – a cohort of expert outsiders – led the pontiffs to devise a new response to this prodigy; it is also striking to see that the intervention of another outsider, the freedman Livius Andronicus, made the fulfilment of the pontiffs' advice possible.

The events following the decision of the pontiffs are even more remarkable. The expiatory ritual was cut short by a prodigy. As the choir of the maidens was rehearsing in the temple of Jupiter Stator, the temple of Juno Regina on the Aventine was hit by lightning; the prodigy was again referred to the haruspices, who argued that it was about the position of the matrons and that a gift had to be offered to the goddess in order to placate her wrath. Since the collection of public funds was needed, the aediles got involved and issued some rules: the favour of Juno was to be sought through a sacrifice and the donation of a golden basin paid for with the offerings of twenty-five matrons. When the process seemed to have reached a felicitous conclusion, another cohort of experts became involved: the *decemuiri* outlined their prescriptions on how to regain the favour of Juno.[77] It is hard to avoid the impression that a Roman priesthood (that is, a priesthood that could be held only by Roman citizens) openly competed with the haruspices and their ritual prescriptions. The earlier idea of the pontiffs to have twenty-seven maidens in the expiatory ritual was salvaged, as the maidens were required to lead a procession in honour of Juno, opened by two images of the goddess. Livy carefully records the itinerary of the procession, which went from the temple of Apollo through the Carmental Gate down to the Forum and eventually to the temple of Juno on the Aventine; more singing was involved when the girls reached the Forum, although it is unclear whether a poet was commissioned to write a new

---

[75] Livy 27.37.5–15.

[76] Livy 27.37.7. The tradition on the life and work of Livius Andronicus is complex and problematic, but Livy's evidence for the hymn of 207 is reliable (Gagé 1955: 229, 353–8; Suerbaum 2002: 96 n. 3c; Welsh 2011: 34–8; Manuwald 2011: 190). Suerbaum 2002: 96 offers a *status quaestionis* on Livius' involvement in 207; the hypothesis that he wrote the *carmen* for the *ludi saeculares* of 249 must be rejected (Suerbaum 2002: 84).

[77] On the role of the matrons in 207 see Schultz 2006a: 34–6, 165.

carmen for the occasion. We do know, however, that the decisive role of the *decemuiri* was openly in the order of the procession itself: they marched right behind the twenty-seven maidens, wearing their *togae praetextae* and sporting laurel on their heads, and they performed the sacrifice of two heifers just before the statues were deposited in the temple of Juno.[78]

This is an unusually detailed account of a complex set of events and rituals, which nonetheless overlooks some important aspects. Livy does not express any views on this peculiar juxtaposition of different ritual responses to the same prodigy, except for saying that the gods had been appropriately appeased.[79] Most importantly, he does not make any reference to the role that the Senate undoubtedly had in the events of 207, from the moment the first prodigy was reported: the decision as to which priestly college was to be entrusted with the *procuratio* of a prodigy fell within its remit. In some cases the choice will have been fairly uncontroversial: both rain showers were addressed with the same decision to call for a *nouemdiale sacrum* (nine days of ritual purification), which was made by the Senate.[80] Other decisions, however, must have been more problematic, especially because they were about the interpretation of prodigies that were reported shortly after a previous prodigy had been allegedly expiated. This is the case, for instance, of the birth of a hermaphrodite and of the lightning on the temple of Juno in the same year. The intervention of the haruspices was in both cases justified by the nature of the prodigy: the Etruscan priests dealt with the birth of hermaphrodites on other occasions and lightning uncontroversially fell within the remit of their *disciplina*.[81] It is certain that the involvement of the haruspices was decided by the Senate and took place in the customary official framework. However, on both occasions it was accompanied by the intervention of a senior Roman priestly college. Most importantly, on both occasions the pontiffs and the *decemuiri* recommended the performance of new rituals. The sources do not make it clear whether these were intended to be re-enacted in the future, although the involvement of the twenty-seven virgins on both occasions suggests that there was a link between the two episodes. The involvement of Livius Andronicus is remarkable too, not

---

[78] Gagé 1955: 357–9 speculates that the *decemuiri* were also involved in the preparation of the *carmen* and argues that Livius' patron, M. Livius Salinator (*cos.* 219 and 207), played an important role in the religious developments of 207 (although there is no evidence that he was a member of the college).

[79] Livy 27.38.1: *deis rite placatis.*   [80] Orlin 1997: 89–90.

[81] Hermaphrodites in Roman *Prodigienwesen*: MacBain 1982: 127–35; Breglia Pulci Doria 1983: 67–110; Allély 2003 (a list at 132–4); Monaca 2005: 141–50; Mangas Manjarrés 2007: 99–100; Brisson 2008: 26–39, 141–4. Legal aspects: Crifò 1999; Cantarella 2005: 6–7; Cuny-Le Callet 2005a: 96–102. Jacobs 2010 discusses the similarities in the handling of abnormal human births in Babylonian, Etruscan and Roman divination and argues for a direct transfer of doctrines from the Near East to Italy.

least because it provides an early example of the role that poets could have in public and religious contexts in Rome, according to a pattern that was widely attested in the Greek world. We can only speculate on the reasons that persuaded the pontiffs to choose him for that task.[82]

It may be excessive to define the events of 207 as a watershed in the history of Roman religion, because the fragmentary state of the evidence does not allow us to rule out the possibility of precedents. This cautionary remark could apply to most 'watersheds' in Roman history. The significance of what happened in 207, however, should not be underestimated. In the same year there were the concomitant interventions of two Roman priestly colleges, the haruspices and the *decemuiri*, on the interpretation and expiation of a number of prodigies, which were reported to Rome by a number of communities at a time of deep political tension. On two occasions divergent and competing advice was given by different cohorts of experts; whatever tensions may have lurked in the background, from Livy's account we learn that both strategies were put in place, and that on both occasions the 'Roman' response (that of the pontiffs or of the *decemuiri*) was given the last word, as it followed that of the haruspices. The final outcome was that the gods were pacified. The reader is left with a powerful demonstration of the ability of Roman public religion to accommodate diversity and to negotiate space and power for different actors, including some that came from outside the city – the cities that reported prodigies to the Senate and the Etruscan experts that were entrusted with the interpretation of several prodigies.

The threats of the *uates*

The *uates* could be a destabilising figure, whose prophecies had the potential to rouse the least educated and least intelligent sectors of the populace against the State or the ruling elites, whether he intended to or not. Destabilisation was not the aim of the *uates* and the *harioli* who spread superstitious fears during the Hannibalic War and led the Senate to act and confiscate a number of prophetic texts. However, Eunus of Apamea, the Syrian leader of the slave revolt in Sicily in 133, did use prophecies to gain support for his cause. Diodorus Siculus gives a heavily critical portrait of Eunus, which probably derives from Posidonius and is inspired by the Stoic theories of divination; it is likely, however, that a similar portrait was

---

[82] Livius Andronicus' position in the religious and intellectual climate of his time is of great interest: cf. Schmidt 1996 on the Hellenising depiction of the Roman gods in the epic poem *Odusia* and Rüpke 2012a: 89 on Livius' theological interests.

also offered by some Latin sources.[83] On other occasions, the responses of *uates* could be used in support of the status quo. In the case of the *carmina Marciana*, the intervention of the Senate, the praetors and the *decemuiri* shaped and controlled the responses of the *uates*. This was possible even if Marcius was not attached to any religious institution and did not belong to any priestly college.

However, other solutions were possible. In 87, the troubled year that witnessed the clash between Cinna and the consul Cn. Octavius, the prophecies of the *uates* Cn. Cornelius Culleolus found a receptive audience in the Roman elite, even if Cicero later qualified them as 'frenzied' (*furibundas*).[84] It is unclear where and how those prophecies were heard, whether in the Senate or elsewhere. Culleolus may well have belonged to a family of some consequence; a L. Culleolus of proconsular rank is among Cicero's correspondents.[85] Whatever the standing of this *uates*, the crisis of 87 called for unusual solutions; Cicero speaks of a *bellum Octauianum*; the Etruscan prophecy of the beginning of a new age dated to the previous year. The premature death of Cn. Pompeius Strabo (*cos.* 89) contributed to an overexcited and volatile climate. According to some accounts, he was struck by lightning; some regarded that as an omen, and his funeral was interrupted by the intervention of the mob, which even dragged the body from the bier.[86] Moreover, Cn. Octavius was very keen to hear from seers of various kinds – including *Chaldaei* and interpreters of Sibylline prophecies. Plutarch gives a sombre comment on how keenly an otherwise sensible man was prepared to follow such misguided advice.[87]

Individual diviners who acted outside the framework of public religion and did not practise an officially recognised *disciplina* could sometimes play their influence right at the top of the ladder of power. According to Plutarch, during the Cimbrian War (104–101 BC) Marius had in his retinue a Syrian woman called Martha, who claimed to be a prophetess, and he used to perform sacrifices when she instructed him to do so. The stages of Martha's rise are especially interesting. First, she sought an audience with the Senate with a view to present her prophecies, but was refused it. She then gained an audience with a group of women, including Marius' wife Julia, to whom she displayed her prophetic skills by predicting the outcome of a gladiatorial stand. It was Marius' wife who sent her to her

---

[83] Diod. Sic. 34/35.2. Montero 1995b: 144–5; Santangelo 2007b: 123.
[84] Cic. *Div.* 1.4. Montero 1997: 113.   [85] Cic. *Fam.* 13.41 and 42; cf. *Att.* 6.3.
[86] App. *B Civ.* 1.80; Oros. 5.19.18; Obseq. 56a; Granius Licinianus 35.36–7; cf. Vell. 2.21.4. Hillard 1996.
[87] Plut. *Mar.* 42.4.

husband, who ostensibly was impressed with her prophetic skills and accorded her a prominent status during the campaign: she was carried in a litter and attended the sacrifices wearing unusually elaborate attire. Marius' enthusiasm for her skills appeared to be great; Plutarch, however, mentions the reservations of some, who questioned that Marius was genuinely impressed with her ability and suggested that he was merely acting a part.[88] Whatever his private views were, Marius' choice to use the services of a Syrian prophetess so prominently in a military endeavour of that significance is a clear illustration of the importance that prophecies could have. It is also striking to see that, according to Plutarch, Martha's prophecies were directly connected to the performance of sacrifice. The existence of a circle of women, no doubt from senatorial families, who became the audience of this prophetess is a reminder of how many avenues were available at this time for the circulation of divinatory lore.

Divination is a practice that has a strong emotional impact on those who resort to it. Lucretius' polemical depiction of the activity of the *uates* offers invaluable elements in this respect. The references to the *uates* come at the end of a long discussion of the liberating power of philosophy, which starts with the portrait of Epicurus who raised his mortal eyes in defiance, while mankind was oppressed by the burden of *religio* (1.62–7):

> *humana ante oculos foede cum uita iaceret*
> *in terris oppressa graui sub religione,*
> *quae caput a caeli regionibus ostendebat*
> *horribili super aspectu mortalibus instans,*
> *primum Graius homo mortalis tollere contra*
> *est oculos ausus primusque obsistere contra.*

> When human life lay grovelling in all men's sight, crushed to the earth under the heavy burden of *religio*, whose grim features loured menacingly from the regions of the sky, a Greek man was first to raise mortal eyes in defiance, first to stand erect and brave the challenge. (trans. R. E. Latham, modified)

Religio is the factor of oppression. The word is often translated as 'superstition' in this context, but this is not the best solution.[89] Lucretius' attack reverberates upon the whole panoply of public religion as a form of social control, in which divination played such an important part. *Caeli regiones* may well be an ironic reference to the Etruscan doctrines on the interpretation of thunder and lightning, which were part of the lore of the

[88] Plut. *Mar.* 17.1–3. Montero 1997: 200–1. Marius' innovative approach to religion: Rawson 1974: 202–6 (= 1991: 158–63).
[89] Lucretius on *religio*: Schiesaro 2002: 52.

haruspices.[90] A more obvious and more important reference to divination comes at the end of the section, after Lucretius has addressed Memmius' possible concerns about the impious nature of philosophy and has argued that *religio*, on the contrary, perpetrated many horrible deeds: *quod contra saepius illa / religio peperit scelerosa atque impia facta* (82–3). This statement is followed by the famous narrative of the sacrifice of Iphigenia (84–101).[91] The *uates* comes under attack immediately after this section, when Lucretius resumes his case in favour of the importance of philosophy and feels the need to resume his attack against *religio*. Memmius is warned against the risk of being intimidated and misled by the words of the *uates* (1.102–11):

> *tutemet a nobis iam quouis tempore uatum*
> *terriloquis uictus dictis desciscere quaeres.*
> *quippe etenim quam multa tibi iam fingere possunt*
> *somnia, quae uitae rationes uertere possint*
> *fortunasque tuas omnis turbare timore!*
> *et merito; nam si certam finem esse uiderent*
> *aerumnarum homines, aliqua ratione ualerent*
> *religionibus atque minis obsistere uatum.*
> *nunc ratio nulla est restandi, nulla facultas,*
> *aeternas quoniam poenas in morte timendum.*

> You yourself, if you surrender your judgement at any time to the blood-curdling words of the *uates*, will want to desert our ranks. Only think what phantoms they can conjure up to overturn the tenor of your life and wreck your happiness with fear. And not without cause. For, if men saw that a term was set to their troubles, they would find strength in some way to withstand the *religiones* and the threats of the *uates*. As it is, they have no way and no power of resistance, because they are haunted by the fear of eternal punishment after death. (trans. R. E. Latham, modified)

Lucretius portrays the *uates* as stalwarts of *religio*; no doubt Cicero would have disagreed. Their prophetic sayings are intended to generate fear. The adjective *terriloquus* strongly points out that to frighten is their main purpose.[92] It is only fear that can keep people away from the pursuit of philosophy and the practice of independent thinking. Lucretius establishes a strong and explicit relationship between religion and intimidation: *religionibus ac minis obsistere uatum*. What makes the threats of the *uates* so

---

[90] Lucretius frequently uses *regio*: Bailey 1947: 609–10.
[91] Minyard 1985: 37 pointed out that in 1.83–101 'Lucretius performs the surgery of separating *pietas* from *religio*'.
[92] Gladigow 1979: 64–5.

strong is the anticipation of horrible suffering after death, which the *uates*
foretell to those who do not pay tribute to the gods. The emphasis is not
on the predictions of the *uates*, but on the stress that they placed on the
fulfilment of religious duties.

T. P. Wiseman gave a ground-breaking discussion of the *uates* attacked
by Lucretius and their social position. As he rightly pointed out, they are
not to be confused with the Augustan 'inspired poets' or 'poet-prophets'.[93]
The word *uates* changed meaning towards the end of the first century BC
and became synonymous with 'poet'. Lucretius, however, refers to a group
of diviners and to figures who are somehow part of the complex machinery
of Roman public religion. Their identity is difficult to establish. Since
in this context *religio* means 'public religion', it is conceivable that the
uates mentioned here are the priests who are involved with divinatory
activities: the haruspices, the *decemuiri*, and especially the augurs, who
base their responses on the observation of the sky.[94] Wiseman suggests, on
the contrary, that Lucretius' reference to the *uates* may apply to the crowds
of public and private diviners who were active in Rome in the first century
BC. This hypothesis is tempting and, even if it were not correct, the central
point of Wiseman's argument certainly is: late Republican Rome was a
place crowded by prophets and prophecies.

This aspect tends to be underestimated, even overlooked, in modern
scholarship. The emphasis is usually on elite control and on the importance of divination in shaping and negotiating political choices. The underlying assumption is that divination was more an instrument of political
manipulation and social cohesion than an important feature of religious
and spiritual life. Moreover, the often repeated assumption that Roman
religion underwent a steady decline in the last century of the Republic
has not encouraged further research in this respect. There is, however,
significant evidence for intense and widespread divinatory activity in the
Republic, both in public and in private contexts. Its range and diversity
are clear symptoms of its success: divination's strength and pervasiveness
lay in defining a specific and meaningful relationship between divine and
human.[95] We cannot explain the success and the extent of divination in
Rome without considering that divination was widely accepted, practised

---

[93] Wiseman 1994a: esp. 50–3 and 2006 (= 2008: 39–51); cf. also Bailey 1947: 617. Different readings in
Hardie 1986: 17 and O'Hara 1987, who correctly established a link between this passage and Lucil.
F 484–98 Marx. Poetry and prophecy: Kugel 1990; Struck 2004: 165–70.
[94] Cf. Ovid's use of *uates* as synonym for *augur*: passages listed in Wiseman 1994a: 138 n. 105 (*Met.*
15.596, where *augur* is used in reference to a haruspex, suggests that terminological accuracy was not
central in Ovid's references to divination).
[95] Ripat 2006: esp. 155–7.

and respected among a significant part of the non-elite population. This is the background against which we can understand the proliferation of divinatory experiences in the late Republic and the competition that could take place around various forms of divination. For most people in first-century BC Rome, divination – in its many varieties – appeared the most reliable and respectable form of prediction available.

A systematic survey of the occurrences of the word *uates* in Augustan poetry would exceed the boundaries of this study and would entail a discussion of the figure of the poet in the period: an issue that has received a great deal of attention.[96] It will suffice to stress that the word acquires a greater semantic complexity in the late first century BC, which is reflected by its greater frequency, not just in poetic texts.[97] We even encounter uses of the word *uates* that go far beyond the range of the familiar meanings. Valerius Maximus refers to the great jurist Q. Mucius Scaevola (*cos.* 95) as *legum clarissimus et certissimus uates* (8.12.1). An association between divination and law seems to be suggested; the exceptional ability of the lawyer is likened to that of the diviner.[98] At the same time, the word *uates* may also imply that the sayings of Mucius were so terse and insightful that they could be compared to poetry. It is to the overlaps between political foresight and divinatory clairvoyance that we shall turn our attention in the next chapter.

---

[96] Wiseman 1994a: 57–8. Runes 1926 is the best discussion; see also Bickel 1951 (comprehensive, but speculative); Newman 1967: 15 (the thesis that the word *uates* went through a process of 'rehabilitation' in the late Republic is surely too simplistic); Newman and Newman 2005: 306–28. O'Hara 1990: 176–84 offers valuable thoughts on the complexity (or indeed 'inherent ambiguity', 181) of the concept of *uates* in Augustan poetry.

[97] Newman 1967; Hardie 1986: 11–32. See esp. Hor. *Epod.* 16.62–6 (Watson 2003: 485, 530; cf. Cavarzere 1994 for the unconvincing view that the voice speaking in the epode is a deranged and unreliable prophet); *Carm.* 1.31.2; Prop. 4.6.1.

[98] Cic. *De or.* 1.200 explicitly compares Mucius to an oracle.

CHAPTER 8

Foresight, prediction and decline
in Cicero's correspondence

In the preceding chapters we have discussed how ubiquitous divination was in late Republican Rome and how central it was in the political debate of the period. We have also discussed how the debate on divination and, more generally, on the prediction and control of the future belonged in the broader context of the intellectual developments of the second and first centuries BC. The following four chapters will develop this approach by focusing on how divination and the prediction of the future are represented and discussed in several late Republican authors. Attention will be devoted to three literary genres – epistolography, biography and historiography – which all address, in different ways, political and religious concerns. The following discussion aims to show that Cicero's discussion of divination and prediction in the *De diuinatione* was not an isolated undertaking. Quite the contrary, it was an intellectual project that addressed issues and concerns that other contemporaries of Cicero shared and developed further, albeit with different interests, strategies and outcomes.

Servius Sulpicius: negotiating despair,
predicting the future

Cicero's interest in philosophy had a fundamental political dimension, but it also had personal and spiritual implications. It became even keener, if at all possible, after the death of his daughter Tullia, in February 45. Philosophy became an increasingly pressing need for a man who had to cope with the sorrow of a tragic personal loss and the bitter disappointment of his political defeat and marginalisation under Caesar. It is in this period that the project of the religious trilogy took shape. In the immediate aftermath of Tullia's death, Cicero must have found little consolation, but perhaps some intellectual pleasure, in a sombre if extremely lucid and impressively well-written letter from Servius Sulpicius Rufus, an old acquaintance, consul in 51 and best known for his invaluable contribution to the formation of

Roman jurisprudence.[1] The letter offers some original thoughts on the problem of the prediction of the future and on the relationship between personal and political events. It deserves some close scrutiny. Sulpicius had managed not to take a clear position in the Civil War, although he certainly considered joining Pompey early in the conflict; at any rate, Caesar brought him back into the fold by assigning him the governorship of Achaia in early 46. The letter was written from Athens. Sulpicius did not claim that his aim was to bring Cicero any consolation, and he presented his views very eloquently. His point is that what Cicero is experiencing should not affect him so deeply. The main challenge that fortune is imposing on him and his contemporaries is the bleak destiny that has fallen upon the Republic: the end of a whole world, brought about by Caesar's victory, should have made Cicero used to this sort of sorrow and made everything else seem of little importance (*omnia minoris existimare*). Tullia, on the contrary, died at a time that already betrayed all the traces of decline and disorder. There was no serious prospect of her leading the life that her talents and condition would have enabled her to live under different circumstances and she would have hardly been able to find a worthy husband in the new generation. Her children, had she borne any, might have been destined to a life of distinction, but in a state where no freedom could be enjoyed. Losing a child is bad enough, of course, but the present destiny of the Republic is much worse to bear.

Much of Sulpicius' thinking was shaped, of course, by the recent political catastrophe that had affected his *partes* and still kept him away from Italy. As is often the case, the surroundings he finds himself in reverberate in his thoughts. Sulpicius recalls his recent journey on the Aegean, in which he sailed past Aegina, Megara, the Piraeus, Corinth: the vision of those ruined cities (surely an overstatement, at least for Aegina and Megara and possibly for the Piraeus too) acted as a reminder of the caducity of things. If even those glorious places met a destiny of decline, surely that has to be the inevitable fortune for all things human. It is unwise for a *homunculus* to hope to resist this law, or even to complain about it. Tullia's death must be understood within this framework. Almost imperceptibly, the focus changes at this point in the letter: a shift from the catastrophe of Roman politics to the comforting wisdom that enables one to come to terms with the ineluctability of death and decline. This was alien wisdom, of course, and it is not fortuitous that the shift in Sulpicius' argument

---

[1] Cic. *Fam.* 4.5. Hutchinson 1998: 65–74; Schiavone 2005: 235–42; Treggiari 2007: 136–7. On Sulpicius' biography and intellectual work see Bauman 1985: 4–65 (48–9 on this letter); on his place in Roman intellectual history see Rawson 1978b: 26–9 (= 1991: 340–5).

coincides with a change of focus from Rome to the Greek ruins that he could see from the Aegean. Sulpicius knew how important Cicero's role had been in developing a Latin version of this set of Hellenistic philosophical knowledge for the perusal of a Roman audience. He therefore urged his friend not to contradict his own teachings and to endure his sorrow bravely.

The final section of the letter is more typically consolatory: time will make sorrow less piercing and Cicero must recover his composure as promptly as he can. There is even room for a brief note of hope. The fatherland might need Cicero's advice and service in the future and it is important for him to be prepared for that moment. What makes the letter memorable, however, is the unreserved pessimism that pervades it, accompanied by the powerful analogy between the decline of the Greek world and the imminent decay of the Roman Republic. Sulpicius is not even interested in seeking the causes of the disaster he sketches, nor does he try to offer an accurate description of the symptoms of decline that he detects. On the one hand, his disgust is so immediate and instinctive that it requires no further elucidation. On the other hand, the abstract, even schematic depiction of Rome's imminent destiny – based on the assumption that everything is bound to pass and disappear, as everything is mortal – seems more than adequate to account for his argument.

Cicero's reply (*Fam.* 4.6) is focused on the themes raised in the second part of the letter, rather than on the argument of the first part, which may well have sounded arrogant or insensitive to him. He pledges to resist and overcome his grief and to keep offering his contribution to the Republic, which is however a source of deep grief in itself.[2] The manifestations of his sorrows are however frequent and explicit, and Cicero states very clearly that Tullia's death has seriously influenced his ability to concentrate on political matters. The next piece of his correspondence with Sulpicius is again concerned with matters of decline and death. In May 45 Sulpicius sent a short letter to Cicero, from Athens, announcing the recent death of their mutual friend M. Claudius Marcellus, the colleague of Sulpicius in the consulship of 51 (*Fam.* 4.12). The two men had met in Greece and were about to set off to Italy together; the night before the departure, however, Marcellus was attacked by his friend P. Magius Cilo with a dagger and died a few hours later. Magius committed suicide shortly afterwards. Sulpicius tells Cicero in some detail about the arrangements to secure a proper burial for Marcellus, which included an unsuccessful attempt to

---

[2] Gildenhard 2007a: 59. The letter should not be read as evidence of Cicero's egocentrism: Hutchinson 1998: 74–7 and Treggiari 2007: 137–8.

persuade the Athenians to allow a burial within the city walls. It is all the more striking to see, then, that nothing is said about the motive of the murder; there is not even a list of conjectural explanations. The only cursory remark that might be read as an attempt to provide an explanation is at the very beginning of the letter and again it has to do with the problem of consolation. Sulpicius knows that his friend is going to find the news distressing, but implies that there is no alternative but to accept it: 'we are dominated by chance and nature' (*casus et natura in nobis dominatur*). As in the letter about Tullia's death, there seems to be no interest in describing the specific causes of the facts and processes under discussion. The focus is entirely on matters of general importance and indeed on some abstract, even vague explanations. As Schiavone notes, the emphasis is all on the external mechanics of the episode: nothing is said even on the immediate causes that brought it about.[3]

Writing and predicting the decline of Rome: Nepos on Cicero and Atticus

In the letter to Caecina that we discussed in Chapter 2 (*Fam.* 6.6), Cicero stresses the significance of the predictions based on experience, on the knowledge of precedents and on the reflective assessment of any situation. This point finds a strikingly close echo in a passage of Cornelius Nepos' *Life of Atticus*. In his survey of Atticus' outstanding qualities, Nepos pays tribute to his ability to make friends and to his special loyalty to Cicero (*Att.* 16.2–5):

> *quamquam eum praecipue dilexit Cicero, ut ne frater quidem ei Quintus carior fuerit aut familiarior. ei rei sunt indicio praeter eos libros, in quibus de eo facit mentionem, qui in uulgus sunt editi, undecim uolumina epistularum ab consulatu eius usque ad extremum tempus ad Atticum missarum; quae qui legat, non multum desideret historiam contextam eorum temporum. sic enim omnia de studiis principum, uitiis ducum, mutationibus rei publicae perscripta sunt, ut nihil in his non appareat et facile existimari possit prudentiam quodam modo esse diuinationem. non enim Cicero ea solum, quae uiuo se acciderunt, futura praedixit, sed etiam, quae nunc usu ueniunt, cecinit ut uates.*

Nevertheless Cicero was especially fond of him, to the extent that not even his brother Quintus was dearer or closer. To prove the point, apart from the books in which Cicero mentions Atticus, which have been published, there are eleven rolls of letters, which were sent to Atticus from the time of

---

[3] Schiavone 2005: 242–3. Cf. White 2010: 54 on the position of the letter in *Fam.* 4.

Cicero's consulship right down to the end: who reads them would hardly need a continuous history of those times. For they offer so full a record of everything to do with the plans of statesmen, the failings of generals, and mutations in the state that nothing does not feature in them, and one may easily think that Cicero's good sense was in some way prophetic, since he not only predicted things which happened in his lifetime, but also sang like a prophet of things that are happening now.[4]

Indeed, according to Nepos, the affection that the orator had for Atticus was even greater than that he had for Quintus – no doubt this is accurate.[5] Nepos had access to a corpus of eleven rolls that differed from the corpus we read today, starting with Cicero's consulship and ending with his death, and possibly gathered by Atticus himself.[6] He fully appreciated the importance of Cicero's letters as historical sources, and even went as far as saying that they are such a comprehensive body of evidence that a historical narrative is bound to become unnecessary: any student of the late Republic knows how inaccurate this prediction was.[7] Nepos' enthusiasm, however, goes even further. He claims that the variety of events documented by the letters, involving both individuals and collective bodies, is almost endless and that the letters show most clearly how prudence and foresight are a form of divination (*quodam modo esse diuinationem*). This is precisely the same point that Cicero made in the letter to Caecina, when he offered his friend 'the authoritativeness of my augural and divinatory expertise' (*auctoritatem augurii et diuinationis meae*); while in Cicero's letter there may have been more than a hint of irony, Nepos is clearly serious here. His praise of Cicero becomes even more lavish in the following sentence, where he says that his ability to predict what would happen in his own lifetime and beyond is so clear that he deserves the qualification of *uates*. Nepos was inaccurate here, as he was on so many occasions, but he was right to stress that the theme of political prediction is present in Cicero's correspondence and in Cicero's later philosophical work.[8] Indeed, it is fair to work on the assumption that, for anyone writing about Cicero in the

---

[4] Moles 1993b: 79; Guillaumont 2000: 103–4; Anselm 2004: 181–2.

[5] This chapter was probably written in Atticus' lifetime, before the end of March 32: Shackleton Bailey 1965: 60 ('probably in 35–34'); Horsfall 1989: 8. Cf. Toher 2002 against the idea that Nepos published two editions of Atticus' biography, one before his friend's death and one after.

[6] Shackleton Bailey 1965: 69; Horsfall 1989: 96. Narducci 1983 (= 2004: 235–7) reads this passage as evidence that Nepos had access to an unpublished version of the *Ad familiares*, a collection in which words like *praedicere, prudentia, diuinatio, diuinare* and *futura* occur on a number of occasions.

[7] In the *De historicis Latinis* (F 58 Marshall) Nepos argued that Cicero was a great historian *manqué*; La Penna 1978: 92–3. Genre-related concerns in Nepos: Geiger 1985a; Moles 1989; Tuplin 2000; Beneker 2009–10.

[8] Osgood 2006: 25–8, esp. 26: '[m]emory . . . mixes with hope in these letters'.

thirties of the first century BC, writing about Cicero and *diuinatio* meant coming to terms with the *De diuinatione*, which had appeared just a decade earlier and was a remarkable and innovative text in so many respects.[9]

Cicero's correspondence shows that he was on friendly terms with Nepos, and not just because they shared Atticus' friendship.[10] There is no evidence, however, that Nepos read Cicero's *Ad familiares* or that he was aware of the letter to Caecina and the point that Cicero made on his *diuinatio* there. It is safer to think that Nepos developed the point independently, or maybe that he reflected insights that were circulating in the intellectual debate of the time and that we can track only with great difficulty. It must be noted that this is not the only occasion when divination features in Atticus' biography. In fact, the link between *prudentia* and *diuinatio* is established as early as Chapter 9, this time with reference to Atticus (*Att.* 9.1):

> *secutum est bellum gestum apud Mutinam. in quo si tantum eum prudentem dicam, minus, quam debeam, praedicem, cum ille potius diuinus fuerit, si diuinatio appellanda est perpetua naturalis bonitas, quae nullis casibus agitur neque minuitur.*

> Next followed the war that was fought at Mutina, in which, if I were only to say that he was wise, I should say less of him than I ought; for he rather proved himself divine, if a constant goodness of nature, which is neither increased nor diminished by the events, may be called divine foresight.[11]

The great man showed remarkable moderation and sympathy towards Antony in the difficult times that followed the battle of Mutina and he supported the escape of some of his supporters from Italy. This attitude proved invaluable to Atticus after Antony's return, but it was a far from obvious course of action when Atticus decided upon it. Nepos remarks that Atticus was more than prudent and that indeed his conduct was similar to that of a seer, since he could foresee what was at the time a very unlikely development. In fact, though, what enabled Atticus to see so far down the road were his naturally good temper and his humanity – something that no revolution or threat could affect.[12]

---

[9] On a declaredly speculative note, Nepos' insistence on Cicero's own ability to make political predictions and his decision to call it *diuinatio* may be read as an endorsement of what Marcus says on the importance of rational political prediction in *Div.* 2.

[10] Cic. *Att.* 16.5.5; *ibid.* 16.14.4. Cf. Gell. *NA* 15.28.1. Geiger 1985b; Anselm 2004: 28–9; White 2010: 32, 188 n. 9.

[11] This translation follows the suggestions of Moles 1993b: 78.

[12] Nepos' portrayal of Atticus: Labate and Narducci 1981; Lindsay 1998; Leppin 2002: 195–200; Narducci 2004: 158–86; Stem 2009–10: 125–34. Atticus as Nepos' ideal reader: Anselm 2004: 175–82. Atticus' biography: Perlwitz 1992; Epicureanism: Benferhat 2005: 98–169.

There is some affinity between the two occurrences of *diuinatio* in Atticus' biography, despite the obvious differences in context and tone. A remarkably sharp ability to predict events can turn into a form of divination, a supernatural ability to foresee the future: *diuinatio*, in other words, is a development of *prudentia*, a further stage in the ability to understand the future. Nepos is unspecific on how this ability may be acquired. The case of Cicero seems to imply that political experience can put one in the position to predict the future more effectively; however, the example of Atticus suggests that natural talents are the main source of divinatory abilities. What makes Atticus so remarkable is the blend of intelligence and good character that was so unique to that remarkable man.

Nepos' interest in and admiration for Atticus' divinatory talent may also be read as part of a broader reflection on the relationship between divination, prediction and history. They feature in the biography of a man who is celebrated for his political intelligence and his wide-ranging learning and who stands out as a model citizen and intellectual – at the same time, an ideal character and a valuable blueprint for the ideal reader of Nepos' work. The issues raised in the biography had a historiographical relevance; the work on Atticus was part of a collection of *Lives of the Latin Historians*. The importance of analysing the present correctly and making sound predictions on the grounds of previous experience must have been central in the economy of the work.[13] A contemporary of Nepos, who chose a completely different kind of historical writing from biography, the Greek historian Diodorus Siculus, started his universal history by arguing that history is not just a source of knowledge and understanding: it is, first of all, the 'prophetess of the truth' (*prophetis tes aletheias*), an intellectual practice that enables people to make informed predictions of the future.[14] Nepos develops the same point from a different perspective: that of a biographer who bases his approach to history on the study of individual personalities and believes in the possibility of understanding the past through the analysis of specific examples and cases. His assessment of Cicero's correspondence should be understood in this light. Nepos says that it is through the study of the flaws of kings, the lives of the great generals and the political changes of the State discussed and analysed in the letters that the *prudentia* of Cicero stands out – it is by discussing concrete historical realities that a

[13] Dionisotti 1988 conclusively shows that Nepos' intellectual project is underpinned by pressing political concerns. Millar 1988 (= 2002: 183–99) stresses the importance of Nepos' text to the understanding of late Republican history. Overview of recent scholarship: Pryzwansky 2009–10.
[14] Diod. Sic. 1.2.2. Santangelo 2007b: 123–5.

reliable prediction of the future may be gained.[15] In this important respect, epistolography and biography share remarkable similarities: they are not grand historical narratives, but they engage with important problems and can provide plenty of food for thought.

[15] A similar point is tangentially made in Cicero's letter to Lucceius on historiography (*Fam.* 5.12.4): Lucceius' knowledge of the mechanics of revolutions and political changes may enable him not just to explain their causes, but to suggest remedies as well.

CHAPTER 9

Between fortune and virtue
Sallust and the decline of Rome

The proemium of Sallust's *Bellum Catilinae* displays a biographical approach to the prediction of the future that has something in common with Nepos' interest in the lives of the great man and in their ability to shed light on the destiny of the states.[1] We are on a different level of intellectual sophistication, of course, but Sallust starts his grand sketch of the history of Rome with a discussion of the balance between body and mind and with how the rulers of the past failed to achieve it, in different ways, in any period of time. Sallust seems to think that the victories of Cyrus marked a turning point in history: it was with the rise of the Persian empire that an unrestrained desire to rule became the leading principle of the world, and men were not happy with their own gifts any longer. The eventual success of Athens and Sparta confirmed this new pattern, which was based on the supremacy of the body's basest instincts over reason and restraint.[2] The energies that were devoted to victory in war were not matched by a comparable effort to be sensible and just in peace. The abilities that make victory possible go under the comprehensive definition of *uirtus* and may be further divided into *labor*, *continentia* and *aequitas* (industry, restraint and equity); their opposites, *desidia*, *lubido* and *superbia* (idleness, wantonness and arrogance), are factors of discord and defeat. Every political failure has an ethical dimension to it: 'fortune changes along with morality' (*fortuna simul cum moribus immutatur*).[3] Therefore, Sallust decides to write a history of the conspiracy of Catiline and to shed light on the political tragedy of the Republic through the story of an individual, who embodied the deep moral and intellectual developments of his time better than anyone else.[4]

---

[1] Cf. Mutschler 2003: 268–78.

[2] *Translatio imperii* in Sall. *Cat.*: Heldmann 1993: 15–69.   [3] Sall. *Cat.* 2.5.

[4] The debate between Cato and Caesar on the destiny of the conspirators plays a crucial role in Sallust's approach to the political and moral decline of the Republic and in his quest for an appropriate conceptual vocabulary: Sklenár 1998.

Decline and Catiline's conspiracy

Sallust's first monograph opens with the bold statement that the lives of the states follow the same rules as the lives of individuals and that the history of mankind may be read by focusing on the individuals who aspire to prominence. The statement is not merely an introduction to the intellectual autobiography that Sallust outlines in the following paragraph to explain and justify his choice to write history. Catiline, whose personality he introduces at the very beginning of his narrative, is a powerful example of the tensions and flaws of his time. His overwhelming, all-consuming ambition is matched by *lubido maxuma*, the unprecedented greed that dominated Roman history after Sulla's rise to power.[5] Catiline is a man of his own time; he belongs to a generation that pays the price of a corruption of public morality that has no precedents and which is based on two different evils, *luxuria atque auaritia*.

The ambitious summary of Roman history that takes up the following chapters is rooted in this 'biographical' and moralistic interpretation of history.[6] After the fall of Carthage the Romans found themselves unable to resist the pressure and temptations of the wealth and luxury secured by their own victories. The extraordinary availability of resources led to a profound moral change, whereby ambition and greed grew unchecked and the cohesion that was typical of the early history of the Republic became increasingly weak. This is a moralistic account of the crisis of the Republic, in which fortune plays only a marginal role. The destiny of the State seems to be determined by human factors, such as the unprecedented concentration of wealth and power in the hands of the Roman elite and the deep changes that the increasing competition within the elite caused. Fortune changes along with human behaviour; it is not the main factor of historical change; on the contrary, its course is determined by factors that are eminently human – the declining *mores*.[7] The very development of the crisis shows that it was typically historical and human. Its spread may be likened to that of a disease, or a plague epidemic, which grows steadily and gradually and against which remedies are increasingly less effective. Ambition was the driving factor in the first phase of the process; after Sulla

---

[5] Osgood 2006: 306–7.   [6] Sall. *Cat.* 6–13.

[7] Stewart 1968: 301–2; Novara 1983: 592–619; Heldmann 1993: 108–10. This approach to the role of *fortuna* in Sallust's historical thought solves the contradiction between the prologues and the rest of the work discussed in Tiffou 1977 (bibliography at 351–2; unlike Tiffou, I do not think we can say anything meaningful about the role of *fortuna* in the *Historiae*); on Sallust's alleged contradictions see also Cupaiuolo 1984: 17–18.

completed the conquest of the Greek East and gained the favour of his soldiers by allowing them to live in luxury, competition for wealth became the rule. As Sallust makes clear after the debate between Cato and Caesar on the destiny of the conspirators, the extent of the moral change entailed a complete change in the structure of the Republic.[8] While the growth of Rome and her empire had been made possible by an exceptionally competent elite, the decline was balanced and contained by the great complexity and efficiency of the *res publica*, which often made up for the incompetence of the elite and even managed to endure the lack of able men throughout several generations. Sallust employs yet another biological analogy, that between the weakness of Rome after decades of victories and conquests and the exhaustion of mothers after childbirth, but he does not give any prediction on the length of the recovery period, or on the chances of a proper, complete recovery.

Sallust does not fail to notice that this shift of values has an important political dimension. The new mansions of the late Republican elite are shameless displays of wealth and power, and their contrast with the simple and solemn temples built by the ancestors, whose main adornment was piety, could not be stronger: the contrast between the piety of the former generations, *religiosissimi mortales*, and the reckless behaviour of the recent generation, *ignauissimi homines*, could hardly be phrased in more explicit terms. The introduction to the monograph on Catiline's conspiracy insists at length on the climate of moral decline and degeneration that was typical of the time it deals with. It prepares the ground for an individual like Catiline, who found his perfect habitat in that atmosphere.

The decline that Sallust discusses is chiefly moral; political disruption is a consequence. There is a reference to the role of fortune, but a series of specific events and longer-term processes is brought to the attention of the reader. There is a passing reference to religious decline and the overall picture of decay and absence of any control shifts emphasis in the same direction. On the whole, however, Sallust produces a reconstruction of the Roman past and present in which the gods seem to play no role whatsoever and references to *fortuna* seem more like casual revisitations of a philosophical and literary commonplace than the development of an important theme of Sallust's historical vision. This interpretation of the past inevitably raises questions about the future and namely the possibility of

---

[8] Sall. *Cat.* 53.2–5. Sallust on the expansion of Rome and its role in the decline of the Republic: Ruch 1972: 832–3; de Blois 1988; Walter 2004: 321–9; Samotta 2009: 104–8.

stopping the decline that he portrays so forcefully. Sallust strongly believes in the power of historiographical writing and in the importance of the civic gesture of writing about the past, either by celebrating it, or by accounting for disruption and decline. He is never explicit, however, about his views on the ability of history to predict the future and to contribute to the education of its readers. He is also quite elusive on the role of prophecies in history or in the political developments of his own time – a surprising omission, in light of the role that prophecies played in late Republican history.[9]

The only reference to the practice of divination in the *Bellum Catilinae* may be found in the summary of the interrogation of the conspirator P. Cornelius Lentulus Sura, in which he was asked to explain the statement he made in conversation that a prophecy of his rise to power was contained in the Sibylline Books, which foretold the rule of Rome by three Cornelii:

> *eadem Galli fatentur ac Lentulum dissimulantem coarguunt praeter litteras sermonibus, quos ille habere solitus erat: ex libris Sibyllinis regnum Romae tribus Corneliis portendi; Cinnam atque Sullam antea, se tertium esse, cui fatum foret urbis potiri; praeterea ab incenso Capitolio illum esse uigesumum annum, quem saepe ex prodigiis haruspices respondissent bello ciuili cruentum fore.*

> The Gauls stated the same and refuted Lentulus' dissimulation on the grounds of the conversations which he used to hold (apart from his letter): he claimed that the Sibylline Books portended kingship at Rome for three Cornelii; that, after Cinna and Sulla, he was the third who was destined to rule over the city; moreover, that that was the twentieth year after the fire of the Capitol, and the haruspices had often responded to prodigies by saying that it would be stained with blood by the civil war.[10]

Lentulus allegedly claimed that he was the third one after Sulla and Cinna; his position was made worse by the fact that the conspiracy took place twenty years after the fire on the Capitol in 83, an event that the haruspices had foretold would be stained with the blood of a civil war (*bello ciuili cruento fore*). The point is also raised in Cicero's speeches against Catiline

---

[9] There is no mention, for instance, of the prodigy of the death of the decurion of Pompeii, M. Herennius, which points to some local involvement in the conspiracy: Plin. *HN* 2.57, with Zevi 1995: 18–24; cf. also Obs. 61. Sallust evokes religious negligence as a symptom of decline: *Cat.* 10.4 (*deos neglegere*); the ancestors are *religiosissimi mortales* (*Cat.* 12.5). Sacchetti 1996: 209–10 suggests that the genre chosen by Sallust exempted him from the duty to report prodigies as was customary in annalistic history.

[10] Sall. *Cat.* 47.2. Cf. also Plut. *Cic.* 17.4; App. *B Civ.* 2.4. H. Flower 2008: 86–7 rightly stresses the lasting impression that the fire on the Capitol made at the time. On *fatum* in this context see Begemann 2012: 331–3.

and it is interesting that Sallust does not insist on it at all, not even to criticise Cicero's handling of the prodigies.[11] He is equally vague on the Sibylline oracles that Lentulus referred to, the status of which is rather uncertain: were they part of the official collection of Sibylline Books that was painstakingly reassembled after the fire of the Capitol, or did Lentulus bring to the fore an apocryphal version of the oracles, which was produced in private circles? The problem is overlooked. Sallust does not deviate from the basic account of the events, which he apparently derived from the minutes of the interrogations kept by four commissioners personally appointed by Cicero.[12] He does not take the time to discuss the use of the prophecies in this context, nor to express views on their reliability. They are merely a factor in the narrative that Sallust provides and not an important enough one to deserve any special comment. Sallust's characteristic lack of interest in religious matters and developments fits very well with the tone of his reconstruction of Roman history, in which religious developments are seen just as a symptom of a change of manners and behaviours that is best explained by social and economic developments.[13]

Sallust on Marius

References to religious themes, however, become more frequent in Sallust's second monograph, the *Bellum Jugurthinum*, although the same attitude of disenchantment and at times open indifference remains apparent. Soon after Q. Caecilius Metellus pitched his camp near Thala, in the build-up to a battle against Jugurtha, a great amount of rain fell on the camp and increased the water supplies of the Romans. In fact, the addition was hardly necessary, since plenty of water had been supplied by the local allies of Rome. However, the soldiers preferred to use rainwater, because they considered it a sign of divine favour; the rain was a major boost to the morale of the troops. Again, Sallust gives no explicit statement on the episode and on the attitude of the soldiers. His detached, even critical approach, however, is apparent from the way he refers to the soldiers' view: *nam rati sese dis immortalibus curae esse* – 'indeed, they thought that they were of some importance to the immortal gods'. It is abundantly clear that this is not the view of Sallust, but that of the soldiers.[14] The juxtaposition of a *uerbum opinandi* like *rati* and the reflexive pronoun *sese* conveys the impression that the whole scheme is a product of the deluded minds of the

---

[11] Cic. *Cat.* 3.9. Ramsey 2007: 181–3.   [12] Evidence in Ramsey 2007: 181.
[13] Cf. Rosenblitt 2011: 406 on Sallust's lack of interest in religion.   [14] Paul 1984: 195–6.

soldiers and finds no support in the reality of things. A similar tone may be detected in the portrait of the overwhelming consensus and support that Marius meets after the battle of Capsa, when he is admired by his men and feared by the enemy and everybody is in awe of his ability to predict the consequences of his actions. All the actions that he had not planned properly, but in which he had nonetheless succeeded, were seen as examples of virtue; people debated whether he possessed a divine mind, or things were revealed to him by the gods. Sallust does not embark on a full-scale critique of this attitude: he is interested in conveying a sense of the admiration that Marius had earned in that period of his career. However, his brief remark that even all the actions that were poorly planned were seen as evidence of a great talent is a very clear sign that Sallust had reservations concerning Marius' ability.[15] A few lines before, there is an even more explicit reference to Marius' recklessness in the Capsa campaign: Sallust bitterly remarks that, as soon as Marius realised the difficulty of getting hold of water supplies in the region, he put his trust in the gods, since his *consilium* could not possibly be an adequate resource in that difficult situation.[16]

This reference to divine involvement is not just another symptom of Sallust's unenthusiastic assessment of Marius' strategy. It is also a link that the historian establishes with another moment of his narrative, which is also the junction of his work where the engagement with religious themes and situations becomes closest. The turning point of Marius' career was the response that he received from a haruspex, as he sacrificed to the gods at Utica: both Plutarch and Sallust report the episode, and the latter's account is especially detailed.[17] The unnamed haruspex who assisted Marius in the fulfilment of his religious duties uttered a prophecy the scope of which went beyond the range of affairs that Marius was handling at the time in his official capacity. The seer advised him that a great career was awaiting him, that it was time for him to put his fortune to the test and to head for a bright future. This response fits the other known late Republican instances of haruspical prophecy. It was a specific, wide-ranging, explicit statement on the future and it was based on a lengthy assessment of Marius' life and career up to that time. In fact, Marius' rise from an unremarkable background to military and political prominence was the clearest evidence of his suitability for the task. Despite being a new man, he was an excellent consul-in-waiting, who just needed to find the resolve

[15] Sall. *Iug.* 92.2: *omnia non bene consulta in uirtutem trahebantur*. Paul 1984: 227.
[16] Paul 1984: 223–4.　　[17] Sall. *Iug.* 63; Plut. *Mar.* 8.4–5.

to stand for election as soon as possible and to break the cycle that had transformed the consulship into a magistracy passed from one member of the nobility to another. It was more than just a prediction of the future; like many prophecies, it was a loaded account of the past. It was a political statement and a historical summary of the factors that made Marius such an extraordinary individual. We do not know from what source it derives, although it was surely a pro-Marian one. The episode is also reported by Plutarch, although much more briefly than in Sallust. He agrees with Sallust on the point that the prophecy was given at Utica, but places it just before Marius' departure to Italy. In Sallust it is given when Marius is still actively involved in the African campaign and the departure to Italy has not been planned yet. Various attempts have been made to resolve this discrepancy. It can be explained by different literary and narrative agendas, which handled the same material – a favourable prophecy received by Marius at Utica – in different ways. While the date of the episode is hard to establish, there is no reason to doubt its historicity: some time before his departure from Africa, at Utica, Marius received a favourable prophecy concerning his political prospects from a haruspex.[18] What the haruspex says, of course, is a free elaboration of the historian.[19] The passage, however, also confirms that Sallust appreciated the importance of religious themes in the rise of Marius and in his self-representation.[20] At the same time, it shows how well Sallust understood the importance of haruspical prophecies in this period and their potentially disrupting impact on the usual dynamics of political competition.

Sallust knew that by developing the prophecy of Marius' rise to power he could forcefully convey one of the leading themes embodied by this character: a sense of promise and urgency, based upon Marius' ability to come across as an alternative to the elite that had been in charge of the Republic for such a long time. The famous speech that Marius delivers before setting off to Africa is perhaps the best illustration of this.[21] Marius opens his address with a denunciation of the inconsistency of the members of the nobility, who are at first humble and industrious, only to become

---

[18] Cf. Paul 1984: 165–6, who suggests that the episode is ultimately 'an invention of pro-Marian propaganda'.

[19] Paul 1984: 165–71. See Gilbert 1973; Tiffou 1977: 354–5.

[20] See also Plut. *Mar.* 38.2–40.3, Val. Max. 1.5.5 and Granius Licinianus 35.3–5 on the omen that preceded Marius' escape from Minturnae in 88, with Wardle 1998: 174–6. Cf. Gaius Piso, *HRR* I², p. 317 = Plut. *Mar.* 45.5: in his final conversation with his friends, Marius allegedly said that no wise man should ever trust fortune. On Marius' association with the Syrian prophetess Martha see Chapter 7.

[21] Sall. *Iug.* 85.

indolent and arrogant once in office, which recalls the emphasis on decline and corruption in the proem of the *Bellum Catilinae*; he then pledges to be consistent and resilient, precisely because he lacks personal ambition, just like the Romans of the old days, according to the portrait that Sallust depicts. The end of the speech conveys an even stronger sense of promise, with Marius' prediction that, with the help of the gods, Rome is going to achieve much more than she already has: *et profecto dis iuuantibus omnia matura sunt, uictoria, praeda, laus* (85.48: 'and surely with the help of the gods everything is ripe for us – victory, booty, praise'). A similar theme is echoed at the end of the monograph, when Sallust remarks that at the end of the war all the hopes (*spes*) and the welfare (*opes*) of Rome rested in Marius: a gloomily ironic statement, in light of what was to follow.[22]

Indeed, Sallust's appreciation of Marius is far from unreserved. Marius' emphasis on the *praeda* ('booty') is the premonition of further misfortunes to come. The historian is well aware of the corruption brought about by the generals' indulgence towards their troops and an instance of the devastations perpetrated by the soldiers can be found a few chapters later, when Marius oversees the sack of a rich and fertile district.[23] The theme is developed most impressively in the account of the capture of the citadel of Moluccha, which Sallust explicitly attributes more to Marius' fortune than to his ability. In fact, the choice of starting the siege was at least questionable: Moluccha was extremely well guarded and its position made it exceptionally difficult to access, let alone conquer. Sallust's disapproval of the strategic choice of Marius is apparent. It was only the fortuitous intervention of a Ligurian soldier (*forte quidam Ligus*), whose name is not recorded (*ex cohortibus auxiliariis miles gregarius*), that overturned the destiny of the siege.[24] As he was looking for snails on the rock of Moluccha, he managed to reach a spot from which he could easily look down into the wall's precinct and take a careful look at the enemy camp. He then reported his findings to Marius, who decided to believe him and so attacked the Numidian stronghold. The leader of the successful attack was again the Ligurian, who, after all, had devised his plan thanks to a chance discovery and because of the natural curiosity that the awareness of being alone and free engendered in him.[25] It was only a fortunate series of circumstances

---

[22] Sall *Iug.* 114.4. Levene 1992: 54–5 stresses the elements of incompleteness and inconclusiveness of the monograph and their role in bringing about a picture of decline and betrayed expectation.

[23] Sall. *Iug.* 87.1.

[24] Sall. *Iug.* 93–4. Brescia 1997. Sallust on Marius' fortune and its possible relationship with the fortune of Sulla: Avery 1967.

[25] Sall. *Iug.* 93.3.

that saved Marius from his recklessness and incompetence; Sallust makes this clear beyond any doubt. It is conceivable, as D. Levene argued, that the point is intended as a deliberate response to the prophecy of the haruspex, which plays such a central role in the narrative.[26] The deed of the Ligurian was brought about by a series of fortunate, and indeed fortuitous, factors: his natural curiosity, his sudden desire to collect and eat some snails creeping out from the rocks and the presence of an oak tree among the rocks, which enabled the Ligurian to reach a perfect vantage point from which he could observe the inside of the fortress. It is tempting to see some similarities between the Ligurian and the haruspex who predicts a future of success and prosperity for Marius. Like the haruspex, the Ligurian bases his prediction on a series of signs that he, unlike Marius, is able to detect and interpret: the haruspex looks into the entrails of an animal and produces a response, while the Ligurian observes the military operations inside the fortress and manages to devise a plan. More importantly, the Etruscan haruspex and the Ligurian are anonymous outsiders. They serve in the Roman ranks, but preserve – partly because of their origins, partly thanks to their anonymity – a distinctive identity that prevents them from assimilating. It is this position of the outsider that enables him to gain such a prominent role in the military developments without posing any threat to Marius; indeed, the general can entrust him with the direction of the whole enterprise without the risk of losing his position within the ranks.

Yet, Sallust's evaluation of Marius and his leadership remains critical; in fact, the events at Moluccha mark the beginning of the decline of Marius' leadership.[27] In many respects, the endeavour undertaken by Marius is completed by Sulla, who has similar qualities and vision to those of his senior commander, and later rival, but is capable of developing them more ruthlessly and more consistently.[28] He is more capable than Marius of deaing with the troops; he achieves the capture of Jugurtha, thanks to his personal relationship with Bocchus. Two decades later, as Sallust points out in the *Bellum Catilinae*, he would make the corruption of the Roman army irredeemable by letting his troops plunder Asia Minor without any control.[29] Sulla's speech to Bocchus contains a restatement of the tension between *uirtus* and *fortuna* that we encounter in the proem of the *Bellum*

---

[26] Sall. *Iug.* 94.7: *sic forte correcta Mari temeritas gloriam ex culpa inuenit* ('thus Marius' recklessness was corrected by chance and found glory out of his wrongdoing'). Levene 1992: 63; Dix 2006: 239–40.
[27] Brescia 1997: 13.
[28] La Penna 1978: 208–11 and, from a different angle, Levene 1992: 58–9, 63–4. Dix 2006: 250–76 explores the similarities between Sulla and Jugurtha.
[29] Sall. *Cat.* 11.5.

Catilinae. Sulla ends his address to the king with a tribute to the role of *fortuna* in human affairs. *Fortuna* rules everything: it has made Bocchus experience both the might and the compassion of the Romans and now gives him the opportunity to take advantage of their generosity by changing side. It is not immediately clear why Sallust used this argument at this stage, especially since he had approached the issue of the role of *fortuna* at the beginning of the monograph and had clearly ruled that the *animus* rules the life of mortals and is capable of directing them onto the path of virtue (*ad gloriam uirtutis*). It is conceivable that he derived this statement on the importance of *fortuna* from Sulla's *Memoirs*, which he undoubtedly knew and used. If that was indeed the case, Sulla's speech anticipated some of the leading themes of his later propaganda: the fascination with the Hellenistic idea of an overarching and dominating *tuche* and the conviction that a great deal of his success was due to a special bond with the gods – hence the adoption of the name *Felix*.[30]

This approach was familiar to Sallust and he may have found it useful in the depiction of Sulla's character, but he chose not to develop it at all. The whole framework of Sallust's historical monographs shows that Sallust set out to write Roman history without invoking the supernatural element as a factor of historical explanation. He was prepared to show his awareness of the importance of some religious factors, such as the responses of the haruspices, but the gods are never invoked as factors of historical causation. Being a keen reader of Thucydides, he knew that there was little need to express vocal dissent or criticism. His views on such issues could be made apparent by some simple, yet powerful stylistic and rhetorical devices.[31] In the next chapter, we shall turn to another historian who worked on similar problems, but chose radically different solutions.

---

[30] Santangelo 2007a: 207–13, with earlier bibliography; Smith 2009; Thein 2009; Wiseman 2009b.

[31] Thucydides and Sallust: Scanlon 1980 and, more specifically on the representation of στάσις and decline, Sklenár 1998: 215–17; Syme 1964: 245–8, 255–6 explores the differences between the two authors, as well as the fundamental similarities.

CHAPTER 10

Divination, religious change
and the future of Rome in Livy

Unlike Sallust, Livy had a keen interest in religion; the importance of his work for a study of divination and prediction in Roman culture is profound. One reason for that is obvious: the *ab Urbe condita libri* are a key source for many aspects of Roman religion, including central features of Roman divination. However, they are much more than an inventory of instructive stories and valuable information. Livy's work was a full-scale account of Roman history, which addressed the problem of the rise of Rome to the status of hegemonic power, and took religious themes and motifs very seriously. It was written at a time of crucial political, cultural and ideological change, by a second-generation Roman citizen, an *eques* from Patavium, an Italian intellectual who moved to Rome when he was in his prime and set out to write a history of Rome from the foundation of the city, using an impressive array of source material.

The stumbling block is the serious deficiency of our knowledge. Very little is known about Livy's life and convictions (political, religious or of any other kind). The composition of his work took at least three decades and Livy must have revised his agenda and, given the enormous changes of those years, it is highly likely that he revisited his views in a number of respects.[1] Augustus' *bon mot* that labelled Livy as a *Pompeianus* has been the object of much debate, but it can hardly be used as a safe guide to Livy's politics.[2] At any rate, the section of the work that dealt with the Civil Wars and the rise and fall of Pompey is lost. This draws attention to the second, major area of ignorance and uncertainty. At the cost of restating the obvious, it must not be overlooked that most of Livy's work is lost; we have access to thirty-five books out of 142, and the surviving narrative breaks off at the beginning of the second century BC. The *Periochae* cannot be used as a meaningful source for Livy's views on religious matters. We do not know what Livy said about the age of the Civil Wars, the religious innovations of Sulla

---

[1] Henderson 1989: 76. Interesting speculation in Liebeschuetz 1967: 54–5.   [2] Tac. *Ann.* 4.34.4.

and Caesar, the destruction and restoration of the Sibylline Books, or the increasingly prominent role of the haruspices.[3] The *Periochae* of the books that covered the late Republic and the early Principate (the summary stops in 9 BC) do not mention a single prodigy. The epitomiser was probably not interested in this aspect of Roman religion or, more probably, he regarded Livy's references to prodigies as an unremarkable feature of his narrative, which occurred every year and had therefore nothing exceptional about it. As we shall see, it is possible to infer what views Livy may have had on the religious developments of his own time, but this is only because of some passing references he made in the narrative of earlier events.

Although only such a relatively small portion of Livy's text survives, the role that religion plays in it and the problem of the author's own views on the matter have attracted considerable attention.[4] This is not surprising, given the importance of Livy's evidence. The focus will not be on Livy and religion in general, but on two specific issues: how Livy handles divination (especially prodigies) and what views he puts forward on Rome's historical prospects and on the possibility of predicting Rome's future. The opening act of the contemporary debate on Livy and religion was the book by I. Kajanto, which offered a comprehensive discussion of religious themes in Livy's work, with special emphasis on the problem of the role of the gods and fate.[5] Kajanto mastered an impressive amount of material and presented a view that ran against the grain of decades of Livian scholarship: Livy was a sceptic at heart, who disapproved of the 'irrational' aspects of Roman religion and did not have any 'belief' in a providential ordering of the universe.[6] This approach was as flawed as it was thought-provoking. It is by now mainstream opinion that concepts like 'irrational' or 'belief' are not especially helpful to the study of Roman religion.[7] Kajanto's conclusions were based on the assumption that Livy was not in any way engaged with, or even aware of, Cicero's work on divination and the contemporary debate on religion. Moreover, Kajanto made no attempt to assess the extent of the debt that Livy may have had towards his sources. More generally, many aspects of Kajanto's analysis

---

[3] Cf. however the suggestion in Woodman 1988: 128–34, 151–4 that the preface was written before Actium. On the dating of Livy's first pentad see also Burton 2000, who argues that the composition of the work began in 33 or early 32.

[4] Krauss 1930: 26–31; Stübler 1941.   [5] Kajanto 1957.

[6] The view was not entirely new: bibliography in Guittard 2007b: 85. Overviews of modern scholarship in Cupaiuolo 1984: 21–2 and Nice 1999: 33–40. The cautionary remarks on Herodotus' alleged scepticism in Harrison 2000: 11–14 may also be applied, *mutatis mutandis*, to Livy.

[7] For a recent, passionate attempt to rehabilitate the use of the concept of 'belief' in the study of religion in the Roman world see King 2003. Cf. the discussion of Ifá divination in Holbraad 2010: 269 for the view that applying the concept of belief to divination is entirely misguided.

are based on a very rigid approach: the discussion of Livy's handling of prodigies, which constantly downplays their function in the narrative, is a typical example.[8] Kajanto's study, however, had two merits: it provided a comprehensive collection of material (drawn not just from Livy) and it outlined a misguided dichotomy between rational and irrational which prompted deconstruction and spurred further debate.

Kajanto's work appeared almost at the same time as an article by P. G. Walsh, who argued that Livy's rationalism was based on an allegiance to Stoicism: a hypothesis that does not stand up to scrutiny, but was nonetheless quite influential.[9] The fullest response to Kajanto's model came several decades later, when D. Levene provided a full-scale study of the place of religion in Livy. The main conclusions of Levene's work may be summarised in two points: first, Livy's work must be analysed not as a repository of historical data, but as a literary work that has a complex and often elusive relationship with a range of precedents, models and sources; secondly, the place of religious themes and problems is consistently central to Livy's work and Rome's relationship with the gods is an essential part of his interpretation of Roman history.[10] Against this background, the polarities established by Kajanto and his faith in Livy's rationalism become irrelevant. The guiding principle for the recent consideration of religion in Livy is the readiness to factor in diversity and nuances and even to allow for the possibility that there may not be a central thesis underpinning Livy's approach to religious matters. The recent, very rewarding studies by A. Nice and J. Davies are based on this very principle.[11] The present discussion will show an obvious debt to this approach, even if it will be more limited in scope than those of Levene and Davies: the focus will be on prediction and divination, rather than on religion as a whole.

As noted above, the incompleteness of Livy's work is a serious obstacle to the understanding of his general historical perspective. Things are further complicated by the elusive and cursory nature of many of the references that Livy makes to religious matters. Nevertheless, Livy does have a precise

---

[8] Kajanto 1957: 46–52, esp. 47: 'I think that if Livy really believed in prodigies, he would put them in causal connection with other events.'

[9] Walsh 1958 (see the brief response to Kajanto at 375); see also Mazza 1966: 132–5. For a convincing refutation of Walsh's hypothesis see Liebeschuetz 1967: 51–3. Overview of the debate in Paschoud 1993: 131–2, 146.

[10] Levene 1993. Similar conclusions in this respect may be found in the inevitably much shorter discussion in Linderski 1993 (= 1995a: 608–25, 679).

[11] Nice 1999: 145–215; Davies 2004: 21–142 (cf. esp. 138: '[r]eligion has emerged as considerably more complex in Livy than has hitherto been thought, as indeed has Livy'). See also Gustafsson 2000: 86–90. This approach was anticipated (with specific reference to plague epidemics) in André 1980.

agenda in the representation of religion and religious behaviour; in fact, it is precisely Livy's agenda that makes his account of religious matters so selective.[12] The preface is the necessary starting point for any attempt to approach the problem; it is all the more important for our purposes because it places the problem of historical prediction at the very centre. It is a multi-layered text, which does not just set out the agenda of a complex and ambitious work, but outlines a version of Livy's historical method, its models and its ambitions.[13] The importance of historical memory is one of its central themes and it is shrewdly linked to the problem of the making of the historical traditions about Rome and especially the problem of its divine origins. As J. Moles has shown, it betrays an immediate and profound debt to Sallust and his historical vision.[14] Livy addresses the same problem that we find at the centre of Sallust's proems: the greatness of Rome, its sustainability, and the very tangible risk of a decline. As he ponders the size and scope of his task, he reflects on the extraordinary development of Rome, which started from inconspicuous beginnings, expanded beyond belief and found itself in a crisis determined by its very greatness.[15] In the following paragraph (§ 5) Livy points out that the main purpose of his work is to convey a sense of the behaviour and the moral principles which made the emergence of the empire possible. Rome's prominence is rooted not in a theological or philosophical scheme, but in a moral consideration: the practice of virtues that have singled out the Roman people as the *princeps terrarum populus*. Livy makes it clear that the main focus of his work is on this moral dimension, no matter how heavy the focus on political and military developments may be.[16] His stated aim is an account of the moral decline of the Republic: the standard of the *mores* was lowered when rigour (*disciplina*) started to decline, first gradually and then without control. Its most serious consequence was the inability of Livy's contemporaries to realise the extent of the crisis and to accept and sustain the effort that could solve it:

> *labente deinde paulatim disciplina uelut desidentes primo mores sequatur animo, deinde ut magis magisque lapsi sint, tum ire coeperint praecipites, donec ad haec tempora quibus nec uitia nostra nec remedia pati possumus peruentum est.*

> Let then him [the reader] follow in his mind how, as discipline gradually broke down, morality at first foundered, then subsided more and more, and

---

[12] Davies 2004: 26–7; Guittard 2007b.
[13] Bibliographical overview in Mazza 2005.   [14] Moles 1993a: 153–62.
[15] Livy *Praef.* 4: *quae ab exiguis profecta initiis eo creuerit ut iam magnitudine laboret sua* ('since it [the State] has grown so large from small beginnings that it now struggles because of its own great size').
[16] Paschoud 1993: 130–5.

then began to fall headlong – until the present time, in which we can endure neither our vices nor the remedies for them.[17]

The point is made more precisely towards the end of the preface, when Livy explains in even more explicitly Sallustian terms that the fall of *disciplina* was caused by the rise of wealth, which in turn brought about greed, and by an increasing licentiousness. The picture may well be conventional, but Livy's conclusion in the preface is clear and forceful: the crisis that Rome is going through is of a moral kind, and various signs suggest that it is not reversible.

Negligence

One of the aims of Livy's work is to convey the distance between past and present and to enable his readers to understand the depth and importance of the crisis to which he is pointing.[18] Augustus is absent from the picture; the solution to the crisis, if there is one at all, can be Livy's work. The preface engages with the problem of predicting the future and especially the course of the crisis. Its final sentence establishes a clear link between the solution of the crisis and the success of Livy's historical project: should Livy be successful in writing a comprehensive political and moral history of the city, his readers may be more inclined to understand and come to terms with the decline that threatens Rome. Livy concludes with an invocation to the gods for the success of his work, which has no parallels in historiography, but is frequent in poetry. It is at this point that the only term with openly divinatory connotations – *omina* – occurs in the Preface: Livy expresses the wish to start his work with good omens, wishes and prayers, rather than the sombre thoughts of the previous paragraphs.

> *sed querellae, ne tum quidem gratae futurae cum forsitan necessariae erunt, ab initio certe tantae ordiendae rei absint: cum bonis potius ominibus uotisque et precationibus deorum dearumque, si, ut poetis, nobis quoque mos esset, libentius inciperemus, ut orsis tantum operis successus prosperos darent.*

> But complaints, which will not be agreeable even in the future, when they will perhaps be necessary, should at least be absent at the beginning of such a great enterprise. Rather, if we too were to take up the practice of poets, we would more gladly begin with good omens, and with vows and prayers to

---

[17] Livy *Praef.* 9. Woodman 1988: 132–4, 152–4 and Mazza 2005: 53–6 use this passage to argue for a pre-Actium dating of the preface.
[18] Miles 1995: 78–9 stresses that Livy's pessimism is not unqualified.

the gods and goddesses that they may grant us success as we embark upon such a great work.[19]

This passing reference shows how clear the link between the writing of history and the prediction of the future was in Livy's mind. Denunciation of the decline of contemporary Rome and historical prediction are also deeply connected to one another, especially in the work of Livy, who was so deeply interested in the moral and moralistic implications of his undertaking. Some allusions to the ways of his contemporaries are instructive. In 3.20 Livy mentions the attempts of some tribunes of the plebs to release the people from an oath that they had pronounced; the consul L. Quinctius Cincinnatus, however, who could have seconded their request, refused to do so. Livy comments that Quinctius' decent behaviour was worthy of a time when there was no disregard of the gods and no attempts were made to bend the laws and oaths to one's favour.[20] The reference to contemporary history is clear. Negligence goes hand in hand with the manipulation of religion and law. In the remote past that Livy depicts in book 3, *mores* were shaped by oaths and laws; in the late first century BC the opposite principle applied. Livy's remark may well be just a passing note inspired by the reading of his source, which has a clearly anti-tribunician tone, but it is certainly not isolated, and also fits well with Livy's more general interest in concord.

The idea of a 'before' and an 'after' in the development of Roman religion reappears in similar terms in his depiction of the Third Samnite War in which divination played an important role (10.40). Before the battle against the Samnites at Aquilonia in 293, the Roman camp was dominated by widespread tension and the soldiers were eager to start fighting. When at night, during the third watch, the consul L. Papirius quietly instructed the *pullarius* – the keeper of the sacred chickens – to take the auspices, he was well aware of the mood that dominated in his ranks. The *pullarius* was eager to fight, like many others in the Roman camp, and he decided to misrepresent the outcome of the ritual.[21] Although the birds had not touched food, he claimed that they had in fact eaten. It was the outcome that the consul expected. Livy does not state that Papirius masterminded the false report, but he says that he was pleased (*laetus*) when the *pullarius* reported that the gods supported the battle. After a brief summary of the preparations for the battle, the *pullarii* disagreed on how the ritual should have been performed. The matter was referred

---

[19] Livy *Praef.* 12–13, with Moles 1993a: 156–8.   [20] Livy 3.20.5.
[21] Scheid 2011: 412 stresses the negative influence that emotions have in this turn of events.

to the nephew of the consul, Spurius Papirius, by some *equites* who had overheard the altercation. Spurius referred the matter to the consul, because he belonged to a generation that did not have contempt for the gods; the consul reassured him promptly, congratulating him on his moral excellence and his diligence (*uirtute diligentiaque*).[22]

Livy employs a stronger concept than religious negligence. He states that the nephew of the consul lived before the time when a doctrine that taught the contempt of the gods emerged. It is unclear to what or to whom he is referring. As is often the case with general moralistic attacks, the target remains vague. It may be a reference to those who deny the existence of the gods outright; or it may be a thinly veiled attack on those who exploit religion for political reasons.[23] The latter hypothesis is likelier, as Livy is here referring to a scruple about a possible manipulation of religious ceremonies. On the other hand, the use of *doctrina* seems to point to a whole intellectual horizon. It is difficult to decide which interpretation should be preferred; at any rate, Livy is taking issue with those who do not have the sort of scruples that Spurius Papirius shared with his uncle and that the *equites* had shared with him before.[24]

The reaction of Papirius to the objections of his nephew must be read in light of the favourable outcome of the battle of Aquilonia. The consul noted that the report of the *pullarius* was binding as far as the Roman magistrate was concerned; if the *pullarius* has indeed lied, he will carry the burden of divine wrath upon himself. He then put the *pullarius* on the front line, with the clear aim of testing the position of the gods. When the *pullarius* was killed in action, he saluted his death as a sign of the participation of the gods in the battle (*di in proelio sunt... habet poenam noxium caput*). The position of the city was corroborated by the sudden appearance of a raven, which marked with a loud cry the support of the gods for the Roman cause. This passage is, first of all, a powerful demonstration of the sophistication of the augural code and its importance to any pursuit of the Roman State.[25] Livy clearly accepts that success in the battle was made possible by the ability of the Roman consul to act within the limits of augural law. Papirius is not just a shrewd commander who understands the mood of his soldiers. He is, most importantly, a competent magistrate

---

[22] Livy 10.40.10–11, with Linderski 2006: 101 (= 2007: 14) and Scheid 2012: 114.

[23] Rüpke 2005a: 1448 (= 2005b: 224) argues that manipulation or the commonplace of priestly deception is not relevant to the understanding of the *auspicium ex tripudiis*; when the ritual was performed, only the announcement of the result was public.

[24] Davies 2004: 23–4.

[25] Linderski 1993: 60–1 (=1995a: 615–16). Cf. also Jocelyn 1966: 101–2 and Scheid 1987–9: 133–4.

who knows his duties and the implications that their fulfilment has for the Republic.[26] His correct understanding of individual and collective responsibility enables him to make the most of a very difficult situation. He does not exploit the response of the *pullarius* for his own purposes without being prepared to face the consequences. He even succeeds in securing the support of the gods for the Roman cause by giving them the opportunity to take prompt revenge on the fraudulent *pullarius*. When the battle begins, the gods are actually on the battlefield alongside the Romans, as is made clear by the punishment of the *pullarius* and by the subsequent arrival of the raven on the battlefield. Livy does not comment on Papirius' own religious convictions. As a consul, he is entrusted with the correct performance of augural rituals, which affect the community, rather than the destiny of an individual. However, Livy does not accuse him of *neglegentia* or impiety. The outcome of his actions makes clear that he is keenly interested in securing the favour of the gods.

Livy's narrative, as we have already noted, is complex, and accommodates a number of different and contrasting viewpoints. There is also room for the straightforward, and indeed simplistic, view that priests can and do manipulate public religion for the sake of their political advantage. In 22.34 the tribune Q. Baebius Herennius launches a vibrant attack against the augurs, blaming them for using their authority to block the elections and prevent the success of his associate C. Terentius Varro. This attack against the augurs is part of a more general attack against the nobility. Livy dismisses the attack as a demagogic pose, which was part of a specific political plan. Most importantly, the development of Livy's narrative shows the consequences of this approach to religious matters: Varro, the man whom Baebius supported when he launched his attack against the augurs, was one of the two consuls that led the Roman army to the terrible defeat at Cannae.[27]

Reporting an incident of divinatory significance is, to Livy's mind, about exploring and understanding piety. The care that L. Papirius took in dealing with the complexity of augural law may be compared to the accuracy that must be expected of a historian. In book 43.13 Livy has a brief digression that is also an editorial note and a statement of great significance (43.13.1–2):

> *non sum nescius ab eadem neglegentia, quia nihil deos portendere uulgo nunc credant, neque nuntiari admodum ulla prodigia in publicum neque in annales*

---

[26] The tradition on the defeat of P. Claudius Pulcher (*cos.* 249) at Drepanum in Sicily (Suet. *Tib.* 2.2; Cic. *Div.* 2.71) provides an example of the dire consequences that disregarding the outcome of the *auspicium ex tripudiis* may have. On this passage see Humm 2012b: 280–1.

[27] Jocelyn 1966: 103; Davies 2004: 72–3.

referri. ceterum et mihi uetustas res scribenti nescio quo pacto antiquus fit animus, et quaedam religio tenet, quae illi prudentissimi uiri publice suscipienda censuerint, ea pro indignis habere, quae in meos annales referam.

I am not unaware that no portents are handled as matters of public interest or recorded in our histories, because of the same negligence that these days leads people in general to believe that the gods do not portend what is to come. Nonetheless, my mind, as I write about past events, becomes in some way ancient; and, apart from that, a certain religious scruple restrains me from deeming unworthy of record events which the very wise men of those days regarded as requiring public action.[28]

Before giving a list of prodigies that occurred in the year 169, Livy concedes that his working method has unwittingly become old-fashioned: in his day, prodigies are not reported publicly and they are not included in the *annales*.[29] This is caused by *neglegentia*: the term recurs, although on this occasion it seems to refer not to the manipulation of public religion, but to an attitude that leads to the overlooking of established traditions. Livy claims that he has not fallen prey to this attitude for two reasons. He is a historian who does justice to his material and empathises with it: as he puts it, when he deals with *uetustas* his mind becomes 'ancient'. He is also bound by a form of religious scruple that prompts him not to overlook the practices followed by previous generations.[30]

This passage is a summary of the difficulties faced when working on Livy's approach to religion. First of all, it is unclear why Livy chose to make this point at this specific place in his narrative, and whether this remark was also made in one of his sources. Moreover, Livy's editorial note refers to the portion of his work that will follow: he alerts the reader to the fact that his sources for the last part of the first century BC do not provide as much information about prodigies as those that he used in the previous sections of his narrative. Julius Obsequens' *De prodigiis*, which is an accurate reflection of the lists of prodigies provided in *AUC*, offers a fairly continuous series of prodigies until 42.[31] The conclusion is that there is no sizeable reduction in the number of reported prodigies in the final

---

[28] Heuss 1983: 208 (= 1995: 1515); Levene 1993: 22–3, 28, 113–15; Linderski 1993: 53–4, 64, 66 (= 1995a: 608–9, 619, 621); Paschoud 1993: 126; Nice 1999: 191–200; Davies 2004: 46–51.

[29] Livy probably alludes to other contemporary historians, since he refers to his own work as *annales* a few lines below.

[30] Livy refers to *prudentissimi uiri* – the choice of the adjective is loaded. The expression also occurs in the account of the Bacchanalia, with reference to the Senate and with clear emphasis on a specific expertise: Livy 39.16.9 (*prudentissimi uiri omnis diuini humanique iuris*); see Pailler 1988: 208. On *prudens* see Chapter 2. *Ciuium neglegentia* was a key concept in Varro's *Antiquitates rerum diuinarum* (F 2a Cardauns).

[31] Obs. 70. Cf. Pina Polo 2011: 252–3.

decades of the Republic. The entry on 44 is even divided into two parts: one on the prodigies that occurred before the Ides of March and one on those that followed the death of Caesar.[32] There is, however, a drastic change after Philippi. Obsequens reports only a few prodigies for the years 17 and 11: an earthquake at Livia's estate in the Apennines, a celestial torch (*fax*) burning in the sky from the south to the north, a meteor and a lightning strike on the tower of Caesar by the Colline Gate are linked with the defeat of Roman troops in Germany in 17; another defeat in 11 is associated with the appearance of a swarm of bees in Drusus' camp, near the tent of the prefect Hostilius Rufus.[33] There is nothing about the thirties, nothing about the aftermath of Octavian's victory, and very little about the remaining part of the Augustan period that was covered by Livy's narrative. Although it cannot be ruled out that Obsequens did not have access to significant portions of the final books of Livy's work, the most reasonable conclusion is that Livy had hardly any prodigies to mention for the period of his own lifetime. The silence of the *Periochae* confirms the same impression, even if its summary must always be used cautiously, as it must have been ruthlessly selective; there is not even a mention of the prodigies that preceded and followed Caesar's death.

However, as we shall see in Chapter 12, there is fairly rich evidence for prodigies that took place in the thirties. Perhaps Livy deliberately overlooked traditions that reported prodigies in the final years of the Republic because they did not serve his historiographical and ideological project. The emphasis on impiety provided Livy with a good strategy for the narrative of the Civil War; but how he may have justified this choice to his contemporary audience remains to be explained.[34] It is likely that in a missing section of his work Livy came back to this problem and confronted it more fully than he did in 43.13. Still, the points that he makes in that passage are of great importance for the purposes of our discussion. On the one hand, Livy states that in his time prodigies were not reported *in publicum*, i.e. handled as a matter of public interest, and that they were not discussed by historians. On the other hand, he says that this is due to widespread lack of interest in religious matters, based on misguided

---

[32] Osgood 2006: 20–2.

[33] Obs. 71–2. The prodigy of the torch is also in Dio 54.17.2, who dates it to 16; Bicknell 1991 argues on astronomical grounds that it was neither a comet nor a meteor, but a fireball that left a bright and persistent train. Prodigy of the bees: Dio 54.33.2–4, who reads it as an unfavourable sign, while Plin. *HN* 11.55 links it with Drusus' victory at Arbalo in 11 and points out that the appearance of bees is not necessarily an unfavourable sign, despite what the haruspices argue; see MacInnes 2000: 64–6.

[34] Nice 1999: 200.

views about the relationship between men and gods. Livy does not just take issue with this theoretical approach and the working method of other historians. He also notes implicitly that prodigies were still being reported in his own time, albeit not at the official level. This makes the task of the historian more difficult than was the case in the past. It does not mean, however, that prodigies no longer occurred, or that they were not noticed and even reported by zealous citizens. It does not even imply that they disappeared from the public discourse altogether. An example from the final years of Augustus' reign is instructive. The *clades Variana*, the loss of three Roman legions in the battle of Teutoburg Forest in AD 9, was preceded and followed by a number of prodigies, which were probably reported in an official context, since they were familiar to Dio's annalistic source. Dio does not record the expiation of these portents; Suetonius mentions the celebration of *ludi magni* in honour of Jupiter Optimus Maximus, which were probably part of the official response. The exceptional situation required a temporary return to traditional practices; divine anger was numbered among the causes of the disaster, along with human incompetence.[35]

Linderski has argued that 43.13 is a thinly veiled attack against Augustus and his ruthless appropriation of public religion, including prodigies: supernatural events were interpreted as signs for the rise of a charismatic leader, rather than as problems that required full understanding and proper ritual action.[36] This may well be true, although it cannot be firmly proved. We do not have Livy's books on the Augustan period and it would be rash to infer such a general point on the general outlook of this section of the work from a mere few lines. Livy recognised Augustus' contribution to the restoration of religious life in Rome: he mentioned the refurbishment of a number of temples and he discussed historical and antiquarian matters with him, such as the year when A. Cornelius Cossus won his spoils and the discrepancies in the tradition.[37] It is doubtful that this generic appreciation can be used as reliable evidence for Livy's attitude to the Augustan settlement. Indeed, Livy's handling of Augustus' version of the story of Cossus' spoils has been intriguingly read as a way of negotiating the ground of the

[35] Manil. *Astr.* 1.901–3; Suet. *Aug.* 23.2; Dio 56.24.2–5. Swan 2004: 272–4; Wardle 2011b: 48–9.
[36] Linderski 1993: 64 (= 1995a: 619).
[37] Livy 4.20, esp. 7 (*Augustum Caesarem, templorum omnium conditorem aut restitutorem*). Ogilvie 1965: 563–6; Linderski 1993: 59, 68 (= 1995a: 614, 623). The more general attitude towards Livy is equally problematic and has been intensely debated. On balance, it seems prudent to accept the solution put forward in Badian 1993: 19: 'Livy had no illusions about Augustus personally, but...he was glad of the peace the Princeps had brought (a sentiment no doubt shared by most Romans) and, after 27, worried that it might not last.'

historian vis-à-vis that of the autocrat, albeit within a framework of general support for the Augustan project.[38]

The concept of *neglegentia* is central in 43.13, but its role within the interpretative framework of Livy's work is hard to establish. Not being mindful of one's religious obligations is a serious flaw: if one fails to fulfil one's duties, there is a risk of causing the wrath of the gods, or at any rate there are not the conditions to create the *pax deum*. Livy says that the main point of the creation of the pontifical college by Numa was to make sure that a proper framework was in place, so that the public rites were not overlooked.[39] The concept resurfaces at another important juncture. In book 5 Camillus repeatedly refers to the importance of being mindful of the religious duties of the community and establishes a clear link between the prosperity of the city and the ability to avoid *neglegentia*.[40] This is a moment in Livy's work at which the special bond between the Romans and the gods is stressed very forcefully, in sharp opposition to the Gauls; *neglegentia* plays a central part in the argument. It is unclear, however, how Livy developed it in the rest of his work. There are, in fact, only two surviving references to religious negligence, which both require some discussion in this context. In 22.9.7 Fabius Maximus argues that Flaminius' major flaw was not incompetence, but negligence of rituals and auspices (*neglegentia caerimoniarum auspiciorumque*).[41] In 28.11.7 there is a cursory reflection upon the consequences of religious *neglegentia*. In 206 the fire in the temple of Vesta extinguished itself. Livy makes it clear that it was not a message from the gods, but a consequence of the negligence of the Vestal who was in charge of the sacred fire – a distraction that had, however, clear religious implications. A ritual expiation was nonetheless arranged, with a series of sacrifices and a supplication at the temple of Vesta.[42] It is unclear whether Livy is putting forward his own interpretation, or that of his source, or if he is reflecting some contemporary perceptions of the incident. At any rate, the view of those who took part in the expiatory rituals is not reflected by Livy's passage.

From what we have seen so far, it is clear that Livy took divination very seriously and viewed it as a crucial force in his narrative. We do not know how he coped with the limitations of his material that he claims

---

[38] Sailor 2006 explores the complexity of this passage and its implications on the relationship between Livy and the Augustan project, although it surely overstates the case for the 'competition' between Augustus' and Livy's *auctoritas*. Cossus' spoils and the tradition on the *spolia opima* and the triumph: H. Flower 1990: 52–3; Hurlet 2001: 165; Beard 2007: 293–4.

[39] Livy 1.20.6.   [40] Livy 5.51.4 and 7; 5.52.4, 9 and 15. Luce 1971: 271–6.

[41] On Flaminius' use of the auspices see Scheid 2012: 117–19.

[42] Livy 28.11.6–7. Davies 2004: 92; Février 2009: 145.

had affected the final part of his work, but it is clear that he credited divination with a very important role when he had enough evidence to do so. On several occasions Livy creates a 'deluge effect' by listing a great number of prodigies that were reported in the same year.[43] It has also been convincingly shown that the ordering of the prodigies is not fortuitous, but is intended to serve specific literary and narrative agendas.[44] One of the most spectacular instances of the significance of prodigy lists is 24.10, where Livy mentions a number of prodigies that took place in 214 in Rome and throughout Italy. Livy opens the list with an interesting remark: the more people who are unsophisticated and religiously observant lend credence to prodigies, the more prodigies tend to be reported.[45] This passage should not be read as a cynical or disenchanted remark on prodigies and the way they are gathered and reported; there are other instances in which Livy distances himself from some representations of religious practice that he found in the tradition.[46]

The interest of this passage lies elsewhere. First, Livy views prodigies as a social phenomenon that can say much about wider approaches to religion and is shaped by a specific religious and intellectual climate. This does not imply that they are meaningless events upon which people just reflected their own concerns and fears. Prodigies are a form of communication between gods and men: no matter how often they occur, they must be recognised and socially shared. It is precisely the social and political negotiation of prodigies that puts them within the framework of *religio*.[47] However, like all social processes, this is an imperfect one. It is possible that some events that may not be considered as prodigies ended up in the official list reported by Livy, although he does not quite say that in this context. An allusion to this may be found in 21.62.1, again at the beginning of a lengthy list of prodigies that took place in the winter of 218, where Livy remarks that many prodigies are announced and believed too hastily at times when people's minds are filled with religious zeal.[48] Again, the central point is

---

[43] Davies 2004: 42–4.

[44] De Saint-Denis 1942. Cf. also, on a similar line, Jimenez Delgado 1961a, 1961b and 1963. Sacchetti 1996: 212–21 stresses the variety of solutions that Livy employs in his accounts of prodigies. Pina Polo 2011: 24–30 and Satterfield 2012b use Livy as evidence that prodigies were always expiated by the consuls at the beginning of their year in office; it is doubtful that general rules may be drawn from the extant evidence.

[45] Livy 24.10.6. Davies 2004: 43–4.

[46] The use of *dicitur* in the account of the *deuotio* reported in 8.6.9 and 8.9.1 is a significant example: Liebeschuetz 1967: 47–8 stresses the psychological effects of the incident on Roman troops.

[47] Cf. *religiosi* in 24.10.6, interestingly associated with *simplices*.

[48] Livy 21.62.1: *Romae aut circa urbem multa ea hieme prodigia facta aut, quod euenire solet motis semel in religionem animis, multa nuntiata et temere credita sunt* ('During that winter many prodigies took

that the prodigy reports must be followed by careful consideration of the course of action that is to be followed. Moreover, the excessive enthusiasm of the populace is explained in terms of *religio* and it seems to be given a positive slant. Livy is keen to style himself as an advocate of *religio* and when he speaks about prodigies he is interested in distinguishing between good practice and aberrations. The list of prodigies at 27.23 provides the clearest example, with the throwaway reference to the incident of the mice that reportedly gnawed the gold stored at the temple of Jupiter in Cumae: Livy deems it a trivial incident that was taken seriously out of *praua religio* ('a perverse religious scruple') and should not have been included in a list of prodigies. In no way should this passage be viewed as evidence for scepticism.[49]

On one occasion Livy spells out a very keen interest in historical causation and its links with divination: in the narrative of the well-known episode of the sacrifice performed by the consul T. Sempronius Gracchus in 212 during a campaign in Lucania.[50] As Gracchus was celebrating a sacrifice, an unfavourable prodigy (*triste prodigium*) disturbed the ritual: two snakes suddenly appeared and devoured the liver of the victim; when the haruspices suggested the repetition of the sacrifice, the same incident occurred twice again.[51] The diviners read the prodigy as an admonishment to beware of hidden enemies. It was an appropriate suggestion, but it bore no fruits: the impending catastrophe could not be avoided by any kind of foresight. In this case, prediction was still possible, but it could in no way change the future. This is no indictment of the haruspices, or indeed of divination.[52]

Reflecting upon the limits of prediction and divination is not incompatible with a general acceptance of the main tenets of divination; Cicero's *De diuinatione* shows that most clearly.[53] However, the acceptance of divination is always qualified, for Livy as well as for Cicero. Telling the history of Rome entails recounting the story of wrong interpretations of omens and prodigies. In the frenzied atmosphere that followed Cannae, two Vestal Virgins were found to have lost their virginity; one committed suicide, while the other was sealed in an underground chamber (*uti mos est*, 'as is the custom'); the *scriba pontificius* L. Cantilius who had committed *stuprum*

---

place in Rome and around the city, or many were reported and rashly believed to have happened, which is what happens when minds are shaken by religious fears'). Gladigow 1979: 74; Rosenberger 1998: 31–2, 176–80.

[49] Davies 2004: 45.   [50] Livy 25.16.1–4. Farney 2007: 152–3.

[51] Snakes and the Gracchi: Santangelo 2005a: 206–9.

[52] Cf. Livy 27.16.15 for a successful haruspical intervention. Davies 2004: 71.

[53] Cf. Davies 2004: 40–1.

with one of them was flogged to death in the Comitium on the orders of the *pontifex maximus*. This extraordinary event (a *nefas*, in Livy's words) was regarded as a prodigy and the live burial of pairs of Greeks and Gauls in the Forum Boarium was decreed.[54] This form of expiation – which, according to Livy, went against established Roman practice – was planned and supervised by the *decemuiri*, who accompanied the human sacrifices with other 'extraordinary' (*extraordinaria*) ceremonies.[55] Livy reports the incident with little enthusiasm and then makes his opinion very clear: the *decemuiri* thought that their expiation had solved the problem, but they were wrong and the destiny of the war did not change.[56] As J. Davies noted, this critical phase of the war ends only in the following book, when Fabius Pictor returned from his official mission to Delphi with an unequivocal response by the oracle.[57] The response consisted of a list of deities to which the Romans were expected to offer supplications, and it included recommendations on the rituals that had to be performed. An offering to the Pythian Apollo was also mentioned, with the recommendation that the god be presented with it after the victory of the Romans. The centrality of this event in Livy's narrative of the war is confirmed by what follows: the return of Mago to Carthage and his announcement of the victory at Cannae. When the Carthaginians are celebrating the highest peak of their military success, the Romans receive the response from Delphi that enables them to restore their relationship with the gods and to restore the destiny of the war. The incident does not cast a shadow on Roman divination or on Roman religion. If anything, it confirms its soundness, as the Roman elite proves able to overcome the earlier mistake of the *decemuiri* by making an appeal to a different religious authority. Fabius goes to Delphi in an official capacity and his specific knowledge makes the translation and the understanding of the oracle's response possible. Moreover, the response makes clear that the observance of purely Roman rituals was not the main issue at stake. The problem was to establish which gods had to be addressed and in what ways; the rituals had to be enacted correctly. Moreover, the response of the oracle was promptly included into the framework of public

---

[54] Livy 22.57. Rosenberger 1998: 137; Davies 2004: 68–9; Várhely 2007; Malloch 2008: 155–7; Schultz 2010: 532–6; Richardson 2011: 99. Human sacrifices at Rome: Grottanelli 1999; Van Haeperen 2005; Schultz 2010; Lacam 2012: 47–50.

[55] Livy 22.57.6: *minime Romano sacro.* Cf. Beard 1994: 732 ('an entirely un-Roman ritual') and Schultz 2010: 533 ('hardly a Roman rite' and 'a rite scarcely Roman'). Várhely 2007: 291 unconvincingly argues that Livy is in fact alluding to the gladiatorial games of 264, which also took place in the Forum Boarium.

[56] Livy 22.57.7: *placatis satis, ut rebantur, deis* ('the gods being, it was supposed, adequately appeased').

[57] Livy 23.11.

religion. It is immediately enforced by Fabius at the sanctuary, it is then shared with the Senate, and finally it is archived, as Livy quotes a Latin text of the oracle that he must have found in his source.

The events surrounding Cannae acutely raise the problem of historical prediction. Romans and Carthaginians made important mistakes before and after the battle and the scale of its consequences prompts questions about the involvement of the gods, or indeed of other supernatural forces. We have already seen that, in Gracchus' case, *fatum* was regarded as a stronger force than human *prouidentia* and than any form of expiation. *Fatum* is also repeatedly mentioned in the narrative of the Hannibalic War. The decision to go into a battle at Cannae was taken by the two consuls, on the proposal of Varro and against the advice of the other consul Paulus. It was a decision taken by majority, which Livy nonetheless regards as a sign of fate's will: *urgente fato*.[58] It has been argued that, in Livy, *fatum* is a force that prevails over the power of the gods.[59] It is doubtful that we can reach such safe conclusions on this point. *Fatum* may be regarded as a force that accompanies the action of the gods and a consequence of the quality of the relationship between men and gods. In Livy's work there was scope for a range of approaches to *fatum*. Early on in his narrative, when he deals with the pregnancy of Rhea Silvia and recounts her difficulty in finding shelter from the king and that neither the gods nor men were helping her, Livy argues that the origin of a great city like Rome was made possible by destiny (*fata*): it is precisely because of a fortuitous event like the flood of the Tiber that the twins were not drowned. However, theological consistency should not be sought: the mention of fate is followed by a generic formula like *forte diuinitus* ('by some divinely sent chance'). There is no reason to think that *fata* are an overarching force that prevails over the gods; they are, however, a force that has been supporting Rome since its origins.

The role of fate becomes all the more significant when the welfare and survival of Rome appear to be under threat. The Hannibalic War is a critical juncture. When one of the soldiers who had taken part in the battle of Cannae addresses the consul Marcellus, Livy provides a different explanation for the defeat. It was not caused by the anger of the gods or by

---

[58] Livy 22.43.8–9: *cum utriusque consulis eadem quae ante semper fuisset sententia, ceterum Varroni fere omnes, Paulo nemo praeter Seruilium, prioris anni consulem, adsentiretur, [ex] maioris partis sententia ad nobilitandas clade Romana Cannas urgente fato profecti sunt* ('Since, as usual, the consuls were each of the same view, and almost everybody supported Varro, while no one spoke in favour of Paulus, except Servilius, consul in the previous year, they left, following the will of the majority, pushed by fate, to render Cannae illustrious because of the Roman defeat'). *Urgente fato* and *urgentibus fatis*: Schmid 1961 (388 on Livy).

[59] Davies 2004: 107–8.

fate, but it was determined by human error (*culpa*) – the mistakes of the generals, rather than of the soldiers.[60] Incidentally, this passage also offers an intriguing definition of what *fatum* is: a force that provides guidance in all human affairs. It is different from the wrath of the gods, but it is not necessarily to be viewed as a force that prevails upon it. Another speech gives a sense of how fluid things could become in Livy's handling of these concepts. Soon after landing at the mouth of the Ebro in 210, Scipio Africanus gives a speech to his soldiers, which is not just the opening act of the great Roman counter-offensive against Carthage, but an assessment of the war and of Roman history as a whole.[61] He begins by saying that fortune (*fortuna*) created a special bond between him and his soldiers even before he took up his province. He continues by saying that the favour (*benignitas*) of the gods will be crucial in securing the expulsion of the Carthaginians from Spain; he then reflects upon the toll that the war has taken upon Rome and his own family and argues that fate (*fatum*) gave Rome a special destiny (*sors*), that of winning great wars after meeting heavy defeats; a series of relevant examples is provided. Just when the reader may be led to think that fate is the dominant force in Roman history after all, the gods reappear a few lines below. They give clear indications through the auspices and the augural signs that victory is at hand. They must be heeded, because they have watchfully presided over the rise of Rome and her empire and because Scipio himself has the same premonition.[62] As he puts it, his own mind has always been the safest *uates* – a loaded word at the time when Livy wrote his work, as we have seen.[63]

The model of Polybius

Livy had earlier called Scipio a *fatalis dux*, as soon as he had entered the narrative, choosing an epithet that he only otherwise used to refer

[60] Livy 25.6.6: *si non deum ira nec fato, cuius lege immobilis rerum humanarum ordo seritur, sed culpa periimus ad Cannas, cuius tandem ea culpa fuit? militum an imperatorum?* ('If it was neither by the anger of the gods, nor by fate, according to whose laws the course of human affairs is unalterably fixed, but by misconduct that we were defeated at Cannae; but whose was that guilt; the soldiers', or that of their generals?'). As Levene 1993: 47–9 notes, the whole account of the battle of Cannae heavily downplays the role of divine interference. This also applies to other aspects of Livy's narrative: cf. 8.10.8, where he argues that whichever side had been led by T. Manlius Torquatus would have been victorious; this implicitly undermines the decisive importation of the *deuotio* of P. Decius Mus in the same battle (see Chapter 3 and Davies 2004: 104).

[61] Livy 26.41.3–25. On this speech see Seguin 1974: 10, 16; Lazarus 1978/9; Feldherr 1998: 66–7.

[62] Cf. also Scipio's evocation of the patronage of Neptune, which is closely intertwined with his leadership qualities, in Polyb. 10.11.6–8 and Livy 26.45.9.

[63] Livy 26.41.19: *animus quoque meus, maximus mihi ad hoc tempus uates, praesagit nostram Hispaniam esse* ('My mind too, always my greatest seer, foretells that Spain will be ours').

to Camillus in the body of work that has survived, again with the aim
of anticipating early on what role the commander was to play in a long
and complex war, which Rome would win only after suffering crushing
defeats.[64] Livy may mean that the commander was chosen by fate to lead
Rome to victory; Scipio is able to understand what fate is planning for
Rome and how the Romans are expected to fulfil their role. However,
fate was by no means the only factor in his success. The gods and *fortuna*
were influential and their actions did not necessarily contrast with what
fate prescribed. Davies has stressed that in Livy the word *fatum* appears
sparingly, and usually evokes an overarching cosmic plan that sets Rome
apart from any other city. This level of explanation is not used to undermine
the role that the gods and their cult play in Livy's work.[65] This argument
is on the whole tenable, but two cautionary remarks are necessary. It is
worth asking whether references to *fatum*, especially in the case of Scipio,
have anything to do with the sources that Livy used; Polybius, with his
frequent references to the role of *tuche*, may well have played a part in
shaping Livy's thinking about the period.[66] Indeed, Polybius' appreciation
of Scipio's achievement was complex and to an extent similar to Livy's.
He takes issue with the widespread popular opinion that Scipio's actions
were divinely inspired and argues that the achievements of Scipio were
based on his talent and his foresight, despite the widespread tendency to
credit 'fortune and the gods' with the success of prominent individuals.[67]
Later in the same book, however, *tuche* appears when Polybius praises the
moderation and good sense that Scipio displayed after his victory in Spain,
despite his young age and the great favour that fortune had shown him.[68]
The reference to *tuche* here is instructive and subtle: on the one hand, the
role of *tuche* in Scipio's rise is acknowledged, in an apparent contradiction
to what was previously stated. On the other hand, Scipio's talent and
resilience are put at the forefront, and come across as more forceful than
tuche. Despite being supported by *tuche*, Scipio chose to rely on other
strengths, namely his own personal qualities.

We do not know how Livy framed the role of *fatum* in the narrative
of the fall of Carthage, or the role of figures like Scipio Aemilianus and

---

[64] Scipio: 22.53.6; Camillus: 5.19.2. Connection of the Cornelii with *fatum*: Paladino 1989: 36–41.
[65] Davies 2004: 114–15.
[66] I write *tuche* without a capital letter, as suggested by Walbank 2007: 349. *Tuche* in the Hellenistic
world: Champeaux 1987: 38–59. Cf. the interesting choice of Clark 2007 of writing the names of
the so-called 'abstract deities' of the Roman pantheon in small capitals (e.g. VIRTUS, HONOS,
etc.), attempting to reflect the indeterminacy between the two possible traditional spellings.
[67] Polyb. 10.5.8.   [68] Polyb. 10.40.6 and 9, with Walbank 1957: 22 n. 4.

Sulla – not to speak of Caesar and Octavian.[69] It is conceivable that *fatum* was discussed at some point, but the emphasis of the preface is all on moral and religious themes, without a single reference to *fatum*. At any rate, it is safe to conclude that the *fatum* of Livy was something very different from that of Virgil's *Aeneid*.[70] Again, the analogy with Polybius is appropriate. *Tuche*, as is well known, plays a very prominent role in Polybius' work: it is frequently mentioned in a variety of contexts and for a number of different purposes.[71] The role of *tuche* leads the reader right to the core of the problem of historical prediction and of the reasons for the writing of history. History is, for Polybius, an attempt to make sense of the past and to teach readers how to interpret the present and use their knowledge to carry out practical actions in the future. However, if *tuche* is the dominant force in historical causation, prediction becomes an unviable exercise, and no useful lessons may be drawn from the past either. The usefulness of historiography itself is thrown into doubt. Polybius is aware of this potential contradiction and he makes the most of the complexity of the concept of *tuche*. He often uses it to refer to imponderable events, which fall outside human control and appear impossible to comprehend. In a discussion of the causes of Roman hegemony, however, he also famously argues that the historian has the specific task not to confine himself to praise the might and power of *tuche*, but to seek the true historical causes (τὰς ἀληθεῖς αἰτίας) that made Roman military success possible.[72] Elsewhere he interestingly draws a distinction between events that escape human understanding, such as heavy rain, drought or frost, and events that are clearly caused by human action or inaction, such as a low birth rate and population decrease. While the first type of events may be attributed to *tuche*, it would be absurd to think that an oracle or a prophet could possibly help with issues that can be addressed by adopting different behaviour and better laws.[73]

There are cases in which *tuche* punishes individuals because of their arrogance, their lack of intelligence or their behaviour. There are also cases when *tuche* seems to act as an overarching cosmic force that determines events a priori, beyond human abilities and talents. We have seen the case of

---

[69] On the religious themes surrounding the fall of Carthage and Scipio Aemilianus' attempt to assert a special connection with the gods see Rawson 1973: 166–74 (= 1991: 88–101).

[70] Cf. Liebeschuetz 1967: 53: Livy 'does not use *fatum* and *fatalis* as sign-posts to a providential interpretation of his history, but for limited literary aims', namely with reference to inevitable calamity and oracles.

[71] A summary of the modern scholarship on the topic in Hau 2011: 183–6. On Polybius' understanding of historical causation see Maier 2012.

[72] Polyb. 18.28.4–5.   [73] Polyb. 36.17. Walbank 1979: 678–83; Parker 1985: 304.

Scipio Africanus; similar points could be made for Hiero and Eumenes.[74] In these cases, however, the reference to *tuche* enables Polybius to make a point that limits its importance and impact. Those men achieved great things because of their personal qualities, not because of the support of *tuche*. In fact, inferring any specific general interpretations on the role of *tuche* in Polybius' work, or indeed in his thought, is a hopeless endeavour.[75] Polybius mainly uses *tuche* as a literary device, which enables the historian to develop certain themes and to stress others in the events with which he deals.[76] Its frequent association with the rhetorical device of 'as if' (ὥσπερ) is a good example of its role in the service of historical explanation, and of Polybius' tendency towards marginalising its influence.[77] Moreover, as is the case with Livy, it must be borne in mind that we have only a portion of Polybius' work and that our appreciation of the significance and development of such themes in the work is bound to be incomplete and provisional.[78]

One negative point, however, can be made with reasonable confidence. Even if the handling of *tuche* by Polybius is comparable to the use of *fatum* in Livy, the context in which it is framed is very different, as Polybius was not interested in portraying religion as a crucial factor in the rise of Rome, or the bond between Rome and the gods as a leading theme in his history. The rise of Rome was due to the ability of the Romans and to the knowledge that they gained by undergoing a number of tests – it was not fortuitous or involuntary.[79] In a famous passage of book 6 Polybius makes clear that he takes the special relationship between the Romans and their gods to be a central aspect of his historical narrative.[80] He recognises that public religion is a crucial factor of cohesion, precisely because it is so tightly controlled by the political elite and it secures its supremacy over the populace. While he does use the Greek word *deisidaimonia*, which is usually translated into Latin as *superstitio*, his recognition of the importance

---

[74] Polyb. 7.8.1; 32.8.4. Walbank 1957: 22.

[75] Brouwer 2011 is an attempt to show that Polybius' use of *tuche* is consistent with Stoic precepts.

[76] Hau 2011: 194–205. [77] Walbank 2007: 352–4, with references.

[78] Walbank 2007: 354 on the 'fluidity' of *tuche* in Polybius. Eidinow 2011: 52, 184 n. 177 argues that Polybius' assessment of the role of *tuche* was not inconsistent; the role of *tuche* and a pragmatic explanation are not mutually exclusive.

[79] Polyb. 1.63.9.

[80] Polyb. 6.56.6–15. Rawson 1973: 161 (= 1991: 81). Vaahtera 2000 notes that what survives of Polybius' work has hardly anything to say about Roman public religion; on his reading, this is deliberate omission, due to Polybius' rationalistic approach. Desideri 2011: 26–31 views Polybius as a committed rationalist, whose critique of δεισιδαιμονία heavily influenced Livy. That Polybius' reflection on Roman public religion made a strong impact on his Roman elite readers is a reasonably safe guess (Beard 1994: 768).

of Roman *religio* is not accompanied by an attempt to explain what makes it so successful, or an appreciation of its intellectual coherence, as we find in Livy or in Cicero. Polybius' approach to the problem is practice-oriented. Significantly, his appraisal of Roman religion features in a discussion of wealth and the control of the malversations of the Roman officials. There is no doubt that this assessment of Roman religion was widely read within Roman intellectual circles from the late second century BC, but we do not know how widely it was debated and how other authors reacted to it. This passage is surely the most prominent example of those (often not very clearly defined) Greek intellectual influences on Roman culture that are often evoked in modern scholarship as the main factor to have prompted a critical revisitation of Roman religion in late Republican culture. However, the agendas of the surviving Roman authors that are known to have discussed religion and divination after Polybius followed quite different lines.

Varro – the man whom Cicero credited with the greatest contribution to the historical understanding of Roman religion – is a case in point.[81] When he wrote the *Antiquitates rerum diuinarum*, his aim was not merely to gather a significant body of information and evidence and to embark on an antiquarian work.[82] He was interested in exploring the profound dynamics of Roman religion: the exploration of the Roman religious tradition was a central feature of this project. Even a hostile reader like Augustine paid tribute to Varro's insight and noted that his work was that of an intellectual who invited his readers to worship the gods by reflecting upon religious tradition and practice.[83] It is to Augustine that we owe the mention of Varro's important statement that he was prepared to accept the names and the characters of the gods as transmitted from antiquity, even when he found them unpersuasive; he thought that his task was to encourage the populace to nurture its religious feelings, rather than to question them. In that context, the choice to override his own views in his discussion was testimony to his piety, because it protected *religio* from disrepute (Aug. *CD* 4.31; cf. Varro *ARD* F 12 Cardauns):

> sed iam quoniam in uetere populo esset, acceptam ab antiquis nominum et cognominum historiam tenere, ut tradita est, debere se dicit, et ad eum finem illa scribere ac perscrutari, ut potius eos magis colere quam despicere uulgus

---

[81] Cic. *Acad. post.* 1.3.9.

[82] Boyancé 1955 (= 1972: 253–82); Cardauns 1976 and 1978; Rawson 1978b: 15–16 (= 1991: 328); Jocelyn 1982–3; Powell 1995a; Tarver 1995; Rüpke 2005c; Van Nuffelen 2010 and 2011: 16–17, 29–37.

[83] August. *De civ. D.* 4.31.7: *auctor acutissimus atque doctissimus.* Augustine's reading of Varro: Ando 2008: 15–18 and esp. Clark 2010. Klingshirn 2005 shows how critical Augustine was of the forms of divination based on a *disciplina*.

uelit. quibus uerbis homo acutissimus satis indicat non se aperire omnia, quae non sibi tantum contemptui essent, sed etiam ipsi uulgo despicienda uiderentur, nisi tacerentur.

But, as it is, since he belongs to an old people, he says that he must keep the narrative of names and surnames as it was trasmitted, and that he writes and researches these topics with the aim that the populace may prefer to worship the gods, rather than despise them. With these words this most intelligent man makes abundantly clear that he has not revealed everything, points that were not only matters of contempt for him, but would also seem despicable to the people themselves, unless they were overlooked.

Therefore, in Varro's view, upholding tradition is not a manipulative use of religion which perpetuates the supremacy of a cynical elite; it is a service to *religio*, which saves the core of the relationship between men and gods.[84] Varro, like some of his contemporaries, thought that public religion was under threat because of the negligence of his fellow-citizens, rather than because of any external pressure. His work was an ambitious intellectual construction that aimed to provide a lifeline for the tenets of public religion. The systematisation that it offered may have entailed omissions and simplifications, but its main aim was to encourage piety in the challenging context of late Republican Rome. We are far away from the reductionistic approach of Polybius.[85]

On the other hand, a Roman author would have no doubt found it easy to agree with Polybius' emphasis on the industriousness and bravery of the Romans. These qualities have significant implications for a discussion of aspects of prediction and divinatory skills. Again, the construction of the character of Scipio in Livy's narrative is especially relevant. In 26.19 Livy interrupts the narrative to present a portrait of Scipio and his qualities, which starts with a celebration of his outstanding ability to persuade and fascinate.[86] Scipio used to claim that he was more capable of understanding and predicting developments than any of his contemporaries, as if he could rely on knowledge imparted by the gods. Livy is rather vague on the sources of Scipio's knowledge: dreams (*per nocturnas species*) or a loosely defined divine inspiration (*diuinitus mente monita*).[87] Most interestingly, he leaves the nature of Scipio's motives for the reader to establish: Scipio may have

[84] It is apparent from August. *De civ. D.* 6.2 that the opposition between *religio* and *superstitio* was central to Varro's concerns and that the *Antiquitates* were intended to provide a thorough discussion and a definition of the remit of *religio*.
[85] *Contra* Jocelyn 1966: 91 and 1982–3: 177–83.   [86] Feldherr 1998: 66–72; Davies 2004: 126–33.
[87] Pelling 1997: 201 notes that Livy's handling of dreams is 'characteristically two-voiced'; consistency is not to be expected.

genuinely possessed a form of prophetic ability (*quadam superstitione*), or else he may have used an oracular tone to corroborate his orders. Livy does not voice open criticism of Scipio's use of his prophetic ability. It is conceivable that the use of the concept of *superstitio*, while perfectly justifiable from a semantic standpoint, may be intended to cast a bad light on Scipio's strategy: Livy certainly knew that the word was often used in opposition to *religio*. Indeed, Scipio's claim to divinatory expertise is precisely the opposite of the traditional construction of public religion: he rejects any filter and mediation, and styles himself as an oracle. On the other hand, he is the legitimate bearer of *imperium*, and it is this legal position that enables him to rely on the support which the gods grant to Rome at a crucial stage of the Hannibalic War.[88] Divine and human causation are never neatly separable in Livy.

Moreover, the very decision to leave the verdict open on a central figure of Republican history is significant; what follows corroborates this critical picture and defines it further. Before embarking on any significant undertaking Scipio used to visit the temple of Jupiter Capitolinus, where he would sit alone. This personal exercise in piety sets him apart from the crowd that takes part in public rituals; his relationship with the gods is, first and foremost, personal, and reflects his exceptional standing. It was precisely his habit of visiting the temple by himself that, according to Livy, was the major cause of the emergence of a widely held belief about Scipio's divine status: the familiar story according to which a snake had been seen in the bedroom of Alexander's mother was also applied to him. Livy rejects it outright, dismissing it as a story that is both silly and baseless (*et uanitate et fabula parem*).[89] It is hard to avoid the impression of an outburst of hostility in his remark that Scipio did nothing either to dismiss this story or to confirm it. He refused to set the record straight on a story that played a crucial role in building an aura of charisma around him and in making his political rise possible. The depiction of Scipio's ability to gain consensus and respect is inextricably linked to the emphasis on his ability to make successful predictions. Livy uses the portrait of Scipio as an opportunity to reflect upon the consequences of unbridled political ambition for the stability of the Republic. The foundation stones of the *iuuenis*' rise are his

---

[88] Feldherr 1998: 66–72 rightly argues that this theme does not appear to have featured in Polybius' narrative of the same events. Cf. also Seguin 1974: 15–16.

[89] Livy 26.19.7: *fabula* as 'myth of the stage'? Cf. also Sil. *Pun.* 13.634–44; Quint. *Inst.* 2.4.19; *De vir. ill.* 49.1–4. The tale has striking similarities to and instructive differences from the traditions on the conception of Augustus (Suet. *Aug.* 94.6; Dio 45.1–2): Lorsch Wildfang 1997. On the impact of this tradition see Lange 2009: 43–5.

special relationship with the gods and his *superstitio* – his quasi-prophetic talent.

No doubt the problem of historical prediction was also discussed elsewhere in Livy's work. While the destiny of an individual may not be necessarily related to his piety and his relationship with the gods, the destiny of a city is easier to determine. This is the message we encounter at the very beginning of book 44, when L. Marcius Philippus gives a speech to his troops on the eve of the war against the Macedonian king Perseus, where he establishes a link between the prospects of the enemy and those of the Romans. While Perseus has planned or perpetrated a number of crimes and inflamed the wrath of the gods, the Romans can base their strength on a special connection with the gods. Their *pietas* and *fides* bode well for the outcome of the war, and also explain previous Roman conquests.[90] This point is made in a speech, but the position it has in the narrative clearly suggests that Livy approves it. We are, after all, at the very beginning of the great transmarine war that completes the Roman conquest of the Eastern Mediterranean and immediately precedes the phase of moral decline that many of Livy's predecessors, from Polybius to Posidonius and Sallust, regarded as a direct consequence of Roman expansion.

One should refrain, however, from applying too rigid an interpretative framework. According to Livy, there were instances of moral decline even before the age of the transmarine wars. During the Hannibalic War, for instance, a Roman hostage attempts to avoid returning to Hannibal's camp by going back to Rome as if he had forgotten something. His name is not even recorded; Livy only states that he was a deeply un-Roman man.[91] He then takes care to specify, at the very end of book 22, that his misdeed was adequately punished by his fellow-citizens: he was handed back to the Carthaginians, either by a unanimous vote of the Senate or by a lengthier procedure at the beginning of the following censorship.[92] Livy notes that his sources were in disagreement, and does not even try to explain why this was the case. At any rate, it is clear that the attitude of the hostage is that of a minority, which does not refrain from exploiting questionable technicalities in order to avoid specific religious duties. By the late third century BC, the system still had the ability to punish and expel members who did not recognise the importance of these obligations.[93]

Some conclusions are in order. Two aspects are central to our purposes: the coexistence and balance between contrasting approaches to divination

---

[90] Livy 44.1.10.   [91] Livy 22.58.8: *minime Romani ingenii homo.*
[92] Livy 22.61.4.   [93] Cf. Davies 2004: 49–50.

and the possibility of inferring Livy's personal views from the complex fabric of his narrative. The two problems are closely related to one another. Livy was not an antiquarian or a priest. We should not expect him to give a meticulously accurate representation of religious problems, or a full summary of rituals. As Linderski noted, in what survives of his work Livy never provides a full outline of the procedure that led to the reporting and interpretation of a prodigy, but chooses to concentrate on the aspects that serve best his own literary agenda.[94]

Livy could also rely on an impressive array of literary evidence, which provided him not just with raw historical data, but also with a range of interpretative approaches. With some of them he will have agreed and with others he will have disagreed; some he will have no doubt reflected in his narrative, albeit to an extent that we are not in a position to determine. Moreover, Livy was acutely aware of the debate on divination that unfolded in his own time, as some of his polemical references to contemporary *neglegentia* suggest. He knew that divination was contested from several different angles, at least in some elite circles, and that its practice was undergoing a process of considerable change. Most importantly, he was aware that each divinatory incident (whether a prodigy or an augural sign) could be debated and scrutinised at an official level, especially by the Senate, and that the very debate on its reliability entailed a debate on the identification of genuine and viable sources of divination and prediction.[95] It is not surprising that some of these arguments resurfaced in Livy's narrative and became part of the interpretative strategy outlined within. Public divination plays a very significant part in Livy's work and is a strong marker of the alliance between the Romans and the gods which Livy identifies as the main cause of the fortunes of the city and her empire. For this reason, religion in Livy is necessarily a political matter that makes sense only if it is practised within specific institutional constraints. Doing justice to the difference between reliable and unreliable forms of religious life is an important task of the historian. As Levene has noted, Livy engages his reader in a complex project aimed at the understanding of Roman history, of which religion is a very important aspect.[96] However, Livy is not presenting his readership with an open agenda, which is fed by unresolved contradictions. On the contrary, he offers a complex assessment of religious practice – including divination – which is based on the importance of public controls and filters, and on the primacy of carefully negotiated and

---

[94] Linderski 1993: 57 (= 1995a: 612); cf. Satterfield 2012b.
[95] Liebeschuetz 1995: 315, discussing Levene 1993.   [96] Levene 1993: 29–30.

codified interpretations. The coexistence of contrasting views and arguments must be understood within this context. History does have a direction and Livy's work is intended to make a meaningful contribution to its interpretation.

Many features of the overall picture inevitably escape us, since so much of Livy's work does not survive. As we noted above, had the narrative of the late Republic and the Augustan age survived, it would have added further, decisive insights into what Livy made of the developments in his own time. The same uncertainty applies to the second problem discussed above, that of Livy's own views on divination. There is agreement among scholars that Livy's 'religiosity' should be separated from the role that Roman religion plays in Livy's work.[97] Indeed, what Livy's own view on religion may have been is essentially a matter for speculation. The debate on Livy curiously mirrors the views of modern scholars on Cicero's *De diuinatione* which have been discussed in Chapter 1. Of course, the views of any author are ultimately inexplorable and should not be expected to emerge clearly from his work. There is no compelling reason, however, to think that Livy held different personal views on prediction and divination from those that he put forward in his work. This takes us back to the problem that was set out at the beginning of this discussion: the surviving portion of Livy's work is too exiguous to allow for a safe conclusion on what his own views were or on how they developed through the decades.

Coda: Livy on the foundation of Rome

Civic cohesion is a fundamental theme in Livy's work and a central concern to an author who set out to write a history of Rome after the season of the Civil Wars. Augury plays an important role in the handling of this problem. Livy's account of the events that led to the foundation of Rome revolves around two augural rites performed by Romulus and Remus on the Palatine and the Aventine.[98] Interestingly, there is a consensus between the two brothers on the purpose of the ritual: their shared aim is to entrust the gods with the choice of the site of their new city through an augural ritual. The conflict arises on the interpretation of the signs received by Romulus and Remus. The ensuing altercation is cut short by Romulus' decision to kill his brother, in anger. Livy's account is intended to confirm the status of augury as the most ancient form of consultation of the gods in Rome, but it may also be constructed as a denunciation of its limit. The

---

[97] Levene 1993: 1–37; Linderski 1993: 54 (= 1995a: 609); Liebeschuetz 1995: 315.   [98] Livy 1.6.4–7.3.

signs of the gods can be confusing and divisive, and their interpretation problematic. Any interpretation can be viable only if there is clear control over it, and if that control is backed up by a formalised body of knowledge – a *disciplina*. Augural law carefully set out which sign was to be followed when a second one opposed a first; indeed, according to Servius, the second sign always prevailed.[99] Moreover, the records of the augural college laid out in detail the signs that were detected in the past and what responses were devised; signs were classified under different grades.[100] However, the dispute between the twins took place before these rules were codified, and it was rooted in the lack of a preliminary agreement on which signs are going to take priority over the others.[101] It is true that Romulus' control over the auspices is accompanied by an act of violence, which is caused by anger and, ultimately, by the inability of either brother to set aside his ambition and desire to rule. However, the story should not be understood as evidence of the gods' intention to give confusing messages to mankind or as an outright condemnation of augury. It is rather a reminder of the fact that augury is effective only in a well-ordered society. Human agency still matters greatly: there are problems that augury cannot solve. On a recent reading of this episode, its implications for Livy's assessment of the Augustan regime are heavy: the reader is led to understand Romulus' victory as a premonition of the unbridled violence of the first century BC.[102] There may be an even stronger case for reading it as a statement of how important consensus and collaboration are if a meaningful and effective relationship with the gods is to be established.

The version of the story chosen by Livy was not the standard one at the time when he wrote his history of Rome. The decision to focus on the dissension between the brothers over augural interpretation and on the fratricide was a deliberate selection made within a complex tradition.[103] In Ennius' *Annales* the foundation of the city takes place *augusto augurio* ('by august augury'), and the signs are received only by Romulus.[104] There is competition between the two brothers, who are accused of aspiring to

---

[99] Cic. *Div.* 1.124; Serv. *ad Ecl.* 9.13; *ad Aen.* 2.691 and 12.183. Wardle 2006: 370, 407.

[100] Serv. *ad Aen.* 3.374, with Linderski 1986a: 2234–6.

[101] Bouché-Leclerq 1882: IV, 218–25 stresses that it was crucial to agree on which augural signs were to prevail if conflicting signs were detected; cf. Green 2009: 152.

[102] Miles 1995: 137–78; Green 2009: 150–3.

[103] Wiseman 1995: 1–17; see esp. 6–9 on the traditions concerning the detection of the augural signs by Romulus and Remus.

[104] Enn. *Ann.* 154–5 Sk. (= Varro *Rust.* 3.1.2–3): *septingenti sunt, paulo plus aut minus, anni / augusto augurio postquam incluta condita Roma est* ('it is seven hundred years, a little more or a little less, since famous Rome was founded by august augury'). Skutsch 1985: 314–16. See also *dant operam simul auspicio augurioque* ('they devote themselves to both auspices and augury'), again referring to

kingship (80–1: *curantes magna cum cura cupientes / regni*), but there is no doubt as to whom the gods favour as the founder of the city and there is no controversy about the interpretation of augural signs. In the account of Dionysius of Halicarnassus the dispute over the augural interpretation causes a tension within the citizen body which goes beyond the control of the two brothers, and Remus dies in the ensuing riot between the two factions. Romulus pays tribute to his memory by burying him at Remoria, the site which Remus had chosen for his new city, and publicly shows his grief. The fratricide does not feature in this tradition, which Dionysius presents along with another one, in which Remus grudgingly surrenders the leadership to Romulus and then crosses the boundaries set by his brother, only to be killed by Romulus' associate Celer.[105] Livy's version emphasises the dispute over the interpretation of the augural signs and has fratricide as its extreme consequence. This is a serious choice, which has a number of implications. While the institution of augury is not put into question, there is an emphasis on the potential ambiguity that underpins the foundation ritual of Rome and it serves as a reminder of the consequences of political division. Reflection upon the correct use of augural signs is at the forefront. Livy – the 'post-war historian', in Sir Ronald Syme's definition – had a lucid understanding of the spirit of his time.[106]

Romulus and Remus, in Enn. *Ann.* 73 Sk. (= Cic. *Div.* 1.107) with Rüpke 2003: 13–15 and 2004: 27–8; Linderski 2006: 98–100 (= 2007: 12–13).

[105] Dion. Hal. *Ant. Rom.* 1.87. Cf. however Dionysius' account of the augural dispute between the twins: Romulus sent messengers to Remus falsely claiming that he had seen the birds and saw the twelve vultures only after Remus had seen six (1.86.3–4, with Wiseman 1995: 8).

[106] Syme was planning an essay entitled 'Livy: a post-war historian' in the final years of his life (Birley 1999: xix n. 29).

CHAPTER II

Signs and prophecies in Virgil

With Livy we have entered – chronologically and, to some extent, ideologically – Augustan territory. In the last chapter of this book we will discuss how the rise of Octavian/Augustus reshaped the practice of divination in Rome and narrowed the diverse range of divinatory experiences that were available in the late Republican period. We will see that the restriction of divination under the patronage of the *princeps* was a central feature of Augustus' agenda. His main aim was not to repress the sources of divination that were available, but to bring them under the patronage and (as far as it was conceivably possible) the control of the new master. The extent of this control is a matter of debate. Against this background, it is not surprising that the open debate on divination and prediction as it had been practised in the late Republic did not find a place. However, the literature of the Augustan period repeatedly engages with problems that are directly relevant to divination and to the relationship between the city, the gods and the future, and it is to a specific aspect of it that our attention will turn first.

Virgil is an invaluable vantage point for a historical discussion like the one that is developed in this book. His work is not commensurable with historical narratives like those of Sallust or Livy, or with a discussion like those we encounter in Cicero's work. Nonetheless, it deserves to be examined in detail, for at least two reasons. Virgil's poems are invaluable documents for the intellectual life of the period; they do engage in highly original ways with contemporary politics, most notably with the Augustan agenda. They also feature a number of divine signs and prophecies. Virgil's handling of these, however, is far from straightforward; he is not an author whom we may expect to offer a depiction of 'regular' religious situations.[1] The relevance of his work to the purposes of this discussion lies chiefly in the contribution that it makes to the understanding of what a recent trend

---

[1] Feeney 2004: 7.

of studies has defined 'ritual in ink'. Virgil depicts a number of divinatory incidents, and in doing so he engages in a critical reflection upon them: he constructs and de-constructs the terms of divination, and reflects on its potential and its boundaries.[2] More generally, he shows a consistent interest in the prediction of the future and the problems that it entails.

Cicero and Virgil

We know little about the publication and reception of the *De diuinatione*. There is little evidence that it was read in the aftermath of Cicero's death and there are no traces of a sustained contemporary debate on Cicero's work. There is, however, a very significant exception. The first book of Virgil's *Georgics* features a famous section devoted to the prodigies that followed the death of Caesar (1.463–97). Virgil somewhat simplifies the complex tradition that surrounded the events, as he overlooks the prodigies that preceded the Ides of March, in order to concentrate on what follows and create a clear link between them and the prodigies that anticipated the Civil War.[3] Virgil lists a series of signs foretelling impending disaster, which closely resemble the signs listed in several passages of the *De diuinatione* and, most notably, in the extensive quote from Cicero's *Consulatus suus* in 1.17–22 (= F 10 Courtney). The correspondence is striking and certainly intentional. This is, in fact, the clearest intertextual use of the *De diuinatione* attested in Latin literature and it cannot be explained just by the intention to establish a link between the Catilinarian conspiracy and the Civil War of the forties.[4] Virgil was certainly aware of the role that the passage played in the debate between Quintus and Marcus. He could appreciate its critical importance to a broader reflection upon the limits of divination and prediction. Virgil mentions the signs surrounding the death of Caesar within a discussion of the link between signs and prediction, straight after a discussion of weather signs and notably of the power of the sun to foretell events.[5] The sun is always a safe guide, in meteorological as well as in political matters. The eclipse in 44 was a sign of divine concern about the destiny of Rome after Caesar's death and a representation of the

---

[2] Cf. Beard 2004: 125–6.

[3] Schiesaro 1997: 75–80. Cf. also the commentary in Thomas 1988: 144–51, which is based on different interpretative premises.

[4] Setaioli 1975 (= 1998: 11–32); Schiesaro 1997: 75–9. It is possible that Virgil directly knew the *Consulatus suus*, but various sections of the *Georgics* suggest a direct knowledge of the *De diuinatione*: Setaioli 1975: 13–15, 22–26 (= 1998: 18–20, 27–31) and 2005: 242–3, 259–61. On the depiction of the triumviral years at the end of *Georgics* 1 see Osgood 2006: 348–9.

[5] Verg. *G.* 1.463–6.

darkness that dominated that period: 'cruel ages dreaded an eternal night'.[6]
That fear proved misplaced. The signs were a symptom of the disgrace that
the last generation of the Republic was already experiencing, rather than
a premonition of further disgrace. A familiar range of prodigies emerges –
ominous birds, volcanic eruptions, comets, floods, earthquakes, land sub-
sidences: it has parallels in Roman history and is closely matched by the
prodigies depicted in Cicero's poem.

Discussing prodigies necessarily entails the problem of their interpretation and their use in averting future disaster. In the *Consulatus suus* the
picture is – at least in this respect – unproblematic: the Muse Urania gives
a list of prodigies and praises Cicero for understanding their significance
and for recognising the importance of divinatory signs to the relationship
between men and gods.[7] In the *Georgics*, the prodigies mark the beginning
of an age of traumatic change and unprecedented violence (esp. 1.487–8),
but it appears that no one is capable at first of understanding their implications and significance. The prodigy list ends with the evocation of Philippi
and the Civil War that accompanied it: the responsibility for that tragedy
is human, but Virgil also specifies that the gods did nothing to prevent
it.[8] His subsequent invocation to the gods, notably Romulus and Vesta,
begs them to allow the young man to save a world in ruins. The present is
not at all peaceful, however, as there are plenty of imminent signs of the
dangerous situation of the empire, from Germany to the Euphrates. The
implication is that no more prodigies are needed to forewarn mortals of
evils ahead – challenges need to be faced and the *iuuenis* is the only one
that can provide a solution, possibly with the guidance and support of the
deified Caesar. This passage is by no means evidence for a negative attitude
towards divination or the reliability or usefulness of prodigies.[9] It ends,
however, with the prodigies almost fading away into a hazy background
and the invocation of a period where the situation will be rectified by a man
who is – or at least appears to be – equipped to gain the necessary support
of the gods. Whatever the outcome of the crisis, the tragic spell marked by
the prodigies that unfolded between the Ides of March and Philippi is over
for good.

[6] Verg. *G.* 1.468: *impiaque aeternam timuerunt saecula noctem.*
[7] Cic. *Div.* 1.17–22 = F 17 Courtney. Courtney 1993: 162–71 and Gildenhard 2011: 294–8.
[8] Verg. *G.* 1.491–2.
[9] 'Pessimistic' approaches: Thomas 1988: 144; Perkell 1989: 154–62. The signs occur after Caesar's
death, but they foretell the civil turmoil that follows the Ides. It is reductive to construct them as 'a
mysterious, unexplained collusion of celestial and terrestrial events' (Perkell 1989: 162); cf. Schiesaro
1997: 76–7.

The dialogue that Virgil builds with Cicero's *De diuinatione* is a complex one. On the one hand, there are intertextual and thematic links, which suggest that Virgil is engaging with the same conceptual framework as Cicero; on the other, Virgil pursues a different agenda, in which *religio* does not appear to be at stake and a different compromise is reached between acceptance and rejection of divination than the strategy envisaged by Cicero. Prodigies do carry specific meanings and may be understood and interpreted in order to avert disgrace; sometimes, however, the spirit of the times can make any positive action impossible and an 'impious' generation may end up misunderstanding the signs of its imminent destiny and head towards a new Civil War. In this important respect the difference between the events of 63 and 44 could not be greater. The failure of the Roman Republic coincides with a failure to read the signs of its imminent demise. Octavian's rise is determined no longer by the ability to interpret the prodigies, but by the moral stature that is required to avoid the crisis of the State and put an end to a season of fear.[10] What is at the forefront is the personal responsibility of the new leader and the moral renewal that he is setting out to enable. Only his success will make the interpretation of divinatory signs once again possible and meaningful. This is, after all, a way of creating the conditions for the restoration of *religio*.

Ambiguity is a concept that is often evoked in modern scholarship on Augustan literature, especially where the assessment of the Augustan regime is concerned. It applies especially to poetry: the modern debate on Virgil's *Aeneid* and the coexistence of different voices in the poem is a case in point. However, in *Georgics* 1 Virgil appears to regard signs as invaluable tools for the understanding of reality and the control of the future, and his discussion is centred on the view that there is a necessary link between divine power and weather-signs. The observation of the sun and the signs it offers is not just relevant to weather forecasting, but may also enable the prediction of events of great political significance: the events of 44 showed it most vividly.[11] Not all signs, however, may be intended as premonitory, or have divinatory value. In a development that already features in the *De diuinatione*, Virgil gives a list of the signs that announce fair weather after rain. Observing the sky is invaluable, for instance. Ravens seem to anticipate the change in the weather, but are not divinely inspired. Their behaviour is, on the contrary, the mere consequence of the change in the

---

[10] Emphasis on security in the Augustan discourse: Kneppe 1994: 218–29.
[11] Verg. *G.* 1.461–6, with Schiesaro 1997: 75.

humidity of the air.[12] The debt of *Georgics* I to the *De diuinatione* is the only evidence we have for the first-century BC reception of the treatise, and it shows what aspects of its argument were debated.[13] The solution that Virgil puts forward in the *Georgics*, of course, is significantly different from that of Cicero, although it shares some of its essential concerns. There is no room for a negative take: divine signs may be read and may enable mankind to attain some knowledge of and control over the future.[14] The gods and the natural elements are not misleading; they need to be interpreted correctly, and the correct boundaries between prodigies and natural signs must be set. Virgil also rejects the idea of a 'double truth' whereby an educated Roman may endorse divination in public and privately reject it, which is set out in explicit terms by Marcus in *Div.* 2. The belief that the world is full of signs and that their correct interpretation is possible and helpful is at the core of Virgil's project. This is a project of piety, first of all, since most signs come directly from the gods. The knowledge that they offer is both empirical and religious, and the perfomance of appropriate rituals is a large part of it.[15]

There is another significant difference from the *De diuinatione*. Virgil develops a case for the centrality of signs and the importance of their expert interpretation to which many members of the late Republican elite (including the author of the *De haruspicum responso*) would have no doubt subscribed. However, he does so under the patronage of Octavian, as he explicitly states at the outset, when he asks the *princeps* to approve his effort to provide *praecepta* to the peasants (1.40–2). It is again with Octavian that the long divinatory excursus of the first book ends, after Virgil has listed the prodigies following the death of Caesar and mourned the catastrophe of Philippi. A prayer is addressed to Romulus not to place any obstacles in the way of the mission of young Caesar, who has come to save an age (*succurrere saeclo*) that has witnessed many destructive events (1.498–514). The danger that the failure of Caesar can represent is powerfully embodied by the image of the chariot dragged off by unrestrained horses, irretrievably

---

[12] Verg. *G.* 1.415–16: *haud equidem credo, quia sit diuinitus illis / ingenium aut rerum fato prudentia maior* ('Not, I believe, that they have wisdom from on high, or from fate a greater foresight of things to come'). It is doubtful that this passage should be read as a statement undermining augury, as this is not an augural context; a different reading in Schiesaro 1997: 73.

[13] Reception of *Div.* from Valerius Maximus to Goethe: Pease 1920: 29–37.

[14] The failure of the seers to perform their rituals and produce a response in the context of the Noric plague (*G.* 3.489–91) does not invalidate this general picture: the seers do not succeed in interpreting unexpected prodigies, which however do have a forceful meaning. 'Pessimistic' reading of this section of *G.* 3.478–566: Perkell 1989: 162–6. Sacrifice in the *Georgics*: Feeney 2004: 7–11.

[15] Schiesaro 1997: 80–9 on the anti-Lucretian features of this agenda. Imitation of Lucretius in the *Georgics*: Hardie 1986: 158–67.

out of control, which embodies the need for the *res publica* to regain a firm direction. The poem sets out to contribute to the effort to bring about a new order.

Signs and prophecies in the *Aeneid*

While the stance on divination and prophecies in the *Georgics* seems clear, establishing how these issues are handled in the *Aeneid* is harder. The numerous occurrences of prophecies and augural practices in the *Aeneid* have often been taken as a vantage point for the understanding of Virgil's construction of the character of Aeneas and the overall agenda of the poem. There is of course a risk underlying the study of poetic texts in this context. While it is fairly uncontroversial that Virgil should be read 'in the light of history', it is less clear how history could and should be read in the light of Virgil, that is how Virgil's use of, or even references to, divination and more generally the relationship between men and gods should be used as evidence for wider historical and cultural developments.[16] The same question could be applied fairly to any Latin poetic text. As D. Feeney argued, the Romans – unlike the Greeks – did not regard poetry as central to their collective reflection upon religion and the role of the gods in human affairs.[17] It is all the more relevant to a work of extraordinary literary, narrative and ideological complexity like the *Aeneid*. The emphasis in this context will be on two aspects: the passages in which Virgil directly engages with specific aspects of Roman divination (e.g. augury), and the role that prophecies play in the poem. Other broader aspects such as the balance between divine and human will, the role of fate in the poem or the agenda of the poem vis-à-vis the Augustan resettlement will not be discussed here, as they fall outside the remit of this study.

It is worth starting from the role of prophecies, which is so pervasive across the poem and has attracted much critical interest. In his study of prophecies in the *Aeneid*, J. O'Hara argued that most of them are optimistic, but are nonetheless not to be taken at face value.[18] Some are based on a limited knowledge of the events; some are deliberately misleading and deceptive, or omit material that would be disturbing for their recipient. The deaths of several friends of Aeneas, for instance, seem to contradict prophecies that were uttered earlier in the poem.[19] On a different note, the poem is marked by the recurrent literary motif of the *si non uana*:

---

[16] Horsfall 1990.   [17] Feeney 1991: 103–5.   [18] O'Hara 1990.
[19] E.g. Orontes (1.390–1), Palinurus (6.343–6) and Pallas (9.241–8): O'Hara 1990: 7–53.

on various occasions a character gives a qualification or limitation to a prediction, saying 'unless divination is useless'. This clause questions the potential of divination, but does not necessarily reflect a critical or negative attitude.[20] Another area of interest is deception: men can produce false prophecies, as Sinon's case powerfully shows, and gods can send deliberately misleading signs to men.[21] A striking case is the prodigy that the nymph Iuturna, Turnus' sister, sends to the Rutulians in order to avoid the duel between Turnus and Aeneas. Juno, the implacable enemy of the Trojans, knows that fate has already decreed the victory of Aeneas, but nonetheless urges Iuturna to make it as hard as it conceivably can be. Juturna too knows that the destiny of her brother is ineluctable, but tries to prevent the direct confrontation between him and Aeneas. She sends to the Rutulians a positive omen which is misleadingly positive, aiming to persuade them to attack Aeneas and distract him from engaging in a duel with Turnus.[22] An eagle drives away the other birds that are on the shore, and then flies down to the sea and snatches away a swan; the other birds, however, react by chasing the eagle, which ultimately is compelled to let the swan go. The Rutulians regard it as a favourable sign, and their augur Tolumnius confirms that interpretation. From a technical standpoint, his reading of the omen was plausible; however, the prediction that derived from it was that the Rutulians would defeat Aeneas: the prediction that derived from the interpretation of the omen was undoubtedly wrong.[23] Questioning the intention behind a divine sign equates to probing the viability itself of divination, and especially of prophecies.

O'Hara's interest in the construction of prediction in the *Aeneid* is directly relevant to the modern debate on the optimistic or pessimistic agenda of the poem, and on the extent of its adherence to the Augustan agenda.[24] The enactment of prophecies in the *Aeneid* should be read as a testing ground for the complex construction of the mythical past of Rome that Virgil conjures up: a story, or indeed a history, where good and evil coexist, and in which sorrow, injustice and violence are fully factored in.

---

[20] O'Hara 1990: 13–14, 55–6; a list of passages at 55.

[21] Sinon quotes a false oracle in his speech to the Trojans: Verg. *Aen.* 2.114–19, with Cowan 2011.

[22] Juno's address to Iuturna: Verg. *Aen.* 12.138–60; prodigy: 12.244–56. Coleman 1982, 152 argues that Juno's intervention is a symptom of her desperation, as by the end of the war she can pursue her aims only through the agency of others; La Penna 2005: 292–3 likens Iuturna's concern for Turnus to that of a mother and establishes an analogy between her and Venus. On Iuturna and her cult in Rome see Aronen 1989.

[23] Verg. *Aen.* 12.244–65, with O'Hara 1990: 85–7; Montero 2006: 28. See also Serv. *ad Aen.* 12.246.

[24] Schiesaro 1993 points out that, despite his declared intentions, O'Hara consistently tends to side with the pessimistic readers' camp and that he fails to appreciate the importance of ambiguity in the overall texture of the poem.

Detailed literary analysis does not fall within the remit of this study. The autonomy of the literary sphere must be borne in mind. Poetry follows rules of its own and should be used only very cautiously for the discussion of wider historical problems.[25] However, it is important to stress the scope of the reflection that Virgil develops on a number of religious issues, and to consider not just the extent of his role in Augustan culture, but also his even more significant debt to the intellectual developments of the first century BC and his grasp of the great historical problems of his time.[26] The *Aeneid* provides clear evidence for Virgil's technical knowledge of haruspicy.[27] Philosophical knowledge will also have played a part. His acquaintance with Epicureanism, for instance, may have shaped his reflection upon the relationship between men and gods. On the other hand, the emphasis on the concept of *fatum*, most notably at the very beginning of the poem (1.2: *fato profugus*), conjures up a strong Stoic resonance, although it cannot be reduced to a philosophical concept derived from the teachings of a specific school: Virgil uses *fatum* and *fata* to convey a range of different meanings, and notably to refer both to 'what is willed' and to the 'will of the gods'.[28] Moreover, the role of fate is intertwined in complex ways with the role of the gods in human affairs. Against the background of such a keen interest in prediction and predestination, it is not surprising that Virgil was familiar with Cicero's *De diuinatione*.

Most of the prophecies that we encounter in the poem come from gods and do not take place in a ritual context that is even vaguely comparable to what happened in the first century BC. On the other hand, the use of prophecies and the creative and critical engagement with their reliability should be viewed as a symptom of a climate in which the viability of prophecies and predictions was debated and questioned. The complexity of the poem and its agenda escapes the dichotomy of an optimistic–pessimistic approach. The same applies to the view that Virgil had on the course of Roman history and the future prospects of Rome. It is more prudent to argue that Virgil was very interested in prophecies, both as worthwhile readings of the history of Rome, her origins and her destiny, and as a fundamental component of Roman public life and of the relationship between the Romans and their gods. He was also well aware of the pitfalls that they

---

[25] M. Flower 2008: 209 argues that it is from prose works, not from poetry that we can glean 'how a divinatory consultation was supposed to work'.

[26] A good example is offered by his reflection on the relationship between Rome, Latium and Italy: Bettini 2005 and 2006; Barchiesi 2008.

[27] Enking 1959; Briquel 1991 and 2008: 116–17. Enking 1959: 90–5 and Hall 1982 argue that Virgil had Etruscan origins.

[28] Pötscher 1978: 409–14; Lyne 1987: 72–3; Gildenhard 2007c: 98–100.

presented. Literary considerations played an important role. Prophecies are traditionally prominent in the epic genre, which is often preoccupied with the relationship between men and gods and the issue of divine intervention in human affairs.

Against this background, it is worth considering in more detail how Virgil deals with two forms of divinatory activity that played an important role in Roman public religion and which also feature prominently in the *Aeneid*, namely the augural lore and the Sibylline prophetic tradition. The first prophecy of the *Aeneid* has a clear augural dimension. Venus, disguised as a huntress, gives Aeneas a response that foretells his imminent arrival in Carthage: twelve swans swimming nearby are put to flight by the arrival of an eagle, and they fly towards the sky; it is a favourable omen, which is confirmed by later developments.[29] There are two important differences with the use of augury in a historical context: the involvement of the swans (which can be explained by the association of this animal with Venus) and, on a more substantial level, the fact that the *augurium* does not come from a priest or any human interpreter, but from the goddess herself. This incident comes before the arrival of Aeneas in Italy and the creation of a statal framework. The intervention of the patron goddess precedes the formation of an organised framework of religious structures.

An augur also intervenes directly in the last book of the poem, after the intervention of Iuturna that we discussed above. The augur Tolumnius is the first to salute it as a benign presage and to thank the gods for their support. This interpretation was based on the misguided assumption that the eagle was a symbol of the Trojans. On the contrary, the development of the battle shows that the Trojans are linked with the swans, and the reader who remembers the augural incident recounted at the beginning of book 1 will have been able to establish that connection.[30] The link with the earlier episode raises the issue that is so often central in the *Aeneid*: the asymmetry between what the narrator, the readers and the characters know. In this case, the reader may be in a position to read the sign correctly, while the Rutulians are misled by it. It has recently been argued that this episode is underpinned by a critical reading of augury.[31] There are some obstacles to this interpretation. First, the position of the augur: Tolumnius' mistake should not be seen as an indictment of augural lore in general, as it is the blunder of an individual. If anything, it draws a contrast between Roman

---

[29] Verg. *Aen.* 1.693–700, with Green 2009: 154–5.

[30] The association between the two passages has often been noticed: O'Hara 1990: 86–7, with bibliography at n. 54.

[31] Green 2009: 155–8.

and Italic augury, and between accurate and fallacious augury, which can also be found in the *De diuinatione*.[32] Secondly, the nature of the sign: it does not take place within the usual context of Roman augury, as it is not sought by men or freely given by Jupiter, the god who is commonly associated with augury.[33] Strictly speaking, therefore, the episode is not even an augural sign: it is the trick of a goddess that the Rutulians fail to discern. The ill-fated reaction of the Rutulians is a reminder of the importance of reading signs correctly. This passage is no evidence for a more general critique of augury and its viability. On the contrary, it may be viewed as a strong assertion of the importance of reading and understanding augural signs correctly, for what they are and for the message they convey. The emphasis on the tragic demise of Tolumnius *augur* at the very beginning of the battle confirms the significance of his incorrect interpretation and the deadly consequences of bad augury.[34]

The Sibyl

Virgil also memorably engages with another strand of Roman divination, the Sibylline tradition, at a crucial juncture of the poem. In depicting the encounter between Aeneas and the Cumaean Sibyl in book 6, Virgil takes an unequivocal line on the nature of Sibylline lore (6.1–155).[35] The first mention of the Sibyl who lives in the cave at Cumae, in the sanctuary of Apollo, defines her as a prophetess, a *uates* inspired by Apollo 'who discloses what will be' (6.11–12: *magnam cui mentem animumque / Delius inspirat uates aperitque futura*).[36] It is in the full confidence of her prophetic abilities that Aeneas consults her, and such confidence is rewarded and confirmed by the future developments of the plot. Before depicting the consultation of the Sibyil, Virgil recounts the aetiology of the sanctuary, which goes back to Daedalus' arrival on the coast of Italy (6.14–33); the Sibyl, who is called Deiphobe and serves as a priestess (6.35: *sacerdos*) of Apollo and Diana, then gives Aeneas a ritual prescription that must be fulfilled before the consultation takes place: the sacrifice of seven bullocks and seven

---

[32] Cic. *Div.* 2.70, 76.

[33] Jupiter's association with augury: Linderski 1986a: 2206–7, 2295–6.

[34] Verg. *Aen.* 12.460; cf. also the bitter irony in the first mention of this character in 11.429 (*felixque Tolumnius*).

[35] Gildenhard 2007c: 89–93. A close reading of the episode in Miller 2009: 133–49. Cumaean Sibyl: Altheim 1938: 351–3; Poccetti 1998: 81–97; Buitenwerf 2003: 114–18.

[36] Coleman 1982: 149 argues that Apollo is a source of reliable prophetic guidance for the Trojans throughout the poem, but does not discuss this passage.

yearling sheep.[37] When the sacrifices are performed, the Sibyl enters an ecstatic trance and urges Aeneas to seek the advice of the god. Aeneas obliges and begins with an invocation to Apollo, whom he asks to rescue the Trojans; he then extends the prayer to all the gods (6.56–65). He subsequently addresses the Sibyil with a request that reveals the concern behind the consultation: he does not ask her for a response directly, even if he admits that she has foreknowledge of what will happen (6.65–6: *o sanctissima uates,* / *praescia uenturi*), but asks her to concede that the Trojans may settle in Italy. The request is backed by a pledge to honour her: he vows to build a temple to Apollo and his sister Diana, where he will place the oracles of the Sibyl and will entrust them to chosen men (6.69–74). This is a direct reference to the Sibylline Books, to the *quindecemuiri*, and to the central role of this institution in Roman religion. It is an aetiology that, as it has been recently noted by I. Gildenhard, deliberately runs against the grain of an established Republican tradition, which credited one of the Tarquins with the introduction of the Books to Rome, on the advice of the augurs, and placed it at the time of the construction of the temple of Jupiter Capitolinus.[38] Aeneas is here credited with the creation of the special relationship between Rome and Sibylline lore; the focus of this relationship is also firmly located at Cumae, rather than with the other centres of Sibylline prophecy that were involved with the reconstruction of the corpus after the fire of 83.[39] The promise that Aeneas offers to the Sibyl contains a strong prophetic element, as it alludes to a key moment in the Augustan resettlement of public religion. On 9 October 28 he presided over the dedication of the temple of Apollo on the Palatine.[40] Virgil also appears to anticipate a later development in Augustan policy: when the emperor took up the supreme pontificate in 12, he promoted a reorganisation of the corpus of the Sibylline Books and had the new collection deposited in two golden cases in the temple of Apollo Palatinus.[41]

---

[37] Sibyl as a priest: Nelis 2004: 63–4. Sibyl as a mystagogue: Quiter 1984: 49–56.

[38] Tarquinius Priscus: Varro *ARD* F 56a (= Lactant. *Div. inst.* 1.6.10–11) and 56c Cardauns (= Serv. *ad Aen.* 6.72); Tarquinius Superbus: Dion. Hal. 4.62; Plin. *HN* 13.88; Gell. *NA* 1.19; Zonar. 7.11; Solin. 2.17; Tzetz. *ad Lycophron* 1279.

[39] Cf. Garstang 1963: 100–1.

[40] Serv. *ad Aen.* 6.69; Hor. *Carm.* 1.31; Prop. 2.31 and 4.6. Barchiesi 2005: 282 points out that Aeneas approaches the Sibyl 'in the guise of a Greek settler looking for a colonization oracle', who promises in return the temple on the Palatine.

[41] Suet. *Aug.* 31.1; see Chapter 6. Austin 1977: 64–5; Bishop 1988: 113. Smith 1913: 444 uses Verg. *Aen.* 6.72 and Tib. 2.5 as evidence that the books were transferred to the Palatine before 19; Gagé 1955: 544 states that Virgil gives a '"préfiguration" assez vague'; Wardle 2011a: 274–6 argues that Virgil's lines should not be used as evidence for the transfer of the Sibylline Books.

There are also, of course, sharp differences with the model of Sibylline Books as it was known and used under the Republic. Firstly, under the Republic the Books were kept in the temple of Jupiter Optimus Maximus on the Capitol, and had no connection with the Palatine. Moreover, the prophecies of the Sibyl are not written – not even on leaves, as Aeneas asks her (6.74–5) – and are delivered in a state of madness, as she is possessed by the god; that is a form of inspired prophecy that had no place in the frame-work of Roman public religion.[42] The Sibyl's prophecies are true, but they envelop the truth with a cloud of obscurity (6.100: *obscuris uera inuoluens*). There are also, however, important analogies. While the first prophecy of the Sibyl is strictly about the future, and what awaits Aeneas and his comrades, the second intervention of the prophetess is a specific piece of advice given in response to a question of Aeneas, in which she shows him the way to the underworld and prescribes the burial of Polydorus as a nec-essary condition for Aeneas' descent. It is a specific prescription like those that were offered by the *quindecemuiri* on the basis of the Sibylline verses. Virgil's engagement with the Sibyl and the Sibylline tradition revolves around these tensions and contradictions with the historical experience.

Prodigies in the *Aeneid*

Virgil also depicts a considerable number of prodigies, which all take place in relation to the foundation of the new community of the Trojans on the Italian shores.[43] Some prodigies occur in book 3, while their fulfilment takes place in books 7 and 8. Virgil could build on a rich tradition of foundation prodigies, which started as early as Lycophron and Fabius Pictor, and which he developed in his own original way. Virgil's crucial innovation is his new depiction of the relationship between prodigies and divine intervention, which does not feature in the parallel tradition. The table-eating prodigy in book 7 is clearly associated with Jupiter, while the prodigy of the sow giving birth to thirty piglets at the site where Aeneas is going to found the new city is linked to Juno by the two figures that prophesy it, notably Helenus and the river-god Tiberinus, who both insist on the need to

---

[42] Splendid discussion of the difference between divine inspiration, ecstasy and frenzy in Lightfoot 2007: 8–11; cf. 8 n. 31 for the point that Aeneas' encounter with the Sibyl resembles a consultation with the Pythia, as the Sibyl usually delivers her message spontaneously. Gildenhard 2007c: 91 n. 101 interestingly reads Aeneas' invitation not to write the prophecy on leaves as a symptom of first-century BC concerns on the circulation of unofficial written prophecies.

[43] Grassmann-Fischer 1966. See also Bailey 1935: 12–28; La Penna 2005: 225–31.

appease the goddess.[44] The close link between the two events is also a Virgilian innovation which does not feature in the tradition: they are both signs that the end of Aeneas' labours is imminent. The significance of these incidents is powerfully marked by the link that Virgil establishes between different sections of the poem. The most striking case is the table-eating prodigy, in which Aeneas, Ascanius and other Trojan leaders are eating bread and keep eating the tables at which they are sitting because they are overcome by hunger. The Harpy Celaeno – *infelix uates* – had prophesied that the Trojans would have to endure hunger and toil before reaching their destination, and Aeneas also recalls a similar prophecy from his father Anchises, which does not appear elsewhere in the poem, but was probably given to Aeneas in one of the nocturnal visits that he received from his father after his death.[45] The reference to Aeneas' father after a prodigy centred around Ascanius gives the scene a whole new dimension: that of an event that embraces three generations and vouches for the survival and continuity of the Trojan stock. Jupiter's support is confirmed by his favourable response to the prayer that Aeneas addresses to him after the prodigy: three thunderclaps from a clear sky. The prophecy of Celaeno is therefore shown to be correct, even if the threatening tone with which it was uttered is turned into a liberating force after the arrival in Latium and the mediation of Anchises. While a 'further voice' may still be heard in the background, the positive one prevails.

This is not the only prodigy in the poem that establishes a link between generations and that may be read in sharply conflicting ways. Ascanius and Anchises are linked by the *mirabile monstrum* that takes place as the Greeks are ravaging Troy and Aeneas is about to join the fighting: a flame appears around the head of Ascanius. Anchises regards it as a sign of Jupiter's favour and dispels the fears of Aeneas and Creusa. He asks for another sign of divine support, which arrives immediately in the form of a shooting star.[46] Anchises regards it as a clear sign that leaving Troy in search of a new motherland is necessary and agrees to follow his son. The same prodigy occurs in book 7, when the head of Lavinia is surrounded by a flame as she is

---

[44] Table-eating prodigy: Verg. *Aen.* 7.107–29 (esp. 110: *sic Iuppiter ipse monebat*). Prodigy of the sow: 3.388–95; 8.41–8. Grassmann-Fischer 1966: 54–63, esp. 62–3 on the close integration between this prodigy and that of the *mensae*. Helenus: 3.388–93; Tiberinus: 8.42–3. See O'Hara 1990: 24–39.

[45] Verg. *Aen.* 3.245–58, evoked in 7.122–7; cf. also Serv. *auct. ad Aen.* 3.246, with discussion of the expression *infelix uates* and a definition of the *dirae*. Boas 1938: 221–49; Grassmann-Fischer 1966: 39–53; Hübner 1970: 61–73; Harrison 1986: 158–62, with a critical discussion of the theory that explains the reference to Anchises with the unfinished state of the poem; Horsfall 2006: 202–8.

[46] Verg. *Aen.* 2.679–704. Grassmann-Fischer 1966: 9–28; West 1993: 8–9, 16 (arguing for a direct reference to the *sidus Iulium*); Horsfall 2008: 480–2 (there was a tradition on Anchises' skill as a seer).

performing a ritual with her father Latinus. The prodigy is interpreted as a sign of future glory for Lavinia and of imminent war for the Latini. Latinus seeks the advice of the prophet Faunus, who foretells that Lavinia will marry a foreigner and that the blood of the Latini will mix with a foreign stock, generating a nation that will subjugate the world.[47] This prodigy is clearly linked to that of Ascanius: the beginning of Aeneas' journey is linked with the beginning of its end; the table-eating prodigy follows only a few lines below. There are, however, other underlying themes: prodigies involving fire were attested elsewhere in the tradition on other figures of the past, such as Servius Tullius and L. Marcius.[48] The association between fire and sacrifice also featured in the account of a prodigy foretelling Augustus' greatness. When his father C. Octavius performed a sacrifice in Thrace in 60, a flame sprang from the wine that he had poured on the altar. A similar prodigy was previously associated with Alexander the Great.[49] It is conceivable, of course, that the prophecy *ex euentu* on Octavian was in fact inspired by the *Aeneid*, or by traditions that Virgil had used.

Faunus' oracle points us to the wider problem of the prophecies uttered by the gods in the *Aeneid*. Their narrative function within the poem is very significant, as they raise the issue of the relationship between men and gods, and of the viewpoint of the voice, or voices, within the poem. While they should not be used for a reconstruction of Virgil's views on divination and on the possibility of predicting the future, they convey a sense of a vision of the direction of the history of Rome at the period, and of how the poem engaged with the question. The relationship between Aeneas and Juno, which mirrors that between Rome and Carthage, is a central concern of the prophecy that Jupiter gives to Venus in the first book.[50] Jupiter is a god who is closely identified with *fatum* throughout the poem, whose will prevails over that of the other gods: he is best placed to reveal the plan of fate and to administer its secrets.[51] His response reassures Venus on the felicitous outcome of the history of Aeneas' descendants, who will

[47] Verg. *Aen.* 7.81–101. Boas 1938: 165–94; Grassmann-Fischer 1966: 67–77; Horsfall 1999: 96–108.

[48] Servius Tullius: Livy 1.39.1–4. L. Marcius: Livy 25.39.16; Val. Max. 1.6.2; Plin. *HN* 2.241; see Wardle 1998: 186–7. Grassmann-Fischer 1966: 27–8 suggests that Virgil was influenced by the annalistic tradition on Servius Tullius.

[49] Suet. *Aug.* 94.5. Engels 2010: 166–7 draws an interesting comparison with a similar story about Seleucus I (App. *Syr.* 284; Paus. 1.16.1). For another parallel with the tradition on Alexander cf. the story of Augustus' conception in *Aug.* 94.6: Lorsch Wildfang 1997.

[50] Verg. *Aen.* 1.254–96. Catalogue of the prophecies on the destiny of Trojans in Bishop 1988: 27–49.

[51] Lyne 1987: 71–99, esp. 71–5 (cf. 74 on the use of *fari*); see also Wilson 1979 (esp. on Jupiter's role in the understanding of *fata* on the part of gods and men); Neri 1986: 1977–80; La Penna 2005: 229–30. *Fatum* and *fata* in the *Aeneid*: Bailey 1935: 204–34; Haury 1981: 229–44.

eventually create an *imperium sine fine* (1.279: 'an empire without end') with the support of the gods, including Juno.

The political implications of this prophecy are clear. At 1.286–8 Jupiter foretells the birth of a Caesar of Trojan ancestry who will oversee the expansion of the empire and mark the beginning of an era of peace.[52] Who this Caesar is has been the subject of intense debate. The obvious hypothesis would be to suggest that he is Augustus, but it is quite possible that Virgil left things deliberately ambiguous; close scrutiny suggests that Julius Caesar may be a good candidate.[53] If this were correct, the passage would open the possibility of an interesting interpretation of Caesar's dictatorship and its aftermath: Jupiter suggests that after the rise of Caesar an age of tranquillity and peace will begin (1.291: *aspera tum positis mitescent saecula bellis*, 'then savage ages shall soften, once the wars have ceased'). The Ides of March can hardly be regarded as the beginning of a golden age; it is perhaps more prudent to accept a recent hypothesis whereby the first part of the response (1.286–90) should be read as a reference to Caesar and the second (1.291–6) as a reference to Augustus.[54]

However, shortly after Caesar's death a memorable event created a sense of promise that was shrewdly exploited by Octavian: the appearance of a comet in the sky during Caesar's funeral games – the so-called *sidus Julium*.[55] The debate on its interpretation takes us back into the political *mêlée*. We are at the core of the Augustan discourse, which will be the main focus of the final chapter of this book.

---

[52] Verg. *Aen.* 1.286–8: *nascetur pulchra Troianus origine Caesar, / imperium Oceano, famam qui terminet astris, / Iulius, a magno demissum nomen Iulo* ('A Caesar shall be born of splendid Trojan descent, to bound his rule by the Ocean and his fame by the stars, Julius, a name derived from the great Iulus').

[53] Dobbin 1995; earlier bibliography at 6–7. *Contra*, see Harrison 1996. Note the clearcut solutions suggested in Kraggerud 1992 (who concludes that the passage univocally refers to Augustus) and West 1993: 16 ('explicit, though contested, reference to Julius Caesar'). White 1988 convincingly argues that the memory of Caesar was not marginalised or removed in the Augustan period, but retained an important role in public discourse; Wardle 2007 explores the prominent role of Caesar in Valerius Maximus' work and its relationship with the Augustan agenda.

[54] Zieske 2010: 131–5.

[55] The expression *sidus Julium* is widely used in modern scholarship; cf. *Iulium sidus* in Hor. *Carm.* 1.12.47 (where Horace is thinking of Augustus himself: Nisbet and Hubbard 1970: 162; Weinstock 1971: 378–9; *contra* see West 1993: 7). Weinstock 1971: 370 prefers *Caesaris astrum* (as in Verg. *Ecl.* 9.47). 'Sense of promise': Osgood 2006: 298–349.

CHAPTER 12

Divination and monarchy

In the late Republic, traditions on divinatory incidents connected with a number of prominent individuals arose, and often featured episodes that did not necessarily enter the domain of public prodigies.[1] Cicero, speaking in the persona of Marcus, relates a curious anecdote concerning Crassus. When the triumvir was about to sail from Brundisium on his way to Parthia, someone was selling figs from Caunus, a city of Caria, in the port: his cry, *Cauneas* ('from Caunus', in the accusative) sounded like *caue ne eas* ('mind you, don't go!'). Had Crassus understood the significance of that utterance and heeded the warning, he would not have suffered a crushing defeat and lost his life at Carrhae. Marcus dismisses the episode as an example of a vain prophecy that cannot be reasonably attributed predictive value. It is significant, however, that a tradition on this episode could take shape: some will have found it a useful strategy to make sense of Crassus' demise.[2]

A few decades earlier, another isolated episode became part of the tradition on the rise and fall of Sertorius. Several ancient sources report the special bond that Sertorius had with a white fawn during his Spanish campaign.[3] Appian interrupts his narrative of the war to insist on how Sertorius connected the presence of the white fawn with his chances of success, and worried whenever the fawn was not close to him. Other authors give a different version, in which Sertorius is not in awe of the animal, but

---

[1] Bayet 1949 discusses the role of omens in Roman culture (see 17–21 on *fortuite dicta* and 30 on the Roman preference for the 'menace "ominale"', rather than for the 'parallélisme rigoureux' between omen and reality favoured by the Greeks). 'Ominous accidental utterances': Lateiner 2005.

[2] Cic. *Div.* 2.84; Plin. *HN* 15.83. Crassus received several omens before his departure and was even cursed by the tribune C. Ateius Capito before crossing the *pomerium* (Cic. *Div.* 1.29–30; Plut. *Crass.* 16; Dio 39.39.6; cf. Dion. Hal. *Ant. Rom.* 2.6.4 and App. *B Civ.* 2.18). Oliphant 1912: 169–70; Simpson 1938; Bayet 1960 (= 1971: 353–65); Kany-Turpin 1999; Wardle 2006: 181–8. C. Ateius Capito's political career and allegiances: Buongiorno 2011: 207–13. For an earlier incident cf. the story of L. Aemilius Paullus, who rejoiced at the news of the death of his daughter's puppy, Persa, as he saw it as an omen of his victory over Perseus (Cic. *Div.* 1.103; Val. Max. 1.5.3).

[3] App. *B Civ.* 1.110; Plut. *Sert.* 11.3–4; Gell. *NA* 15.22.1–4; Val. Max. 1.2.4; Frontin. *Str.* 1.11.13.

uses it to manipulate his allies: the fawn was a present to Sertorius from the Lusitanians, who donated it to him when they joined his forces; Sertorius readily claimed that the animal was a sign of his special bond with the gods, especially with Diana. His critics argued that he merely exploited the animal to consolidate his supremacy over the 'naïve' and 'superstitious' Iberian people.[4] The two versions are not strictly incompatible. The connection with the white fawn shows, at any rate, that a divinatory motif could play a part even in the biography of an outsider, or indeed an outcast like Sertorius, and could be explored in different ways and from different angles. The existence of such traditions is already an instructive fact in itself, and proof of the importance and attractiveness of these motifs to late Republican public opinion.[5] This process became more intense in the final years of the Republic and with the rise of Octavian to monarchic power.

The death of Caesar

Caesar's sparing references to the supernatural in the *Commentarii* did not prevent the development of traditions on the role of the supernatural in his life.[6] The most striking instance is arguably the crossing of the Rubicon, which is glossed over in the *Commentarii de bello ciuili*, but became a defining moment in Caesar's life in a part of the tradition, and the scene of a prodigy in Suetonius' narrative.[7] In this version, a creature of splendid size and beauty appeared to Caesar at the Rubicon, playing music on a reed; he then seized a trumpet from one of Caesar's soldiers, sounded the call to arms, and crossed to the other bank, telling Caesar that the gods had shown him the way and prompting the famous remark that the die was cast – *iacta est alea*.[8] Lucan may have been aware of this tradition and

---

[4] Spann 1987: 63; Konrad 1994: 123–4; Wardle 1998: 141. Cf. also Moeller 1975: 407–8, although the portrait of Sertorius as a 'one-eyed magician shaman' is speculative.

[5] Lehmann 1999: 255–6.

[6] As La Penna 1978: 176–7 notes, the references to *fortuna* in the *Commentarii* should not be used as evidence for Caesar's approach to the supernatural, but are best understood within the framework of a historiographical tradition that goes as far back as to Thucydides (most recently explored in Bowden 2005: 73–7 and Eidinow 2011: 93–142, 195–204).

[7] Tucker 1988; Weber 2000: 261–4.

[8] Suet. *Iul.* 32–3; cf. Plut. *Caes.* 32.5–8, *Pomp.* 60.4–5; App. *B Civ.* 2.35. Gascou 1984: 446–7; Montero 2010: 286–7; Pelling 2011: 312–21. Cf. Beard 2011: 96–8 on the use of the dice metaphor in this context. Weber 2000: 261 n. 92 notes that Suetonius does not define the identity of this figure as human: *quidam eximia magnitudine et forma*. There have been attempts to identify it with a deity: Herrmann 1935 (Apollo) and Wiseman 1998a: 62 (Pan). Canfora 1999: 160–1 envisages a 'messinscena', in which Caesar employed a 'gigantesco Gallo' chosen among his prisoners. Montero 2010: 287 notes that the god blew into the trumpet, and that the sound of a trumpet was also heard in Rome in 88 when the haruspices predicted the end of an age; the connection is very weak.

may have turned it against Caesar: in his depiction of the crossing a 'vision of the anxious motherland' tries to persuade Caesar not to embark on a civil war.[9] It is unclear how this tradition took shape. Asinius Pollio was an eyewitness of the crossing of the Rubicon, and his historical account was used by Suetonius, Plutarch and Appian; it has been plausibly suggested, however, that the prodigy is an invention of Suetonius.[10]

The death of Caesar, as is well known, was announced by a number of portents.[11] In the *De diuinatione*, which was finished a few months after Caesar's death, Cicero puts at the forefront an event that happened shortly before the Ides, 'on the first occasion when he sat in a golden throne and wore a purple robe in public': an ox which he was sacrificing was found to be without a heart; the haruspex Spurinna regarded it as a bad omen, but Caesar allegedly overlooked it. On the following day the outcome was similar: the liver of the animal that was sacrificed was found to have no lobe.[12] The various imperial sources that record the event add a number of different prophecies. Valerius Maximus mentioned Augustus' account of the premonitory dream that Calpurnia had the night before the Ides of March, which Caesar chose to overlook.[13] It is likely that Calpurnia's dream was mentioned in Augustus' *De uita sua*, and quite possibly this was the source of later versions of the story. Velleius mentions the sacrifice (with a generic reference to the haruspices) and Calpurnia's dream and adds a reference to some *libelli* denouncing the conspiracy which Caesar received and overlooked.[14]

---

[9] Luc. 1.185–203, esp. 186: *patriae trepidantis imago*. Marinoni 2002: 283–5; Roche 2009: 206–7.

[10] Hohl 1952. *Contra* Jal 1961: 398–9, who speculates that the tradition on this episode was devised by Caesar, who needed religious legitimacy to support his involvement in the Civil War, and Wiseman 1998a: 60–2, 188, who argues that the source of the episode was a dramatic play, possibly performed at the *ludi scaenici* organised in Rome by C. Vibius Pansa (the figure that Caesar saw on the bank of the river may be Pan; and Pansa's cognomen was appropriate for a putative appearance of the god).

[11] Overviews and discussion in Montero 2000 and Ripat 2006: 167–73. Bell 1994: 226 is unhelpful.

[12] Cic. *Div.* 1.119: *postero die caput in iecore non fuit* ('On the next day there was no lobe to the liver'); cf. the dismissive reply in *Div.* 2.36–7, which includes some details on how spreading emmer and wine may cause the disappearance of the internal organs of a sacrificial victim. Other accounts of the same episode: Val. Max. 1.6.13 (with a more favourable emphasis towards Caesar; see Wardle 1998: 210–11); Plin. *HN* 11.186 (which corresponds almost verbatim to Cicero's account). An unusually large *caput iecinoris* was regarded as an eminently favourable sign (Guittard 2006: 75–7); on its significance in Roman extispicy see Blecher 1905: 25–7. The narrative of Caesar ignoring the omens of his death is closely paralleled by the narrative of the moments preceding the death of Tiberius Gracchus in Plut. *Ti. Gracch.* 17 (but note the decisive role of Blossius of Cumae).

[13] Val. Max. 1.7.2; Plut. *Caes.* 63.8–9. Montero 1998: 382–3; Wardle 1998: 220; Pelling 2011: 471–2. Harris 2009: 92 finds it 'obvious' that the episode is an invention.

[14] Vell. 2.57.2. Velleius interprets Caesar's decision as evidence for fate's intention to blind those whom it intends to defeat (*sed profecto ineluctabilis fatorum uis, cuiuscumque fortunam mutare constituit, consilia corrumpit*); it is a very different approach from that of Cicero in *Div.* 1.119, who argues that

The accounts of Plutarch and Suetonius contain by far the most prodigies. Plutarch gives the following sequence, which he derives from several
different sources: a series of meteorological events (lightning in the sky,
crashing sounds); birds flying in the forum; multitudes of men all on fire;
the episode of the ox with the missing heart (the two latter episodes were
derived from a historical work of Strabo); a story 'that was told by many',
the famous encounter with a seer (*mantis*) who warned him of an imminent
danger that would happen on the Ides of March, to whom Caesar pointed
out that the Ides of March had come, only to hear that they had not yet
passed; some versions of Calpurnia's dream, including the version given
by Livy; and, finally, a generic reference to the warning of the responses
of the 'seers', who 'after many sacrifices' (63.12: *polla katathusantes*) nearly
persuaded Caesar to call off the Senate session on the Ides.[15]

Suetonius reports the incident of the ox without heart in his summary of
the instances of Caesar's arrogance in the final part of his life, mentioning
the pun on the word *cor*, but without relating it to the Ides of March.[16] The
list of prodigies is quite different from Plutarch's. It starts with a prodigy
from Capua, the discovery of a prophetic text in the tomb of Capys,
which was reported by Caesar's associate L. Cornelius Balbus;[17] it then
continues with the story of the horses that Caesar had dedicated to the river
Rubicon, which were refusing to graze and weeping; a sacrifice celebrated
by Spurinna, who warned Caesar against the threat of the Ides of March;
birds flying in the forum and in the Curia of Pompey; a prophetic dream
of Caesar; and a version of Calpurnia's dream which closely resembles
Plutarch's.[18]

Appian's narrative is much drier. It is focused on the rumours that
preceded the conspiracy and especially on the figure of the Greek diviner
Artemidorus, who is also mentioned by Plutarch.[19] Its only reference to a
divinatory incident is the narrative of the sacrifice performed by Spurinna
on the day, in which the ox was found to be without a heart and the
victims that were sacrificed subsequently did not give more favourable

---

the aim of the prodigy was to warn Caesar of his imminent death, without enabling him to avoid
it (*ut uideret interitum, non ut caueret*).

[15] Plut. *Caes.* 63, with Pelling 2011: 465–73. Cf. Bloch 1964: 98–9 on the 'présages figuratifs déterminants'
before the Ides.

[16] Suet. *Iul.* 77.4: the word *cor* can mean both 'heart' and 'intelligence'. See also Polyaen. 8.23.33.

[17] *HRR* II, F 1 = Suet. *Iul.* 81.1–2; cf. Serv. *auct. ad Aen.* 2.35. Farney 2007: 205–6 reads this episode as
a Capuan attempt to engage in a dialogue with Caesar which may be understood as an instance of
kinship diplomacy.

[18] Suet. *Iul.* 81.4–7. The sacrifice was performed in Caesar's house, and was private, albeit related to
Caesar's public activity (Scheid 2005: 272–3).

[19] App. *B Civ.* 2.116; cf. Plut. *Caes.* 65.

auspices. Despite the advice of the diviner (*mantis*) who performed the sacrifices, Caesar decided not to postpone the Senate's meeting. Appian argues that fate wanted Caesar to meet a violent death: the combination of Caesar's arrogance, his reluctance to keep the Senate waiting and the devious machinations of his enemies led him to a fatal decision. Finally, the version of Cassius Dio consists of a summary of familiar occurrences, and features two unique details.[20] We find the responses of the seers and the dreams of Caesar and Calpurnia, but there is also room for some prodigies that take place in Caesar's house: the opening of the doors of the bedroom, the noise coming from the so-called arms of Mars (*ta te gar opla ta Areia*; the *Ancilia*) which were kept in the residence of the *pontifex maximus*; and the curious incident of a statue of Caesar which the dictator put in the vestibule of his house and which fell and broke into pieces as soon as he left the house. These two episodes, which are not attested elsewhere, are likely to derive from the same source.

This brief survey shows several patterns at work. First, the sequence of prodigies that took place before the death of Caesar consists of several stages: bad omens that Caesar received during official ceremonies that were performed before or on the Ides of March, mainly involving the haruspex Spurinna; bad omens that visited Calpurnia and Caesar in their dreams; bad omens that occurred in Caesar's house; bad omens that took place in the city of Rome or in the territory of Capua. Only the first group of prodigies features in Cicero's *De diuinatione*, which was begun before Caesar's death and concluded a few months later, and engages directly with the problem of divination in general and with the events that anticipated Caesar's death in particular. For once, an argument *e silentio* may be used with some confidence. Arguably Cicero was not aware of other prodigies when he wrote the *De diuinatione*: had this been the case, he would have addressed them directly in other sections of his work, which deal with a great variety of allegedly premonitory events. This argument of silence, if correct, would corroborate the view of N. Horsfall, who noted that none of the omens that occurred on the Ides of March was significant enough to prompt the cancellation of a Senate meeting.[21] The series of the prodigies surrounding the death of Caesar was constructed not long after the Ides of March and certainly not just by one source. It is likely that prodigy reports were collected in both favourable and hostile quarters. The names of four lost sources survive: Livy, Strabo, about whose views on Caesar's death we do not know anything, and two men who had profound debts to the

---

[20] Dio 44.17–18.   [21] Horsfall 1974a: 197–9.

former dictator, Cornelius Balbus and Augustus.[22] According to Valerius Maximus, Augustus knew about Calpurnia's dream, and may have alluded to it in his account of the dream that Artorius had before the battle of Philippi. Valerius Maximus' account switches the focus from Caesar's lack of regard for hostile prodigies to his concern not to let the superstitious concerns of his wife affect the political process; this interpretation might well have derived from Augustus himself.[23]

Octavian's victory

The advent of the Second Triumvirate arguably coincides with the emergence of the most diverse and confusing range of divinatory responses in Republican history. This is hardly surprising, if we think that the build-up to the Civil War was in many ways the implosion of the State and the crisis of the systems that regulated and controlled public divination. More strikingly, while there is evidence that a number of prophecies and prodigies circulated in this period, detail is rather scarce. The clearest picture of the climate in 43 may be found in Cassius Dio, at a crucial juncture of the triumviral narrative.[24] A number of prodigies were reported, but the Senate was unable to expiate them effectively; it was not even able to observe the *dies nefasti*. The list of prodigies was impressive: thunderbolts on the temple of Jupiter Capitolinus, an earthquake, a windstorm that hit temples of Saturn and Minerva; the fall of a statue of Minerva on the Capitol in that same storm was regarded as a premonition of the death of Cicero, who had put it up after his return from exile. Most significantly for our purposes, Dio adds that a number of oracles were circulating at the time, all foreseeing the imminent fall of the State. No detail is given on the source of those oracular prophecies, the context in which they were produced and circulated, or their contents. This is all the more striking since the rest of the chapter continues with more mentions of prodigies: crows flying into the Senate house, a drought of the Po which let loose a great number of snakes from the bed of the river, a plague epidemic and finally the death of a lictor of the consul when the opening sacrifice of the year was being performed. Dio, or indeed his source, is clearly well informed about the events of this year; the aspect of the narrative that is strikingly underdeveloped is the reference to the oracles. It is conceivable that Dio

[22] Livy: Plut. *Caes.* 63.9; Strabo: Plut. *Caes.* 63.3; Balbus: Suet. *Iul.* 81.3; Augustus: Val. Max. 1.7.2.
[23] Cf. Wardle 1998: 218–21.
[24] Dio 45.17. Cf. Obs. 68. Manuwald 1979: 46–7, 188–90; Vigourt 2001a: 270–1 n. 80.

did not have access to them. We cannot tell whether or how these oracles were recorded and collected.

What can be established, however, is that Octavian's victory marked a clear discontinuity with that chaotic and troubled period. It is again by Dio that we are told about a decision that Agrippa took during his aedileship in 33: 'the astrologers and the sorcerers' were expelled from the city.[25] We do not know how lasting the effects of this measure were, but we can read this passage as clear evidence of Octavian's interest in bringing non-State supervised divinatory practices under his direct control.

'Astrologers and sorcerers' were only one aspect of a wider problem. Even a literary tradition that is mainly concentrated on political and military developments does not fail to convey a sense of the plurality and diversity of the divinatory practices that were available in the city. Again, a passage of Cassius Dio gives a measure of the complexity.[26] In 38 a revolt of the populace against tax-collectors marked a moment of great tension in the city. It was preceded by many prodigies, of which Dio singles out three: a stream of oil spontaneously flowing from the bank of the Tiber; the destruction of Romulus' hut (the *casa Romuli*) during a ceremony performed by the pontiffs; and the fall of a statue of Virtus by one of the city gates.[27] Nothing else is said about the first two episodes, while the incident of the statue receives more attention. Some followers of the Magna Mater claimed (but in what context?) that the goddess was angry with the city; the Sibylline Books were consulted and found to be in agreement with that assessment: a prophecy that was produced in a private context and yet had a clear political significance was introduced into the public sphere by the *quindecemuiri*. The narrative continues with a brief description of the expiation ritual that was prescribed by the Books, which involved the purification of the statue in sea water. The felicitous conclusion of the process was marked by the growth of four palm trees near the temple of Victoria and in the Forum. Dio's narrative can then move on to the wedding of Octavian and Livia. The fire at the *casa Romuli* is not attested elsewhere, but the incident of the stream of oil is mentioned by several Christian sources, again without any reference to an official handling of

---

[25] Dio 49.43.5: τοὺς ἀστρολόγους τούς τε γόητας. On the marginality of the *goes* and his lack of intellectual recognition (there is no such thing as *goetike*) see Struck 2007: 4–5. Associations with necromancy: Ogden 2001: 110–12.

[26] Dio 48.43.4–6. Vigourt 2001a: 282–3.

[27] It is unclear whether the *casa Romuli* mentioned here was that on the Palatine or that on the Capitol (Coarelli 1993b: 241).

the prodigy.[28] There is no evidence that the prodigy was ever dealt with in an official context.

As we saw in Chapter 10, Livy's statement on the lack of interest in prodigies in his time and their recording (43.13.1–2) should not be taken at face value. It is true that the evidence for prodigies becomes sketchier and less comprehensive for this period and the silence of an author like Obsequens on the prodigies in the late Republic suggests that they played a less central role in the narratives on this period, including Livy's. However, they were not entirely overlooked or omitted in the historical record. Dio's account of the fall of the Republic and the war between Octavian and Antony includes a number of prodigies that play a significant role in shaping the political climate, and also shed light on aspects of the use of divination in the period.[29] Dio usually lists clusters of prodigies that occurred at particular times; he clearly had access to lists of prodigies that related them to specific historical occurrences and possibly interpreted them within the context of a narrative. An impressive range of prodigies is recorded in the build-up to Actium: a whole chapter is devoted to a number of incidents which foretold the war that was about to begin.[30] All the portents stressed that the relationship between the city and the gods was under strain, and they were all related to areas and spaces of cult: an ape enters the temple of Ceres, an owl flies into several temples, the chariot of Jupiter in the Circus is damaged and a statue of Victory falls from the theatre during a storm that also destroys the wooden bridge on the Tiber. Most of the prodigies took place in Rome, anticipating a development that became clearer under the Principate, when prodigies concerning power tend to be set in Rome and to be closely associated with the city.[31] However, a portent involving a snake was reported in Etruria, and the whole of Italy was affected by the climate of expectation and tension that preceded the conflict. Dio makes it clear that the prodigies were addressed to the whole community and not to a particular side. Only one incident anticipated the imminent disgrace of Antony: a marble statue of the triumvir, located on the Alban Mount, cried tears of blood. Moreover, Dio reports an episode that cannot be defined as a prodigy, but does have some predictive value: two gangs of young boys formed in Rome, the Caesarians and the Antonians, and the Caesarians

---

[28] Jer. *Chron.* ad a. 38 a.C.; Oros. 6.18.34, 20.6; Paul. Diac. *Hist. Rom.* 7.8. *Fons olei*: De Spirito 1995; discrepancies among the sources: Manuwald 1979: 223–4 n. 362. Cf. Osgood 2006: 197 for the suggestion that the story of the 'fountain of oil' bursting by the Tiber was originally developed by the Jewish community based in the area.

[29] On Dio's views on religion and historical causation, which appear to be broadly informed by Stoic tendencies, see Gowing 1992: 28–30 and Swan 2004: 8–13.

[30] Dio 50.8.   [31] Vigourt 2001b.

won after two days of fighting. Dio records a closely similar episode after Caesar's departure for Greece in 49. On that occasion too the outcome of the street-fight mirrored that of the war: the Caesariani defeated the Pompeiani.[32]

Dio uses the prodigies to flesh out his picture of a tense period, dominated by emotional tension and uncertainty. It is unclear what his main source was in this section of his work; while it is likely that the contemporary tradition on these prodigies was shaped by Octavian – who was in control of Italy by that time – and his associates, Dio gives the impression of using and organising his material independently and selectively, without pursuing a narrow ideological agenda.[33] Things appear to change after Octavian's victory: the explanation must be sought not in Dio's method, but in the material that he had at hand. On the night after Octavian was granted the name Augustus, on 16 January 27, the Tiber overflowed and flooded a considerable part of Rome: the 'seers' (*hoi manteis*: the haruspices, no doubt) interpreted the event as a sign that Augustus' power over Rome would be unrivalled.[34] Dio does not comment on its striking implication: while the storm of 31 was interpreted as a negative prodigy, this inundation was seen as a favourable omen. A significant interpretative shift had intervened, and it must be explained by Augustus' new dominant position.[35] Dio fails to note that, but interestingly follows this passage with a reference to those who went to great lengths to flatter the *princeps*, perhaps hinting that the interpretation of the haruspices was regarded as part of that climate.

Dio does not offer any comments even when, a few chapters below, he reports another case in which a flood was regarded as a negative omen. In 23, when the new constitutional settlement of Augustus' powers was

---

[32] Dio 41.39.4.

[33] Swan 1997 discusses the sources and methods of Cassius Dio 51–6 and convincingly argues that 'urban annalistic' traditions are clearly recognisable in the narrative; see also Swan 2004: 17–23.

[34] Dio 53.20.1; see Rich 1990: 153 (who speculates that the interpretation was given by private diviners); Linderski 1993: 64 (= 1995a: 619); Vigourt 2001a: 123–5; Montero 2007: 67–70 and 2012: 275–81; Kearsley 2009: 166. Swan 2004: 362–3 points out that Dio's reports on Tiber floods are reliable. Montero 2010: 302–9 and 2012: 292–300 argues that the *quindecemviri* had a special expertise on the interpretation and expiation of the floodings of the Tiber. Bakhouche 2012: 67 sees a link between Augustus' bond with Capricorn and the decision to take up the title of Augustus in January 27.

[35] Becher 1985: 474–6; Vigourt 2001b: 285; Champeaux 2003: 30. Mazzarino 1966: 622–3 suggests that Dio's use of αὔξήσοι is a reference to Augustus. Montero 2007: 68–9 notes that the haruspex who advised the Romans during the war with Veii (Livy 5.15.4) regarded the imminent exundation of the Alban Lake as a prodigy favourable to Veii and that the Romans would never get hold of Veii until the water had been drawn off from the lake. It is conceivable that the involvement of haruspices in 27 was decided because their *disciplina* allowed a favourable interpretation of the prodigy.

completed, a number of prodigies took place.[36] Dio is not clear about
the exact chronological sequence. The events are quite similar to those
reported in 31: wild animals in the city (a wolf, on this occasion), a fire
and a storm, which caused the river to rise and which destroyed (again)
the wooden bridge. Dio does not explicitly elaborate on the atmosphere
of tension and instability, but the structure of his narrative shows that
the prodigies raised serious problems. Book 54 opens with a series of
prodigies that continues that at the end of Book 53. The year 22 is again
marked by a flood, accompanied by a storm and thunderbolts that hit the
statues in the Pantheon – even that of Augustus, which lost its spear. An
epidemic of plague throughout Italy completes the picture.[37] Dio makes
no mention of rituals that were staged to address the crisis; he states that
those events led the Romans to understand that their disgrace was caused
by the fact that Augustus was no longer consul. Hence they offered him
the dictatorship and the *cura annonae*; he accepted only the latter. In this
context, the handling of public prodigies is effectively under the control
of the *princeps* and his associates, who sit in the priestly colleges and steer
their action.[38] The role of the priests is just unacknowledged in Dio's
narrative, which makes room for a general, loosely defined popular will –
a sort of elusive counterpart of the *princeps*. The simplification of the
political context and the shift from republic to *de facto* monarchy appears
matched by a simplification of the religious machinery that presides over
public divination.

However, the minimal involvement of the priestly colleges in the
handling of the prodigies in Dio's account should not be accepted without
qualifications. As P. A. Brunt showed in his study of the Senate under
Augustus, the surviving sources for the early Principate appear to be strikingly uninterested in the details of institutional history.[39] Other accounts
of the period show that the haruspices (who admittedly were not one of
the great priestly colleges) were involved on a number of occasions. Suetonius mentions a response of the haruspices that again marked the special
position of Augustus: when lightning hit a part of his house, they ruled
that the gods had declared their interest in it and Augustus incorporated
it into the temple of Apollo.[40] It is unclear whether the haruspices from
whom advice was sought on that occasion were consulted as an *ordo* or

---

[36] Dio 53.33.5, with Becher 1985: 477–8.   [37] Dio 54.1.1–2.

[38] Vigourt 2001b: 284–9. See *RG* 25.3 and cf. the composition of the pontifical and augural colleges in
22 (Rüpke 2005a: 148–9), with the close associates of the *princeps* Cn. Domitius Calvinus (*cos.* 53
and 50), M. Titius (*cos.* 31) and M. Tullius Cicero (*cos. suff.* 30) serving as pontiffs, and T. Statilius
Taurus (*cos. suff.* 37 and *cos.* 26), M. Iunius Silanus (*cos.* 25), M. Valerius Messalla Corvinus (*cos. suff.*
31), and Sex. Appuleius (*cos.* 29) holding the augurate.

[39] Brunt 1984.   [40] Suet. *Aug.* 29.4. Augustus and Apollo: Lange 2009: 166–90; Miller 2009.

because of their personal association with the emperor. Those who assisted him during his military operations in Umbria in the forties were no doubt members of his official retinue, according to a pattern that is already well attested in the late Republic.

They gave him impressively creative advice. In January 43 at Spoletium the livers of the sacrificial victims were found to be doubled inwards at the bottom (*iocinera replicata intrinsecus ab ima fibra*); the haruspices readily saw it as a sign that Octavian's power would double within the year.[41] During the siege of Perusia, in the early months of 40, Octavian failed to obtain *litatio* and ordered the slaughter of more victims; at that point the enemies stormed out of the city walls and carried off the sacrifical apparatus. The seers stated that the bad omens announced by those victims would fall upon those who had taken them.[42] Significantly, Suetonius reports this episode within a wider discussion of Augustus' ability to predict the outcome of all the wars in which he was involved – another instance of the proximity between prediction and divination: in all the cases that he mentions, specific events enable Augustus to understand – sometimes independently, sometimes with the help of others – how things will develop. At any rate, Augustus is always in a position to understand the situation and make correct predictions. Not even Suetonius gives a full account of the traditions on the omens that accompanied Octavian's rise. He has an anecdote on Actium – the encounter with the donkey Nicon and his owner Eutychos – but does not mention the likely involvement of the haruspices in the sacrifice that Octavian performed just before the battle: he found a double gall bladder in the victim, which the doctrine of the haruspices linked to Neptune and the influence of water.[43] The tradition on Augustus' special connection with the gods was extensive and favourable prodigies and portents played a very important part in it. While Augustus may have managed to exercise greater control over the functioning of divination within Roman state religion, he did not (and probably could not) affect the widespread interest in recording and discussing an event of such importance.

The evidence for the direct association of the *princeps* with divination is sparse, but very instructive. The work that he did on this area of public life was intensive and had far-reaching consequences. Suetonius acknowledges the importance of religious themes in the Augustan discourse, and his evidence is invaluable. A whole section of the biography is devoted to

---

[41] Plin. *HN* 11.190; Suet. *Aug.* 95.2; Dio 46.35.4. Guittard 2002/3: 123–4.
[42] Suet. *Aug.* 96.3; cf. 14.3. Sordi 1993; Guittard 1998: 60. Octavian could rely on significant support in Etruria since the early stages of his career: Rawson 1978a: 146–8 (= 1991: 312–16).
[43] Plin. *HN* 11.195.

portents, premonitory signs and augural matters, and is included within
the broader discussion of Augustus' attitude to religion.[44] This theme
was deliberately singled out by the biographer: no other life features a
comparably conspicuous section. The very body of evidence that Suetonius
presents shows how rich the tradition about it was: most of it, especially
for the events up to 24, was probably based on material gathered and
organised by Augustus himself in the *De uita sua*. While it is apparent that
Suetonius used a considerable range of sources, his account chiefly reflects
a contemporary Augustan viewpoint.

His main interest is in Augustus' own attitude to religion: his fear of
thunder and lightning (90), his attitude to dreams (91) and his handling of
some specific omens (92). The evidence is mainly anecdotal, as one would
expect of a biographical source, but it refers the reader to some moments of
Augustus' life, such as the battle of Philippi and the foundation of the temple of Jupiter the Thunderer on the Capitol.[45] Suetonius conveys well the
sense of how comprehensive and thorough Augustus' interest in religious
matters was. The discussion then becomes more specific in two important
respects. First, Suetonius emphasises Augustus' respect for old and established religious practices, and his contempt of more recent ones:[46] far from
falling prey to any form of *superstitio*, Augustus shapes his approach to
religion on the basis of a principle of careful selection. Secondly, Suetonius
gives a survey of the omens that preceded Augustus' birth and accompanied his life. As the biographer makes clear, the information underpinning
his account was derived from a wide range of sources: local traditions of
Velitrae, Julius Marathus and Asclepiades of Mendes all provided information on the prodigies that preceded the birth.[47] The tradition in which
he worked was pervasive – *et pour cause*. Let us consider its distinctive
features.

Augustan stars

The birth of Octavian, like the death of Caesar, is an episode for which a
number of conflicting accounts survive. Suetonius and Cassius Dio report
as a well-known fact (albeit with some variants) that Nigidius Figulus told

---

[44] Suet. *Aug.* 90–7, esp. 90–2.
[45] Foundation of the temple: Suet. *Aug.* 29.5, referring to an episode of the Cantabrian campaign
which possibly played a role in building Augustus' fear of thunder and lightning, and 91.4, which
mentions a dream that Augustus had on one of his many visits to the temple.
[46] Wardle 2011a.
[47] Local tradition of Velitrae: Suet. *Aug.* 94.2; Julius Marathus: 94.3 (Gascou 1984: 461); Asclepiades:
94.4.

Octavius, shortly after the birth of his son, that the ruler of the world had been born, apparently just on the basis of the time of the birth.[48] It is unclear why Nigidius would have been especially interested in the birth of the son of Octavius, with whom he is not known to have had any personal or political connections; in the account of Suetonius and Dio the two men met at the Senate house on the day when the destiny of the twelve conspirators was debated. Moreover, Nigidius' eventual opposition to Julius Caesar is a well-known fact. The likelihood that this information is a later construction is great, especially in light of Augustus' interest in and use of horoscopes.[49] The tale is matched by the anecdote of the visit of Octavian and Agrippa to the astrologer Theogenes during their stay at Apollonia: a defining moment in Octavian's life, which coincided with Caesar's death, marked in this version is by the confirmation of his predestination. Suetonius views this episode as the moment which marked the beginning of Octavian's faith in his own destiny. In his account, it was after consulting Theogenes that Octavian made his horoscope such a significant part of his self-representation: a strategy that he pursued with the publication of his horoscope and the striking of a coin issue with the symbol of Capricorn.[50] These two initiatives must be discussed separately and appreciated in their own right, but they can only be understood in light of an important, slightly earlier incident: the appearance of the so-called *sidus Julium*.[51]

According to Pliny the Elder, who based his account on Augustus' *De uita sua*, the *sidus* was visible for a week and the populace readily saw it as a sign of Caesar's rise to heaven. Octavian endorsed this interpretation in his memoirs, but in private he claimed that it was a sign of his own rising power.[52] Cassius Dio reports the same episode without mentioning the interpretation of the *sidus* that Octavian gave in private, but confirming the link between its appearance and the deification of Caesar. Since the majority of the populace thought that the comet was a sign of Caesar's rise to heaven, Octavian took the opportunity to give that theme an official expression and install a statue of Caesar in the temple of Venus with a star

---

[48] Suet. *Aug.* 94.7; Dio 45.1.3–5 (in this version Octavius seeks to kill his baby after receiving the prophecy, but is stopped by Nigidius). Detailed discussion in Bertrand-Écanvil 1994.

[49] Della Casa 1962: 17–18, 24–5; Schmid 2005: 20 n. 6; Volk 2009: 132–3 (perhaps an attempt to rehabilitate Nigidius posthumously?); Engels 2010: 171. *Contra*, see DuQuesnay 1984: 39 (the prophecy was first used by anti-Octavian propaganda); Bertrand-Écanvil 1994: 492–3; Vigourt 2001a: 402–3.

[50] A full reconsideration of this episode in Wardle forthcoming.

[51] Bechtold 2011: 161–225 provides the fullest modern discussion and a comprehensive overview of previous scholarship.

[52] Plin. *HN* 2.94 (= *HRR* II, F 4 = F 1 Smith).

above his head.[53] The passage of the *De uita sua* quoted by Pliny gives a slightly different version, in which the emblem of the *sidus* was first added to a bust of Caesar that was soon afterwards consecrated in the forum.

The appearance of the star in the sky above Rome in 44 may be implicitly referred to in the prophecy of Jupiter in the first book of the *Aeneid*, where the beginning of a new era of peace and stability is foretold. However, as we saw in Chapter 11, it remains a matter of debate whether the prophecy refers to Caesar or Augustus.[54] Virgil's use of the word *saeculum* in this context was surely not an innocent choice.[55] The *sidus Julium* was viewed by the haruspex Vulcatius as a sign that the ninth Etruscan *saeculum* was about to end, and the tenth and last one was imminent; speculation on the number of *saecula* that were allocated to Rome was intense. Jupiter's prophecy disposed of the apocalyptic implications of this theme and suggested that the new age, hailed by the *sidus Julium*, was the beginning of several *saecula* of prosperity.[56] Virgil's reference to an *imperium sine fine* may have been a response to the idea that the sequence of the *saecula* would some day come to an end, and that even Rome would have to fall.[57] We are not in a position to infer what Virgil made of that model; what seems fairly clear, however, is that Octavian played a crucial role in shaping this interpretation of the *sidus Julium* and the version of Roman history after Caesar's death that was based on that interpretation.

The theme of the star is very prominent in Augustan iconography, and the emphasis on the beginning of a new age emerges most powerfully from the solemn celebration of the *ludi saeculares* in 17: a ritual that was more about securing the protection of the gods for the city in the new *saeculum* than about merely marking the beginning of the new age.[58] As we have seen in Chapter 5, there were conflicting versions in the tradition on the sequence of the *ludi saeculares* under the Republic and on the interval of time that was supposed to lapse between two performances of the *ludi*.

[53] Dio 45.7.1–2. See Weinstock 1971: 371. Plut. *Caes.* 69.4–5 mentions the comet along with the dimming of the sun's rays, which had an impact on the harvest of that year: this might be interpreted as evidence for a negative interpretation of the portent (Powell 2009: 175–6).

[54] Verg. *Aen.* 1.286–96, esp. 291.

[55] *Saec(u)lum* in Virgil: Angeli Bertinelli 1988. Zetzel 1989: 276–84 has an excellent discussion of the place of this theme in *Aen.* 6.

[56] The *sidus* and the ancient debate on the *saecula*: Weinstock 1971: 194–7; Massa-Pairault 1991: 6–9; Fabre-Serris 1991: 83–4; Ramsey and Licht 1997: 140–2; Bechtold 2011: 213–21. West 1993 provides an optimistic survey of all the possible references to the *sidus* in Augustan poetry; Williams 2003 seeks to demonstrate that the iconography of the *sidus Julium* had a direct influence on many sections of the *Aeneid*.

[57] Dobbin 1995: 28–31; Williams 2003: 14–15.

[58] On the rituals performed during the *ludi* see Schnegg-Köhler 2002: 115–54, 186–200, 244–62; Habinek 2005: 150–7; Cooley 2006: 230–7.

The evidence of Censorinus and Zosimus suggests that there were two competing and mutually exclusive systems: one in which the *ludi* took place every 100 years, and another in which there was an interval of 110 years.[59] When he decided that the *ludi saeculares* were to be celebrated in 17, Augustus chose the latter framework. Zosimus suggests that the main advisor to the *princeps* on this occasion was C. Ateius Capito (*cos. suff.* AD 5), the great expert in pontifical law, who may have drawn up the necessary instructions for the *quindecemuiri*.[60] The historical tradition on the *ludi* had to be accommodated accordingly. A new series of four festivals that supposedly took place during the Republic, in 456, 346, 236 and 126 was invented, and the Augustan *ludi* were listed as the fifth celebration of the series. The details were incorporated into the text of the *Fasti Consulares Capitolini* after the Augustan games had taken place.[61] Moreover, Phlegon and Zosimus record the text of a Sibylline oracle that prescribed the celebration of the *ludi*: thirty-eight lines in Greek hexameter, only partly written in acrostics, which appear to be a patchwork of different oracles assembled for a specific political purpose, and which open with an explicit reference to a cycle of 110 years.[62]

Ancient discussions of the *sidus Julium* centre on the oscillation between star and comet that can be seen in the ancient sources. Comets were usually regarded as unfavourable signs, while stars did not carry negative associations. Two conflicting interpretations of the *sidus* circulated in Rome immediately after its appearance. Octavian's opponents, and more widely those who were opposed to the deification of Caesar, viewed the *sidus* as a negative omen. The prophecy of Vulcatius must be understood in that context. Octavian, on the other hand, very ably provided an alternative, positive interpretation of the *sidus*, whereby it was not a comet, but a star.[63] The issue, however, remained controversial for some time. The

[59] Cens. *DN* 17.8–9; Zos. 2.4, with Paschoud 2000: 197–8 nn. 5–6. See Weiss 1973: 207–12 and Schnegg-Köhler 2002: 164–70 on the analogies and differences between the *saecula* of the *ludi* and the Etruscan ones: the Roman festivals were not based on a fully fledged theory on the sequence of different ages. Mommsen 1859: 172–94 remains an important discussion.

[60] Zos. 2.4.2, with Gagé 1955: 623–4 and Horsfall 1974b: 252–3. See also Scheid 2000: 646–51 and Schnegg-Köhler 2002: 201–20 on the central role of the *quindecemuiri s.f.* in the *ludi saeculares*, which however (*pace* Gagé) were not predominantly associated with Apollo.

[61] *CIL* 1.1², p. 29. On this invented tradition see Schnegg-Köhler 2002: 156–7. Cf. also Taylor 1934: 105–6; Weiss 1973: 207; Fuhrmann 1987: 134–6; Gladigow 1989: 268–9.

[62] *FGrHist* 257 F 37 = Phlegon *Macr.* 99.4 = Zos. 2.6. English translation in Hansen 1996: 56–7. See Paschoud 2000: 201–3; Guittard 2007a: 268–75; Satterfield 2008: 233–4.

[63] Gurval 1997, esp. 61–2; Ramsey and Licht 1997: 143–5; Guittard 2006: 81; Bechtold 2011: 218–21. Wiseman 2009b: 116–17 rightly emphasises the emotional impact that prophecies on the beginning and ending of *saecula* must have had on the Roman populace. On emotions in Roman religion cf. Scheid 2011.

numismatic evidence shows that the theme of the *sidus* was not pursued by Mark Antony; however, Octavian placed a star above the statues of Caesar as early as in the summer of 44, shortly after the appearance of the *sidus*.[64] Stars were a familiar sign of divinity in Hellenistic iconography, and the presence of this motif is related to the recognition of the apotheosis of Caesar on Octavian's part. They clearly precede the emergence of the theme of the comet – a star with a tail – which appears for the first time on two Augustan coin types from the late 20s.[65] It is tempting to accept the idea that the comet became the mainstream version only in this period, when the Civil War was over, and that its revival was masterminded by Augustus himself: the comet carried Caesar to the heavens. The ideal venue to air that version was no doubt Augustus' *De uita sua*, which was published in the late 20s.[66] The whole work was marked by a deep interest in the supernatural and featured a considerable number of prodigies. The extant fragments give a sense of the diversity of the episodes recorded by Augustus; 'oblative', 'unsolicited' signs are well represented.[67] Augustus reported the prophecy of the haruspex Vulcatius on the meaning of Caesar's comet and the end of the ninth *saeculum*. He also reported a dream that allegedly Cicero had when the future emperor was still a child, 'merely Iulius Octavius', in which he foresaw that the child would one day become Augustus and would bring the civil wars to an end. It is unclear on what grounds Augustus based his account of this prophecy; this may not have been the only prophecy of the future greatness of the young boy included in the *De uita sua*.[68] The dream of M. Artorius, a friend of Octavian, which persuaded him to leave his camp just before an attack by the Liberators, played a prominent role in the narrative and it had great resonance among later authors.[69] There was also room for trivial incidents that could be constructed as premonitory. Augustus cared to report that on the day when a military mutiny almost overthrew him he had put his left shoe on the wrong foot.[70] One of the key aims of the *De uita sua* was to present and discuss a version of the

---

[64] The position of the star (above, behind or in front of Caesar's head) varied over time: evidence and discussion in Weinstock 1971: 378.

[65] *RIC* I².37 a–b and 38 a–b, with Gurval 1997: 59.

[66] Hahn 1983 provides a thorough survey of the shifting interpretations of the *sidus* from star to comet, and from sign concerning Julius Caesar to sign foretelling Octavian's greatness; see esp. 61–4.

[67] Boas 1938: 93.

[68] Tert. *De anim.* 46.7 (= *HRR* II, F 2 = F 4 Smith). The story of Nigidius' horoscope may also derive from Augustus' *De uita sua*.

[69] Plut. *Brut.* 41.5; *Ant.* 22.2; App. *B Civ.* 4.110 (= *HRR* II, F 10 = F 7 Smith). A reminiscence of Sulla's autobiography, where dreams were notoriously prominent, no doubt played a part.

[70] Plin. *HN* 2.24 (= *HRR* II, F 20 = F 18 Smith). Cf. the omen of Tiberius Gracchus bashing his foot against the threshold of his house, shortly before his death: Plut. *Ti. Gracch.* 17.3.

events that accompanied the rise of Octavian, no doubt cutting across a number of controversial issues and presenting versions that were intended to provide an unequivocal narrative 'from the top'. Caesar's death featured prominently in this narrative, not least because it was so divisive; moreover, Octavian will have been aware of the series of portents that had purportedly taken place before and after the Ides, including the star that appeared in the north part of the sky, which 'some called a comet', according to Dio.[71] The comet was conceivably included in this account, perhaps in association with the motif of the star. A complex network of astrological themes took shape at a crucial stage in the definition and self-representation of Augustus' power.

The *princeps'* interest in astrology did not fade away throughout his long reign, as the publication of his horoscope in AD 11 shows. That initiative was part of a broader plan for the control and containment of various forms of prediction and divination, but it must also be understood in the tense atmosphere of the final part of Augustus' rule, and with the intention to allay concerns over the possible imminent death of the elderly emperor.[72] Cassius Dio mentions it along with Augustus' decision to outlaw prophecies in private contexts and prophecies foretelling the death of an individual, and makes it clear that Augustus' interest in the horoscope was determined by its prophetic dimension.[73] The horoscope was published as a decree: according to Dio, it was a text that outlined the disposition of the stars at the time of Augustus' birth. This aspect has sparked intense scholarly debate, since Augustus was born on 23 September and would not therefore have had Capricorn as his star sign.[74] Some scholars have tried to remove the difficulty by postulating that the horoscope referred to the moment on the day when Augustus was conceived.[75] However, this suggestion is not compatible with the texts of Dio and Suetonius; on balance, it is more likely that Capricorn was the location of the Moon and the Lot of Fortune when Augustus was born.[76] However, the choice of Capricon as Augustus' favourite star sign was determined by a number of concomitant and independent factors, some of which lay outside his own horoscope. Capricorn is an amphibious sign, which chimes well with Augustus' emphatic

---

[71] Dio 45.7.1: καὶ αὐτὸ κομήτην τέ τινων καλούντων.

[72] Cramer 1954: 99; MacMullen 1966: 129; Wardle forthcoming.   [73] Cramer 1954: 97.

[74] Overviews of the possible solutions and summaries of the earlier debate in Brind'Amour 1983: 62–76; Barton 1994a: 40–5, 192–4 and 1995 (bibliography at 37–8); Orth 1996: 109–12, 124–9; Terio 2006: 155–221; Volk 2009: 146–51; Bakhouche 2012; Wardle forthcoming.

[75] See e.g. Bowersock 1990: 385–7; Le Bœuffle 1999: 277–80.

[76] Lewis 2008: 313, with earlier bibliography. See also *ibid.* 330–4 on the significance of Virgo in Augustus' horoscope. Lot of Fortune: Barton 1995: 39–40; Beck 2007: 89–90.

celebration of his victories on land and sea (*terra marique*). According to an Egyptian and Hellenistic tradition Capricorn was the sign that ruled over the Western regions, like Spain, Gaul and Germany; in the 30s it coincided with Octavian's triumviral assignment.[77] Moreover, it is the sign in which the Sun begins to rise after the winter solstice, and hence is ideally suited to a discourse that emphasises the beginning of a new age of peace and concord.[78] It is very likely that the determination of these elements of interest was made possible by the intervention of at least one expert astrologer advising Augustus.[79] Three fundamental provisos must be borne in mind: there were a number of competing systems in ancient astrology, which generated considerable disagreement among practitioners; astrology may have been a highly technical discipline, but it also allowed plenty of scope for creativity, and indeed internal contradiction; and many competing but not mutually exclusive associations could be established between a complex figure like Augustus and Capricorn.[80]

The *princeps'* interest in horoscopes was not isolated or unprecedented. Varro consulted the mathematician and astrologer L. Tarutius, from Firmum, whom he asked to determine the day and hour of Romulus' birth. Tarutius reviewed the events of Romulus' life and the circumstances surrounding his death and concluded his investigation by producing three dates: that of Romulus' conception, that of his birth and that of the foundation of Rome, all expressed in the months and days of the Egyptian calendar.[81] Tarutius was no obscure figure. Cicero numbered him among his *familiares* and engaged critically in *Div.* 2 with the horoscope of the date of the foundation of Rome that he had produced. Marcus denies that there was any link between the foundation of the city and the Palilia, and dismissed the idea that the stars and the moon could have any influence on the foundation of a city as ludicrous. Still, Tarutius' views had an appeal and a significance that could not be underestimated. Cicero conceded that the expertise of this *municipalis* from Picenum was based on a thorough knowledge of Near Eastern lore (the *Chaldaicae rationes*, as Cicero calls them). Mastering it and securing its control was a necessity for the new regime.

Babylonian astrology was no novelty in the religious and intellectual landscape of late Republican Rome and Italy. It also had a considerable

---

[77] Manil. *Astr.* 4.791–4, with Wardle forthcoming.   [78] Barton 1994a: 41 and 1994b: 40.
[79] Schmid 2005: 341–60.   [80] Barton 1995: 39–48. Cf. also Bakhouche 2012: 59.
[81] Plut. *Rom.* 12; Cic. *Div.* 2.98–9; Solin. 1.32; Lyd. *Mens.* 1.14. Bergk 1860: ix–x (= 1884: 242–4); Brind'Amour 1983: 240–8; Rawson 1985: 244–5; Grafton and Swerdlow 1985: 456–60 and 1986; Domenicucci 1996: 126–30; Abry 1996; Wiseman forthcoming.

impact on the doctrine of the Etruscan haruspices. The interpretation of lightning, codified in the so-called *libri fulgurales*, was influenced by Chaldaean lore, especially through the writings of Berossus, a Babylonian astrologer whose Greek works circulated widely in the Hellenistic world. Hellenistic astrology was deeply indebted to the Babylonian craft. It was a lively, diverse and highly technical discipline, the practitioners of which shared a keen interest in the prediction of the future, even if they did not all use the same approaches and methods.[82] Etruscan extispicy, the art of reading the entrails of animals for divinatory purposes, was probably also influenced by Babylonian doctrines, although it was not necessarily an Eastern import.[83] A most unusual artefact sheds some light on this problem. The Piacenza liver is a bronze model of a stylized sheep's liver that was ostensibly used by a haruspex as a guide to the reading of the entrails, and perhaps also used as a teaching tool. It was found at Settima di Gossolengo near Piacenza, but was probably made at Chiusi or Cortona, around 100.[84] Its archaeological context is bound to remain elusive, but there has been intense debate on the sectors into which it is divided and the inscriptions that cover it.[85] If the reconstruction of M. Maggiani is correct, the Piacenza liver reflects a doctrine that was the outcome of a conscious blend of Etruscan, Greek and Chaldaean elements. Extispicy and astrology are inextricably linked in this context. Chaldaean influences

---

[82] Cramer 1954: 3–28; Gundel and Gundel 1966: 75–121; Long 1982; Barton 1994b: 9–63; Lehoux 2007: 55–69; Beck 2007; Gieseler Greenbaum 2010. See Long 1982: 170 n. 19 for the conceptual differentiation between 'hard' and 'soft' astrology: in the 'hard' version of the discipline, 'heavenly bodies are both signs and causes of human affairs', while in the 'soft' one 'heavenly bodies only are signs of human affairs without also attributing a causal role to the heavenly bodies'.

[83] Plin. *HN* 11.186 points to a specific development in the practice of extispicy: in 275 the haruspices started to examine the heart of the victim (North 1989: 577). As Cic. *Div.* 2.28 points out, extispicy was widely practised throughout the ancient Mediterranean, but there was no unifying method regulating its practice (*nec esse unam omnium disciplinam*); see Montero 1995a: 158–62. An overview of Babylonian divination in Maul 2003. Gadd 1966: 30–4 discusses the affinities between ancient Babylonian extispicy and astrology. Links between Babylonian and Etruscan extispicy: Blecher 1905; Clemen 1936: 266–71 (sceptical); Bloch 1966: 159; and esp. Nougayrol 1955, a ground-breaking study based on the study of the clay liver from Falerii Veteres (third century BC).

[84] Excellent description of the artefact (with illustrations) in van der Meer 1987: 3–18; see also Thulin 1906b: 7–30 and Maggiani 2005: 55–9. On the position of the haruspex during the ritual cf. van der Meer 1979. Turfa and Gettys 2009 offer a tentative explanation for the reliance on sheep livers in Etruscan extispicy: the inspection of this organ may have revealed the spread of serious diseases that became apparent in the sheep some time before they did in humans.

[85] The surface of the liver is divided into sixteen parts, and names of Etruscan deities are inscribed on each. In the *De nuptiis Philologiae et Mercurii* the fifth-century AD author Martianus Capella (1.41–61) gives a list of sixteen deities, each one residing in a different region of the heavens. The analogies with the Piacenza liver are significant: see the classic discussions in Thulin 1906b and Weinstock 1946. On the epistemological analogies between augury and extispicy see Vernant 1948: 304–5.

on the Etruscan *disciplina* may go as far back as the fourth century BC.[86] The analogy between astronomy and extispicy is developed systematically by Manilius, who wrote the didactic poem *Astronomica* in the second decade of the first century AD.[87] Both disciplines are based on the principle that the universe has a corporeality, which can be studied and understood in detail.[88]

The attempt to secure tighter political control over the practice of astrology was matched by the decision that accompanied the publication of the horoscope. Limitations and occasional prohibitions were not a novelty.[89] In 33 Agrippa, during his aedileship, outlawed astrology from the city of Rome; the first known measure prohibiting astrology, however, dates back to 139 and was set out in an edict of the praetor Cornelius Hispalus, which also included a clause on the expulsion of the Jews.[90] It is likely that both these decisions were temporary and were discontinued when the magistrates that took them left office.[91] It was only under Tiberius that the measures against the professional practice of astrology in private contexts were endorsed by two *senatusconsulta* in AD 16 and 17, no doubt because they were intended as long-term decisions.[92] Moreover, establishing who these astrologers were in the late Republican period, how they practised their craft, and how homogeneous a group they were, is an impossible task.[93] There is no evidence for a systematic repression of astrology in the late Republic and early Principate. Neither was there an attempt to provide legal definitions of the astrological practices that were not socially

---

[86] Maggiani 1982: 73–7, 84–8; cf. also Dumézil 1966: 621–6; Linderski 1990: 71 (= 1995a: 599); Assmann 1992: 248–51; Montero 2001: 239–48. *Contra*, van der Meer 1987: 153–66.

[87] Volk 2011: 4–5 summarises the debate on the dating of Manilius' poem.

[88] Manil. *Astr.* 4.908–14 is a key passage; see Guillaumont 1991: 106–7; Habinek 2007. Cf. Habinek 2011 and Mann 2011 on the Stoic undercurrents of Manilius' project.

[89] Cramer 1954: 58–99; Volk 2009: 127–37; Green 2011: 129–35.

[90] Expulsion of 33: Dio 49.43.5. Expulsion of 139: Val. Max. 1.3.3, with Wardle 1998: 148–9 and Mueller 2002: 100–1. Treggiari 1969: 204 links the presence of the *Chaldaei* in Rome with the coming of Syrian slaves after the war with Antiochus III; cf. the reference to the freedman Manilius Antiochus as *conditor astrologiae* in Plin. *HN* 35.199 (Bakhouche 2002: 35 and Volk 2009: 4 place him in the first half of the first century BC). See also Cramer 1951: 16–21 and 1954: 234–7; Desanti 1990: 17–19; Ando 2008: 107; Orlin 2010: 182–6; Ripat 2011: 118. Cf. A. Alföldi's speculative if thought-provoking view that in 139 the beginning of a new *saeculum* was widely expected (Alföldi 1971 = 1997: 15–32 and 1973 = 1997: 33–45); for a general reassessment of Alföldi's work on late Republican religion and culture see Santangelo forthcoming.

[91] However, Wardle 1998: 151 remarks that these expulsions may have still featured in the largely tralatician praetorian edict for some time after 139.

[92] Tac. *Ann.* 2.32; Suet. *Tib.* 36; Ulp. 15.2.1; Dio 57.15.8–9. Cramer 1951: 21–9; Ripat 2011: 118–21. Cf. Tiberius' ban on private haruspices: Suet. *Tib.* 63.2, with Ripat 2011: 131. Green 2011 interestingly argues that Manilius' poem reflects this 'imperial nervousness surrounding astrology', which in turn undermines its didactic mission.

[93] Ripat 2011: 129.

acceptable. The infrequency of the expulsions of the astrologers in this period is instructive. The strategy of the Roman government was reactive, not inquisitory.[94] Whatever the legal framework in which these decisions were taken, it was certainly clear to Augustus that the invaluable weapon that was astrology had to be under the firm control of the emperor. The late Republican theme of the good fortune of the great man found a new systematisation in the framework provided by the horoscope, which provided a further development to the problem of predestination. The favour of the stars was a manifestation of the favour of the gods for the *princeps*.[95]

There is no doubt that Augustus played a crucial role in promoting astrology as a practice of great political significance and, one would assume, of deep intellectual value.[96] However, the practice of astrology was already widespread in late Republican Rome, as a *scientia peregrina* keenly sought after by some. C. Sulpicius Galus (pr. 169), an associate of L. Aemilius Paullus, used his astrological expertise to reassure the soldiers who were terrified by an eclipse before the battle of Pydna; his main source was Archimedes.[97] In the nineties, during his tenure in Cilicia, Sulla took the advice of Chaldaean seers, albeit in what appears to have been a private context.[98] The consul of 87, Cn. Octavius, had a keen interest in astrology, and some Chaldaean seers told him that he would be successful in the struggle against Marius and Cinna; when he was killed an astrological chart (*diagramma Chaldaikon*) was found on his body.[99] Cicero's interest in Aratus' *Phaenomena* led him to explore the teachings of Hellenistic debates on astrology, and the *De diuinatione* shows some engagement with astrology.[100] The terms of his friend Nigidius' work in this area are difficult to define, but it is certain that he wrote about astrological matters.[101]

---

[94] Phillips 1991: esp. 263–4.   [95] Schmid 2005: 245–303.

[96] Barton 1994b: 40–2; Orth 1996: 104; Rehak 2006: 69–74; Wallace-Hadrill 2008: 251; Volk 2009: 135–6. Cf. Montero 2001: 249–59 on the competition between astrology and haruspicy under the Principate.

[97] Cic. *Rep.* 1.21–3, with Gallagher 2001: 510; Livy 44.37.5–9; Val. Max. 8.11.1; Plin. *HN* 2.53. See Rawson 1985: 306–11; cf. Rawson 1973: 162 (= 1991: 82); Guillaumont 1996: 56–7; Vigourt 2001a: 127–8. On the eclipse see Brind'Amour 1983: 151–6.

[98] Plut. *Sull.* 5.11; Vell. 2.24.3. Thein 2009: 92–3.   [99] Plut. *Mar.* 42.4–5.

[100] See e.g. Cic. *Div.* 1.85, 2.88, 146. Cicero wrote the *Aratea*, his translation of the *Phaenomena*, in the early eighties; however, he probably revised it at later stages and came back to the themes of Aratus' poem in various parts of his philosophical work: Gee 2001. Astronomical language and imagery in the *De re publica*: Gallagher 2001.

[101] Barton 1994a: 38–9 (he tried to 'compare and perhaps combine' haruspicy and astrology); Schmid 2005: 183–94. Liuzzi 1983: 83 rightly points out that the known titles of Nigidius' works are more instructive than the fragments that have survived. Guillaumont 1986: 124 notes that the evidence for Cicero's intellectual debt to Nigidius is practically non-existent. The nature of Nigidius' intellectual ties with Varro is hard to establish (Swoboda 1889: 27–8).

Augustus' innovation was to understand the potential of astrology for building the grand narrative underpinning his political agenda; this was not done, however, at the expense of other divinatory practices.[102] One of the factors that made astrology so attractive was its predictive potential. Like the responses of the haruspices, it did not just offer an assessment of the position of the gods on a given matter, but provided fully fledged prophecies about the future, including some on the distant future. The analogy with the Etruscan *disciplina* also applies on another important level: astrology was a complex set of doctrines that applied principles to a complex body of material and was practised by a range of professional trained experts. Control over its practice was a crucial aspect of the strategy deployed by Augustus.

There is, however, an important difference between astrology and the other forms of divination that were practised in the late Republic. Astrology took the interpretation of signs – whether actively sought (*impetratiua*) or interpreted after they had presented themselves (*oblatiua*) – to an altogether new level. Any astrological prediction produced concerning the destiny of an individual was based on the observation of the position and movements of the stars at a given moment. The response of the astrologer was not the interpretation of several signs, but a narrative that followed specific rules and was based on a specific set of evidence, which – unlike the signs interpreted by augurs and haruspices – was already *in re*. With its powerful message, a horoscope could be constructed as a sign, which already provided its audience with a strategy for its interpretation. The practicalities of the publication of Augustus' horoscope are unclear, except for the important detail that it was made public by decree. It is unclear, for example, whether a copy of the horoscope was displayed in a public place, like the map of the world commissioned by Agrippa.[103] It is also unclear how widely the implications of the horoscope were understood; this reservation also applies to the most educated members of the elite. Moreover, different interpretations could be produced for the same horoscope: the symbolic possibilities that it opened up made such disagreement inevitable.[104] These very possibilities were, of course, one of the factors that made astrology so attractive to Augustus.

The horoscope is not the only aspect of Augustus' interest in astrological matters, and not even the most prominent one. The symbol of Capricorn

[102] A different assessment in Wallace-Hadrill 2008: 250–1.   [103] Plin. *HN* 3.16–17. Abry 2011: 232–4.
[104] Barton 1995: 42 notes that this potential for confusion is also reflected in the disagreement that dominates in modern scholarship.

featured on a wide range of material produced in the Augustan period, especially after Actium: coinage, of course, but also glass-pastes, cameos, temple antefixes, and more.[105] Capricorn was probably used first on motifs featuring in private contexts; there is evidence for its appearance on coins since 41/40, but it appears on Octavian's own coinage only in 28, in tune with post-Actium rhetoric of victory and conquest.[106] It is also significant that this motif usually appeared in association with other themes, such as the cornucopia or the globe, and it conjured up associations with good fortune and stability, which Nigidius Figulus spelled out in his treatise *Sphaera Graecanica*.[107] An association with the concept of the *imperium* as a territorial entity encompassing the earth and the sea was no doubt also part of the picture, since Capricorn is both a terrestrial and a marine creature.[108] The prominence of Capricorn in the iconography of this period can be explained as a symptom of the widespread echo of public themes that is typical of the Augustan period. With its distinctive connotations, Capricorn was a clear and forceful symbol of association with the imperial power that was appealing in private iconography too.

Astrological themes featured very prominently in an aspect of the monumental reorganisation of Rome masterminded by Augustus. The obelisk taken to Rome by Augustus after the conquest of Egypt and erected in the Campus Martius in 10 (now in Piazza Monte Citorio) was long regarded as a sundial forming part of a broader complex, the so-called *Horologium Augusti*. This interpretation, developed by the German archaeologist E. Buchner after his excavation of the area on the basis of a passage of Pliny the Elder, has been shown to be fallacious: the obelisk was part not of a sundial, but of a solar meridian line, which was intended to mark the unfolding of the solar year through the zodiac signs. There was no such thing as a *Horologium*.[109] Although there was a clear relationship between the obelisk, the *Ara Pacis*, which was perpendicular to it, and the Mausoleum of Augustus, the three monuments were not integrated into a tool

---

[105] An exhaustive inventory in Terio 2006: 221–65.

[106] Evidence and discussion in Barton 1994a: 41–3.

[107] Nigidius Figulus, *De Capricorno* (from the *De sphaera*), in F LXXXXVIII Swoboda. Dwyer 1973: 61–6; Abry 1988, esp. 114–21. Nigidius' contribution to Roman astrology: Cramer 1954: 63–5; Gundel and Gundel 1966: 137–9.

[108] On the development of the concept of *imperium* in the Augustan period see Richardson 2008: 117–45.

[109] Plin. *HN* 36.72–3. Buchner 1982; cf. Bowersock 1990, 383–8; Rehak 2001: 200–1, 207–8 and 2006: 80–6; Haselberger 2007: 169–70 n. 220 and 2011; Alföldy 2011; Hannah 2011. Critical discussions in Schütz 1990; Barton 1994a: 45–6; Barton 1995: 44–6; Schmid 2005: 305–13; Lange 2009: 6–7; Abry 2011: 230–1; Schütz 2011; and esp. Heslin 2007: 1–16 and 2011.

for the measurement of time.[110] However, the design of the monumental complex is underpinned by an expert use of astrological lore and an impressive spatial awareness. The intention was to celebrate Augustus and his family and to emphasise a number of central themes in the Augustan discourse: the conquest of Egypt, the opposition between East and West, the leading role of Augustus in Roman religion, and the centrality of the *gens Julia*. The whole project can be safely dated to a specific phase of Augustus' principate, between 13 (when the construction of the *Ara Pacis* was decreed) and 9 (the date of its dedication). Crucially, the obelisk was erected in 10, two years after Augustus' rise to the highest pontificate, which marked the full accomplishment of his hegemony over Roman public religion.[111] The monumental landscape of the Campus Martius forcefully asserted that a new era had begun.

Augury in the Augustan discourse

The use and promotion of astrological themes must be appreciated within the broader context of the importance of religious themes in the Augustan discourse and especially in the construction of the public persona of the *princeps*. Suetonius' account makes it clear that a tradition took shape around the premonitory signs that Octavius received concerning the success of his son; the prediction of Father Liber in Thrace poses equally serious problems.[112] Indeed, the tradition was complex. Suetonius mentions dreams by Q. Lutatius Catulus and Cicero that foretold the rise of young Octavius, and another episode at the battle of Munda, when Julius Caesar saw a sign that foretold Octavian's rise.[113] Predestination is deeply connected to the ability to predict events and developments, not just by rational inference, but also through the reading of premonitory signs. Suetonius mentions events that preceded all the main battles of the Civil War, and maintains that Octavian was unfailingly able to understand their premonitory meaning. He does not just celebrate Octavian's piety

---

[110] Heslin 2007: 6–8. Moreover, the Mausoleum was closely integrated with another Augustan monument: Agrippa's Pantheon was half a Roman mile (some 740 metres) south of the Mausoleum on an alignment determined by the Pole Star (Wardle 2008: 359–66, with previous bibliography; Rehak 2006: 22 argues that 'the two structures were not precisely aligned, even if they were connected by lines of sight').

[111] Heslin 2007: 15–16. *Contra* cf. Rehak 2006: 89, who argues that the *Horologium* and the *Ara Pacis* were planned as early as in 17.

[112] Suet. *Aug.* 94.8.

[113] Suet. *Aug.* 94.12–14, 17–18. Dreams of Catullus and Cicero: Dio 45.2.2–4; on Cicero's cf. also Plut. *Cic.* 44.2–5. Gascou 1984: 356, 777–8; Moles 1988: 195; Lorsch Wildfang 2000a: 48–51; Wardle 2005b.

or divinatory ability; most importantly, he conveys a picture of constant divine interest in the affairs of the *princeps*, which is the clearest testimony to the exceptional qualities and merits of the man, and accompanies him down to the end of his life. Therefore, Suetonius' excursus on Augustus and religion ends with a lengthy discussion of the events that preceded his death.[114]

Suetonius' discussion is wide ranging and well informed, but it is by no means comprehensive – nor should it be expected to be so.[115] It says hardly anything about Augustus' use of augury and augural themes, which was a very important aspect of his strategy, as we shall see; it does not even include all the relevant events of which Suetonius was aware. At the beginning of the *Life of Galba*, Suetonius mentions a prodigy that occurred to Livia and was connected to Augustus and the Julio-Claudians. He does not record it in the *Life of Augustus*, but finds it relevant to explain the fall of Nero and the rise of Galba.[116] Immediately after Livia's marriage to Augustus, as she was at her estate near Veii, an eagle which flew by dropped into her lap a white hen, holding a wreath of laurel in its beak. Livia decided to rear the chicken and to plant the laurel: a breed of chicks was born, and a grove of laurel sprang up on the site. The villa was soon named *ad Gallinas Albas* ('White Hens Villa'); most interestingly, the laurel that was used in the triumphs of the members of the imperial family since that time came from that grove.[117] The story is told with some variations by Pliny the Elder, who claims that all the emperors wore a wreath and carried a branch taken from the grove. According to Suetonius, the grove died at the end of Nero's reign, therefore pointing to an exclusive connection with the Julio-Claudian dynasty.[118] Whatever version one chooses and whatever the relationship of the Julio-Claudian dynasty to the grove was, the episode is certainly linked to the rise of monarchy, and to the restriction of the prerogative to celebrate a triumph to the members of imperial family.[119] Cassius Dio includes it among the disquieting signs that occurred during the Civil War, and adds that the prodigy was regarded by some as a premonition of Livia's dominating influence over her husband.[120] His version has the merit of placing the

---

[114] Suet. *Aug.* 97–8.

[115] Suetonius on religion: Wallace-Hadrill 1983: 189–97; Gascou 1984: 728–33; Fögen 1993: 113–26. Suetonius on haruspicy: Champeaux 1995.

[116] Suet. *Galb.* 1. Same approach in Dio 63.29.3. Martin 1986: 19, 38; Vigourt 2001b: 271–2; Montero 2006: 102–7. Livia's association with inductive divination: Montero 1994b.

[117] On the villa see Messineo 2001 and Clark Reeder 2001.

[118] Plin. *HN* 15.136–7. Poulle 1999: 37–8 speculates that the death of the chickens (*gallinae*) may be a sign of the imminent revolt in Gaul (*Gallia*).

[119] Beard 2007: 287–8.   [120] Dio 48.52.3–4.

episode within a broader historical context, but does not mention the venue where it took place. The setting is very significant, because it happens to be Livia's villa at Prima Porta, where the famous statue of Augustus was discovered. A connection between the prodigy, the iconography of the statue and especially of Augustus' cuirass, and the underground complex of the villa-garden has been plausibly argued.[121]

The use of augural motifs should be viewed as an aspect of a broader political and ideological programme, which had the control of the religious scene as one of its central concerns.[122] In 28 Octavian banned the Egyptian cults within the *pomerium* of the city of Rome.[123] As has been convincingly shown, this was not an attempt to isolate, marginalise or repress Egyptian cults in Rome.[124] There is, in fact, evidence that Octavian supported the cults of Isis and Sarapis in the city, notably by promoting the reconstruction of temples of both deities.[125] This ran against the grain of decades of hostility and at times open repression of Egyptian cults on the part of the Roman senatorial elite. The haruspices played a central role in shaping that climate. When in 48 some bees settled next to a statue of Hercules on the Capitol, they prescribed the digging up of all the sites where Isis was worshipped; the reason for that response was that some sacrifices in honour of Isis had been performed near the statue.[126] Five years earlier, a decree of the Senate had ordered the destruction of the temples of Isis and Serapis that had been built by private individuals at their own expense.[127] Octavian had a more sophisticated strategy: placing the Egyptian cults outside the *pomerium*, but within the boundaries of the city, was not just part of the *princeps'* grand plan to secure his control of the religious life in the city. It was not merely a Machiavellian power strategy either. That decision was part of a wider process of definition of what was and was not Roman. Establishing boundaries or using existing ones, including a physical one like the *pomerium*, was a crucial part of the process.[128]

In 28, according to the *Res Gestae*, Octavian was also entrusted by the Senate with the restoration of eighty-two temples in the city of Rome that needed repair.[129] Roman religion was a 'religion of place' and taking charge of a series of interventions on such a great number of sites afforded Augustus the unique opportunity to redesign the religious and ritual landscape of the city.[130] Even the order in which the temples were rebuilt served to

---

[121] Clark Reeder 1997.   [122] Hurlet 2001.   [123] Dio 53.2.
[124] Orlin 2008 and 2010: 211–12.   [125] Dio 53.2.4.   [126] Dio 42.26.1.   [127] Dio 40.47.
[128] Orlin 2008: 244–5. Sandberg 2009: 150–9 argues that the cult of Isis had always been extra-pomerial.
[129] *RG* 20.4.
[130] 'Religion of place': Price 1996. Cf. also Cancik 1985/6 on Rome as a sacred landscape.

present specific messages and build specific associations, both with cults and with the history of the city.[131] On the Nones of February of the same year he carried out the strengthening of the city's walls, an act that was directly associated to the precedent of Romulus.[132] The resonance of augural themes becomes even stronger after the settlement of 27.[133] The name 'Augustus', of course, had an obvious connection with augury, and with the theme of a new foundation and a new beginning for the city. It also conjured up the idea of the growth and the expansion of the city and its dignity: in itself a firm response to the rhetoric of decline that was so prominent in the last decades of the Republic.[134] The most striking instance of Augustus' innovative use of augury, however, was the decision to perform the *augurium salutis* in 29. Cassius Dio describes this as a decision taken by the Senate as part of the set of honours decreed to Octavian during his fifth consulship, which accompanied the closing of the gates of the temple of Janus in the same year.[135] Dio portrays both gestures as signs that an age of peace was beginning: he also argues that they were autonomous decisions of the Senate, and two of the few honours that Octavian did not turn down in that year.

In early 29 Octavian was still in the Greek East and did not attend the ritual.[136] Nonetheless, it may be safely ruled out that the decision was made without his involvement. The antiquarian flavour of the *augurium salutis* fits well in the typically Augustan pattern of rediscovery and restaging of early rituals, which had begun already in the thirties. Dio himself stresses that it was an important political and symbolic decision, which was intended to make the very specific point that peace had come: the *augurium* was performed even if the claim that the whole of the empire was at peace was not quite accurate. Dio's interest in this ritual is apparent, and emerges even more clearly in his account of its previous performance. The last occasion when the *augurium salutis* had been performed was in 63, after Pompey's victory in the East.[137] Dio explains that the *augurium*

---

[131] Orlin 2007: esp. 81–5.   [132] Ov. *Fast.* 2.133–4. Kearsley 2009: 159–60; Robinson 2010: 149–50.

[133] Cf. Hurlet 2001: 167–80.

[134] Suet. *Aug.* 7; Serv. *ad Aen.* 1.292. Montero 2006: 145–8; Todisco 2007. Wiseman forthcoming discusses the role that Varro's work may have had in shaping Augustus' augural interests and expertise.

[135] Dio 51.20.4; see also Suet. *Aug.* 31.4. Liegle 1942: 297–8; Lange 2009: 131. On Janus' augural connotation cf. Taylor 2000: 11–26.

[136] He was on Samos when he took up his fifth consulship: Suet. *Aug.* 26.6.

[137] Dio 37.24.1–2. On the context of the *augurium salutis* of 63 see Havas 2000: 77–8. It is unclear who presided over the ceremony in Octavian's absence; the view that the eldest augur (M. Valerius Messalla Rufus, on that occasion: Rüpke 2005a: 143) presided over the college and had the title of *augur maximus* is unsupported by the evidence (Linderski 1986a: 2154–5 n. 26).

was performed only when no Roman troops were deployed or were being mobilised, and for this reason there were hardly any occasions when the ritual could be performed.[138] This explanation is surely off the mark, and it even seems to suggest that the Romans felt some sort of guilt for waging war; however, there is no reason to question the fundamental accuracy of Dio's account. The end of the Eastern campaign, in which Mithridates, the long-standing enemy of Rome, was defeated and the threat of piracy was purportedly removed, could rightly be regarded as a major moment. There are, indeed, only two previous attestations of this ritual, in 235 (which is doubtful) and in 160.[139]

It is unclear what input Pompey himself had in the decision to perform the ritual, which was probably taken by the Senate. It is apparent, however, that it was a controversial process, as the outcome of the ritual showed: some birds appeared in an unfavourable quarter of the sky and the procedure had to be repeated. An echo of this episode can be found in Cicero's *De diuinatione*, where the controversy on the success of the *augurium* is linked to the preparation of Catiline's conspiracy.[140] There is no evidence that a controversy arose around the *augurium salutis* of 29. A time-honoured ritual, which had seldom been used before and never in the recent past, was rediscovered and reused to serve the agenda of a new political context. A useful parallel may be found in the revisitation of the fetial procedure in 32, at the beginning of the war with Antony and Cleopatra, which was based on a series of minor but significant changes to the old ceremony and also conveyed the message that the war was an external, not a civil one.[141]

The *augurium salutis* of 29 attained the twofold aim of conveying the message that peace had come and of restating the commitment of Octavian and the new regime to the centrality of augury in Roman public religion. A further implication may be suggested. Although the role of Pompey in planning the *augurium* of 63 is not entirely clear, it is a fair guess that the ritual was inextricably associated with the greatest deed of the great man, the victory in the East. Octavian's decision to revive it suggests that he did not fear to portray himself as the continuator of an important aspect

---

[138] According to Cic. *Div.* 1.105, Appius Claudius questioned the validity of the *augurium* of 63 and predicted that internecine war would soon follow (Vaahtera 2001: 133–6; Wardle 2006: 359–60).

[139] Overviews: Blumenthal 1914; Liegle 1942; Rüpke 1990: 141–3. Liegle 1942: 297–305 and Montero 2006: 127–30 on the ceremony celebrated by Octavian in 29; see also Catalano 1960: 335–46 and Linderski 1986a: 2253–6 on ritual aspects.

[140] Cic. *Div.* 1.105. Wardle 2006: 359–60.   [141] Dio 50.4.4–5. Santangelo 2008: 86–8.

of Pompey's legacy and that, therefore, his agenda went beyond the remit of Caesar's legacy. The civil wars were truly over if Octavian could attach himself so explicity to the finest hour of the greatest enemy of his father. At any rate, the close link with augural themes was a fundamental aspect of the strategy of Octavian/Augustus, which cannot be explained with short-term propagandistic aims. The ritual of 29 was not an isolated exception. The importance of the *augurium salutis* to the Augustan ideological construction is confirmed by the epigraphical evidence for the celebration of the *augurium* in AD 3 in an inscription from Rome, which strongly suggests that by that time the rite had become a regular occurrence.[142]

The most impressive echo of augural themes in this period is perhaps to be found in an iconographical source: the relief on a small altar set up in honour of the Lares by the *magistri* of the *uicus Sandaliarius*, a neighbourhood in the vicinity of the Forum of Augustus in Rome (Figure 12.1).[143]

The relief can be safely dated to 2 BC, and portrays three figures: two are safely identified respectively as Augustus, standing in the centre dressed as an augur and holding a *lituus* (i.e. a curved staff carried by the augurs), and as Gaius Caesar, standing on the left, holding a roll that may be interpreted as a military *itinerarium*. We are on the eve of the latter's departure to a campaign against the Parthians: Augustus' attire is, first of all, a reference to Gaius Caesar's command and its full legitimacy, but it also carries a resonance that reverberates upon the outcome of the mission. The scene depicts the moment of the augural ritual that is known as *tripudium*, in which the augur observes the sacred chickens eating and determines whether a campaign that is about to begin has divine support.[144] Various gods were usually invoked during this ritual. The identification of the third figure, standing on the right, is crucial. B. Rose has suggested a convincing solution to the lengthy scholarly debate and argued that she is neither a goddess nor Livia (as was previously argued by other scholars) but a priestess of Cybele/Magna Mater.[145] Far from being an awkward combination of traditional augural practices and Eastern cults, the association suggested by this relief is a powerful attempt to redefine the boundaries of the Augustan

---

[142] *CIL* 6.36841. Wardle 2011a: 282–3.
[143] Description of the altar: Scott Ryberg 1955: 60–1. Iconographic and historical discussion: Rose 2005: 47–50, with a full survey of previous scholarship.
[144] On the *tripudium* in the last two centuries of the Republic see Scheid 2012: 113–17 and cf. above, Chapter 1.
[145] Rose 2005: 47–9.

Figure 12.1 Altar for the *Lares Augusti* given to the *uicus Sandaliarius* in Rome by
four *magistri uici* in 2 BC. Front showing the emperor flanked by Gaius Caesar and
a priestess of Magna Mater. Florence, Uffizi, inv. 972. Singer © Neg. D-DAI-ROM
72.159.

discourse. Cybele is a goddess who had a strong link with the Roman
conquest of the East, since her coming to Rome from Pessinus in 205 BC. It
was, however, an even stronger sign of the allegiance to the goddess at times
when the defence of the city was a crucial concern. The creation of the cult
of Magna Mater played an important role in the tense religious climate
of the Hannibalic War, and the oracle of Pessinus also sent reassuring
messages to Rome in 102, when the Cimbrians were posing a threat to
Italy that some considered similar to Hannibal's.[146] The presence of the
priestess of Cybele in this context and her association with Augustus in
his augural capacity develop both these points. On the one hand, they
reassert the strong bond of patronage between the goddess and Rome,
which was accompanied and confirmed by the presence of augural symbols
that ensured the relationship between Rome and the gods: Western and

[146] Diod. 36.13; Plut. *Mar.* 17.5–6.

Eastern gods were all important to the city, which was – like Troy – both Western and Eastern. On the other hand, the support of Cybele completed the military message conveyed by the augural signs: if an Eastern goddess supported the Roman general at the inception of an Eastern campaign, the forthcoming victory was guaranteed and predicted by the combination of military might and divine support. The other face of the altar completed the message by portraying the goddess Victoria placing spoils on a trophy: success is there to be obtained, already foretold in the iconography of the altar.[147]

Augustus remains central even in a context that appears to be dominated by Cybele, and not just visually. He makes Cybele's support to Gaius Caesar possible through the augural ritual that he performs and guarantees. Cybele is important to Gaius' mission because of her Eastern and Trojan connections and because of the role that she played in making Aeneas' journey to Italy possible. It is only appropriate that she should now aid the journey in the opposite direction of a member of the *gens Julia*, who descends from the Trojan hero. The association of the altar with the cult of the Lares reinforced the connection with Aeneas. The spatial association with the Forum of Augustus and the allusion to the theme of the revenge on the Parthians, forcefully conveyed by the spoils scene, also linked the altar to the neighbouring temple of Mars Ultor. This combination of multi-faceted, strikingly experimental themes is quintessentially Augustan. So is the approach to the prediction and the control of the future. The relief is all about a promise of success, which is backed by the correct performance of the augural ritual and the presence of the priestess, and is spelled out by the depiction of Victoria. The outcome is a prophecy that is not conveyed by an oracular response or an extract of the Sibylline Books. It is presented in images, and it is set out as an unfalsifiable truth. Augustus makes it possible with his presence and guarantees it through his priestly and imperial roles. Augury is central, whilst being part of a wider discourse that gains further resonance through a number of symbolic and ideological associations. At the same time, it is firmly placed within a specific spatial and topographical context, which is intrinsically associated with the *princeps*, while at the same time offering scope to the advertisement of the piety and *religio* of specific groups, such as the inhabitants of the *uicus Sandaliarius*. By the time the altar was dedicated, the project of monarchic control on prophecies in

[147] Wiseman 1984: 125–8, 227–9 has an excellent discussion of the association between Cybele and Victoria and of its relevance for the Augustan agenda; cf. also the hypothesis at 127 and 229 that the goddess portrayed behind Augustus in the Gemma Augustea may be Cybele, rather than Oikoumene.

the public discourse was fully accomplished. In a world where prophecies were planned, controlled and circulated by *sapientissimus et unus*, debate on prediction and divination had become a thing of the past, because the problem of their control had been given a solution.[148]

[148] Tac. *Dial.* 41.4: 'the wisest man, and the only one'. Imperial and late antique developments: MacMullen 1966: 128–62, 325–36; Grodzynski 1974; Hopkins 1978: 231–42; Desanti 1990: 31–206; Fögen 1993: Potter 1994; Sfameni Gasparro 2002: 23–60. Prodigies, especially those foretelling the rise of an emperor to power: Vigourt 2001a and Requena 2001 (cf. also Martin 1986). Haruspicy: Montero 1991; Briquel 1997a: 27–118, 139–204; Ramelli 2003: 85–150. Astrology: Cramer 1954: 99–231, 237–81; Barton 1994a: 54–69, 196–200; Barton 1994b: 41–85.

Away from the future

In book 52 of Cassius Dio's *History of Rome*, Maecenas addresses a speech to Augustus, in which he gives advice on how to run the State and how to set up a monarchic regime. He also offers some prescriptive comments on religion, and notably on divination.[1] Any deviation from established ancestral religious practice must be curtailed, as it is both offensive towards the gods and politically dangerous. No one must be allowed to be an atheist (*atheos*) or a sorcerer (*goes*; there is also mention of *mageutai* a couple of lines below). A clear distinction is then made between magic, which cannot in any way be accepted, and divination (*mantike*), a craft that Maecenas explicitly deems useful to the state. Augustus is urged to allow (*apodeixon*) the people who are to practise divination (diviners and augurs: *hieroptai* and *oionistai*) to hold the priesthoods, so that they can be consulted by people who are interested in accessing their advice.[2] The importance of keeping magic and philosophy in check is restated; the boundaries between divination and magic are blurry. Rather surprisingly, the Etruscan Maecenas has nothing to say about the position of haruspicy under the new regime.

The historical value of this text is at best relative. Dio, who wrote in the first quarter of the third century AD, used the fictional debate between Agrippa and Maecenas as an attempt to reflect on the foundations of the Augustan regime.[3] The arguments put forward by Augustus' advisors should not be regarded as evidence for views that were argued and debated in the last quarter of the the first century BC. The apparent confusion between divination and magic reflects concerns that had wider currency in the later imperial period than in the early Augustan age.[4] Significantly,

---

[1] Dio 52.36.

[2] Ἱερόπτης is unique to Dio; cf. also 64.5.3. *Apodeiknumi* in Maecenas' speech is best understood as '*probare, recipere, retinere*', 'guarantee, accept, officially recognise, admit' (Favuzzi 1996: 277–8).

[3] Swan 1997: 2549–56 gives an overview of the scholarly debate on the chronology of Dio's work.

[4] Sordi 2002b: 474–5. Reinhold 1986: 208 sees possible 'hostility to the orgiastic cults brought in by Elagabalus'. See Bleicken 1962 (= 1998: 876–99) and esp. Millar 1964: 107 on the third-century

however, Dio included control over divination among the fundamental tenets of the Principate. The emphasis on the emperor's overseeing of the priesthoods that were involved with public divination finds indirect confirmation in the evidence that was discussed in the previous chapter. A number of associates of Augustus belonged to the great priestly colleges, notably the pontiffs and the augurs. The *princeps*' decision to hold a number of priesthoods emphatically reasserted his commitment to *religio* and corroborated his control over it. The *ordo* of the haruspices was the inevitable exception, since it had eluded a straightforward inclusion into the framework of Roman public religion throughout the Republican period; there was, however, intense collaboration between Augustus and the haruspices as early as in the mid thirties. The focus of Augustus' efforts was on public divination, upon which he secured an increasingly strong control; private divination was also regulated as long as it could pose a threat to the authority of the *princeps*. Along with asserting his loyalty and commitment to traditional forms of divination, Augustus was the promoter of an important innovation: the strong presence of astrology in the public discourse. It was a craft that ran against the established practice of Roman public divination, had nothing to do with the prodigy system, included a strong predictive element, and was based on a set of complex, specialised techniques.

Augustus' reliance on astrology does not contradict or overshadow his interest in ancestral religion. With his wide-ranging interventions Augustus responded to two fundamental trends in late Republican history: the fragmentation of religious expertise and the increasing disruption and tension within civic religion. Several chapters of this book have fleshed out this picture. Rules on the functioning of public religion mattered even at times of extreme political disruption, as the story of Antony's response to the election of Dolabella shows, and growing concern over the future played an important role in the emergence of a number of forms of divination. Some of these belonged in the framework of State religion; an important role was also played by independent diviners who did not hold priesthoods and were not attached to a college – the *uates*, *harioli* and *sacrificuli* that are mentioned in a number of sources. Many of these diviners will have had non-elite backgrounds, especially in the city of Rome; but there were exceptions. The story of C. Fulvius Salvis from Ostia stands out. Fulvius

concerns that are reflected in Maecenas' speech. Dorandi 1985 draws attention to some philosophical commonplaces. Struck 2007: 4–5 points out that confusing divination and magic is misleading; an opposite view in Cryer 1994: 229–34. Johnston 2008: 175–9 explores the areas of overlap.

must have been a man of considerable standing if he could afford to commission such an impressive monument. In the dedicatory inscription he defined himself as a haruspex, but he chose to assert his very close association with a cleromantic oracle. This was a world where a choice between mutually incompatible practices and views on the gods was not expected or required. The 'market model' may be applied with the important proviso that the available choices were not among narrowly defined, mutually incompatible options.[5] This also applies to theoretical reflection. The three kinds of theology that Varro set out, apparently building on the precedent of the pontiff and jurist Q. Mucius Scaevola, that of the poets, of the philosophers and of the political communities, are meant to be integrated with each other.

During the last century of the Republic increasing intellectual complexity and sophistication coexisted with fear and disruption on many levels, and were accompanied by a growing interest in the future on the one hand, and in the terms of divine involvement in human affairs on the other. Cicero's dialogue on divination must be understood within a wider effort to define the boundaries of this problem. His philosophical work as a whole must be understood against the background of an increasingly intense reflection over terminology and structures of Roman religion. In the first chapter we have suggested that the dialogue carries a specific interpretation of divination and its relevance to Rome; that the voice of Marcus carries more weight than that of Quintus. There is also, however, some common ground between the two characters: a commitment towards defining the terms of socially mediated and politically accepted religious cult (*religio*) and unreflective and unregulated practice (*superstitio*). Focusing on terminology is instructive, and not just because Cicero's philosophical work is constantly concerned with refining the vocabulary of theoretical reflection. The history of the words *religio* and *superstitio*, and indeed that of *diuinatio* and *prudentia*, are a reminder of how lively the reflection on religion was, and how deep its roots were into the development of Roman culture. There were different outcomes, some of which were strikingly creative. *Prudentia* – foresight – is coterminous with practical knowledge and specialised expertise, and Cicero's *diuinatio* does not quite correspond to the set of practices that we usually term Roman divination.

There is another important point on which both speakers of the *De diuinatione* agree: the rejection of prophetic divination. The *De diuinatione* does not undermine *religio*; quite the contrary, it suggests strategies to put

---

[5] Cf. Price 2003: 193–7 (= 2011: 267–73); Steuernagel 2007: 144.

it on a safer footing. The emergence of prophetic divination is not a development of the age of the Civil Wars. It is a trend that begins in the first half of the second century BC, after an early appearance in the age of the Punic Wars, and is closely linked to the emergence of the haruspices as an increasingly prominent presence in Roman public divination. The rise of prophetic divination in the last two centuries of the Republic is not surprising at times of deep historical change and danger, in which there was increasing interest in the future and the discussion of the itinerary of Roman history. Securing the preservation of piety was part of the project of ensuring the survival of Rome. The resonances of this ambition are apparent both in some literary genres and in the work of diviners. There is evidence for a debate on the sequence of ages that were allocated to Rome and to the Etruscan people: reflection on these themes was rife both in the public domain – the haruspical prophecies on the end of the *saecula* in 88 and 43 – and in the intellectual reflection about time, in which Varro played such an important role. On the other hand, contemporary literature repeatedly engaged with the problem of the direction of Roman history and the issue of historical causation. Sallust and Livy put forward broadly similar diagnoses and strikingly different solutions; although they both viewed the decline of Rome – whether real or perceived – as a central problem of their historical work, they suggested different solutions on the role of the gods and of religion. The discourse on the future and the prospects of Rome was an important feature in the development of late Republican culture in general, and was not confined to historiography. The control of the future, the power of prophecy and the involvement of the gods in human affairs are significant themes in the *Aeneid*: a work that is a strong testimony to how complex were the reflections on these issues in the Augustan period.

The victory of Octavian and the emergence of monarchy marked a clear discontinuity with the past. A wide range of divinatory practice was effectively contained under imperial patronage and control. Public prodigies became less prominent a feature of public debate, although they kept being reported and expiated; the emphasis of the surviving evidence is on signs and omens that pertained to the person of the emperor or members of the imperial family. Much of the history of the imperial engagement with divination is one of antagonism, as the legal texts from the Principate show, and at the same time of systematic engagement. Moreover, no real debate takes place in Roman culture on the remit of divination and prediction after the Augustan period; the same applies to the debate on religion. The later history of the word *superstitio* is instructive: rather than indicating deviant forms of religious practice, it is increasingly frequently used to refer to forms of foreign religious practice. The debate on the sequence of *saecula* and ages in the history of Rome and its progression disappears in the first century AD, and leaves room for concerns on how to preserve ancestral piety and the bond between the city and the gods.

A haruspical intervention at the end of another civil war strikingly reveals the extent of the change that intervened in the position of divination in public discourse. In AD 70, the *eques* L. Vestinus was entrusted by Vespasian with the reconstruction of the Capitol after the fire of December 69, and consulted the haruspices before undertaking the task.[6] According to Tacitus, who provides a detailed account of their intervention, the haruspices carefully confined themselves to ritual prescriptions, albeit significant. The ruins of the destroyed temple had to be removed and a new shrine had to be built on exactly the same site, as the gods forbade a change of plan.[7] The haruspices also warned against using stone or gold intended for any other purpose; in the ceremony of the dedication of the temple, which took place on 21 June 70, large quantities of unworked silver and gold were thrown into the foundations of the temple. The only deviation from previous practice that was allowed was an increase in the height of the temple.

The history of the late Republic shows that in different times an event of that magnitude would have caused a very different response on the part of the haruspices. Prophecies on the hidden meaning of the event and the future direction of history would have been produced. The fire on the Capitol occurred barely more than 110 years after the appearance of the *sidus Julium* in the summer of 44. According to a well-established Etruscan doctrine, the length of an age could be between 100 and 120 years, and an event of those proportions could have been a very suitable warning of an imminent change of age. As far as we know, that prophecy was not voiced in AD 70. A possible explanation may be that the beginning of the tenth era, according to the tradition outlined by the haruspex Vulcatius in 44, foretold the end of the Etruscan people, something that it would have probably been convenient for the haruspices to gloss over. The most significant factor, however, was the changed political context, in which the haruspices and their lore were under the patronage and control of the new emperor. The focus of the response, therefore, was on the construction of a ritual that was intended to emphasise the revival of consensus and

---

[6] On the fire see Plin. *HN* 34.38; Jos. *BJ* 4.647–9; Tac. *Hist.* 3.69–75; Dio 65.17.3, with Barzanò 1984.
[7] Tac. *Hist.* 4.53; commentary in Chilver 1985: 63–6. Detailed discussion in Wardle 1996.

the restoration of the orderly government; a ritual in which the whole city took part, and was made possible by the initiative and leadership of one man. The recommendation of the haruspices tellingly emphasised continuity with the past as the factor that could secure the renewed support of the gods. They were fully integrated within *religio*, and their bond with the emperor enabled that connection and guaranteed it.[8] The balance in the struggle for power over divine signs had decisively shifted since the age of the Roman revolution.

Immediately after the account of the haruspical intervention, Tacitus discusses the reactions that the fire on the Capitol triggered in Transalpine Gaul.[9] The Druids saw a connection between the destruction of the temple and the imminent demise of Rome. On their reading, the sanctuary of Jupiter had survived the Gallic sack because of the divine protection on which Rome could rely; the fire of AD 69 was a sign of the anger of the gods and of the imminent rise of the people beyond the Alps to supremacy. Tacitus has no time for that misguided prediction, which he dismisses as inspired by a 'vain superstition' (*superstitione uana*).[10] The boundaries between *religio* and *superstitio* were still relevant.[11] The late Republican reflection on divination, prediction and the involvement of the gods in human affairs had left a conspicuous legacy even in what had become a very different world.

---

[8] On imperial haruspices as 'fonctionnaires' cf. Haack 2003: 108; see also Briquel 1997a: 27–40.

[9] Tac. *Hist.* 4.54.

[10] Zecchini 1984 explores the political and ideological background of the prophecy. On prodigies as motivating factors in Tacitus' narrative see Kröger 1940: 51–4.

[11] Cf. Scheid 1985a.

Mark Antony the augur and the election
of Dolabella

In the Introduction we touched upon Antony's use of his augural prerogatives in 44 and the account that Cicero gives of it in the *Philippics*. We discussed them as an instance of the profound and enduring significance that divination retained at the end of the Roman Republic. This appendix will provide a close discussion of the importance of this episode, of the options that were available to its protagonists, and of the choices that they made.

In the *Philippics* the argument that Antony acts against the auspices and the tenets of the augural law, both intentionally and out of ignorance, is often canvassed. The account of the rise of P. Cornelius Dolabella to the consulship in 44 is especially instructive for a number of reasons: for the arguments used by Cicero in his depiction of the affair, for the terminology that he uses, and for the possible motives for Antony's conduct (*Phil.* 2.79–84).[1] On 1 January 44 Caesar stated before the Senate that he intended to step down from the consulship later in the year, just before setting off for the Parthian campaign, and that he supported the election of Dolabella as *consul suffectus*, with a view to his taking up the consulship upon Caesar's departure.[2] Antony stated publicly (probably during the same meeting) that he would use his position as augur to prevent Dolabella's election.[3] In the

---

[1] The fullest modern discussion remains Denniston 1926: 144–9, 180–6. See also Valeton 1891: 95–6; McDonald 1929: 168–71, 175; Weinstock 1937: 221–2; Tucker 1976: 176–7; Cristofoli 2004: 208–15; Rüpke 2005a: 1451–3 (= 2005b: 228–30); Montero 2006: 64–6; Manuwald 2007: 355–6.

[2] Despite the wording of Cic. *Phil.* 2.79 (*iussus es renuntiari consul, et quidem cum ipso,* 'you were ordered to be returned as consul, and what is more together with him'), it is likely that this was merely a recommendation, a *commendatio* on Caesar's part; Cicero also suggests that Caesar had promised Dolabella the consulship for 44 and that he eventually changed his mind; this is unlikely (Ramsey 2003: 275). The procedure for the election of a *consul suffectus* in this period is not entirely clear (Sumi 2005: 181). At the time Caesar held a ten-year dictatorship; he became *dictator perpetuo* in February 44 (see Jehne 1987: 15–38); the decision to hold the consulship in 45 and 44 must be explained with the attempt to equal other great figures of Roman history, like Marius, who held more consulships than he did (*ibid.*: 39–42).

[3] On the reasons for their enmity see Cristofoli 2004: 209.

Second Philippic – which was composed in October 44 and is constructed as a fictional speech delivered to the Senate on 19 September 44 – Cicero uses this statement and Antony's later behaviour as evidence for his lack of intellect and knowledge (*stupiditatem hominis cognoscite*).[4] Antony was not just an augur at that time but was also Caesar's colleague in the consulship, and he could have more easily stopped Dolabella's election in that capacity by performing a *spectio* (an inspection of the sky) and by claiming to have detected a *uitium* (a forbidding or hindering sign).[5] As Cicero reminds his audience, the augurs had only the right to perform a *nuntiatio*, i.e. to report what they saw in the sky, while the consuls also had the right to perform a *spectio*, i.e. to observe the sky and report unfavourable signs to another presiding magistrate (as Bibulus did in 59 in his clash with Caesar). The argument was based on the crucial distinction between impetrative signs, i.e. signs that were actively looked for by looking at the sky, and oblative signs, i.e. those that were observed without being actively solicited.[6] In Cicero's view, Antony's ignorance was combined with arrogance, because he had pointedly stated his intentions before the Senate months before the assembly which was supposed to elect Dolabella: this was against the spirit of the augural priesthood.[7] Cicero may well have had a point, but different interpretations are possible, as we shall see.

Cicero's terminology is instructive: *quisquamne diuinare potest, quod uitii in auspiciis futurum sit, nisi qui de caelo seruare constituit?*[8] It is not possible to divine what the auspices will show; as Marcus states in the *De diuinatione*, augury is not about predicting the future, but about acknowledging the will of the gods on a specific occasion. Altering this fact leads to a betrayal of the priesthood and a fraudulent use of the augural lore. It is conceivable that in *Philippics* 2 Cicero is presenting a partisan view of what Antony did. We know that there was no consensus within the augural college on the divinatory or prophetic remit of augury. The account continues with the day of the election of the *consul suffectus*: Dolabella stood for election with Caesar's support and a clear prospect of victory; Antony announced his opposition at the end of the voting procedure, after Dolabella had secured

---

[4] Composition and the chronology of the speech: Ramsey 2003: 157–8.

[5] Paschall 1936: 227 (the whole paper is important).

[6] Linderski 1986a: 2198 and 1986b: 332–5 (= 1995a: 487–90).

[7] On that meeting cf. *Phil.* 2.99 (*frequentissimo senatu*). Weinrib 1970: 403 n. 33 rightly doubts that Antony was so incompetent in augural matters; *contra* see Rubino 1839: 57 n. 2; McDonald 1929: 169–70; Cristofoli 2004: 213.

[8] 'Who can divine what flaw there will be in the auspices, except for the man who has decided to inspect the sky?' On the expression *de caelo seruare* and the difference between *seruatio* and *obnuntiatio* see De Libero 1992: 57–59, with the important provisos of Linderski 1969–70: 320–1 (= 1995a: 455–6) and 1995b: 193 (= 2007: 521).

a sufficient number of votes to be elected.[9] He claimed that he had seen an unfavourable sign during the voting operations. Cicero argues that, in fact, he had not even bothered to inspect the sky. Antony's intervention was based on the principle that an augur could intervene during a voting assembly if he happened to see a prohibitive sign during the proceedings; the law, however, did not allow a consul to use *obnuntiatio* during a voting assembly. The assembly was thus brought to a close by Antony's uttering the sentence *alio die* ('on another day'), which was the formula that augurs usually pronounced when they prevented or interrupted an assembly on grounds of an unfavourable sign. Again Cicero uses some divinatory terminology in his polemic against Antony: the consul of 44 did just what he had foreseen (*prouideras*) he would do at the beginning of the year and announced a long time before (*et tanto ante praedixeras*).[10] The language of prediction is counterpoised by the vocabulary of falsification with which Cicero dismisses Antony's work as augur: *tua . . . ementitus es auspicia* ('you have falsified the auspices').[11] The process that Antony's intervention initiated is destructive, according to Cicero: however, even if the argument and the procedure he used were illegitimate, the prohibition against the election of Dolabella remains in force until the augural college have looked into it. As Cicero says a few chapters below (88), it is necessary to obey even fraudulent auspices.[12]

Leaving aside Cicero's hostile account for a moment, Antony's decision to intervene in his augural capacity requires an explanation. First of all, it must be noted that there was a recent precedent for the intervention of an augur who was at the same time consul to stop a voting assembly; the rule prohibiting the *obnuntiatio* of consuls during the voting assemblies was probably part of the *lex Clodia* of 58 that overrode the *leges Aelia et Fufia*.[13]

---

[9] The date of the assembly in which Dolabella was voted cannot be firmly established, but it must have taken place not long before the Ides of March (Jehne 1987: 118 n. 34).

[10] Cf. also the reference to *prudentia* in 2.81, paired with *impudentia* to create a 'pleasing aural effect' (Ramsey 2003: 278): *nec enim est ab homine numquam sobrio postulanda prudentia; sed uidete impudentiam* ('for good sense may not be expected from a man who is never sober; but do note his shamelessness').

[11] *Ementita auspicia*: Cic. *Div.* 1.29 and Denniston 1926: 148–9; Schäublin 1986, esp. 175–8; Kany-Turpin 1999; Wardle 2006: 184 (who translates 'falsify the auspices'; cf. also 177 on the correct understanding of *auspicia*: 'the procedure of seeking the gods' will in relation to the timing of an action, an indication valid only for one day'). Cf. Shackleton Bailey in the Loeb Classical Library: 'thus you lied about the auspices'; Manuwald's translation of *Phil.* 3.9: 'a colleague whose status he himself had flawed by announcing false auspices'.

[12] Cic. *Phil.* 2.88: *de ementitis auspiciis, quibus tamen parere necesse erat* ('on the falsified auspices, which nevertheless had to be obeyed'). See also *Phil.* 3.9.

[13] On the *leges Aelia et Fufia* see Weinrib 1970. A full overview of the evidence for Clodius' law is in Fezzi 1995: 302–5. The nature and scope of Clodius' legislation on religious matter is debated. Gruen

In 55 the consul Pompey prevented the election of Cato the Younger to the praetorship by interrupting the assembly as the vote was taking place; his colleague Crassus was presiding over it.[14] Cicero interestingly overlooks this episode. Antony's motives may be understood from the procedure that he decided to follow. The first one is political. Antony's intention was to interfere with the process as it was unfolding or indeed straight after its completion, and not before its beginning (as he would have had to do had he been a consul). Dolabella was the only candidate for the consulship, he was supported by Caesar, and Antony knew that he had no real chance to prevent his election.[15] However, he could use his augural opposition to delay the election, compelling Dolabella to reckon with him and acknowledge his role and influence if he wanted his consulship to be fully recognised. Dolabella was – to all practical purposes – elected to the consulship: that was the outcome which Caesar favoured and the political situation made inevitable. However, Antony's opposition was an obstacle that had to be overcome if clarity was to be reached on Dolabella's constitutional position.[16] This put Antony in a strong position: if Dolabella wanted to remove a potentially fatal hurdle to his holding the magistracy, he had to come to an arrangement with Antony.

This is exactly what happened a few months later, when Dolabella took up the consulship immediately after the death of Caesar. At the Senate meeting of 17 March there was a spectacular rapprochement between Antony and Dolabella.[17] Dolabella had taken up the trappings of the

---

1974: 255–7 and Mitchell 1986 provide favourable assessments; De Libero 1992: 67–8 unconvincingly argues that the law was never enforced after 58. Weinstock 1937: 221 speculates that it was annulled shortly after it was passed, but that it was reinstated by a law of Julius Caesar. Comprehensive bibliography in Fezzi 1995: 297–301; at 328, the law is linked to Clodius' ambition to strengthen his control over the assemblies and to his ambitious legislative programme. Rüpke 2005a: 1456 (= 2005b: 233) argues that late Republican legislation on *obnuntiatio* should be viewed as a symptom of contemporary concerns over augural 'Verhandlungsoptionen'; see also Rüpke 2012a: 123.

[14] Plut. *Cat. Min.* 42.4; *Pomp.* 52.4. See Valeton 1891: 95 (Pompey probably waited for the vote of the *centuria praerogatiua*); Burckhardt 1988: 203.

[15] *Contra*, cf. Rüpke 2005a: 1451–2 (= 2005b: 228–9), who views Antony's use of his augural prerogatives as a decision to 'opt out' of the political process. Denniston 1926: 149 argues (against Plut. *Ant.* 11) that the election of Dolabella was carried out, although its validity was questioned. Cf. the suggestion of Valeton 1891: 96, who argued that Antony did not envisage the possibility of a deal with Dolabella at a later stage, but waited to see how Caesar would react to the election of Dolabella; had Caesar rejected it, he would have kept quiet; had Caesar accepted it, he would have put forward his opposition. A similar assessment in Denniston 1926: 185–6.

[16] Gotter 1996: 36: '[o]b er höchster römischer Beamter sein würde oder Privatmann, war eine Frage der momentanen Machtverhältnisse'. According to Rüpke 2005a: 1452 (= 2005b: 229), Antony's acceptance of Dolabella's election was merely an arbitrary act. Burckhardt 1988: 207 n. 116 notes that the use of religious opposition to the election of a magistrate was seldom used after Caesar's dictatorship: two more cases are reported, and in both cases they are tribunician interventions; see Valeton 1891: 96–7, 99–100.

[17] Cic. *Phil.* 1.31; App. *B Civ.* 2.129, 132; Dio 44.53.1. Gotter 1996: 24–5.

consulship immediately after the death of the dictator and had shown a willingness to co-operate with the Liberators; Antony swiftly offered him the chance of an understanding and accepted him as his consular colleague. It is a fair guess that Dolabella welcomed this opportunity for a complete recognition of his right to be in office. Antony's move worked: their reconciliation was the beginning of a political partnership that lasted until Dolabella's death in the following year during the Syrian campaign.[18] This fact, however, did not remove the problem that Antony's opposition had created two months earlier; a shadow was cast on the political and constitutional process of the whole year. After his decision to collaborate with Dolabella, Antony had started to put forward legislation along with a consul whose election he had declared (and thus *made*) invalid; the ratification of the *acta Caesaris* was the first item on the agenda of the consular pair.[19]

Cicero anticipates that the issue will have to be looked at by the college of augurs and that Antony's conduct will have to be thoroughly scrutinised in due course. He even rhetorically asks his opponent about the meaning of his interdiction and he speculates that he may not have been sober when he gave it. A further religious argument is deployed. It is to be hoped that, by his illegitimate conduct on a crucial religious matter, Antony has brought disgrace only upon himself, and not on the whole Roman people (*tua potius quam rei publicae calamitate*). The whole city, however, remains bound to the unlawful religious acts he has taken. A few months earlier Cicero had expressed a different viewpoint in the *De diuinatione*, albeit through the persona of Quintus. In 50 Appius Claudius Pulcher, augur and censor, prompted the expulsion of C. Ateius Capito from the Senate with the allegation that he produced false auspices shortly before Crassus' departure for the Parthian campaign and that the Roman people had suffered a great disaster because of his actions.[20] Quintus takes issue with this interpretation on the basis that the person who reported an inauspicious oblative sign was not responsible for the misfortune that came to pass, but that the burden was on the magistrate who had to act in order to avert the misfortune. Moreover, the later developments proved that the announcement was an accurate warning that Crassus did not accept.[21]

---

[18] Gotter 1996: 37–8.

[19] Cic. *Phil.* 3.9: *seruabant auspicia reges; quae hic consul augurque neglexit* ('The kings used to respect the auspices, which this consul and augur neglected').

[20] Cic. *Div.* 1.29–30. Kany-Turpin 1999: 265 and 2003b: 72; Wardle 2006: 184–5.

[21] There is an important difference between the alleged false auspices of Antony and those of Ateius: the intervention of the latter was not legally binding, unlike that of a consul (*Div.* 1.30, with Wardle 2006: 186–7).

A religious aspect should also be considered as among the motives for Antony's decision to oppose Dolabella's election. Using his position as augur enabled him to mount a weightier opposition, which he was entitled to use anyway as consul; adding a further dimension to his move, which involved both his priestly status and the expertise that derived from it, gave his move a force that it could not have possibly had otherwise. It is interesting to see that, in the *First Philippic*, which he delivered in Antony's absence on 2 September 44, Cicero used different tones on Antony's decision to accept Dolabella as consul, portraying Antony's move as a magnanimous gesture of reconciliation that freed the city from the threat of civil strife (*Phil.* 1.31).[22] His decision to set aside the augural obstruction to the election is evoked along with the decision to set aside personal enmity. The fact that the obstruction had come from Antony as augur is not used against Antony, but – if anything – seems to suggest that there would have been weighty reasons to hold on to that prohibition, because Antony the augur knew what he was doing. Cicero's change of heart on this matter should not surprise and is not the object of the present discussion. What matters is the subtext of this conciliatory assessment of Antony's rapprochement with Dolabella. Even Cicero seems to recognise that, in a case of that nature, the *nuntiatio* of an augur can have more weight than the *spectio* of a consul, and that the religious and the political levels did not coincide. Moreover, his reference to the decision of Antony suggests that the authority of a priest could have a resonance that the authority of a consul could not have in these matters. Antony was an augur, and therefore he could claim a further level of authority that a magistrate who did not have a comparable priestly position could not reasonably claim. Finally, by choosing to intervene as augur, and not as consul, Antony was shifting the controversy from the political level to the religious one. This enabled him to diffuse the tension with Caesar, who was the backer of Dolabella; more generally, it enabled him to place himself on a level that was not that of the partisan controversy, but pertained to the relationship between the city and its gods. The dispute over the election of Dolabella was a factor of tension between Caesar and his junior partner Antony. Antony's intervention at the end of the *comitia* was no doubt intended to turn it into a matter of disagreement between the augurs, Caesar and Antony.

---

[22] On the meaning of *auspicia* as 'signs announced by the augurs' see Linderski 1986a: 2202. Stevenson 2009 convincingly argues that *Phil.* 1 is a powerful attack against Antony and an attempt to characterise him as a tyrant, despite its seemingly conciliatory attitude.

Glossary

The following glossary provides brief definitions of some terms pertaining to Roman divination, which are used in the text.

aeromancy (*aeromantis*): either a byword for augury or a form of divination which relied on the movement of air.

augurium (plur. *auguria*): divinatory ritual in which (a) divine sign(s) expressing divine permission or opposition concerning an envisaged act was (were) sought. Its outcome was the inauguration of an individual (e.g. a magistrate) or a place (e.g. a temple). Their validity had no time limit. It could be carried out only by an augur.

augurs (*augures*): Roman official diviners, who formed one of the most senior priestly colleges; they advised on a number of religious matters, assisted the magistrates in taking the auspices, and were entitled to make binding announcements of adverse signs on important public occasions.

auspices (*auspicia*; sing. *auspicium*): divinatory ritual in which (a) divine sign(s) expressing divine permission or opposition concerning an envisaged act was (were) sought; such signs had to be sought before any important public occasion (e.g. a voting assembly, a battle), but they could sometimes appear without being solicited. They were valid for one day only.

cleromancy: a form of divination based on the drawing of the lot or on the throwing of the dice.

coniector, coniectrix: dream interpreter.

extispicy: the technique of reading of the entrails of a sacrificial victim for divinatory purposes.

geomancy (*geomantis*): probably a form of cleromancy practised with stones and pebbles.

hariolus, hariola: diviner, normally acting as a free agent.

haruspex (plur. *haruspices*): Etruscan diviner, especially trained in the reading of animal entrails and in the interpretation of lightning and
thunder.

hydromancy: literally, 'divination by water'. Water was used in several
divinatory rituals: e.g. the diviner could base his response from the
movement of the water in a bowl.

impetratiua (*signa*): divinatory signs that were actively besought by the
diviner before producing a response (e.g. a sign that an augur detected
in the sky).

litatio: the successful completion of a sacrifice and its acceptance on the
part of the gods, which was normally detected when the entrails of
the victim appeared to be on inspection flawless.

lituus: a staff carried by the augurs, curved into the form of a crook,
which was frequently associated with their authority in the literary
and iconographic evidence.

nuntiatio: report of an inspection of the sky by an augur, which could be
announced only if he was asked to do so by a magistrate.

oblatiua (*signa*): divinatory signs that presented themselves without being
solicited and required prompt interpretation and expiation (e.g.
prodigies).

obnuntiatio: report of a prohibitive sign by an augur.

ornithomancy: a form of divination based on the observation of the flight,
position, cries and number of certain kinds of birds.

procuratio: set of ceremonies of expiation following a prodigy.

pullarius: the keeper of the birds (usually chickens, *pulli*) that were used
in the augural ritual known as *tripudium*. He was entrusted to feed
them during the performance of the ritual and assisted the magistrate
who was responsible for it.

pyromancy (*pyromantis*): a form of divination based on the observation of
the movement of a flame and its smoke, usually during a sacrifice, or
on the reaction of the flesh of the victim.

(*quin*)*decemuiri sacris faciundis*: a body of ten (and, after Sulla, at least
fifteen) priests who were entrusted with the preservation, consultation
and interpretation of the Sibylline Books.

Sibylline Books: a collection of Greek prophetic texts that were preserved
on the Capitol in the Republican period and were consulted by a
priestly college, the (*quin*)*decemuiri s.f.*, under instruction of the Senate when a prodigy required interpretation.

sors: lot used for cleromantic purposes.

spectio: ritual inspection of the sky by a consul.

tripudium solistimum (or *sollistimum*): augural ritual in which success was measured according to whether a bird that was fed in a cage let drop some of the food that it was given; the contact of the food with the ground was regarded as an eminently favourable sign.

Bibliography

Aberson, M. (1994) *Temples votifs et butin de guerre dans la Rome républicaine.* Bibliotheca Helvetica Romana 26. Rome.

Abry, J.-H. (1988) 'Auguste, la Balance et le Capricorne', *REL* 66: 103–21.

  (1996) 'L'horoscope de Rome (Cicéron, *Div.*, ii, 98–99)', in *Les astres. Actes du colloque international de Montpellier, 23–25 mars 1995, Séminaire d'études des mentalités antiques. 2, Les correspondances entre le ciel, la terre et l'homme, les survivances de l'astrologie*, ed. B. Bakhouche, A. Moreau and J.-C. Turpin. Montpellier: 121–40.

  (2011) 'Cosmos and imperium. Politicized digressions in Manilius' *Astronomica*', in Green and Volk (eds.): 222–34.

Adams, J. N. (2003) *Bilingualism and the Latin Language.* Cambridge.

Aigner-Foresti, L. (2000) 'Gli Etruschi e la politica di Cesare', in Urso (ed.): 11–34.

Aigner-Foresti, L. (ed.) (1998) *Die Integration der Etrusker und das Weiterwirken etruskischen Kulturgutes im republikanischen und kaiserzeitlichen Rom.* Vienna.

Alexandratos, L. (2009) 'Gli agrimensori romani e l'astronomia', *Maia* 61: 285–305.

Alföldi, A. (1971) '*Redeunt Saturnia regna*: l'attente du roi-sauveur à Rome', *RN* s. 6, 13: 76–89.

  (1973) '*Redeunt Saturnia regna* ii: an iconographic pattern heralding the return of the Golden Age in or around 139 bc', *Chiron* 3: 131–42.

  (1975) '*Redeunt Saturnia regna* iv: Apollo und die Sibylle in der Epoche der Bürgerkriege', *Chiron* 5: 165–92.

  (1997) *Redeunt Saturnia Regna*, trans. E. Alföldi-Rosenbaum. Antiquitas s. 3, 36. Bonn.

Alföldy, G. (2011) 'The Horologium of Augustus and its model at Alexandria', *JRA* 24: 96–8.

Allély, A. (2003) 'Les enfants malformés et considerés comme "prodigia" à Rome et en Italie sous la République', *REA* 105: 127–56.

Allen, J. (2008) *Inference from Signs. Ancient Debates about the Nature of Evidence.* Cambridge.

Altheim, F. (1938) *A History of Roman Religion*, trans. H. Mattingly. London.

Ampolo, C. (1990–1) 'Lotte sociali in Italia centrale. Un documento controverso: il calendario brontoscopico attribuito a Nigidio Figulo', *Opus* 9–10: 185–97.

Ando, C. (2008) *The Matter of the Gods. Religion and the Roman Empire.* The Transformation of the Classical Heritage 44. Berkeley, Los Angeles and London.

(2010) 'The ontology of religious institutions', *History of Religions* 50: 54–79.

(2011) *Law, Language, and Empire in the Roman Tradition.* Philadelphia.

André, J.-M. (1975) 'La philosophie religieuse de Cicéron', in Michel and Verdière (eds.): 11–21.

(1980) 'La notion de *pestilentia* à Rome: du tabou religieux à l'interprétation préscientifique', *Latomus* 39: 3–16.

(1991) 'Conclusions', in Briquel and Guittard (eds.): 116–31.

Angeli Bertinelli, M. G. (1988) 'Saec(u)lum', in *Enciclopedia virgiliana* III, ed. F. Della Corte. Rome: 637–41.

Angeli Bertinelli, M. G., Manfredini, M., Piccirilli, L. and Pisani, G. (eds.) (1997) *Plutarco. Le vite di Lisandro e di Silla.* Milan.

Annus, A. (ed.) (2010) *Divination and Interpretation of Signs in the Ancient World.* Chicago.

Anselm, S. (2004) *Struktur und Trasparenz. Eine literaturwissenschaftliche Analyse der Feldherrnviten des Cornelius Nepos.* Altertumswissenschaftliches Kolloquium II. Stuttgart.

Arena, V. (2011) 'Tolerance, intolerance and religious liberty at Rome: an investigation in the history of ideas', in *Politiche religiose nel mondo antico e tardoantico. Poteri e indirizzi, forme del controllo, idee e prassi di tolleranza*, ed. G. A. Cecconi and C. Gabrielli. Munera 33. Bari: 147–64.

Armisen-Marchetti, M. (2000) 'Sénèque et la divination', in *Seneca e il suo tempo*, ed. P. Parroni. Biblioteca di 'Filologia e critica' 6. Rome: 193–214.

Aronen, J. (1989) 'Giuturna e il suo culto', in *Lacus Iuturnae* I, ed. E. M. Steinby. Lavori e studi di archeologia pubblicati dalla Soprintendenza Archeologica di Roma 12. Rome: 57–75.

Assmann, J. (1992) *Das kulturelle Gedächtnis. Schrift, Erinnerung und politische Identität in frühen Hochkulturen.* Munich.

Austin, R. G. (ed.) (1977) *P. Vergili Maronis Aeneidos liber sextus.* Oxford.

Avery, H. C. (1967) '*Marius felix* (Sallust, *Jug.* 92–94)', *Hermes* 95: 324–30.

Badian, E. (1972) 'Ennius and his friends', in *Ennius*, ed. O. Skutsch. Entretiens Hardt 17. Vandoeuvres: 149–208.

(1993) 'Livy and Augustus', in Schuller (ed.): 9–38.

Bagnasco Gianni, G. (2001) 'Le *sortes* etrusche', in Cordano and Grottanelli (eds.): 197–220.

Baier, T. (1997) *Werk und Wirkung Varros im Spiegel seiner Zeitgenossen von Cicero bis Ovid. Hermes* Einzelschriften 75. Stuttgart.

Bailey, C. (1935) *Religion in Virgil.* Oxford.

Bailey, C. (ed.) (1947) *Titi Lucreti Cari De rerum natura libri sex.* Oxford.

Bakhouche, B. (2002) *L'astrologie à Rome.* Bibliothèque d'études classiques 29. Leuven, Paris and Sterling, VA.

(2012) '*Augustus*: les astres et la mutation de l'autorité à Rome', *REA* 114: 47–72.

Baraz, Y. (2012) *A Written Republic. Cicero's Philosophical Politics.* Princeton.

Barchiesi, A. (1994) *Il poeta e il principe. Ovidio e il discorso augusteo.* Rome and Bari.

(1997) *The Poet and the Prince. Ovid and Augustan Discourse.* Berkeley, Los Angeles and London.

(2002) 'Martial arts. Mars Ultor in the Forum Augustum: a verbal monument with a vengeance', in *Ovid's Fasti. Historical Readings at its Bimillennium*, ed. G. Herbert-Brown. Oxford: 1–22.

(2005) 'Learned eyes: poets, viewers, image makers', in *The Cambridge Companion to the Age of Augustus*, ed. K. Galinsky. Cambridge: 281–305.

(2008) '*Bellum Italicum*: l'unificazione dell'Italia nell'*Eneide*', in Urso (ed.): 243–60.

Barchiesi, A., Rüpke, J. and Stephens, S. (eds.) (2004) *Rituals in Ink. A Conference on Religion and Literary Production in Ancient Rome.* PAwB 10. Stuttgart.

Barnes, J., Brunschwig, J., Burnyeat, M. and Schofield, M. (eds.) (1982) *Science and Speculation. Studies in Hellenistic Theory and Practice.* Cambridge and Paris.

Barrett, J. L. (2007) 'Gods', in Whitehouse and Laidlaw (eds.): 179–207.

Barton, T. S. (1994a) *Power and Knowledge. Astrology, Physiognomics, and Medicine under the Roman Empire.* Ann Arbor.

(1994b) *Ancient Astrology.* London and New York.

(1995) 'Augustus and Capricorn: astrological polyvalency and imperial rhetoric', *JRS* 85: 33–51.

Barwick, K. (1938) *Caesars Commentarii und das Corpus Caesarianum. Philologus* Supplementband 31.2. Leipzig.

Barzanò, A. (1984) 'La distruzione del Campidoglio nell'anno 69 d.C.', in Sordi (ed.): 107–20.

Baudou, A. (1995) 'Censorinus et le *saeculum* pisonien', *RPh* 69: 15–37.

Bauman, R. A. (1983) *Lawyers in Roman Republican Politics. A Study of the Roman Jurists in their Political Setting, 316–82 BC.* Münchener Beiträge zur Papyrusforschung und antiken Rechtsgeschichte 75. Munich.

(1985) *Lawyers in Roman Transitional Politics. A Study of the Roman Jurists in their Political Setting in the Late Republic and Triumvirate.* Münchener Beiträge zur Papyrusforschung und antiken Rechtsgeschichte 79. Munich.

Bayet, J. (1949) 'La croyance romaine aux présages déterminants: aspects littéraires et chronologie', in *Hommages à Joseph Bidez et à Franz Cumont.* Collection Latomus 2. Brussels: 13–30.

(1960) 'Les malédictions du tribun C. Ateius Capito', in *Hommages à Georges Dumézil.* Collection Latomus 45. Brussels: 31–45.

(1969) *Histoire politique et psychologique de la religion romaine*, 2nd. edn. Paris.

(1971) *Croyances et rites dans la religion romaine antique.* Paris.

Beard, M. (1986) 'Cicero and divination: the formation of a Latin discourse', *JRS* 76: 33–46.

(1987) 'A complex of times: no more sheep on Romulus' birthday', *PCPS* 213: 1–15.

(1994) 'Religion', in *Cambridge Ancient History* ix. Cambridge: 729–68.

(2004) 'Writing ritual: the triumph of Ovid', in Barchiesi, Rüpke and Stephens (eds.): 115–26.

(2007) *The Roman Triumph*. Cambridge, MA and London.

(2011) 'Risk and the humanities. *Alea iacta est*', in Skinns, Scott and Cox (eds.): 85–108.

(2012) 'Cicero's "Response of the *haruspices*" and the voice of the gods', *JRS* 102: 20–39.

Beard, M., North, J. and Price, S. (1998) *Religions of Rome*. 2 vols. Cambridge.

Becatti, G. (1939) 'Il culto di Ercole ad Ostia ed un nuovo rilievo votivo', *BCAR* 67: 37–60.

(1942) 'Nuovo documento del culto di Ercole ad Ostia', *BCAR* 70: 115–20.

Becher, I. (1985) 'Tiberüberschwemmungen. Die Interpretation von Prodigien in augusteischer Zeit', *Klio* 67: 471–9.

Bechtold, C. (2011) *Gott und Gestirn als Präsenzformen des toten Kaisers. Apotheose und Katasterismos in der politischen Kommunikation der römischen Kaiserzeit und ihre Anknüpfungspunkte im Hellenismus*. Schriften zur politischen Kommunikation 9. Göttingen.

Beck, R. (2006) 'The religious market of the Roman Empire. Rodney Stark and Christianity's pagan competition', in *Religious Rivalries in the Early Roman Empire and the Rise of Christianity*, ed. L. E. Vaage. Studies in Christianity and Judaism/Études sur le christianisme et le judaïsme 18. Waterloo, Ont.: 233–52.

(2007) *A Brief History of Ancient Astrology*. Oxford and Malden, MA.

Begemann, E. (2012) *Schicksal als Argument. Ciceros Rede vom fatum in der späten Republik*. PAwB 37. Stuttgart.

Belardi, W. (1976) *Superstitio*. Biblioteca di ricerche linguistiche e filologiche 5. Rome.

Belayche, N. (2007) 'Les dieux "nomothètes". Oracles et prescriptions religieuses à l'époque romaine impériale', *RHR* 224: 171–91.

Belayche, N. and Rüpke, J. (2007) 'Divination et révélation dans les mondes grec et romain. Présentation', *RHR* 224: 139–47.

Bell, A. A. (1994) 'Fact and *exemplum* in accounts of the deaths of Pompey and Caesar', *Latomus* 53: 824–36.

Bell, C. (1992) *Ritual Theory, Ritual Practice*. New York and Oxford.

(2000) 'Pragmatic theory', in Jense and Rothstein (eds.): 9–20.

Bendlin, A. E. (1998) 'Social complexity and religion at Rome in the second and first centuries BCE'. Diss. Oxford.

(2000) 'Looking beyond the civic compromise: religious pluralism in late Republican Rome', in Bispham and Smith (eds.): 115–35, 167–71.

(2008) 'Vom Nutzen und Nachteil der Mantik: Orakel im Medium von Handlung und Literatur in der Zeit der Zweiten Sophistik', in *Texte als Medium und Reflexion von Religion im römischen Reich*, ed. D. Elm von der Osten, J. Rüpke and K. Waldner. PAwB 14. Stuttgart: 159–207.

(2009) 'Einleitung', in Bendlin and Rüpke (eds.): 7–15.

(2011) 'On the uses and disadvantages of divination. Oracles and their literary representations in the time of the Second Sophistic', in North and Price (eds.): 175–250 (English translation of Bendlin 2008).

Bendlin, A. and Rüpke, J. (eds.) (2009) *Römische Religion im historischen Wandel. Diskursentwicklung von Plautus bis Ovid.* PAwB 17. Stuttgart.

Beneker, J. (2009–10) 'Nepos' biographical method in the *Lives of foreign generals*', *CJ* 105: 109–21.

Benferhat, Y. (2005) Ciues Epicurei. *Les Épicuriens et l'idée de monarchie à Rome et en Italie de Sylla à Octave.* Collection Latomus 292. Brussels.

Benoist, S. (1999) *La fête à Rome au premier siècle de l'Empire. Recherches sur l'univers festif sous les règnes d'Auguste et des Julio-Claudiens.* Collection Latomus 248. Brussels.

Benveniste, E. (1969) *Le vocabulaire des institutions indo-européennes. 2. Pouvoir, droit, religion.* Paris.

Bergemann, C. (1992) *Politik und Religion im spätrepublikanischen Rom.* Palingenesia 38. Stuttgart.

Bergk, T. (1860) *Quaestionum Ennianarum specimen novum.* Halle, reprinted in Bergk 1884: 235–46.

(1884) *Kleine philologische Schriften* I, ed. R. Peppmüller. Halle.

Bernett, M. (1995) Causarum cognitio. *Ciceros Analyse zur politischen Krise der späten römischen Republik.* Palingenesia 51. Stuttgart.

Bernstein, F. (1998) Ludi publici. *Untersuchungen zur Entstehung und Entwicklung der öffentlichen Spiele im republikanischen Rom. Historia* Einzelschriften 119. Stuttgart.

Berry, D. H. and Erskine, A. (eds.) (2010) *Form and Function in Roman Oratory.* Cambridge.

Berthelet, Y. (2011) 'Le rôle des pontifes dans l'expiation des prodiges à Rome, sous la République: le cas des "procurations" anonymes', *Cahiers 'Mondes anciens'* 2 (available at http://mondesanciens.revues.org/index348.html, last accessed 29.08.12).

Bertrand-Écanvil, E. (1994) 'Présages et propagande idéologique: à propos d'une liste concernant Octavien Auguste', *MEFRA* 106: 487–531.

Bettini, M. (2005) 'Un'identità troppo compiuta. Troiani, Latini, Romani e Iulii nell'*Eneide*', *MD* 55: 77–102.

(2006) 'Forging identities. Trojans and Latins, Romans and Julians in the *Aeneid*', in *Herrschaft ohne Integration? Rom und Italien in republikanischer Zeit*, ed. M. Jehne and R. Pfeilschifter. Studien zur Alten Geschichte 4. Frankfurt: 269–91.

(2008) 'Mighty words, suspect speech: *fari* in Roman culture', *Arethusa* 41: 313–74.

Bickel, E. (1951) 'Vates bei Varro und Vergil', *RhM* 94: 257–314.

Bicknell, R. J. (1991) 'The celestial torch of 17 B.C.', *AHB* 5: 123–8.

Birley, A. R. (1999) 'Editor's introduction', in R. Syme, *The Provincial at Rome and Rome and the Balkans 80 BC–AD 14*, ed. A. Birley. Exeter: xi–xx.

Bishop, J. D. (1948) 'Augustus and A. Cornelius Cossus cos.', *Latomus* 7: 187–91.

Bishop, J. H. (1988) *The Cost of Power. Studies in the Aeneid of Virgil*. University of New England Monographs 4. Armidale.

Bispham, E. and Smith, C. (eds.) (2000) *Religion in Archaic and Republican Rome and Italy. Evidence and Experience*. Edinburgh.

Blänsdorf, J. (1991) 'Augurenlächeln. Ciceros Kritik an der römischen Mantik', in *Zur Erschliessung von Zukunft in den Religionen. Zukunftshoffnung und Gegenwartsbewältigung in der Religionsgeschichte*, ed. H. Wissmann. Würzburg: 45–65.

Blecher, G. (1905) *De extispicio capita tria*. Giessen.

Bleicken, J. (1962) 'Der politische Standpunkt Dios gegenüber der Monarchie: die Rede des Maecenas Buch 52, 14–40', *Hermes* 90: 444–67, reprinted in Bleicken 1998: 876–99.

(1998) *Gesammelte Schriften*. 2 vols. Stuttgart.

Bloch, M. (1989) *Ritual, History and Power. Selected Papers in Anthropology*. London School of Economics, Monographs on Social Anthropology 58. London and Atlantic Highlands, NJ.

Bloch, R. (1940) 'Origines étrusques des Livres Sibyllins', in *Mélanges de philologie, de littérature et d'histoire anciennes offerts à Alfred Ernout*. Paris: 21–8.

(1962) 'La divination romaine et les Livres Sibyllins', *REL* 40: 118–20.

(1963) *Les prodiges dans l'antiquité classique (Grèce, Étrurie et Rome)*. Paris.

(1964) 'Liberté et déterminisme dans la divination romaine', in *Hommages à Jean Bayet*, ed. M. Renard and R. Schilling. Collection Latomus 70. Brussels: 89–100.

(1965a) 'L'origine des Livres Sibyllins à Rome: méthode de recherches et critique du récit des annalistes anciens', in *Neue Beiträge zur Geschichte der alten Welt II*, ed. E. C. Welskopf. Berlin: 281–92.

(1965b) 'Liberté et déterminisme dans la divination étrusque', in *Studi in onore di Luisa Banti*. Rome: 63–8.

(1966) 'Liberté et déterminisme dans la divination étrusque et romaine', in *La divination en Mésopotamie ancienne et dans les regions voisines*. Paris: 159–70.

(1968) 'La divination en Etrurie et à Rome', in *La divination*, ed. A. Caquot and M. Leibovici, I, Paris: 197–232.

de Blois, L. (1988) 'The perception of expansion in the works of Sallust', *Latomus* 47: 604–19.

Blumenthal, F. (1914) '*Auguria salutis*', *Hermes* 49: 246–52.

Boas, H. (1938) *Aeneas' Arrival in Latium. Observations on Legends, History, Religion. Topography and Related Subjects in Vergil, Aeneid VII, 1–135*. Amsterdam.

Bobzien, S. (1998) *Determinism and Freedom in Stoic Philosophy*. Oxford.

Boes, J. (1981) 'À propos du *de divinatione*, ironie de Cicéron sur le *nomen* et l'*omen* de Brutus', *REL* 59: 164–76.

Borgeaud, P. (1987) 'Du mythe à l'idéologie: la tête du Capitole', *MH* 44: 86–100.

Bottéro, J. (1974) 'Symptômes, signes, écritures en Mésopotamie ancienne', in Vernant (ed.): 70–197.

Bouché-Leclerq, A. (1879–82) *Histoire de la divination dans l'Antiquité*, 4 vols. Paris.

(1892) '*Divinatio*', in *Dictionnaire des antiquités grecques et romaines*, ed. C. Daremberg and E. Saglio, II.I. Paris: 292–319.

Bouquet, M. and Morzadec, F. (eds.) (2004) *La Sibylle. Parole et representation*. Rennes.

Bowden, H. (2003) 'Oracles for sale', in *Herodotus and His World. Essays from a Conference in Memory of George Forrest*, ed. P. Derow and R. Parker. Oxford: 256–74.

(2005) *Classical Athens and the Delphic Oracle. Divination and Democracy*. Cambridge.

Bowersock, G. W. (1990) 'The pontificate of Augustus', in *Between Republic and Empire. Interpretations of Augustus and His Principate*, ed. K. A. Raaflaub and M. Toher. Berkeley, Los Angeles and Oxford: 380–94.

(2006) 'Le tre Rome', *Studi Storici* 47: 977–91.

Boyancé, P. (1955) 'Sur la théologie de Varron', *REA* 57: 57–84, reprinted in Boyancé 1972: 253–82.

(1972) *Études sur la religion romaine*. CEFR II. Rome.

(1976) 'Les implications philosophiques des recherches de Varron sur la religion romaine', in *Atti del Congresso internazionale di studi varroniani*. Rieti: 137–61.

Boyce, A. (1937) 'The expiatory rites of 207 B.C.', *TAPA* 68: 157–71.

Bradley, G. (2000) *Ancient Umbria. State, Culture, and Identity in Central Italy from the Iron Age to the Augustan Era*. Oxford.

Breglia Pulci Doria, L. (1983) *Oracoli sibillini tra rituali e propaganda (Studi su Flegonte di Tralles)*. Naples.

(1998) 'Libri sibyllini e dominio di Roma', in Chirassi Colombo and Seppilli (eds.): 277–304.

Bremmer, J. N. (1993) 'Prophets, seers and politics in Greece, Israel and early modern Europe', *Numen* 40: 150–83.

Brendel, O. (1960) 'Two *Fortunae*, Antium and Praeneste', *AJA* s. 2, 64: 41–7.

Brescia, G. (1997) *La 'scalata' del Ligure. Saggio di commento a Sallustio, Bellum Iugurthinum 92–94*. Scrinia II. Bari.

Brind'Amour, P. (1978) 'L'origine des Jeux Séculaires', *ANRW* 2.16.3: 1334–1417.

(1983) *Le Calendrier romain. Recherches chronologiques*. Collection d'études anciennes de l'Université d'Ottawa 2. Ottawa.

Bringmann, K. (1971) *Untersuchungen zum späten Cicero*. Hypomnemata 29. Göttingen.

Briquel, D. (1986a) 'À propos d'un oracle de Preneste', in Briquel and Guittard (eds.): 114–20.

(1986b) 'Art augural et *Etrusca disciplina*: le débat sur l'origine de l'augurat romain', in Briquel and Guittard (eds.): 68–100.

(1990a) 'Les changements de siècles en Étrurie', in *Fin de siècles*, ed. P. Citti. Bordeaux: 61–76.

(1990b) 'Le paradoxe étrusque: une parole inspirée sans oracles prophétiques', *Kernos* 3: 67–75.

(1991) 'Virgile et l'*Etrusca disciplina*', in Briquel and Guittard (eds.): 33–52.

(1993) 'A proposito della profezia dell'aruspice veiente', in Sordi (ed.): 169–85.

(1995a) 'Cicéron et les Étrusques', *ACUSD* 31: 21–32.

(1995b) 'Sur un fragment d'Umbricius Melior. L'interprétation par un haruspice de la légende de fondation de Rome?', in Briquel and Guittard (eds.): 17–26.

(1997a) *Chrétiens et haruspices. La religion étrusque, dernier rempart du paganisme romain*. Paris.

(1997b) 'Le cas étrusque: le prophétisme rejeté aux origines', in Heintz (ed.): 439–55.

(1998) 'Ancora sulla cattura dell'aruspice veiente', *Annali della Fondazione per il Museo 'Claudio Faina'* 5: 69–82.

(1999) 'Les présages de royauté de la divination étrusque', in Smadja and Geny (eds.): 185–204.

(2001) 'Millenarismo e secoli etruschi', *Minerva* 15: 263–78.

(2008) 'Il ruolo della componente etrusca nella difesa della religione nazionale dei Romani contro le *externae superstitiones*', in Urso (ed.): 115–33.

Briquel, D. and Guittard, C. (eds.) (1985) *La divination dans le monde étrusco-italique. Caesarodunum* Supplément 52. Tours.

(1986a) *La divination dans le monde étrusco-italique (II). Caesarodunum* Supplément 54. Tours.

(1986b) *La divination dans le monde étrusco-italique (III). Caesarodunum* Supplément 56. Tours.

(1991) *Les écrivains du siècle d'Auguste et l'Etrusca Disciplina. La divination dans le monde étrusco-italique (IV). Caesarodunum* Supplément 61. Tours.

(1993) *Les écrivains du siècle d'Auguste et l'Etrusca Disciplina II. La divination dans le monde étrusco-italique (V). Caesarodunum* Supplément 63. Tours.

(1995) *Les écrivains et l'Etrusca Disciplina de Claude à Trajan. La divination dans le monde étrusco-italique (VI). Caesarodunum* Supplément 64. Tours.

(1996) *Les écrivains du deuxième siècle et l'Etrusca Disciplina. La divination dans le monde étrusco-italique (VII). Caesarodunum* Supplément 65. Tours.

Brisson, L. (2008) *Le sexe incertain. Androgynie et hermaphrodisme dans l'Antiquité gréco-romaine*, 2nd edn. Paris.

Brouwer, R. (2011) 'Polybius and Stoic *Tyche*', *GRBS* 51: 111–32.

Brown, P. (1981) *The Cult of the Saints. Its Rise and Function in Latin Christianity*. The Haskell Lectures on History of Religions n.s. 2. Chicago.

Brunt, P. A. (1984) 'The role of the Senate in the Augustan regime', *CQ* 34: 423–44.

(1989) 'Philosophy and religion in the late Republic', in *Philosophia Togata. Essays on Philosophy and Roman Society*, ed. J. Barnes and M. T. Griffin. Oxford: 174–98.

Buchet, E. (2012) 'Tiburnus, Albunea, Hercules Victor: the cults of Tibur between integration and assertion of local identity', in *Processes of Integration and Identity Formation in the Roman Republic*, ed. S. T. Roselaar. *Mnemosyne* Supplement 342. Leiden and Boston: 355–64.

Buchner, E. (1982) *Die Sonnenuhr des Augustus. Nachdruck aus* Römische Mitteilungen *1976 und 1980 und Nachtrag über die Ausgrabung 1980/1981*, Mainz.

Buitenwerf, R. (2003) *Book III of the Sibylline Oracles and its Social Setting with an Introduction, Translation, and Commentary.* Studia in Veteris Testamenti Pseudepigrapha 17. Leiden and Boston.

Bunse, R. (2002) 'Entstehung und Funktion der Losung (*sortitio*) unter den *magistratus maiores* der römischen Republik', *Hermes* 130: 416–32.

Buongiorno, P. (2011) '*Ateii Capitones*', *Iura* 59: 195–216.

Burckhardt, L. A. (1988) *Politischen Strategien der Optimaten in der späten römischen Republik. Historia* Einzelschriften 57. Stuttgart.

Burkert, W. (1965) 'Cicero als Platoniker und Skeptiker. Zum Platonverständnis der Neuen Akademie', *Gymnasium* 72: 175–200.

   (1996) *Creation of the Sacred. Tracks of Biology in Early Religions.* Cambridge, MA and London.

   (2005) 'Signs, command, and knowledge: ancient divination between enigma and epiphany', in Johnston and Struck (eds.): 29–49.

Burton, P. J. (2000) 'The last Republican historian: a new date for the composition of Livy's first pentad', *Historia* 49: 429–46.

Caerols, J. J. (1989) Los Libros Sibilinos en la historiografía latina. Diss. Madrid (available at http://eprints.ucm.es/12197/1/T15374.pdf, last accessed 29.08.12).

   (2006) '*Sacrificuli ac uates ceperant hominum mentes* (Liu. 25.1.8): religión, miedo y política en Roma', in Urso (ed.): 89–136.

Calderone, S. (1972) '*Superstitio*', *ANRW* 1.2: 376–96.

Campbell, B. (2000) *The Writings of the Roman Land Surveyors. Introduction, Text, Translation and Commentary. JRS* Monographs 9. London.

Cancik, H. (1985/6) 'Rome as sacred landscape. Varro and the end of Republican religion in Rome', *Visible Religion* 4/5: 250–65.

   (1989) '*Libri fatales*. Römische Offenbarungsliteratur und Geschichtstheologie', in *Apocalypticism in the Mediterranean World and the Near East*, ed. D. Hellholm. Tübingen: 549–76.

   (1995) 'M. Tullius Cicero als Kommentator. Zur Formgeschichte von Ciceros Schriften "Über den Bescheid der haruspices" (56 v. Chr.) und "Über die Gesetze II" (ca. 52 v. Chr.)', in *Text und Kommentar*, ed. J. Assmann and B. Gladigow. Beiträge zur Archäologie der literarischen Kommunikation 4. Munich: 293–310.

   (1999a) '*Idolum* and *imago*: Roman dreams and dream theories', in *Dream Cultures. Explorations in the Comparative History of Dreaming*, ed. D. Shulman and G. G. Stroumsa. Oxford: 169–88.

   (1999b) 'The reception of Greek cults in Rome. A precondition of the emergence of an "imperial religion"', *ARG* 1: 161–73.

Cancik, H. (ed.) (1996) *Geschichte – Tradition – Reflexion. Festschrift für Martin Hengel zum 70. Geburtstag* II. Tübingen.

Canfora, L. (1999) *Giulio Cesare. Il dittatore democratico.* Rome and Bari.

Cantarella, E. (2005) 'The androgynous and bisexuality in ancient legal codes', *Diogenes* 52: 5–14.

Capdeville, G. (1993) 'Les sources de la connaissance de l'*Etrusca disciplina* chez les écrivains du siècle d'Auguste', in Briquel and Guittard (eds.): 2–30.

(1994) 'Le vocabulaire technique dans les traités d'*Etrusca Disciplina* en langue latine', *RPh* 68: 51–75.

(1997) 'Les livres sacrés des Etrusques', in Heintz (ed.): 457–508.

(1998) 'Die Rezeption der etruskischen Disziplin durch die gelehrten Römer', in Aigner-Foresti (ed.): 385–419.

Cardauns, B. (1978) 'Varro und die römische Religion. Zur Theologie, Wirkungs-geschichte und Leistung der "Antiquitates Rerum Divinarum"', *ANRW* 2.16.1: 80–103.

Cardauns, B. (ed.) (1960) *Varros Logistoricus über die Götterverehrung (Curio de cultu deorum)*. Würzburg.

(1976) *M. Terentius Varro. Antiquitates Rerum Divinarum*. 2 vols. Mainz and Wiesbaden.

Catalano, P. (1960) *Contributi allo studio del diritto augurale I*. Università di Torino. Memorie dell'Istituto Giuridico s. 2, 107. Turin.

Cavarzere, A. (1994) '*Vate me*. L'ambiguo sigillo dell'Epodo XVI', *Aevum Antiquum* 7: 171–90.

Cèbe, J.-P. (ed.) (1996) *Varron, Satires ménippées* XI. CEFR 9. Rome.

Cébeillac-Gervasoni, M., Caldelli, M.-L. and Zevi, F. (2010) *Epigrafia latina. Ostia: cento iscrizioni in contesto*. Rome.

Champeaux, J. (1982) *Fortuna. Recherches sur le culte de la Fortune à Rome et dans le monde romain des origines à la mort de César. I. Fortuna dans la religion archaïque*. CEFR 64. Rome.

(1986) 'Oracles institutionnels et formes populaires de la divination italique', in Briquel and Guittard (eds.): 90–113.

(1987) *Fortuna. Recherches sur le culte de la Fortune à Rome et dans le monde romain des origines à la mort de César. II. Les transformations de Fortuna sous la République* (CEFR 64). Rome.

(1988) 'Sur trois passages de Tite-Live (21, 62, 5 et 8; 22, 1, 11). Les "sorts" de Caere et de Faleries', *Philologus* 133: 63–74.

(1990a) '"*Sors oraculi*": les oracles en Italie sous la République et l'Empire', *MEFRA* 102: 271–302.

(1990b) '"Sorts" et divination inspirée. Pour une préhistoire des oracles italiques', *MEFRA* 102: 801–28.

(1990c) 'Les oracles de l'Italie antique: hellénisme et italicité', *Kernos* 3: 103–11.

(1991) 'Horace et la divination étrusco-italique', in Briquel and Guittard (eds.): 53–72.

(1995) 'L'*Etrusca disciplina* dans Suétone, *Vies des douze Césars*', in Briquel and Guittard (eds.): 63–87.

(1996a) 'Pontifes, haruspices et décemvirs: l'expiation des prodiges de 207', *REL* 74: 67–91.

(1996b) 'L'*Etrusca disciplina* et l'image de l'Étrurie chez Plutarque', in Briquel and Guittard (eds.): 37–65.

(1997) 'De la parole à l'écriture. Essai sur le langage des oracles', in Heintz (ed.): 405–38.

(2003) 'Le Tibre, le pont et les pontifes. Contribution à l'histoire du prodige romain', *REL* 81: 25–42.

(2005) 'Permission, monition, prédiction: les signes de la divination romaine', in Kany-Turpin (ed.): 211–22.

Chilver, G. E. F. (1985) *A Historical Commentary on Tacitus' Histories IV and V*, ed. G. B. Townend. Oxford.

Chirassi Colombo, I. (2012) '*Teras* ou les modalités du prodige dans le discours divinatoire grec: une perspective comparatiste', in Georgoudi, Koch Piettre and Schmidt (eds.): 221–51.

Chirassi Colombo, I. and Seppilli, T. (eds.) (1998) *Sibille e linguaggi oracolari. Mito Storia Tradizione*. Ichnia 3. Pisa and Rome.

Citroni Marchetti, S. (2008) 'Tiberio Gracco, Cornelia e i due serpenti (Cic. *div.* 1, 36; 2, 62; Val. Max. 4, 6, 1; Plut. *Ti. Gracch.*1.4–5; Plin. *nat.* 7.122)', *MD* 60: 39–68, reprinted in Citroni Marchetti 2011: 203–27.

(2011) *La scienza della natura per un intellettuale romano. Studi su Plinio il Vecchio*. Biblioteca di *MD* 22. Pisa and Rome.

Clark, A. (2007) *Divine Qualities. Cult and Community in Republican Rome*. Oxford.

Clark, G. (2010) 'Augustine's Varro and pagan monotheism', in *Monotheism between Pagans and Christians in Late Antiquity*, ed. S. Mitchell and P. van Nuffelen. Interdisciplinary Studies in Ancient Culture and Religion 12. Leuven and Walpole, MA: 181–201.

Clark Reeder, J. (1997) 'The statue of Augustus from Prima Porta, the underground complex, and the omen of the *gallina alba*', *AJP* 118: 89–118.

(2001) *The Villa of Livia* ad Gallinas Albas. *A Study in the Augustan Villa and Garden*. Archaeologia Transatlantica 20. Providence.

Clausen, W. (1990) 'Virgil's Messianic eclogue', in Kugel (ed.): 65–74.

Clauss, M. (2011) 'Kein Aberglaube in Hispellum', *Klio* 93: 429–45.

Clemen, C. (1928) 'Die etruskische Säkularrechnung', *SMSR* 4: 235–42.

(1936) 'Les rapports de la religion étrusque avec les religions du Proche-Orient', *AC* 5: 263–71.

Coarelli, F. (1987) *I santuari del Lazio in età repubblicana*. Studi NIS Archeologia 7. Rome.

(1993a) 'Note sui *ludi saeculares*', in *Spectacles sportifs et scéniques dans le monde étrusco-italique*. CEFR 172. Rome: 211–45.

(1993b) 'Casa Romuli (Cermalus)', in *Lexicon topographicum urbis Romae* I, ed. E. M. Steinby. Rome: 241–2.

Coleman, R. (1982) 'The gods in Aeneid', *G&R* 29: 143–68.

Connerton, P. (1989) *How Societies Remember*. Cambridge.

Cooley, A. E. (2006) 'Beyond Rome and Latium: Roman religion in the age of Augustus', in Schultz and Harvey (eds.): 228–52.

Corbeill, A. (2009) 'Weeping statues, weeping gods and prodigies from Republican to Early-Christian Rome', in *Tears in the Graeco-Roman World*, ed. T. Fögen. Berlin and New York: 297–310.

    (2010a) 'The function of a divinely inspired text in Cicero's *De haruspicum responsis*', in Berry and Erskine (eds.): 139–54.

    (2010b) 'Dreams and the prodigy process in Republican Rome', in Scioli and Walde (eds.): 81–101.

    (2012) 'Cicero and the Etruscan *haruspices*', *PLLS* 15: 243–66.

Cordano, F. and Grottanelli, C. (eds.) (2001) *Sorteggio pubblico e cleromanzia dall'antichità all'età moderna*. Milan.

Cornell, T. J. (1978) '*Principes* of Tarquinia', *JRS* 68: 167–73.

    (1981) 'Some observations on the "crimen incesti"', in *Le Délit religieux dans la cité antique*. CEFR 48. Rome: 27–37.

Courtney, E. (1960) 'Notes on Cicero', *CR* 10: 95–9.

    (1993) *The Fragmentary Latin Poets*. Oxford.

Cowan, R. (2011) 'Sinon and the case of the hypermetric oracle', *Phoenix* 65: 361–70.

Cramer, F. C. (1951) 'Expulsion of astrologers from ancient Rome', *CM* 12: 9–50.

    (1954) *Astrology in Roman Law and Politics*. Philadelphia.

Crampon, M. (2002) 'Les caractères formels du songe de pouvoir sous la République romaine', in Fartzoff, Smadja and Geny (eds.): 97–124.

Crawford, M. H. (ed.) (1996) *Roman Statutes* I. BICS Supplement 64. London.

Crifò, G. (1999) '"*Prodigium*" e diritto: il caso dell'ermafrodita', *Index* 27: 113–20.

Cristofoli, R. (2004) *Cicerone e la II Filippica. Circostanze, stile e ideologia di un'orazione mai pronunciata*. Rome.

Cryer, F. H. (1994) *Divination in Ancient Israel and its Near Eastern Environment. A Socio-Historical Investigation. JSOT* Supplement Series 142. Sheffield.

Cugusi, P. and Sblendorio Cugusi, M. T. (eds.) (2001) *Opere di Marco Porcio Catone Censore*. Turin.

Cuny-Le Callet, B. (2005a) *Rome et ses monstres. Naissance d'un concept philosophique et rhétorique*. Paris.

    (2005b) 'La lettre de Cicéron à Cécina: vers une divination rationelle?', in Kany-Turpin (ed.): 223–39.

Cupaiuolo, F. (1984) 'Caso, fato e fortuna nel pensiero di alcuni storici latini: spunti e appunti', *BSL* 14: 3–38.

Curry, P. (2010a) 'Introduction', in Curry (ed.): 1–9.

    (2010b) 'Embodiment, alterity and agency: negotiating antinomies in divination', in Curry (ed.): 85–117.

Curry, P. (ed.) (2010) *Divination. Perspectives for a New Millennium*. Farnham and Burlington, VT.

Dahlmann, H. (1948) 'Vates', *Philologus* 97: 337–53.

    (1963) 'Zu Varros Literaturforschung, besonders in "De poetis"', in *Varron*, ed. O. Reverdin. Entretiens sur l'antiquité classique 9. Vandœuvres and Geneva: 3–20.

Dangel, J. (1995) *Lucius Accius. Œuvres. Fragments*. Paris.

Dart, C. J. (2012) 'The address of Italian portents by Rome and the *Ager Publicus*', *AC* 81: 111–24.

Davies, J. P. (2004) *Rome's Religious History. Livy, Tacitus and Ammianus on their Gods*. Cambridge.

DeFilippo, J. G. (2000) 'Cicero vs. Cotta in *De natura deorum*', *Ancient Philosophy* 20: 169–87.

De Libero, L. (1992) *Obstruktion. Politische Praktiken im Senat und in der Volksversammlung der ausgehenden römischen Republik (70–49 v. Chr.)*. Hermes Einzelschriften 59. Stuttgart.

Della Casa, A. (1962) *Nigidio Figulo*. Rome.

Della Corte, F. (1974) 'Numa e le streghe', *Maia* 26: 3–20.

Denniston, J. D. (ed.) (1926) *M. Tulli Ciceronis in M. Antonium orationes Philippicae prima et secunda*. Oxford.

Denyer, N. (1985) 'The case against divination: an examination of Cicero's *de divinatione*', *PCPS* n.s. 31: 1–10.

Desanti, F. (1990) *Sileat omnibus perpetuo divinandi curiositas. Indovini e sanzioni nel mondo romano*. Pubblicazioni della Facoltà Giuridica dell'Università di Ferrara s. 2, 26. Milan.

Desideri, P. (2011) 'Punti di vista greci e romani su religione e politica in Roma repubblicana', *Politica antica* 1: 25–38.

De Spirito, G. (1995) 'Fons olei', in *LTUR* II. Rome: 260.

Develin, R. (1978) 'Religion and politics at Rome during the third century BC', *JRH* 10: 3–19.

Díaz Fernández, A. (2011) '*L. Culleolus proconsul*: Cic., *Fam.* XIII, 41–42', *Latomus* 70: 664–75.

Diehl, E. (1934) 'Das *saeculum*, seine Rite und Gebete', *RhM* 83: 255–72, 348–72.

Diels, H. (1890) *Sibyllinische Blätter*. Berlin.

Dihle, A. (1996) 'Die Theologia tripertita bei Augustin', in Cancik (ed.): 183–202.

Dionisotti, A. C. (1988) 'Nepos and the generals', *JRS* 78: 35–49.

Dix, C. V. (2006) *Virtutes und* vitia. *Interpretationen der Charakterzeichnung in Sallusts Bellum Iugurthinum*. Bochumer Altertumswissenschaftliches Colloquium 70. Trier.

Dobbin, R. F. (1995) 'Julius Caesar in Jupiter's prophecy, *Aeneid*, Book 1', *CA* 14: 5–40.

Domenici, I. (2009) *Etruscae fabulae. Mito e rappresentazione*. Archaeologica 156. Rome.

Domenici, I. (ed.) (2007) *Giovanni Lido. Sui segni celesti*. Milan.

Domenicucci, P. (1996) *Astra Caesarum. Astronomia, astrologia e catasterismo da Cesare a Domiziano*. Testi e studi di cultura classica 16. Pisa.

Dorandi, T. (1985) 'Der "gute König" bei Philodem und die Rede des Maecenas vor Octavian (Cassius Dio LII, 14–40)', *Klio* 67: 56–60.

Douglas, M. (1966) *Purity and Danger. An Analysis of the Concepts of Pollution and Taboo*. London and New York.

Dumézil, G. (1966) *La religion romaine archaïque avec un Appendice sur la religion des Étrusques*. Paris.

Dunsch, B. (2009) 'Religion in der römischen Komödie: Einige programmatische Überlegungen', in Bendlin and Rüpke (eds.): 17–56.

DuQuesnay, I. M. Le M. (1984) 'Horace and Maecenas: the propaganda value of *Sermones* I', in *Poetry and Politics in the Age of Augustus*, ed. T. Woodman and D. West. Cambridge: 19–58.

Dyck, A. R. (1998) 'Cicero the dramaturge: verisimilitude and consistency of characterization in some of his dialogues', in *Qui miscuit utile dulci. Festschrift Essays for Paul Lachlan MacKendrick*, ed. G. Schmeling and J. D. Mikalson. Wauconda, IL: 151–64.

Dyck, A. R. (ed.) (2003) *Cicero De natura deorum Liber I*. Cambridge.

(2004) *A Commentary on Cicero*, De Legibus. Ann Arbor.

(2008) *Cicero. Catilinarians*. Cambridge.

Dwyer, E. J. (1973) 'Augustus and the Capricorn', *RM* 80: 59–67.

Ehrenberg, V. (1927) 'Losung', *RE* 13: 1451–1504.

Eidinow, E. (2007) *Oracles, Curses, and Risk among the Ancient Greeks*. Oxford.

(2011) *Luck, Fate and Fortune. Antiquity and its Legacy*. London and New York.

Eidinow, E. and Taylor, C. (2010) 'Lead-letter days: communication and crisis in the ancient Greek world', *CQ* 60: 30–62.

van der Eijk, P. (1993) 'Aristotelian elements in Cicero's "De divinatione"', *Philologus* 137: 223–31.

Engels, D. (2007) *Das römische Vorzeichenwesen (753–27 v.Chr.). Quellen, Terminologie, Kommentar, historische Entwicklung*. PAwB 22. Stuttgart.

(2009) 'Déterminisme historique et perceptions de déchéance sous la république tardive et le principat', *Latomus* 68: 859–94.

(2010) 'Prodigies and religious propaganda: Seleucus and Augustus', in *Studies in Latin Literature and Roman History* XV, ed. C. Deroux. Collection Latomus 323. Brussels: 153–77.

(2012) 'Dionysius of Halicarnassus on Roman religion, divination and prodigies', in *Studies in Latin Literature and Roman History* XVI, ed. C. Deroux. Brussels.

Enking, R. (1959) 'P. Vergilius Maro vates Etruscus', *RM* 66: 65–96.

Escobar, A. (2002) 'Humor, sarcasmo e intolerancia en la literatura religiosa tardorrepublicana', in *Religión y propaganda política en el mundo romano*, ed. F. Marco Simón, F. Pina Polo and J. Remesal Rodríguez. Instrumenta 12. Barcelona: 41–55.

Evans-Pritchard, E. E. (1937) *Witchcraft, Oracles and Magic among the Azande*. Oxford.

Fabre-Serris, J. (1991) 'Ovide et l'*Etrusca disciplina*', in Briquel and Guittard (eds.): 73–88.

Fantham, E. (1995) 'Recent readings of Ovid's *Fasti*', *CP* 90: 367–78.

Farney, G. D. (2007) *Ethnic Identity and Aristocratic Competition in Republican Rome*. Cambridge.

Fartzoff, M., Smadja, E. and Geny, E. (eds.) (2002) *Pouvoir des hommes, signes des dieux dans le monde antique*. Besançon and Paris.

Fauth, W. (1976) 'Der Traum des Tarquinius. Spuren einer etruskisch-mediterranen Widder-Sonnensymbolik bei Accius (fr. 212 D.)', *Latomus* 35: 469–503.

(1978) 'Römische Religion im Spiegel der "Fasti" des Ovid', *ANRW* 2.16.1: 104–86.

Favuzzi, A. (1996) 'Osservazioni su alcune proposte di Mecenate nel libro LII di Cassio Dione', in *Epigrafia e territorio IV. Temi di antichità romane*, ed. M. Pani. Documenti e studi 19. Bari: 273–83.

Feeney, D. C. (1991) *The Gods in Epic. Poets and Critics of the Classical Tradition.* Oxford.

(1998) *Literature and Religion at Rome. Cultures, Contexts, and Beliefs.* Cambridge.

(1999) '*Mea tempora*: patterning of time in the *Metamorphoses*', in *Ovidian Transformations. Essays on Ovid's* Metamorphoses *and its Reception*, ed. P. Hardie, A. Barchiesi and S. Hinds. Cambridge Philological Society. Supplementary Volume 23. Cambridge: 13–30.

(2004) 'Interpreting sacrificial ritual in Roman poetry: disciplines and their models', in Barchiesi, Rüpke and Stephens (eds.): 1–21.

(2007) *Caesar's Calendar. Ancient Time and the Beginnings of History.* Sather Classical Lectures 65. Berkeley and London.

Feil, E. (1986) Religio. *Die Geschichte eines neuzeitlichen Grundbegriffs von Frühchristentum bis zur Reformation.* Forschungen zur Kirchen- und Dogmengeschichte 36. Göttingen.

Feldherr, A. (1998) *Spectacle and Society in Livy's* History. Berkeley, Los Angeles and London.

Ferrary, J.-L. (1988) *Philhellénisme et impérialisme: aspects idéologiques de la conquête romaine du monde hellénistique, de la seconde guerre de Macedoine à la guerre contre Mithridate.* BEFRA 271. Rome.

(2007) 'Le droit naturel dans les exposés sur les parties du droit des traités de rhétorique', in *Testi e problemi del giusnaturalismo romano*, ed. D. Mantovani and A. Schiavone. Pubblicazioni del Cedant 3. Pavia: 75–94.

Février, C. (2004) 'Le double langage de la Sibylle de l'oracle grec au rituel romain', in Bouquet and Morzadec (eds.): 17–27.

(2009) Supplicare deis. *La supplication expiatoire à Rome. Recherches sur les rhetoriques religieuses* 10. Turnhout.

Fezzi, L. (1995) '*Lex Clodia de iure et tempore legum rogandarum*', *SCO* 45: 297–328.

Fine, G. A. (2007) *Authors of the Storm. Meteorologists and the Culture of Prediction.* Chicago.

Finger, P. (1929) 'Die zwei mantischen Systeme in Ciceros Schrift über die Weissagung (*de divinatione* 1)', *RhM* 78: 371–97.

Firpo, G. (1998) 'La polemica sugli etruschi nei poeti dell'età augustea', in Aigner-Foresti (ed.): 251–98.

Flower, H. I. (1990) 'The tradition of the *spolia opima*: M. Claudius Marcellus and Augustus', *CA* 19: 34–64.

(2008) 'Remembering and forgetting temple destruction. The destruction of the temple of Jupiter Optimus Maximus in 83 BC', in *Antiquity in Antiquity: Jewish and Christian Pasts in the Greco-Roman World*, ed. G. Gardner and K. L. Osterloh. Texte und Studien zum antiken Judentum 123. Tübingen: 74–92.

Flower, M. A. (2008) *The Seer in Ancient Greece*. Berkeley, Los Angeles and London.

Fögen, M. T. (1993) *Die Enteignung der Wahrsager. Studien zum kaiserlichen Wissensmonopol in der Spätantike*. Frankfurt.

Fögen, T. (2000) *Patrii sermonis egestas. Einstellungen lateinischer Autoren zu ihrer Muttersprache*. Beiträge zur Altertumskunde 150. Munich and Leipzig.

Fontaine, M. (2010) *Funny Words in Plautine Comedy*. Oxford.

Fontanella, F. (1997) 'Introduzione al *De legibus* di Cicerone. I', *Athenaeum* 85: 487–530.

Fortenbaugh, W. W. and Pender, E. (eds.) (2009) *Heraclides of Pontus. Discussion*. Rutgers University Studies in Classical Humanities 15. New Brunswick.

Fortes, M. (1966) 'Religious premisses and logical technique in divinatory ritual', *Philosophical Transactions of the Royal Society* 251: 409–22.

Fortin, E. L. (1980) 'Augustine and Roman civil religion: some critical reflections', *REAug* 26: 238–56.

Foti, G. (2011) 'Funzioni e caratteri del "pullarius" in età repubblicana e imperiale', *Acme* 64: 89–121.

Fox, M. (2007) *Cicero's Philosophy of History*. Oxford.

(2009) 'Heraclides of Pontus and the philosophical dialogue', in Fortenbaugh and Pender (eds.): 41–67.

Fraenkel, E. (1957) *Horace*. Oxford.

Frank, H. (1992) Ratio *bei Cicero*. Studien zur klassischen Philologie 75. Frankfurt, Berlin, Berne, New York, Paris and Vienna.

Fraschetti, A. (1990) *Roma e il principe*. Rome and Bari.

Frassinetti, P. (1953) *Fabula Atellana. Saggio sul teatro popolare latino*. Pubblicazioni dell'Istituto di filologia classica 4. Genoa.

(1967) *Atellanae fabulae*. Poetarum Latinorum Reliquae 6.1. Rome.

Fromentin, V. (1996) 'Appien, les Étrusques et l'*Etrusca disciplina*', in Briquel and Guittard (eds.): 81–95.

Fuhrmann, M. (1987) 'Erneuerung als Wiederherstellung. Zur Funktion antiquarischer Forschung im spätrepublikanischen Rom', in *Epochenschwelle und Epochenbewusstsein*, ed. R. Herzog and R. Koselleck. Munich: 131–51.

Gadd, C. J. (1966) 'Some Babylonian divinatory methods and their inter-relations', in *La divination en Mésopotamie ancienne et dans les régions voisines*. Paris: 21–34.

Gagé, J. (1955) *Apollon romain. Essai sur le culte d'Apollon et le développement du "ritus Graecus" à Rome des origines à Auguste*. BEFAR 82. Rome.

Galinsky, K. (1996) *Augustan Culture. An Interpretive Introduction*. Princeton.

Gallagher, R. L. (2001) 'Metaphor in Cicero's *de re publica*', *CQ* 51: 509–19.

Garbarino, G. (2010) 'Cesare e la cultura filosofica del suo tempo', in Urso (ed.): 207–21.

García de la Fuente, O. (1973) 'La observación de las aves en Roma', *Helmantica* 24: 135–57.

Gargola, D. J. (1995) *Lands, Laws, & Gods. Magistrates & Ceremony in the Regulation of Public Lands in Republican Rome*. Chapel Hill and London.

(2004) 'The ritual of centuriation', in Konrad (ed.): 123–49.

Garstang, J. B. (1963) 'Aeneas and the Sibyls', *CJ* 59: 97–101.

Gascou, J. (1984) *Suétone historien*. BEFAR 255. Rome.

Gee, E. (2000) *Ovid, Aratus and Augustus. Astronomy in Ovid's* Fasti. Cambridge.

(2001) 'Cicero's astronomy', *CQ* 51: 520–36.

Geertz, A. (2000) 'Analytical theorizing in the secular study of religion', in Jense and Rothstein (eds.): 21–31.

Geiger, J. (1985a) *Cornelius Nepos and Ancient Political Biography*. Historia Einzelschriften 47. Stuttgart.

(1985b) 'Cicero and Nepos', *Latomus* 44: 264–70.

Georgoudi, S., Koch Piettre, R. and Schmidt, F. (eds.) (2012) *La raison des signes. Présages, rites, destin dans les sociétés de la Méditerranée ancienne*. RGRW 174. Leiden and Boston.

Geraci, G. (1983) *Genesi della provincia romana d'Egitto*. Studi di storia antica 9. Bologna.

Giardina, A. (2008) 'Metis in Rome: a Greek dream of Sulla', in *East & West. Papers in Ancient History Presented to Glen W. Bowersock*, ed. T. C. Brennan and H. Flower. Cambridge, MA: 61–84.

(2010) 'Cesare vs Silla', in Urso (ed.): 31–46.

Gieseler Greenbaum, D. (2010) 'Arrows, aiming and divination: astrology as a stochastic art', in Curry (ed.): 179–209.

Gigandet, A. (2005) 'Le signe dans les *Questions naturelles* de Senèque', in Kany-Turpin (ed.): 85–95.

Gigon, O. (1978) 'Cicero und die griechische Philosophie', *ANRW* I.4: 226–61.

Gilbert, C. D. (1973) 'Marius and Fortuna', *CQ* 23: 104–7.

Gildenhard, I. (2003) 'The "annalist" before the annalists. Ennius and his Annales', in *Formen römischer Geschichtsschreibung von den Anfängen bis Livius. Gattungen–Autoren–Kontexte*, ed. U. Eigler, U. Gotter, N. Luraghi and U. Walter. Darmstadt: 93–114.

(2007a) *Paideia Romana. Cicero's* Tusculan Disputations. CCJ-PCPS Supplementary Volume 30. Cambridge.

(2007b) 'Greek auxiliaries: tragedy and philosophy in Ciceronian invective', in *Cicero on the Attack. Invective and Subversion in the Orations and Beyond*, ed. J. Booth. Swansea: 149–82.

(2007c) 'Virgil vs. Ennius or: the undoing of the annalist', in Ennius perennis. *The Annals and Beyond*, ed. W. Fitzgerald and E. Gowers. PCPS Supplementary Volume 31. Cambridge: 73–102.

(2009) 'Gelegenheitsmetaphysik. Religiöse Semantik in Reden Ciceros', in Bendlin and Rüpke (eds.): 89–114.

(2011) *Creative Eloquence. The Construction of Reality in Cicero's Speeches.* Oxford.

Ginzburg, C. (1986) *Miti emblemi spie. Morfologia e storia.* Piccola biblioteca Einaudi 567. Turin.

Girardet, K. M. (2012) 'Das Verbot von "betrügerischen Machenschaften" beim Kaiserkult in Hispellum (CIL xi 5265/ILS 705)', *ZPE* 182: 297–311.

Gladigow, B. (1979) 'Konkrete Angst und offene Furcht. Am Beispiel des Prodigienwesens in Rom', in *Angst und Gewalt. Ihre Präsenz und ihre Bewältigung in den Religionen*, ed. H. von Stietencron. Düsseldorf: 61–77.

(1989) 'Aetas, aevum und saeclorum ordo. Zur Struktur zeitlicher Deutungssysteme', in *Apocalypticism in the Mediterranean World and the Near East*, ed. D. Hellholm. Tübingen: 255–71.

Glassner, J.-J. (2012) 'La fabrique des présages en Mésopotamie: la sémiologie des devins', in Georgoudi, Koch Piettre and Schmidt (eds.): 29–53.

Glucker, J. (1978) *Antiochus and the Late Academy.* Hypomnemata 56. Göttingen.

(1999) 'A Platonic cento in Cicero', *Phronesis* 44: 30–44.

Goar, R. J. (1968) 'The purpose of *de divinatione*', *TAPA* 99: 241–8.

(1972) *Cicero and the State Religion.* Amsterdam.

Goldberg, S. M. (1995) *Epic in Republican Rome.* Oxford.

(2011) 'Roman comedy gets back to the basics', *JRS* 101: 206–21.

Goldschmidt, V. (1978) 'Remarques sur l'origine épicurienne de la "prenotion"', in *Les Stoiciens et leur logique*, ed. V. Goldschmidt, Paris: 155–69.

Gordon, R. (2008) '*Superstitio*, superstition and religious repression in the late Roman Republic and Principate (100 bce–300 ce)', in *The Religion of Fools? Superstition Past and Present*, ed. S. A. Smith and A. Knight. *Past & Present* Supplement 3. Oxford and New York: 72–94.

Gotter, U. (1996) *Der Diktator ist tot! Politik im Rom zwischen den Iden des März und der Begründung des Zweiten Triumvirats. Historia.* Einzelschriften 110. Stuttgart.

(2001) *Griechenland in Rom? Die römische Rede über Hellas und ihre Kontexte (3.–1. Jh. V.Chr.).* Habilitationsschrift Freiburg.

Gourinat, J.-B. (2012) 'Les signes du futur dans le Stoïcisme: problèmes logiques et philosophiques', in Georgoudi, Koch Piettre and Schmidt (eds.): 557–75.

Gowing, A. M. (1992) *The Triumviral Narratives of Appian and Cassius Dio.* Ann Arbor.

Gradel, I. (2002) *Emperor Worship and Roman Religion.* Oxford.

Grafton, A. T. and Swerdlow, N. M. (1985) 'Technical chronology and astrological history in Varro, Censorinus and others', *CQ* 35: 454–65.

(1986) 'The horoscope of the foundation of Rome', *CP* 81: 148–53.

Grandazzi, A. (1993) '"Intermortua jam et sepulta verba" (Festus, 242 L). Les mots de la divination chez Verrius Flaccus', in Briquel and Guittard (eds.): 31–92.

Grassmann-Fischer, B. (1966) *Die Prodigien in Vergils Aeneis.* Studia et testimonia antiqua 3. Munich.

Green, S. J. (2009) 'Malevolent gods and Promethean birds: contesting augury in Augustus's Rome', *TAPA* 139: 147–67.

(2011) '*Arduum ad astra*. The poetics and politics of horoscopic failure in Manilius' *Astronomica*', in Green and Volk (eds.): 120–38.

Green, S. J. and Volk, K. (eds.) (2011) *Forgotten Stars. Rediscovering Manilius'* Astronomica. Oxford.

Griffin, M. T. (1995) 'Philosophical badinage in Cicero's letters to his friends', in Powell (ed.) (1995): 325–46.

Grilli, A. (1996) '*Superstitiosi vates* (Enn. *sc.* 321 v.²)', in *Studi in onore di Albino Garzetti*, ed. C. Stella and A. Valvo. Brescia: 227–30.

Grodzynski, D. (1974) 'Par la bouche de l'empereur', in Vernant (ed.): 267–94.

Gros, P. (1993) 'Apollo Palatinus', in *LTUR* I, ed. E. M. Steinby. Rome: 54–7.

Grottanelli, C. (1999) 'Ideologie del sacrificio umano: Roma e Cartagine', *ARG* 1: 41–59.

(2005) '*Sorte unica pro casibus pluribus enotata*. Literary texts and lot inscriptions as sources for ancient kleromancy', in Johnston and Struck (eds.): 129–46.

Gruen, E. S. (1974) *The Last Generation of the Roman Republic*. Berkeley, Los Angeles and London.

(1990) *Studies in Greek Culture and Roman Policy*. Leiden, Boston and Cologne.

Günther, C. (1964) 'Der politische und ideologische Kampf in der römischen Religion in den letzen zwei Jahrhunderten v.u.Z.', *Klio* 42: 209–97.

Gugel, H. (1970) 'Caesars Tod (Sueton, *Div. Iul.* 81, 4–82, 3). Aspekte zur Darstellungskunst und zum Caesarbild Suetons', *Gymnasium* 77: 5–22.

Guillaumont, F. (1984) *Philosophe et augure. Recherches sur la théorie cicéronienne de la divination*. Collection Latomus 184. Brussels.

(1986) 'Cicéron et les techniques de l'haruspicine', in Briquel and Guittard (eds.): 121–35.

(1988) 'Naissance et développement d'une légende: les "Decii"', in *Hommages à Henri Le Bonniec. Res Sacrae*, ed. D. Porte and J.-P. Néraudau. Collection Latomus 201. Brussels: 256–66.

(1991) 'Manilius et l'*Etrusca disciplina*', in Briquel and Guittard (eds.): 100–15.

(1992) 'Aulu-Gelle lecteur du *De Divinatione*', in *Au miroir de la culture antique. Mélanges offerts au président René Marache par ses collègues, ses étudiants et ses amis*. Rennes: 259–68.

(1996) 'La nature et les prodiges dans la religion et la philosophie romaines', in *Le concept de nature à Rome. La physique*, ed. C. Lévy. Études de littérature ancienne 6. Paris: 43–64.

(2000) 'Divination et prévision rationnelle dans la correspondance de Cicéron', in *Epistulae Antiquae. Actes du Ier colloque "Le genre épistolaire antique et ses prolongements"*, ed. L. Nadjo and E. Gavoille. Leuven and Paris: 103–15.

(2002) 'Les philosophes grecs dans la correspondance de Cicéron', in *Epistulae Antiquae II. Actes du IIe colloque international 'Le genre épistolaire antique et ses prolongements européens'*, ed. L. Nadjo and E. Gavoille. Leuven and Paris: 61–76.

(2006) *Le De diuinatione de Cicéron et les théories antiques de la divination.* Collection Latomus 296. Brussels.

Guittard, C. (1985) 'La tradition oraculaire étrusco-latine dans ses rapports avec le vers saturnien et le "carmen" primitif', in Briquel and Guittard (eds.): 33–55.

(1986a) 'Le songe de Tarquin (Accius, *Brutus*, fr. I–II S. R. F. Klotz)', in Briquel and Guittard (eds.): 47–67.

(1986b) 'Haruspicine et "devotio": "caput iocineris a familiari parte caesum" (Tite-Live, VIII, 9, I)', in Briquel and Guittard (eds.): 49–67.

(1988) 'Naissance et développement d'une légende: les Decii', in *Hommages à Henri Le Bonniec: Res Sacrae*, ed. D. Porte and J.-P. Néraudeau. Collection Latomus 201. Brussels: 256–66.

(1996) 'Le témoignage de Phlégon de Tralles', in Briquel and Guittard (eds.): 123–33.

(1998) '"Auctoritas extorum": haruspicine et rituel d'"evocatio"', *Annali della Fondazione per il Museo 'Claudio Faina'* 5: 55–67.

(2002/3) '*Etrusca disciplina* et *regnum*: actualité des signes rélatifs au pouvoir royal à la fin de la République', *ACUSD* 38–9: 103–25.

(2003) 'Les calendiers brontoscopiques dans le monde étrusco-romaine', in *Météorologie dans l'antiquité. Entre science et croyance*, ed. C. Cusset. Saint-Étienne: 455–66.

(2004) 'Reflets étrusques sur la Sibylle. "Libri Sibyllini" et "libri Vegoici"', in Bouquet and Morzadec (eds.): 29–42.

(2006) 'Signes du destin et pouvoir dans les pratiques étrusco-italiques', in Fartzoff, Geny and Smadja (eds.): 71–82.

(2007a) *Carmen et prophéties à Rome.* Recherches sur les rhétoriques religieuses 6. Turnhout.

(2007b) 'Tite-Live, historien de la religion romaine?', *LEC* 75: 79–91.

Gundel, W. and Gundel, H. G. (1966) *Astrologumena. Die astrologische Literatur in der Antike und ihre Geschichte.* Sudhoffs Archiv Beihefte 6. Wiesbaden.

Gurval, R. (1997) 'Caesar's comet: the politics and poetics of an Augustan myth', *MAAR* 42: 39–71.

Gustafsson, G. (2000) *Evocatio deorum. Historical and Mythical Interpretations of Ritualised Conquests in the Expansion of Ancient Rome.* Historia Religionum 16. Uppsala.

Haack, M.-L. (2002) 'Haruspices publics et privés: tentative d'une distinction', *REA* 104: III–33.

(2003) *Les haruspices dans le monde romain.* Scripta Antiqua 6. Bordeaux.

(2006) *Prosopographie des haruspices romains.* Biblioteca di *SE* 42. Pisa and Rome.

Habinek, T. (1994) 'Ideology for an empire in the prefaces to Cicero's dialogues', *Ramus* 23: 55–67.

(2002) 'Ovid and empire', in *The Cambridge Companion to Ovid*, ed. P. Hardie. Cambridge: 46–61.

(2005) *The World of Roman Song. From Ritualized Speech to Social Order.* Baltimore and London.

(2006) 'The wisdom of Ennius', *Arethusa* 39: 471–88.

(2007) 'Probing the entrails of the universe: astrology as bodily knowledge in Manilius' Astronomica', in *Ordering Knowledge in the Roman Empire*, ed. J. König and T. Whitmarsh. Cambridge: 229–40.

(2011) 'Manilius' conflicted Stoicism', in Green and Volk (eds.): 32–44.

Habinek, T. and Schiesaro, A. (eds.) (1997) *The Roman Cultural Revolution*. Cambridge.

Hadas-Lebel, J. (2004) *Le bilinguisme étrusco-latin. Contribution à l'étude de la romanisation de l'Étrurie*. Bibliothèque d'études classiques 41. Leuven, Paris and Dudley, MA.

Hahn, I. (1968) 'Zur Interpretation der Vulcatius-Prophetie', *AAAHung*: 239–46.

(1983) 'Die augusteischen Interpretationen des *sidus Iulium*', *ACUSD* 19: 57–66.

Hall, J. (2009) *Politeness and Politics in Cicero's Letters*. Oxford.

Hall, J. F. (1982) 'P. Vergilius Maro: *vates Etruscus*', *Vergilius* 28: 44–50.

(1986) 'The *saeculum novum* of Augustus and its Etruscan antecedents', *ANRW* 2.16.3: 2564–89.

Haltenhoff, A., Heil, A. and Mutschler, F.-H. (eds.) (2003) *O tempora, o mores! Römische Werte und römische Literatur in den letzten Jahrzehnten der Republik*. Beiträge zur Altertumskunde 171. Munich and Leipzig.

Hankinson, R. J. (1988) 'Stoicism, science, and divination', *Apeiron* 21: 123–60.

Hannah, R. (1996) 'Lucan *Bellum Civile* 1.649–65: the astrology of P. Nigidius Figulus revisited', *PLILS* 9: 175–90.

(2011) 'The Horologium of Augustus as a sundial', *JRA* 24: 87–95.

Hano, M. (1986) '*Haruspex* et *vates* chez Tite-Live', in Briquel and Guittard (eds.): 101–21.

Hansen, W. (1996) *Phlegon of Tralles' Book of Marvels*. Exeter.

Hardie, P. (1986) *Virgil's Aeneid. Cosmos and Imperium*. Oxford.

(1987) 'Aeneas and the omen of the swans (Verg. *Aen.* 1.393–400)', *CP* 82: 145–50.

Harries, J. (2006) *Cicero and the Jurists. From Citizens' Law to the Lawful State*. London.

Harris, W. V. (1971) *Rome in Etruria and Umbria*. Oxford.

(1979) *War and Imperialism in Republican Rome 327–70 B.C.* Oxford.

(2003) 'Roman opinions about the truthfulness of dreams', *JRS* 93: 18–34.

(2009) *Dreams and Experience in Classical Antiquity*. Cambridge, MA and London.

Harrison, E. L. (1986) 'Foundation prodigies in the *Aeneid*', *PLLS* 5: 131–64.

Harrison, S. J. (1996) '*Aeneid* 1.286: Julius Caesar or Augustus?', *PLLS* 9: 127–33.

Harrison, T. (2000) *Divinity and History. The Religion of Herodotus*. Oxford.

(2006) 'Religion and the rationality of the Greek city', in *Rethinking Revolutions through Ancient Greece*, ed. S. Goldhill and R. Osborne. Cambridge: 124–40.

Haselberger, L. (2007) *Urbem adornare. Die Stadt Rom und ihre Gestaltumwandlung unter Augustus. Rome's Metamorphosis under Augustus*. *JRA* Supplementary Series 64. Portsmouth, RI.

(2011) 'A debate on the Horologium of Augustus: controversy and clarifications', *JRA* 24: 47–73.

Hau, L. I. (2011) '*Tychê* in Polybios: narrative answers to a philosophical question', *Histos* 5: 183–207.

Haury, A. (1955) *L'ironie et l'humour chez Cicéron*. Leiden.

(1966) 'Une querelle de clocher: augures contre haruspices', in *Mélanges d'archéologie et d'histoire offerts à André Piganiol*, ed. R. Chevalier. Paris: 1623–33.

(1981) 'La faute de Didon', *REA* 83: 227–54.

Havas, L. (2000) 'Romulus Arpinas. Ein wenig bekanntes Kapitel in der römischen Geschichte des saeculum-Gedankens', *ACUSD* 36: 71–88.

Heibges, U. (1969) 'Cicero, a hypocrite in religion?', *AJP* 90: 304–12.

Heimlich, E. (2010) 'Darwin's fortune, Jonah's shipmates and the persistence of chance', in Curry (ed.): 143–77.

Heintz, J.-G. (ed.) (1997) *Oracles et prophéties dans l'antiquité*. Travaux du Centre de recherche sur le Proche-Orient et la Grèce antiques 15. Strasbourg.

Hekster, O. and Rich, J. (2006) 'Octavian and the thunderbolt: the temple of Apollo Palatinus and Roman traditions of temple building', *CQ* 56: 149–68.

Heldmann, K. (1993) *Sallust über die römische Weltherrschaft. Ein Geschichtsmodell im Catilina und seine Tradition in der hellenistischen Historiographie*. Beiträge zur Altertumskunde 34. Stuttgart.

Hellegouarc'h, J. (1963) *Le vocabulaire latin des relations et des partis politiques sous la République*. Publications de la Faculté des Lettres et Sciences Humaines de l'Université de Lille 11. Paris.

Henderson, J. (1989) 'Livy and the invention of history', in *History as Text. The Writing of Ancient History*, ed. A. Cameron. London: 66–85.

Henry, E. (1989) *The Vigour of Prophecy. A Study of Virgil's Aeneid*. Carbondale and Edwardsville.

Herrmann, L. (1935) 'Le Prodige du Rubicon', *REA* 37: 435–7.

(1960) 'Carmina Marciana', in *Hommages à Georges Dumézil*. Collection Latomus 45. Brussels: 117–23.

Heslin, P. J. (2007) 'Augustus, Domitian and the so-called Horologium Augusti', *JRS* 97: 1–20.

(2011) 'The Augustus Code: a response to L. Haselberger', *JRA* 24: 74–7.

Heurgon, J. (1959) 'The date of Vegoia's prophecy', *JRS* 49: 41–5.

Heuss, A. (1983) 'Zur inneren Zeitform bei Livius', in *Livius. Werk und Rezeption. Festschrift für Erich Burck zum 80. Geburtstag*, ed. E. Lefèvre and E. Olshausen. Munich: 175–215.

(1995) *Gesammelte Schriften*. Stuttgart.

Hickson, F. V. (1991) 'Augustus *triumphator*: manipulation of the triumphal theme in the political program of Augustus', *Latomus* 50: 124–38.

Hillard, T. W. (1996) 'Death by lightning, Pompeius Strabo and the people', *RhM* 139: 135–45.

(2005) 'Scipio Aemilianus and a prophecy of Clunia', *Historia* 54: 344–8.

Hine, H. M. (1981) *An Edition with Commentary of Seneca Natural Questions, Book Two*. New York.

Hoffmann, W. (1933) 'Wandel und Herkunft der Sibyllinischen Bücher in Rom'. Diss. Leipzig.

Hoffmann, Z. (1985/8) 'Wahrsager und Wahrsagung bei Plautus', *AAntHung* 31: 367–79.

Hohl, E. (1952) 'Caesar am Rubico', *Hermes* 80: 246–9.

Hohti, P. (1975) 'Aulus Caecina the Volaterran. Romanization of an Etruscan', in *Studies in the Romanization of Etruria*. Acta Instituti Romani Finlandiae 5. Rome: 405–33.

Holbraad, M. (2010) 'Afterword. Of ises and oughts: an endnote on divinatory obligation', in Curry (ed.): 265–74.

Hopkins, K. (1978) *Conquerors and Slaves. Sociological Studies in Roman History* 1. Cambridge.

Horsfall, N. (1973/4) 'Dido in the light of history', *PVS* 13: 1–13, reprinted in *Oxford Readings in Virgil's* Aeneid, ed. S. J. Harrison. Oxford, 1990: 127–44.

(1974a) 'The Ides of March: some new problems', *G&R* 21: 191–9.

(1974b) 'Labeo and Capito', *Historia* 23: 252–4.

(1983) 'Some problems in the "Laudatio Turiae"', *BICS* 30: 85–98.

(1989) *Cornelius Nepos, a Selection, Including the Lives of Cato and Atticus*. Oxford.

(1999) *Virgil, Aeneid 7. A Commentary. Mnemosyne* Supplement 198. Leiden, Boston and Cologne.

(2003) *The Culture of the Roman Plebs*. London.

(2006) *Virgil*, Aeneid 3. *A Commentary. Mnemosyne* Supplement 273. Leiden and Boston.

(2008) *Virgil*, Aeneid 2. *A Commentary. Mnemosyne* Supplement 299. Leiden and Boston.

Hose, M. (1995) 'Cicero als hellenistischer Epiker', *Hermes* 123: 455–69.

Hübner, W. (1970) *Dirae in römischen Epos. Über das Verhältnis von Vogeldämonen und Prodigien*. Spudasmata 21. Hildesheim and New York.

Humm, M. (2004) 'Numa et Pythagore: vie et mort d'un mythe', in *Images d'origines, origines d'une image. Hommages à Jacques Poucet*, ed. P.-A. Deproost and A. Meurant. Louvain-la-Neuve: 125–37.

(2012a) 'The curiate law and the religious nature of the power of Roman magistrates', in *Law and Religion in the Roman Republic*, ed. O. Tellegen-Couperus. *Mnemosyne* Supplements 336. Leiden and Boston: 57–84.

(2012b) 'Silence et bruits autour de la prise des auspices', in *Les sons du pouvoir dans les mondes anciens*, ed. M. T. Schettino and S. Pittia. Besançon: 275–95.

Hurlet, F. (2001) 'Les auspices d'Octavien/Auguste', *CCGG* 12: 155–80.

Hutchinson, G. O. (1998) *Cicero's Correspondence. A Literary Study*. Oxford.

Itgenshorst, T. (2008) 'Der Princeps triumphiert nicht: Vom Verschwinden des Siegesrituals in augusteischer Zeit', in *Triplici invectus triumpho. Der römische Triumph in augusteischer Zeit*, ed. H. Krasser, D. Pausch and I. Petrovic. PAwB 25. Stuttgart: 27–53.

Jacobs, J. (2010) 'Traces of the Umma series *Šumma Izbu* in Cicero, *De divinatione*', in Annus (ed.): 317–39.

Jaillard, D. and Prescendi, F. (2008) 'Pourquoi et comment connaître la volonté des dieux? Divination et possession à Rome et en Grèce', in *Religions antiques. Une introduction comparée. Égypte – Grèce – Prôche-Orient – Rome*, ed. P. Borgeaud and F. Prescendi. Geneva: 75–99.

Jakobi, R. (1990) '*Superstitio* bei Donat, Servius und Isidor', *Hermes* 118: 252–3.

Jal, P. (1961) 'La propagande religieuse à Rome au cours des guerres civiles de la fin de la République', *AC* 30: 395–414.

(1962) 'Les dieux et les guerres civiles', *REL* 40: 170–200.

(1963) *La guerre civile à Rome. Étude littéraire et morale*. Publications de la Faculté des Lettres et Sciences Humaines de Paris, Série 'Recherches' 6. Paris.

Jambon, E. (2012) 'Les signes de la nature dans l'Égypte pharaonique', in Georgoudi, Koch Piettre and Schmidt (eds.): 131–56.

Jannot, J.-R. (1998) *Devins, dieux et démons. Regards sur la religion de l'Étrurie antique*. Paris.

Janssen, L. F. (1975) 'Die Bedeutungsentwicklung von *superstitio/superstes*', *Mnemosyne* s. 4, 28: 135–88.

Jehne, M. (1987) *Der Staat des Dictators Caesar*. Passauer historische Forschungen 3. Cologne and Vienna.

Jense, T. and Rothstein, M. (eds.) (2000) *Secular Theories on Religion. Current Perspectives*. Copenhagen.

Jimenez Delgado, J. (1961a) 'Importancia de los prodigios en Tito Livio', *Helmantica* 12: 27–46.

(1961b) 'Clasificación de los prodigios titolivianos', *Helmantica* 12: 441–61.

(1963) 'Postura de Livio frente al prodigio', *Helmantica* 14: 381–419.

Jocelyn, H. D. (1966) 'The Roman nobility and the religion of the Republican state', *JRH* 4: 89–104.

(1967) *The Tragedies of Ennius. The Fragments Edited with an Introduction and Commentary*. Cambridge Classical Texts and Commentaries 10. Cambridge.

(1982–3) 'Varro's *Antiquitates rerum diuinarum* and religious affairs in the late Roman Republic', *Bulletin of the John Rylands University Library* 65: 148–205.

Johnston, S. I. (2003) 'Lost in the shuffle: Roman sortition and its discontents', *ARG* 5: 146–56.

(2005) 'Introduction: divining divination', in Johnston and Struck (eds.): 1–28.

(2008) *Ancient Greek Divination*. Malden, MA and Oxford.

Johnston, S. I. and Struck, P. T. (eds.) (2005) *Mantikê. Studies in Ancient Divination*. RGRW 155. Leiden and Boston.

Kajanto, I. (1957) *God and Fate in Livy*. Turun Yliopiston julkaisuja, sarja B, osa 64. Turku.

Kany-Turpin, J. (1999) 'Fonction de la vérité dans un énoncé augural. Le paradoxe du menteur Ateius Capito', in *Conceptions latines du sens et de la signification*, ed. M. Baratin and C. Moussy. Paris: 255–66.

(2003a) 'Météorologie et signes divinatoires dans le *De diuinatione* de Cicéron', in *Météorologie dans l'antiquité. Entre science et croyance*, ed. C. Cusset. Saint-Étienne: 367–78.

(2003b) 'La divination augurale romaine, une science des signes?', in *Ars et ratio. Sciences, art et métiers dans la philosophie hellénistique et romaine*, ed. C. Lévy, B. Besnier and A. Gigandet. Collection Latomus 273. Brussels: 61–74.

(2004) *Cicéron. De la divination. De diuinatione*. Paris.

Kany-Turpin, J. (ed.) (2005) *Signe et prédiction dans l'Antiquité*. Centre Jean Palerne Mémoires 29. Saint-Étienne.

Kany-Turpin, J. and Pellegrin, P. (1989) 'Cicero and the Aristotelian theory of divination by dreams', in *Cicero's Knowledge of the Peripatos*, ed. W. W. Fortenbaugh and P. Steinmetz. New Brunswick and London: 220–45.

Kearsley, R. (2009) 'Octavian and augury: the years 30–28 B.C.', *CQ* 59: 147–66.

Ker, J. (2009) 'Drinking from the water-clock: time and speech in Imperial Rome', *Arethusa* 42: 279–302.

Kienast, D. (1982) *Augustus. Prinzeps und Monarch*. Darmstadt.

King, C. (2003) 'The organization of Roman religious beliefs', *CA* 22: 275–312.

Kirov, J. (2010) 'Der Umgang mit Abweichungen in der römischen Republik', *HZ* 290: 297–320.

Klingshirn, W. E. (2005) 'Divination and the disciplines of knowledge according to Augustine', in *Augustine and the Disciplines. From Cassiciacum to* Confessions, ed. K. Pollmann and M. Vessey. Oxford: 113–40.

(2006) 'Inventing the *sortilegus*: lot divination and cultural identity in Italy, Rome, and the provinces', in Schultz and Harvey (eds.): 137–61.

Klynne, A. and Liljenstoppe, P. (2000) 'Where to put Augustus? A note on the placement of the Prima Porta statue', *AJP* 121: 121–8.

Kneppe, A. (1994) *Metus temporum. Zur Bedeutung von Angst in Politik und Gesellschaft der römischen Kaiserzeit des 1. und 2. Jhdts. n. Chr.* Stuttgart.

Koch, U. S. (2010) 'Three strikes and you're out! A view on cognitive theory and the first-millennium extispicy ritual', in Annus (ed.): 43–59.

Köves-Zulauf, T. (1997) 'Die Vorzeichen der Catilinarischen Verschwörung', *ACUSD* 33: 219–27.

Konrad, C. F. (1994) *Plutarch's Sertorius: A Historical Commentary*. Chapel Hill.

Konrad, C. F. (ed.) (2004) *Augusto augurio. Rerum humanarum et divinarum commentationes in honorem Jerzy Linderski*. Stuttgart.

Korenjak, M. (1999) '*Vates: a vi mentis*. Eine Etymologie Varros und ihr Schicksal in der lateinischen Literatur der frühen Kaiserzeit', *GFA* 1: 1–4.

Kragelund, P. (2001) 'Dreams, religion and politics in Republican Rome', *Historia* 50: 53–95.

Kraggerud, E. (1992) 'Which Julius Caesar? On *Aen*. 1.286–296', *SO* 67: 103–12.

Kranemann, B. and Rüpke, J. (eds.) (2003). *Das Gedächtnis des Gedächtnisses. Zur Präsenz von Ritualen in beschreibenden und reflektierenden Texten*. Europäische Religionsgeschichte 2. Marburg.

Krauss, F. B. (1930) 'An interpretation of the omens, portents, and prodigies recorded by Livy, Tacitus and Suetonius'. Diss. Philadelphia.

Krenkel, W. A. (ed.) (2002) *Marcus Terentius Varro. Saturae Menippeae* III. Subsidia Classica 6. St. Katharinen.

Kröger, H. (1940) 'Die Prodigien bei Tacitus'. Diss. Münster.

Krostenko, B. A. (2000) 'Beyond (dis)belief: rhetorical form and religious symbol in Cicero's *de Divinatione*', *TAPA* 130: 353–91.

Kroymann, J. (1975) 'Cicero und die römische Religion', in Michel and Verdière (eds.): 116–28.

Kugel, J. L. (ed.) (1990) *Poetry and Prophecy. The Beginnings of a Literary Tradition.* Ithaca and London.

Kumaniecki, K. (1959) 'Ciceros Rede de haruspicum responso', *Klio* 37: 135–52.

(1962) 'Cicerone e Varrone. Storia di una conoscenza', *Athenaeum* 40: 221–43.

Kurczyk, S. (2006) *Cicero und die Inszenierung der eigenen Vergangenheit. Autobiographisches Schreiben in der späten römischen Republik.* Europäische Geschichtsdarstellungen 8. Cologne, Weimar and Vienna.

Kurfeß, A. and Gauger, J.-D. (1998) *Sibyllinische Weissagungen. Griechisch–Deutsch*, 2nd edn. Düsseldorf and Zurich.

Kuttner, A. (1991) 'A third century BC Latin census on a Praenestine cist', *RM* 98: 141–61.

Labate, M. and Narducci, E. (1981) 'Mobilità dei modelli etici e relativismo dei valori: il "personaggio" di Attico', in *Società romana e produzione schiavistica. III. Modelli etici, diritto e trasformazioni sociali*, ed. A. Giardina and A. Schiavone. Rome and Bari: 127–82, 386–400.

Lacam, J.-C. (2010) *Variations rituelles. Les pratiques religieuses en Italie centrale et méridionale au temps de la Deuxième Guerre Punique.* CEFR 430. Rome.

Laidlaw, J. (2007) 'A well-disposed social anthropologist's problems with the "cognitive science of religion"', in Whitehouse and Laidlaw (eds.): 211–46.

Lange, C. H. (2009) *Res Publica Constituta. Actium, Apollo and the Accomplishment of the Triumviral Assignment.* Impact of Empire 10. Leiden and Boston.

Langlands, R. (2011) 'Roman *exempla* and situation ethics: Valerius Maximus and Cicero *de officiis*', *JRS* 101: 100–22.

Lantella, L. (1984) '"Finem fore nominis Etrusci"', in *Sodalitas: scritti in onore di Antonio Guarino* v, ed. V. Giuffrè. Naples: 2155–73.

La Penna, A. (1978) *Aspetti del pensiero storico latino.* Piccola biblioteca Einaudi 354. Turin.

(2005) *L'impossibile giustificazione della storia. Un'interpretazione di Virgilio.* Rome and Bari.

Lateiner, D. (2005) 'Signifying names and other ominous accidental utterances in classical historiography', *GRBS* 45: 35–57.

Latte, K. (1960) *Römische Religionsgeschichte.* Handbuch der Altertumswissenschaft 5.4. Munich.

Lausberg, M. (1970) *Untersuchungen zu Senecas Fragmenten.* Untersuchungen zur antiken Literatur und Geschichte 7. Berlin.

Lazarus, F. M. (1978–9) 'Fortune and rhetorical structure in Livy', *CJ* 74: 128–31.

Le Bœuffle, A. (1999) 'Le pouvoir et la "rétro-prédestination" ou l'art de la déformation . . . astrologique', in Smadja and Geny (eds.): 273–82.

Leeman, A. D., Pinkster, H. and Nelson, H. L. W. (1985) *M. Tullius Cicero de Oratore libri III. Kommentar.* Heidelberg.

Le Glay, M. (1976) 'Magie et sorcellerie à Rome au dernier siècle de la République', in *Mélanges offerts à Jacques Heurgon. L'Italie préromaine et la Rome républicaine* I. CEFR 27. Rome: 525–50.

Lehmann, Y. (1999) 'Comment échapper au destin: signes auguraux et pouvoir politique à Rome', in Smadja and Geny (eds.): 259–72.

Lehoux, D. (2007) *Astronomy, Weather, and Calendars in the Ancient World.* Parapegmata *and Related Texts in Classical and Near-Eastern Societies.* Cambridge.

(2012) *What Did the Romans Know? An Inquiry into Science and Worldmaking.* Chicago and London.

Lenaghan, J. O. (1969) *A Commentary on Cicero's Oration* De haruspicum responso. Amsterdam.

Leonhardt, J. (1999) *Ciceros Kritik der Philosophenschulen.* Zetemata 103. Munich.

Leppin, H. (2002) 'Atticus – zum Wertewandel in der späten römischen Republik', in *Res publica reperta. Zur Verfassung und Gesellschaft der römischen Republik und des frühen Prinzipats. Festschrift für Jochen Bleicken zum 75. Geburtstag,* ed. J. Spielvogel. Stuttgart: 192–202.

Levene, D. S. (1992) 'Sallust's *Jugurtha*: an "historical" fragment', *JRS* 82: 53–70.

(1993) *Religion in Livy. Mnemosyne Supplementum* 127. Leiden, Boston and Cologne.

(2012) 'Defining the divine in Rome', *TAPA* 142: 41–81.

Levick, B. (1982) 'Morals, politics, and the fall of the Roman Republic', *G&R* 29: 53–62.

Lévy, C. (1992) *Cicero Academicus. Recherches sur les Académiques et sur la philosophie cicéronienne.* CEFR 162. Rome.

(1997) 'De Chrysippe à Posidonius: variations stoïciennes sur le thème de la divination', in Heintz (ed.): 321–43.

Lewis, A. M. (2008) 'Augustus and his horoscope reconsidered', *Phoenix* 62: 308–37.

Liberman, G. (1998) 'Les documents sacerdotaux du collège sacris faciundis', in Moatti (ed.): 65–74.

Liébert, Y. (2006) *Regards sur la truphé étrusque.* Limoges.

Liebeschuetz, J. H. W. G. (1967) 'The religious position of Livy's history', *JRS* 57: 45–55.

(1979) *Continuity and Change in Roman Religion.* Oxford.

(1995) Review of Levene 1993, *JRS* 85: 314–15.

Liegle, J. (1942) 'L. Aemilius Paullus als Augur Maximus im Jahre 160 und das Augurium des Heils', *Hermes* 77: 249–312.

Lightfoot, J. L. (2007) *The Sibylline Oracles, with Introduction, Translation, and Commentary on the First and Second Books.* Oxford.

Linderski, J. (1969–70) 'Römischer Staat und Götterzeichen: zum Problem der obnuntiatio', *Jahrbuch der Universität Düsseldorf:* 309–22, reprinted in Linderski 1995a: 444–57.

(1982) 'Cicero and Roman divination', *PP* 37: 12–38, reprinted in Linderski 1995a: 458–84.

(1986a) 'The augural law', *ANRW* 2.16.3: 2146–2312.

(1986b) 'Watching the birds: Cicero the augur and the augural *templa*', *CP* 81: 330–40, reprinted in Linderski 1995a: 485–95.

(1989) 'Garden parlors: nobles and birds', in *Studia Pompeiana et Classica in Honor of Wilhelmina F. Jashemski. II: Classica*, ed. R. I. Curtis. New Rochelle, NY: 105–27, reprinted in Linderski 1995a: 44–66.

(1990) Review of van der Meer 1987, *CR* 85: 67–71, reprinted in Linderski 1995a: 595–9.

(1993) 'Roman religion in Livy', in Schuller (ed.): 53–70, reprinted in Linderski 1995a: 608–25.

(1995a) *Roman Questions: Selected Papers*. HABES 20. Stuttgart.

(1995b) Review of Bergemann 1992 and de Libero 1992, *CP* 90: 192–5, reprinted in Linderski 2007: 520–4.

(1996) 'Q. Scipio Imperator', in *Imperium sine fine: T. R. S. Broughton and the Roman Republic*, ed. J. Linderski. *Historia* Einzelschriften 105. Stuttgart: 145–85; reprinted in Linderski 2007: 130–74.

(2001) 'Updating the *CIL* for Italy: part 5', *JRA* 14: 513–35, reprinted in Linderski 2007: 424–57.

(2006) 'Founding the city', in *Ten Years of the Agnes Kirsopp Lake Michels Lectures at Bryn Mawr College*, ed. S. B. Faris and L. E. Lundeen. Bryn Mawr, PA: 88–107, reprinted in Linderski 2007: 3–19.

(2007) *Roman Questions II: Selected Papers*. HABES 44. Stuttgart.

Lindsay, H. (1998) 'The biography of Atticus: Cornelius Nepos on the philosophical and ethical background of Pomponius Atticus', *Latomus* 57: 324–36.

Linke, B. (2000) '*Religio* und *res publica*. Religiöser Glaube und gesellschaftliches Handeln im republikanischen Rom', in Mos maiorum. *Untersuchungen zu den Formen der Identitätsstiftung und Stabilisierung in der römischen Republik.*, ed. B. Linke and M. Stemmler. *Historia* Einzelschriften 141. Stuttgart: 269–98.

Lintott, A. W. (1972) 'Imperial expansion and moral decline in the Roman Republic', *Historia* 21: 626–38.

(2008) *Cicero as Evidence. A Historian's Companion*. Oxford.

Lisdorf, A. (2007) 'The dissemination of divination in Roman Republican times – a cognitive approach'. Diss. Copenhagen (available at www.csr-arc.com/view.php?arc=21, last accessed 29.08.12).

Liuzzi, D. (1983) *Nigidio Figulo, 'astrologo e mago'. Testimonianze e frammenti*. Lecce.

Long, A. A. (1982) 'Astrology: arguments *pro* and *contra*', in Barnes, Brunschwig, Burnyeat and Schofield (eds.): 165–92.

Lorsch Wildfang, R. S. (1997) 'Augustus' conception and the heroic tradition', *Latomus* 56: 790–9.

(2000a) 'The propaganda of omens: six dreams involving Augustus', in Lorsch Wildfang and Isager (eds.): 43–55.

(2000b) '*Fulgura et fulmina*: or what it portends when the family tomb is struck by a *fulmen quod decussit*', in Lorsch Wildfang and Isager (eds.): 67–78.

Lorsch Wildfang, R. and Isager, J. (eds.) (2000) *Divination and Portents in the Roman World.* Odense University Classical Studies 21. Odense.

Luce, T. J. (1971) 'Design and structure in Livy: 5.32–55', *TAPA* 102: 265–302.

Luciani, S. (2010) *Temps et éternité dans l'œuvre philosophique de Cicéron.* Paris.

Luhmann, N. (2004) *Law as a Social System,* trans. K. A. Ziegert. Oxford.

Lundgreen, C. (2011) *Regelkonflikte in der römischen Republik. Geltung und Gewichtung von Normen in politischen Entscheidungsprozessen. Historia* Einzelschriften 221. Stuttgart.

Luterbacher, F. (1904) *Der Prodigienglaube und Prodigienstil der Römer. Eine historisch-philologische Abhandlung.* Burgdorf.

Lyne, R. O. A. M. (1987) *Further Voices in Vergil's Aeneid.* Oxford.

Maas, M. (1992) *John Lydus and the Roman Past. Antiquarianism and Politics in the Age of Justinian.* London and New York.

MacBain, B. (1982) *Prodigy and Expiation. A Study in Religion and Politics in Republican Rome.* Collection Latomus 177. Brussels.

McDonald, W. F. (1929) 'Clodius and the *lex Aelia Fufia*', *JRS* 19: 164–79.

McGing, B. C. (1986) *The Foreign Policy of Mithridates VI Eupator King of Pontus. Mnemosyne* Supplementum 89. Leiden.

MacInnes, D. (2000) '*Dirum ostentum*: bee swarm prodigies at Roman military camps', in *Studies in Latin Literature and Roman History* x, ed. C. Deroux. Collection Latomus 254. Brussels: 56–69.

MacKendrick, P. L. (1989) *The Philosophical Books of Cicero.* London.

MacMullen, R. (1966) *Enemies of the Roman Order. Treason, Unrest, and Alienation in the Empire.* Cambridge, MA and London.

(1971) 'Social history in astrology', *AncSoc* 2: 105–16.

(1990) *Changes in the Roman Empire. Essays in the Ordinary.* Princeton.

Maffi, A. (2001) 'Nomina per sorteggio degli ambasciatori nel mondo romano', in Cordano and Grottanelli (eds.): 137–8.

Maggiani, A. (1982) 'Qualche osservazione sul fegato di Piacenza', *SE* 50: 53–88.

(2005) 'La divinazione in Etruria', in *ThesCRA* III. Los Angeles: 52–78.

Magotteaux, E. (1956) 'L'augure des douze vautours', *AC* 25: 106–11.

Magris, A. (1995) '"A che serve pregare, se il destino è immutabile?". Un problema del pensiero antico', *Elenchos* 11: 51–76.

Maier, F. K. (2012) 'Learning from history *para doxan*: a new approach to Polybius' manifold view of the past', *Histos* 6: 144–68.

Malloch, S. J. V. (2008) '*Scriba pontificius* (Livy 22.57.3 and SHA Opil. 7.2)', *Philologus* 152: 155–8.

Maltby, R. (1991) *A Lexicon of Ancient Latin Etymologies.* ARCA Classical and Medieval Texts, Papers and Monographs 25. Leeds.

Manetti, G. (1987) *Teorie del segno nell'antichità classica.* Milan.

(1993) *Theories of the Sign in Classical Antiquity,* trans. C. Richardson. Bloomington and Indianapolis.

Mangas Manjarrés, J. (2007) 'Los niños y la adivinación en la Roma antigua', in Sánchez-León (ed.): 89–110.

Mann, W.-R. (2011) 'On two Stoic "paradoxes" in Manilius', in Green and Volk (eds.): 85–103.

Mansuelli, G. A. (1998) 'Etrusca disciplina e pensiero scientifico', *Annali della Fondazione per il Museo 'Claudio Faina'* 5: 105–18.

Mantovani, D. (2009) '"Quaerere", "quaestio". Inchiesta lessicale e semantica', *Index* 37: 25–67.

Manuwald, B. (1979) *Cassius Dio und Augustus. Philologische Untersuchungen zu den Büchern 45–56 des Dionischen Geschichtswerkes.* Palingenesia 14. Wiesbaden.

Manuwald, G. (2007) *Cicero*, Philippics *3–9.* Texte und Kommentare 30. Berlin and New York.

   (2011) *Roman Republican Theatre.* Cambridge.

Manzo, A. (1969) Facete Dicta Tulliana. *Ricerca–analisi–illustrazione dei facete dicta nell'epistolario di Marco Tullio Cicerone.* Biblioteca della Rivista di Studi Classici. Saggi Vari 5. Turin.

Marastoni, S. (2008) 'Fulminare i nemici: Silla, Postumio e l'*ars fulguratoria*', *Klio* 90: 323–33.

Marinoni, E. (2002) 'Cesare al Rubicone. L'elemento soprannaturale', in *Logios aner. Studi di antichità in memoria di Mario Attilio Levi*, ed. P. G. Michelotto. Quaderni di *Acme* 55. Milan: 277–85.

Martin, D. B. (2004) *Inventing Superstition. From the Hippocratics to the Christians.* Cambridge, MA and London.

Martin, J.-P. (1982) Providentia deorum. *Recherches sur certains aspects religieux du pouvoir impérial romain.* CEFR 61. Rome.

   (1986) 'Les signes de souveraineté échus aux rois de la Rome étrusque – traditions et résurgences', in Briquel and Guittard (eds.): 16–46.

Martínez-Pinna, J. (2001) 'El "saeculum" etrusco y el final de la historia', in *El milenarismo. La percepción del tiempo en las culturas antiguas*, ed. J. Mangas and S. Montero. Madrid: 81–102, 211–17.

   (2007) 'Los Etruscos y la adivinación', in Sánchez-León (ed.): 51–88.

Massa-Pairault, F.-H. (1985) 'La divination en Étrurie. Le ɪvème siècle, période critique', in Briquel and Guittard (eds.): 56–115.

   (1991) 'Octavien, Auguste et l'*Etrusca disciplina*', in Briquel and Guittard (eds.): 5–32.

Massaro, M. (1977) '*Aniles fabellae*', *SIFC* 49: 104–35.

Mastandrea, P. (1979) *Un neoplatonico latino. Cornelio Labeone (Testimonianze e frammenti).* Études préliminaires aux religions orientales dans l'Empire romain 77. Leiden.

Mastrocinque, A. (2005) 'L'incendio del Campidoglio e la fine del saeculum etrusco', *Gerión* 23: 137–42.

Maul, S. M. (1994) 'How the Babylonians protected themselves against calamities announced by omens', in *Mesopotamian Magic. Textual, Historical and Interpretive Perspectives*, ed. T. Absuck and K. van der Toorn. Studies in Ancient Magic and Divination 1. Groningen: 123–9.

(2003) 'Omina und Orakel. A. Mesopotamien', in *Reallexicon der Assyriologie* x. Berlin and New York: 45–88.

Mayer, M. (1975) 'Sobre el fragmento 4 ed. Swoboda de Publio Nigidio Figulo', *CFC* 5: 319–28.

Mayor, A. (2010) *The Poison King. The Life and Legend of Mithradates, Rome's Deadliest Enemy*. Princeton and Oxford.

Mazurek, T. (2004) 'The *decemviri sacris faciundis*: supplication and prediction', in Konrad (ed.): 151–68.

Mazza, M. (1966) *Storia e ideologia in Tito Livio. Per un'analisi storiografica della Praefatio ai Libri ab Urbe Condita*. Testi e studi di storia antica 1. Catania.

(2005) 'La *praefatio* di Livio: una rivisitazione', in *La cultura storica nei primi due secoli dell'impero romano*, ed. L. Troiani and G. Zecchini. Monografie del Centro ricerche di documentazione sull'antichità classica 24. Rome: 41–59.

Mazzarino, S. (1957) 'Sociologia del mondo etrusco e problemi della tarda etruscità', *Historia* 6: 98–122, reprinted in Mazzarino 1980: 258–94.

(1962) 'Le alluvioni 54 a.C./23 a.C., il cognome *Augustus*, e la data di Hor. *Carm.* 1 2', *Helikon* 6: 621–4.

(1966) *Il pensiero storico classico* 1. Bari.

(1980) *Antico, tardoantico ed èra costantiniana. Volume secondo*. Bari.

van der Meer, L. B. (1979) 'Iecur Placentinum and the orientation of the Etruscan haruspex', *BABesch* 54: 49–64.

(1987) *The Bronze Liver of Piacenza. Analysis of a Polytheistic Structure*. Dutch Monographs on Ancient History and Archaeology 22. Amsterdam.

Messineo, G. (ed.) (2001) Ad Gallinas Albas. *Villa di Livia*. BCAR Supplementi 8. Rome.

Meyer, E. A. (2004) *Legitimacy and Law in the Roman World*. Tabulae *in Roman Belief and Practice*. Cambridge.

Meyer, J. C. (2002) 'Omens, prophecies and oracles in ancient decision-making', in *Ancient History Matters. Studies Presented to Jens Erik Skydsgaard on his Seventieth Birthday*, ed. K. Ascani, V. Gabrielsen, K. Kvist and A. H. Rasmussen. *ARID* Supplementum 30. Rome: 173–83.

Michel, A. and Verdière, R. (eds.) (1975) *Ciceroniana. Hommages à Kazimierz Kumaniecki*. Roma Aeterna 9. Leiden.

Michels, A. K. (1976) 'The versatility of *religio*', in *The Mediterranean World. Papers Presented in Honour of Gilbert Bagnani*. Peterborough, Ont.: 36–77.

Milani, C. (1993) 'Note sul lessico della divinazione nel mondo classico', in Sordi (ed.): 31–49.

Miles, G. B. (1995) *Livy. Reconstructing Early Rome*. Ithaca and London.

Millar, F. (1964) *A Study of Cassius Dio*. Oxford.

(1988) 'Cornelius Nepos, "Atticus," and the Roman Revolution', *G&R* 35: 40–55, reprinted in Millar 2002: 183–99.

(2002) *Rome, the Greek World, and the East 1: The Roman Republic and the Augustan Revolution*. Chapel Hill.

Miller, J. F. (2009) *Apollo, Augustus, and the Poets*. Cambridge.

Minyard, J. D. (1985) *Lucretius and the Late Republic. An Essay in Roman Intellectual History. Mnemosyne* Supplements 90. Leiden.

Mitchell, T. N. (1986) 'The *leges Clodiae* and *obnuntiatio*', *CQ* 36: 172–6.

(1991) *Cicero, the Senior Statesman.* New Haven.

Moatti, C. (1997) *La raison de Rome. Naissance de l'esprit critique à la fin de la République (IIe–Ier siècle avant Jesus-Christ).* Paris.

(2003) 'Experts, mémoire et pouvoir à Rome, à la fin de la République', *RH* 626: 303–25.

Moatti, C. (ed.) *La mémoire perdue. Recherches sur l'administration romaine.* CEFR 243. Rome.

Moeller, W. O. (1975) 'Once more the one-eyed man against Rome', *Historia* 24: 402–10.

Moles, J. L. (1983) 'Fate, Apollo, and M. Iunius Brutus', *AJP* 104: 249–56.

(1988) *Plutarch. The Life of Cicero.* Warminster.

(1989) Review of Geiger 1985, *CR* 39: 229–33.

(1993a) 'Livy's Preface', *PCPS* 39: 141–68.

(1993b) 'On reading Cornelius Nepos with Nicholas Horsfall', *LCM* 18: 76–80.

Momigliano, A. (1984) 'The theological efforts of the Roman upper classes in the first century B.C.', *CP* 79: 199–211, reprinted in Momigliano 1987: 261–77.

(1987) *Ottavo contributo alla storia degli studi classici e del mondo antico.* Storia e letteratura 169. Rome.

(1988) 'From the Pagan to the Christian Sibyl: prophecy as history of religion', in *The Uses of Greek and Latin. Historical Essays*, ed. A. C. Dionisotti, A. Grafton and J. Kraye. Warburg Institute Surveys and Texts 16. London: 3–18, reprinted in Momigliano 1992: 725–44.

(1992) *Nono contributo alla storia degli studi classici e del mondo antico*, ed. R. Di Donato. Storia e letteratura 180. Rome.

Mommsen, T. (1853) 'Theodori Mommsenii epistula re Romanorum prodigiis at Ottonem Jahnium', in *T. Livi ab urbe condita librorum CXLII periochae. Iulii Obsequentis ab anno urbis conditae DV prodigiorum liber*, ed. O. Jahn. Leipzig: XVIII–XXVI, reprinted in Mommsen 1909: 168–74.

(1859) *Die römische Chronologie bis auf Caesar*, 2nd edn. Berlin.

(1909) *Gesammelte Schriften VII. Philologische Schriften.* Berlin.

Monaca, M. (2005) *La Sibilla a Roma. I Libri Sibillini fra religione e politica. Hierá.* Collana di studi-storico religiosi 8. Cosenza.

Montero, S. (1991) *Política y adivinación en el bajo imperio romano. Emperadores y harúspices (193 D.C. – 408 D.C.).* Collection Latomus 211. Brussels.

(1993a) 'Mántica inspirada y demonología: los *harioli*', *AC* 62: 115–29.

(1993b) 'Los harúspices y la moralidad de la mujer romana', *Athenaeum* 81: 647–58.

(1993c) 'Plauto, *Mil.* 694 y los primeros *metoscopi* latinos', *Dioniso* 63: 77–82.

(1994a) *Diosas y adivinas. Mujer y adivinación en la Roma antigua.* Paradigmas 4. Madrid.

(1994b) 'Livia y la adivinación inductiva', *Polis* 6: 255–67.

(1995a) 'La interpretación romana de las prácticas hepatoscópicas extranjeras', *Gerión* 13: 155–67.

(1995b) 'Adivinación y esclavitud en la Roma antigua', *Ilu* 0: 141–56.

(1997) *Diccionario de adivinos, magos y astrólogos de la Antigüedad*. Madrid.

(1998) 'Aruspici contro donne: due tecniche divinatorie a confronto', in Aigner-Foresti (ed.): 369–84.

(2000) 'Los prodigios en la vida del ultimo Cesar', in Urso (ed.): 231–44.

(2001) 'Astrología y *Etrusca disciplina*: contactos y rivalidad', *MHNH* 1: 239–60.

(2003) 'Tiempo y espacio en los Libros Sibilinos romanos', in *Transcurrir y recorrer. La categoría espacio-temporal en las religiónes del mundo clásico*, ed. D. Segarra Crespo. Serie histórica 3. Rome and Madrid: 187–208.

(2006) *Augusto y las aves. Las aves en la Roma del Principado: prodigio, exhibición y consumo*. Colleció instrumenta 22. Barcelona.

(2007) 'Los desbordamientos del Tíber a su paso por Roma en época de Augusto', in *El agua y las ciudades romanas*, ed. J. Mangas and S. Martínez Caballero. Serie Antigüedad 2. Mostoles: 66–72.

(2010) 'César y la sacralidad de las aguas', in Urso: 285–310.

(2012) *El Emperador y los ríos. Religión, ingeniería y política en el Imperio romano*. Madrid.

Mora, F. (2003) '"Irrazionalismo" nazionalistico nel pensiero teologico di Cicerone', *BSL* 33: 3–26.

Morandi Tarabella, M. (2004) Prosopographia Etrusca. 1. *Corpus. 1. Etruria meridionale*. Studia Archaeologica 135. Rome.

Morani, M. (1984) '*Augurium augur augustus*: una questione di metodo', *Glotta* 62: 65–71.

Morelli, A. M. (2000) *L'epigramma latino prima di Catullo*. Cassino.

Morgan, L. W. G. (1997) '*Levi quidem de re* . . . : Julius Caesar as tyrant and pedant', *JRS* 87: 23–40.

Moussy, C. (1977) 'Esquisse de l'histoire de *monstrum*', *REL* 55: 345–69.

Mueller, H.-F. (2002) *Roman Religion in Valerius Maximus*. London and New York.

Murphy, T. (1998) 'Cicero's first readers: epistolary evidence for the dissemination of his works', *CQ* 48: 492–505.

Muth, R. (1978) 'Von Wesen römischer *religio*', *ANRW* 2.16.1: 290–354.

Mutschler, F.-H. (2003) 'Geschichtsbetrachtung und Werteorientierung bei Nepos und Sallust', in Haltenhoff, Heil and Mutschler (eds.): 259–85.

Naether, F. (2010) *Die Sortes Astrampsychi. Problemlosungsstrategien durch Orakel im römischen Ägypten*. Orientalische Religionen in der Antike 3. Tübingen.

Nagy, A. A. (2002) '*Superstitio* et *coniuratio*', *Numen* 49: 178–92.

Narducci, E. (1983) 'La più antica citazione delle *familiares* di Cicerone', *Maia* 35: 20–1, reprinted in Narducci 2004: 235–7.

(2004) *Cicerone e i suoi interpreti. Studi sull'Opera e la Fortuna*. Testi e studi di cultura classica 29. Pisa.

Nasse, C. (1999) 'Zum Begriff *hostia consultatoria* (Macr. Sat. 3,5,5)', in *Zwischen Krise und Alltag. Antike Religionen im Mittelmeerraum = Conflit et normalité. Religions anciennes dans l'espace méditerranéen*, ed. C. Batsch, U. Egelhaaf-Gaiser and R. Stepper. PAwB 1. Stuttgart: 111–24.

Nelis, D. P. (2004) 'La Sibylle et Médée: Virgile et la tradition argonautique', in Bouquet and Mozadec (eds.): 61–74.

Neri, V. (1986) 'Dei, Fato e divinazione nella letteratura Latina del 1 sec. d.C.', in *ANRW* 2.16.3: 1974–2051.

Newlands, C. E. (1995) *Playing with Time. Ovid and the Fasti*. Ithaca and London.

Newman, J. K. (1967) *The Concept of Vates in Augustan Poetry*. Collection Latomus 89. Brussels.

Newman, J. K. and Newman, F. S. (2005) *Troy's Children. Lost Generations in Virgil's Aeneid*. Spudasmata 101. Hildesheim and New York.

Nice, A. T. (1999) 'Divination and Roman historiography'. Diss. Exeter.

(2001) 'Ennius or Cicero? The disreputable diviners at Cic. *De Div.* 1.132', *AClass* 44: 153–66.

(forthcoming) 'Understanding religious competition in the later Roman Republic', in *Competition and Religion in Antiquity*, ed. D. Engels and P. Van Nuffelen.

Nisbet, R. G. M. (1978) 'Virgil's Fourth *Eclogue*: Easterners and Westerners', *BICS* 25: 59–78, reprinted in Nisbet 1995: 47–75.

(1995) *Collected Papers on Latin Literature*, ed. S. J. Harrison. Oxford.

Nisbet, R. G. M. and Hubbard, M. (1970) *A Commentary on Horace: Odes Book 1*. Oxford.

Noreña, C. F. (2011) *Imperial Ideals in the Roman West. Representation, Circulation, Power*. Cambridge.

North, J. A. (1967) 'The inter-relation of state religion and politics in Roman public life from the end of the Second Punic War to the time of Sulla'. Diss. Oxford (available at www.homepages.ucl.ac.uk/~ucrajan/, last accessed 29.08.12).

(1976) 'Conservatism and change in Roman religion', *PBSR* 44: 1–12.

(1979) 'Religious toleration in Republican Rome', *PCPS* 25: 85–103.

(1989) 'Religion in Republican Rome', in *Cambridge Ancient History* VII. Cambridge: 573–624.

(1990) 'Diviners and divination at Rome', in *Pagan Priests*, ed. M. Beard and J. North. London: 51–71.

(2000a) 'Prophet and text in the third century BC', in Bispham and Smith (eds.): 92–107, 164–6.

(2000b) *Roman Religion. Greece & Rome*. New Surveys in the Classics 30. Oxford.

(2008) 'Action and ritual in Roman historians; or how Horatius held the door-post', in *Religion and Society. Rituals, Resources and Identity in the Ancient Graeco-Roman World*, ed. A. H. Rasmussen and S. W. Rasmussen. *ARID* Supplementum 40. Rome: 23–36.

North, J. A. and Price, S. R. F. (eds.) (2011) *The Religious History of the Roman Empire. Pagans, Jews, and Christians*. Oxford.

Nougayrol, J. (1955) 'Les rapports des haruspicines étrusque et assyro-babylonienne, et le foie d'argile de *Falerii Veteres* (Villa Giulia 3786)', *CRAI* 99: 509–17.

Novak, M. G. (1991) 'Adivinhação, supersticão e religião no ultimo século da República (Cícero e Lucrécio)', *Classica* 4: 145–61.

Novara, A. (1982 and 1983) *Les idées romaines sur le progrès d'après les écrivains de la République (essai sur le sens latin du progrès)*. 2 vols. Publications de la Sorbonne. Histoire ancienne et médiévale 9–10. Paris.

Oakley, S. P. (1998) *A Commentary in Livy. Books VI–X. Volume II: Books VII–VIII*. Oxford.

Obbink, D. (1992) '"What all men believe – must be true": common conceptions and *consensio omnium* in Aristotle and Hellenistic philosophy', *OSAP* 10: 193–231.

Ogden, D. (2001) *Greek and Roman Necromancy*. Princeton and Oxford.

Ogilvie, R. M. (1965) *A Commentary on Livy Books 1–5*. Oxford.

O'Hara, J. (1987) '*Somnia ficta* in Lucretius and Lucilius', *CQ* 37: 517–19.

(1990) *Death and the Optimistic Prophecy in Vergil's Aeneid*. Princeton.

(1996) *True Names. Vergil and the Alexandrian Tradition of Etymological Wordplay*. Ann Arbor.

Oliphant, S. G. (1912) 'The use of the omen in Plautus and Terence', *CJ* 7: 165–73.

Opsomer, J. (1996) 'Divination and academic "scepticism" according to Plutarch', in *Plutarchea Lovaniensia*, ed. L. Van der Stockt. Studia Hellenistica 32. Leuven: 165–94.

Orlin, E. M. (1997) *Temples, Religion, and Politics in the Roman Republic. Mnemosyne* Supplementum 164. Leiden and Boston.

(2002) 'Foreign cults in Republican Rome: rethinking the Pomerial rule', *MAAR* 47 (2002), 1–18.

(2007) 'Augustan religion and the reshaping of Roman memory', *Arethusa* 40: 73–92.

(2008) 'Octavian and Egyptian cults: redrawing the boundaries of Romanness', *AJP* 129: 231–53.

(2010) *Foreign Cults in Rome. Creating a Roman Empire*. Oxford.

Orth, W. (1994) 'Verstorbene werden zu Sternen. Geistesgeschichtlicher Hintergrund und politische Implikationen des Kasterismos in der frühen römischen Kaiserzeit', *Laverna* 5: 148–66.

(1996) 'Astrologie und Öffentlichkeit in der frühen römischen Kaiserzeit', in *Kommunikation in politischen und kultischen Gemeinschaften. Stätten und Formen der Kommunikation im Altertum* v, ed. G. Binder and K. Ehlich. Bochumer Altertumswissenschaftliches Colloquium 24. Trier: 99–132.

Osgood, J. (2006) *Caesar's Legacy. Civil War and the Emergence of the Roman Empire*. Cambridge.

Otto, W. F. (1909) '*Religio* und *superstitio*', *Archiv für Religionswissenschaft* 12: 533–54.

(1913) 'Hirpi Sorani', *RE* VIII.2. Stuttgart: 1933–5.

Paden, W. E. (2000) 'Religion, world, plurality', in Jense and Rothstein (eds.): 193–209.

Pailler, J.-M. (1988) *Bacchanalia. La répression de 186 av. J.-C. à Rome et en Italie: vestiges, images, tradition*. BEFAR 270. Rome.

Paladino, I. (1989) 'Modello "fatale" e modello funzionale nel comportamento delle *gentes*', *SMSR* 55: 31–43.

Palmer, R. E. A. (1970) *The Archaic Community of the Romans*. Cambridge.

Palombi, D. (1993) 'Columna rostrata M. Aemilii Paulli', in *LTUR* I, ed. E. M. Steinby. Rome: 307–8.

Panayotakis, C. (2010) *Decimus Laberius. The Fragments*. Cambridge Classical Texts and Commentaries 46. Cambridge.

Parke, H. W. (1988) *Sibyls and Sibylline Prophecy in Classical Antiquity*. London and New York.

Parker, R. C. T. (1985) 'Greek states and Greek oracles', in *CRUX. Essays in Greek History Presented to G. E. M. de Ste. Croix*, ed. P. A. Cartledge and F. D. Harvey. London: 298–326.

(2012) 'Divination: Greek', in *The Oxford Classical Dictionary*, ed. S. Hornblower, A. J. S. Spawforth and E. Eidinow, 4th edn. Oxford: 469–70.

Paschall, D. (1936) 'The origin and semantic development of Latin *vitium*', *TAPA* 67: 219–31.

Paschoud, F. (1993) 'Réflexions sur quelques aspects de l'idéologie patriotique romaine de Tite-Live', in Schuller (ed.): 125–49.

Paschoud, F. (ed.) (2000) *Zosime. Histoire nouvelle. Tome I. Livres I–II*. Paris.

Pasco-Pranger, M. (2000) '*Vates operosus*: vatic poetics and antiquarianism in Ovid's *Fasti*', *CW* 93: 275–91.

(2002) 'A Varronian vatic numa? Ovid's *Fasti* and Plutarch's *Life of Numa*', in *Clio and the Poets. Augustan Poetry and the Traditions of Ancient Historiography*, ed. D. S. Levene and D. P. Nelis. *Mnemosyne* Supplement 224. Leiden, Boston and Cologne: 291–312.

Patera, M. (2012) 'Le corbeau: un signe dans le monde grec?', in Georgoudi, Koch Piettre and Schmidt (eds.): 157–75.

Paul, G. M. (1984) *A Historical Commentary on Sallust's* Bellum Jugurthinum. ARCA, Classical and Medieval Texts, Papers, and Monographs 13. Liverpool.

Pavis d'Escurac, H. (1981) 'La pratique augurale romaine à la fin de la République: scepticisme, tradition', in *Religion et culture dans la cité italienne de l'Antiquité à nos jours. Actes du colloque du Centre interdisciplinaire de recherches sur l'Italie, des 8–9–10 Novembre 1979*, Strasbourg: 27–39.

(1993) 'Siècle et jeux séculaires', *Ktema* 18: 79–89.

Pease, A. S. (1920) *M. Tulli Ciceronis De Divinatione Liber Primus*. University of Illinois Studies in Language and Literature 6.2. Urbana.

(1923) *M. Tulli Ciceronis De Divinatione Liber Secundus*. University of Illinois Studies in Language and Literature 8.2. Urbana.

(1958) *M. Tulli Ciceronis De Natura Deorum Libri Secundus et Tertius*. Cambridge, MA.

Peglau, M. (2003) 'Varro, ein Antiquar zwischen Tradition und Aufklärung', in Haltenhoff, Heil and Mutschler (eds.): 137–64.

Pelling, C. (1997) 'Tragical dreamer. Some dreams in the Roman historians', *G&R* 44: 197–212.

(2011) *Plutarch, Caesar.* Oxford.

Pentikäinen, J. (2010) 'Central Asian and northern European shamanism', in Curry (ed.): 47–67.

Peppel, M. (2007) '"Nicht für das römische Volk, sondern für alle guten und starken Völker" (Cicero): Die Universalisierung von Religion in der späten römischen Republik', in *Antike Religionsgeschichte in räumlicher Perspektive*, ed. J. Rüpke. Tübingen: 18–22.

Perfigli, M. (2004) Indigitamenta. *Divinità funzionali e funzionalità divina nella religione romana.* Anthropoi 2. Pisa.

Perkell, C. G. (1989) *The Poet's Truth. A Study of the Poet in Virgil's* Georgics. Berkeley, Los Angeles and London.

Perlwitz, O. (1992) *Titus Pomponius Atticus. Untersuchungen zur Person eines einflußreichen Ritters in der ausgehenden römischen Republik. Hermes Einzelschriften* 58. Stuttgart.

Pfaff-Reydellet, M. (2009) 'Ovids Fasti: Der Kaiser tritt in den öffentlichen Kalender ein', in Bendlin and Rüpke (eds.): 156–69.

Pfeffer, F. (1976) *Studien zur Mantik in der Philosophie der Antike.* Beiträge zur klassichen Philologie. Meisenheim am Glan.

Pfiffig, A. J. (1961) 'Eine etruskische Prophezeiung', *Gymnasium* 68: 55–64.

(1964) *Religio Iguvina. Philologische und religionsgeschichtliche Studien zu den Tabulae Iguvinae.* Österreichische Akademie der Wissenschaften. Philosophisch-historische Klasse. Denkschriften 84. Vienna.

Phillips III, C. R. (1991) '*Nullum crimen sine lege*: socioreligious sanctions on magic', in *Magika Hiera. Ancient Greek Magic and Religion*, ed. C. A. Faraone and D. Obbink. Oxford: 260–76.

Piccaluga, G. (1976) 'I Marsi e gli Hirpi. Due diversi modi di sistemare le minoranze etniche', in Magia, *Studi di storia delle religioni in memoria di Raffaela Garosi*, ed. P. Xella. Rome: 207–31.

Piganiol, A. (1951) 'Sur le calendrier brontoscopique de Nigidius Figulus', in *Studies in Roman Economic and Social History in Honor of Allan Chester Johnson*, ed. P. R. Coleman-Norton. Princeton: 79–87, reprinted in Piganiol 1973: 48–55.

(1973) *Scripta varia II. Les origines de Rome et la République.* Collection Latomus 132. Brussels.

Pighi, I. B. (ed.) (1965) *De ludis saecularibus populi Romani Quiritium: libri sex,* 2nd edn. Amsterdam.

Pina Polo, F. (2011) *The Consul at Rome. The Civil Functions of the Consuls in the Roman Republic.* Cambridge.

Plasberg, O. and Ax, W. (eds.) (1933) *De natura deorum.* 2nd edition, Stuttgart.

Poccetti, P. (1998) '"*Fata canit foliisque notas et nomina mandat*". Scrittura e forme oracolari nell'Italia antica', in Chirassi Colombo and Seppilli (eds.): 75–105.

Pötscher, W. (1978) 'Das römische Fatum – Begriff und Verwendung', *ANRW* 2.16.1: 393–424.

Pollard, J. (1977) *Birds in Greek Life and Myth*. London.

Potter, D. S. (1990) *Prophecy and History in the Crisis of the Roman Empire. A Historical Commentary on the* Thirteenth Sibylline Oracle. Oxford.

(1994) *Prophets and Emperors. Human and Divine Authority from Augustus to Theodosius*. Revealing Antiquity 7. Cambridge, MA.

Poulle, B. (1999) 'Les présages de l'arrivée de Galba au pouvoir', in Smadja and Geny (eds.): 33–42.

Powell, A. (2009) 'Augustus' age of apology: an analysis of the Memoirs – and an argument for two further fragments', in Smith and Powell: 173–94.

Powell, J. G. F. (1995a) Response to Tarver 1995, in Sommerstein (ed.): 59–64.

(1995b) 'Cicero's translations from the Greek', in Powell (ed.): 273–300.

Powell, J. G. F. (ed.) (1995) *Cicero the Philosopher. Twelve Papers*. Oxford.

Prescendi, F. (2000) *Frühzeit und Gegenwart. Eine Studie zur Auffassung und Gestaltung der Vergangenheit in Ovids* Fastorum libri. Studien zur klassischen Philologie 116. Frankfurt.

(2007) *Décrire et comprendre le sacrifice. Les réflexions des Romains sur leur propre religion à partir de la littérature antiquaire*. PAwB 19. Stuttgart.

Prescendi, F. and Volokhine, Y. (eds.) (2011) *Dans le laboratoire de l'historien des religions. Mélanges offerts à Philippe Borgeaud*. Geneva.

Price, S. R. F. (1996) 'The place of religion: Rome in the early Empire', in *Cambridge Ancient History* X, 2nd edn. Cambridge: 812–47.

(2003) 'Homogénéité et diversité dans les religions à Rome', *ARG* 5: 180–97.

(2011) 'Homogeneity and diversity in the religions of Rome', in North and Price (eds.): 253–75 (English translation of Price 2003).

Prosdocimi, A. L. (1972) 'Redazione e struttura testuale delle Tavole iguvine', *ANRW* 1.2: 593–699.

Pryzwansky, M. M. (2009–10) 'Cornelius Nepos: key issues and critical approaches', *CJ* 105: 97–108.

Purcell, N. (1995) 'Literate games: Roman urban society and the game of alea', *PP* 147: 3–37.

Quiter, R. J. (1984) *Aeneas und die Sibylle. Die rituellen Motive im sechsten Buch der Aeneis*. Beiträge zur klassischen Philologie 162. Königstein.

Rambaud, M. (1966) *L'art de la déformation historique dans les Commentaires de César*, 2nd edn. Paris.

Ramelli, I. (2003) *Cultura e religione etrusca nel mondo romano. La cultura etrusca dalla fine dell'indipendenza*. Studi di storia greca e romana 8. Alessandria.

Ramsey, J. T. (2000) '"Beware the Ides of March!": an astrological prediction?', *CQ* 50: 440–54.

(2003) *Cicero. Philippics I–II*. Cambridge.

(2007) *Sallust's* Bellum Catilinae, 2nd edn. Oxford.

Ramsey, J. T. and Licht, A. L. (1997) *The Comet of 44 BC and Caesar's Funeral Games*. APA American Classical Studies 39. Atlanta.

Rasmussen, S. W. (2000) 'Cicero's stand on prodigies. A non-existent dilemma?', in Lorsch Wildfang and Isager (eds.): 9–24.

(2003) *Public Portents in Republican Rome. ARID* Supplementum 34. Rome.

Rawson, E. (1971) 'Prodigy lists and the use of the Annales Maximi', *CQ* 21: 158–69, reprinted in Rawson 1991: 1–15.

(1973) 'Scipio, Laelius, Furius and the ancestral religion', *JRS* 63: 161–74, reprinted in Rawson 1991: 80–101.

(1974) 'Religion and politics in the late second century B.C. at Rome', *Phoenix* 28: 193–212, reprinted in Rawson 1991: 149–68.

(1978a) 'Caesar, Etruria and the disciplina Etrusca', *JRS* 68: 132–52, reprinted in Rawson 1991: 290–323.

(1978b) 'The introduction of logical organization in Roman prose literature', *PBSR* 46: 12–34, reprinted in Rawson 1991: 324–51.

(1985) *Intellectual Life in the Late Roman Republic.* London.

(1991) *Roman Culture and Society.* Oxford.

Regell, P. (1878) 'De augurum publicorum libris part. I'. Diss. Wroclaw.

(1881) 'Die Schautempla der Augurn', *Neue Jahrbücher für klassische Philologie* 12: 597–637.

(1882) 'Fragmenta auguralia', *Programm, Königliches Gymnasium zu Hirschberg* 164: 3–19.

(1893) 'Commentarii in librorum auguralium fragmenta specimen', *Programm, Königliches Gymnasium zu Hirschberg* 189: 3–22.

(1904) 'Beiträge zur antiken Auguralliteratur', *Programm, Königliches Gymnasium zu Hirschberg* 226: 3–10.

Reggi, G. (2002) 'Cesare, *de bello civili* III 105, 3–6', *PP* 57: 216–26.

Rehak, P. (2001) 'Aeneas or Numa? Rethinking the meaning of the Ara Pacis Augustae', *ABull* 83: 190–208.

(2006) *Imperium and Cosmos. Augustus and the Northern Campus Martius*, ed. J. G. Younger. Madison.

Reinhold, M. (1986) *From Republic to Principate. An Historical Commentary on Cassius Dio's Roman History Books 49–52 (36–29 B.C.).* American Philological Association Monograph Series 34. Atlanta.

Repici, L. (1991) 'Aristotele, gli Stoici e il libro dei sogni nel *De divinatione* di Cicerone', *Métis* 6: 167–203.

(1995) 'Gli Stoici e la divinazione secondo Cicerone', *Hermes* 123: 175–92.

(1996) 'Il sapiente stoico, la divinazione, la città', *QS* 44: 41–69.

Requena, M. (2001) *El emperador predestinado. Los presagios de poder en época imperial romana.* Madrid.

Rich, J. W. (1990) *Cassius Dio. The Augustan Settlement (Roman History 53–55.9).* Warminster.

Richardson, J. H. (2011) 'The Vestal Virgins and the use of the *Annales Maximi*', in Richardson and Santangelo (eds.): 91–106.

Richardson, J. H. and Santangelo, F. (eds.) (2011) *Priests and State in the Roman World.* PAwB 33. Stuttgart.

Richardson, J. S. (2008) *The Language of Empire. Rome and the Idea of Empire from the Third Century BC to the Second Century AD*. Cambridge.

Ripat, P. (2006) 'Roman omens, Roman audiences, and Roman history', *G&R* 53: 155–74.

(2011) 'Expelling misconceptions: astrologers at Rome', *CP* 106: 115–54.

Rives, J. (1995) 'Human sacrifice among pagans and Christians', *JRS* 85: 65–85.

Rizzo, G. E. (1932) 'La base di Augusto', *BCAR* 60: 7–109.

Robinson, M. (2010) A *Commentary on Ovid's* Fasti, *Book 2*. Oxford.

Roche, P. (2009) *Lucan De bello ciuili Book 1*. Oxford.

Roller, M. B. (2004) 'Exemplarity in Roman culture: the cases of Horatius Cocles and Cornelia', *CP* 99: 1–56.

Romano, E. (2008) 'Oracoli divini e responsi di giuristi. Note sulla *interpretatio* enniana nell'Euhemerus', in *Amicitiae templa serena. Studi in onore di Giuseppe Aricò* II, ed. L. Castagna and C. Riboldi. Milan: 1433–48.

(2009–10) 'Senso del passato e paradigma dell'antico: per una rilettura del *De legibus* di Cicerone', *Incontri triestini di filologia classica* 9: 1–44.

Ronca, I. (1992) 'What's in two names: old and new thoughts on the history and etymology of *religio* and *superstitio*', *RPL* 15: 43–60.

Rose, C. B. (2005) 'The Parthians in Augustan Rome', *AJA* 109: 21–75.

Rosen, K. (1985) 'Die falschen Numabücher. Politik, Religion und Literatur in Rom 181 v. Chr.', *Chiron* 15: 65–90.

Rosenberger, V. (1998) *Gezähmte Götter. Das Prodigienwesen der römischen Republik*. HABES 27. Stuttgart.

(2003) 'Die verschwundene Leiche. Überlegungen zur Auffindung des Sarkophags Numas im Jahre 181 v. Chr.', in Kranemann and Rüpke (eds.): 39–59.

(2005) 'Prodigien aus Italien: geographische Verteilung und religiöse Kommunikation', *CCGG* 16: 235–57.

(2007) 'Republican *nobiles*: controlling the *res publica*', in *A Companion to Roman Religion*, ed. J. Rüpke. Oxford and Malden, MA: 292–303.

Rosenblitt, J. A. (2011) 'The "*devotio*" of Sallust's Cotta', *AJP* 132: 397–427.

Rosenstein, N. (1995) 'Sorting out the lot in Republican Rome', *AJP* 116: 43–75.

Ross, R. C. (1969) '*Superstitio*', *CJ* 64: 354–8.

Rossi, A. (2004a) *Contexts of War. Manipulation of Genre in Virgilian Battle Narrative*. Ann Arbor.

(2004b) 'Parallel lives: Hannibal and Scipio in Livy's Third Decade', *TAPA* 134: 359–81.

Rubino, J. (1839) *Untersuchungen über römische Verfassung und Geschichte I, 1*. Cassel.

Ruch, M. (1958) *Le préambule dans les œuvres philosophiques de Cicéron. Essai sur la genèse et l'art du dialogue*. Publications de la Faculté des Lettres de l'Université de Strasbourg 136. Paris.

(1966) 'La capture du devin (Livius v 15)', *REL* 44: 333–50.

(1972) 'Le thème de la croissance organique dans la pensée historique des Romains, de Caton à Florus', *ANRW* 1.2: 827–41.

Runes, M. (1926) 'Geschichte des Wortes *vates*', in *Festschrift für Universitäts-Professor Paul Kretschmer. Beiträge zur griechischen und lateinischen Sprachforschung*. Vienna, Leipzig and New York: 202–16.

Rüpke, J. (1990) *Domi militiae. Die religiöse Konstruktion des Krieges in Rom*. Stuttgart.

   (1995) *Kalender und Öffentlichkeit. Die Geschichte der Repräsentation und religiösen Qualifikation von Zeit in Rom*. Religionsgeschichtliche Versuche und Vorarbeiten 40. Berlin and New York.

   (1996a) 'Controllers and professionals: analyzing religious specialists', *Numen* 43: 241–62.

   (1996b) '*Quis vetat et stellas . . . ?* Les levers des étoiles et la tradition calendaire chez Ovide', in *Les astres 1. Les astres et les mythes, la description du ciel*, ed. B. Bakhouche, A. Moreau and J.-C. Turpin. Montpellier: 293–306.

   (2001) *Die Religion der Römer*. Munich.

   (2002) 'Accius als Theologe', in *Accius und seine Zeit*, ed. S. Faller and G. Manuwald. Identitäten und Alteritäten 13. Würzburg: 255–70.

   (2003) 'Acta aut agenda. Schrift–Performanz–Beziehungen in der römischen Religionsgeschichte', in Kranemann and Rüpke (eds.): 11–38.

   (2004) 'Acta aut agenda: relations of script and performance', in Barchiesi, Rüpke and Stephens (eds.): 23–43.

   (2005a) *Fasti sacerdotum. Die Mitglieder der Priesterschaften und das sakrale Funktionspersonal römischer, griechischer, orientalischer und jüdisch-christlicher Kulte in der Stadt Rom von 300 v. Chr. bis 499 n. Chr.* PAwB 12. Stuttgart.

   (2005b) 'Divination et décisions politiques dans la République romaine', *CCGG* 16: 217–33.

   (2005c) 'Varro's *tria genera theologiae*: religious thinking in the Late Republic', *Ordia prima* 4: 107–29.

   (2006) 'Ennius's *Fasti* in Fulvius's temple: Greek rationality and Roman tradition', *Arethusa* 39: 489–512.

   (2007a) 'Literatur als Medium und als Spiegel der Verbreitung von Religion im römischen Reich', in *Antike Religionsgeschichte in räumlicher Perspektive*, ed. J. Rüpke. Tübingen: 125–34.

   (2007b) '*Religio* and *religiones* in Roman thinking', *LEC* 75: 67–78.

   (2009a) 'Antiquar und Theologe: systematisierende Beschreibung römischer Religion bei Varro', in Bendlin and Rüpke (eds.): 73–88.

   (2009b) 'Between rationalism and ritualism: on the origins of religious discourse in the late Roman Republic', *ARG* 11: 123–43.

   (2010a) 'Religious pluralism', in *The Oxford Handbook of Roman Studies*, ed. A. Barchiesi and W. Scheidel. Oxford: 748–66.

   (2010b) 'Zwischen Rationalismus und Ritualismus: zur Entstehung des Diskurses "Religion" in der späten römischen Republik', in *Religion und Bildung. Medien und Funktionen religiösen Wissens in der Kaiserzeit*, ed. C. Frateantonio and H. Krasser. PAwB 30. Stuttgart: 29–45.

(2011a) *The Roman Calendar from Numa to Constantine. Time, History and the Fasti*, trans. D. M. B. Richardson. Oxford and Malden, MA.

(2011b) *Von Jupiter zu Christus. Religionsgeschichte in römischer Zeit.* Darmstadt.

(2011c) 'Reichsreligion? Überlegungen zur Religionsgeschichte des antiken Mittelmeerraums in der römischen Zeit', *HZ* 292: 297–322.

(2011d) 'Rationalité grecque et société romaine: contextes politiques et intellectuels de la religion de la République tardive', in Prescendi and Volokhine (eds.): 385–405.

(2012a) *Religion in Republican Rome. Rationalization and Religious Change.* Philadelphia.

(2012b) 'Divination romaine et rationalité grecque dans la Rome du IIe siècle avant notre ère', in Georgoudi, Koch Piettre and Schmidt (eds.): 479–500.

Rüpke, J. and Belayche, N. (eds.) (2005) 'Divination romaine', in *ThesCRA* III. Los Angeles: 79–104.

Russo, F. (2005) 'I *carmina Marciana* e le tradizioni sui Marcii', *PP* 60: 5–32.

(2008) 'Su alcuni aspetti dei *ludi saeculares* del 249 a.C.', *SCO* 54: 115–35.

(2012) 'Kinship in Roman–Italian relationships: diverse traditions, perspectives and interpretations in Velleius Paterculus and other Roman and Greek historical writers', *Histos* 6: 228–56.

Sabbatucci, G. (1989) *Divinazione e cosmologia.* La Cultura 92. Milan.

Sacchetti, L. (1996) 'Prodigi e cronaca religiosa. Uno studio sulla storiografia latina arcaica', *MAL* ser. 9, 8: 153–258.

Sachot, M. (1991) '"Religio/Superstitio". Historique d'une subversion et d'un retournement', *RHR* 208: 355–94.

Sailor, D. (2006) 'Dirty linen, fabrication, and the authorities of Livy and Augustus', *TAPA* 136: 329–88.

de Saint-Denis, E. (1942) 'Les énumérations des prodiges dans l'œuvre de Tite-Live', *RPh* 16: 126–42.

de Ste. Croix, G. E. M. (2006) *Christian Persecution, Martyrdom, and Orthodoxy*, ed. M. Whitby and J. Streeter. Oxford.

Samotta, I. (2009) *Das Vorbild der Vergangenheit. Geschichtsbild und Reformvorschläge bei Cicero und Sallust. Historia* Einzelschriften 204. Stuttgart.

Sánchez-León, M. L. (ed.) (2007) *L'endevinació al món clàssic.* Religions del món antic 6. Palma.

Sandberg, K. (2009) 'Isis Capitolina and the *pomerium*. Notes on the augural topography of the Capitolium', *Arctos* 43: 141–60.

Santangelo, F. (2005a) 'The religious tradition of the Gracchi', *ARG* 7: 198–214.

(2005b) 'Prodigies at Privernum. A note on Cicero, *div.* 1 97', *AncSoc* 35: 167–73.

(2007a) *Sulla, the Elites and the Empire. A Study of Roman Policies in Italy and the Greek East.* Impact of Empire 8. Leiden and Boston.

(2007b) 'Prediction and divination in Diodorus', *DHA* 33: 115–26.

(2008) 'The fetials and their *ius*', *BICS* 51: 63–93.

(2011) '*Pax deorum* and pontiffs', in Richardson and Santangelo (eds.): 161–86.

(2012) 'Law and divination in the late Roman Republic', in *Law and Religion in the Roman Republic*, ed. O. Tellegen-Couperus. *Mnemosyne* Supplements 336. Leiden and Boston: 31–54.

(forthcoming) '*Saturnia regna* revisited', in *Andreas Alföldi in the Twenty-First Century*, ed. J. H. Richardson and F. Santangelo.

Santi, C. (2000) 'I libri sibyllini e il problema delle prime consultazioni', *SMSR* 66: 21–32.

Santini, C. (1988) 'Letteratura prodigiale e *sermo prodigialis* in Giulio Ossequente', *Philologus* 132: 210–26.

Satterfield, S. (2008) 'Rome's Own Sibyl. The Sibylline Books in the Roman Republic and Early Empire'. Diss. Princeton.

(2011) 'Notes on Phlegon's hermaphrodite oracle and the publication of oracles in Rome', *RhM* 154: 117–24.

(2012a) 'Intention and exoticism in Magna Mater's introduction to Rome', *Latomus* 71: 373–91.

(2012b) 'Livy and the timing of expiation in the Roman year', *Histos* 6: 67–90.

Scanlon, T. F. (1980) *The Influence of Thucydides on Sallust*. Heidelberg.

Schaefer, H. (1977) '*Divinatio*. Die antike Bedeutung des Begriffs und sein Gebrauch in der neuzeitlichen Philologie', *Archiv für Begriffsgeschichte* 21: 188–225.

Schäublin, C. (1986) 'Ementita Auspicia', *WS* 20: 165–81.

(1991) *Marcus Tullius Cicero. Über die Wahrsagung. De Divinatione. Lateinisch–Deutsch*. Munich and Zurich.

Schallenberg, M. (2008) *Freiheit und Determinismus. Ein philosophischer Kommentar zu Ciceros Schrift De fato*. Quellen und Studien zur Philosophie 75. Berlin and New York.

Scheid, J. (1985a) 'Religion et superstition à l'époque de Tacite: quelques réflexions', in *Religión, superstición y magia en el mundo romano*. Cadiz: 19–34.

(1985b) 'Numa et Jupiter, ou les dieux citoyens de Rome', *Archives des sciences sociales des religions* 59: 41–53.

(1987–9) 'La parole des dieux. L'originalité du dialogue des Romains avec leurs dieux', *Opus* 6–8: 125–36.

(1992) 'Myth, cult and reality in Ovid's *Fasti*', *PCPS* 38: 118–31.

(1995) '*Graeco ritu*: a typically Roman way of honoring the gods', *HSCP* 97: 15–31.

(1997) 'La religion des Romains à la fin de la République et au début de l'Empire. Un problème généralement mal posé', in *Die späte römische Republik/La fin de la République romaine. Un débat franco-allemand d'histoire et d'historiographie*, ed. H. Bruhns, J.-M. David and W. Nippel. CEFR 235. Rome: 127–39.

(1998a) *La religion des Romains*. Paris.

(1998b) 'Les Livres Sibyllins et les archives des quindécemvirs', in Moatti (ed.): 11–26.

(1999a) 'Auguste et le grand pontificat. Politique et droit sacré au début du Principat', *RHD* 77: 1–19.

(1999b) 'The expiation of impieties committed without intention and the formation of Roman theology', in *Transformations of the Inner Self in Ancient Religions*, ed. J. Assmann and G. Stroumsa. Studies in the History of Religions 83. Leiden, Boston and Cologne: 331–48.

(2000) 'Dell'importanza di scegliere bene le fonti. L'esempio dei *ludi* secolari', *Scienze dell'Antichità* 10: 645–57.

(2001a) *Religion et piété à Rome*, 2nd edn. Paris.

(2001b) 'Honorer le prince et vénérer les dieux: culte public, cultes des quartiers et culte impérial dans la Rome augustéenne', in *Rome, les Césars et la ville aux deux premiers siècles de notre ère*, ed. N. Belayche. Rennes: 85–105.

(2005) 'Les sénateurs et le religieux: obligations publiques et convictions privées', in *Senatores populi Romani. Realität und mediale Präsentation einer Führungsschicht*, ed. W. Eck and M. Heil. HABES 40. Stuttgart: 271–82.

(2006a) 'Oral tradition and written tradition in the formation of sacred law in Rome', in *Religion and Law in Classical and Christian Rome*, ed. C. Ando and J. Rüpke. PAwB 19. Stuttgart: 14–33.

(2006b) 'Rome et les grands lieux de culte d'Italie', in *Pouvoir et religion dans le monde romain en hommage à J.-P. Martin*, ed. A. Vigourt, X. Loriot, A. Bérenger-Badel and B. Klein. Paris: 75–86.

(2011) 'Les émotions dans la religion romaine', in Prescendi and Volokhine (eds.): 406–15.

(2012) 'Le rite des auspices à Rome: quelle évolution? Réflexions sur la transformation de la divination publique des Romains entre le IIIe et Ier siècle avant notre ère', in Georgoudi, Koch Piettre and Schmidt (eds.): 109–28.

Schiavone, A. (2005) *Ius. L'invenzione del diritto in Occidente*. Biblioteca di cultura storica 254. Turin.

Schiesaro, A. (1993) Review of O'Hara 1990, *CP* 88: 285–93.

(1997) 'The boundaries of knowledge in Virgil's Georgics', in Habinek and Schiesaro (eds.): 63–89.

(2002) 'Ovid and the professional discourses of scholarship, religion, rhetoric', in *The Cambridge Companion to Ovid*, ed. P. Hardie. Cambridge: 62–75.

(2003) 'Rhétorique, politique et *didaxis* chez Lucrèce', in *Le jardin romain. Épicurisme et poésie à Rome. Mélanges offerts à Mayotte Bollack*, ed. A. Monet. Lille: 57–75.

(2007) 'Lucretius and Roman politics and history', in *The Cambridge Companion to Lucretius*, ed. S. Gillespie and P. Hardie. Cambridge: 41–58.

Schilling, R. (1962) 'À propos des "exta": l'extispicine étrusque et la "litatio" romaine', in *Hommages à Albert Grenier*, ed. M. Renard. Collection Latomus 58. Brussels: 1371–8, reprinted in Schilling 1979: 183–90.

(1971) 'L'originalité du vocabulaire religieux latin', *RBPH* 49: 31–54.

(1972) 'Le Romain de la fin de la République et du début de l'Empire en face de la religion', *AC* 41: 540–62.

(1979) *Rites, cultes, dieux de Rome*. Études et commentaires 92. Paris.

Schmid, A. (2005) *Augustus und die Macht der Sterne. Antike Astrologie und die Etablierung der Monarchie in Rom*. Cologne, Weimar and Vienna.

Schmid, W. (1961) '*Urgentibus imperii fatis* (Tac. *Germ.* 33)', in *Didascaliae. Studies in Honor of Anselm M. Albareda, Prefect of the Vatican Library, Presented by a Group of American Scholars*, ed. S. Prete. New York: 383–92.

Schmidt, E. (1996) 'Römische Theologie in der Odusia des Livius Andronicus', in Cancik (ed.): 287–303.

Schmidt, P. L. (1968) 'Iulius Obsequens und das Problem der Livius-Epitome. Ein Beitrag zur Geschichte der lateinischen Prodigienliteratur', *Akademie der Wissenschaften und der Literatur. Abhandlungen der Geistes- und Sozialwissenschaftlichen Klasse* 5: 155–242.

  (1978–9) 'Cicero's place in Roman philosophy: a study of his prefaces', *CJ* 74: 115–27.

Schmitz, H.-G. (1993) 'Fiktion und Divination. Fünf Studien zur stoischen Semiotik des Orakels, wie Cicero sie entfaltet', *Philosophisches Jahrbuch* 100: 172–86.

Schnegg-Köhler, B. (2002) *Die augusteische Säkularspiele. ARG* 4. Munich and Leipzig.

Schneider, M. (2004) *Cicero 'haruspex'. Political Prognostication and the Viscera of a Deceased Body Politic*. Gorgias Dissertations 10. Piscataway.

Schofield, M. (1986) 'Cicero for and against divination', *JRS* 76: 47–65.

  (2008) 'Ciceronian dialogue', in *The End of Dialogue in Antiquity*, ed. S. Goldhill. Cambridge: 63–84.

Schütz, M. (1990) 'Zur Sonnenuhr des Augustus auf dem Marsfeld. Eine Auseinandersetzung mit E. Buchners Rekonstruktion und seiner Deutung der Ausgrabungsergebnisse, aus der Sicht einer Physikers', *Gymnasium* 97: 432–57.

  (2011) 'The Horologium on the Campus Martius reconsidered', *JRA* 24: 78–86.

Schuller, W. (ed.) (1993) *Livius. Aspekte seines Werkes*. Xenia 31. Konstanz.

Schultz, C. E. (2006a) *Women's Religious Activity in the Roman Republic*. Chapel Hill.

  (2006b) 'Juno Sospita and Roman insecurity in the Social War', in Schultz and Harvey (eds.): 207–27.

  (2009) 'Argument and anecdote in Cicero's *De Divinatione*', in *Maxima debetur magistro reverentia. Essays on Rome and the Roman Tradition in Honor of Russell T. Scott*, ed. P. B. Harvey, Jr. and C. Conybeare. Biblioteca di *Athenaeum* 54. Como: 193–206.

  (2010) 'The Romans and ritual murder', *Journal of the American Academy of Religion* 78: 516–41.

Schultz, C. E. and Harvey, P. B. Jr. (eds.) (2006) *Religion in Republican Italy*. Yale Classical Studies 33. Cambridge.

Sciarrino, E. (2004) 'A temple for the professional Muse: the *Aedes Herculis Musarum* and cultural shifts in second-century B.C. Rome', in Barchiesi, Rüpke and Stephens (eds.): 45–56.

  (2011) *Cato the Censor and the Beginning of Latin Prose. From Poetic Translation to Elite Transcription*. Columbus, OH.

Scioli, E. and Walde, C. (eds.) (2010) Sub imagine somni. *Nighttime Phenomena in Greco-Roman Culture*. Testi e studi di cultura classica 16. Pisa.

Scott Ryberg, I. (1955) *Rites of the State Religion in Roman Art*, ed. L. R. Taylor. *MAAR* 22. Rome.

Sedley, D. (1982) 'On signs', in Barnes, Brunschwig, Burnyeat and Schofield (eds.): 239–72.

Seguin, P. (1974) 'La religion de Scipion l'Africain', *Latomus* 33: 3–21.

Sehlmeyer, M. (2009) 'Auseinandersetzungen mit Religion in antiquarischer Literatur von M. Fulvius Nobilior bis L. Iulius Caesar', in Bendlin and Rüpke (eds.): 57–72.

Setaioli, A. (1975) 'Un influsso ciceroniano in Virgilio', *SIFC* 47: 5–26, reprinted in Setaioli 1998: 11–32.

(1998) *Si tantus amor . . . Studi virgiliani*. Testi e manuali per l'insegnamento universitario del latino 53. Bologna.

(2005) 'Le fragment II Soubiran du *De consulatu* de Cicéron, le *De diuinatione* et leur lecture par Virgile', in Kany-Turpin (ed.): 241–63.

(2007) 'Seneca and the divine: Stoic tradition and personal developments', *IJCT* 13: 333–68.

Sfameni Gasparro, G. (2002) *Oracoli profeti sibille. Rivelazione e salvezza nel mondo antico*. Biblioteca di scienze religiose 171. Rome.

Shackleton Bailey, D. R. (1965) *Cicero's Letters to Atticus I. 68–59 B.C.* Cambridge. (1971) *Cicero*. London.

Sharples, R. W. (1995) 'Causes and necessary conditions in the *Topica* and *De Fato*', in Powell (ed.): 247–71.

Sharples, R. W. (ed.) (1991) *Cicero: On Fate (De Fato) & Boethius: The Consolation of Philosophy IV.5–7, V (Philosophiae Consolationis)*. Warminster.

Simpson, A. D. (1938) 'The departure of Crassus for Parthia', *TAPA* 68: 532–41.

Skinns, L., Scott, M. and Cox, T. (eds.) (2011) *Risk*. The Darwin College Lectures 24. Cambridge.

Sklenár, R. (1998) '*La république des signes*: Caesar, Cato, and the language of Sallustian morality', *TAPA* 128: 205–20.

Skutsch, O. (1985) *The Annals of Ennius*. Oxford.

Slater, N. W. (2000) 'The market in sooth: supernatural discourse in Plautus', in *Dramatische Wäldchen. Festschrift für Eckard Lefèvre*, ed. E. Stärk and G. Vogt-Spira. Spudasmata 80. Hildesheim: 345–61.

(2011) 'Plautus the theologian', in *Sacred Words. Orality, Literacy and Religion. Orality and Literacy in the Ancient World* VIII, ed. A. P. M. H. Lardinois, J. H. Blok and M. G. M. van der Poel. *Mnemosyne* Supplement 332. Leiden and Boston: 297–310.

Sluiter, I. (1997) 'The Greek tradition', in *The Emergence of Semantics in Four Linguistic Traditions: Hebrew, Sanskrit, Greek, Arabic*. Studies in the History of the Language Sciences 82. Amsterdam and Philadelphia: 149–224.

Smadja, E. and Geny, E. (eds.) (1999) *Pouvoir, divination, prédestination dans le monde antique*. Besançon and Paris.

Small, J. P. (1982) *Cacus and Marsyas in Etrusco-Roman Legend*. Princeton.

Smith, C. (2009) 'Sulla's *Memoirs*', in Smith and Powell (eds.): 65–85.

Smith, C. and Powell, A. (eds.) (2009) *The Lost Memoirs of Augustus and the Development of Roman Autobiography*. Swansea.

Smith, K. F. (1913) *The Elegies of Albius Tibullus*. New York, Cincinnati and Chicago.

Solmsen, F. (1944) 'Cicero on *religio* and *superstitio*', *Classical Weekly* 37: 159–60.

Sommerstein, A. (ed.) (1995) *Religion and Superstition in Latin Literature*. Nottingham Classical Literature Studies 3. Bari.

Sordi, M. (1972) 'L'idea di crisi e di rinnovamento nella concezione romano-etrusca della storia', *ANRW* 1.2: 781–93, reprinted in Sordi 1995: 175–87.

(1993) 'Il sacrificio interrotto e l'espropriazione degli "omina"', in Sordi (ed.): 187–92.

(1995) *Prospettive di storia etrusca*. Biblioteca di *Athenaeum* 26. Como.

(2002a) 'I *saecula* degli Etruschi e gli *ostenta*', *RSI* 114: 715–25.

(2002b) 'Il problema religioso nel discorso di Mecenate ad Augusto. Cassio Dione 52, 35, 3–36,3', in Michelotto (ed.): 469–75.

(2006) 'L'ira di Atena: terrorismo e miracolistica fra il 196 e il 191 a.C.', in Urso (ed.): 137–42.

(2008) 'Il paradosso etrusco: il "diverso" nelle radici profonde di Roma e dell'Italia romana', in Urso (ed.): 89–97.

Sordi, M. (ed.) (1984) *I santuari e la guerra nel mondo classico*. Contributi dell'Istituto di storia antica 10. Milan.

(1993) *La profezia nel mondo antico*. Contributi dell'Istituto di storia antica 19. Milan.

Spahlinger, L. (2005) *Tulliana simplicitas. Zu Form und Funktion des Zitats in den philosophischen Dialogen Ciceros*. Hypomnemata 159. Göttingen.

Spann, P. O. (1987) *Quintus Sertorius and the Legacy of Sulla*. Fayetteville.

Stark, R. (1996) *The Rise of Christianity. A Sociologist Reconsiders History*. Princeton.

Steel, C. E. W. (2001) *Cicero, Rhetoric and Empire*. Oxford.

Stem, R. (2009–10) 'Shared virtue and the limits of relativism in Nepos' *Epaminondas* and *Atticus*', *CJ* 105: 123–36.

Steuernagel, D. (2007) 'Ancient harbour towns – religious market places? Formation and social functions of voluntary associations in Roman Ostia', *Hephaistos* 25: 141–51.

Stevenson, T. (2009) 'Antony as "tyrant" in Cicero's *First Philippic*', *Ramus* 38: 174–86.

Stewart, D. J. (1968) 'Sallust and *Fortuna*', *History and Theory* 7: 298–317.

Stewart, R. (1998) *Public Office in Early Rome. Ritual Procedure and Political Practice*. Ann Arbor.

Stok, F. (2010) 'Cicerone e la politica del sogno', in Scioli and Walde (2010): 103–17.

Storchi Marino, A. (1992) 'C. Marcio Censorino, la lotta politica intorno al pontificato e la formazione della tradizione liviana su Numa', *AION* 14: 105–47.

(1999) *Numa e Pitagora*. Sapientia constituendae civitatis. Pubblicazioni del Dipartimento di discipline storiche 10. Naples.

Strasburger, H. (1999) *Ciceros philosophische Spätwerk als Aufruf gegen die Herrschaft Caesars.* Spudasmata 45. 2nd edn. Zurich and New York.

Stroh, W. (2004) '*De Domo Sua*: legal problem and structure', in *Cicero the Advocate*, ed. J. Powell and J. Paterson. Oxford: 313–70.

Strothmann, M. (2010) 'Himmel und Erde im Einklang. Augustus und der eine Gott', in *Zwischen Monarchie und Republik. Gesellschaftliche Stabilierungsleistungen und politische Trasformationspotentiale in den antiken Stadtstaaten*, ed. B. Linke, M. Meier and M. Strothmann. *Historia* Einzelschriften 217. Stuttgart: 213–29.

Struck, P. T. (2003) 'The ordeal of the divine sign: divination and manliness in Archaic and Classical Greece', in *Andreia. Studies in Manliness and Courage in Classical Antiquity*, ed. R. M. Rosen and I. Sluiter. *Mnemosyne* Supplement 238. Leiden and Boston: 167–86.

(2004) *Birth of the Symbol. Ancient Readers and the Limits of their Texts.* Princeton and Oxford.

(2005) 'Divination and literary criticism', in Johnston and Struck (eds.): 147–65.

(2007) 'A world full of signs: understanding ancient divination in ancient Stoicism', in *Seeing with Different Eyes. Essays in Astrology and Divination*, ed. P. Curry and A. Voss. Newcastle: 3–20.

(2010) 'Allegory and ascent in Neoplatonism', in *The Cambridge Companion to Allegory*, ed. R. Copeland and P. T. Struck. Cambridge: 57–70.

Stübler, G. (1941) *Die Religiosität des Livius.* Tübinger Beiträge zur Altertumswissenschaft 35. Stuttgart.

Suárez de la Torre, E. (2007) 'Tradizione profetica, composizione poetica e identità nazionale: Asia ed Europa negli *Oracoli Sibillini* giudaici', in *Tra Oriente e Occidente. Indigeni, Greci e Romani in Asia Minore*, ed. G. Urso. I Convegni della Fondazione Niccolò Canussio 6. Pisa: 61–78.

Sudhaus, S. (1901) 'Jahrhundertfeier in Rom und messianische Weissagungen', *RhM* 56: 37–54.

Suerbaum, W. (2002) 'Livius Andronicus', in *Handbuch der lateinischen Literatur der Antike. Erster Band: Die archaische Literatur. Von den Anfängen bis zu Sullas Tod. Die vorliterarische Periode und die Zeit von 240 bis 78 v. Chr.*, ed. W. Suerbaum. Handbuch der Altertumswissenschaft 8.1. Munich: 93–104.

Sumi, G. S. (2005) *Ceremony and Power. Performing Politics in Rome between Republic and Empire.* Ann Arbor.

Swan, P. M. (1987) 'Cassius Dio and Augustus: a poverty of annalistic sources?', *Phoenix* 41: 272–91.

(1997) 'How Cassius Dio composed his Augustan books: four studies', *ANRW* 2.34.3: 2524–57.

(2004) *The Augustan Succession. An Historical Commentary on Cassius Dio's Roman History Books 55–56 (9 B.C.–A.D. 14).* American Classical Studies 47. Oxford.

Swoboda, A. (1889) *P. Nigidii Figuli operum reliquiae.* Vienna and Prague.

Syme, R. (1964) *Sallust.* Berkeley and Los Angeles.

Taisne, A.-M. (1995) 'Stace et l'*Etrusca disciplina*', in Briquel and Guittard (eds.): 115–27.

Takács, S. A. (2003) 'Forging a past: the Sibylline Books and the making of Rome', in *Cultures of Forgery. Making Nations, Making Selves*, ed. J. Ryan and A. Thomas. New York and London: 15–27, reprinted in Takács 2008: 60–70, 159–61.

(2008) *Vestal Virgins, Sibyls, and Matrons. Women in Roman Religion*. Austin.

Talamanca, M. (1987) 'Développements socio-économiques et jurisprudence romaine à la fin de la République', in *Studi in onore di Cesare Sanfilippo*. Pubblicazioni della Facoltà di giurisprudenza dell'Università di Catania 96.7. Milan: 773–91.

Tarán, L. (1987) 'Cicero's attitude towards Stoicism and Skepticism in the *De natura deorum*', in *Florilegium Colombianum. Essays in Honor of Paul Oskar Kristeller*, New York: 1–22, reprinted in Tarán 2001: 455–77.

(2001) *Collected Papers (1962–1999)*. Leiden, Boston and Cologne.

Tarpin, M. (2003) 'M. Licinius Crassus *imperator* et les dépouilles opimes de la République', *RPh* 77: 275–310.

Tarrant, H. (2000) 'Recollection and prophecy in the *De Divinatione*', *Phronesis* 45: 64–76.

Tarver, T. (1995) 'Varro, Caesar, and the Roman calendar: a study in late Republican religion', in Sommerstein (ed.): 39–57.

(1997) 'Varro and the antiquarianism of philosophy', in *Philosophia togata II. Plato and Aristotle at Rome*, ed. J. Barnes and M. Griffin. Oxford: 130–64.

Tatum, W. J. (1993) 'Ritual and personal morality in Roman religion', *SyllClass* 4: 13–20.

(1999a) *The Patrician Tribune. Publius Clodius Pulcher*. Chapel Hill and London.

(1999b) 'Roman religion: fragments and further questions', in *Veritatis amicitiaeque causa. Essays in Honor of Anna Lydia Motto and John R. Clark*, ed. S. N. Byrne and E. P. Cueva. Wauconda, IL: 273–91.

Taub, L. (2003) *Ancient Meteorology*. London and New York.

Taylor, L. R. (1934) 'New light on the history of the Secular Games', *AJP* 55: 101–20.

(1949) *Party Politics in the Age of Caesar*. Berkeley, Los Angeles and London.

Taylor, R. (2000) 'Watching the skies: Janus, auspication, and the shrine in the Roman Forum', *MAAR* 45: 1–40.

Tedlock, B. (2010) 'Theorizing divinatory acts: the integrative discourse of dream oracles', in Curry (ed.): 11–23.

Tels-de Jong, L. L. (1959) *Sur quelques divinités romaines de la naissance et de la prophétie*. Delft.

Tempest, K. (2011) 'Combating the odium of self-praise: Cicero's *Divinatio in Caecilium*', in *Praise and Blame in Roman Republican Rhetoric*, ed. C. Smith and R. Covino. Swansea: 145–63.

Terio, S. (2006) *Der Steinbock als Herrschaftszeichen des Augustus*. Orbis antiquus 41. Münster.

Thein (2009) '*Felicitas* and the Memoirs of Sulla and Augustus', in Smith and Powell (eds.): 87–109.

(forthcoming) 'Capitoline Jupiter and the historiography of Roman world rule'. *Histos.*

Themann-Steinke, A. (2008) *Valerius Maximus. Ein Kommentar zum zweiten Buch der* Facta *et* Dicta memorabilia. Bochumer Altertumswissenschaftliches Colloquium 77. Trier.

Thomas, J. F. (2002) *Gloria et laus. Étude sémantique.* Bibliothèque d'études classiques 31. Leuven and Dudley, MA.

Thomas, K. (1971) *Religion and the Decline of Magic. Studies in Popular Beliefs in Sixteenth- and Seventeenth-Century England.* London.

Thomas, R. F. (1988) *Virgil. Georgics. Volume I: Books I–II.* Cambridge.

Thulin, C. (1905a) *Die etruskische Disciplin* I. Göteborgs Högskolas Årsskrift 11. Gothenburg.

(1905b) 'Synonyma quaedam latina (*Prodigium, portentum, ostentum, monstrum*)', in *Commentationes philologae in honorem Iohannis Paulson scripserunt cultores et amici.* Lund: 194–213.

(1906a) *Die etruskische Disciplin* II. Göteborgs Högskolas Årsskrift 12. Gothenburg.

(1906b) *Die Götter des Martianus Capella und der Bronzeleber von Piacenza.* Religionsgeschichtliche Vorarbeiten und Versuche 3.1. Giessen.

(1909) *Die etruskische Disciplin* III. Göteborgs Högskolas Årsskrift 15. Gothenburg.

Tiffou, E. (1977) 'Salluste et la Fortuna', *Phoenix* 31: 349–60.

Timpanaro, S. (1978) *Contributi di filologia e di storia della lingua latina.* Ricerche di storia della lingua latina 13. Rome.

(1988) *Cicerone. Della divinazione. Introduzione, traduzione e note.* Milan.

(1994) 'Alcuni fraintendimenti del *de divinatione*', in *Nuovi contributi di filologia e storia della lingua latina.* Testi e manuali per l'insegnamento universitario del latino 38. Bologna: 241–64.

Todisco, E. (2007) 'Il nome *Augustus* e la "fondazione" ideologica del Principato', in *Antidoron. Studi in onore di Barbara Scardigli Foster*, ed. P. Desideri, M. Moggi and M. Pani. Studi e testi di storia antica 17. Pisa: 441–62.

Toher, M. (2002) 'Nepos' second edition', *Philologus* 146: 139–49.

Toner, J. (2009) *Popular Culture in Ancient Rome.* Cambridge.

Torelli, M. (1975) *Elogia Tarquiniensia.* Studi e materiali di Etruscologia e Antichità italiche 15. Florence.

(2011) 'The *haruspices* of the Emperor: Tarquitius Priscus and Sejanus' conspiracy', in Richardson and Santangelo (eds.): 137–59.

Traill, A. (2004) 'A haruspicy joke in Plautus', *CQ* 54: 117–27.

Trampedach, K. (2011) 'Götterzeichen im Heiligtum: das Beispiel Delphi', in *Griechische Heiligtümer als Erinnerungsorte. Von der Archaik bis in den Hellenismus*, ed. M. Haake and M. Jung. Stuttgart: 29–43.

Treggiari, S. (1969) *Roman Freedmen during the Late Republic.* Oxford.

(2007) *Terentia, Tullia and Publilia. The Women of Cicero's Family*. London and New York.

Troiani, L. (1984) 'La religione e Cicerone', *RSI* 96: 920–52.

Tromp, S. P. C. (1921) 'De Romanorum piaculis'. Diss. Leiden.

Tucker, C. W. (1976) 'Cicero, Augur, *De iure augurali*', *CW* 70: 171–80.

Tucker, R. A. (1988) 'What actually happened at the Rubicon?', *Historia* 37: 245–8.

Tuplin, C. (2000) 'Nepos and the origins of political biography', in *Studies in Latin Literature and Roman History* x, ed. C. Deroux. Collection Latomus 254. Brussels: 124–61.

Turcan, R. (1976) 'Encore la prophétie de Végoia', in *Mélanges offerts à Jacques Heurgon. L'Italie préromaine et la Rome républicaine* ii. Rome: 1009–19.

Turfa, J. M. (2006) 'Etruscan religion at the watershed: before and after the fourth century BCE', in Schultz and Harvey (eds.): 62–89.

    (2007) 'The Etruscan brontoscopic calendar and modern archaeological discoveries', *Etruscan Studies* 10: 163–73.

    (2012) *Divining the Etruscan World. The* Brontoscopic Calendar *and Religious Practice*. Cambridge.

Turfa, J. M. and Gettys, S. (2009) 'The skill of the Etruscan haruspex. A biological basis for successful divination?', *BABesch* 84: 41–52.

Turner, V. W. (1967) *The Forest of Symbols. Aspects of Ndembu Ritual*. Ithaca and London.

    (1968) *The Drums of Affliction. A Study of Religious Processes among the Ndembu of Zambia*. Oxford.

    (1995) *The Ritual Process. Structure and Anti-Structure*. New York.

Urso, G. (1994) 'Il concetto di "alienigena" nella guerra annibalica', in *Emigrazione e immigrazione nel mondo antico*, ed. M. Sordi. CISA 20. Milan: 223–36.

Urso, G. (ed.) (2000) *L'ultimo Cesare. Scritti riforme progetti poteri congiure*. Monografie – Centro ricerche e documentazione sull'Antichità Classica 20. Rome.

    (2006) Terror et pavor. *Violenza, intimidazione, clandestinità nel mondo antico*. I convegni della Fondazione Niccolò Canussio 5. Pisa.

    (2008) Patria diversis gentibus una? *Unità politica e identità etniche nell'Italia antica*. I convegni della Fondazione Niccolò Canussio 7. Pisa.

    (2010) *Cesare: precursore o visionario?* I convegni della Fondazione Niccolò Canussio 9. Pisa.

Vaahtera, J. E. (2000) 'Roman religion and the Polybian *politeia*', in *The Roman Middle Republic. Politics, Religion and Historiography c. 400–133 B.C.*, ed. C. Bruun. Acta Instituti Romani Finlandiae 23. Rome: 251–64.

    (2001) *Roman Augural Lore in Greek Historiography. A Study of the Theory and Terminology*. Historia Einzelschriften 156. Stuttgart.

Valeton, I. M. J. (1891) 'De iure obnuntiandi comitiis et conciliis', *Mnemosyne* 19: 75–113, 229–70.

Valvo, A. (1988) *La 'profezia di Vegoia'. Proprietà fondiaria e aruspicina in Etruria nel I secolo a.C.* Studi pubblicati dall'Istituto italiano per la storia antica 43. Rome.

Vandermeersch, L. (1974) 'De la tortue à l'achillée', in Vernant (ed.): 29–69.

Van Haeperen, F. (2005) 'Mises à mort rituelles et violences politiques à Rome sous la République et l'Empire', *Res antiquae* 2: 327–46.

Van Nuffelen, P. (2010) 'Varro's *Divine Antiquities*: Roman religion as an image of truth', *CP* 105: 162–88.

(2011) *Rethinking the Gods. Philosophical Readings of Religion in the Post-Hellenistic Period*. Cambridge.

Várhely, Z. (2007) 'The specters of Roman imperialism: the live burials of Gauls and Greeks at Rome', *CA* 26: 277–304.

(2010) *The Religion of Senators in the Roman Empire. Power and the Beyond*. Cambridge.

Vernant, J. (1948) 'La divination. Contexte et sens psychologiques des rites et des doctrines', *Journal de psychologie normale et pathologique* 41: 299–325.

Vernant, J.-P. (ed.) (1974) *Divination et rationalité*. Paris.

Veyne, P. (1983) *Les Grecs ont-ils cru à leurs mythes?* Paris.

(1999) 'Prodiges, divination et peur des dieux chez Plutarque', *RHR* 216: 387–442.

Vigourt, A. (2001a) *Les présages impériaux d'Auguste à Domitien*. Paris.

(2001b) 'La représentation de Rome dans les présages concernant le pouvoir de la mort de César à celle de Domitien', in *Rome, les Césars et la ville aux deux premiers siècles de notre ère*, ed. N. Belayche. Rennes: 267–89.

Volk, K. (2009) *Manilius and his Intellectual Background*. Oxford.

(2011) 'Introduction. A century of Manilian scholarship', in Green and Volk (eds.): 1–10.

Wagenvoort, H. (1956) *Studies in Roman Literature, Culture and Religion*. Leiden.

(1972) 'Wesenzüge altrömischer Religion', *ANRW* 1.2: 348–76.

Walbank, F. W. (1957) *A Historical Commentary on Polybius* I, *Commentary on Books I–VI*. Oxford.

(1979) *A Historical Commentary on Polybius* III. Oxford.

(2007) 'Fortune (*tychē*) in Polybius', in *A Companion to Greek and Roman Historiography* II, ed. J. Marincola. Malden, MA and Oxford: 349–55.

Walde, C. (2001) *Die Traumdarstellungen in der griechisch-römischen Dichtung*. Munich and Leipzig.

Wallace-Hadrill, A. (1983) *Suetonius. The Scholar and his Caesars*. London.

(1987) 'Time for Augustus: Ovid, Augustus and the *Fasti*', in Homo viator. *Classical Essays for John Bramble*, ed. M. Whitby, P. Hardie and M. Whitby. Bristol and Oak Park: 221–30.

(1989) 'Rome's cultural revolution', *JRS* 79: 157–64.

(2008) *Rome's Cultural Revolution*. Cambridge.

Walsh, P. G. (1958) 'Livy and Stoicism', *AJP* 79: 355–75.

Walter, U. (2004) Memoria *und* res publica. *Zur Geschichtskultur im republikanischen Rom*. Studien zur alten Geschichte 1. Frankfurt.

Walton, F. R. (1965) 'A neglected historical text', *Historia* 14: 236–51.

Warde Fowler, W. (1911) *The Religious Experience of the Roman People*. London.

(1920) *Roman Essays and Interpretations*. Oxford.

Wardle, D. (1996) 'Vespasian, Helvidius Priscus and the restoration of the Capitol', *Historia* 45: 208–22.

(1997) '"The sainted Julius": Valerius Maximus and the dictator', *CP* 92: 323–45.

(1998) *Valerius Maximus. Memorable Deeds and Sayings Book 1*. Oxford.

(2005a) 'Valerius Maximus and the end of the First Punic War', *Latomus* 64: 376–84.

(2005b) 'Unimpeachable sponsors of imperial autocracy, or Augustus' dream team (Suetonius *Divus Augustus* 94.8–9 and Dio Cassius 45.2.2–4)', *Antichthon* 39: 29–47.

(2006) *Cicero: On Divination. Book 1*. Oxford.

(2007) '"The Sainted Julius". Valerius Maximus and the Dictator', *CP* 92: 323–45.

(2008) 'Initial indications of Augustus' imminent (im)mortality (Suet. *DA* 97.1)', *Athenaeum* 96: 355–67.

(2009) 'Caesar and religion', in *A Companion to Julius Caesar*, ed. M. Griffin. Malden, MA and Oxford: 100–11.

(2011a) 'Augustus and the priesthoods of Rome: the evidence of Suetonius', in Richardson and Santangelo (eds.): 271–89.

(2011b) 'The blame game: an aspect of handling military defeat in the early Principate', *Hermes* 139: 42–50.

(forthcoming) 'The "legend" and publication of Augustus' horoscope'.

Wardman, A. (1982) *Religion and Statecraft among the Romans*. London.

Waßmuth, O. (2011) *Sibyllinische Orakel 1–2. Studien und Kommentar*. Ancient Judaism and Early Christianity 76. Leiden and Boston.

Watson, L. C. (2003) *A Commentary on Horace's Epodes*. Oxford.

Weber, G. (2000) *Kaiser, Träume und Visionen in Prinzipat und Spätantike. Historia* Einzelschriften 143. Stuttgart.

Weinrib, E. J. (1970) '*Obnuntiatio*: two problems', *ZSS* 87: 395–425.

Weinstock, S. (1937) 'Clodius and the *lex Aelia Fufia*', *JRS* 27: 215–22.

(1946) 'Martianus Capella and the cosmic system of the Etruscans', *JRS* 36: 101–29.

(1950) 'C. Fonteius Capito and the *libri Tagetici*', *PBSR* 18: 44–9.

(1951) 'Libri fulgurales', *PBSR* 19: 122–53.

(1971) *Divus Julius*. Oxford.

Weiss, P. (1973) 'Die "Sakuläre" der Republik, eine annalistische Fiktion? Ein Beitrag zum Verständnis der kaiserzeitlichen Ludi saeculares', *RM* 80: 205–17.

Wells, J. C. (2004) *De religionibus sacris et caerimoniis est contionatus*. 'Piety and public life in Republican Rome'. Diss. Ohio State (available at http://drc.ohiolink.edu/handle/2374.OX/4619, last accessed 29.08.12).

Welsh, J. T. (2011) 'Accius, Porcius Licinus, and the beginning of Latin literature', *JRS* 101: 31–50.

West, D. (1993) 'On serial narration and on the Julian Star', *PVS* 21: 1–16.

White, P. (1988) 'Julius Caesar in Augustan Rome', *Phoenix* 42: 334–56.

(2010) *Cicero in Letters. Epistolary Relations of the Late Republic*. Oxford.

Whitehouse, H. and Laidlaw, J. (eds.) (2007) *Religion, Anthropology, and Cognitive Science*. Durham, NC.

Wifstrand Schiebe, M. (2006) 'Sinn und Wahrheitsgehalt der Kultbilder aus der Sicht der antiken Philosophie. Zur antiken Debatte an Hand des Beispiels Marcus Terentius Varro', in *Suncharmata. Studies in Honour of Jan Fredrik Kindstrand*, ed. S. Uklund. Acta Universitatis Upsaliensis. Studia Graeca Upsaliensia 21. Uppsala: 189–209.

Wilkins, J. B. (1994) 'The Iguvine Tables: problems in the interpretation of the text', in *Territory, Time and State. The Archaeological Development of the Gubbio Basin*, ed. C. Malone and S. Stoddart. Cambridge: 152–72.

Willi, A. (1998) 'Numa's dangerous books. The exegetic history of a Roman forgery', *MH* 55: 139–72.

Williams, M. F. (2003) 'The *sidus Julium*, the divinity of men, and the Golden Age in Virgil's *Aeneid*', *LICS* 2.1 (available at www.lics.leeds.ac.uk/2003/200301.pdf, last accessed 29.08.12).

Wilson, C. H. (1979) 'Jupiter and the Fates in the *Aeneid*', *CQ* 29: 361–71.

Wiseman, T. P. (1966) 'The ambitions of Quintus Cicero', *JRS* 56: 108–15.

(1971) *New Men in the Roman Senate, 139 B.C.–A.D. 14*. Oxford.

(1984) 'Cybele, Virgil and Augustus', in *Poetry and Politics in the Age of Augustus*, ed. T. Woodman and D. West. Cambridge: 117–28, 225–9.

(1994a) 'Lucretius, Catiline, and the survival of prophecy', in *Historiography and Imagination. Eight Essays on Roman Culture*. Exeter Studies in History 33. Exeter: 49–67 (originally published in *Ostraka* 1 (1992), 7–18).

(1994b) 'Caesar, Pompey and Rome, 59–50 B.C.', in *Cambridge Ancient History* IX, 2nd edn. Cambridge: 368–423.

(1995) *Remus. A Roman Myth*. Cambridge.

(1998a) *Roman Drama and Roman History*. Exeter.

(1998b) 'The publication of the *De Bello Gallico*', in *Julius Caesar as Artful Reporter. The War Commentaries as Political Instruments*, ed. K. Welch and A. Powell. London: 1–9.

(2006) 'Fauns, prophets, and Ennius's *Annales*', *Arethusa* 39: 513–29, reprinted in Wiseman 2008: 39–51.

(2008) *Unwritten Rome*. Exeter.

(2009a) *Remembering the Roman People. Essays on Late-Republican Politics and Literature*. Oxford.

(2009b) 'Augustus, Sulla and the supernatural', in Smith and Powell (eds.): 111–23.

(forthcoming) 'Rome on the balance: Varro and the foundation of Rome', in *The Works of Varro Reatinus*, ed. D. Butterfield.

Wissowa, G. (1912) *Religion und Kultus der Römer*. Handbuch der klassischen Altertumswissenschaft 5.4. 2nd edn. Munich.

Woodman, A. J. (1988) *Rhetoric in Classical Historiography. Four Studies*. London and Sydney.

Wülker, L. (1903) 'Die geschichtliche Entwicklung des Prodigienwesens bei den
    Römern. Studien zur Geschichte und Überlieferung der Staatsprodigien'.
    Diss. Leipzig.
Zancan, L. (1939) 'Il frammento di Vegoia e il "novissimum saeculum"', *A&R* 7:
    203–19.
Zanker, P. (1988) *The Power of Images in the Age of Augustus*. Jerome Lectures 16.
    Ann Arbor.
Zecchini, G. (1984) 'La profezia dei druidi sull'incendio del Campidoglio nel 69
    d.C.', in Sordi (ed.): 121–31.
    (2001) *Cesare e il* mos maiorum. *Historia* Einzelschriften 151. Stuttgart.
Zetzel, J. E. G. (1989) '*Romane memento*: justice and judgment in *Aeneid* 6', *TAPA*
    119: 263–84.
    (1994) 'Looking backward. Past and present in the late Roman Republic', *Pegasus*
    37: 20–32.
    (1995) *Cicero. De re publica. Selections*. Cambridge.
Zevi, F. (1982) 'Oracoli alfabetici, Praeneste e Cuma', in *Aparchai. Nuove ricerche
    e studi sulla Magna Grecia e la Sicilia antica in onore di Paolo Enrico Arias*, ed.
    M. L. Gualandi, L. Massei and S. Settis. Biblioteca di studi antichi 35. Pisa:
    605–9.
    (1992) 'Note prenestine', in *Kotinos. Festschrift für Erika Simon*, ed. H. Froning,
    T. Hölscher and H. Mielsch. Mainz: 356–65.
    (1995) 'Personaggi della Pompei sillana', *PBSR* 63: 1–24.
Zieske, L. (2010) 'Iulius Caesar in Vergils Aeneis. Ein Beitrag zu Vergils dichter-
    ischer Haltung', *Gymnasium* 117: 129–40.

Index locorum

INSCRIPTIONS

COINS

General index

CPSIA information can be obtained
at www.ICGtesting.com
Printed in the USA
LVHW080509120922
728111LV00006B/196

9 781009 296359